MIS
Concepts and Design

ROBERT G. MURDICK

Florida Atlantic University

MIS CONCEPTS AND DESIGN

PRENTICE-HALL, INC., *Englewood Cliffs, New Jersey 07632*

Library of Congress Cataloging in Publication Data

MURDICK, ROBERT G
  MIS, concepts and design.

  Includes bibliographies and index.
  1. Management information systems. I. Title.
T58.6.M88 1980   658.4'03   79-24702
ISBN 0-13-585331-1

Printed in the United States of America

10 9 8 7 6 5 4 3 2 1

Editorial production/supervision and interior design by Sonia Meyer
Cover design by Philip J. Gibson
Page layout by Rita Kaye Schwartz
Manufacturing buyer: Anthony Caruso

PRENTICE-HALL INTERNATIONAL, INC., *London*
PRENTICE-HALL OF AUSTRALIA PTY. LIMITED, *Sydney*
PRENTICE-HALL OF CANADA, LTD., *Toronto*
PRENTICE-HALL OF INDIA PRIVATE LIMITED, *New Delhi*
PRENTICE-HALL OF JAPAN INC., *Tokyo*
PRENTICE-HALL OF SOUTHEAST ASIA PTE. LTD., *Singapore*
WHITEHALL BOOKS LIMITED, *Wellington, New Zealand*

Contents

part 3

ADVANCED CONCEPTS FOR MIS

CASES

Foreword

The concept and practice of management information systems (MIS) have been around for almost twenty years. Despite a few detractors and a slow beginning, the movement has gained momentum and now promises to take its place alongside the great managerial innovations of the century. Indeed, MIS is viewed by many as the mortar that holds together the bricks of the modern management movement.

The essential ingredient of both technical and general management is information. It is central to organized activity. The contribution of MIS is the *integration* of the often unrelated information subsystems of technical and general management into a systems approach that facilitates the output of the whole rather than a focus on the parts. This synergistic approach, combined with the computer, promises a new frontier in management planning and control. What double entry accounting did for financial information, the computer and MIS can now do for the entire company.

Despite the advances in the state-of-the-art of computer application to the management process, the future holds even greater promise, limited only by the imagination and design talent of interested individuals. Modeling of the firm and other sophisticated management science applications for decision making will continue to advance, so that future emphasis will be on the quality rather than the quantity of information.

· Dr. Robert Murdick, colleague and coauthor, has been a leader in the rapidly changing field of MIS. In this book he brings new dimensions to the subject. He not only provides the conceptual background for present and future thinking about the topic but also makes the transition from theory to practice. More importantly, he avoids the technical data processing approach in favor of a treatment that focuses on decision making and the managerial process. This book is truly a substantial contribution to the field.

Joel E. Ross

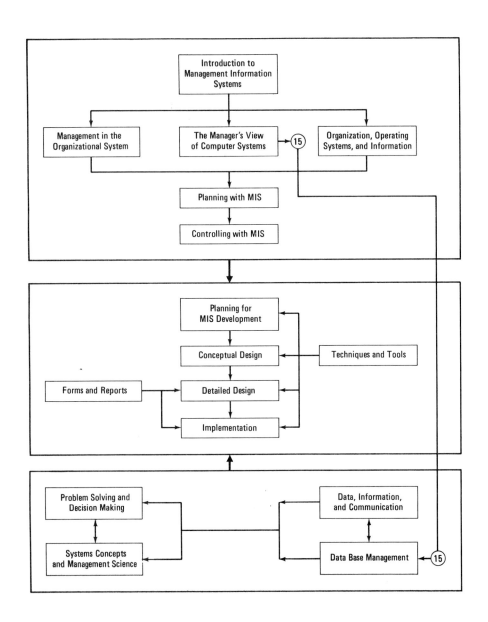

Preface

Knowledge and practice in the functional areas of business have matured. In an increasingly complex and often hostile environment, business today emphasizes strategic planning, balanced control, and rapid response. The consequence is a constant demand by managers for better and more timely information. A systems approach to management requires that this demand be met by information systems.

There is probably no more challenging and diversified subject than management information systems. It ranges through management theory, organizational behavior, systems theory, communication theory, and computer science. A thorough treatment of the subjects involved in MIS design would require volumes; this book provides the basics.

I have tested the approaches in this text during ten years of teaching at Florida Atlantic University. During this period the students have been assigned to projects working with a wide variety of companies, and many companies have progressed from the question "What's an MIS?" to the implementation of companywide systems.

ORGANIZATION OF THE BOOK

Three major concepts divide this text. Part 1 provides an insight into the systems view of management in a computerized world. Part 2 is a how-to-do-it section. Part 3 presents the underlying theory of MIS in more depth for more advanced students. For an undergraduate course Part 3 may be omitted.

The questions and problems at the end of each chapter have been designed for the convenience of the students and instructor. A set of fill-in and matching questions for review of the text are followed by discussion questions and mini-cases for mind-expanding.

Major cases at the end of the book provide a variety of challenges. The Van Dam case has questions keyed into each chapter and could be the basis of the entire course. Each instructor, choosing among the variety of alternatives offered, should be able to find a good basis for his or her course.

ACKNOWLEDGMENTS

I am grateful to the reviewers who read the manuscript and offered many suggestions which made this a stronger text. In addition, I appreciate the kindness of The Center for Information Systems Research, Alfred P. Sloan School of Management, Massachusetts Institute of Technology; the Center for Information Studies, Graduate School of Management, University of California at Los Angeles; and the Management Information Systems Research Center, Graduate School of Business Administration, University of Minnesota, for sharing with me the research of their scholars in the form of working papers.

The special contributions of Mr. Gene Giannotti and the management of the Western Division of GTE Sylvania, Dr. Robert E. Markland, Dr. L. Douglas Smith, and Dr. John C. Munson are gratefully acknowledged.

This book could not have been put together without the dedication of Emily Murdick in editing, prompt and frequent retyping, preparation of artwork, and managing of the many backstage tasks that go into the preparation of a new text. I also wish to thank Jerry Rosen for his assistance with production; and, at Prentice-Hall, my thanks to Ron Ledwith, Sonia Meyer, and Robert Lentz, for their interest, help, and consistent hard work in seeing the book through to its completion.

Robert G. Murdick

part 1

MANAGEMENT, INFORMATION, AND SYSTEMS

chapter 1

Introduction
to MIS

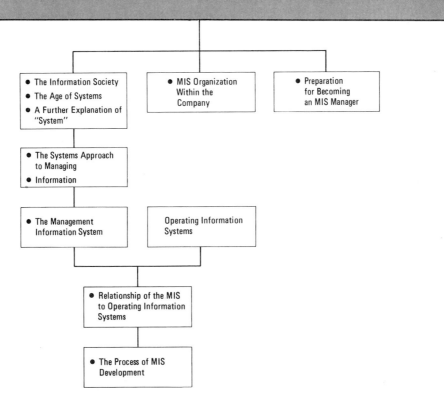

- The Information Society
- The Age of Systems
- A Further Explanation of "System"

- MIS Organization Within the Company

- Preparation for Becoming an MIS Manager

- The Systems Approach to Managing
- Information

- The Management Information System

Operating Information Systems

- Relationship of the MIS to Operating Information Systems

- The Process of MIS Development

PURPOSE: To provide the student with a broad view of MIS in society and business.

The Prisoner: What do you want?
   Number 2:   Information! We want information!

From the TV series, The Prisoner, *starring Patrick McGoohan*

THE INFORMATION SOCIETY

Over 100 million checks are cleared every day. Over 30 *billion* pieces of paper are processed each year in the United States. Over $50 billion was spent worldwide on data processing equipment, personnel, and supplies in 1978. Seventy-five percent of all the information available to mankind has been developed within the last two decades. With 72 billion new pieces of information being generated annually, how can we comprehend it, let alone use it?

When we read the newspapers, there appear to be shortages everywhere—shortages of energy, shortages of food, shortages of housing, shortages of health care. In contrast, one resource that is growing at a tremendous rate is data. Today's managers are supplied with bushels of data, which can be translated into overwhelming amounts of information. The United States has in fact changed from an industrial to an information society. This transformation was documented in 1950, when the employment of U.S. workers in information jobs surpassed that of workers in the industrial sector (Figure 1.1). In the 1980s, information workers will probably outnumber workers in all the other three sectors—agriculture, industry, and services—combined!

Modern societies are changing their characteristics at an accelerating rate. Such developments must be monitored by political, business, and not-for-profit

Figure 1.1 Four sector aggregation of the U.S. workforce
(1860-1980)

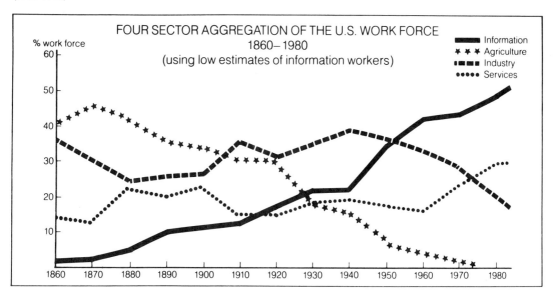

Source: Jeanne Binstock, "Dr. Spock's Babies Take Charge," **Planning Review**,
September, 1977, p. 15.

organization leaders. As the quantity of available information increases, its flow
to such leaders must be increasingly selective. Sophisticated information systems
are required to supply both environmental and internally generated information to
modern managers. Some environmental changes and their effects on information
systems for management are listed in Table 1.1.

THE AGE OF SYSTEMS

The Industrial Revolution transformed mercantile and agrarian economies of the
Western world to industrial economies. The change from cottage and artisan
production to factory production introduced the production *system*. *A system is
essentially a group of things that function together to achieve common objectives.* The factory brought together people, money, machines, materials, and
facilities for the purpose of producing goods. As the Industrial Revolution
advanced, automation linked the factors of production closer. The concept of
interchangeable parts, made practical by Eli Whitney in 1800, and of continuous
production, proposed by Oliver Evans in 1785, provided the foundation for such
automation. The late nineteenth and early twentieth centuries witnessed the
growth of large corporations through mergers and trusts.

The Age of Systems was born during World War II. The production of
hundreds of thousands of war planes annually by an economy that had produced
only a few hundred was truly a revolution in management. The development of
the atom bomb represented an integrated effort of scientists and laboratories all

Table 1.1 Some possible innovations and trends affecting management information systems

Factors	Changes	Impact on MIS
Economic	Global business systems Worldwide inflation Sudden energy crises Growing shortages of many vital national resources Control of key resources by new third-world countries Taxation inhibiting capital formation in basic U.S. industries High interest rates Unfunded pension plans growing beyond control Declining growth in productivity	Increased monitoring and prompt reporting of worldwide events Need for rapid reporting for rapid response to currency fluctuations Increasing need for forecasting resources and costs Better models of the firm in terms of plant locations to reduce taxes Better forecasts of interest rates for borrowing Use of MIS for controlling productivity
Technological	Tremendous increase in computer capabilities at rapidly decreasing cost for functions Radical changes in communications systems such as satellites Video word processing developments Replacement of the U.S. Postal Service	Increased ability to model complex systems Ability to process masses of data, such as global currency transactions Expansion of real-time MIS Better management reports Growth of number of MIS workers
Social	Higher level of education Health care Reduced age and sex discrimination Pollution Computers in the home Privacy threats	Higher quality of personnel available over a longer life span Managers always available or "on call" day and night Legal challenges to information gathering and storage Obstacles to linking government and private data bases
Political-legal	Government trend towards "Big Brother" as data bases grow Standards Privacy laws Liability laws	Concern for keeping corporate data bases inaccessible to governments. Possible reduction of innovation but improved compatibility of hardware Increased liability hazards
Management and organization	Increased importance of systems people relative to managers Development of organizational systems theory Greater reliance for decisions on individual workers rather than on managers	A larger role for MIS in decision assisting Better trade-offs in decision making Supplying of more information by MIS to lower-level managers and key specialists

over the country. National systems of airlines, roads, defense, and social security came into being.

The latter decades of the twentieth century have seen the rise of world systems, such as the World Bank and multinational corporations, which transcend all national political boundaries. Such systems require a flow of information that was not even envisioned a few decades ago. This book deals with *management information systems (MIS),* which make it possible for people to manage all types of complex systems such as businesses, service organizations, or government agencies.

Stateless Money System

Instead of local banks dealing in a single currency in a national marketplace—as banking used to be—there is now a vast, integrated global money and capital system, almost totally outside government regulation, that can send billions of Eurodollars, Euromarks, and other "stateless" currencies hurtling around the world 24 hours a day. . . .

Tying together the vast new supranational banking system is a technology that has outpaced not only the ability of nations to deal with it but even the perception by government officials that a new banking order has been created.[1]

A FURTHER EXPLANATION OF "SYSTEM"

Very simply, a system is a set of elements, such as people and things, that are related to achieve mutual goals. Systems that we deal with have inputs from the environment and send outputs into the environment. The system itself is a *processor* that changes inputs into outputs. Figure 1.1 summarizes this. What we cannot show in Figure 1.1 without making it unreadable is the network of communications among system elements, i.e., the information systems.

We may now show the essentials of the system for a number of managed institutions to make the meaning of *system* clearer. We have tabulated these essentials in Table 1.2. In the case of a business firm, remember that goals vary from producing or selling products to generating consulting reports to training people for careers. We have given the example of a manufacturing firm in Figure 1.2.

[1]Reprinted from the August 21, 1978, issue of *Business Week* by special permission, © 1978 by McGraw-Hill, Inc., New York. All rights reserved.

Figure 1.2
The system as a processor.

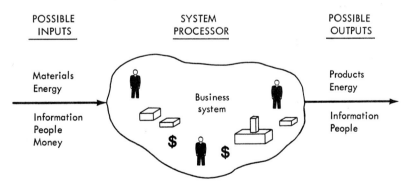

| POSSIBLE INPUTS | SYSTEM PROCESSOR | POSSIBLE OUTPUTS |

Materials
Energy

Information
People
Money

Business system

Products
Energy

Information
People

(Elements: People, machines, buildings, money)

Table 1.2 Some systems and their basic characteristics

System	Basic Goals	Elements	Inputs	Outputs
1. Department store	Provide the right goods at the right time	People, buildings, machines, money	Purchased goods, money, energy, information	Goods, services, information
2. Bank	Store money for customers, provide loans, trust services, checking services, and credit	People, buildings, machines, money	Money, information, energy	Money, services, information
3. Management consulting firm	Provide advice to customers	People, buildings, machines	Information, money, energy	Reports, services
4. University	Generate and disseminate information, develop leaders, provide community services	People, buildings, machines	People, money, information, energy	People, information, services
5. Electric utility	Provide energy in the form of electricity	People, buildings, machines	Energy, information	Energy in the form of electricity
6. Hospital	Provide health care, conduct research, teach doctors and nurses	People, buildings, machines	People, materials, energy, money, information	People, bodies, reports, services

THE SYSTEMS APPROACH TO MANAGING

The integration of so many human activities into systems means that there are many more complex systems to be managed. Modern managers must learn how to manage *systems,* rather than groups of fragmented operations. This new approach to managing is called, appropriately, the *systems approach.* The systems approach to managing involves the design of business operations and information flow as an integrated system.

The fundamental concept of the systems approach to organization and management is the interrelationship of the parts or subsystems of the organization. The approach begins with a set of objectives, and it focuses on the design of the whole as distinct from the design of components or subsystems. The *synergistic* characteristic of the systems approach is all-important. Organizational and information systems are designed to achieve *synergism*—the simultaneous action of separate but interrelated parts producing a total effect greater than the sum of the effects taken independently. The results obtained by a team or a "system" of eleven football players are greater than those achieved by eleven individual players performing without integrated effort. The analogy for a business organization is clear.

In the past, business organizations lost much of their effectiveness by failing to relate the parts or functions (subsystems) to each other and to the whole. The sales function was sometimes performed without adequate regard for the manufacturing function; production control was not coordinated with financial or personnel planning; and the classic management information system was concerned largely with the production of ex post facto information for financial statements, not with forward-looking management decision making.

This focus on separate functions and failure to interrelate the parts into a unified whole can be attributed to a variety of causes, primarily the narrow view of the specialist (i.e., engineer, accountant, inventory clerk) who cannot or will not relate his specialty or his "box" on the organization chart to the remainder of the organization. Other causes are improper organization, poor planning, or dominating specialist managers. Focus on the design of the whole as distinct from the design of components and subsystems—a fundamental premise of the systems approach—is illustrated in Figure 1.3. The heavy solid line indicates the authority relationships and hierarchical structure of the classical organization; concern is with formal authority relationships and the chain of command rather than with the interrelationship of the parts. The dotted lines show the same organizational structure with the parts joined in a system by means of information flow and the systems approach to organization and management.

We should not conclude from Fig. 1.3 that the distinction between the "classical" and "systems" approaches is clear and absolute. Indeed, the classical approach has always provided for the routine exchange of information across the chain of command. Copies of sales orders have gone to the credit, production scheduling, shipping, and accounts receivable departments. Budgets have looked to the future and have included the separate parts of the organization. However, these devices, while providing some coordination, did not provide the close coupling of departments, the subordination of departmental goals to total organizational goals, and cost/benefit trade-offs among departments to optimize total business performance.

The systems approach has been described by Thome and Willard thus:

> The Systems Approach is an orderly way of appraising a human need of a complex nature, in a let's-stand-back-and-look-at-this-situation-from-all-its-angles frame of mind, asking oneself: How many distinguishable elements are there in this seeming problem? What cause-and-effect relationships exist among these elements? What functions need to be performed in each case? What trade-offs may be required among resources once they are defined?[2]

Because the systems approach focuses on the design of the whole, it deals with relationships before perfecting components. To illustrate this point, consider the Saturday Nite Disco. In the old, component, approach, the management sought to:

---

[2]P. G. Thome and R. G. Willard, "The Systems Approach, A Useful Concept of Planning," *Aerospace Management* (General Electric Company), Fall/Winter 1966, p. 25.

1. Optimize the bandstand and dance floor operation

2. Optimize the bar area operation

3. Optimize the seating and serving area.

By this approach, the customer might have good service at the bar but have to leave his or her drink to walk through the seating area to the dance floor fifty

Figure 1.3 The classical and systems approach to organization and information flow

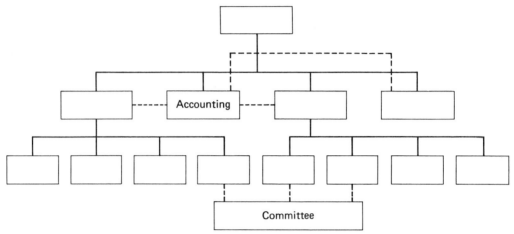

a. Classical authority approach to managing

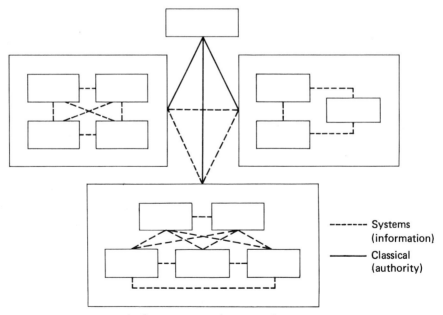

b. Systems approach to managing

------- Systems (information)

——— Classical (authority)

feet away. Alternatively, the seating area might be large and comfortable, but the adjacent dance floor small and the band playing loudly right next to the tables.

In the systems approach, the disco stated its objectives first. This was to maximize profits by providing the best balance of bar service, table service, and dancing area. Thus, the dance floor was placed centrally, with seating and bar forming the perimeter. The dance floor was made to correspond in size to the capacity of patrons at the bar and in the seated area. The bar and seated areas were balanced to provide the most satisfaction in terms of the higher revenues provided by bar customers. Thus, on *peak* nights, some customer dissatisfaction could be expected, but the higher bar revenues would be attained without long-term loss of customers.

INFORMATION

Information is a sign or set of signs which predispose a person to action. It is distinguished from data, because data are not a stimulus to action but merely a string of characters or uninterpreted patterns. For example, symbols (data) stored in a file cabinet or computer base represent data. A computer printout which a manager reads but whose significance cannot be interpreted because the figures are unorganized represents data. On the other hand, an organized analysis of sales or a graphical trend line of costs will affect the behavior of the manager and therefore is information.

Management decision making, a step taken which leads to action, is based upon information. Uncertainty about the future and lack of knowledge about the current situation cause the manager to seek information. Information may therefore be further defined as organized data which reduce uncertainty in decision making.

The rapidly changing environment and the increasing size and complexity of managed systems have increased the managers' needs for information. The cost of poor decisions has become exorbitant. The premium for really good strategic decisions in turn has become enormous. There is clearly a necessity for a good system to supply managers with timely, appropriate, and concise information in all types of organizations.

THE MANAGEMENT INFORMATION SYSTEM

The system which monitors and retrieves data from the environment, which captures data from transactions and operations within the firm, and which filters, organizes, and selects data and presents them as information to managers is called the management information system (MIS). Managers have always sought and utilized information. In the past, they have been forced to rely on miscellaneous—haphazard—sources. They processed the information on a personal basis, so that different managers operated on different perceptions about their environment.

Three changes are now occurring in progressive companies:

1. *Management* has become system-oriented and more sophisticated in management techniques.
2. *Information* is planned for and made available to managers as needed.
3. A *system* of information ties planning and control by managers to operational systems of implementation.

The combined result of these concepts is the management information system (MIS). The purpose of an MIS is to raise the process of managing from the level of piecemeal spotty information, intuitive guesswork, and isolated problem solving to the level of systems insights, systems information, sophisticated data processing, and systems problem solving. Managers have always had "sources" of information; the MIS provides a *system* of information. It thus is a powerful method for aiding managers in solving problems and making decisions. Figure 1.4 displays *the basic meaning of an MIS*.

As shown in Figure 1.4, the MIS is related to three components: managers, operating systems, and information. The system which captures both internal and external data and converts them to information for management decision making is the MIS. While all workers make decisions, managers' decisions are concerned with planning for, directing, and controlling work groups. Individual workers in the systems block of Figure 1.4 make decisions for directing their own work rather than the work of others. In addition, managers make decisions on longer-term and broader-scale issues than do the individual machine operators, clerks, technicians, professionals, and staff consultants.

The MIS not only provides information to assist managers in making decisions, but it also may be designed to *provide decisions* for repetitive classes of problems. The MIS, by providing a common set of data and information available to all managers, integrates the management of the company. Thus the company as a whole may be truly operated as a *system*, with all elements working toward common objectives.

Figure 1.4 Basic meaning of an MIS

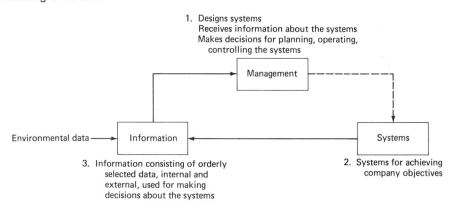

The beginning of a system for providing management with information for planning and control of the total business was the historical accounting system. This originated with the concept of double entry bookkeeping published by Luca Pacioli, a Venetian professor of mathematics, in 1494. Three threads of historical development have intertwined to bring about the modern MIS. These are the development of accounting theory, the development of management theory, and the introduction of the electronic computer. Management information system development was extremely slow until the twentieth century. With the advent of the high-speed, high-storage-capacity electronic computers at midcentury, the development and application of MIS concepts soared. Figure 1.5 indicates the growth of MIS theory in terms of the three contributing factors.

An Example of an MIS

The Ralston Purina Company produces foods for people and for pets. The entire marketing, planning, and budgeting process at the Consumer Products Group of Ralston Purina takes place each year in the spring and summer. This group developed an MIS that processes raw *data* into reports containing meaningful *information*. With this information, managers at the division level and group level find out how different promotional budgets and product recipes will affect profits and cash flow.

Inputs to the MIS consist of data on proposed new products and sales, which go into the brand accrual models shown in Figure 1.6.

The output of the brand accrual models consists of the monthly sales volume for each product and brand for the year ahead. Also costs and dollar sales are computed by the mathematical formulas of the model when it is stored in the computer. Next the computer consolidates the data for each brand into a projected earnings statement for product managers to evaluate.

The data on all the brands in a single division are combined, and selected information is prepared in the form of reports for the division manager.

Finally, the assumptions and consequences developed by all the division managers are brought together for the Consumer Products Group manager.

OPERATING INFORMATION SYSTEMS

For our purposes, the company is the total system. This total system is composed of subsystems designed to carry out the activities leading to company objectives. For example, in a manufacturing company we find a production subsystem. This in turn is composed of subsystems such as production control and quality control. Similarly, in a bank we may find the commercial loan subsystem or the credit card system. These subsystems all have two parts: the physical handling of materials and the processing of information. The processing of information is called an operating information system. Without the operating information system to tie together the people and machines, there could be no operating system.

Let us illustrate how operations are connected in a simple version of an order processing system. The purpose of the order processing system is to accept

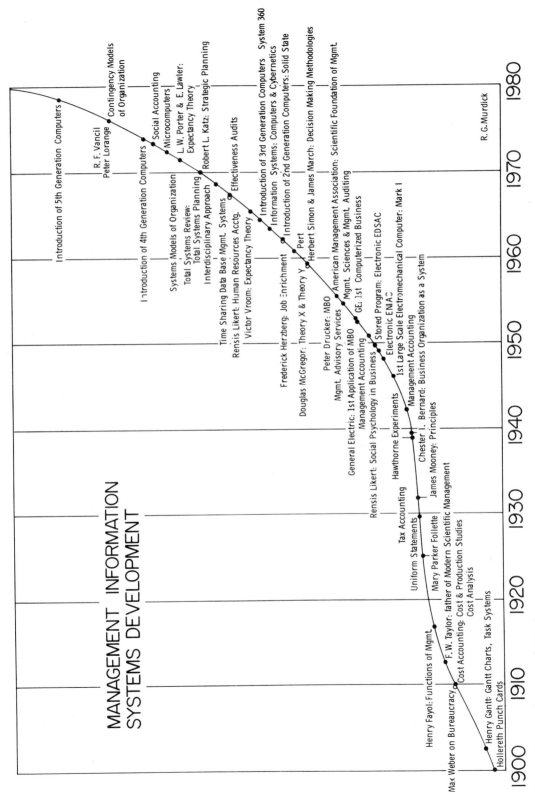

MANAGEMENT INFORMATION SYSTEMS DEVELOPMENT

Introduction of 5th Generation Computers

R. F. Vancil
Peter Lorange — Contingency Models of Organization

Introduction of 4th Generation Computers

Social Accounting
Microcomputers
L. W. Porter & E. Lawler: Expectancy Theory

Robert L. Katz: Strategic Planning

Systems Models of Organization
Total Systems Review:
Total Systems Planning
Interdisciplinary Approach

Effectiveness Audits

Time Sharing Data Base Mgmt. Systems
Rensis Likert: Human Resources Acctg.

Victor Vroom: Expectancy Theory

Introduction of 3rd Generation Computers   System 360
Information Systems: Computers & Cybernetics

Introduction of 2nd Generation Computers: Solid State

Frederick Herzberg: Job Enrichment

Pert
Herbert Simon & James March: Decision Making Methodologies

Douglas McGregor: Theory X & Theory Y

Peter Drucker: MBO
Mgmt. Advisory Services

American Management Association: Scientific Foundation of Mgmt.
Mgmt. Sciences & Mgmt. Auditing
GE: 1st Computerized Business

General Electric: 1st Application of MBO
Management Accounting

Stored Program: Electronic EDSAC

Electronic ENIAC
1st Large Scale Electromechanical Computer: Mark I

Rensis Likert: Social Psychology in Business

Hawthorne Experiments

Chester I. Bernard: Business Organization as a System

Tax Accounting

Management Accounting

Uniform Statements

James Mooney: Principles

Mary Parker Follette

Henry Fayol: Functions of Mgmt.

F. W. Taylor: father of Modern Scientific Management
Cost Accounting: Cost & Production Studies
Cost Analysis

Max Weber on Bureaucracy

Henry Gantt: Gantt Charts, Task Systems
Hollereth Punch Cards

R. G. Murdick

1900   1910   1920   1930   1940   1950   1960   1970   1980

Figure 1.5 Development of MIS theory

14

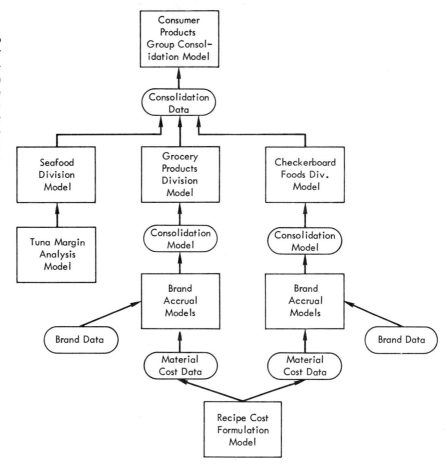

Figure 1.6 Consumer products on-line decision system for the Ralston Purina Company (courtesy of the Ralston Purina Company)

orders from customers (usually through sales people) and to arrange to ship and bill promptly, accurately, and completely. Figure 1.7 shows how this works. Information is fed into each operation and information is produced as an output of each operation, as shown in Table 1.3.

RELATIONSHIP OF THE MIS TO OPERATING INFORMATION SYSTEMS

The operating systems carry out individual operations and transactions required for the day-to-day conduct of business. There are literally thousands of such transactions daily in even medium-size companies. Yet management must somehow be aware of what is going on. The operating information systems must be so designed that they capture and store needed data to be converted into information useful to managers. The MIS employs this bank of data as a basis for preparing summary reports and "trouble" reports for management. Thus the MIS is connected to every operating information system but does not monitor every detailed transaction. The MIS is for *managers*. This concept is further amplified by Figure 1.8. Here we see operating systems interacting with the data bank to supply internal data. These internal data as well as external data are

15

Table 1.3 Information inputs/outputs to operations

Operation	Information Input	Information Output
1. Collect orders from sales people and customers and put on standard forms.	Order forms, telegrams, purchase orders, phone calls	Customers' orders on standard forms
2. Extend and compute prices with discounts. Edit orders for completeness. Segregate items in inventory from those that must be manufactured.	Prices Discounts allowed Customer name and address Items available in inventory	Units to be made and shipped Amount customer owes Production request
3. Prepare and mail invoices	Prices; discounts allowed Number and kind of units available to be shipped to customers within 30 days Customer's address	Invoice to customer Invoice copies to required departments in the company

processed by the computer and staff specialists to convert them into the kinds of reports needed by managers.

THE PROCESS OF MIS DEVELOPMENT

The study of MIS covers two important subjects: (1) the theory or conceptual foundation of MIS, (2) the action-oriented, normative procedures for the design of the MIS. This chapter and this book as a whole treat these two subjects. Table 1.4 outlines the steps in MIS development. These steps will be elaborated in later chapters.

Figure 1.7 Order processing and information flow

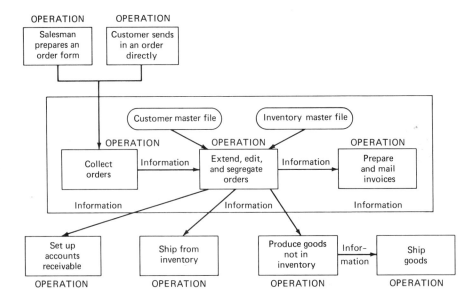

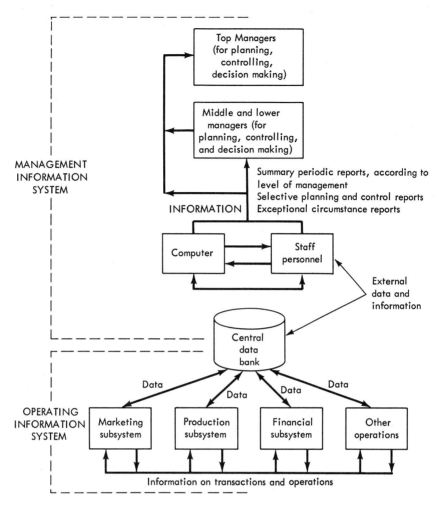

Figure 1.8
MIS related to operating information systems

MANAGEMENT
INFORMATION
SYSTEM

Top Managers
(for planning,
controlling,
decision making)

Middle and lower
managers (for
planning, controlling,
and decision making)

Summary periodic reports, according to
level of management
Selective planning and control reports
Exceptional circumstance reports

INFORMATION

Computer

Staff
personnel

External
data and
information

Central
data
bank

Data   Data   Data   Data

OPERATING
INFORMATION
SYSTEM

Marketing
subsystem

Production
subsystem

Financial
subsystem

Other
operations

Information on transactions and operations

Table 1.4 Steps in MIS development

Step	Examples
1. Find out the *information needs* of all managers.	Study the position description for the marketing manager. This manager says that some of his/her needs are for monthly information about sales by product and area for the company and for competitors.
2. Write down the *objectives* of the MIS based upon the needs of all managers, the costs, and the anticipated benefits.	One objective will be to supply managers with productivity analyses at the end of each month. Another objective will be to make financial and cost reports available within three days after the end of each month.
3. Prepare a *plan* and *proposal* for the design of the MIS including schedule and estimated cost.	A revised financial and new marketing MIS will be completed in preliminary form by May 17, 1980. The estimated cost is $57,500.

(continued on next page)

Table 1.4 (Cont'd.)

Step	Examples
4. Prepare a preliminary, *conceptual* design of the MIS.	A table listing each manager, his/her responsibilities, his/her information needs, and source of such information. An outline of files and records. General computer configuration.
5. Prepare the *detailed* design of all aspects of the MIS.	Specific report received by each manager. The customer-record file. A flow chart of the environmental scanning system. Computer programs. Hardware architecture. (Obviously, the detailed design of the MIS is a very lengthy document.)
6. Put the new MIS into operation. Prior testing may be desirable to see that all parts work together. Imagine the problems that could arise in a company if the old system were abandoned and a computer program in the new system did not work.	Replace a small part of the old system with the new system and check out the new system.
7. Monitor and maintain the new system. That is, needed changes in procedures or the structure of the data files must be made to meet changing inputs and changing management needs.	The company changes its inventory accounting from FIFO to LIFO. This requires a change in procedure, computer program, and management reports. The company reorganizes product line responsibilities so that each division manager is responsible for a new mix of products.

MIS ORGANIZATION WITHIN THE COMPANY

Although managers and many specialists in the functional areas participate in the design of the MIS, the responsibility for the design must be assigned to the MIS manager. Having this important responsibility, the MIS manager must be given high enough status to command the attention of managers at all levels. Since the MIS activities are companywide and often strategic in scope and time, the MIS manager should be close to top management.

Placement of the MIS Organization

In practice, the manager of MIS generally reports to a vice president of administrative services or senior vice president for corporate planning and control. In many companies a vice president of MIS may report directly to the president. One variant of this arrangement is found at Northwest Industries, Inc. Here a small staff organization under Jay P. Thomas, Vice President—Management Information Services, provides advice and consultation to the operating divisions of the company [Figure 1.9(a)].

In another arrangement, all MIS activities are centralized at the corporate level. The MIS manager is on the same level as the top line officers, as shown in Fig. 1.9(b). In the case of a functionally organized company such as Levitz Furniture Corp., the VP of MIS reports to the president along with the VP's of operations, marketing, and personnel, the controller, the treasurer, and the secretary.

In some companies the MIS manager reports to the controller, the VP of finance, or the data processing manager. These are very poor arrangements, because MIS will be dominated by the bias of the particular organization it is in. The MIS perspective is companywide and should not be subject to limitations imposed by a single functional specialty. Further, MIS is pushed one level lower in the organization by such an arrangement, so that its influence is weakened.

Figure 1.9 Placement of the MIS function within the company

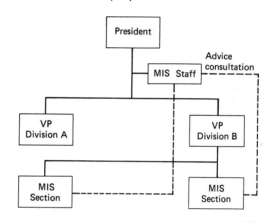

(a) Good influence with managers

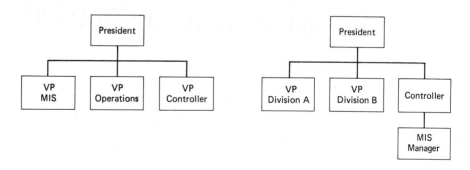

(b) Good access to managers   (c) No good

SYSTEMS SERVICES

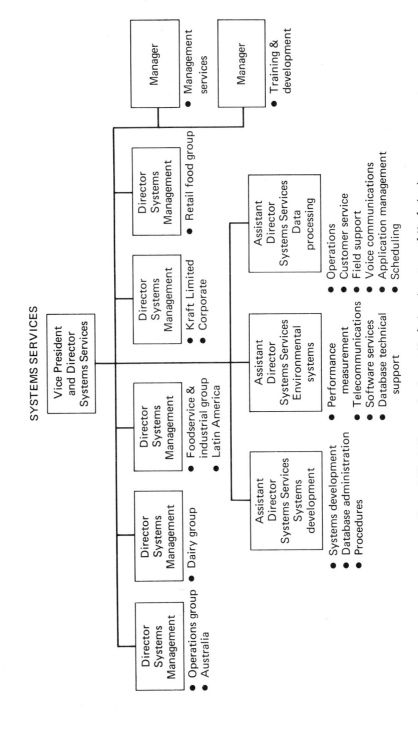

Figure 1.10 MIS organization at Kraft, Inc. (courtesy of Kraft, Inc.)

Vice President and Director Systems Services

Director Systems Management
- Operations group
- Australia

Director Systems Management
- Dairy group

Director Systems Management
- Foodservice & industrial group
- Latin America

Director Systems Management
- Kraft Limited
- Corporate

Director Systems Management
- Retail food group

Manager
- Management services

Manager
- Training & development

Assistant Director Systems Services Systems development
- Systems development
- Database administration
- Procedures

Assistant Director Systems Services Environmental systems
- Performance measurement
- Telecommunications
- Software services
- Database technical support

Assistant Director Systems Services Data processing
- Operations
- Customer service
- Field support
- Voice communications
- Application management
- Scheduling

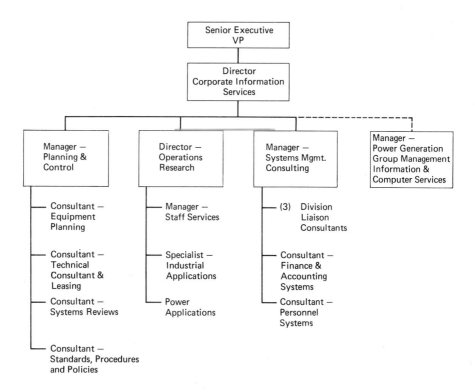

Figure 1.11 Management information services at the Babcock and Wilcox Company (courtesy of Babcock and Wilcox Company, a wholly owned subsidiary of J. Ray McDermott & Co., Inc.)

Organization Within the MIS Function

For a major first-time MIS effort, a company steering committee consisting of the MIS manager, the sales manager, the production manager, the finance manager, and the engineering manager may guide the systems effort. A special project team composed of representatives from each of the functional areas plus the technical systems people carry out the design effort with heavy managerial involvement. Once the first MIS has been installed, there must be an organization that monitors it, keeps it running smoothly, and redesigns it at times.

The permanent MIS organization usually includes systems analysts (designers), computer and data communications specialists, and, sometimes, management scientists. The last develop mathematical relationships for processing raw data into useful information such as sales forecasts, inventory reorder levels, and capital expenditure evaluations.

Three examples of the MIS organization in actual companies, Kraftco, Babcock and Wilcox, and the Continental Group, are shown in Figures 1.10, 1.11, and 1.12. Note that in Kraftco, systems development and data processing are at the same level of the organization but brought together under the Director—Systems Services.

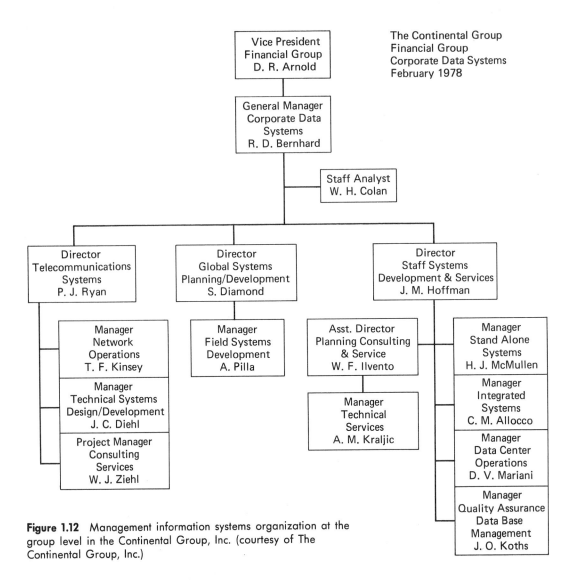

Figure 1.12 Management information systems organization at the group level in the Continental Group, Inc. (courtesy of The Continental Group, Inc.)

PREPARATION FOR BECOMING AN MIS MANAGER

The position of MIS manager or VP—Management Information Systems is a very responsible one. The salaries may range from $30,000 to around $100,000 per year. While many career paths may lead to the position of MIS manager, the two basic routes are (1) through line management transfer and (2) by working up through the MIS organization. In the first case, an unusually broad, analytical, manager in finance, production, or marketing may be transferred or promoted to head the MIS organization. In the second case, a young person may enter the MIS organization near the bottom, Figure 1.13, and work up through one of the many paths possible.

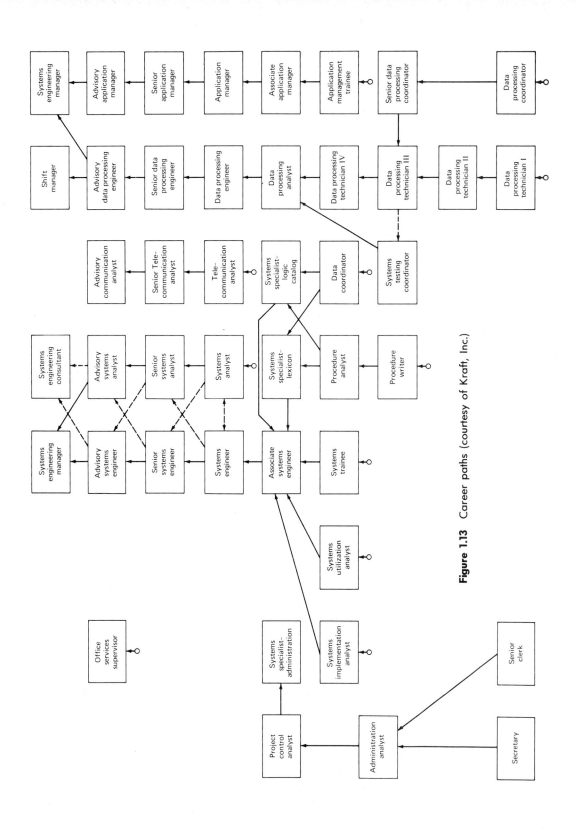

Figure 1.13 Career paths (courtesy of Kraft, Inc.)

Table 1.5
Skills needed
by the MIS
manager

Skill	Ranked by MIS Executives	Ranked by General Management Executives
Knowledge of total company and its objectives	2	1
Ability to communicate effectively, orally and in writing	6	2
Relationships with heads of other business departments that utilize the system's functions	1	3
Ability to manage projects	4	4
Relationships with top management	3	5
Relationships with subordinates	5	6
Knowledge of information processing and data communications technology	8	7
Ability to design and judge the design of systems	6	8

The best preparation that a person may have consists of three forms of experience: (1) formal college education in MIS subject matter, (2) on-the-job systems design experience, and (3) line management experience at the middle management level. Education and experience alone are not enough for the ideal manager. Skills in dealing with people are extremely important. Table 1.5 shows the results of a survey in which both line managers and MIS managers rate the importance of skills needed by MIS managers.

Today, all business graduates should have a good idea of the nature of management of information. A survey of the New Orleans chapter of Data Processing Management Association and the Association for Systems Management rated information knowledge and skills as very important.[3] Table 1.6 summarizes the ratings.

[3]Barry Render and Ralph M. Stair, Jr., "Future Managers Need DP Training," *Infosystems,* October 1975, p. 42.

Table 1.6
Importance of
information
knowledge and
skills to the
business
graduate

AREA	PERCENT RESPONDING		
	Very Important	Somewhat Important	Not Important
Programming language and software	34%	62%	4%
Operation of DP equipment	19	53	28
Management information systems	68	32	0
Organization and operation of DP department	47	45	8
Computerized business applications	79	19	2
Systems analysis and design	64	34	2

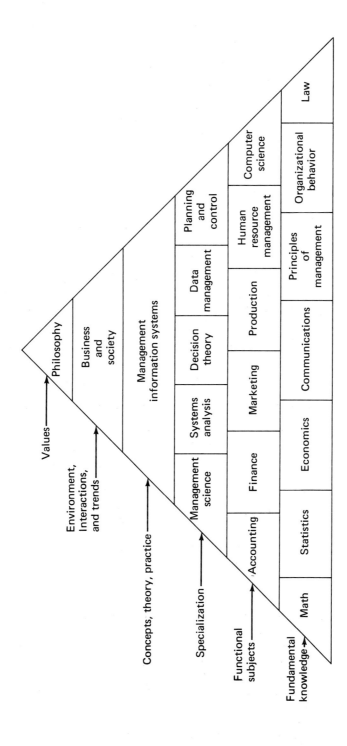

Figure 1.14 College subject areas for the prospective MIS manager

Figure 1.15
Position guide:
responsibilities
of the MIS
manager

THE BABCOCK & WILCOX COMPANY
(CMIS)
Corporate Management Information Services
(Division or Subsidiary)
POSITION DESCRIPTION

Title: Manager, Systems Management Consulting *Level:*
Depart-   *FLSA Status:* Exempt
ment: Systems Management Consulting (SMC)   *Date:*   April 6, 1978
Section: *Location:*   New York, N.Y.
Reports To: Director, Corporate MIS

Major Responsibilities:

Exercises CMIS functional responsibility for all division MIS&DP organizations as delegated by Director, Corporate MIS. This includes supervising approval of development
of major systems in the divisions and expenditure for computer-related equipment and
software; supervising consulting with division MIS&DP organizations regarding development of MIS&DP plans and support strategies; supervising assistance to divisions in
developing specific systems solutions to meet division operating objectives; and coordinating inter-divisional cooperation and interfaces where advantageous for division
and company operations. Responsible for requirements analysis and development of
company headquarters and companywide systems applications.

Representative Responsibilities:

Maintains an awareness of computer application plans throughout the company. Coordinates inter-divisional plans and activities to utilize total company expertise/experience
and minimize redundant efforts.

Supervises the review and approval of division requests: (1) to develop major systems
within divisions, and (2) to acquire computers and related equipment, procure software
and outside MIS&DP services. Recommends final approval or disapproval to Director,
Corporate MIS.

Supervises the company's internal consulting regarding advice and counsel to the
divisions in the use of MIS&DP resources, systems and management methods and
systems strategies. Emphasis is on helping divisions realize more effective use of their
MIS&DP resources and in utilizing these resources to meet operating objectives.

Supervises systems project managers in performing systems studies and development
for company headquarters or companywide systems as directed by executive management.

Keeps abreast of state-of-the-art in computer processing techniques and systems applications. Translates these advancements into practical applications, techniques and
programs for use within the company.

Responds to special requests for systems or data processing consulting, special studies, or special assignments.

Approved _____

Date _____

(Courtesy of Babcock & Wilcox Company, a wholly owned subsidiary of J. Ray McDermott & Co., Inc.)

Based on various studies, curricula, and management opinions, we propose a number of key courses in a program for a person wishing to make a career in the management of information. The general hierarchical representation of these courses is given in Figure 1.14 on page 25. The starting courses represent general skills and knowledge. At the next level are business subjects. Following these courses is specialization in MIS areas. Finally, the student needs a broadening course or set of courses in order to relate the business system to the environment. An increasingly important role of the MIS is to monitor and interpret the environment of the business. The student also needs an understanding of value systems in order to understand the basis for management decision making. In the final analysis, all decisions incorporate values in assumptions or objectives.

Finally, what do you do when you reach the top of the MIS organization? The position guide shown in Figure 1.15 suggests responsibilities of the MIS manager.

SUMMARY   More U.S. workers are employed in information processing jobs than in agriculture, industry, or services. The development of information processing has grown with the rapid development of large systems since World War II.

A system is a set of elements or components related by structure or communication, working toward achieving common goals. Practical systems interact with the environment, receiving inputs from it and transmitting outputs to it.

System elements in organizations are coordinated by the communication of information. Information consists of signs meaningful to the receiver. Data are not information, because data are not an immediate stimulus to action.

The systems approach to managing is derived from systems concepts and information flow. The systems approach focuses on the organization as a whole and the interrelationship of parts.

A management information system is a system whose elements are people, equipment, procedures, and information designed to supply timely, reliable, accurate, and concise information to managers to assist them in decision making. In some cases the MIS actually makes "programmed" or routine decisions for managers.

Operating information systems consist of systems designed to achieve the many objectives of the firm. The flow of information which ties together the components (people and equipment) of an operating system is an operating information system. The data (transactions and operations) captured by these information systems are the source of information for the MIS. If the operating information systems do not capture certain data, then the MIS has no way of monitoring, processing, or converting such data for management planning and control.

The basic steps in the development of an MIS consist of:

1. Determining information needs
2. Setting MIS objectives
3. Developing an MIS plan and a proposal for management approval
4. Preparing a general conceptual design
5. Expanding upon the conceptual design to prepare a detailed design

6. Implementing the design by converting it to the working MIS, checking it out, and operating it

7. Monitoring the MIS in operation and making changes to correct, update, or expand it.

The MIS is a companywide service. Therefore, the manager of MIS should report to top-level management. The MIS group should not be reporting to the manager of a specialized function.

Careers in MIS are very attractive from a financial, intellectual, and practical viewpoint. Many positions offer great challenge for people who like to solve complex, unstructured problems and who are capable of teamwork.

QUESTIONS AND PROBLEMS

1. To describe a system, we must identify or define the items in the left column below. For a manufacturing company, match the elements in the left column with the descriptions.

_____ Objectives	a. President, VP, functional managers
_____ Elements	b. Money, materials, information
_____ Process performed	c. Produce desired products at a profit and achieve worker satisfactions
_____ Structure	d. People, facilities, equipment, money, materials
_____ Inputs	e. Products, information, services
_____ Outputs	f. Convert parts and raw materials to finished goods, provide services and information

2. Set up a table with headings across the top as shown in Table 1.2. Complete the table for the following systems:

a. A marketing system within a manufacturing company
b. The order processing system of Fig. 1.7
c. A quality control system in a manufacturing company
d. A restaurant
e. One of the "Big Eight" accounting firms

3. Classify the following as data or management information by entering a checkmark in the proper column.

Item	Data	Management Information
a. Computer printout of 3572 customers' names	_____	_____
b. Accounting journal entry	_____	_____
c. Profit trend over the past years for the firm	_____	_____
d. Obsolete policy guide	_____	_____
e. A 500-page report on material handling	_____	_____
f. A COBOL program	_____	_____

Item	Data	Management Information
g. Report on a shortage of metal used in production	_____	_____
h. Variance report on productivity	_____	_____
i. Union contract	_____	_____

4. MIS relates three concepts: _____ _____ _____

5. The United States became an information society in about the year

   a. 1960   b. 1950   c. 1975   _____

6. The MIS function should report to

   a. Controller   b. DP manager   c. Administrative VP
   d. Production manager   _____

7. By placing the appropriate letters opposite the numbers below, indicate the sequence of basic MIS steps:

		Sequence of steps
a. Put the MIS into operation		1. _____
b. Prepare the detailed design		2. _____
c. Determine information needs of managers		3. _____
d. Prepare a plan and proposal		4. _____
e. Write down the objectives of the MIS		5. _____
f. Monitor and maintain the MIS		6. _____
g. Prepare a conceptual design of the MIS		7. _____

8. Using the headings of Table 1.1, identify one change and its impact on the MIS for the following factors:

Factor	Changes	Impact on MIS
Economic		
Technological		
Social		
Political-legal		
Management		

9. Discuss whether the systems approach is applied to

   a. Management of the Postal Service
   b. Management of an airline company
   c. Design of homes
   d. Management of a university
   e. Design of an automobile

10. What impact would (1) the technological revolution, (2) the information explosion, (3) modern management techniques have on the need for information by the following organizations?

    a. Bank   c. University
    b. Hospital   d. Chain of department stores

11. Develop a more complete and rigorous definition of "system" by considering the role of information, structure, objectives, inputs, outputs, materials, energy, facilities, money, people, equipment, procedures, and operations. Consider empirical systems and abstract systems such as philosophy.

12. Figure 1.5, illustrating the development of MIS theory, brings together three threads of vital importance to MIS. Identify these and discuss their role and importance to the modern MIS.

13. The president of one of the nation's largest food manufacturing companies declared, "Our information system gives us the edge we need over our competitors." Describe ways in which an information system could provide a competitive edge for this company.

14. Develop the concept of the systems approach to solving problems of the real world or to design of a product or service.

15. It has been said that power resides with the person who possesses and controls information.

    a. Discuss the power relationships among levels of management in the 1950s and now in a company with a sophisticated MIS.
    b. Discuss how decision making may change as MIS puts more complete information in the hands of all managers in a company.

16. Distinguish between accounting systems before the advent of MIS and today in terms of management decision making.

17. Why has accounting occupied a special role in MIS in the past, as well as the present?

18. Discuss the accountant's function with regard to:

    a. Data processing
    b. Data collection
    c. Reporting
    d. Controlling the accuracy and validity of information

19. Phil Mallon has decided to establish a nursery for landscaping on a five-acre plot. He will employ about five people and purchase two trucks. He will need to have various flowers, shrubs, and trees available throughout the year.

    a. Describe the business as a system.
    b. List information needs of Phil Mallon.
    c. List about five transactions that must be recorded.
    d. Describe two reports that Mallon would require. Specify the number of times per year or month that he will need these reports.

SELECTED REFERENCES

ALTER, STEVEN L., "How Effective Managers Use Information Systems," *Harvard Business Review,* November–December 1976.

BENTON, LEWIS, ed., *Management for the Future.* New York: McGraw-Hill, 1978.

BRANDON, DICK H., ARNOLD D. PALLEY, and A. MICHAEL O'REILLY, *Data Processing Management: Methods and Standards.* New York: Macmillan, 1975, chap. 9, "Personnel Requirements."

DAVIS, GORDON B., *Management Information Systems.* New York: McGraw-Hill, 1974.

HANOLD, TERRANCE, "An Executive View of MIS," *Datamation,* November 1972.

HERNANDEZ, WILLIAM H., "Is the Controller an Endangered Species?" *Management Accounting,* August 1978.

IDEMA, THOMAS H., "Systems Career Path Development," *Journal of Systems Management,* April 1978.

JOHNSON, RICHARD A., FREMONT E. KAST, and JAMES E. ROSENZWEIG *The Theory and Management of Systems,* 3d ed. New York: McGraw-Hill, 1973.

KATCH, DAVID, "What Is a Management Information System?" *Infosystems,* June 1978.

MURDICK, ROBERT G., and JOEL E. ROSS, *MIS in Action.* St. Paul, Minn.: West Publishing Company, 1975.

PAYNE, EUGENE E., JOEL E. ROSS, and ROBERT G. MURDICK, *The Scope of Management Information Systems.* Atlanta: American Institute of Industrial Engineers, 1975.

ROSS, JOEL E., *Modern Management and Information Systems.* Reston, Va.: Reston, 1976.

STODDARD, F. DON, "The Accountant's Role in Management," *Management Accounting,* July 1978.

VOICH, DAN, JR., HOMER J. MOTTICE, and WILLIAM A. SCHRODE, *Information Systems for Operations and Management.* Cincinnati: South-Western Publishing Co., 1975.

chapter 2

Management
in the
Organization System

- Managers and their Responsibilities
- Classical Model of Managing/Organizing

- Behavioral Theory
- Motivation
- Leadership

- The Systems View of Organization and Management

- Application of Organizational Behavior to MIS

PURPOSE: To develop the concepts and theory underlying managerial and organizational functioning in a systems framework.

Future managers will reach solutions to problems on the basis of analytical and integrating skills and information systems rather than the exercise of formal power and intuition.

In order to develop the concepts of MIS, we must first study the nature of organizations and managements. We need to understand what the functions and responsibilities of managers are, how managers relate to other organizational elements, and how information networks may be structured in organizations.

To deal with these concepts, four main topics are covered here: (1) management tasks, (2) classical management principles, (3) organizational behavior including motivation and leadership, and (4) a systems view of organization. A single chapter can barely outline the general nature of such broad and diverse material, so that the selected references at the end of the chapter are of special importance to the serious student.

MANAGERS AND THEIR RESPONSIBILITIES

When a number of people join together to work toward mutual objectives, their effectiveness is tremendously increased if their work is coordinated. In business, the type of worker who performs such a function is called a manager. Thus, managers may be identified as those persons who have responsibility for an objective that requires the efforts of other people.

In the Egyptian Dynasty IV, over 4000 years ago, the divine kings of three generations constructed the great pyramid of Khufu. This structure on the west bank of the Nile river covers more than 12 acres. Ten years were required to build the pyramid, and 100,000 laborers worked more than 20 years to complete the tomb. Each side extended 756 feet, and the pyramid rose majestically to 451 feet. When we stand in awe of this gigantic engineering and management feat, we become aware that management is as old as civilization.

Today, for several reasons, the managing of projects and organizations has become complex. First, a given organization is affected by many other organizations and institutions. That is, companies depend upon actions of government, competitors, vendors, the general public, and customers. A second source of complications is the use of power, sophisticated equipment, and complex technological systems of production. A third is the development of new management techniques and of large, educated, work forces. The management of 380,000 employees of General Electric Company dispersed throughout the world and performing a myriad of diverse activities is far more demanding than the management of architects, engineers, and laborers working at one location on a single pyramid.

A manager, in theory, should not be performing operations or technical duties such as engineering, accounting, and selling. Rather, he or she should be performing *managerial* functions:

1. Defining organizational objectives
2. Planning
3. Organizing resources
4. Initiating organizational action
5. Controlling
6. Communicating organizational activities.

Unfortunately, there is no simple formula or set of principles that tells us what to do to be an effective manager. We can, however, bring together the contributions from history and research to help us define the characteristics of organizations and the functions of managers from a systems view. We will then be able to relate MIS concepts and design to managers and organizations in future chapters.

CLASSICAL MODEL OF MANAGING / ORGANIZING

The basic tenets attributed to classical theorists such as Henri Fayol,[1] Frederick W. Taylor,[2] L. Gulick and Lyndall Urwick,[3] and J. D. Mooney[4] are:

[1]Henri Fayol, *Administration Industrielle et Generale* (1916) (Translated, London: Sir Isaac Pitman & Sons, Ltd., 1949).

[2]Frederick W. Taylor, *Scientific Management* (New York: Harper & Row, Pub., 1947).

[3]L. Gulick and Lyndall Urwick, eds., *Papers on the Science of Administration* (New York: Institute of Public Administration, 1937).

[4]J. D. Mooney and A. C. Riley, *The Principles of Organization* (New York: Harper & Row, Pub., 1943).

1. Clear lines of authority. Every individual should be related through a chain of command to the top manager (scalar chain).
2. Specialization of labor. Breaking work down into small tasks that are easily learned leads to greater productivity. The company can then be departmentalized on the basis of grouping of similar tasks.
3. Unity of command. No person should report to more than one manager or supervisor.
4. Span of control. The number of people reporting to a manager should be limited by the nature of the tasks. Many articles argued whether span should be broad or narrow and tried to establish an ideal number.
5. Clear separation of line and staff. The staff members (or managers) are to act as *advisors* to line managers and not to influence other organizational members directly.

Despite much criticism, changed environment, and a wealth of research, we find all of the above principles a matter of concern in today's organizations. It would be unfair to state that the early pioneers neglected the human side of management. It was a matter of first things first—the need to develop a usable framework for managing to satisfy the needs of the time. In addition, sophisticated techniques and human resources to conduct behavioral research were simply not available in those days.

BEHAVIORAL THEORY

Behavioral contributions to the theory of management were boosted by the Hawthorne experiments of 1927 to 1932 reported by Elton Mayo and F. J. Roethlisberger. This research indicated that employee attitudes could be more important to productivity than the technical and physical environment. The modification of classical tenets by means of a strong emphasis on needs of workers (human relations) produced the neo-classical theory of management.

Informal Organization

Behavioral research progressed from "human relations" concepts of communication, trust, and delegation of responsibility to modern organizational behavior research. A major factor in the behavior of people in organizations has been found to be the "informal organization."

Social organizations arise and persist because of man's need for interaction with other humans. Two or more people who share activities, sentiments, or interactions form a social system. People gather into groups to satisfy needs of affiliation, security, identity, and power. The term *group dynamics* was popularized by Kurt Lewin, a social psychologist, to designate the forces and behavior that occur within a group. The linking groups and subgroups of members of a business organization form the *informal organization*. "The informal organization is the total of member-initiated institutions existing without the sanction of formal authority."[5] The informal and the formal organizations modify, supplement, and reinforce or weaken each other.

Sociologists have identified six types of informal groups:

1. The *total organization* consists of all the many interlocking groups or subsystems in the entire organization.
2. *Large groups* form over some issue of internal politics. Typical of these groups might be production versus marketing factions, one aggressive young executive and his followers versus an old-line executive and his followers, or nonunion groups versus union groups.
3. *Primary cliques* form when workers are located together for work purposes or when employees have similar jobs and hence common interests. The workmen in a maintenance crew, the top executives who work together and dine together in the executive dining room, and the professional accountants dispersed throughout the company are examples of primary cliques.
4. *Cliques* include any small group that forms to gain some special power or social advantage.
5. *Friendship-kinship groups* form in many companies in which generation after generation of the same families become employees. Kinship groups form from relatives. Friendship groups form because of close social and neighborhood ties.
6. *Isolates* are the individuals who are loners and do not attach themselves to any group, or shift from group to group.

Informal groups are composed of people who share the same values. Acceptance in the group is achieved through acceptance by all people in the group, not by just an individual. Informal groups arise based upon physical location of members, similar occupations or interests, or special issues.

Informal organizations assume certain characteristics that are different from those of formal, structured organizations; these must be taken into account when managing in a climate of informal groups.

1. *Informal organizations* act as agents of *social control,* generating a culture that demands conformity from group members.
2. *Human interactions* are quite different from those in the formal organization, and different techniques of analysis are required.
3. *Status and communication* systems exist quite apart from the formal structure.
4. Informal organizations *resist change.*
5. The group has an *informal leader* who is not necessarily the formally appointed one.

[5]Albert H. Rubenstein and Chadwick J. Haberstroh, eds., *Some Theories of Organization* (Homewood, Ill.: The Dorsey Press, Inc., 1960), p. 63.

Because organizations are made up of people, not boxes on organization charts, managers and systems designers must not isolate themselves from the actual organizational dynamics. Management must utilize information about social groups in the design of systems and must acknowledge the realities of organization as indicated in Figure 2.1.

Figure 2.1
Organization
structure

Source: Reproduced from the Professional Systems Course, copyrighted by Leslie H. Matties. Published by Systemation, Inc., P.O. Box 2555, Littleton, Colorado 80161

Group Standards and Norms

The informal organization exerts strong pressures for conformity through social control methods. Implicitly, a new member in a social group accepts the norms and standards of the group, which are communicated to him by example, anecdote, expressions of attitude, and other behavior. Pressure for conformity of attitude and of action are brought to bear upon group initiates.

Group norms may restrict work output or increase it. If management wishes to change group norms, it must find people who are accepted by the group or who are influential within the group and change their attitudes. Obviously, this is not easy.

Within an informal group, each member achieves identity through his role, a role determined by the behavior expectations of others in the group. Informal leadership is assumed by those who exert more influence on the group than other individuals do, since role and status within the organization are closely related. Further on, we will discuss these topics in terms of power and accommodation.

Communication

One of the major functions of the informal organization is to provide for communication outside of the lengthy, rigid, formal chain of responsibility. Employees communicate with each other both laterally and vertically as necessary to get their jobs done, but this occurs according to the informal contacts they have in different parts of the organization. Such communication makes possible much more rapid response to job and situation requirements. The informal means for rapid spread of information or rumor throughout the organization is called the grapevine.

Communication also serves to relieve the monotony on boring, repetitive jobs. It may not be in the form of conversation only, but in behavior and role activities. Donald F. Roy describes how such communication and social interaction kept the four workers isolated in the clicking room from "going nuts" in his classic article, "Banana Time."[6]

Power and Authority

Social psychologists and political scientists have contributed further to our understanding of organizational behavior by their studies of power, authority, influence, conflict, and decision making. Power and authority are derived from both the formal and informal organizations in complex ways. In order to understand how these influences are related, we will discuss some basic concepts, admitting at the start that scholars disagree among themselves about the meaning of authority and power and their relationship to acceptance, responsibility, accountability, and control.

Authority may be considered, roughly, the "legitimate" right to command and to apply sanctions. Thus authority is derived from the formal organization. Authority represents the expression of a consensus of the group and hence acceptance by the individual who defers to that authority. Power is at the other end of the spectrum in that the person with power can satisfy his or her wants despite resistance from the person controlled. Power implies the capacity to exercise coercion or even force—the hangman's rope, the club, the threat of firing, of disgrace, or of economic ruin. To the extent that authority is permitted some degree of sanctions, it contains some elements of power. The limits of authority and power are the points at which people refuse to obey and willingly take the consequences.

There are a number of explanations concerning the source of authority. Some of the most commonly accepted are:

1. Institutional approach
2. Subordinate approach
3. Authority of the situation
4. Organizational relationship
5. Personal acceptance or consultative authority
6. Identification
7. Sanctions
8. Legal decree.

[6]Donald F. Roy, "Banana Time—Job Satisfaction and Informal Interaction," *Human Organizations,* 18 (1960), 158–68. Reprinted in a number of books of readings.

In the institutional theory, authority is derived from accepted cultural institutions—traditional, legal, or theological. Thus the concept of private ownership of property bestows upon the owners the authority to use the property as they see fit within general constraints imposed by society.

The subordinate acceptance school of thought states that a manager has authority to the degree that his subordinates accept his decisions. Authority thus flows from the bottom of the organization upward and is gained by the manager through his leadership and ability to win support from his subordinates.

The concept of the "authority of the situation" represents an attempt to integrate the goals of the organization with the goals of the individuals involved. Mary Parker Follett describes it thus:

> True authority springs from only the intrinsic competence, worthiness, and strength of one in a place of authority. To be called authority, it must be spontaneously and tacitly acquiesced to by the workers. Authority does not leap forth from the commands of those at the top simply because the organization charts say so. It arises out of "the law of the situation."

In application, the manager and his subordinate get together, assemble the facts of the situation, discuss alternate solutions to the problem at hand, and weigh the pros and cons. Through full discussion and mutual understanding, it is believed, one preferable course of action will be seen to be called for by the situation. The views of the manager (organization's goals) and of the subordinate (individual's goals) are thus integrated into a single course of action.

Authority is often considered to be based upon the organizational position or organizational relationships that have been established. Here the individual receives his authority by virtue of the authority of the position.

Personal acceptance or consultative authority arises because of recognition of the leader. Recognition may be due to the leader's popularity, his past achievements, his integrity, or his skill and knowledge. In an organization, such a man may not have any formal authority (authority by position), but his recommendations may carry such weight that he appears to have extensive authority. Max Weber's charisma classification of authority would fall under this heading. Charismatic legitimacy is based upon irrational faith in the values and goals of the leaders.

One view holds that authority is derived from group "belongingness." According to this view, people will accept decisions that have been agreed upon by the group to which they belong, thereby delegating authority to the group. People who are strongly associated with the group making the decision will more readily accept the authority of the group. Therefore, the society in which we live is a source of authority, and society may thus be defined as the most comprehensive group to which an individual feels he "belongs." At the other end of the scale is the *ad hoc* committee that a manager appoints to develop a recommendation or make a decision where there is likely to be considerable resistance to any recommendation or decision. The committee participants, by taking part in the decision making, identify themselves with this group and accept its authority.

Authority is often identified with possession of sanctions, the rewards or punishment that one person may mete out to another. In almost all types of organizations, those with authority possess some sanctions that they can apply, such as slowdowns in work, carelessness in treating the organization's property, or starting unfavorable rumors.

Authority by legal decree is commonly found in the government. The law grants authority so that enforcement of the statutes may be carried out.

Table 2.1 gives an excellent comparison of the technical, social, and power subsystems of the organization. Note how the technical subsystem reflects the classical theory concepts. Also note that the power subsystem appears to grow out of the social subsystem. Information supplied to managers should also be included as a source of power in the power subsystem.

Conflict and Cooperation

Conflict occurs within groups and between groups in both the formal and informal organization. Conflict is related to both power and cooperation: conflict brings shifts in power and is often resolved by power (influence); cooperation is often the end result of conflict.

Cooperation is a stronger need for individuals with greater needs for affiliation and stability. However, for those who covertly seek power, cooperation is necessitated by mutual goals.

In the past, conflict was often considered harmful and destructive of organizational goals. Modern administrative thought takes the view that there is much constructive potential in conflict. In business, this is achieved through "controlled competition" among individuals and groups.

Solutions of conflict, other than integration and cooperation, are: (1) victory/defeat, (2) compromise, (3) avoidance of the subject, and (4) deadlock with varying ultimate consequences. Because the design and implementation of new systems often face group pressures against change, the designer and manager should be aware of methods for handling constructively the conflict of organizational and informal group goals.

Decision Making

Completely objective rational decision making would require complete information about all possible alternative courses of actions and their outcomes. Herbert Simon, James G. March, R. M. Cyert, and others have pointed out that human information-processing ability and limits on information available put bounds upon the extent of rationality in decision making (bounded rationality). Bounded rationality explains decision making as (1) sequential consideration of alternatives, (2) heuristics to limit the alternatives considered, and (3) "satisficing."

Heuristics, the second characteristic of bounded rationality, refers to rules which reduce many alternatives to a few. For example, specifying a minimum and maximum size for a new office building eliminates many possibilities. *Satisficing* (satisfying and sufficient) is a search for the optimal solution that stops when some alternative meets specified minimum requirements.

Table 2.1
Technical, social, and power subsystems

Characteristics	Technical Subsystem	Social Subsystem	Power Subsystem
1. Origin	Deliberate employment and arrangement of men and capital to perform tasks required by formal objectives.	Arises spontaneously from social interactions and shared values of men placed in contact with each other.	Arises as people use the various sources of power to acquire things that are judged valuable by others and successfully implement decisions.
2. Processes	Decision, communication, and action.	Interaction, sentiments, and activity.	Politics, decision implementation, and maintenance of order.
3. Structure	Arrangement of jobs in relation to each other. Process and authority relations.	Differentiation based on expressions of sentiments of members for each other. Friendship relations.	Differentiation based on the number of behavior areas controlled.
4. Status	Man* holds status because of his ability to meet the job requirements. Status is same as job in importance in the technical structure.	Man holds status because of the sentiments of others in the system. For example, the leader is liked most in the group.	Man holds status because of degree of success attained in implementing his decisions.
5. Roles	Man plays role according to job requirements	Man plays role according to sentiments, beliefs, attitudes, and social mores.	Man plays opportunistic role.
6. Sources of authority and power	Directly related to the job and is delegated from those who have higher authority.	Informal authority is derived from those who are its subjects. Based on sentiments.	Official position, location, job importance, expertise, interest and tenure, personal characteristics, and coalitions.
7. Norms	Job descriptions, written policies, procedures, and rules.	Values and accepted norms of behavior. Unwritten tacit agreements.	Expediency. That behavior which sustains power. People who are objects of power follow orders of power holder to obtain desired values.

Note: The word "Man" in this table is used generically. We understand "Man" here to mean humans of both sexes.

Source: Rocco Carzo and John N. Yanouzas, **Formal Organization: A Systems Approach** (Homewood, Ill.: Richard D. Irwin, 1967), p. 240. © 1967 by Richard D. Irwin, Inc.

The explanation of why people behave as they do in organizational settings is a major concern of management. Managers would like to know how they can influence people to be both more productive and more satisfied on the job. In particular, the MIS manager is concerned with how to get individual and organizational support for the design and implementation of the MIS. The MIS itself must be designed so that people will be motivated to perform primary and related tasks.

There are numerous explanations of motivation in organizations, each with varying amounts of supporting and conflicting research evidence. We will describe briefly the three salient approaches. As we will show, the manager will carry out pretty much the same activities to modify the behavior of subordinates regardless of the underlying theory.

Needs Models

Cognitive approaches to motivation emphasize how and why people behave. They assume, generally, that people seek pleasure and avoid pain. In Figure 2.2 we note the relationship of needs to behavior.

A *need* is a tension produced within a person by a deprivation. Some condition entailing pleasure or some condition causing pain is presented by the environment. The person is alerted to things in the environment that will satisfy the resulting need, and he or she feels a desire to attain these things. In Fig. 2.2 the person desires to obtain food. This desire directs activity toward obtaining the food and eating it. After the food has been eaten, satisfaction (elimination of need) or reduction of need occurs.

Figure 2.2
Needs model
of motivation

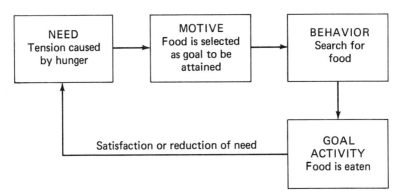

Abraham Maslow, a psychologist, proposed a hierarchy of needs. He felt people attempt to satisfy, in an ascending order, a sequence of needs starting from the physiological and continuing to higher-level acquired needs, as shown in Table 2.2. David C. McClelland and J. W. Atkinson, with support from their own and others' research, identified three basic motives: need for achievement, need for affiliation, and need for power.

Table 2.2 "Needs" in motivation theories	Maslow's Hierarchy[a]	McClelland and Atkinson[b]	Herzberg[c]
	Physiological needs:	Achievement need	Hygiene needs:
	Food	Affiliation need	Working conditions
	Water	Power need	Interpersonal relationships
	Rest		Salary
	Warmth		Supervisor's skill
	Sex		Company policy and admin-
	Safety needs:		istration
	Injury avoidance		Motivators:
	Long-term security		Recognition
	Social needs:		Achievement
	Affiliation with groups		Advancement
	Friendship		Responsibility
	Love		Nature of the work
	Ego needs:		Opportunity for growth
	Self-esteem		
	Strength		
	Power		
	Freedom		
	Status		
	Respect		
	Self-fullfilment needs:		
	Realizing one's full		
	potential		

[a]Abraham Maslow, **Motivation and Personality** (New York: Harper & Row, Pub., 1954).
[b]David C. McClelland, **The Achieving Society** (New York: Van Nostrand Reinhold, 1961), and J. W. Atkinson, **An Introduction to Motivation** (New York: Van Nostrand Reinhold, 1964).
[c]Frederick Herzberg, Bernard Mausner, and Barbara Blosh Snyderman, **Motivation to Work** (New York: John Wiley, 1959).

Frederick Herzberg developed a two-factor theory of dominant needs (Table 2.2):

1. *Hygiene factors*—dissatisfiers or maintenance factors in the work
2. *Motivators*—factors which lead to satisfaction and greater productivity.

Table 2.2 lists the needs defined by the foregoing three theories so that the reader may make comparisons. There are many other possible needs that in some particular person and situation will produce goal-directed behavior.

Expectancy Model

Victor Vroom proposed that motivational force depends upon the desirability of the goal (valence) and the "expectancy" that each action will lead to each outcome.[7] Further research by L. W. Porter and E. E. Lawler yielded the model shown in Figure 2.3. In this model, the individual perceives the outcome of efforts connected to desired rewards through the link of performance. The

[7]Victor H. Vroom, *Work and Motivation* (New York: John Wiley, 1964).

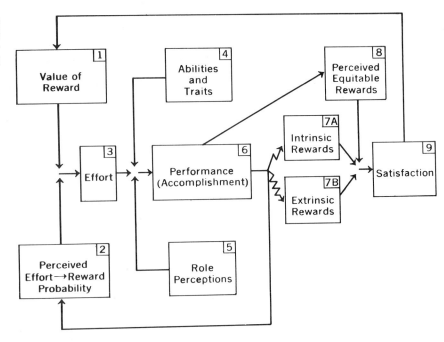

Figure 2.3
The revised
Porter-Lawler
model

Source: Lyman Porter and Edward Lawler, III, **Managerial Attitudes and Performance** (Homewood, Ill.: Richard D. Irwin, 1968), p. 165. © 1968 by Richard D. Irwin, Inc.

expectancy of rewards resulting from performance may be high or low. Three types of rewards lead to satisfaction. Intrinsic rewards come from the nature of the work itself. Extrinsic rewards are rewards given out by management. Perceived equity in rewards is also heavily affected by management.

The degree to which perceived effort matches reward probability influences the individual's effort (behavior), as does the total value of the reward (valence) to the individual. Because so much influence on effort is determined by the individual's perceptions, the manager may heavily influence behavior by good communication and leadership.

Operant Conditioning

Operant (behavior) conditioning is the process of modifying behavior by changing the consequences. B. F. Skinner, the leading advocate, says that people are not autonomous but are simply organisms responding to their environment. The psychological concepts of what goes on in the mind are irrelevant to a scientific theory of human behavior, since there is no scientific way of measuring and testing mental processes. Behavior is determined by its consequences. Therefore, when desired behavior occurs, the manager should reinforce it (as soon as possible) with rewards ranging from praise to promotion or bonuses. Undesirable behavior should not lead to discipline or punishment except as a last resort.

Managers, Motivation, and MIS

Regardless of which theory we subscribe to, the managers' function will be the same. That is, once organizational objectives have been established, the managers will modify each worker's environment to reinforce desired behavior through a system of intrinsic and extrinsic rewards.

In the development of the MIS, management must consider whether the task-information assignment to each worker is suitable. In other words, we cannot design an MIS that is technically excellent and then present it to the organization to be implemented. We must work with the people in the organization so that the MIS duties and outputs will result in motivating the organizational members involved to achieve company objectives.

LEADERSHIP

An important factor in the worker's environment is the leadership exerted by his or her manager. Leadership is influencing others to work enthusiastically toward established objectives. Leaders provide the focus of action for the other members of the group. A good leader will induce his or her group to go "all out."

Leadership is a part of managing. It is concerned with interpersonal relationships between the manager and his or her subordinates. Managing is broader in scope and includes all processes—mental, physical, and interpersonal—which the manager applies to achieve organizational goals.

Formal and Informal Leaders

Managers in organizations have official positions which allow them to officially reward and penalize subordinates. Because of their authority over members of the group they are called *formal* leaders. A formal leader is held accountable for the behavior of the group.

Informal leaders arise within informal groups. The informal leader influences other members of the group by means of personal attributes such as expert knowledge, personality, charisma, persuasiveness, identification with the members of the informal group, or courage to speak out. Informal leaders are not held accountable for mistakes or misjudgments, and they remain leaders as long as their groups accept them.

It is apparent that informal leaders may do much to resist successful development of the MIS. For this reason, management must identify such leaders and win them over early.

Identification of Leaders

Early attempts to identify leaders focused on traits common to all leaders. Generally, the idea that leaders could be identified by traits has been rejected. There is some evidence, however, that successful managers are more intelligent, better educated, more original, more fluent, and highly motivated. Some recent research suggests also that while there is no universal set of traits for leaders, a certain set of traits may lead to increased leadership effectiveness in a particular situation.

Behavioral Theory of Leadership

In the late 1940s, researchers began to abandon the trait theory and to examine leadership in terms of relationships between the leader and followers. From the late 1940s to early 1960s several large research programs were conducted. Studies at Ohio State University, as well as later studies elsewhere, identified two orthogonal dimensions of leader behavior: consideration and initiating structure. Closely allied terms of other researchers are people-orientation and task- or production-orientation. *Consideration* refers to leader behavior indicating friendship, mutual trust, respect, and warmth. *Initiating structure* means that the leader organizes and defines the relationships between himself or herself and the other members of the organization.

Further studies showed that different combinations of consideration and initiating structure were more effective in different situations. That is, high consideration together with high initiating structure was not always the best combination.

Situational Theory

When it was discovered that the situation (type of worker, urgency, type of work, and so on) reacted with the consideration and initiating structure combination, situational theory became the focus of research. F. E. Fiedler developed his contingency theory of leadership. Fiedler states that leaders derive their satisfactions from interpersonal relations and work accomplishment. He developed the *least preferred coworker (LPC)* scoring means for rating leaders. Task-oriented (low-LPC) leaders will be most effective in high favorable or highly unfavorable situations. Relations-oriented (high-LPC) leaders will be most effective in moderately favorable situations.

In summary, various situational approaches to leadership theory say that the leader's success depends upon (1) the leader's traits, (2) the nature of the subordinates, (3) the nature of the tasks, and (4) the nature of the situation. It was once believed that managers had to be either task-oriented (for high production) *or* people-oriented (to give high worker satisfaction). It is now believed that good managers can be task- *and* people-oriented leaders who are highly effective in both respects.

With development of management information systems, it is likely that analytical managers who are able to adapt well will be able to handle a wider variety of situations and tasks.

Normative Leadership Implications

The abandonment of the trait theory meant that we could not select future leaders on the basis of trait tests. Since current leadership theory suggests that

Figure 2.4
The managerial grid

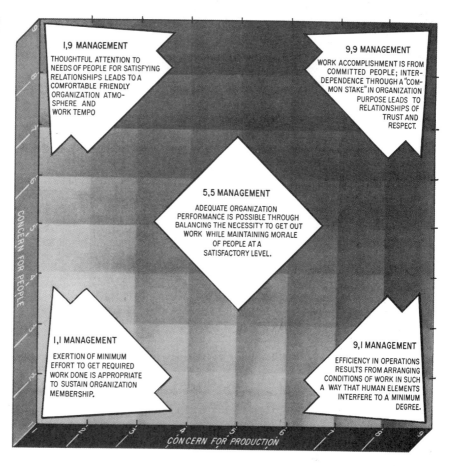

effective leadership is related to the specific situation, and since situations are constantly changing, present forms of leadership training may be largely useless.

For a normative approach we need to analyze the situation and modify the manager's behavior, if we can. Robert R. Blake and Jane S. Mouton developed the *managerial grid* (Figure 2.4) to analyze and evaluate managers' styles in terms of concern for people and concern for production. This analysis is used as part of a program for developing managers' sensitivity to interpersonal relations.

W. J. Reddin extended the concept of the managerial grid by adding a dimension for effectiveness.[8] Finally, Jeffrey C. Barrow proposed the three dimensions for measuring leadership effectiveness shown in Figure 2.5.

[8]W. J. Reddin, *Managerial Effectiveness* (New York: McGraw-Hill, 1970).

Figure 2.5
Leadership
effectiveness
framework.

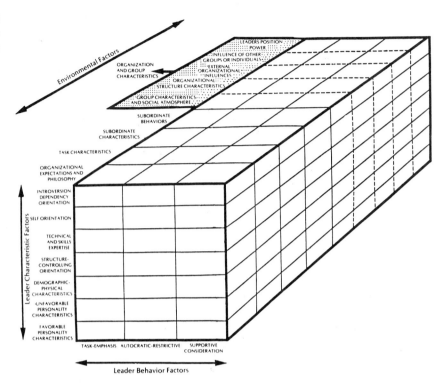

Leader Behavior Factors

Source: Jeffrey C. Barrow, "The Variables of Leadership: a Review and Conceptual Framework," **The Academy of Management Review,** April, 1977, p. 242.

THE SYSTEMS VIEW OF ORGANIZATION AND MANAGEMENT

In the systems approach to design or analysis, we must identify the system by answering the following questions:

1. What are the system's objectives?
2. What are the elements and subsystems?
3. What are the integrating links or processes?
4. What is the structure?

The Organization as a System

Organizational objectives are determined by management when it sets the basic mission, the strategic objectives, and the operating objectives. No general statements can be made about these other than that objectives relate to the survival of the company. We will cover structure for organizations in Chapter 4, because structure and operations are so closely related.

Let us look now at the elements and subsystems of the organization relevant to MIS.

Managers

Managers occupy a unique position in an organization. They are essentially the people responsible for its perpetuation. They also carry out integrating activities. Managers are "change agents" because they are responsible for the organization's direction, missions, and objectives. They bring about changes in direction to adapt the organization to the environment. Management is also the principal control system in the organization. It establishes methods and procedures for making sure that the organization pursues its general objectives efficiently.

The functions of managers themselves are integrated to form the subsystem of activities shown in Figure 2.6.

Individual Contributors

There are several classes of individual contributors, performing a wide variety of tasks. Professional workers are those who are well educated and perform mental tasks of considerable variety and complexity. Technicians are skilled specialists such as engineering assistants, laboratory workers, or computer programmers. Data processors are clerical personnel who deal with transactions or transmission of data. Finally, operating personnel perform work that is primarily physical, such as machine operation, monitoring, and maintenance.

Physical Elements

Although some writers refer to tasks, we list the *physical elements related to tasks* as elements of the organization. Tasks are concepts or processes, whereas we wish to identify concrete elements. Physical elements such as buildings and equipment support the objectives of the organization. The nature of office and plant layout affects the functioning of the organization. People interact with much modern sophisticated equipment, such as computers or production machinery. Thus, by our definition, the human elements and physical elements are both part of the organizational system.

Subsystems

The important *subsystems* are the formal organizations and the informal organizations comprising individuals, goals, and relationships as discussed earlier. Figure 2.7 diagrams the subsystems, elements, and the integrating processes. Let us look now at the integrating processes.

Information Systems

Formal information systems are established by management. These consist of prescribed flows, official reports, and physical means for communicating. Informal systems consist of the company grapevine, casual or unplanned contacts among workers, and routine or ritualistic communication within and among informal organizational groups.

Figure 2.6 The systems view of the managerial process. © R.G. Murdick 1974.

	SET OBJECTIVES	PLAN	ORGANIZE RESOURCES	INITIATE	CONTROL	COMMUNICATE
SET OBJECTIVES	**D**	Set objectives for the company	Match objectives to available resources	Develop objectives at the level of management	Develop key objectives for control	Set objectives for communication at each level of the organization
PLAN	Plan around basic objectives	**E**	Plan the company organization and allocation of resources	Plan the sequence and schedule of the organization of resources	Plan for standards and procedures for control	Plan procedures for communications throughout the organization
ORGANIZE RESOURCES	Organize the hierarchy of objectives	Organize for planning	**C**	Organize the system for action	Organize a control system	Organize resources to provide for communication
INITIATE	Take action to establish objectives	Initiate the planning process	Start the organization of human and other resources for conduct of the business	**I**	Start the control of objectives, plans, action, standards, and communication	Keep communications flowing freely at all stages and for all processes
CONTROL	Control the setting of objectives to suit the nature of the organization	Control the setting of plans to ensure plans are properly prepared on time	Control the mix of resources to achieve a balance	Control the process of directing action	**D**	Control the communication of standards / Control the communication performance for corrective action
COMMUNICATE	Communicate objectives to attain a unified sense of direction	Communicate plans in the proper detail to each person in the company	Communicate through organization charts, manuals, and reports: the distribution of resources	Communicate to initiate action at the proper time	Communicate standards of performance / Communicate performance to responsible individuals for corrective action	**E**

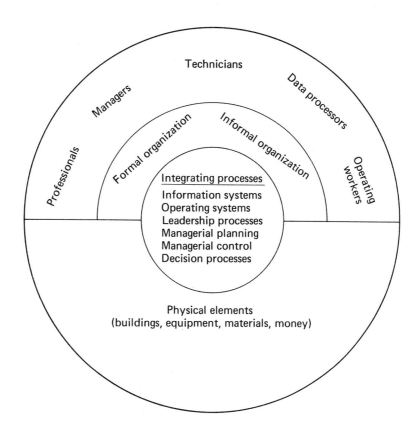

Figure 2.7 Elements and integrating processes of the organization

Operating Systems

Operating systems consist of patterns of work flow, tasks, and procedures established either formally or informally to achieve some set of related objectives. Examples are (a) the order processing system, (b) the purchasing system, and (c) the production control system.

Leadership Processes

We have discussed leadership in more detail earlier. Basically, leadership consists of activities which produce motivation and organizational unity in working for objectives.

Managerial Planning

The preparation of written plans for the organization as a whole and for each managed component requires integration of all activities. The dissemination of plans, and of task objectives and schedules contained in plans, contributes to coordinated activity by all personnel.

Managerial Control

Managerial control is the monitoring and measuring of performance of the organization for comparison with preestablished plans and standards. It also means taking corrective action if performance deviates too far from plans and standards. It thus integrates activities by keeping them all within the bounds established.

Decision Processes

Managerial decision making must take account of all major impacts of alternative courses of action. Decisions should be made in the interests of the organization as a whole, not just those of the component immediately concerned. (Unfortunately, not many decisions are made on this systems basis in real life!)

SUMMARY OF MAJOR CONTRIBUTORS TO ORGANIZATION / MANAGEMENT CONCEPTS

Although some significant and lasting contributions were made by earlier pioneers, modern organization/management concepts have evolved mainly since 1900. In the present century, theory has progressed from individual speculation to research-based conclusions. People from many disciplines have shaped the current framework. A limited listing of pioneers is shown in Table 2.3. Table 2.4 indicates the general area of contribution for some of the better-known scholars and practitioners.

APPLICATION OF ORGANIZATIONAL BEHAVIOR TO MIS

The best *technically* designed MIS is doomed to failure unless it is modified for human behavior. The attempt to develop and introduce an MIS is apt to meet with resistance, because it usually means changes in tasks, organization structure, and roles of managers and individual contributors. As a result, the behavior of present personnel will need to be modified, or new managers with different kinds of skills may have to be brought into the organization.

Resistance to Changes Entailed by the MIS

People do not resist change automatically. We see people making changes every day to make their work easier or more pleasant. Managers constantly work for changes such as improved methods, more responsibilities for themselves, and bigger jobs. The changes entailed by introduction of an MIS may be classed as *technological* and *social,* and often they do meet with resistance.

Usually management focuses on the technological change through training programs. Both management and the training programs overlook the breaking up of informal groups, the challenge to group norms, and the responses of informal leaders.

Table 2.3 Development of management thought

	Management Process	Behavioral Theory	Management Technology	Organization Theory
1885			Henry C. Metcalf Henry R. Towne	
1910		Max Weber	Frederick W. Taylor	
	Henry Fayol		Frank & Lillian Gilbreth	
1920				
	Oliver Sheldon	Mary P. Follett		
1930		G. Elton Mayo		
			Harry A. Hopf	Chester Barnard
1940		Fritz Roethlisberger		
	Lyndall F. Urwick James D. Mooney	Rensis Likert B. F. Skinner		
1950		George Homans		Ernest Dale
	Peter Drucker	Abraham Maslow Chris Argyris		Joan Woodward

1960	Harold Koontz	Douglas McGregor
		Frederick Herzberg
		R. R. Blake &
		  J. S. Mouton
		Victor H. Vroom
		L. W. Porter &
		  E. E. Lawler
			Robert McNamara &
			Charles T. Hitch
				Systems and Contingency Models
				
				P. R. Lawrence &
				  J. W. Lorsch
				James D. Thompson

1970	William H. Newman			Fremont E. Kast &
				  James E. Rosenzweig
				Leonard R. Sayles &
				  Margaret K. Chandler
				
				Henry L. Tosi &
				  W. Clay Hamner
				James R. Galbraith

Table 2.4
Contributors to
management
thought

Approx. Time	Individual	A Major Management Contribution
1900s	Henry L. Gantt	Humanistic approach to labor. Task and bonus system. Gantt Chart for planning and control
1900s	Max Weber	Defined principles of bureaucracy. Applied social psychology to organization theory
1910s	Henri Fayol	First attempt at a complete theory of management. Developed a list of the functions of management
1910s	Frederick W. Taylor	Scientific management. Need for cooperation between labor and management. Methods studies
1920s	Mary Parker Follette	Concept of integrating viewpoints in group problem solving
1930s	Elton Mayo, Fritz J. Roethlisberger	Social forces rather than economic forces provide basic motivation in industry. Originated the human relations approach to managing
1930s	Chester I. Barnard	Logical analysis of organization structure and application of sociological concepts to managing
1930s	James D. Mooney	Outlined universal principles of organizations
1940s 1960s	Rensis Likert	Applied psychology and social psychology in research on organizational theory. Originated the concept of human resource accounting
1950s	Peter Drucker	Purpose of business is to serve customers. Management by objectives. Management as a practice
1950s	Douglas McGregor	Theory X and Theory Y. Assumption that people wish to do their best will lead to greater motivation
1950s 1960s	Herbert A. Simon & James G. March	Placed emphasis on human behavior in decision making
1960s	Frederick Herzberg	Two-factor theory of motivation. Some factors in the environment do not motivate but are necessary. Self-fulfillment factors lead to motivation
1960s	Victor Vroom	Expectancy theory of motivation
1970s	L. W. Porter & E. E. Lawlor	Expectancy theory of motivation including equity theory
1970s	Robert L. Katz	Strategic planning concepts and process
1970s	R. F. Vancil, Peter Lorange	Strategic planning processes

Here are some common reasons that people resist change:

1. Threat to status: a supervisor is converted to a technician in the new system.
2. Threat to ego: job as bookkeeper is eliminated.
3. Economic threat: automation of job reduces worker to lower-paid monitoring position or takes away his job entirely.
4. Job complexity: supervisor is required to hire and supervise new types of technical specialists.

5. Insecurity: top manager is deprived of "personal" information and made dependent on computer output.

6. Superior-subordinate relationships are changed as a new information system produces new balances of power.

7. Clearer job definitions and better information require higher degrees of analytical skills.

8. Time pressures increase: the MIS requires coordinated action and provides the information to achieve it.

9. Interpersonal relationships are changed: both working relationships and informal groups are altered.

How to Avoid Resistance to Change

The way to avoid resistance to change is to communicate in advance with all employees affected and enlist their participation in bringing change about. In the long run, the company should create a climate for change. It does this by constantly rewarding new useful ideas put into action. The company also may assign "change agents" to some groups to stimulate change. These may be good managers, innovative specialists, or highly successful informal leaders who are rotated to different job assignments. Special training in MIS may be given to such people. Finally, the organization and MIS may be modified to fit the needs of employees.

Overcoming Resistance to Change

Avoiding resistance to change is obviously more desirable than *overcoming* resistance. However, systems are often installed too quickly to allow completing programs to avoid resistance. In such cases, special efforts must be made to identify resistance and reduce it before the MIS is made to appear unworkable.

The formula for overcoming resistance is simple to state. First, identify targets for behavior modification, such as key individuals, formal organization components, and informal groups. Second, increase the present forces for change and reduce the forces opposing change. Figure 2.8 shows this latter process.

Figure 2.8
Overcoming
resistance
to MIS
implementation

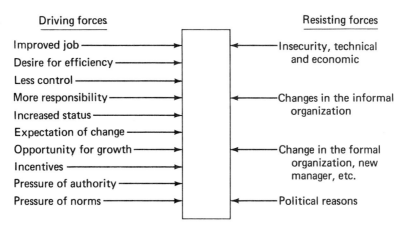

Driving forces	Resisting forces
Improved job	Insecurity, technical and economic
Desire for efficiency	
Less control	
More responsibility	Changes in the informal organization
Increased status	
Expectation of change	
Opportunity for growth	Change in the formal organization, new manager, etc.
Incentives	
Pressure of authority	
Pressure of norms	Political reasons

SUMMARY   The development of MIS is founded on the role and functions of management in the organizational system. Managers (1) define objectives, (2) plan, (3) organize resources, (4) initiate action, (5) control, and (6) provide for organizational communications. Classical principles of organization and management still provide a basis for many modern hierarchical organizations:

1. Clear lines of authority
2. Specialization of labor
3. Unity of command
4. Span of control
5. Clear separation of line and staff.

Behavioral concepts have provided us with further insights as to how organizations actually function and respond to inputs. Behavioral concepts that have modified the purely classical model include:

1. Informal organization
2. Group norms
3. Communication
4. Power and authority
5. Conflict and cooperation
6. Decision processes.

Concepts of power and authority are of particular interest, because managers must influence organizational behavior to achieve organizational objectives.

Managers influence organizational behavior by applying knowledge of both leadership and motivation. Three classes of motivation theory are (1) needs theory, (2) operant conditioning, and (3) expectancy models; the latter have the widest current acceptance.

Leadership, the reverse side of the coin from motivation, has been intensively researched. The situational or contingency approach has the greatest currency. According to this theory, effective leadership depends upon the leadership style, the nature of the followers, and the task situation. Diagnostic tools are needed for analysis of these factors. Blake and Mouton have provided a tested approach, while Reddin and also Barrow have proposed others.

Rather than viewing organization and management from technical (classical) and behavioral perspectives, we may take a systems viewpoint. We identify the elements, the integrating relationships, their functions, and total system goals. We examine inputs, outputs, and ways to modify the system to provide desired outputs. This does not mean that we reject the earlier concepts, but rather, we relate them to the systems perspective. The advantage of the systems perspective is that it provides an integrating framework for understanding what is really a system—the business organization. The MIS provides managers with the means to plan and control the functioning of this system.

1. Companies are dependent upon the actions of external agencies. Match the following:

   a. Ecology demonstration in front of company headquarters   (1) Government   _____

   b. Purchase of foreign automobiles   (2) Competitors   _____

   c. ICC, CAB, OSHA   (3) Vendors   _____

   d. Late deliveries   (4) Public   _____

   e. Intensive TV sales promotion   (5) Customers   _____

2. For the basic tenets of classical management, match the following:

   a. Breaking work down into small similar tasks   (1) Scalar chain   _____

   b. Specialists act as advisors   (2) Specialization of labor   _____

   c. Clear lines of authority from bottom to top of the organization   (3) Unity of command _____

   d. Each person reports to only one manager

   e. The number of people who report to a manager   (4) Span of control   _____

       (5) Separation of line and staff   _____

3. Six types of informal groups are:

   (1)   (4)

   (2)   (5)

   (3)   (6)

4. Match the following:

   a. Mary Parker Follett   (1) Group norm   _____

   b. Satisficing   (2) Authority   _____

   c. Owner-manager   (3) Consultative authority   _____

   d. Rules-of-thumb to reduce alternatives

   e. Legitimate right to command   (4) Authority of the situation   _____

   f. Ability to hurt someone   (5) Bounded rationality   _____

   g. Rate setting by the informal group

   h. "Grapevine"   (6) Conflict   _____

   i. MIS systems expert   (7) Communication   _____

   j. Controlled competition   (8) Heuristics   _____

       (9) Power   _____

       (10) Institutional authority   _____

5. Complete the diagram by analogy to Fig. 2.2.

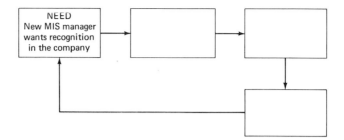

6. Complete the following table by listing "needs."

Maslow	McClelland/Atkinson	Herzberg
1	1	1
2	2	2
3	3	
4		
5		

7. The "optimal image of man for systems theory" is B. F. Skinner's hypothesis of operant conditioning as determining behavior. Show how this model works by completing the figure below. Specify inputs, outputs, etc.

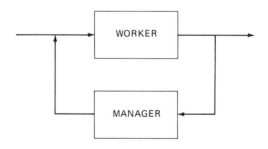

8. Recommend a leadership style for the MIS manager in the situations on the following page by putting the appropriate code in the blanks:

a. Autocratic
b. Custodial
c. Supportive
d. Collegial

Leader's Traits	Nature of Subordinates	Task	Situation	Leadership Style
(1) Hard-driving, task-oriented	Ambitious, experienced in MIS projects	Design a strategic planning MIS	Old-line conservative company	_____
(2) Quiet, analytical, systematic	Ambitious, hard-driving	Evaluate the MIS which has been in place for five years	Many costly foul-ups are occurring. Company is losing money	_____
(3) Easy-going, people-oriented	Some ambitious, some deadwood	Overhaul the financial information system	New, demanding top management team	_____
(4) Intellectual, analytical, both task- and people-oriented	Highly educated and experienced, creative	Redesign the entire MIS	Progressive, profitable, high-technology company	_____
(5) Not-too-bright, experienced, but somewhat obsolete	Young, highly educated, ambitious competent	Develop a new MIS based upon the latest computer technology	Much manual work, high office costs, poor records. Need for audit and control	_____
(6) Competent, task-oriented	Young, inexperienced	Develop a marketing information system	Aggressive competition is cutting the firm's market share	_____

9. For a bank viewed as a system complete the following:

   Inputs: _____ _____ _____

   Elements: _____ _____ _____

   Integrating process: _____ _____ _____

   _____ _____ _____

10. Distinguish between the classical and the modern theories of organization.

11. a. Is management an art, science, profession or practice, or a combination?
    b. On the basis of your answer, show the application of your concept to the MIS manager.

12. Peter Drucker stated that management is the most important activity in our society. Discuss.

13. How can an MIS reduce conflict in an organization?

14. Draw a diagram which shows the communication role of accounting with respect to the other functional areas.

15. Compare expectance theory of motivation with Herzberg's theory.

16. Describe 10 examples of possible resistance to change when an MIS is being introduced.

17. The Star Bank is organized with the operations manager, installment loan manager, commercial loan manager, marketing manager, and personnel manager reporting to the president. The president decides to reorganize to include data processing and an MIS manager.

    a. Draw an organization chart for the bank.
    b. Prepare a simple position description for the MIS manager.

18. The manager—manufacturing for the Triad Pump Co., Mr. Ives, at age 60 was appointed manager of the new MIS function. Triad had over $100 million in annual sales, over 2300 customer accounts, and employed over 3000 people. Mr. Ives knew all operations of the company well. He and two assistants analyzed information needs by examining position guides, developed a system for processing data, and with the approval of top management, purchased computer hardware.

    When the new MIS was being installed, transfers to new jobs were made and new forms and procedures were revealed. Workers grew confused and angry. Within a week, conditions were chaotic despite Mr. Ives' carefully planned installation.

    a. What did Mr. Ives fail to do?
    b. How should Mr. Ives proceed at this point?

19. Read the following excerpt and then answer the questions below.

> *Volvo: Taking the Monotony Out of the Production Line.* Volvo has only one auto-assembly plant, at Kalmar, that was built without a conventional assembly line, an arrangement that eliminates most of the noise, monotony, and pressure for haste that autoworkers find repugnant. Though the plant cost 10 percent more than one with a conventional assembly line, workers' morale improved, and there is less costly personnel turnover and absenteeism than at other Volvo factories. Most important, many of the Kalmar innovations have been successfully applied at older plants.
>
> On the mile-long assembly line at Volvo's largest auto plant outside Gothenburg, workers have the option of organizing into groups of six or more and working as teams. For example, one group of women injects a sealing compound in all seams and installs sound-dampening insulation. They rotate the group's fifteen functions so that no one gets a sore back from having to reach for long periods into remote crevices or grows too bored performing the same job.
>
> Since the line creeps ahead at an almost imperceptible pace, the teams generally finish their assigned work before the next batch of cars reaches them. During the waiting time, they are free to go for coffee or read a book.
>
> Women, who make up 18 percent of Volvo's work force in Sweden, can handle auto-assembly jobs easily because Pehr Gyllenhammar, Volvo's inno-

vative boss, has redesigned the work so that no special physical strength is required. When the bottom of the auto is being worked on, for example, the car is tipped sideways for easy accessibility. The tools have also been redesigned to operate so quietly that the workers can converse in normal conversational tones or listen to pop songs on their cassette players. Volvo's system is disdained by most other automakers as inapplicable to mass production of low-priced vehicles, but Gyllenhammar argues: "We have to change the organization so the job itself provides more for the individual." And he vows: "We will never build another production line as long as I am in command at Volvo."[9]

a. Discuss cliques and informal leaders for the assembly process.
b. Discuss the development of possible norms and their influence on the assembly process.
c. Who would be apt to have the most authority, the informal leaders or the first-line manager? What is the source of authority of each?
d. In terms of the Porter-Lawler model, describe how management, by changing the nature of the work situation, hopes that workers will be motivated to be more productive.
e. Explain how operant conditioning could be applied in this new arrangement to gain greater productivity.
f. What type of leadership do you believe would be most effective in the production plant and why?
g. What type of leadership is the CEO of Volvo, Pehr Gyllenhammar, exercising? Read the complete article that is referenced and then state what, in your opinion, is the basis for his authority.

SELECTED REFERENCES

ARGYRIS, CHRIS, "Management Information Systems: The Challenge of Rationality and Emotionality," *Management Science,* February 1971.

BARROW, JEFFREY C., "The Variables of Leadership: A Review and Conceptual Framework," *Academy of Management Review,* April 1977.

BEHLING, ORLANDO, and CHESTER SCHRIESHEIM, *Organizational Behavior: Theory, Research and Application.* Boston: Allyn & Bacon, 1976.

BURNS, JAMES MACGREGOR, *Leadership.* New York: Harper & Row, Pub., 1978.

CHANDLER, ALFRED D., JR., *The Visible Hand: The Managerial Revolution in American Business.* Cambridge, Mass.: Belknap Press of Harvard University Press, 1977.

DRUCKER, PETER F., *Management: Tasks, Responsibilities, Practices.* New York: Harper & Row, Pub., 1974.

GALBRAITH, JAY R., *Organization Design.* Reading, Mass.: Addison-Wesley, 1977.

GRIMES, A. J., "Authority, Influence, and Social Control: A Theoretical Synthesis," *Academy of Management Review,* October 1978.

HARE, A. PAUL, *Handbook of Small Group Research.* New York: The Free Press, 1976.

HART, DAVID K., and WILLIAM G. SCOTT, "The Optimal Image of Man for Systems Theory," *Academy of Management Journal,* December 1972.

[9]David B. Tinnin, "Why Volvo Is Staking Its Future on Norway's Oil," *Fortune,* February 1979, p. 112, by permission.

KARMEL, BARBARA, "Leadership: A Challenge to Traditional Research Methods and Assumptions," *Academy of Management Review,* July 1978.

KAST, FREMONT E., and JAMES E. ROSENZWEIG, *Organization and Management: A Systems Approach.* New York: McGraw-Hill, 1970.

PERROW, CHARLES, "The Short and Glorious History of Organizational Theory," *Organizational Dynamics,* Summer 1973.

SCHRIESHEIM, CHESTER A., JAMES M. TOLLIVER, and ORLANDO C. BEHLING, "Leadership Theory: Some Implications for Managers," *MSC Business Topics,* Summer 1978.

STIEGLITZ, HAROLD, "On Concepts of Corporate Structure," *The Conference Board RECORD,* February 1974.

TOSI, HENRY L., and STEPHEN J. CARROLL, *Management: Contingencies, Structure, and Process.* Chicago: St. Clair Press, 1976.

VROOM, VICTOR H., and PHILIP W. YETTON, *Leadership and Decision-making.* Pittsburgh: University of Pittsburgh Press, 1973.

WREN, DANIEL A., *The Evolution of Management Thought,* 2d ed. New York: John Wiley, 1979.

ZALTMAN, GERALD, ROBERT DUNCAN, and JONNY HOLBEK, *Innovations and Organizations.* New York: John Wiley, 1973.

chapter 3

The Manager's View of Computer Systems

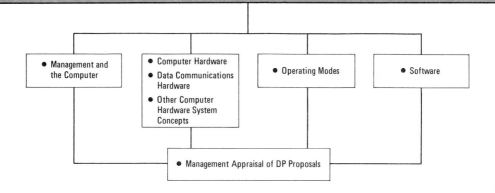

- Management and the Computer

- Computer Hardware
- Data Communications Hardware
- Other Computer Hardware System Concepts

- Operating Modes

- Software

- Management Appraisal of DP Proposals

PURPOSE: To present major computer concepts so that the MIS designer and manager can understand and evaluate computer alternatives for the MIS

Infosystems, May 1978, p. 99. By permission.

Not since the invention of writing in about 3000 B.C. has there been such an advance in information processing as that provided by electronic computer equipment. Jumps in computer technology are occurring faster than textbooks can come off the press. While minicomputers are still newcomers on the scene, *micro*computers, which also give promise of matching early giant computers, already are pushing minicomputers from the spotlight.

Today, computers separated by great distances talk with each other. Computer output microfilmers translate data into readable language and microfilms 100 times faster than paper printers can do. Paper printers are not exactly slow, either, printing over 3000 lines per minute. A computer may store over 1 billion characters internally. On-line storage capacity may be expanded to nearly one-half *trillion* characters. In comparison, the average human, living 70 years, stores information equivalent to 1 trillion *words*.

Multiplication operations have gone from 2000 per second in 1952 to over 2 million per second today. In 1952 the cost of 100,000 multiplications on an IBM computer was $1.26. By 1978 the cost had declined to $0.007. When we consider the millions of transactions carried out annually by large firms, the computer's impact on operations formerly performed manually is mind-boggling.

This chapter was prepared in collaboration with Dr. John C. Munson, Florida Atlantic University.

Table 3.1
World revenues
for U.S.
computer firms

	1976 ($ MILLIONS IN 1976 DOLLARS)			1981 ($ MILLIONS IN 1976 DOLLARS)
	U.S.	Overseas	World Total	World Total
Equipment:				
General-purpose computers	9,500	7,000	16,500	28,000
Mini and dedicated application computers	1,200	800	2,000	7,000
Peripherals:				
Data entry and terminal equip. from mainframe manufacturers	1,000	800	1,800	4,000
Data entry and terminal equip. from independent suppliers	1,600	600	2,200	5,000
Machine room peripherals from independent suppliers	1,000	400	1,400	2,500
Leasing	1,000	100	1,100	1,500
Used computer sales	100	*	100	300
Services:				
Batch	1,700	200	1,900	2,400
On-line	1,400	300	1,700	5,600
Software	1,100	500	1,600	5,000
Education	60	*	60	*
Supplies	1,200	300	1,500	2,700
Totals	20,860	11,000	31,860	64,000

*Negligible.

Source: AFIPS. Adapted from Pender M. McCarter, "Where Is the Industry Going?" **Datamation,** February 1978, p. 101. Reprinted With Permission of DATAMATION© magazine, © Copyright by TECHNICAL PUBLISHING COMPANY, A Division of DUN-DONNELLEY PUBLISHING CORPORATION, A DUN & BRADSTREET COMPANY, 1978—all rights reserved.

It has been said that if Detroit had done for the automobile what the computer industry has done for the computer, cars would now cost $1 and travel at the speed of light.

The growth of the computer industry has been phenomenal. Starting from essentially zero in 1945, worldwide computer revenues reached $31.8 billion in 1976 and were expected to reach $64 billion in 1981 (Table 3.1). Total U.S. employment of data processing (DP) personnel was expected to exceed 1 million or about 1% of the total work force (Figure 3.1) in 1981.

In the United States the top 50 computer companies obtain more than 95% of data processing industry revenues. The top seven U.S. companies had revenues totaling over $23 billion in 1977 (Figure 3.2),[1] accounting for over 75% of U.S. industry sales. The industry is so volatile, however, that it would be difficult to predict its makeup in 1985. We can only be sure that innovations and growth will continue to be astounding.

[1]Oscar H. Rothenbuecher, "The Top 50 U.S. Companies in the Data Processing Industry," *Datamation,* June 1978.

Figure 3.1
U.S. employment of data processing personnel

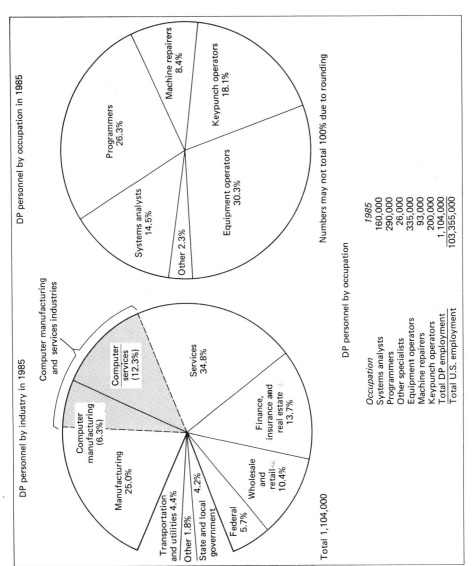

DP personnel by industry in 1985

Computer manufacturing and services industries

Computer services (12.3%)

Computer manufacturing (6.3%)

Services 34.8%

Manufacturing 25.0%

Finance, insurance and real estate 13.7%

Transportation and utilities 4.4%

Other 1.8%

State and local government 4.2%

Federal 5.7%

Wholesale and retail 10.4%

Total 1,104,000

DP personnel by occupation in 1985

Programmers 26.3%

Machine repairers 8.4%

Keypunch operators 18.1%

Systems analysts 14.5%

Other 2.3%

Equipment operators 30.3%

Numbers may not total 100% due to rounding

DP personnel by occupation

Occupation	1985
Systems analysts	160,000
Programmers	290,000
Other specialists	26,000
Equipment operators	335,000
Machine repairers	93,000
Keypunch operators	200,000
Total DP employment	1,104,000
Total U.S. employment	103,355,000

Source: AFIPS, based on data supplied by the Bureau of Labor Statistics, U.S. Department of Labor, 1977. Adapted from Pender M. McCarter, "Where Is the Industry Going?" **Datamation,** February 1978, p. 104. Reprinted With Permission of DATAMATION© magazine, © Copyright by TECHNICAL PUB-LISHING COMPANY, A Division of DUN-DONNELLEY PUBLISHING CORPORATION, A DUN & BRADSTREET COMPANY, 1978—all rights reserved.

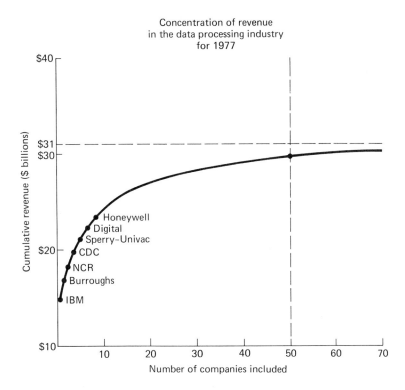

Figure 3.2
Revenues of the top seven U.S. computer companies

Concentration of revenue in the data processing industry for 1977

Source: Oscar H. Rothenbuecher, "The Top 50 U.S. Companies in the Data Processing Industry," **Datamation,** June 1978, p. 87. Reprinted With Permission of DATAMATION© magazine, © Copyright by TECHNICAL PUBLISHING COMPANY, A Division of DUN-DONNELLEY PUBLISHING CORPORA-TION, A DUN & BRADSTREET COMPANY, 1978—all rights reserved.

MANAGEMENT AND THE COMPUTER

Use of the Computer

Management has tended to view the computer as a number cruncher, a substitute for clerical operations. In some organizations such as banks and hospitals this employment is very evident. The payoff from converting manual to computer operations is fairly measurable, so that managers feel comfortable with such applications.

For several reasons, the use of computers to assist managers with planning, controlling, and decision making has not been accepted so easily. First, managers do not know in advance what information they need to fulfill their responsibilities. This makes the design of the MIS difficult. The introduction of a system which supplies more information means that managers must adopt a different style, a more analytical approach, to decision making. Not all managers are able or ready to change their style of managing. Another factor is that the art of modeling the firm and its environment has developed more slowly than anticipated. Managers have felt that the models were too unrealistic and have lacked confidence in them. Also, many managers have not understood what went on in the models. With experience, however, both managers and models have become more sophisticated. Another drawback is that it is difficult or impossible in most cases to measure the value of the computer for decision-supporting applications.

Despite these obstacles, the use of computers to assist managers with planning, controlling, and decision making is rising rapidly. Managers have found that computers allow them to consider quickly many alternatives for annual and long-range planning. When they find that competitors are successfully using company models, they respond in order to survive. The computer's power to monitor millions of transactions and operations and report on significant variations from standards has made its use for control a necessity. Increased demands upon executives' time have led to the use of the computer for "programmed" decision making in recurring situations.

Responsibility for the Computer Systems

Management is responsible to the owners of the company for the best use of resources. The purchase and the operation of a computer system represent large expenditures. Assailed by the mystique and jargon of computer specialists and vendor salespeople, management must not be intimidated. It is management's clear responsibility to learn enough about computer systems to ask probing questions, to demand alternative proposals, and to require both economic and noneconomic justification for the purchase of equipment and hiring of employees. To clarify these matters for present and future managers, this chapter describes the basic concepts and issues in the use of computer systems.

Baffled by Snow Job

I've seen the ablest and toughest of executives insist on increased productivity by a plant manager, lean on accounting for improved performance, and lay it on purchasing in no uncertain terms to cut its staff. But when these same executives turn to EDP they stumble to an uncertain halt, baffled by the snow job and the blizzard of computer jargon. They accept the presumed sophistication and differences that are said to make EDP activities somehow immune from normal management demands. They are stopped by all this nonsense, uncertain about what's reasonable to expect, what they can insist upon. They become confused and then retreat, muttering about how to get a handle on this blasted situation.[2]

Components of a Computer-based MIS

There are several prerequisites for a computer-based MIS. First, there must be a *management system*—the organizational structure, the organizational objectives and operations, and the managerial procedures for planning and control.

---

[2]Harry T. Larson, "EDP, a 20-Year Ripoff," *Infosystems,* November 1974, p. 27.

Second, sources of internal data must be available concerning the company's objectives, resources, transactions, and operations as well as competitive and environmental data. Third, it is necessary to have a computer system to process the data and convert them to information. The computer system must (1) provide economic and rapid storage and retrieval of data, (2) process the data economically and rapidly, (3) present information in easily understood formats and in a variety of mediums.

The Computer System

The computer system consists of three major blocks or subsystems:

1. *Hardware*—if you kick it, you might hurt your toe.
2. *Software*—instructions telling the computer what to do.
3. *People*—to do those things that the particular computer can't do.

To some degree, the functions of these subsystems are interchangeable, so that trade-offs may be made to move toward an optimal computer system. For example, the hardware may contain circuits whch perform certain operations, *or* the circuits may be omitted and software (programs) may be used. Similarly, instructions may be written for the computer, *or* the operator may instruct the computer step by step. Other possible exchanges among the three elements may be easily shown.

Our objective in this chapter is to describe briefly the principal elements of the three computer subsystems. The subject of data-base management systems is so important, however, that we have expanded it in detail in Chapter 15 as an advanced concept. We will also give special emphasis to the hardware subsystem in order to remove its mystique.

COMPUTER HARDWARE

For the old days, and for simple computer configurations today, the analogy between a manual data processing system and a computerized system is easily shown. There are inputs to the system, a processor, data storage devices, and outputs. The analogy is as follows:

	Manual System	Computer System
1. Input	Documents, voice reports, etc.	Card readers, terminals
2. Data processor	Human	Central processing unit
3. Storage or memory	File cabinets, rotary files, notebooks, human memory	Punched cards, magnetic tapes, magnetic cores, magnetic disks, etc.
4. Outputs	Documents, typed reports, drawings, voice reports, etc.	Computer printout sheets, video displays, punched cards, magnetic tapes, microfilms, etc.

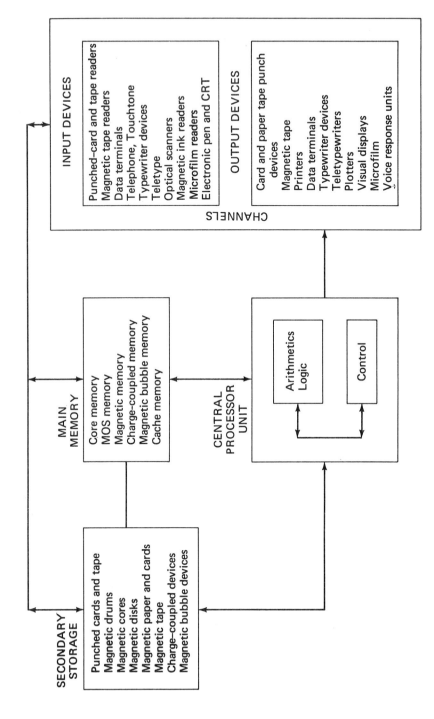

Figure 3.3 Computer components (except for data transmission equipment)

The computer system here consists of the key unit, the central processing unit (CPU), the main and secondary memories, an input and an output end device. In Figure 3.3 we have included channels (programmable transmission devices), which are required if there are several input or output end devices.

The kinds of situations which make computer systems complex are (1) the need to handle masses of data in the data base, (2) the addition of more input/output (I/O) end devices per CPU, (3) the use of networks of CPU's, storage devices, and I/O end devices, and (4) the technology and economics of data communications among dispersed computer components. The computer hardware for such complex systems is expanded to the following list.

Computer Components	Communications Components
CPU	I/O end devices
Primary storage	Telecommunications
Secondary memory	Modems
I/O channel, or back-end computer	Front-end computers
	Concentrators and multiplexors

In order to discuss computer hardware (and software), we need to understand the binary number system.

The Binary Number System

Numbers, letters, and symbols that we are all familiar with are represented by numerical codes for the computer to work with. The number system that the computer works with has a base of 2. Let us look briefly at this system.

In our everyday (decimal) number system, the number 2742 means:

$$2 \times 10^3 + 7 \times 10^2 + 4 \times 10^1 + 2 \times 10^0$$

In the binary system, instead of 10 digits there are only two digits, 0 and 1. Therefore, the number 1011 means:

$$1 \times 2^3 + 0 \times 2^2 + 1 \times 2^1 + 1 \times 2^0$$

which converts to 11 in the decimal system. Here are some examples of binary and decimal equivalents:

Binary	Decimal
0000	0
0001	1
0010	2
0011	3
0100	4
0101	5
0110	6
0111	7
1000	8
1001	9

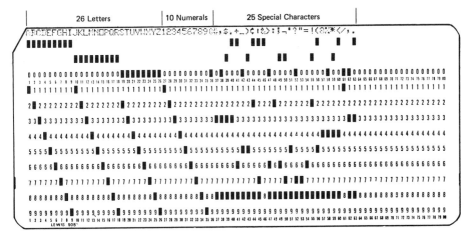

Figure 3.4 Business data input

The binary system is good for electronic equipment because the two numbers may be represented by any on-off alternatives. For example, a position in a card is not punched or it is punched. A particular storage position in a magnetic device may not be magnetized or it may be magnetized. Any storage position may therefore represent either 0 or 1 corresponding to its magnetized or nonmagnetized condition. These codings are called *bits* (for binary digit).

Although we have shown how our decimal system may be converted to machine language, how are letters and symbols translated into machine language? The answer is that they are coded into a sequence of zeros and ones. Generally, 10 decimal digits, 26 alphabetic characters, and 25 special symbols are used as coded in the 80-column punched card in Figure 3.4.

The eight *bits* which represent a *character* (alpha, numeric, or special) are, in total, called a *byte* (pronounced as "bite") of information.

Central Processing Unit

The central processing unit (CPU) is the most significant component of the computer system. It contains a *control* section which coordinates system components and controls the sequence of execution of program instructions being processed by the arithmetic/logic unit. The main or primary memory provides the working storage for the CPU. Essentially, everything the CPU does is based upon adding, subtracting, comparing the relative size of two numbers, and determining whether two characters are the same or different. From these elementary operations, division, multiplication, and higher-level operations are built into the machine. More complicated operations appear to be part of the computer when programs are stored in main memory.

A simple application of the central processor is illustrated in the inventory accounting system of Figure 3.5. In secondary or external storage, the inventory of raw materials is maintained. When a foreman withdraws some material, he prepares a material requisition. The information on the requisition is keypunched onto cards. At the end of the day, all requisition cards are read by an

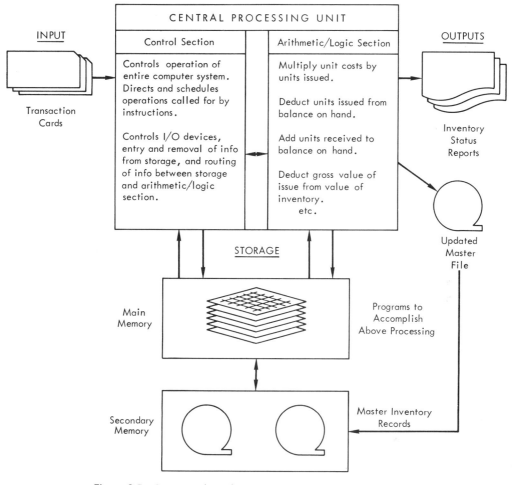

Figure 3.5 Computer-based inventory accounting system

inventory update program, which will update an existing materials file to develop a revised master file of raw materials on hand. The master file is shown as stored on magnetic tape in Fig. 3.5, although it could be stored on punched cards or some other medium.

Storage Components

The computer system has two types of storage: *main* memory and *secondary* storage. The main memory is the working memory. Programs and data in the main memory are utilized as needed by the arithmetic/logic section under the supervision of the control section. The brain's memory is the analogy in the human. Humans also require data that are not immediately available, such as data in an encyclopedia or textbook. The human has to look up needed data and transfer them to the brain, primary storage, before they can be processed or used. Similarly, the computer system contains secondary storage of data on magnetic tapes, disks, punched cards, and the like (Fig. 3.3) which must be "read" into main memory before the CPU can process it.

The main memory can be made to seem almost limitless by a system called *virtual memory (VM)*. A program which exceeds the main memory is brought into the main memory in what we may call "pages" as needed. Data are also brought in as needed. When these pages are not needed, they are temporarily stored in secondary storage.

Storage of a bit may be (1) mechanical, as the hole or absence of a hole in a punched card, (2) electronic, as on-off in a semiconductor, or (3) magnetic

Figure 3.6
Memory
capacity vs.
access time

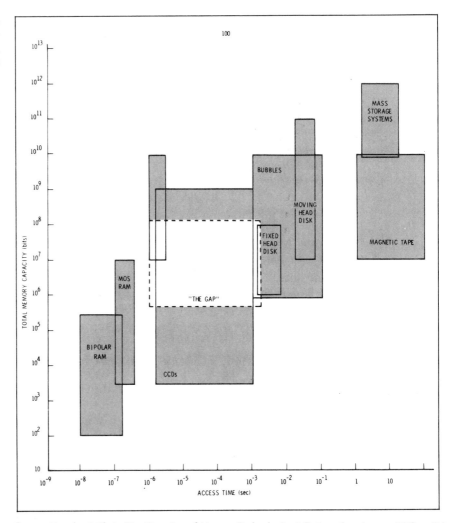

Source: Douglas J. Theis, "An Overview of Memory Technologies," **Datamation,** January 1978, p. 114. Reprinted With Permission of DATAMATION© magazine, © Copyright by TECHNICAL PUBLISHING COMPANY, A Division of DUN-DONNELLEY PUBLISHING CORPORATION, A DUN & BRADSTREET COMPANY, 1978—all rights reserved.

charge *or* polarization, as for magnetic drums, magnetic tape, disks, and bubble memories.

Capacity, access speed, and cost per bit of storage are three variables of concern to management. In serial access, such as magnetic tape, the computer must proceed along the length of the tape until it reaches the item it wants to retrieve—a slow process. In random access memory (RAM), such as for disks, drums, or cores, the computer is directed to the item by means of a key or code. This is an expensive process, because the key addresses utilize valuable storage space. Such space not devoted to useful data is called, appropriately, *overhead*. Figure 3.6 shows the relationship between memory capacity and access time.

Most computer hardware is now packaged in cabinets such that only labels can distinguish among them. The memory units inside appear as shown in Figure 3.7. Drum storage, shown in Fig. 3.7(a), consists of rotating metal drums whose surfaces are divided into tracks. The tracks are magnetized to identify information by phase encoding. A row of electrical heads read data onto the drum.

In Fig. 3.7(b) a magnetic tape and drive are shown in the background. Magnetic tapes are about 2400 to 3600 feet long and are wound on reels. Tapes are one-half inch in width. Data are recorded as magnetized spots along "channels" (of which there may be seven or nine) across the tape for closer packing up to about 6200 characters per inch. Records are stored on the tapes serially, and blocks of records are separated by interblock gaps, which contain no data but permit the tape to get up to speed or to decelerate before and after entering operations.

A disk pack is shown in Fig. 3.7(c). Basically, disks are made of metal with a special magnetizable coating, are about 1½ to 3 feet in diameter, and are stacked with space between read/write heads to move back and forth across the surface. Tiny tracks on both sides of the disk (except top and bottom disks) are magnetized to represent data. Disk stacks vary from 1 to 100 disks.

Storage devices may be compared in terms of the following characteristics:

1. Storage capacity in millions of bits, bytes, or words
2. Average time to position head over proper track ("seek time")
3. Average rotational time
4. Addressable positions per disk or drum
5. Number of tracks per cylinder
6. Number of cylinders per pack or unit
7. Cylinder capacity
8. Transfer rate for reading or writing
9. Number of channels for access
10. Recording density in bits per inch
11. Recording code
12. Data format
13. Maximum number of units per system
14. Total storage capacity of entire system
15. Number of reading heads
16. Maximum number of tracks one head must read.[3]

[3]Alton R. Kindred, *Data Systems and Management* (Englewood Cliffs, N.J.: Prentice-Hall, Inc. 1973), p. 156.

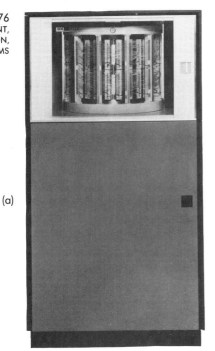

(a)

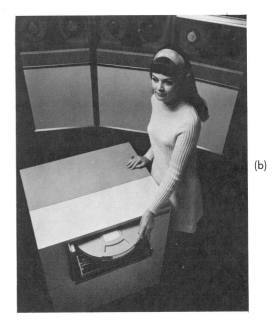

(b)

Figure 3.7 Storage devices: (a) IBM 2303 drum storage (Courtesy of International Business Machines Corporation); (b) desk storage drive with removable cartridge and magnetic tape drive in background (Courtesy of Mohawk Data Sciences); (c) B 9974-7 disk pack for B 9383-18 subsystem drive (Courtesy of Burroughs Corporation)

(c)

I/O Channel

An I/O channel is an electronic device that transmits information between main storage and I/O terminals. With present-day mass storage, the operating system of the CPU would be tied up performing input/output processing for the relatively slow I/O terminals. For this reason the I/O channel was developed to handle the large volume of requests made upon the data base. The I/O channel is

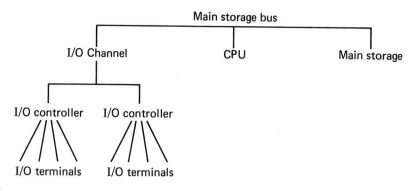

Figure 3.8 Computer system with mass storage and multiple I/O terminals

essentially a specialized computer. It is linked to I/O end-devices (user terminals) through control units as shown in Figure 3.8.

I/O Controllers

I/O end-devices or user terminals require different control signals depending upon their design, function, and the medium used. The variety of such devices is indicated in Fig. 3.3. Control units are placed between the I/O channel and the terminal devices to supply control signals and permit simultaneous operation of the various devices. (See Fig. 3.8.)

I/O End-devices (Terminals)

Business data frequently appear first on forms or other written records. In order to get such data into the computer for storage or for processing, we must enter them through an input device. To get data from the computer we require an output device.

End-use devices consist of such equipment as card readers, OCR and MICR devices, keyboard terminals, electronic pen CRT terminals, point-of-purchase registers, and printers. In some cases, data preparation devices such as card punchers are required. In addition, input and output may be stored (on tapes, disks, etc.) as an intermediate step.

Today, manned terminals, where data are typed and read into computer storage simultaneously, are becoming widely used. These terminals have video displays (cathode ray tubes, called CRT's) as shown in Figure 3.9. They also serve as output devices in that the computer causes the "typewriter" to type output and produces displays on the video screen. Such terminals might be classified as "dumb," "somewhat smart," and "very smart" (intelligent) terminals. Dumb terminals simply accept/transmit data to a CPU and receive data. Somewhat smart terminals perform some data processing and have some memory as well. Very smart terminals have considerable computing and memory capacity and can "stand alone" for most of their operations. All terminals allow the user to "interact" with the computer in the sense that transmission and response are like two people conversing.

Figure 3.9
Manned
terminals with
video displays

HARRIS 1670 distributed processing system offers local or remote batch processing, data entry, and local and remote interaction concurrently. CRT's are individually switchable between local and host files.
Courtesy of Harris Corporation.

Figure 3.10
Interactive
graphics

GT41, 17 inch refresh graphics scope, solid-state light-pen, and display processor.
Courtesy of Digital Equipment Corporation.

Figure 3.11
Graphic output
printer

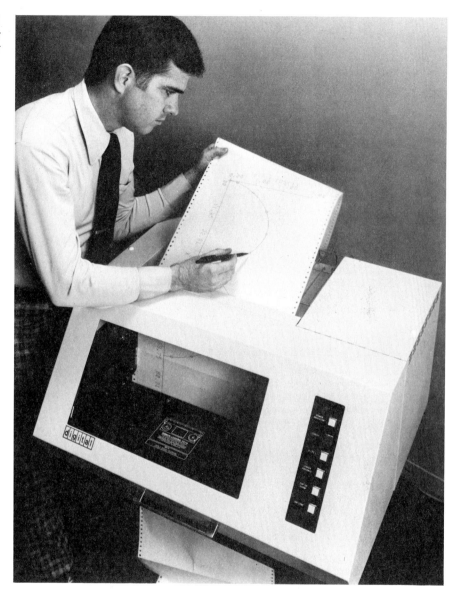

LXY11 printer-plotter. Courtesy of Digital Equipment Corporation.

Another input device that provides visual interaction is the solid-state light-pen and associated terminal shown in Figure 3.10. A graphic output device is shown in Figure 3.11.

For high-speed text output, impact printing devices (Figure 3.12) and laser graphic devices are used. Such printers produce reports at the rate of 3000 or more lines per minute.

Examples of applications of various classes of terminals are listed in Table 3.2.

Table 3.2
Examples of application by terminal class

Primary Application	Secondary Application
Display	
Teletype replacement	
Interactive time-shared	Minicomputer console
computer access	
Interactive display	
File access/interrogation	Airline reservation
Data edit, entry, storage and	Computer-assisted instruction
retrieval (IRS example)	Plotting—limited graphics
	Stock quotation
Graphics	
Engineering design	Production of movies—cartoons
Manufacturing simulation	Computer-assisted instruction—
Medical simulation	pattern recognition
Air traffic control	
Data reduction	
Keyboard Printer	
Teleprinter	
Record communications and	File inquiry
messages	Minicomputer console
Interactive time-shared	Order entry
computer access	Invoicing
	Data logging
	Computer-assisted instruction
Remote Batch	
Remote media entry	Satellite mode (free-standing
Remote media output	operation)
Remote computing with	Limited inquiry—response
centralized system control	
Intelligent	
Decentralization of work	Accommodation to host central
functions from CPU to terminal	processor communication
Control of local data base	disciplines
Localized error correction	Emulation of hardwired
and input data editing	terminals
Localized processing of data in	Manufacturer's flexibility in
event of communications failure	changing functionability
Industry-oriented	
Normal terminal features plus	Some specific functions not
specific functionality to a	allied with data transfer or
market segment and application	control such as:
such as:	Incorporation of cash drawers
Automobile rentals	Merchandise dispensers (i.e.,
Commercial and savings bank	tickets, vouchers, cash,
teller stations	stamps)
Credit authorization	Passbook printers
Factory data collection	
Medical services	
Point of sale	

Source: Harold N. Wells and Anthony B. Ragozzino, "Remote Terminals," in the Diebold Group, Inc., ed., **Automatic Data Processing Handbook** (New York: McGraw-Hill, 1977), p. 2-132.

Figure 3.12
IMPACT 3000
Printer.

IMPACT 3000, rated at 3,000 lines per minute, uses a 48-character set.
Courtesy of Documation, Incorporated.

DATA COMMUNICATIONS HARDWARE

Data Communications and Remote Computing Networks

The development of on-line terminals at the same site as the central (or "host") computer was the start of computer data communication systems. The additional hardware required was primarily switching and control equipment. Since then, terminals have been established at sites remote from the computers, terminals have become small computers, and both large and small computers have become linked in networks extending over great distances. This evolution has been made possible by the development of communications equipment that transports data at a cost below that of duplicating complete computer systems at the various sites in the network.

The development of such remote computing networks has made possible:

1. Remote timesharing—a number of remote users may interact with a computer concurrently.
2. Computer job load sharing—a number of computers in a system may share the data processing load.

Data Transmission

Transmission of data may be designed for one direction only (simplex); both directions, but not at the same time (half-duplex); and both directions at the same time (full-duplex). Transmission may be made by hardwire (such as telephone lines) or electromagnetic waves (with radio, microwaves, or satellite equipment). Data may be transmitted by varying the amplitude, frequency, or phase of such waves.

Data are usually transmitted in bits in serial fashion, although in some instances they may be transmitted in parallel. When one character is transmitted at a time with start and stop gaps between, the transmission is called *asynchronous*. For higher-speed applications, 2000 bits/sec and more, *synchronous* transmission is employed. Here a constant-rate clocking device determines the exact time bits are sent and received and, by synchronizing this information, it eliminates the need for start and stop gaps. Three common asynchronous codes to represent characters in transmission are Baudot, binary-coded decimal, and American Code for Information Interchange.

Transmission speeds are often measured in baud/sec. A *baud* is a change in line condition or a pulse. With modern modems (see the next section), two or three bits may be assigned to a baud. For clarity, therefore, transmission speeds should be expressed in bits/sec.

Transmission channels may be either common carrier, such as AT&T, or private, as established by independent companies. Different grades of service available are low-speed (subvoice-grade such as for teletype), medium-speed (voice-grade), and high-speed (broadband). Figure 3.13 provides an overall view of these services.

Figure 3.13 Types of communications services

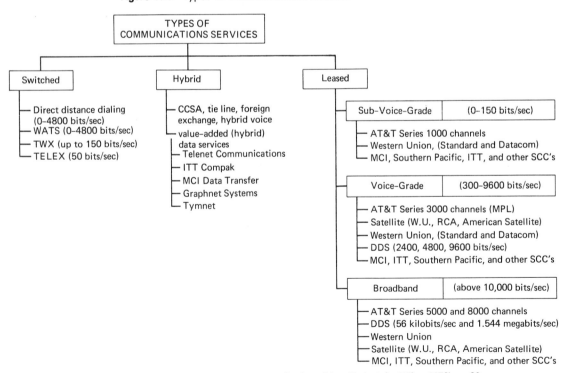

Source: Dixon R. Doll, **Data Communications** (New York: John Wiley, 1978), p. 80.

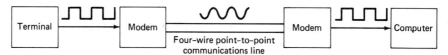

Figure 3.14 Modems in data transmission

Modems

Data enter or leave digital computers or terminals in binary form. However, for minimum distortion, transmission by telecommunication must be in the form of sine waves. Therefore, as shown in Figure 3.14, the square digital pulses at the sending end must be converted to sine waves, which are modulated in terms of either amplitude, frequency, or phase (Figure 3.15). When the modulated wave signal is received, it must be demodulated to be acceptable to the computer. Devices that modulate and demodulate are called *modems*.

Figure 3.15 Transmission of the binary number 01001011000100 over a telephone line bit by bit: (a) two-level signal, (b) amplitude modulation, (c) frequency modulation, (d) phase modulation.

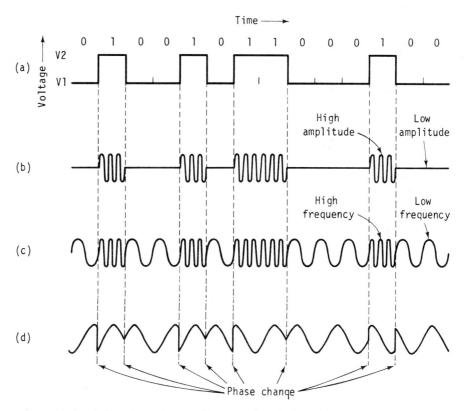

Source: Andrew S. Tanenbaum, **Structured Computer Organization** (Englewood Cliffs, N.J.: Prentice-Hall, Inc., 1976), p. 44. Reprinted by permission of Prentice-Hall, Inc., Englewood Cliffs, New Jersey.

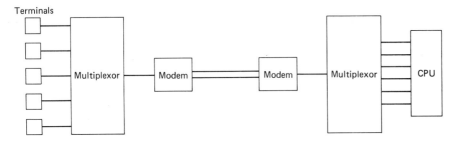

Figure 3.16 Multiplexors in telecommunications

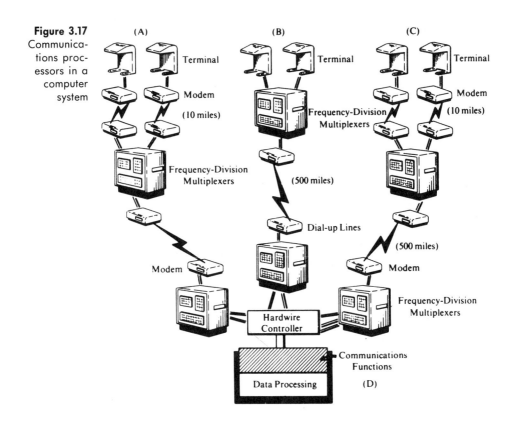

Figure 3.17 Communications processors in a computer system

This system has been configured without communications processors—relying on hardware multiplexing devices to realize efficiencies in transmission line utilization. The inefficiencies of the system are that (1) line costs are not minimized (especially when messages are switched from one terminal group to another) and (2) a considerable portion of the host computer resources (central processing time and core memory utilization) is required to perform network control functions.

Source: Kenneth W. Ford, "About Communications Processors," **Infosystems,** February 1973, p. 47. © Copyright Hitchcock Publishing Company, Wheaton, Illinois.

Multiplexors and Concentrators

Economics of scale in the cost of bandwidth can be gained when a number of low-speed or low-activity remote terminals are connected on-line to a computer. Multiplexors are devices which allow one voice-band grade channel to substitute for a number of subvoice-grade channels, as shown in Figures 3.16 and 3.17.

In frequency-division multiplexing (FDM), the lower-speed terminals are each assigned a portion of the frequencies of the voice-grade band. In synchronous time-division multiplexing (STDM), a permanently dedicated time-slot for each terminal is created. On the other hand, asynchronous or statistical TDM's allocate the output of the terminals to the transmission channel on a dynamic statistical basis.

Concentrators, which also permit a reduction in telecommunication channels, operate on a different basis. Suppose that there are 10 end-devices but only four transmission channels. The concentrator polls each terminal as a channel becomes available. The first terminal transmitting gets the channel. If a terminal wishes to transmit and all channels are being used, it gets a busy signal.

Front-end Devices (Communications Controllers)

When there are a number of terminals and the data processing activity from the terminals is high, the computer control program becomes tied up in message switching, data storage and retrieval, handling protocols for different devices, and generally controlling other aspects of dialogs between the terminals and the host CPU. Front-end devices, which are in reality either general-purpose or dedicated computers, are connected between the host CPU and the local modems to remove such tasks from the CPU. They serve, in addition, as concentrators. The following list presents typical applications of front-end devices:

1. Message switching
2. Store-and-forward
3. Data collection
4. Interface to mass storage
5. Code and terminal conversion
6. Data validation and prescanning
7. Terminal or system security
8. Audit trailing
9. Stand-alone operation
10. Device polling—rotary or special (priority)
11. Character and message assembly
12. Translation to a common code
13. Line recovery
14. Automatic error detection and correction
15. Dynamic line reassignment
16. Network monitoring
17. System regeneration capability.[4]

---

[4]Richard J. Stenger, "Telecommunication Techniques," *Journal of Systems Management,* April 1973, p. 13.

Large computers, called mainframe computers, dominated the early history of computer hardware. Rapid changes in technology keep putting more computing power into smaller packages at less cost. Today, desk-size "minicomputers" far outperform early mainframe computers, which occupied an entire room. In fact, the line between mainframes and minis is becoming harder to define.

Originally, minis were distinguished by their low cost relative to mainframes. One author defines a mini as a programmable computer with a word length of up to 16 bits.[5] The typical main memory associated with a mainframe computer is of the order of 10,000,000 bytes (at 8 bits per byte), while it is around 500,000 bytes for a mini. The central processor unit cycle time is only about 80 nanoseconds (billionths of a second) for a mainframe compared to about 300 nanoseconds for a mini. Although you can put any job on a mini that you can put on a mainframe, throughput times on minis are longer because they lack the resources of the large computers.[6] Figure 3.18 shows what different sizes of computers look like.

[5]Joe E. Frazier, "Off-the-shelf Minis," *Automation,* February 1974.

[6]For a more complete comparison, see Gerald J. Burnett and Richard L. Nolan, "At Last, Major Roles for Minicomputers," *Harvard Business Review,* May-June 1975.

Figure 3.18 (a) Components of a medium-to-large-scale computer system (NCR Century 300) (Courtesy of the NCR Corporation) (b) Components of a large-scale computer system (Burroughs B4800) (Courtesy of Burroughs Corporation) (c) Components of a small computer system (Courtesy of International Business Machines Corporation)

(a)

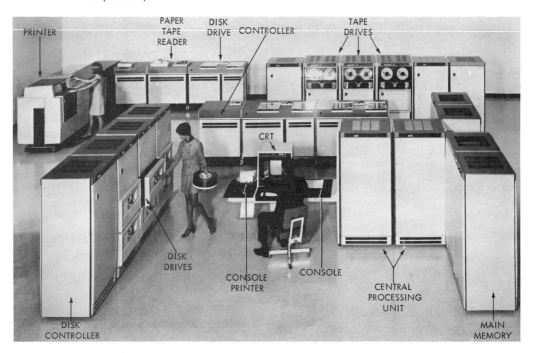

(b)

(c)

The development of minis led to the concept of *distributed processing.* The use of centralized computers often led to data input bottlenecks and lengthy delays in feedback of business information. By the placing of minicomputers in the user organization, greater flexibility in programming and better interaction with the computer is obtained. In addition, a network of minicomputers may be established to share data bases or mainframe computer power.

For specific limited applications, *microcomputers,* or computers on a chip, may be used. The technology of microcomputers is advancing rapidly and includes programmed instructions and increasing address space.[7]

[7]See Tomlinson G. Rauscher, "A Unified Approach to Microcomputer Software Development," *Computer,* June 1978.

Table 3.3 Word processing major features and applications

EQUIPMENT CLASS	MAJOR FEATURES						MAJOR APPLICATIONS				
	CPU	Printer	Keyboard	Display	Storage Medium	Price Range	Text Input	Text Editing	Communications	Electronic Files	Decentralized Data Processing
Stand-alone, Nonvisual	Hard wired	Selective	Yes	No	Mag card or tape	5,000-12,000	Keyed	Simple	No	No	No
Stand-alone, visual	Hard wired	Selective	Yes	Yes 8-1924 chars.	Mag card or tape	9,000-39,000	Keyed	Complex	Not usually	Not usually	No
Cluster, Shared Logic	Micro processor or mini computer	Daisy wheel	Yes	Yes, usually full page	Floppy disk	30,000 up	Keyed	Complex	Yes	Yes	Yes
Cluster, Distributed Logic	Micro processor or mini computer	Daisy wheel	Yes	Yes, usually full page	Floppy disk	26,000 up	Keyed	Complex	Yes	Yes	Yes

Source: Harold F. Doolittle, Jr., "What Management Should Know about Word Processing," **Infosystems,** October 1978, p. 76. © Copyright, Hitchcock Publishing Company, Wheaton, Illinois.

Another area of computer hardware that ties into minicomputers and offers great promise for increased office productivity is word processing. Mechanical word processing in the office has evolved slowly to the present use of electric typewriters and dictating networks with central typing pools. We are now at the very beginning of a revolution of office automation. Image handling, intelligence, file capabilities, and communications are destined to produce a giant leap forward in the productivity of office and knowledge workers.

While the present diversity of equipment and innovation makes the field seem chaotic, eventually *systems* will be developed. The tie-in of the computer with a wide range of devices will be the key factor. Some of the current devices and systems are text editing machines, image and text retrieval systems, computer output microfilming, letter writers based upon computer storage paragraphs, copying equipment, and computer voice recognition. Major features of word processing equipment are outlined in Table 3.3.

OPERATING MODES

The general modes of operation of computer systems are (1) batch processing, (2) multiprogramming, (3) timesharing, and (4) multiprocessing. Not every computer system configuration can operate in all of these modes. Therefore selection of a configuration should take into account the mode suitable for the particular company and its computer application.

In *batch processing*, a collection, or batch, of related transactions is accumulated over a period of time and processed as a group. For example, in a raw materials inventory system, receipts and withdrawals of materials might be entered on cards or in a log during the day. At the end of the day, all these changes in inventory may be gathered, entered on punched cards or magnetic tape, and then run, as a batch, through an inventory-update program and accounts receivable program as shown in Figure 3.19.

Batch processing allows flexibility in scheduling the computer. When decisions are made only once a month or once a year, continual updating rather than batch updating of decision-supporting information is likely to be inefficient.

Multiprogramming means running two programs concurrently in the same processor by interleaving the data processing or performing I/O activities for one while processing the other. Figure 3.20 illustrates how computer facilities might be allocated three programs. The advantage of multiprogramming is efficient use of the computer. In this mode of operation, when one program is waiting for input from a very slow-speed device, another program can be using the machine's resources.

Multiprocessing is the use of several CPU's to service a collection of users' requests. The requests may be assigned to a CPU either as they come through or on the basis of type of request or program. When the CPU's perform the same functions, multiprocessing provides reliability, because if one breaks down the load will be shifted to the working computer. In this mode also the total CPU power is increased.

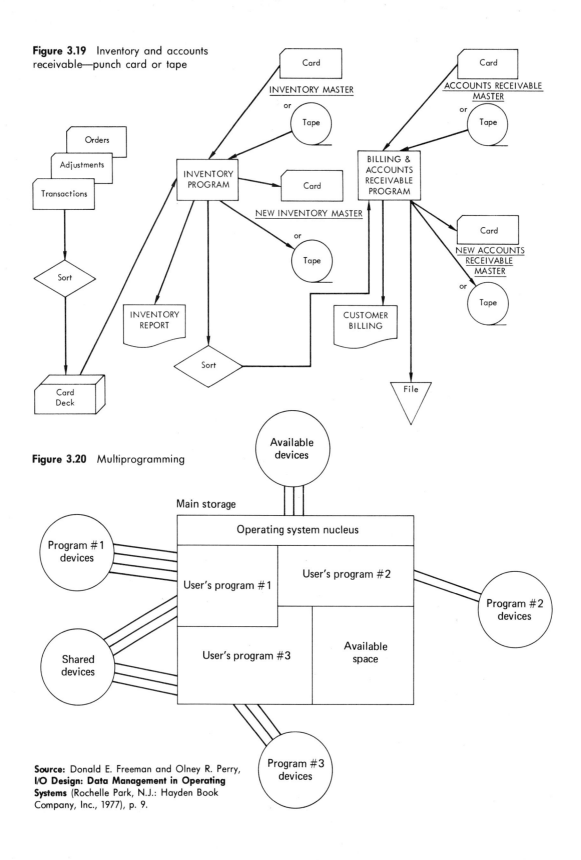

Figure 3.19 Inventory and accounts receivable—punch card or tape

Card
INVENTORY MASTER
or
Tape

Card
ACCOUNTS RECEIVABLE MASTER
or
Tape

Orders
Adjustments
Transactions

INVENTORY PROGRAM

BILLING & ACCOUNTS RECEIVABLE PROGRAM

Card
NEW INVENTORY MASTER
or
Tape

Card
NEW ACCOUNTS RECEIVABLE MASTER
or
Tape

Sort

INVENTORY REPORT

CUSTOMER BILLING

Sort

File

Card Deck

Figure 3.20 Multiprogramming

Available devices

Main storage

Operating system nucleus

Program #1 devices

User's program #1

User's program #2

Program #2 devices

Shared devices

User's program #3

Available space

Program #3 devices

Source: Donald E. Freeman and Olney R. Perry, **I/O Design: Data Management in Operating Systems** (Rochelle Park, N.J.: Hayden Book Company, Inc., 1977), p. 9.

Timesharing allows a number of users to process simple service requests where response time of a few seconds to a few minutes is acceptable. The advantage is making the power of the processor available to a number of users at the same time.

SOFTWARE

Software consists of computer programs. A computer program is a sequence of instructions for the computer to execute. There are two levels of software: (1) the microprogram, which runs the machine, and (2) the user machine language programs, which are eventually interpreted by the microprogram.

Machine Language

The most primitive language in which it is possible for people to communicate with a computer is *machine language*. The execution of a microprogram (Level 1), written in machine language, requires changing the wiring and circuitry. Because, obviously, this is not desirable, a higher-level set of instructions, Level 2, is stored in the computer's working storage to supplement the machine language. Level 2 is called the conventional machine level.

Compilers and Assembly Languages

In the 1950s, *compilers* were developed to ease the programmer's task. These were basic or frequently used routines that were entered in the computer or, if feasible, stored in the computer.

Assembly languages such as FORTRAN and COBOL were developed at about the same time. These languages were more conversational than machine-like and were interpreted for execution by several lower levels of language, as listed in Table 3.4.

Table 3.4
Commonly used computer programming languages for business applications

Acronym	Language	Description
ALGOL	Algorithmic Language	Developed jointly by users in the U.S. and Europe, this language is suitable for expressing solutions to problems requiring numeric computations for some logical processes.
APL	A Programming Language	A general language with complex notation and unusual but powerful operations. Notation is exceptionally compact.
BASIC	Beginner's All-Purpose Symbolic Instruction Code	A very simple language for use in solving numeric and business problems developed in on-line systems. Frequently used by nontechnical users.
COBOL	Common Business-Oriented Language	This is an English-like language that is the most widespread in use for business data processing problems.

(continued on next page)

Table 3.4
(Cont'd.)

Acronym	Language	Description
FORTRAN	Formula Translator	Developed about 1957, this was the first language to be widely used for solving numeric problems. It is perhaps the most widely used language prior to 1970 and has been implemented on almost all computers. It is oriented to specific kinds of problems. For example, the solution to the problem: area of a circle = r^2 was written PI*R**2. Subsequent "generations" of FORTRAN have been FORTRAN II, IV, etc.
GPSS	General-Purpose Systems Simulator	A language for discrete simulation problems based on a block diagram approach.
PL/1		In wide use. Generally limited to IBM equipment. For scientific, business, on-line, real-time.
RPG-II	Report Program Generator	A language to generate programs to prepare reports (usually only once) from existing data in the system.
SIMSCRIPT		Another language for doing discrete simulation problems. Based on FORTRAN.
SIMULA	Simulation Language	ALGOL-based language widely used by international manufacturers of DP equipment.
PASCAL		A generalized programming language, easy to use, very powerful, and similar to ALGOL.

Operating Systems

We have delayed until now a discussion of the operating system because of its important place in computer operation. As A. S. Tanenbaum indicates in Figure 3.21, the interpreter that supports the Level 3 system is called the *operating system*. It does the work originally carried out by computer operators.

An operating system (OS) is a complex and large collection of computer instructions, running, possibly, from 30,000 to 700,000 instructions. The purpose of the OS is to save the programmer's time—an enormous amount of it—and achieve efficient control over computer processing. These objectives are achieved by three principal control programs which each manufacturer supplies with its machine: control (or executive, monitor, or supervisor), job control, and initial program loader.

D. E. Freeman and O. R. Perry describe the major activities of an operating system:

Scheduling Jobs. An operating system accepts jobs and schedules the system resources to satisfy these jobs. Some systems simply schedule jobs in the order of their receipt, that is, first in, first out (FIFO). Others recognize a priority code furnished by the user as an expression of the urgency of the job. Job scheduling involves not only recognition of priorities, but also availability of necessary resources. The resources required for a particular job may not be immediately available because they are being used for another job, or because they are undergoing maintenance. A comprehensive operating system will defer running of jobs when possible within priority constraints to effect efficient use of resources.

Figure 3.21
Five levels
present on
most modern
computers

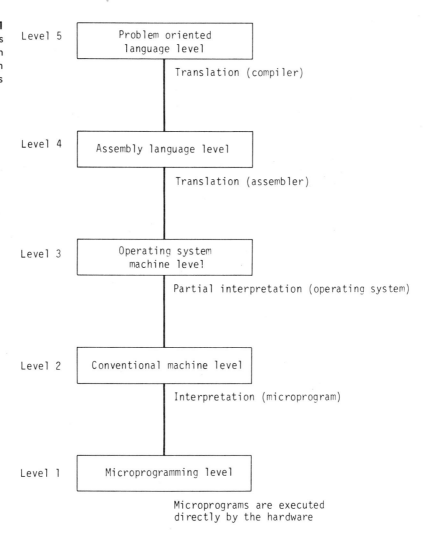

The method by which each level is supported is indicated below it, along with the name of the supporting program in parentheses.

Allocating Resources. The resources of a computing system include main storage space, I/O devices, and files of data. An operating system controls the use of all of these resources. For example, an operating system allocates a particular direct access storage device (DASD) to be used in processing a particular storage volume. Both the DASD and the files recorded on the storage volume are considered system resources.

Dispatching Programs. One very special resource that an operating system controls is central processing unit (CPU) time. At the beginning of an interval of time to be used by a particular program, the operating system takes the necessary steps to start or restart CPU activity for that program. The process of preparing the system for executing a particular program and transferring control of the CPU to that program is called dispatching. The system dispatches programs in the same sense that a clerk might dispatch errand boys.

Communicating with the Operator. Philosophically, the computer-system operator should serve only one purpose: to be the hands for the computer, doing those things that require the mobility and dexterity of a human. This goal was suggested by Doctor Frederick Brooks in about 1968. Practically, operating systems have been unable to achieve the desired level of autonomy, so operators still serve as overall supervisors. In this role, they cancel improper service requests, reassign priorities, or even stop the system entirely when it appears that the operating system has lost control. Examples of communications from the system to the operator include requesting the operator to mount or demount storage volumes, notifying the operator of start and completion of each job, and apprising the operator of any unusual conditions, such as a high frequency of I/O device errors.

Recovering from Incidents. Computer systems, and particularly the I/O devices included within systems, are subject to a variety of unexpected (but not unanticipated) conditions. A comprehensive operating system must be prepared to deal with unexpected conditions at all times. Typical unexpected conditions include intermittent I/O device failure, permanent I/O device failure, operator error, improper action by a user's program, and intermittent main storage or CPU failure. The finesse with which an operating system deals with unexpected conditions is one very important measure of its value. A good system can diagnose many situations and recover with modest loss of work in process.

Recording of Statistics. The recording of operating statistics is unproductive and time-consuming, but it is essential for distributing costs to users and for analyzing system performance. In comprehensive systems, noteworthy events occur at such a rate that even simple counting of events in main storage tables with occasional copying of the tables to auxiliary storage may require as much as 1 or 2 percent of all available CPU time.

Storing and Retrieving Data. The I/O system, a major component of an operating system, is responsible for data storage and retrieval. Because the main body of this book dwells on I/O activity, no more will be said about it in this preliminary section. (These programs are called *utility* programs.)[8]

---

[8]Donald E. Freeman and Olney R. Perry, *I/O Design: Data Management in Operating Systems* (Rochelle Park, N.J.: Hayden Book Co., 1977), pp. 5–7.

Applications Software

Application programs are those developed for an ongoing company operation—for example, an accounts receivable program, an order processing program, and a human resource update program. One special application program is a *data-base management system* program, which maintains the company data base and makes data available to users. Chapter 15 is devoted to this topic.

ORGANIZATION FOR DATA PROCESSING

The data processing (DP) function is a companywide service which supports the MIS and functional operations. Therefore, it should not be reporting to a functional manager such as the controller. Historically, accounting was the first application of the new computer. Management also has always been concerned with obtaining financial data promptly. As a result, DP still reports to the financial executive in about one-third of companies (Table 3.5).

Table 3.5
Executive to which the DP function reports

President, Owner, General Manager	27.7%
Vice President	24.9
Financial Officer Controller	31.1
Director of Information Systems (MIS, etc.)	5.4
Data Base Administrator	.2
Other	10.7

Source: "1979 DP Salaries Report," **Infosystems,** June 1979.
Copyright © Hitchcock Publishing Company, Wheaton, Illinois.

With proper planning, priority setting, and scheduling, there is no need for this concern about prompt financial reporting. The cost of placing the DP function under the financial officer is that computer applications to the company's other needs are neglected or distorted.

The DP organization includes three general activities: systems analysis, programming, and computer operations. Job titles are:

Project Team Leader

Data-Base Administrator

Manager—Computer Systems Analysis and Programming

Lead Computer Systems Analyst and Programmer

Senior Computer Systems Analyst and Programmer

Junior Computer Systems Analyst and Programmer

Manager—Computer Systems Analysis

Lead Computer Systems Analyst

Senior Computer Systems Analyst

Junior Computer Systems Analyst

Manager—Programming

Lead Programmer

Senior Programmer

Junior Programmer

Programmer Trainee.

Figure 3.22 Composition of computer department of McDonald's

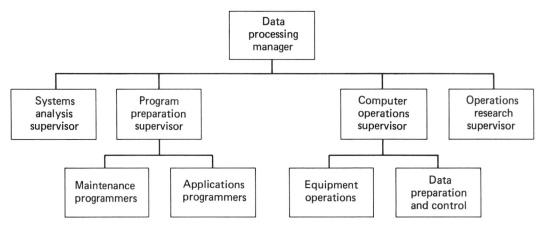

Courtesy of McDonald Corporation

An example of a DP organization (for McDonald's) is shown in Figure 3.22. In a larger and more complex company the following functions may be found:

1. Operations
   a. Operators
   b. Librarians
   c. Security specialists
   d. DP management
2. Systems analysis and design
   a. Systems analysts
   b. Management scientists
   c. Data-base management specialists
   d. MIS liaison personnel
3. Programming
   a. Systems programmers
   b. Development programmers
   c. Maintenance programmers.

One new alternative to the internal organization described is *facilities management*. Independent companies provide the entire computer service on site.

MANAGEMENT APPRAISAL OF DP PROPOSALS

From management's view, acquisition of DP equipment should be no different than acquisition of a large machine, a plant, or a new business. An economic analysis should be made that will show whether incremental benefits exceed incremental costs over the life cycle of the system.

Table 3.6 Applications approach to computer configuration

Application	Master File: Medium—Key	File Size: Records—Characters	Processing Frequency	Transactions Per Run
Order entry	Disc-order no.	10,000-150	Daily	1,000
Sales analysis	Tape-cust. no.	2800-90	Weekly	7,000
Inventory	Tape-prod. no.	2500-120	Daily	7,000
Distribution schedule	Network program	—	Daily	—
Production schedule	Linear program	—	Weekly	—
Payroll	Tape-employee no.	1000-400	Weekly	5,000
Accts receivable	Tape-cust. no.	3000-260	Daily	500
Accts payable	Tape-vendor no.	3000-260	Daily	100
Vendor analysis	Analysis program	—	Monthly	—
General ledger	Tape-account	120-1000	Monthly	3,000
Purchasing	Disc-P.O. no.	600-200	Daily	600
(Other applications)				

Sometimes a proposal for a vast system may appear cost effective. Management should try to bring such proposals down to earth. A simple analysis as shown in Table 3.6 may indicate that a simple batch processing system will be adequate for the next three years.

On the other hand, if a large distributed processing system seems needed, management should demand presentation of a more complete analysis. Table 3.7, for example, is a checklist suggested by Raytheon, allowing management to compare Raytheon equipment with alternatives.

Two other simple guidelines may help management in the review of proposals. The first relates rental range of equipment to DP and total employees of the company (Table 3.8). The second shows percent of DP budget expended for various DP categories (Table 3.9). While certainly some companies may require wide deviations from these averages, management should make certain that they can be justified.

Table 3.7 Raytheon's 54-point checklist for distributed processing systems

FEATURE	TYPICAL CONFIGURATION	PRODUCT CAPABILITIES		IMPORTANCE OF FEATURE
		PTS/1200	Brand X	
Intelligence	✔ Dependent totally on host processor	N/A		Intelligence is based upon the amount of available pro-
	✔ Stand-alone (non-shareable) intelligence in each station	All resources shareable by all sta-tions		grammable memory a system possesses. Its pur-pose is to facilitate local application development
	✔ Small-cluster (shared by 1–8 stations)	64K to 128K bytes		and execution. The larger the available memory the
	✔ Large-cluster (shared by 1–24 or more stations)	64K to 128K bytes		better the applications free-dom.

(Continued on next page)

Table 3.7 (Cont'd.)

FEATURE	TYPICAL CONFIGURATION	PRODUCT CAPABILITIES		IMPORTANCE OF FEATURE
		PTS/1200	*Brand X*	
Controller	✔ Word size	16-bit		The controller is the central
	✔ Number of operator stations per controller	1–8 stations, or 1–24 stations		processor of a distributed system. Its power in terms of word size, attachment
	✔ Number of peripheral attachments per controller	1–4 peripherals, or 1–20 peripherals		capacities, programmability and ability to perform multiple tasks concurrently is
	✔ Availability of high-level languages	Yes, MACROL. COBOL in the future		the key limiting factor in its ultimate performance.
	✔ Ability to perform multitasking	Yes Up to 32 tasks concurrently on one controller		
Terminals	✔ Variety of screen sizes	960 or 1920		The terminal is the point of operator interface and
	✔ Variety of keyboard options	3270 typewriter data entry		should be capable of being comfortable to use, easy to use, and easily matched to
	✔ Availability of user-definable function keys	16 program function keys plus any key programmable		one or many different applications through customizing.
	✔ Ability to provide operator prompting	Yes by screen, audio and light indicators		
	✔ Ability to attach remote terminals on phone line	Yes		
Peripheral Attachments	✔ Number of attachments per controller	1–4 or 1–20, any combination		The ability to attach a variety of peripheral equipment of various speeds and capaci-
	✔ Low-speed printer devices	45–165 CPS, 3 models		ties is a measure of the range of work a system can
	✔ High-speed printer devices	300 LPM and 600 LPM		do.
	✔ Card reading devices	300 CPM		
	✔ Magnetic tape transports	800 and 1600 BPI		
	✔ Printers word processing quality	Yes		

Table 3.7 (Cont'd.)

FEATURE	TYPICAL CONFIGURATION	PRODUCT CAPABILITIES		IMPORTANCE OF FEATURE
		PTS/1200	*Brand X*	
Communications Protocols	✔ Asynchronous	Yes, TTY RS-232		The ability to support more than one protocol—at the same time on the same system—adds immeasurably to the number of tasks and number of networks a system can work in without additional user development effort.
	✔ Synchronous	Yes		
	✔ Binary synchronous —Batch —Interactive	Yes Yes		
	✔ Synchronous data link control (SDLC)	Yes, in 1979		
Intelligent 3270 Operations	✔ Local format storage	Yes		This feature assures that the system can work immediately and easily with the most popular terminal devices in use today, and extend the performance of those devices in a variety of ways.
	✔ Local printing	Yes		
	✔ Ability to access and update local data bases	Yes		
	✔ Transactions stored locally, batched for transmission to host	Yes		
	✔ Field verification at each terminal location	Yes		
	✔ Application program decides when to go to host	Yes		
Emulation Capabilities	✔ 3270 interactive (dumb)	Yes		Emulators are software tools that permit a system to operate as a look-alike under other vendors' protocols and procedures. Their advantage is to permit direct and immediate attachment to networks using a specific device protocol.
	✔ 3270 interactive (intelligent)	Yes		
	✔ 2780 batch	Yes		
	✔ 3780 batch	Yes		
	✔ SDLC batch/interactive	Yes, in 1979		
	✔ HASP remote job entry	Yes		
	✔ Non-IBM protocols	Yes		
	✔ Specialized protocols	Yes		
Data Base Storage	✔ Multiple disk storage capacities	Yes, from 10 to 320MB		Local data base storage under sound memory management techniques assures powerful local filing, easy offloading of large central files and elimination of unnecessary communications to and from host.
	✔ Memory management software	Yes		
	✔ Ability to expand to very large local storage	Yes, to 320MB per system		

Table 3.7 (Cont'd.)

FEATURE	TYPICAL CONFIGURATION	PRODUCT CAPABILITIES		IMPORTANCE OF FEATURE
		PTS/1200	*Brand X*	
Software Language	✔ Assembly language	Yes, not needed by user personnel		Language is the facility that makes it possible to tap the power of the basic system by allowing applications to be written easily. Simple but rich high-level language that can be learned easily by programmers or used by non-programmers extend a system's reach that much further.
	✔ Strong macro command repertoire	Yes, 150 instructions		
	✔ High-level compiler language(s)	MACROL now, COBOL in 1979		
	✔ Easy to learn and use	Yes		
	✔ Numerous screen manipulation and interactive programming aids	Yes		
	✔ Parameter-driven aids where required	Yes, for format creation and source data entry		
Network Enhancements	✔ Concurrent communications operation	Yes, batch and interactive at same line		
	✔ Downline control of multipoint networks	Yes, up to 10 drops per controller		
	✔ Remote program development support for mainframe in any language	Yes		
	✔ Teleprinter network on terminal lines	Yes, on same lines at same time		
	✔ Downline program debugging	Yes		
	✔ Downline terminal loading	Yes		
	✔ High-speed data transmission rates	To 9600 BPS		

Courtesy of Raytheon Data Systems

Table 3.8
Number of
employees
in DP
vs. company
(by equipment)

Rental Range Per Month	Average Number in DP	Average Number in Company
Under $3,000	8.9	2345
$3,000–$4,499	8.7	1793
$4,500–$5,999	12.0	505
$6,000–$8,999	8.6	617
$9,000–$11,999	17.1	795
$12,000–$14,999	15.5	1028
$15,000–$17,999	14.4	3663
$18,000–$24,999	21.4	4950
$25,000–$49,999	39.3	2594
$50,000–$74,999	59.1	3706
$75,000–$99,999	80.0	4563
$100,000–$149,999	86.7	3895
$150,000 or more	197.2	12507
Not available	36.5	2722
Total	24.1	1900

Source: "1979 DP Salaries Report," **Infosystems,** June 1979. Copyright © Hitchcock Publishing Company, Wheaton, Illinois.

Table 3.9
Allocation
of 1979
DP budget

Expense	Average Percent
Services and software	14.1
Hardware	29.6
Personnel	43.8
Supplies	8.0
Other	4.5
Total	100.0

Source: "1979 DP Salaries Report, **Infosystems,** June 1979. Copyright © Hitchcock Publishing Company, Wheaton, Illinois.

SUMMARY

The technological development of computer and data transmission systems is continuing at a tremendous pace. The computer, first seen by management as a potent tool for processing data, is now envisioned as a powerful assistant in decision making, planning, and control. Line management must learn enough about computer hardware and software to be able to evaluate well-prepared proposals of technicians. Such proposals should be based on a management system and a computer system.

An analogy between manual systems and computer systems provides a starting point for management understanding of computer systems. In addition, management should have a primitive understanding of the binary number system.

The computer system consists essentially of (a) a central processing unit for execution of instructions and control, (2) main memory and secondary storage, (3) I/O (input/output) channels to transmit information between main storage and I/O devices, (4) I/O controllers to provide control signals for simultaneous operation of I/O, and (5) I/O end-devices (terminals).

There has been a trend for adding a variety of user terminals at locations remote from processing units. This has resulted in rapid development of data communications technology and hardware. Data transmission may be simplex (in one direction only), half-duplex (both directions, but not simultaneously), or full-duplex. Transmission channels may be common carrier or private. Available grades of service are low-speed (subvoice grade), medium speed (voice grade), and high-speed (broadband).

Modems are required at each end of a data transmission system to modulate square waves (digit wave forms) for transmission and demodulate them upon reception. Multiplexors and concentrators permit transmission of multiple terminal outputs concurrently (although, in the strict sense, not simultaneously). In addition, front-end devices, or communications controllers, relieve the CPU of message switching, data storage and retrieval activities, handling protocols, etc. These devices actually are general-purpose or dedicated computers themselves.

The development of powerful minicomputers, along with data communications systems, has led to distributed processing. Often distributed processing systems are more economical than a large, centralized CPU. Other hardware units being incorporated in systems are word processing units, computer output microfilming, and computer voice recognition.

Finally, the manager should be familiar with the concepts of operating modes for computer systems: batch processing, multiprogramming, timesharing, and multiprocessing.

While the cost of hardware is going down, expenditures for software are increasing. Software consists of computer programs—sequences of instructions for the computer to execute. A hierarchy of software languages from machine level to user level is making user-machine dialog easier.

Organizational concepts for the computer systems group are also a concern of management. Job titles and examples of organizations are given in this chapter.

With a general knowledge of hardware, software, system, and organizational concepts, the line managers should be able to evaluate EDP proposals with the same confidence that they evaluate proposals for other complex machinery or facilities.

QUESTIONS AND PROBLEMS

1. Match the following:

_____ (1) Input	a.	Binary digit
_____ (2) 111, base 2	b.	Overhead
_____ (3) CPU	c.	Modulator-demodulator
_____ (4) Multiprogramming	d.	Text editing
_____ (5) Bit	e.	Document
_____ (6) Protocol	f.	Six
_____ (7) Modem	g.	Batch processing
_____ (8) Word processing	h.	Concurrent programs
_____ (9) Operating mode	i.	Random access memory
_____ (10) RAM	j.	Central processing unit

2. Identify the components in the diagrammed system by placing the correct letters in the symbols for the components.

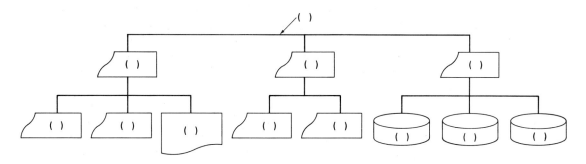

a. Printer   b. Interprocessor bus   c. User work station
d. Data base   e. Application processor

3. Define the following terms:

   a. Computer architecture
   b. Computer operating system
   c. Protocol
   d. Multiplexor
   e. Concentrator

   f. Bit
   g. Overhead (computer program)
   h. Multiprogramming
   i. Multiprocessing.

4. Compare and contrast "computer operating system" with "management operating system."

5. Give a series of steps for selecting a computer system. Make clear the role that management plays.

6. The self-fulfilling prophecy suggests that an event will come true because we believe it will and act accordingly. Discuss the problems of a negative managerial attitude with regard to computerized modeling in terms of self-fulfilling prophecy.

7. How might the term "overhead" be applied to computer hardware and software?

8. Take the role of Jim Booth and respond to the following memo.

   From: R. G. Gill, General Manager
   To: J. Booth, DP Manager

   Jim, I know that we have one of the largest computer processors around. I keep hearing how mini computers and microprocessors are replacing big computers. Will you give me a one or two page writeup telling me what these new devices are and what they could do for us?

9. The Strongarm Company has had a computer installed for about six months. The Controller is on his way down to the Data Processing Department when he happens to bump into the Data Processing Manager, and the following dialog takes place:

   Controller: Hi Bill.
   DP Mgr.:   Oh, hi John. How are you? Hey listen, I'm sorry you missed our department meeting the other day. You know we threw a party when

the System arrived and my wife, that cute little thing, she made a cake in the form of a System. Why, it was one of the cutest little things I ever saw. I told her the key-punch operator just simply loved it.

Controller: Yes, I'm sorry I missed that, Bill, but as you know I was away at a meeting on the boat with Joe, the President.

DP Mgr.: Yes, I know. You seem to have an awful lot of meetings out there on that boat with the President.

Controller: Well, we find the boat very conducive to our meetings. After all, there are no telephones or other distractions to interrupt us.

DP Mgr.: Well, that's very nice, John. By the way, I've made some cards with your kids' names on them. I thought they could use these for trading cards the same way they use the football cards from bubble gum.

Controller: (under his breath) You mean I'm spending over $2000 a month simply to get cards with my kids' names on them? (aloud) Well, Bill, I just thought I'd stop by to find out how things are going in the area of accounts receivable.

DP Mgr.: Accounts receivable? Well, John, we are not doing accounts receivable.

Controller: What do you mean, you are not doing accounts receivable?

DP Mgr.: Just what I said, John. We are not doing accounts receivable. You see, there is something you don't seem to understand. In order to do accounts receivable or any application on a computer system, we have to have what is called "machine readable input." Now, if I were to do accounts receivable first, as you have suggested, I would, first of all, have to take the orders as they come in and give them to the girls at the Order Desk. They would then have to type up the invoices on a typewriter. All right, that's one job function. Then my key-punch operator, Tilly, would have to take those invoices over to Data Processing, where she would key-punch them onto a punch card so they could be put into the computer. You see, John, that is duplication of effort and it is redundant. And so, I am going to be doing billing first so that I capture the data at the source.

Controller: Billing first? But what we wanted was accounts receivable. We don't want billing.

DP Mgr.: I know, John, but what I said is that we are going to be doing billing first because we have to have that in order to do accounts receivable.

Controller: But I thought the computer could do anything. That's what I was told.

DP Mgr.: It can. John, don't worry about it. We will get to accounts receivable, but right now, we are only doing billing and, by the way, it is going just great. The way I am handling the special pricing and the back orders is terrific.

Controller: That brings up a question, Bill. How are you handling the back orders?

DP Mgr.: Well, John, I am glad you asked me that, because here is how I see it. What I am going to do is that if we have the item in the warehouse when we receive the order, I'm going to go ahead and ship that item. Then, if we don't have the item in the warehouse, what I am going to do out on my disk is to flag that item.

Controller: You are going to do what?

DP Mgr.: I am going to flag it.

Controller: Flag it?

DP Mgr.: Yes, flag it. That way at the end of a day, John, I can give you a report that shows you everything we couldn't ship.

Controller: Let me see if I understand what you are telling me. You are telling me that at the end of a day, I am going to get a report that will show me everything I couldn't ship.

DP Mgr.: That's right. That's called "management information."

Controller: That's not what I call it. Listen, Bill, we wanted to have the back orders on the invoices when they went out to the customers. That way, they knew we properly received their order and we also knew that we would have out-of-stock items on back order for them. I don't want to receive a report at the end of the day that shows me everything we couldn't ship.

DP Mgr.: Well, look, John, I just assumed that was the way you wanted things. After all, I didn't know you wanted the back order on the invoice.

Controller: Well, why didn't you ask somebody?

DP Mgr.: Because, John, you are never around. You are always on that boat. I mean, after all, if you want me to go ahead and put the back order on the invoice the way you want to do it, I mean, I would blow core. I would have to go from my 3000's to my 4000's and I would completely destroy the interface to my I/O module. I mean, it simply cannot be done.

Controller: There you go again, telling me it can't be done. I thought this computer could do anything.

DP Mgr.: John, I just assumed . . . .

Controller: Again, Bill, you cannot go around assuming things.

DP Mgr.: Well, if you think you know so much about system design and everything, John, here it is. Here's the entire system. You go ahead and make any changes that you want to make.

Controller: You know I don't understand anything about that kind of stuff.

DP Mgr.: That's my point exactly, John, you don't understand. After all, that's why you hired me. You know, I was number one in my school.

Controller: Yes, I know. We are all very proud of that simple little fact.

DP Mgr.: All right, John, I understand you are upset. Don't worry. I am in control of things. I will go ahead and take it from here and try. I will see if I can arrest this back-order problem and put it on the invoices' without having to upgrade my equipment. But it may require some more funding in the area of Data Processing.

Controller: Oh, gosh, there we go. More money in Data Processing.

DP Mgr.: That's all right, John, don't worry about it. I am in control.

Controller: Speaking about control, tell me, Bill, how are you coming along on your house hunting?

DP Mgr.: Boy, am I glad you asked me that question! You know, I now know why they call this the Gold Coast down here. Do you know how expensive things are? I was wondering, John, if you had a couple of minutes if we could talk about my raise.

Controller: Raise? Look, Bill, I am already late for a meeting out on the boat with the President. But, if I were you looking at houses, I wouldn't rush into any quick closings.

a. Discuss how the controller could handle the "time problem" of meetings on the boat and demands of subordinates.

b. What do you think of the DP manager's production of "trading cards"?

c. Does the controller appear to have a good perspective of computer applications? Discuss.

d. Do you think the DP manager is tactful or not? Why?

e. Would you follow the same line of system development as the DP manager is doing?

f. What is the basic problem illustrated by this case, and how could it be remedied?

10. The Astrodyne Co. located in New York City wishes to provide connections to 12 terminals in its major branch office in Chicago. The distance between buildings is 750 miles. The terminals operate at 300 bits/sec. Three options are being considered: (1) individual leased lines, (2) two frequency-division multiplexors per line on two leased lines, with 6 terminals/leased line, or (3) two time-division multiplexors on one leased line. Astrodyne has investigated and found the following costs:

FDM equipment $32/month/channel end
TDM equipment $260/month fixed cost
                            plus $23/month per low speed port
Modem equipment $10/month for 300 bits/sec. units
                            $55/month for 2400 bits/sec. units
                            $110/month for 4800 bits/sec. units
                            $220/month for 9600 bits/sec. units
Cost of voice-grade lines—leased $750

Evaluate the following three alternatives:

a. CPU–modem–individual voice-grade lines for the 12 circuits–modem–terminal

b. Frequency-division multiplexing with the arrangement of CPU–FDM–voice-grade line–FDM–terminals.

c. Time-division multiplexing with the arrangement of CPU–TDM–modem–voice-grade line–modem–TDM–terminals.

GLOSSARY OF COMPUTER ACRONYMS

ACS	advanced communication service (of AT&T)
ADP	automatic data processing
ANSI	American National Standards Institute
ASCII	American standard code for information interchange
BCD	binary-coded decimal
BPI	bytes per inch
CAD	computer automated design
CAM	computer automated manufacturing
CBI	computer-based instruction

COM	computer output microfilm
CPS	cycles per second
CPU	central processing unit
CRT	cathode ray tube
DASD	direct-access storage device
DBMS	data-base management system
DDD	direct distance dialing
DDS	digital data service
DOS	disk operating system
DP	data processing
DPS	distributed processing system
EBCDIC	extended BCD interchange code
EDP	electronic data processing
EFT	electronic fund transfer
FDM	frequency-division multiplexing
FM	facilities management
Hz	hertz (cycles/sec)
IBG	interblock gap (between records on magnetic tape)
IC	integrated circuit
I/O	input/output
IOCS	input/output control system
IPS	inches per second (tapes)
KHz	kilohertz
LPM	lines per minute
LSI	large-scale integration
MICR	magnetic ink character recognition
MOS	metal oxide semiconductor
MUX	multiplexor
MVX	virtual storage
OCR	optical character recognition
OCS	optical character scanner
OS	operating system
PIN	personal identification number
PPS	page printing system
RAM	random access memory
RCN	remote computing networks
RDOS	real-time disc operating system
RTOS	real-time operating system
SNA	systems network architecture
STDM	synchronous time-division multiplexing
TDM	time-division multiplexing
TTY	teletype
TWX	typewriter exchange service
UPS	uninterruptible power supply
VM	virtual memory
WATS	wide-area telephone service

SELECTED REFERENCES

ASTEN, K. J., *Data Communications for Business Information Systems.* New York: Macmillan, 1973.

BERGLUND, RALPH G., "Comparing Network Architectures," *Datamation,* February 1978.

BOEHM, BARRY W., "Software and Its Impact: A Quantitative Assessment," *Datamation,* May 1973.

BURCH, JOHN G., JR., FELIX R. STRATER, and GARY GRUDNITSKI. *Information Systems: Theory and Practice* (2nd ed.). New York: John Wiley, 1979.

BURNS, J. CHRISTOPHER, "The Evolution of Office Information Systems," *Datamation,* April 1977.

DIEBOLD GROUP, INC., THE, eds., *Automated Data Processing Handbook.* New York: McGraw-Hill, 1977.

DOLL, DIXON R., *Data Communications.* New York: John Wiley, 1978.

ENSLOW, PHILIP H., JR., "Multiprocessor Organization—A Survey," *Computer Surveys,* March 1977.

FLORES, IVAN, *Peripheral Devices.* Englewood Cliffs, N.J.: Prentice-Hall, Inc., 1973.

FOSS, W. B., "Guidelines for Computer Selection," *Journal of Systems Management,* March 1976.

FRANK, HOWARD, "Tomorrow's People to Determine DDP's Price Tags," *Data Communications,* September 1977.

FREEMAN, DONALD E., and OLNEY R. PERRY, *I/O Design: Data Management in Operating Systems.* Rochelle Park, N.J.: Hayden Book Co., 1977.

HANSEN, JOHN R., "Word Processing More Power to the User," *Infosystems,* April 1977.

JOY, JAMES, J., "Pricing DP Services," *Journal of Systems Management,* November 1977.

MAHMOUD, SAMY A., and K. C. TOTH, "A Modelling Approach to Systems Analysis of Processing Networks," *Canadian Datasystems,* April 1977.

MCNAMARA, JOHN E., *Technical Aspects of Communication.* Maynard, Mass.: Digital Equipment Corp., 1977.

MILLER, FREDERICK W., "Talk It Over With Your Computer," *Infosystems,* August 1978.

"Minicomputers Challenge the Big Machines," *Business Week,* April 26, 1976.

NOLAN, RICHARD L., "Business Needs a New Breed of EDP Manager," *Harvard Business Review,* March–April 1976.

PERRY, WILLIAM E., "Internal Auditing of DP," *Infosystems,* August 1977.

SHARPE, WILLIAM F., *The Economics of Computers.* New York: Columbia University Press, 1969.

STIMLER, SAUL, *Data Processing Systems: Their Performance, Evaluation, Measurement, and Improvement.* Trenton, N.J.: Motivational Learning Programs, Inc., 1974.

TANENBAUM, ANDREW S., *Structured Computer Organization.* Englewood Cliffs, N.J.: Prentice-Hall, 1976.

THEIS, DOUGLAS, "An Overview of Memory Technologies," *Datamation,* January 1978.

THIERAUF, ROBERT J., *Distributed Processing Systems.* Englewood Cliffs, N.J.: Prentice-Hall, 1978.

WEISSMAN, CLARK, "Tradeoff Considerations in Security System Design," *Data Management,* April 1972. Reprinted in Robert G. Murdick and Joel E. Ross, *MIS in Action.* St. Paul, Minn.: West Publishing Company, 1975.

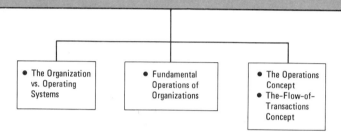

chapter 4

Organization, Operating Systems, and Information

- The Organization vs. Operating Systems
- Fundamental Operations of Organizations
- The Operations Concept
- The-Flow-of-Transactions Concept

PURPOSE: To demonstrate the concepts of organizational structure, operating subsystems, information flows, and the level of data-capture for operations and transactions.

An organization is not a hierarchy of boxes connected by lines; it is a set of problem-solving systems whose structures are described by information flows.

The design of the MIS must be related to the structure of the organization and vice versa. The organizational structure depends generally upon the purpose of the company, its size, and the industry to which the organization belongs. In this chapter we examine the nature of operating systems as the bases for information systems. Our examination includes a discussion of the level at which data are recorded in terms of operations and transactions.

THE ORGANIZATION VS. OPERATING SYSTEMS

One of the major difficulties faced by large organizations is that the authority/responsibility structure is not congruent with the problem-solving systems. For example, new product development consists of an operating system which includes people from engineering, marketing, manufacturing, and accounting. This new product development system cuts across the traditional functional structure of organization.

Two other examples are worth mentioning: the order processing system and the capital budgeting system. The objectives of the order processing system are to accept orders from customers and/or salespersons, follow up on orders to see that they are filled accurately and promptly, and notify the customer of any problems. People from the production, accounting, warehouse, and shipping organizations are all involved in this operation. This system clearly requires a wide lateral system of information flow rather than the vertical system associated with the functional organization structure.

Even more complex, perhaps, is the capital budgeting system of large organizations. In the typical functional organization this system involves many people both laterally and vertically (Figure 4.1). Once again, the operating system is mismatched with the basic authority/responsibility structure.

One usual difficulty is that many persons in an organization provide functional specialties to a number of operating systems. In essence, they must be responsible to their functional managers and to the managers responsible for the operating system (if anyone is responsible for the system). This violates the tradition of unity of command. In the next section, we shall see how companies use patchwork devices to overcome this problem. Since the MIS must serve both the hierarchical responsibility structure and the operating (and decision) systems, this organizational problem is also an MIS problem.

Figure 4.1 Capital budgeting system

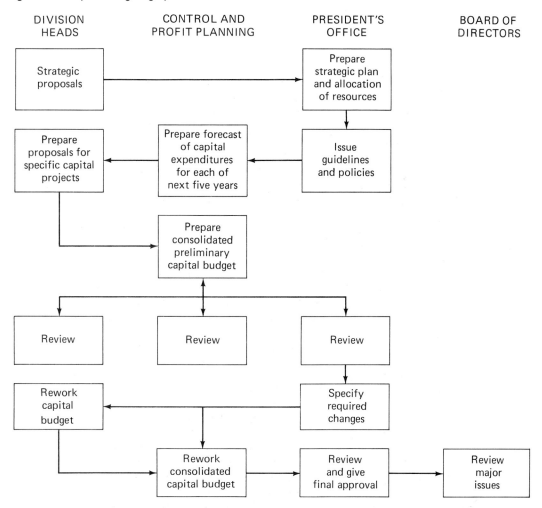

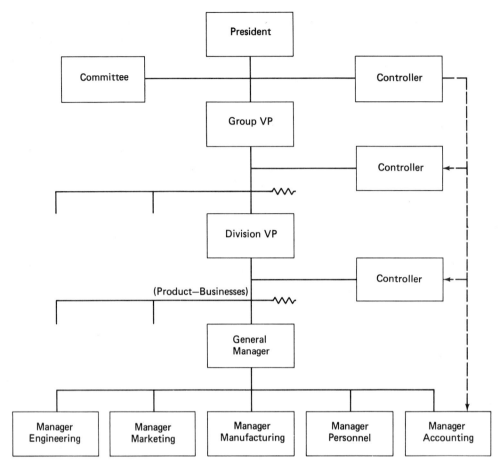

Figure 4.2 Staff coordination

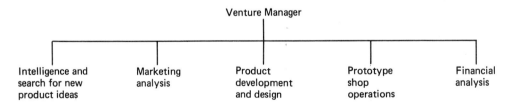

Figure 4.3 Venture team

Functional-Traditional Structure

In Chapter 2 we covered the classical principles of organization. The classical concepts of division of labor and organization around specialties or disciplines led to a hierarchical structure. Information flow in such organizations is designed to be primarily vertical, modified only through lateral relationships that may develop informally. The more important the problem that arises at a low level between two units, the higher up in the organization information must flow before a solution flows back down to coordinate the two units.

For day-to-day problem solving and coordination, the flow of information shown in Fig. 4.1 is obviously too slow and cumbersome. The more people that are in the communications channel, the more distorted the information is likely to become. In practice, informal relationships develop among members at each level of such organizations. However, since there is no *formal* lateral information flow, such informal systems may fail. When they do, responsibility for such failures may be placed upon managers who were not kept informed.

Line-Staff-Committee Structures

The introduction of staff executives and staff groups meant that line managers throughout the organization gained access to technical expertise. Staff managers, by their contacts with managers throughout the company, became an information storage bank of good ideas and common problems. They prepared policies and procedures for top management to issue to coordinate practices for the company as a whole.

Staff influence in the accounting area has grown so that middle line management is bypassed completely in many instances. Figure 4.2 shows by dotted lines the flow of information from top-level staff to the accounting managers at lower levels. Policies, procedures, directives, and informal conversations are the means for exercising this authority.

Teams, Task Forces, and Projects

In an effort to align formal authority with operating systems, the grouping of individuals from various functional areas has been tried. Teams, task forces, and projects have been formed, usually on a temporary basis, to operate a system until specific objectives have been accomplished. In Figure 4.3 we see a venture management team which has been established for a long-term series of venture developments. The venture team contains all specialists required to develop a new product. In some cases the venture teams must initially market the new product. In this case, the organization is matched to the operations to be performed.

Organization Trends

The introduction of teams and task forces has been an attempt to formalize lateral and network information flows required to solve system problems. One trend has been to partition the firm along several dimensions and place respon-

Areas (Profit Centers)

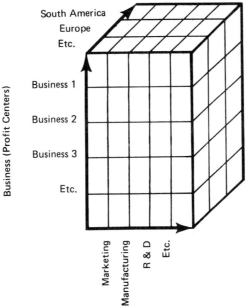

Figure 4.4
Three-dimensional organization

South America
Europe
Etc.

Business (Profit Centers)

Business 1

Business 2

Business 3

Etc.

Marketing
Manufacturing
R & D
Etc.

Source: William C. Goggin, "How the Multidimensional Structure Works at Dow Corning," **Harvard Business Review,** January-February 1974.

Functions (Cost Centers)

sibility with managers for each dimension. For example, William C. Goggin, CEO of Dow Corning Corporation, presented a four-dimensional design of organization at Dow Corning. Three dimensions, shown in Figure 4.4, are:

1. Business profit centers—the different businesses that the company is engaged in. The businesses are product lines that serve a related group of industries, markets, or customers.
2. Cost centers, such as the functional activities of marketing, manufacturing, and finance. Support cost centers such as corporate planning, corporate communications, and legal services are also included here.
3. Geographical area.

The fourth dimension is *time,* in which the organization changes form.[1]

If we examine the main concerns of large businesses, we may anticipate the extension of Dow Corning's multidimensional organization structure to five dimensions (plus a sixth, time, if we wish). Figures 4.5(a) through (e) show these dimensions and the systems to be managed in each dimension. The dimensions are

1. Strategic business units
2. Cost centers

[1]William C. Goggin, "How the Multidimensional Structure Works at Dow Corning," *Harvard Business Review,* January–February 1974.

3. Phase systems

4. Resource systems

5. Geographical area systems.

At present, companies *do* manage along these dimensions in a hodgepodge fashion. The organization structure is usually hierarchical along product lines and ultimately along functional lines. Responsibility for human resources, capital assets, and so on is often assigned to committees or diffused throughout the organization. Responsibility for the phase systems is so compartmentalized that it is a wonder that products drift through the company and into the market.

Companies need to be organized in terms of the five dimensions of Fig. 4.5. Managers should be assigned specific responsibility for each dimension and for each system of each dimension. Information flows in the MIS should be developed to aid in the planning and controlling of each dimension and each system. Managers should be rotated so that they may learn the problems in each organizational dimension.

Figure 4.5 Dimensions of organization for business

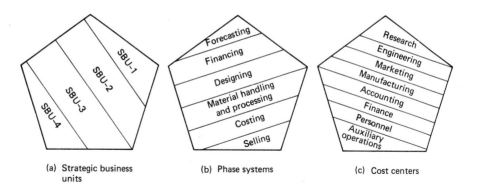

(a) Strategic business units

(b) Phase systems

(c) Cost centers

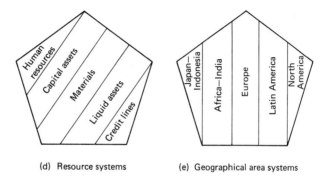

(d) Resource systems

(e) Geographical area systems

Organizations in our society vary widely in terms of primary purpose or mission. Business firms may be classified according to industry, as shown in Table 4.1. These industries are subdivided further in the full seven-digit SIC classification. The chain of fundamental operations of firms varies from industry to industry because of the differences in purpose. In Table 4.2 we may see these activity chains and examples of each. To a great extent, companies organize around these activities.

Supporting financial operations for the primary operations of Table 4.2 are billing, collecting, and disbursing. We have shown the interrelations among the basic operations in Figure 4.6.

Table 4.1
SIC classification of firms according to industry

DIVISION A	Agriculture, Forestry, and Fisheries
DIVISION B	Mining
DIVISION C	Contract Construction
DIVISION D	Manufacturing

19	ordnance and accessories
20	food and kindred products
21	tobacco manufacturers
22	textile mill products
23	apparel and other finished products made from fabrics and other similar materials
24	lumber and wood products except furniture
25	furniture and fixtures
26	paper and allied products
27	printing, publishing, and allied industries
28	chemicals and allied industries
29	petroleum refining and related industries
30	rubber and miscellaneous plastic products
31	leather and leather products
32	stone, clay, and glass products
33	primary metal industries
34	fabricated metal products, except ordnance, machinery, and transportation equipment
35	machinery, except electrical
36	electrical machinery, equipment
37	transportation equipment
38	professional, scientific, and controlling instruments photographic, optical, watches and clocks
39	miscellaneous manufacturing industries

DIVISION E	Transportation, Communication, Electrical, Gas, and Sanitary Services
DIVISION F	Wholesale and Retail Trade
DIVISION G	Finance, Insurance, and Real Estate
DIVISION H	Services
DIVISION I	Government
DIVISION J	Nonclassifiable Establishments

Table 4.2
Activity chains

Activity Chains	Typical Organizations
Design a service ... Provide the service	Not-for-profit and government agencies
Design ... Sell ... Provide the service	Service companies and some not-for-profit organizations
Purchase ... Store ... Sell ... (Ship)	Retail and wholesale firms, some not-for-profit organizations
Sell ... Design ... Purchase ... Store ... Manufacture ... Store ... Ship	Custom manufacturers, shipbuilders, military defense components, manufacturers, machine tool manufacturers
Design ... Purchase ... Store ... Manufacture ... Store ... Sell ... Ship	Mass production and batch production; manufacturers of consumer goods

Figure 4.6 Basic operations

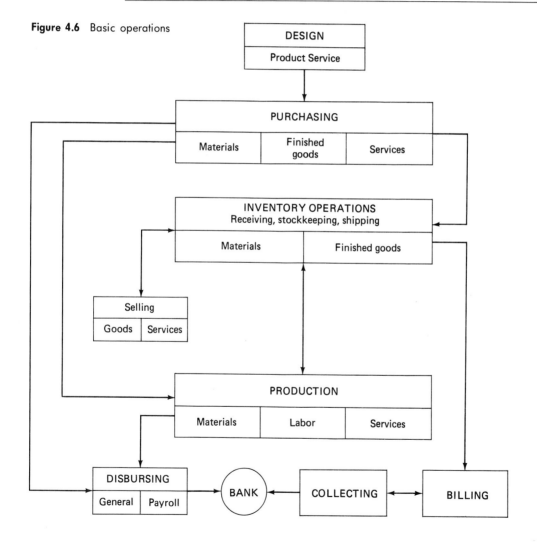

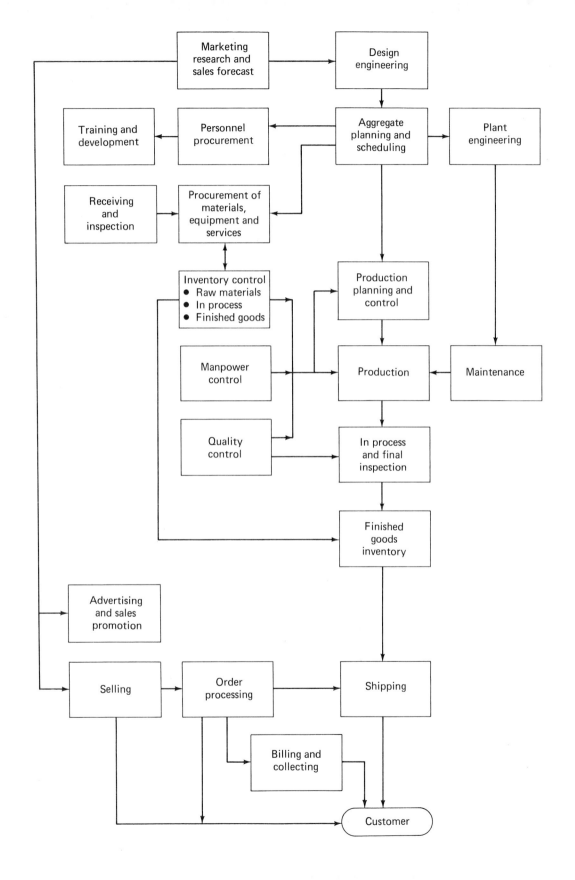

Manufacturing Company Operating System

The fundamental operating systems of Figure 4.6 may be developed more specifically for each industry. In addition, the typical subsystems making up the entire company may be shown along with their interrelationships. In Fig. 4.7 we have presented the operating subsystems in a manufacturing company. This is a simplified figure because only major relationships among subsystems are shown. For example, personnel procurement is related to all operating systems, because all the systems employ human resources. As another example, the design engineering system may be broken down into a number of subsystems such as design analysis, laboratory testing, and drafting. In addition, we have omitted the administrative and the financial systems.

Department Store Operations

Department store chains may vary from three stores in a single state to hundreds of stores throughout the country. Generally, there is centralized planning and controlling of merchandising, advertising, and human resources. While there may be intermediate levels of regional management, local store management is the primary focus of operations.

In Figure 4.8, the aggregate planning for all stores in a chain is carried out by top management. A number of operating subsystems deal with specific areas of the total planning and controlling, as shown in Fig. 4.8. For each store, the fundamental systems for acquiring merchandise, selling, controlling costs, and handling personnel activities are essentially the same. Operations at a store are usually closely limited by policies and procedures developed by corporate-level management.

Bank Operations

Banks differ from manufacturing and many other types of organizations because of the diversity of "mainstream" operations they perform. Manufacturing companies generally do no more than produce and sell a product. Department stores buy and sell. Banks, however, supply a variety of services beyond the two typical ones of storing and loaning money. Figure 4.9 shows operating systems separately. These systems are integrated by top management review of net return on each dollar available. Control of cash and securities is also a strong integrating operation for a bank.

Hospital Operations

Hospitals, like banks, supply services. While banks operate on money, hospitals process people. Figure 4.10, on page 122, shows the typical operations of a hospital.

Figure 4.7 (Opposite) Operating systems in a manufacturing company

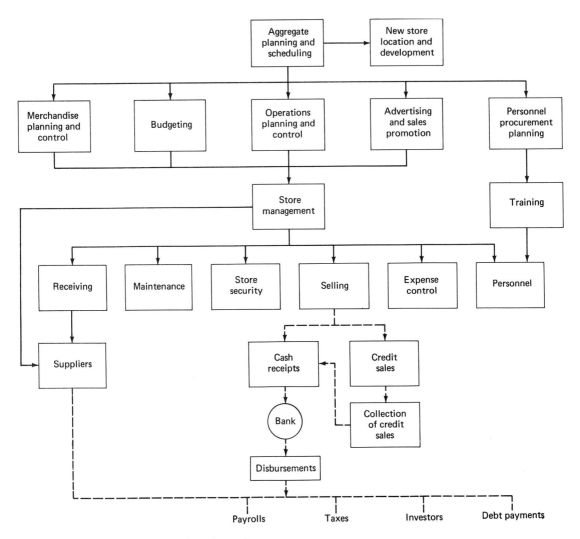

Figure 4.8 Operations flow chart for a department store

Figure 4.9 (Opposite) Bank operations
Source: Expanded from Robert G. Murdick et al.,
Accounting Information Systems (Englewood Cliffs,
N.J.: Prentice-Hall, 1978), p. 82.

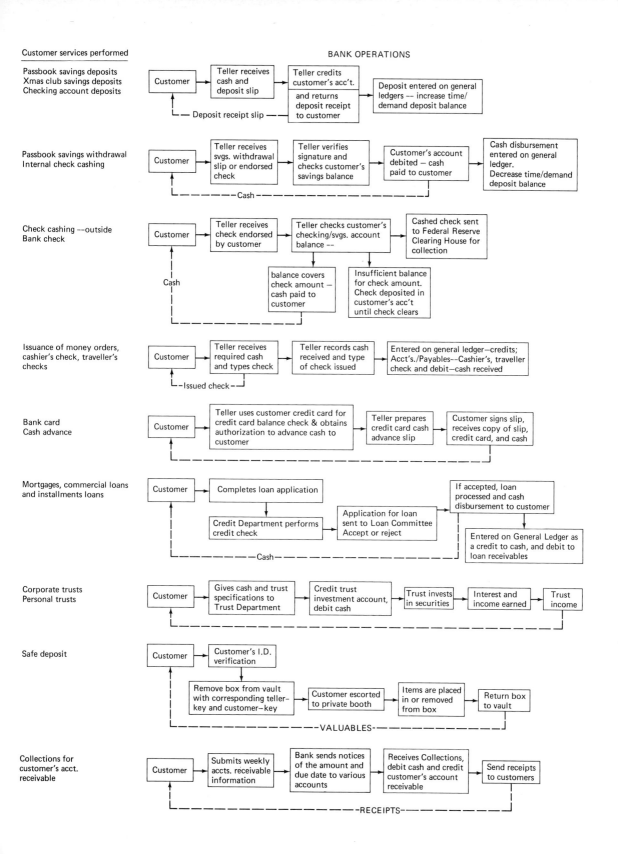

Figure 4.10 Hospital operations flow chart

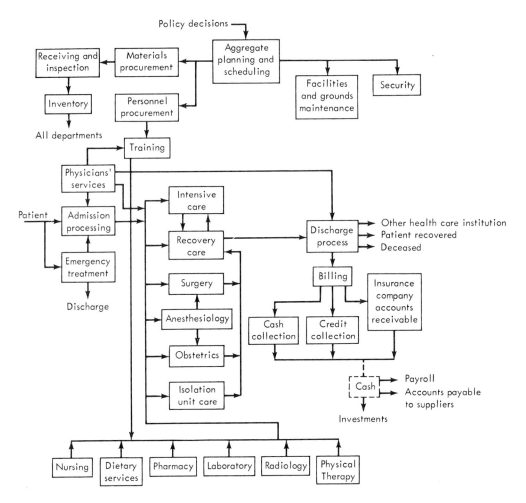

Source: Robert G. Murdick et al., **Accounting Information Systems** (Englewood Cliffs, N.J.: Prentice-Hall, 1978), p. 83. Reprinted by permission of Prentice-Hall, Inc., Englewood Cliffs, New Jersey.

Airline Operations

Airline companies have immense time pressures because of airplane schedules and interconnections with other airlines. In addition, large sums of capital must be raised and allocated to new generations of planes. As a result, management must have a very good MIS for both short- and long-term problems. The operational systems which must be monitored by the MIS are shown, with some simplification, in Figure 4.11.

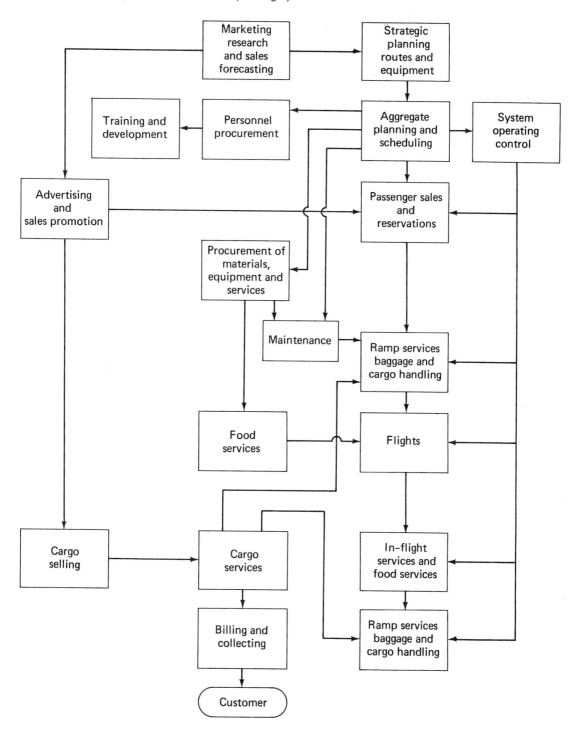

Figure 4.11 An airline operating system

Table 4.3
Subsystems
in a
manufacturing
company

MANAGEMENT OPERATIONS AND INFORMATION SYSTEMS

Environmental monitoring system
Strategic planning
Organization
Acquisitions and divestitures
Policies
Managerial and financial audit and control
Government, stockholder, and public relations
Management audit

MAINSTREAM OPERATIONS AND INFORMATION SYSTEMS

Engineering	*Marketing*	*Production*
Engineering design	Marketing research	Production planning
Engineering change	Marketing intelligence	Raw materials and goods-in-process inventory control
Bill of materials	New product planning	
Engineering and production control	Sales forecasting	
Product testing	Spare parts sales forecasting	Order release (dispatching)
Engineering standards and specifications	Advertising and sales promotion	Plant monitoring and control
Drafting	Personal selling	Tool control
New product development (advance engineering)	Channels of distribution	Equipment maintenance
Engineering administration	Warehousing and inventory management	Materials handling
	Pricing	Production
	Order processing	Quality control
	Customer service	Methods and time standards
		Value analysis
		Operations and standards
		Receiving
		Shipping

SUPPORTING OPERATIONS AND INFORMATION SYSTEMS

Financial and Accounting

Profit planning and expense budgets   Accounts receivable
Capital budgets   Accounts payable
Cash flow and cash investment   Credit
Cost center planning and budgeting   Billing
Internal control and audit   Payroll

Human Resources

Manpower planning   Health and safety
Recruiting and staffing   Employee benefits
Organizational development and change   Labor relations
Wage and salary administration   Personnel administration

Administrative

Purchasing   Physical facilities and maintenance
Physical distribution and traffic   Security
EDP system   Internal mail
MIS   Document reproduction
Office planning and work flow

We have discussed the general outline of operating systems for various types of companies. Now we will look at the subsystems found in practice for a manufacturing company. We will also give examples showing the combined operating (process) system and information system. We recall at this point that the operations diagram shows a process or series of tasks to be performed. The information system shows the relationships among the elements of the operating system—that is, the structure of the system.

Subsystems and Organizational Objectives

A company may be divided conceptually into a set of subsystems along any of the five dimensions we have discussed. The subsystems corresponding to the cost centers—the functional organizational components—are the easiest to present. In a manufacturing company, the objectives of these subsystems are the well-established objectives of engineering, marketing, production, finance, and personnel.

Typical Subsystems of the Manufacturing Company

When we attempt to list systems (operating or information) along the functional or cost center dimension, we find that some fit neatly into the organization and some cut across organizational boundaries. We may start with the following grouping of subsystems for a manufacturing firm:

1. Management
2. Engineering
3. Marketing
4. Manufacturing.

The following are supporting groups of systems:

5. Financial/accounting
6. Administrative
7. Human resources.

Table 4.3 summarizes the subsystems which make up these seven major systems for a manufacturing company. While many of these subsystems may be found in other types of organizations, it is apparent that there are differences among organizations within industries and between industries.

Examples of Information System Flow Charts

Operating systems depend on information systems which are interwoven with the operations. Three types of flow charts are useful to the systems analyst:

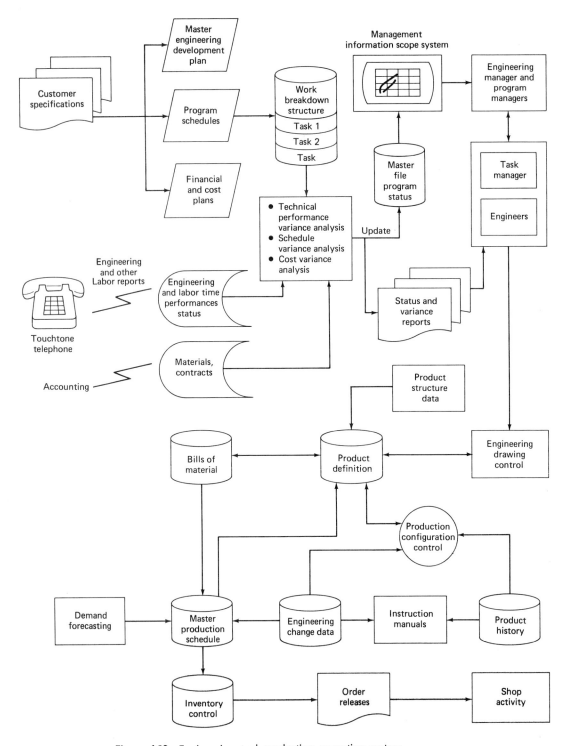

Figure 4.12 Engineering and production operating system

1. Operations or process charts. These charts show only the activities or steps in performing a process. They are useful for analyzing the type of work done and the sequence of work.
2. Information and document flow charts. These are useful in analyzing dissemination of information (or lack of it) for operating and control purposes.
3. Combinations of operations and information flow charts. These present a more nearly complete picture of the operation being studied and the critical documents or information.

Engineering and production control

Let us start with the design and manufacture of a product. An example of the flow chart for these operations is shown in Figure 4.12. Engineering processes may differ according to product and company, but all engineering leads to product specifications. The definition of the product in terms of structure, parts list, materials, and standards must be supplied to a production planning and control organization. Production planning and control makes available the equipment, materials, and human resources according to scheduled needs. Shop activities, directed by foremen, carry out the actual production of goods.

Inventory control

Part of the production system is the inventory control system, illustrated by a simplified flow chart in Figure 4.13. This is an important system because production hinges on having materials available when needed, yet the cost of

Figure 4.13 Inventory control system

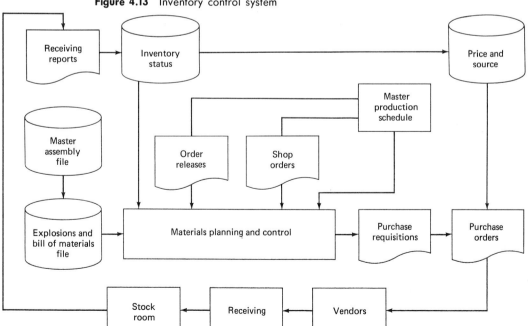

maintaining inventory may be large. The materials planning and control group tries to avoid stockouts, minimize the number of orders placed, take advantage of volume discounts, and minimize inventory on hand. Since all of these objectives cannot be achieved, the materials group tries to minimize *total system* costs by making trade-offs among these objectives.

The inventory system consists essentially of inventory on hand and changes due to additions and withdrawals. Current production requirements, planned

Figure 4.14 Marketing system

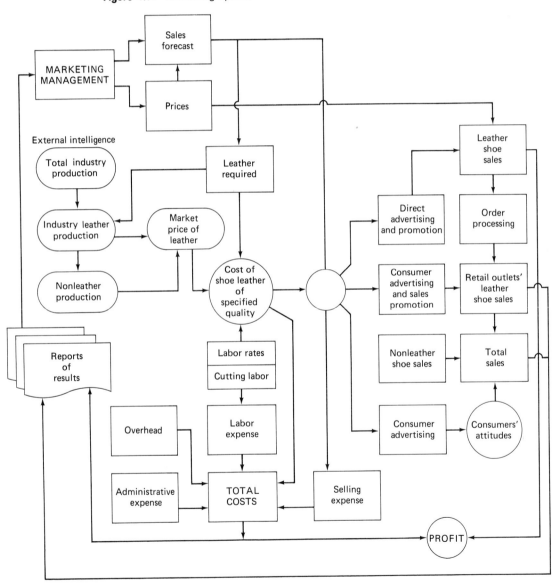

production activities, receipts of goods, and forecasts of goods to be received are inputs to the materials planning and control activity.

Marketing system

Marketing systems can be quite complex because they combine external information, a variety of marketing functions, cost data, and a wide variety of reports. A simplified flow chart for a manufacturer of leather shoes is shown in Figure 4.14.

In business, all plans start with the company's sales forecast. The sales forecast depends upon the product's competitive edge, the price established by the company, the company's promotional efforts, customer preferences, and service level offered by the company. In Fig. 4.14 we see that the company's demand for leather affects the cost of the leather to the company. The budgets for promotion to retailers and to consumers will be based upon the revenues estimated from the sales forecast. The channel of distribution selected by marketing is the retail store.

Marketing must obtain cost information from production, through accounting, to insure that the price established covers cost of sales as well as marketing and administrative expense. Total retail sales are made up of leather and non-leather shoe sales as determined by consumers' preferences. Reports of both types of sales are important to marketing management.

Order processing system

The order processing system is sometimes viewed as containing elements from accounting and finished goods inventory systems as well as marketing. If we attempt to limit the system to marketing elements, we might draw a flow chart such as that shown in Figure 4.15. As orders arrive, they must be edited (checked for completeness and accuracy). The customer, if a new one, must be checked for his credit rating. Order processing is responsible for seeing that the order is filled promptly and that the customer is billed. Note that the handy worksheet of Fig. 4.15 makes flow-charting easier.

Human resources management system

The traditional personnel system which still exists in many companies today concerns itself primarily with hiring and wage administration. The expanding complexity of managing human resources in today's environment has added many other responsibilities to the job of human resources managers, such as training, motivating, advising on legal implications, participating in labor negotiations, organizational development, and developing data-base systems for employee histories and fringe benefit administration. These responsibilities have required that management develop a systems approach to the many human resource management activities. An overall view of such a system is shown in Figure 4.16. One of the subsystems, the staffing system, is shown in Figure 4.17 on page 132.

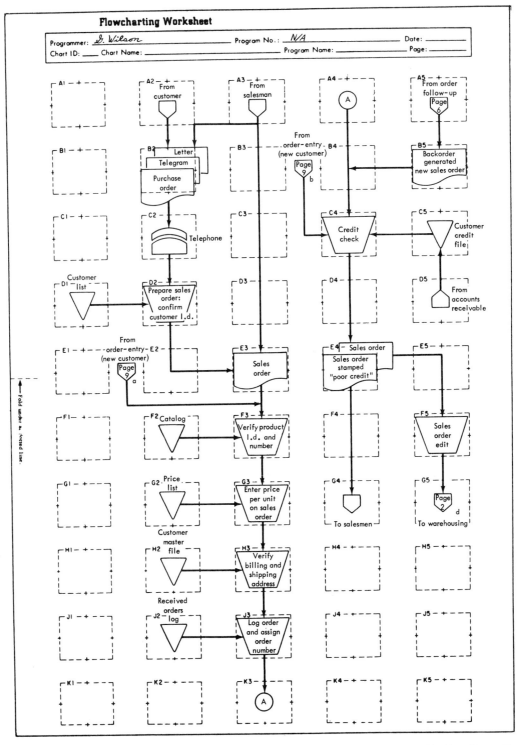

Figure 4.15 Order-entry flow chart   Courtesy of International Business Machines Corporation

Accounts receivable system

The common accounting systems are:

1. Personnel, labor costing and payroll
2. Net-change material requirements planning
3. Accounts payable
4. Accounts receivable
5. General ledger and financial reporting system.

Many commercial computer programs are available for these systems.

Figure 4.16 The human resource system in the business environment

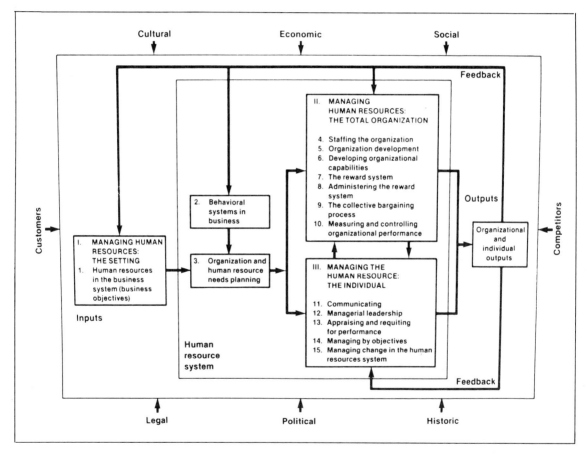

Source: Lawrence A. Klatt, Robert G. Murdick, and Fred E. Schuster,
Human Resource Management: A Behavioral Systems Approach
(Homewood, Ill.: Richard D. Irwin, 1978), p. 13.
© 1978 by Richard D. Irwin, Inc.

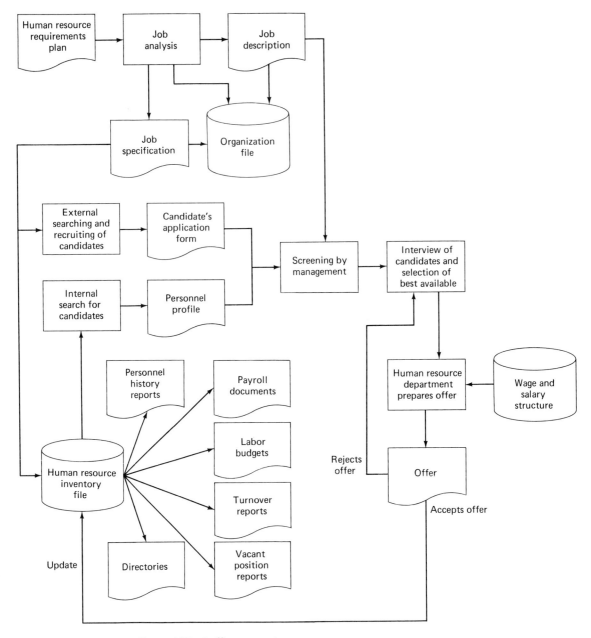

Figure 4.17 Staffing operation

Let us look at the accounts receivable system (A/R) in particular. We may view it as consisting of three major cycles or types of activities: the posting of accounts receivable because of goods shipped or services performed; an inquiry or information-as-required cycle; and the production of reports at the end of the established reporting period.

In Figure 4.18 we may study the flow chart for the posting cycle. Let us review the steps in this cycle:

1. Load A/R transactions.
2. Edit the A/R by checking each against the customer file, the A/R master file, and the cross-reference file.
3. Update A/R transactions.
4. Update transfer transactions.
5. Distribute A/R transactions.
6. Recreate cross-reference master file.
7. Print A/R maintenance report.
8. Print A/R edit listing.
9. Print A/R register.
10. Print report of customers exceeding credit limit.
11. Print cash edit listing.
12. Print "cash register."
13. Print unauthorized discount book.
14. Print charge-back report.
15. Print A/R batch control report.
16. Print A/R summary of suspense items.

Cycle-subsystems of a Manufacturing Company

Besides looking at the company as a set of functional subsystems, we may view the company as a set of cycles of economic events. Four of these cycles represent phases of business, while the fifth is a reporting cycle.These cycles are as follows:

1. *Treasury activity.*
   a. Capital funds are received from investors and creditors.
   b. Capital funds are temporarily invested.
   c. Investments are turned to cash needed for operations.
2. *Expenditure activity.* Cash is exchanged for goods and services supplied by vendors and employees.
3. *Conversion activity.* Resources are held, used, or transformed over a period of time.
4. *Revenue activity.* Resources are distributed to outsiders in exchange for cash.
5. *Financial reporting.* Management's activities in planning, measuring, and controlling the other four cycles.

Expenditure cycles and revenue cycles each have an additional step in many cases which involves a promise to pay. This means that cash is not exchanged for goods and services directly.

Figure 4.18 Accounts receivable posting cycle

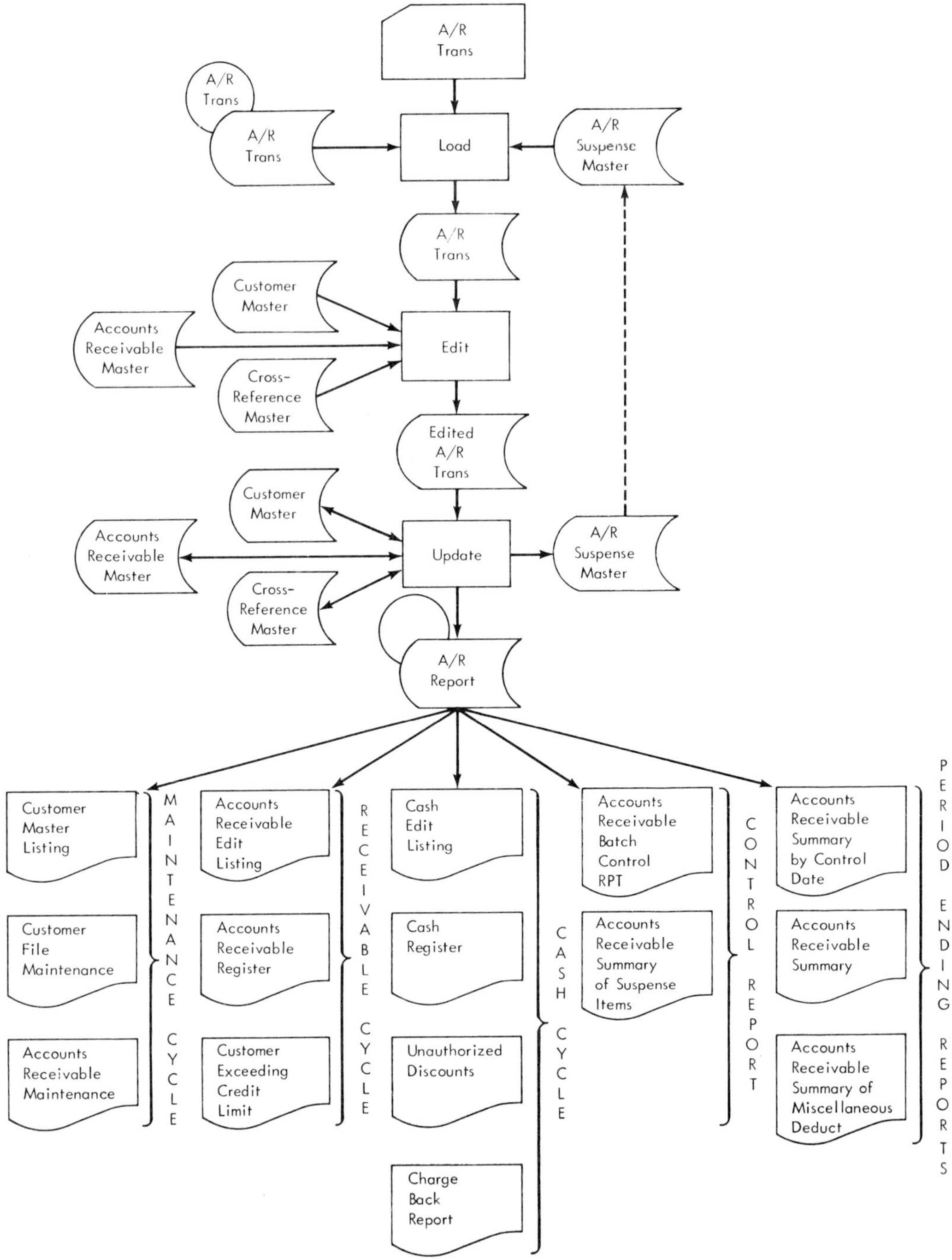

Courtesy of Software International, Andover, Mass.

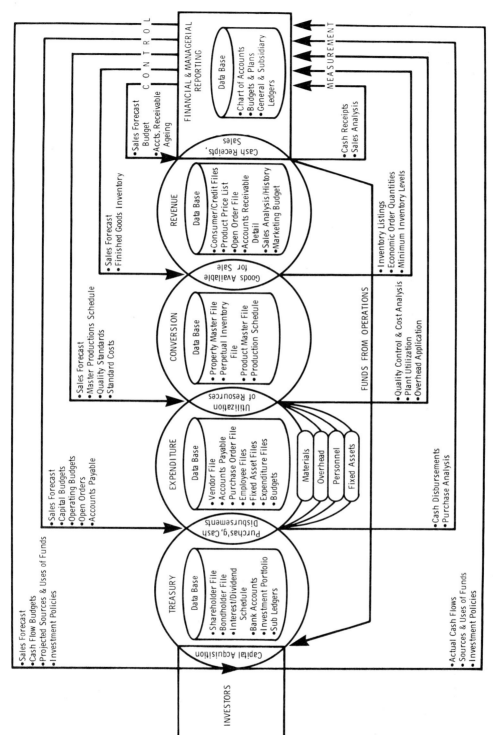

Figure 4.19 Subsystem cycles of a business

135

The overall relationships among these cycle-subsystems is shown in Figure 4.19 on page 135. This figure shows the flow of goods and services, the related flow of cash, and major management information flows.

THE OPERATIONS CONCEPT

A firm could conceivably record every minute transaction, or it could record only major operations and transactions. The level of detail which a firm selects for initial recording is both an economic and information choice. If utilization of labor at the micromotion level were always recorded, the quality control might be good, but the cost might be exorbitant. On the other hand, if we recorded only total labor for the month, control might be poor but record keeping would be inexpensive. It is apparent that we should define the various possible levels of detail of operations so that we may define the transaction level to be recorded.

First, we need a general idea of the meaning of *operation* so that we can break it down into a hierarchy of more detailed operations. An operation describes something that is done. This "something" may be a physical act, a mental activity, or a combination. Some examples are:

Physical	Mental	Combined
Change the form of material	Plan	Communicate
Assemble or disassemble	Decide	Construct a radio
Arrange materials for the next operation	Conceive of a new product	Obtain the correct model from a storeroom
Transport	Perform a calculation	Operate a complex machine
Inspect	Appraise a subordinate's work	Check the circuit on a production line
File	Classify	Place a folder in a filing cabinet
Record	Code	Enter an amount in accounts payable ledger

From this concept we construct a hierarchy of definitions.

The concept of *operation* may be constructed from the smallest element of physical work, the micromotion. A *micromotion* is a movement of a portion of the hands or other part of the body which takes time of the order of 0.005 to 0.001 minute.

A *work element* is a simple motion more extensive than a micromotion. It must be carried out in less than 0.03 minute and must be combined with another element for visual observation or stopwatch timing.

An *operation* is a set of work elements which leads to the intentional change of an object in any of its physical or chemical characteristics, the assembly or disassembly of components, the arrangement for another operation, or the transportation, inspection, or filing of an object or the recording of data. An operation also occurs when mental effort is applied to an elementary part of a complex problem or to a simple problem.

A *task* is a set of operations, often unique or single-time, with a predetermined problem or product objective, performed at one or more work stations. At the lowest level, a task is a portion of a *position* at a work station.

A *job* is a cycle of operations performed at one work station; it describes a group of positions which are identical with respect to their major tasks.

At the macro level, a *process* is the set of all operations required for completing the objectives of a subsystem or total system.

THE FLOW-OF-TRANSACTIONS CONCEPT

Eventually all operations must be aggregated into or identified as a transaction in order for us to describe the financial position and results of operations.

The Auditing Executive Committee of the AICPA has defined transactions in Statement of Auditing Standards No. 1,[2] Section 320, paragraph 20, on the following page:

[2]*Statement on Auditing Standards*, No. 1 (New York: AICPA, 1973). © 1973 by the American Institute of Certified Public Accountants, Inc.

Table 4.4 Accountability function, following the change in custody as assets flow through the firm

| EVENT | CHANGE IN CUSTODY | | RECORD ENTRY |
	From	*To*	
Purchase of raw materials	Treasurer (cash)	Inventory control (raw materials)	A. Debit: Raw materials inventory Credit: Accounts payable B. Debit: Accounts payable Credit: Cash
Requisition of raw materials by production control	Inventory control (raw materials)	Production control (raw materials)	Debit: Work in process Credit: Raw materials inventory
Application of overhead expenses	Assignment of expenses based on machine-hours, man-hours, units of production, etc.	Value added to work in process	Debit: Work in process Credit: Factory overhead expense
Completion of production function	Production control (finished goods)	Finished goods inventory control (finished goods)	Debit: Finished goods inventory Credit: Work in process
Sale of finished product	Finished goods inventory control	Customer	A. Debit: Accounts receivable Credit: Sales B. Debit: Cost of goods sold Credit: Finished goods inventory
Payment for product	Customer (cash)	Treasurer (cash)	Debit: Cash Credit: Accounts receivable

Transactions are the basic components of business operations and, therefore, are the primary subject matter of internal control. In the context of this section, transactions include exchanges of assets or services with parties outside the business entity and transfers or use of assets or services within it. The primary functions involved in the flow of transactions and related assets include the authorization, execution, and recording of transactions and the accountability for resulting assets.

The Committee goes on to state in paragraphs 21 through 25 that there are four parts to a complete transaction: authorization, execution, recording, and accountability. See Table 4.4 (page 137) for an illustration of the accountability function.

SUMMARY This chapter points out the need for integration of organization, operating systems, and information flow. In most organizations the authority structure and the operating systems are not matched. The reason is that companies tend to be organized on the basis of one-dimensional hierarchies, whereas the operating systems cut across such organizations in many ways.

Attempts to manage the subsystems of a business have led first to line-staff organization, then to project management, and finally to multidimensional structures. Management information systems which are based upon systems and managers' needs also represent a fluidity of organization not shown on the traditional, static organization charts.

In order to study information systems and MIS, we must first be familiar with typical operations of a variety of companies. This chapter shows the total operating system in flow-chart form for a manufacturing company, department store, bank, hospital, and airline. Amplification of the manufacturing operations is given through examples of subsystems.

Finally, the conceptual underpinnings of *transactions* and *operations* are developed. The importance of these concepts is not usually recognized. The cycle-subsystems, or cash-to-cash subsystems, clarify the series of operations and transactions that must be performed. They provide the basis for historical measurement, for control, and for planning. In addition, the meanings of "operation" and "transaction" have great economic significance. Management that understands these terms can make explicit decisions on the level and source of data to be captured (recorded).

1. Check all functions that are involved in the systems below.

	FUNCTION						
SYSTEM	General Management	Marketing	Manufacturing	Engineering	Accounting	Finance	Personnel
a. Capital budgeting							
b. Order processing							
c. Quality control							
d. Raw materials inventory control							
e. Recruiting							

2. Match the manager responsible with the systems of a business.

a. Manufacturing manager	(1) Strategic business unit	_____
b. Capital budgeting committee	(2) Forecasting	_____
c. Division VP	(3) Material processing	_____
d. Treasurer	(4) Costing	_____
e. Corporate economist	(5) Research	_____
f. Director of R & D	(6) Capital expenditures	_____
g. European VP	(7) Human resources	_____
h. Personnel manager	(8) Materials	_____
i. Accounting	(9) Liquid assets	_____
j. Management	(10) European division	_____
k. Nobody		

3. Indicate activities which *may be* functions of committees and those which *are* functions of line managers only.

	Committee	Line Manager
a. Hire an individual	_____	_____
b. Interchange ideas among departments	_____	_____
c. Formulate companywide standards	_____	_____
d. Make an operating decision	_____	_____

e. Prepare a functional plan ⸻ ⸻

f. Prepare a strategic plan ⸻ ⸻

g. Review operations and make recommendations ⸻ ⸻

h. Make studies of important companywide crises ⸻ ⸻

4. Indicate which of the lettered individuals are line and which are staff.

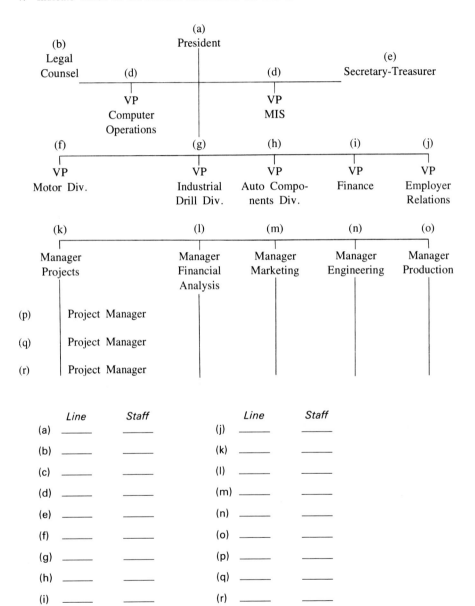

	Line	Staff		Line	Staff
(a)	⸻	⸻	(j)	⸻	⸻
(b)	⸻	⸻	(k)	⸻	⸻
(c)	⸻	⸻	(l)	⸻	⸻
(d)	⸻	⸻	(m)	⸻	⸻
(e)	⸻	⸻	(n)	⸻	⸻
(f)	⸻	⸻	(o)	⸻	⸻
(g)	⸻	⸻	(p)	⸻	⸻
(h)	⸻	⸻	(q)	⸻	⸻
(i)	⸻	⸻	(r)	⸻	⸻

5. Check the appropriate activities for the firms below.

	Sell	Design	Buy	Store	Service or Make	Store	Sell	Ship
(a) Shipbuilder	___	___	___	___	___	___	___	___
(b) Restaurant	___	___	___	___	___	___	___	___
(c) Hospital	___	___	___	___	___	___	___	___
(d) Bank	___	___	___	___	___	___	___	___
(e) Food store	___	___	___	___	___	___	___	___
(f) University	___	___	___	___	___	___	___	___

6. Draw a flow diagram showing operations and information flow for a training department program in a large manufacturing company.

7. Develop a flow chart for an accounts payable system.

8. Develop a description of the cycle-subsystems for a department store by analogy with Fig. 4.19.

9. For each of the following give an example of a possible transaction.

	Example	Possible Transaction
Operation	_____	_____
Task	_____	_____
Job	_____	_____
Process	_____	_____

10. Obtain an organization chart of the following:

   a. A city
   b. A bank
   c. A large department store
   d. A hospital
   e. An oil company
   f. One of the "Big Eight" accounting firms.

   (a) Discuss similarities and differences.
   (b) Identify line and staff managers.
   (c) Can you identify matrix management and organization?
   (d) Where do MIS and computer operations appear on the charts? Why?

11. Scott Sims has just been named tennis pro and recreation director at a new club, the South Winds. The club has eight outdoor tennis courts and a swimming pool. Sims plans to have the following subsystems:

   a. Swimming competition once a week
   b. Tennis shop
   c. Men's tennis leagues, A players and B players
   d. Women's tennis leagues, A players and B players.

A league will be composed of four groups of players. Each week each of the groups will play against another group. Thus it will take three weeks for a particular group to play against all others. The pro charges a small fee each week to each player to cover the cost of balls and to bring in revenue.

1. Prepare an operations flow chart for each of the above subsystems as you would establish them.

2. At what level of operations and transactions should Sims capture and record data for planning and control for each of the subsystems?

SELECTED REFERENCES

CHASE, RICHARD B., and NICHOLAS J. AQUILANO, *Production and Operations Management.* Homewood, Ill.: Richard D. Irwin, 1973.

DRUCKER, PETER F., "New Templates for Today's Organizations," *Harvard Business Review,* January–February 1974.

Financial Accounting Standards Board, *Objectives of Financial Reporting and Elements of Financial Statements of Business Enterprises,* December 29, 1977.

FIORE, MICHAEL V., "Out of the Frying Pan and Into the Matrix," *Personnel Administration,* July–August 1970.

GALBRAITH, JAY R., *Organization Design.* Reading, Mass.: Addison-Wesley, 1977.

Guide for Studying and Evaluating Internal Accounting Controls, A. Chicago, Ill.: Arthur Andersen & Co., 1978.

HARRILL, E. REECE, "The Transaction Concept," *PMM & Co./Management Controls,* July 1971.

HINRICHS, JOHN R., "Restructuring the Organization for Tomorrow's Needs," *Personnel,* March–April 1974.

MAYNARD, H. B., ed., *Industrial Engineering Handbook,* 3d ed. New York: McGraw-Hill, 1971.

MELCHER, ARLYN J., *Structure and Process of Organizations: A Systems Approach.* Englewood Cliffs, N.J.: Prentice-Hall, 1976.

MURDICK, ROBERT G., "MIS for MBO," *Journal of Systems Management,* March 1977.

MURDICK, ROBERT G., et al., *Accounting Information Systems.* Englewood Cliffs, N.J.: Prentice-Hall, 1978.

MURDICK, ROBERT G., and THOMAS C. FULLER, "Subsystem Cycles for MIS," *Journal of Systems Management, June 1979.*

Statement on Auditing Standards, No. 1. New York: AICPA, 1973.

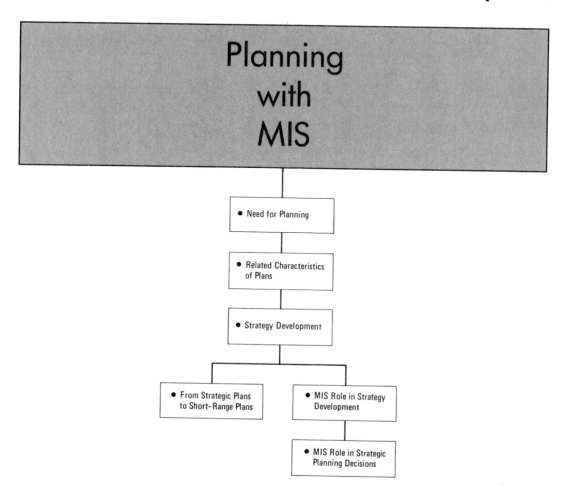

chapter 5

Planning
with
MIS

- Need for Planning

- Related Characteristics of Plans

- Strategy Development

- From Strategic Plans to Short-Range Plans

- MIS Role in Strategy Development

- MIS Role in Strategic Planning Decisions

PURPOSE: To outline the nature of strategic planning and MIS as a decision support system for planning

A planning and control system pervades the entire organizational structure at IBM. It serves as a primary communication link between corporate and operating unit management for establishing unit objectives and strategic direction, negotiating plan commitments, and measuring performance against plan.[1]

A fundamental tenet underlying Business Systems Planning is that information systems must be integrated with the business plan and should be developed from the point of view of top management and with their active participation.[2]

Managing starts with planning. All managers at all levels conduct planning, and the successful performance of the other management functions depends on this activity. Planning is deciding in advance what has to be done, how it is to be done, when it is to be done, and who is to do it. Planning bridges the gap from where we are now to where we want to be at future dates. All people at work plan to some extent, but managerial planning is distinctive. Managers plan for the allocation of all resources and the work of organizations; the nonmanager does not plan for the allocation of human resources and plans only for his own activities.

NEED FOR PLANNING

A business that survives is an adaptive system, one that adjusts to changes in the environment. Changes in the environment are occurring at a traumatic rate. For example, world population is doubling every 30 years. The speed of communication increased 10,000,000-fold in the last 100 years. In 1946, the first computer

[1]Abraham Katz, Director of Planning Systems, IBM, "There's No Room for Guesswork at IBM," *Planning Review,* November 1977, p. 3.

[2]*Business Systems Planning/Information Systems Planning Guide,* IBM, 1975, GE-20-0527-1, p. 1.

(ENIAC) was introduced; in 1980, about $57 billion will be spent on data processing hardware, software, personnel, and services. In the five-year period from 1972 to 1975, inflation reduced the purchasing power of the dollar by 41%.

Large, multiproduct corporations cannot respond instantaneously to changes outside at the instant they become aware of them. Rather, companies need early warning information and time to prepare for action to minimize threats and seize new opportunities. The planning process, supported by an effective MIS, provides the means for companies to adapt before disaster strikes.

The complexity of companies today, as well as their size, requires increasingly sophisticated methods for integrating all activities. The many employees need guidelines that simply cannot be supplied efficiently by constant personal direction. Plans supply these guidelines and directions so that all efforts are coordinated.

RELATED CHARACTERISTICS OF PLANS

The work of an organization starts with a major mission and is then broken down into a hierarchy of smaller tasks at each lower level. This work breakdown structure is paralleled by the structure of plans. At the corporate level, the definition of mission and strategy leads to the development of strategic, system, long-range plans. At the next lower level, the division level in large companies, constrained strategic plans are developed which must be consistent with the corporate system plan. In smaller companies, the next lower level may be that of functional or geographic managers, whose plans have more operating emphasis than strategic perspective. Finally, at the lowest levels, weekly, monthly, and annual plans are prepared based upon fairly specific objectives in the higher-level plans.

All of these plans may be described in terms of a set of related characteristics and information requirements:

Purpose	Time span
Level	Information requirements
Scope	

Table 5.1 shows the structural relationships of plans by means of these characteristics. Broad, strategic plans for the company provide the direction and limitations for the objectives developed in the lower-level plans, and so on. This nesting of plans at successively lower levels insures integration of all plans into a system of plans.

The strategic level of planning is so important that we will give it some special attention. The development of an MIS to assist top management in creating new and critical strategies is one of the great challenges for the MIS manager. The payoff from maintaining a viable direction for the firm is far greater than that of simply mechanizing data processing for routine cyclical transactions.

Table 5.1 Characteristics and information requirements for plans

	CHARACTERISTICS			
Purpose	Level	Scope	Time Span	Information Requirements
Strategy	Corporate	Companywide Posture planning Portfolio planning	5 to 20 years	Environmental scan Companywide data base
Strategy	Divisions	Divisionwide or strategic business unit Choose product lines and assess environmental changes	5 years	Environmental scan Division data base Corporate policy and strategy
Operating plans	Middle management	Plantwide or business profit center	1 to 3 years	Environmental scan Division data base Division policy and strategy Company standards
Functional plans	Functional and first-line managers	Function of a business profit center, such as production, marketing, finance	1 week to 1 year	Routinized environmental scan Plant or business profit center data base Plant or profit center policy and plans Division standards

STRATEGY DEVELOPMENT

The strategic planning process consists of two phases: (1) developing the *strategy* and (2) formulating the steps, timing, and costs required to achieve the strategy. The expression of these steps, timing, and costs is called the strategic plan (or, often, the long-range plan).

Definition of Strategy

"Corporate strategy deals mainly with the continuous definition of corporate identity."[3] Strategy is the desired configuration of the firm at a future specified date.[4] Although some authors include plans as a part of strategy, there are advantages in defining strategy as objectives for the firm. The separation is easy to make in any case; for example: "Strategy is: the concept of the business, the set of goals and objectives it is to pursue, including the plans, policies, and standards of conduct, and the courses of action, the allocation of resources,

---

[3]R. Hal Mason, Jerome Harris, John McLoughlin, "Corporate Strategy: A Point of View," *California Management Review*, Spring 1971.

[4]See Robert L. Katz, *Cases and Concepts in Corporate Strategy* (Englewood Cliffs, N.J.: Prentice-Hall, 1970).

authorizations, and tasks which are pursued for at least one cycle in the rhythm of planning in that business."[5]

The desired shape, configuration, posture, or identity of the firm at a future date essentially represents a set of objectives to be attained. The configuration may be described in terms of:

1. Scope: products, customers, markets, price/quality relationships of products, and product characteristics.
2. Competitive edge: special market position or supply position, unique product advantages, special financial strength or credit lines, unique management or technical talents, or capacity for rapid response to competitive moves.
3. Specifications of targets: quantitative statements of acceptable and desired goals such as size of the company, market share, profitability, return on investment, assets, and trade-off between risk and reward.
4. Assignment of resources: allocation of long-term capital, investment and disinvestment, emphasis on particular activities such as marketing, engineering, production, management development, geographic regions, market segments, etc.
5. Level of risk-taking or "exposure": ratio of project investment to company equity at a specified probability of success, on the average.[6]

As an example, let us look briefly at Eaton Corporation's strategy as expressed by strategic objectives. Eaton has annual sales of over $2 billion. Its major product categories are

Auto components
Truck components
Off-highway vehicle components
Industrial vehicles
Construction and woodland vehicles
Industrial drives and power transmissions
Security products

In its *Annual Report* (p. 7),[7] Eaton lists some objectives for the 1980s. Let us see how these may fit into the components of strategy that have just been listed:

---

[5]Melvin E. Salveson, "The Management of Strategy," *Long Range Planning,* February 1974.

[6]See Robert L. Katz, *Management of the Total Enterprise* (Englewood Cliffs, N.J.: Prentice-Hall, 1970). See also J. Thomas Cannon, *Business Strategy and Policy* (New York: Harcourt Brace Jovanovich, Inc., 1968).

[7]The material here and on the following pages is from Eaton Corporation's 1977 *Annual Report.* Courtesy of Eaton Corporation.

Eaton's Objective	Components of Strategy
Pursue selective business line acquisitions or divestitures to enlarge, redirect or dispose of existing businesses where internal development alone will not serve return on asset or cash generation objectives	Scope, allocation of resources
Expand Eaton through acquisition, or merger, with one or more large companies in markets beyond those already heavily served by the company	Assignment of resources, scope
Achieve a mix of businesses which would provide increased growth in earnings per share	Scope
Add businesses that would lessen Eaton's vulnerability to short-term declines in the world economy	Risk, scope
Establish Eaton's presence in selected new markets	Scope
Supplement Eaton's professional skills in management, marketing, engineering, and manufacturing	Allocation of resources
Maintain strong supplier relationships to assure continuous flow of purchased materials, permitting capital resources to be concentrated on market expansion and market share improvement	Allocation of resources
Achieve a steady reduction in the assets required to generate sales	Specification of targets (when rate of reduction is filled in)
Increase worldwide exports to adjust to demand peaks and to achieve more sales in developing and less-developed countries	Scope
Achieve increased productivity through innovative employee relations practices which encourage and develop employee involvement	Assignment of resources
Strengthen programs to identify and develop tomorrow's management talent, increasing the depth behind each management position	Assignment of resources
Maintain a dividend payout which coupled with stock appreciation will provide shareholders a combined return that exceeds returns on comparable investments	Specification of targets (when data are added)
Achieve the following corporate operating results:	Specifications of targets
Pretax profit on sales — 12.0% After-tax profit on sales — 6.2% Pretax profit on average assets employed — 17.0% After-tax profit on equity — 18.5%	

Steps in the Development of Strategy

In Figure 5.1 the steps in the development of strategy, as defined by the components above, are summarized and related. The steps in strategy development, illustrated by some excerpts from Eaton's *1977 Annual Report,* are as follows:

1. *Analyze the environment.* Identify existing conditions in the environment that have an influence on the company. Look for early warning signals of sudden changes in the future. Consider possible scenarios of the future. Classify information under the headings of (1) events, (2) trends, and (3) constituent demands.

The purpose of this step is to identify *new opportunities* for new products and new markets and to identify *threats* to continuing operations. Eaton's *Report* states:

> The Strategic Plan for Eaton's businesses is more than a series of projections of past trends and financial schedules. Through it, management analyzes and evaluates the total environment in which the company operates—today and in the future.

2. *Identify company strengths and weaknesses.* Evaluate the products, markets, processes, personnel, plant and equipment, and financial resources. Look for strengths and weaknesses, particularly with other firms in the industry. Relate strengths and weaknesses to possible future opportunities for new products, new markets, and profit growth.

Figure 5.1 Strategic planning process

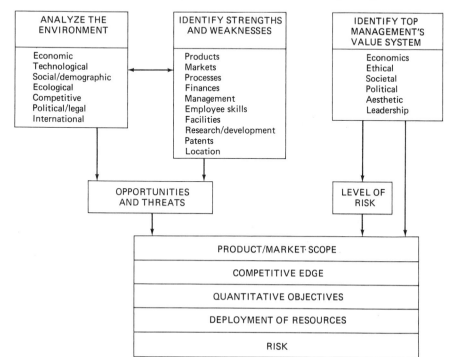

Eaton's *Report* says of this step:

It includes an assessment of external business factors and internal operating strengths and weaknesses—in marketing strategy, pricing, design, quality, manufacturing capacity and efficiency as well as customer and supplier relationships.

The plan includes an analysis of market share and an evaluation of competitors' strengths and weaknesses. This analysis outlines a product's expected life cycle, capital expenditure trends, technological trends, economic conditions, availability of manpower and even social and political pressures.

3. *Clarify the personal values of top management.* The profit-orientation, social responsibility beliefs, philosophy regarding employees and customers, and ethical beliefs must be forged into a guiding set of principles and constraints. This value system, once agreed upon, will likely affect all future major decisions relative to strategy.

Eaton's *Report* makes the following assertion:

Operate as a concerned, enlightened, and socially responsible corporate citizen of the world community.

We continue to take strong public stands concerning regulation and legislation affecting our business and our way of life. We have encouraged Eaton people to become involved in the political process to influence public policy and to select and to elect qualified candidates for public office at every level of government. During 1977, an Eaton Public Policy Association was formed for management employees who want to help elect candidates who support fiscal responsibility in government and understand the importance of preserving the free enterprise system.

Eaton's efforts at economic education have been expanded to include a unique teacher work/learn program that enables teachers to take a realistic understanding of the business system back to their classrooms.

Recognizing the social as well as the business and economic consequences of the energy crisis, we have undertaken numerous programs to conserve energy in our operations and to develop a wide range of products that are energy-efficient.

4. *Establish the level of risk* to be taken in decisions involving resources. This level will be affected by the value system, above, and economic considerations.

Eaton's *Report* observes:

These objectives will change as the mix of Eaton's businesses changes because of different market growth rates and investment allocations. They also will change as profitability and risks are modified due to external, political, and economic forces.

5. *Identify opportunities to be exploited.* By matching company strengths to future opportunities, the company should now be able to identify specific niches to be filled. The shape of the company at a future time

may now be developed. The constraints will be the value system and the specified risk level.

In Eaton's *Report*:

Strategic planning has determined that the growth areas of Eaton's automobile components businesses lie in products that will help the automobile manufacturer meet the lighter weight and higher fuel efficiency characteristics of the vehicles of the 1980s.

6. *Define the product/market scope.* The results of steps 1 through 5 make it possible for management to specify the range of products, the future markets to be exploited, and scope of company activities.

Careful definition of the product/market scope reduces the time and complexity of decisions regarding acquisitions, new investments, and other components of company development. It promotes integration of the divisions of the company into a companywide system. Further, it allows the firm to focus on decisions and actions that take advantage of the competitive edge.

Eaton's *Report* gives the following description:

The strategic planning process is organized around the corporation's basic building blocks, called product-market segments or businesses. In all, Eaton has more than 400 product-market segments, many of them closely related. The precise management of a $2 billion company is aided by understanding the detailed nature of these basic units of the corporation.

Product-market segments consist of a single product or a family of related products which go into a well-defined and unified market. Each of these businesses generates its own revenues, operating costs, investments and strategic action plans. For example, Eaton's Engine Components operations manufacture and market engine valves. The engine valve businesses consist of a number of product-market segments including passenger car valves, aircraft valves and heavy-duty truck valves. Businesses take on geographic limits too, such as passenger car valves-North America, or -Europe, or -Latin America.

In time, Eaton's businesses may be made larger or smaller. Some will be discarded. New ones will be conceived and created within the corporation. Or, entirely new businesses may be acquired.

7. *Define the competitive edge.* The competitive edge comprises those qualities of service, price, trust, image, location, and so on which appear unique to the customers and fit his needs. The definition answers the customer's question, "Why should I buy from this firm instead of one of the competitors?"

Management should try to set competitive edges for the future. Competitors are constantly trying to close the current gap. Eaton's *Report* defines the firm's intentions as follows:

Eaton will build on its balanced skills in engineering, manufacturing and marketing with ongoing emphasis on product leadership attained through increased research, engineering programs, product development and testing. High value will continue to be placed on an entrepreneurial approach to selected new businesses. Strong emphasis on planning and the vigorous execution of plans will mark Eaton's thrust into the next decade.

8. *Establish quantitative objectives and measures of performance.* Although creativity and innovation are very important in developing scope and competitive edge, quantitative specifications sharpen the definition of all components of strategy. Such specifications may be established for sales, profits, return on investment, market share, number of employees, value of human and capital assets, debt, and desired trend rates.

9. *Establish deployment of resources.* Should resources be applied to internal growth or to acquisitions? How should resources be divided between new product research and advertising? To what major problems should top management devote its time? Should more resources be devoted to acquiring equipment or upgrading human resources? Every company has limited resources, and decisions as to their application must be considered from the strategic view, not just on an *ad hoc* basis.

The Eaton *Report* asserts:

Effective strategic planning demands that we constantly evaluate our current businesses and their performance against planned objectives. Those which after a reasonable time do not meet long-term objectives, become candidates for phase-out or divestiture. In the past two years we have disposed of several small product lines including our construction equipment business in Brazil in the summer of 1977.

MIS ROLE IN STRATEGY DEVELOPMENT

The MIS plays an important role in the development of corporate strategy because it provides a continuous, formalized, and structured gathering of information, both internal and external. The MIS uses organized inputs from managers given specific responsibilities in certain areas as well as information based on manipulation of transaction data and models. Let us look more closely now at the components of the MIS and their contributions to development of strategy.

Overview of the MIS-User Relationship in Formulation of Strategy

Figure 5.2 shows an overview of the MIS in support of management's function of strategy development. The major groupings of components are:

1. Management-users (incorporating the value system)
2. Consolidation system for strategic business units

3. Environmental analysis system
4. Transaction-capturing and input system
5. Data management system
6. Modeling systems
7. Reporting and query system.

These components are interactive with each other and particularly with management throughout the company. These systems and information flows will be discussed in more detail.

Figure 5.2 MIS Role in corporate strategic development system

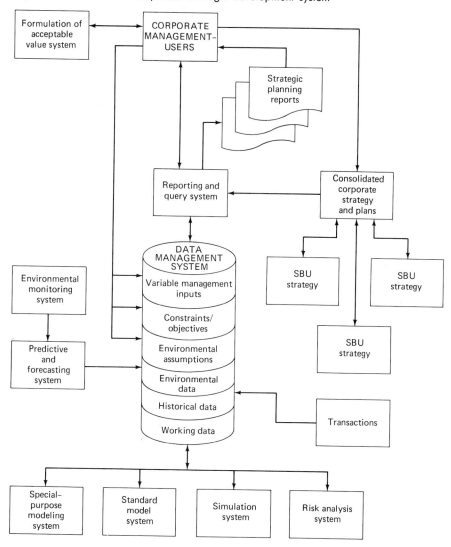

Environmental Analysis System

Increasingly rapid changes in the last two decades suggest even more startling and sudden changes in the years ahead. Some of these recent changes are the youth movement, the consumer protection movement, the ecology movement, the civil rights movement, the women's liberation movement, world energy and resource depletion, world inflation, the population explosion, and the rise of "third world" countries.

In most companies, information about the environment filters in to management as a result of casual, undirected reading by managers. Some executives may subscribe to business periodicals to keep themselves generally abreast of the world. What is needed, however, is a formalized and planned approach to scanning the environment. A necessary second step is a formalized method for analyzing environmental data and converting it to useful information for managerial planning. Figure 5.2 shows the incorporation of these two steps in the MIS.

Briefly, we note that the environmental monitoring system consists of executives who are assigned specific responsibilities for monitoring external factors and developing files on the variety of topics shown in Table 5.2. The predictive and forecasting system consists of line and staff executives, assisted by the modeling systems of Fig. 5.2 when needed. This predictive and forecasting system attempts to develop alternative scenarios of the future through such methods as scenario building, Delphi techniques, or trend analysis.

Table 5.2
Environmental
Data Files

INTERNATIONAL

Balance of trade	Investment
World energy	Political situations
World mineral resources	Taxes
Food production	World Bank activities
Technology	Productivity

UNITED STATES

Economic	*Government*
GNP	Antitrust activities
Expenditures by GNP segments	Law enforcement
Construction, commercial and	Consumer interests
residential	Credit
Disposable personal income	Employment:
Personal savings	Equal opportunity
Corporate profits and cash flow	Discrimination
Federal government expenditures	Ethical practices
Local and state expenditures	FCC
Employment rate	ICC
Money supply	IRS
Inflation rate	OSHA
Economic indicators	Postal service
Interest rate	Privacy
Productivity	Resource restrictions
Wage levels	Taxes
Hourly work week	Education
Personal debt	Research in science

Table 5.2
(Cont'd.)

Corporate debt
Pension funds
Taxes
Physical distribution
Land use
Farm subsidies

Social and cultural
Categories of spending
Dwelling types
Leisure interests
Lifestyles
Mobility
Purchase of services
Shopping habits
Workweek

Demographic
Age distribution
Age of workers
Education
Education of workers
Income distribution
Income levels
Labor force size
Occupations
Part-time workers
Population concentrations
Population size
Urban suburban proportions
Women workers

Technology
Scientific research policy and funding
Alternate energy sources
Mass transportation
Weather modification
Medicine and health care
Communications
Food
Home construction
Defense

Resources
Coal
Electricity
Fabrics
Fertilizer
Food
Gas
Metals
Oil
Outdated sources
Scarce material restrictions
Transportation systems (people)

Monetary policy
Fiscal policy
Defense expenditures
Foreign aid
Ecology
Inner-city development
Medical and health

Public Attitudes
Work:
  Benefits
  Trade and professional unions
  Working conditions
  Hours
  Retirement
  Women/minority managers
Business:
  Profits
  Ethics
  Products
  Disclosure
Consumerism:
  Advertising
  Pricing
  Privacy
  Packaging (labeling)
  Product quality
  Product safety
  Product type
  Service quality
Economic conditions:
  Income
  Taxes
  Economy in general
  Inflation
Education:
  Cost
  Effectiveness of system
  Benefits
Environment:
  Air, water, noise
  Energy, resources
  Land use
  Material resources
  Solid waste
Equal opportunity
Government:
  Regulation of business
  Regulation of individuals
  Effectiveness
  Honesty of leaders
  Competence of leaders
  Belief in institutions
  Law enforcement
Inner cities
Quality of life

For the more likely scenarios, forecasts of the economy, the industry, and the company are developed. These forecasts concern such items in the economy as GNP, income distribution, inflation, interest rates, consumer and capital spending, demographics, and transportation. Forecasts for the industry touch on market shares, total production, legal impacts, costs, and profits. Forecasts for the company deal with unit sales, revenue, market share, new products, and capital expansion, cash flow, and profits. Outputs of the environmental analysis system are stored in the data management system to provide reports and answers to queries to management.

Transaction System

The transaction system supplies data on internal operations as the basis for trend and position analysis.

The Data Management System

The data management system consists primarily of the computer's CPU, supporting data storage systems, and data-base system software. It stores and retrieves the variety of data and information required for the development of strategy. In addition, it produces reports and answers queries of users about data stored in the system.

Modeling Systems

The modeling systems involve managers, management scientists, model banks, and the computer system. Special-purpose models are one-time models developed to solve some special aspect of strategy. For example, a model may be developed by an oil company to estimate world supply of oil from known and unknown sources over the next ten years. Or a model may be constructed to evaluate a merger on company performance for the next five years.

Standard models may be retained in storage to project trends, model the economy, or forecast population shifts. Optimization models such as linear programming also are typical of standard models.

Simulation systems permit the solution of complicated models made up of numerous equations which are functions of time and other variables. For example, national resources, pollution, food supply, and population may be linked and, starting from the present, forecast year by year for 20 years. Incremental time periods form the basis for the step-by-step calculations.

Risk analysis looks at the probabilities of events. Probability distributions of input variables to models yield a probability distribution for the output. Thus, instead of estimating market share of competitors five years hence as a single value for each, we would obtain for each competitor a set of probabilities associated with a set of market-share values.

In summary, modeling systems serve to represent, in approximate fashion, the real world. They do this by means of mathematical relationships. Input data from operations and managerial estimates help define the models and provide initial conditions. The models may lead to predictions of the future, suggest optimum allocations of resources, simulate time-dependent conditions, or provide probabilistic descriptions of the future. Results from models assist managers by dealing with complex manipulations. The limitation on models is that they cannot deal with the full complexity of the real world.

MIS ROLE IN STRATEGIC PLANNING DECISIONS

Once the desired specifications of the firm of the future have been established, major decisions must be made as to the best ways of achieving these specifications. That is, we must develop a long-range plan to achieve our strategy. Major decisions must be made which may concern capital equipment, alternatives, acquisitions/divestments/mergers, new product development, contract bids, marketing expansion, tax planning, and executive compensation plans. These decisions are obviously very complex, so that we may only touch here upon the problems they entail. Our purpose is only to get an idea of how the MIS supports management in these problem areas of strategic planning.

Capital Equipment Alternatives

Capital equipment purchases represent long-term commitments of company resources. Thus they are strategic choices. In comparing alternatives, management needs such information as:

Equipment characteristics:
    Degree of newness of the process
    Service life of the equipment
    Disposal value
    Operating costs of the equipment over its life cycle
    Quality of output
Cost:
    Purchase price
Net cost of installation:
    Special tooling costs
    Debugging costs
    Special training costs
    Special insurance costs
    Special costs such as severance pay for released workers
Interest rates
Taxes and depreciation
Sources of funds and capital structure
Sources of equipment
Working capital required
Cash-flow budget
Inflationary price changes
Noneconomic factors such as safety and working conditions

Table 5.3 Blocking variables, complements, and supplements

Acquisition Blocking Factors	Complementary Factors
B1. Sales must be over $500,000,000 annually	C1. Countercyclical sales pattern
B2. The company must have been profitable over the past five years	C2. Large cash position
B3. There must be no competition with our own existing customers	C3. Strong brand name
B4. No history of labor trouble	C4. National distribution network
B5. Must be a high-technology company	C5. Needed technology and laboratory
B6. No dominant firm in the industry to which the company belongs	
B7. No antitrust implications	

Divestiture Blocking Factors	Supplementary Factors
B1. High intangible assets	S1. Manufacturing facilities
B2. High capacity utilization	S2. Marketing capabilities
B3. Highly specialized equipment	S3. Product scope
B4. Industry is at rock bottom	S4. Middle-management strength
B5. Very low market share	S5. Technological strength
B6. Unions on strike	
B7. Government litigation	

Much of this information may be stored in the MIS. The MIS, using the modeling system previously discussed, can provide economic comparisons of alternatives.

Large companies continuously review their portfolio of business to determine whether new businesses should be acquired or present ones sold. The method for evaluation can be standardized so that the MIS can provide relevant information in a standard format to assist managerial decision making.

For the acquisition/merger decision, blocking criteria, complementary variables, and supplementary variables need to be considered.[8] *Blocking criteria* are imposed by management to make sure that only firms with certain financial, marketing, and other relevant characteristics will be considered. These may be readily programmed for initial go, no-go, decisions on acquisitions.

After the elimination of candidates who do not pass the blocking screening, complement-variables may be considered. A *complement* is a characteristic of a candidate firm that will compensate for weakness in the acquiring firm. For example, a cyclical sales pattern that evens out the sales pattern of the acquiring firm, a large supply of cash, or a strong R & D organization may be the complementary characteristic.

Finally, *supplements*—variables that reinforce existing strengths of the acquiring firm—must be identified. Examples of blocking variables, complements, and supplements are shown in Table 5.3.

It is apparent that a rating system may be established for complements and supplements. When a firm is to be considered for acquisition, management rates

[8]See Arthur L. Herrmann, "A Decision Model for Mergers and Acquisitions," *Mergers and Acquisitions*, Spring 1976.

Table 5.4
Evaluating a
candidate for
acquisition

Blocking Factors	Not Effective	Rank (1–10)	Weight (1–10)	Points
Sales over $200 million	X			
No labor trouble	X			
High technology	X			
Complementary variables				
Strong brand name		10	5	50
Investor appeal		7	3	21
Countercyclical sales		7	10	70
National distribution		6	9	54
Supplementary variables				
Manufacturing facilities		10	8	80
Middle-management fit		8	3	24
Customer fit		3	6	18
Product scope		5	7	35
			Total	352

the firm on each variable (properly weighted). A simple model in the MIS can combine the ratings to give an overall rating for the candidate. A very simple example is shown in Table 5.4.

Divestitures face similar barriers (Table 5.3). Going out of a business by discontinuing operations or selling the business may have adverse effects that make divestiture difficult. Once again, a rating system needs to be established for evaluating the impact of certain exit barriers.[9]

New Product Development

Although management inputs are required, the analysis of new-product candidates can be programmed. One of the largest manufacturing companies in the United States has identified a number of factors it considers important for selection of a product for development. It has attached weights to each of these to be combined with management's evaluations. These criteria include, of course, a pro forma estimate of earnings and of the risk involved. The reports on new product evaluations are part of the MIS.[10]

Tax Planning

Tax planning has become an important factor in strategic planning of multinational firms. Tax laws and structures of various countries should be picked up on a continuing basis by the environmental scanning system. The impact of tax structures on plant locations, banking and investments, and shipping may then be analyzed by MIS modeling systems to aid decision making.

[9]See Michael E. Porter, "Please Note Location of Nearest Exit," *California Management Review,* Winter 1976.

[10]See, for example, Delmar W. Karger and Robert G. Murdick, *New Product Venture Management* (New York: Gordon and Breach, 1972).

Executive and Nonexecutive Compensation Plans

Compensation plans represent strategic decisions about the allocation of company resources. That is, compensation plans should represent a philosophy of management and the fulfillment of expectations upon which people accept employment in the long run. Compensation plans also determine special strengths of the company. They determine the quality of people who join and stay with the company as well as affecting motivation. The MIS can, by means of its modeling system, help management make a systems decision involving many variables such as the following:

1. Salary structure
2. Level of compensation structure relative to that of local competitors and the industry as a whole
3. Fringe benefits such as paid vacations and holidays, pensions, medical benefits, insurance, illness and personal leave time
4. Flexitime
5. Commissions
6. Bonuses
7. Stock ownership plan
8. Executive bonuses
9. Executive stock options
10. Other executive perquisites such as company car and aircraft.

Management may utilize the outputs of the MIS to evaluate costs and benefits of various mixes of compensation. "What if . . . ?" queries are also very appropriate for decisions on mixes of compensation.

FROM STRATEGIC PLANS TO SHORT-RANGE PLANS

The choice of strategy is converted into a long-range plan by developing major steps (or milestones) to be achieved. These steps are themselves the result of creative approaches, careful analysis, and final decision making. Costs and benefits may be computed by MIS models as guides to management. Finally, the plan is prepared as a description of what is to be done, when it is to be done, by whom it will be done, and expected results. The further out in time, the more approximate must be the descriptions. It is an amazing fact that some large companies project revenues and earnings *five years ahead to the nearest dollar!*

Short-Range Planning and the MIS

Figure 5.3 shows how strategic planning guides the annual operating and functional plans. Once objectives for (supporting) operations and functional programs are established, the tasks may be identified. Then budgets and a profit plan for the year are developed.

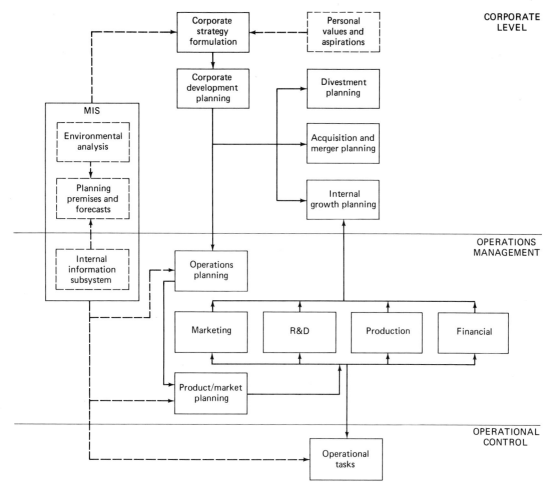

Figure 5.3 Short-range plans from strategic plans

Operations planning deals with all short-range activities starting with resource utilization, product selection, market research, and planning for marketing, R & D, production, and financial operations. Note that both operations planning and implementation (operational tasks) are assisted by the MIS.

In the short-range planning process, each manager develops *work packages* for all the significant tasks which make up his or her programs. These work packages describe the work to be done, the resources to be used (labor and materials), and the estimated monthly rate. The MIS planning model then combines all such information to produce a set of reports which form the basis of the annual plan. Form this original plan, a revised plan is produced to incorporate desired changes. Changes may occur because of the need to reallocate funds, reduce expenditures, or change the timing of expenditures throughout the year. Comparison with previous years' budgets may uncover discontinuities which require explanation or change in the budget. Typical inputs and reports

Figure 5.4
From inputs
to plans

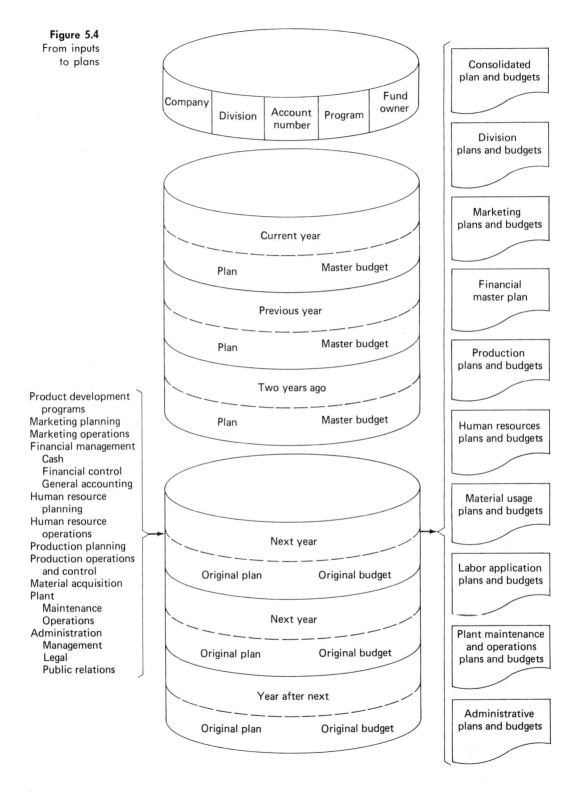

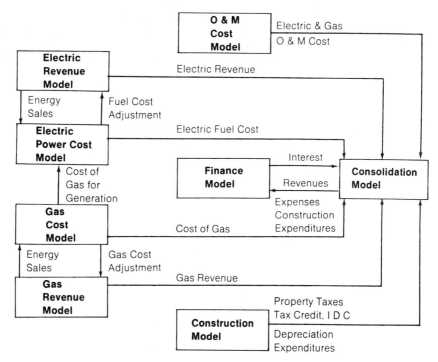

Figure 5.5
Planning
system,
Iowa Power
and
Light Company

Source: Dwight H. Swanson, "Planning for Electricity to Avoid a Shock,"
Planning Review, November 1976.

are shown in Fig. 5.4. In Figure 5.5, a simple model for the Iowa Power and
Light Company shows how interrelationships among inputs lead to the final
consolidated plan.

MIS Planning Models

While a wide variety of planning models may be incorporated in the MIS,
a few of direct significance to top management should be mentioned.

1. *Consolidated profit model.* This is the annual profit plan for the company as a whole.
2. *Division profit models.* These show more detail than the first, since they
   focus on parts of the company rather than the company as a whole.
3. *Profit center or investment center models.* These focus on parts of the
   company headed by a manager who has full responsibility for profits
   (and investments, in the latter case).
4. *Cost center models.* These are models for planning functional activities
   such as marketing, production, engineering, and corporate staff activities such as economic forecasting, training and development, and public
   relations.

5. *Product models.* These planning models show the anticipated resources applied and the costs and revenues for product lines or major products.

6. *Resource models.* These deal with the planning for the acquisition, storage, and use of materials, companywide, by material. Similarly, plans for human resources including staffing, developing, and costing may be modeled.

7. *Strategic Business Unit models.* These deal with plans for matched product–market segments.

SUMMARY

The most valuable application of the MIS is to assist managers with planning. This chapter deals with the role of MIS in strategic and short-range planning.

The need for planning is constantly increasing, since the time in which the firm must adapt to its environment is growing shorter. In addition, changes in the environment are occurring more rapidly. In fact, discontinuities are appearing, such as oil shortages, social and value changes, world power shifts, and technological breakthroughs.

Plans may be described in terms of purpose, level, scope, time span, and information requirements. Strategic planning is very important, because it provides the integrating structure for all other plans. Strategic planning determines the future "shape" of the company: the scope, competitive edge, allocation of resources, quantitative objectives, and level of risk-taking. The MIS provides information to management in every phase of developing the strategy.

The MIS involves interaction with the manager-users in developing strategy. The components of this system therefore are: manager-users, consolidation systems for SBU's, environmental analysis system, transaction capturing and input system, data management system, modeling system, and reporting and query system.

The MIS helps managers specifically to make major strategic planning decisions. Some of these decisions relate to capital equipment investment, acquisition or divestiture of subsidiaries, new product development, tax planning, and compensation plans.

Short-range plans deal more with the specifics of programs such as costs, revenues, and timing. The annual plan requires the "spreading" of such data over a year on a month-by-month basis. Computer modeling of the plans, particularly the financial plans, allows management to make revisions easily and quickly until a satisfactory plan is worked out.

QUESTIONS AND PROBLEMS

1. Complete the following table in the same way as Table 5.1.

Item	Purpose	Level	Example of Information Requirement
a. Mars, Inc., diversifies beyond candy to other food-related business			
b. Ford designs its annual model change for the Pinto			
c. Chock Full o' Nuts Corp. buys Rheingold Beer			

d. New plant layout at Texfi
   Industries' North Carolina plant
e. Annual profit plan for Macy's
   Albany store

2. Complete the following table as indicated by the example.

Item in the Strategic Plan	Possible Item in the Short-Range Plan	Sample Item of Information Required
a. Eliminate 161 company-owned fast food outlets	Develop a franchise program for picking 17 outlets next year	Sales and profit history of each store
b. Xerox plans to enter the computerized word processing field		
c. Boise Cascade: "Another element of our strategic plan is to grow as a converter and distributor of wood products."		
d. NCR: "Become a full-line supplier of data processing terminals and systems, as well as specialized equipment for banks and retail stores."		

3. What form of information is the following?

   Code: (a) Environmental   (b) Competitive   (c) Internal

   _____ (1) Xerox learns of IBM's development of an office copier.

   _____ (2) Lubrizol's monomer plant in Bayport, Texas, will cost an estimated $8 million and be completed in 1980.

   _____ (3) "Pressures are building up in the foreign exchange markets to a dangerous degree. . . ." *Business Week,* August 28, 1978.

   _____ (4) Motorcycle demand took a surprising turn toward heavyweights in 1978. Honda learns of increased sales of Harley-Davidson Motor Co.

   _____ (5) CR Madden, CEO of Potlatch: "Field managers most responsible for annual plans were making different assumptions from those of the division and corporate managers working on the strategic plan." *Business Week,* Nov. 10, 1975.

   _____ (6) Arthur B. Hall, Crocker Bank VP: "There was expense budgeting but no profit planning. And the directors were receiving financial reports that were not particularly germane to this century." *Business Week,* Aug. 11, 1975.

   _____ (7) Mexico estimates its oil reserves exceed those of Saudi Arabia.

4. Match the following:

(a) Manager estimates probability of new product success as .80

(b) Economic model of the economy

(c) Add digital telephone switches to electronics product line

(d) Choosing purchase of computer processors

(e) Probability distribution for next year's profit

(f) Company contributes to universities annually

(g) Record labor cost for machining operation

(h) What if we double manufacturing capacity?

(i) Linear programming model

(j) ICC rate ruling

(1) Transaction _____

(2) Management input _____

(3) Constraint _____

(4) Forecasting system _____

(5) Standard model system _____

(6) Risk analysis system _____

(7) Query system _____

(8) SBU strategy _____

(9) Value system _____

(10) Capital investment analysis _____

5. Complete the following table.

Management problem	Operating or strategic problem?	How can an MIS assist management to find a solution or make a decision?
a. Company is a "me-too" firm and lacks a competitive edge.		
b. Excessive stockouts and back orders for a staple product		
c. Company has not identified its strengths		
d. Measures of performance have been established, but management does not get reports of variance because no standards have been established.		
e. Poor scheduling of people and machines in production.		
f. Should the firm purchase or lease a $500,000 machine?		
g. What is an optimum executive compensation package?		

6. Obtain a good annual report of some company. From it, deduce two examples for each of the following blocks.

| Environmental events impacting the firm 1. 2. | Strengths 1. Weaknesses 2. | Management's values 1. 2. |

| Opportunity 1. Threat 2. | Level of risk |

| Product/market scope 1. 2. |
| Competitive edge 1. 2. |
| Quantitative objectives 1. 2. |
| Deployment of resources 1. 2. |

7. Discuss the part the MIS can play in preparation of a written strategic-plan report.

8. Discuss the nature of the annual profit plan and how the MIS may assist management in modifying the plan to answer "what if . . ." questions.

9. The MIS, including management inputs, may assist management with the evaluation and screening of new product concepts. Develop a flow chart and description of a process for estimating the impact of a new product on the company's earnings statement.

10. By means of a block diagram and a narrative, develop a simple consolidation model for some company. (This may be based upon an annual report of the company.)

11. Pan American World Airways was concerned with acquiring National Airlines in 1979. List:

a. Acquisition blocking factors

(1)

(2)

(3)

b. Complementary factors

(1)

(2)

(3)

c. Supplementary factors

(1)

(2)

(3)

12. The following is excerpted from an ad by Boise Cascade Corporation. (The rationale for each strategy has been omitted.)

No businessman likes to talk very specifically in advertising about future plans. Too much of what's to come is beyond his control. And yet we think a company that seeks to convince you of its potential ought to do so. So we've decided to share our long term growth strategies with you.

Strategy Number 1. We plan to concentrate on our two basic businesses—building materials and paper products.

We plan to invest $1.1 billion in them between 1974 and 1978 while holding to our target debt to equity ratio of 0.6:1.

We plan to generate an average annual return on total investment of at least 12% after taxes on each project within the $850 million we're using to improve and expand our businesses. (The remaining $250 million are being used to keep our facilities well maintained, safe and environmentally sound.)

Strategy Number 2. We plan to invest 27% of our capital dollars in our converting and distributing operations in order to maximize the earning power of our forest-originated products.

Strategy Number 3. We plan to divide our capital investment about equally between our paper and building materials operations in order to maintain our relatively equal balance between the two.[11]

a. Prepare a table listing the five components of strategy. List the elements of Boise Cascade's strategies that make up each component.
b. Discuss the role that the MIS could perform for Boise Cascade in developing strategic components more fully.

SELECTED REFERENCES

AGUILAR, FRANCIS JOSEPH, *Scanning the Business Environment.* New York: Macmillan, 1967.

ANSOFF, H. IGOR, ROGER P. DECLERCK, and ROBERT L. HAYES, eds., *From Strategic Planning to Strategic Management.* New York: John Wiley, 1976.

BARNETT, JOHN S., "Corporate Foreign Exposure Strategy Formulation," *Columbia Journal of World Business,* Winter 1976.

[11]Courtesy of Boise Cascade Corporation.

CHEN, KUANG-CHIAN, "A Conceptual Structure of Corporate Strategic Planning Information Systems," *Managerial Planning,* September–October 1977.

FAIRAIZL, ALAN F., and SATINDER K. MULLICK, "A Corporate Planning System," *Management Accounting,* December 1975.

GALE, BRADLEY T., "Planning for Profit," *Planning Review,* January 1978. [Gives an overview of profit impact of market strategy (PIMS) programs.]

HAMILTON, WILLIAM F., and MICHAEL A. MOSES, "A Computer-Based Corporate Planning System," *Management Science,* October 1974.

HERRMANN, ARTHUR L., "A Decision Model for Mergers and Acquisitions," *Mergers & Acquisitions,* Spring 1976.

HOFER, CHARLES W., "Towards a Contingency Theory of Business Strategy," *Academy of Management Journal,* December 1975.

KASHYAP, R. N., "Management Information Systems for Corporate Planning and Control," *Long-Range Planning,* June 1972.

KATZ, ROBERT L., *Cases and Concepts in Corporate Strategy.* Englewood Cliffs, N.J.: Prentice-Hall, 1970.

KILMAN, RALPH H., and KYUBG-IL GHYMN, "The MAPS Design Technology: Designing Strategic Intelligence Systems for MNC's," *Columbia Journal of World Business,* Summer 1976.

McCARTHY, DANIEL J., and CHARLES A. MORRISSEY, "Using the Systems Analyst in Preparing Corporate Financial Models," *Financial Executive,* June 1972.

MENDELL, JAY S., and ALFRED W. MUELLER, "Social and Technological Assessment," *Technological Assessment,* 2:1 (1973).

MURDICK, ROBERT G., "MIS for MBO," *Journal of Systems Management,* March 1977.

NEUBAUER, F. FRIEDRICH, and NORMAN B. SOLOMON, "A Managerial Approach to Environmental Assessment," *Long-Range Planning,* April 1977.

O'CONNOR, ROCHELLE, *Corporate Guides to Long-Range Planning.* New York: The Conference Board, 1973.

REED, STANLEY FOSTER, "Corporate Growth by Strategic Planning," *Mergers & Acquisitions,* Summer, Fall, and Winter, 1977.

SCHENDEL, DAN E., and CHARLES W. HOFER (eds.). *Strategic Management.* Boston: Little Brown & Co., 1979.

THORELLI, HANS B., ed., *Strategy + Structure = Performance.* Bloomington, Ind.: Indiana University Press, 1977.

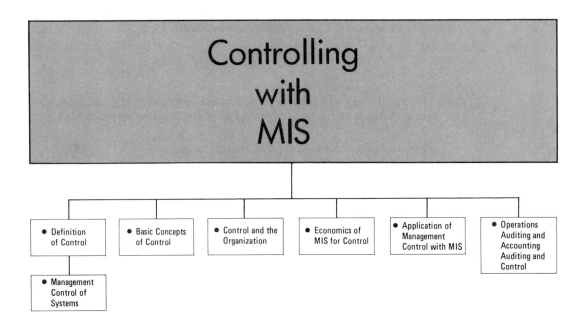

chapter 6

Controlling
with
MIS

- Definition of Control
- Basic Concepts of Control
- Control and the Organization
- Economics of MIS for Control
- Application of Management Control with MIS
- Operations Auditing and Accounting Auditing and Control
- Management Control of Systems

PURPOSE: To explain the nature of control,
relate control to the organization,
outline the economics of MIS for control,
and cover applications of managerial control including auditing

"... in my humble opinion ..." THAVES

Wall Street Journal, Dec. 4, 1972, p. 14.

The best-defined application of the MIS is for the managerial function of controlling. The MIS can be designed to capture any information about company operations and present it to management. While this process is simple in concept, decisions required to implement the process are not. Questions must be answered such as:

1. What types of control systems are possible?
2. What do we measure and when?
3. How much information does management need to control?
4. What is controlled?
5. What techniques for control may be incorporated in the MIS?
6. How is the quality of information controlled?

Our discussion will center on these ideas. The fact that managerial control hinges on the flow of information in a formally designed system will become obvious.

DEFINITION OF CONTROL

Control means bringing or maintaining

1. the performance of an individual, group, machine, or facility, *or*
2. the characteristics of an individual, group, machine, or facility, *or*
3. the characteristics or value of a variable

within prescribed limits.

More specifically, control may be applied to some environmental factor, organizational components, individuals within the organization, functional or specialized activities such as inventory control or product reliability, and mechanical processors such as lathes or elevators. In brief, control means causing events to conform to the desires or plan of the controller.

Table 6.1 lists some examples of items to be controlled, such as people, equipment, or effort, and the measure of performance or characteristic that is to be kept within desired limits. The role of the MIS is to inform management whether the limits have been exceeded or are likely to be exceeded. At this point, we may view controlling as (1) setting standards of performance, (2) measuring performance against standards, and (3) taking corrective action to reduce deviations from standards.

Table 6.1
Examples of control

Item to Be Controlled	Output or Characterisic	Limits	MIS Report
Sales person	Weekly sales expense	$53 to $72	Sales Expense
Sheet metal department	Applied hours	250 to 300 hours	Attendance or Labor Hours
Division manager	Profitability of decisions	11.5% minimum ROI after taxes	Earnings Statement
Total work force	Years of formal schooling	12 years minimum and 14 years average	Personnel Profile Summary
Lathe	Tolerance	± 0.0015″	Quality Control
Capital equipment	Average age	6 to 8 years	Capital Equipment Summary
Pollution	Investment per year	0 to $5 million	Impact Study

MANAGEMENT CONTROL OF SYSTEMS

Control as a Requirement of Business Systems

Control is a requirement for the business as a whole and for the subsystems. Without control of the subsystems, resources may be wasted and objectives never achieved. While planning could be conducted, without control the plans might never be achieved. Each subsystem could diverge from plans without limit. Thus planning and control are meaningless alone. The MIS ties the two together by reports to management.

Information as a Requirement for Control

Whether we are talking about individuals, organizations, or equipment, the idea of control means that someone or something is exercising control. The controller requires information about the process, its performance, and the standard or goal to be achieved. Therefore, if managers are to fulfill their control responsibilities, they require relevant, timely, and clear information about the systems they are to control. The MIS is the formal system which supplies information to management for control purposes.

BASIC CONCEPTS OF CONTROL

If we were to simply look at the flow of reports to managers in a firm as the control system, we would have a very shallow understanding of what is really happening. In order to understand the requirements for good control with the MIS, we will need to examine some basic concepts of control.

Open and Closed Loops

An *open-loop* system is one with just inputs, processes, and outputs with no connection or information flow from the process or outputs back to the inputs. Figure 6.1 gives a simple example. In the open-loop system, the control depends upon the inputs and the processes being correct. Nobody gathers data to compare actual sales and actual expenses with quotas and budgets.

Figure 6.1
Open-loop
control

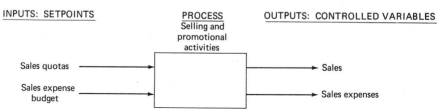

INPUTS: SETPOINTS   PROCESS   OUTPUTS: CONTROLLED VARIABLES
                           Selling and
                           promotional
                           activities

Sales quotas ⟶   ⟶ Sales

Sales expense ⟶   ⟶ Sales expenses
  budget

In *closed-loop* systems, information about the process and/or about the outputs is fed back to a controller who adjusts the inputs and system as necessary. Figure 6.2 shows these feedback and control elements applied to sales expenses in Fig. 6.1. This concept of feedback is so important that we will give special attention to it.

Figure 6.2
Closed-loop
control

Sales expense budget ⟶ ⊗ —Error→ Manager —Controller output→ Selling process ⟶ Sales expense

Measured sales expense

Feedback Control Systems

Feedback control is the most widely used method of control in business. A major objective of any MIS is to feed information on results back to managers so that any needed corrective action may be taken. Feedback control results in a closed-loop system. It is customary to say that the process of feedback control consists of (a) setting a standard of performance, (b) measurement of performance against standards, and (c) reducing deviations of performance from the standard.

A more rigorous managerial view indicates that establishing feedback control requires:

1. Establishing or identifying a system
2. Identifying the objectives of the system
3. Establishing an index for measurement of output (objectives)
4. Establishing a measure for the index to be used as a standard
5. Reporting the measurement of performance to the controller
6. Acting on the inputs or process to reduce deviations of performance from standards.

Table 6.2 Examples of the control process

System	A System Objective	Index of Measurement	Standard Measure	Report	Management Action
Production	Meet demand requirements for number of units	Units produced divided by units demanded	100%	Production output report each week	If the measure of output is less than 100%, investigate cause and take action such as training, providing better equipment, or going overtime
Order processing	See that customer orders are filled within 10 days	Percent of orders filled within 10 days	95%	Age of open orders	Special action is taken on orders over 10 days of age to fill immediately
Inventory control	No stockout at minimum cost	Number of stockouts	Zero	Standard material cost of production	If stockouts occur, get immediate delivery of materials and increase buffer stock or reorder level
		Inventory system cost per period	$21,500		
Processing of insurance claims	Zero errors	Errors as a percent of claims	Zero	Customer complaint report	Identify individuals who make errors and retrain or shift to different job, or change procedure

In Table 6.2 we have translated this general control process into several examples. In the first example, the production system, one obvious objective is to produce a number of units of product equal to the scheduled demand. We could use an index such as number of units produced, but in this case we have chosen a ratio of output to required as an index. In order to set a standard, we must give a desired value to this index. Since we don't want to produce any extra for inventory, the standard value is 100%. A weekly production report is prepared by accumulating all the completed job tickets and organizing much material which is relevant to production. This production report will include this index and will be sent (as feedback) to the foreperson and the production manager. If the index is below (or above) 100%, then management must determine the cause and take action to match production to demand.

Operation of a feedback control system

Let us now show the operation of a feedback control system by means of a block diagram. The system selected is the maintenance operation in a large machine shop. The system's objective is to repair machines at a minimum cost, where there is a trade-off between size of the work crew and cost of downtime of machines. The output of the systems is measured by the number of machines repaired per hour, and the standard is three machines per hour. Feedback is in the form of a daily report to the maintenance foreman prepared by the production control group. Figure 6.3 shows how this system works.

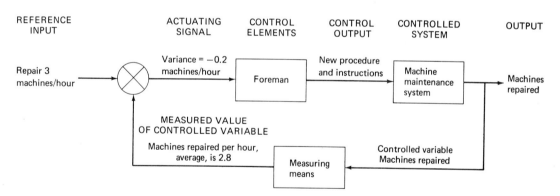

Figure 6.3 Feedback control of a machine maintenance system

Time is a very important factor in feedback control systems. To illustrate this, assume that in Fig. 6.3 the maintenance crew is going along smoothly repairing three machines per hour, day after day. One of the experienced crewmen retires and is replaced by a young and not fully trained person. Instantly, the rate of repair drops to an average of 2.8 per hour. However, the report prepared by production control always lags the events by one day. When the foreman gets the report in the morning two days after the day in question, he must consider what action is to be taken. Not until three days after the low productivity occurred does the foreman take action.

Figure 6.4
Some feedback
loops for top
management
control

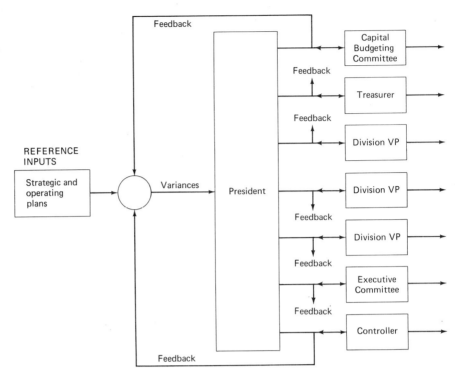

A top management feedback control system

The previous example is a very simple representation of feedback control. The president of a company receives formal feedback from many sources by means of the MIS. In Fig. 6.4 we note some of the principal feedback loops. A complete presentation would depend upon the total MIS in the company. In the schematic, we note that the president receives reports from his division vice presidents, his staff, and key committees. Other staff, such as legal and public relations, usually would appear, and there may be many more committees as well as the board of directors. Because of the long-range implication of decisions and the many feedback systems in which the president is involved, the time lag in adjusting the business to a change in the environment is usually a relatively long one. The fact that all of the people reporting to the president are also involved in systems with feedback loops with time delays accentuates the problem. A well-designed MIS contains feedback loops that notify the president as well as other lower-level managers simultaneously when major events occur that require the president's attention.

Steering Control

Most management information systems are based on feedback control that involves a time delay between the occurrence of events (or undesirable results) and corrective action. A system may be kept right on standard, however, if the response to disturbances or changes can be anticipated so that the system may be

Figure 6.5
Steering control

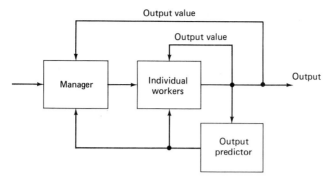

changed in anticipation. This type of control is called *steering control*. It requires a sophisticated MIS which measures not only change, but rates and directions of change. The MIS must provide information not only to the manager of the system but to all elements of the system which perform operations. The feedback must be on a real-time basis. From Fig. 6.5 we may see that the system is not driven by an error signal as in Figs. 6.3 and 6.4, but rather by current and anticipated values of output fed directly to the system.

To illustrate steering control, we might use the example of a person steering a car by turning the steering wheel to go around a curve. We will need to simplify a business system to illustrate the concept in our area of interest, however. The system to be studied is the inventory system of Fig. 6.6. The objective of the system is to maintain a constant inventory level, called the buffer stock. The buffer stock is a sort of insurance against stockout if our system breaks down.

Two variables over which we have no control are demand and the lead time—the time between placement of an order and receipt of goods. Our system must adapt to anticipate both of these variables. Two models are built into the MIS to assist us. One is the demand forecast model; the other is the lead-time forecast model. The demand forecast model requires both historical demand and

Figure 6.6
Steering control
of an inventory
system

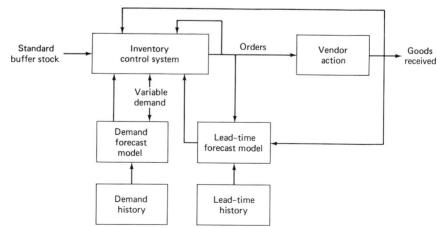

177

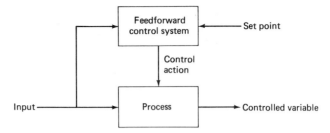

Figure 6.7 Feedforward control system

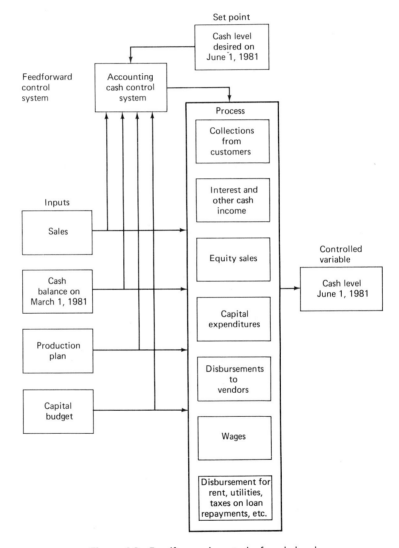

Figure 6.8 Feedforward control of cash level

most-recent demand as inputs. Similar inputs are required for the lead-time forecast model. The inventory system adjusts to place orders that will anticipate changing inventory demands based upon orders, goods received, predicted lead time, and predicted demand.

In practice, the predicted values produce the weakness in steering control. Nevertheless, such systems often maintain very small deviations of performance from standard, so that feedback control can be applied even more effectively.

Feedforward Control

Feedforward control is another form of anticipatory control. It takes effect before the anticipated deviation of performance from standard can occur. This requires control of the inputs and/or the process. Figure 6.7 shows a schematic of control of the process to overcome variations in inputs. Figure 6.8 illustrates feedforward control for a cash-flow system. Components of the process are shown inside the process block.

An idea of the importance of the MIS for feedforward control can be gleaned from a study of Fig. 6.8. The variability and uncertainty of sales, the many process components and their interrelationships, the uncertainty of collections and interest rates, and the periodic change of the setpoint require a very responsive control system. The computerized MIS will alert management to required inputs and required adjustments of the process of cash flow in order to have the needed cash on hand at any given date.

Yes-No Control

All business operations, transactions, and decisions should be bounded. At the lowest level, say, an inspection process determines whether bolts are too long or too short. The result is either a "go" or "no-go" decision. At the top level of management, in contrast, suppose that a vice president is considering authorizing the construction of a two-million-dollar plant. The company's policy guide states that he can only spend up to $500,000 without approval of the president and the board of directors. His desired action is no-go because it exceeds control limits. Therefore he must go through an approval procedure. The policy guide is the MIS source of most of the no-go restrictions.

Levels of Control Complexity

We are now able to describe control systems at increasing levels of complexity. In all cases, information flow is a necessity. The four levels are:

1. Fixed setting control
2. Self-regulatory control (homeostasis)
3. Optimal control
4. Adaptive control.

The features of each, with an example, are given in Table 6.3.

Table 6.3 Levels of control

Level of Control	Features	Examples	MIS Control Information
1. Fixed setting	Procedure or task provided	a. Automatic shutoff on sprinkler system	—
		b. Assignment of men to load a truck	Man-hours required per loading
2. Self-regulatory control	Feedback control, continuous or on-off control of system	a. Heating system with thermostat control based on feedback of temperature of the house	—
		b. The sales manager increases his sales force and provides training to meet objectives set forth in the annual operating plan. Sales reports lead to further training or adjustment of territory	Annual sales plan and sales performance, along with exceptionally high deviations. (The high deviations are feedback causing the manager to take action.)
3. Optimal control	Feedback control. May also have feedforward, and yes-no control	a. A demand forecasting model (such as exponential smoothing) where the smoothing constant changes with each forecast to take into account new data	Performance of the model is feedback to management
		b. Plant operations are geared to the annual operating plan. A "rolling forecast" of month-by-month performance is prepared each month. Adjustments are made to all activities to bring the year-end results forecasted monthly into line with the original plan	Annual plan Rolling forecasts Variances of functional groups Budget variances
4. Adaptive control	Feedback control. Steering control. May also have feedforward control	a. The human being as a worker adapts to work environment	—
		b. Viable organizations change objectives, structures, methods, operations, and size	Environmental, particularly competitive information Needed organizational, structural, and strategy changes Total system performance

CONTROL AND THE ORGANIZATION

Control and Organizational Structure

Strategy, organizational structure, and control are linked very tightly in the business firm. Strategy and the resultant long-range and short-range plans establish the objectives or standards of the business system. Research has shown that a change in strategy requires a change in structure. Conversely, if the organizational structure is changed materially, the strategy of the company will change.

Control of company activities depends upon the location of "controllers," i.e., managers. The control system reflects the management structure. The MIS, in turn, includes the control and planning system information flows.

Control in the traditional hierarchical organization is easily explained. Summary reports, variance reports, and exceptional activity reports proceed up the organization. Responsibility for breakdowns and corrective action is clearly defined. In modern complex organizations, information flows to many managers, who often share responsibility for decisions and performance. In such multi-dimensional organizations, the big problem is isolating responsibility for control. This places a larger burden upon the MIS: that of keeping all participating managers in each function or activity well informed. Such information as will prompt their spontaneous action to control their complex systems is necessary.

Management by Objectives

Management by objectives (MBO) means establishing measurable and verifiable objectives for managers (and other workers). These objectives form a hierarchy which corresponds to the hierarchy of plans. They include the objectives of the annual plan, but they also include short-term (one- to three-month) objectives which build flexibility into implementation of plans.

In MBO, the manager negotiates with his or her superior the objectives and schedule of achievement. The manager then negotiates with each subordinate the objectives and schedule for the subordinate. This participation by subordinates in defining their own work is intended to lead to greater motivation. Further, each person knows exactly what he or she will be appraised on and rewarded for. With verifiable objectives, performance can be measured reasonably well. Before MBO, workers were appraised on their traits and methods, not on achievement of objectives.

Unfortunately, traditional MBO tends to focus on the hierarchy of managers rather than the objectives of systems.[1] Control based on system objectives depends upon identifying the key systems of the company. A manufacturing company may be divided into five sets of systems:

1. Product systems
2. Area profit or investment centers
3. Functional, or cost, systems
4. Resource systems
5. Major phase systems.

[1]See Robert G. Murdick, "MIS for MBO," *Journal of Systems Management,* March 1977.

	Possible Sharing of Responsibility for the Resource	Typical MIS Reports
Table 6.4 Typical responsibilities and MIS reports related to company resources		
Human resources	Line managers at each level of the organization Corporate staff development and training executives Personnel department managers Personnel department specialists Labor relations negotiators	Manpower planning. Response to manpower inventory queries. Turnover. Attitude survey summaries. Labor costs Promotion-potential charts Organization charts
Capital assets	Line managers Industrial engineers Executive committee Capital budget committee Board of directors Controller	Average age of equipment Financial analysis of alternatives Justification of need for new capital items or disposition of old items Summaries of present capital assets Capital budgets
Materials	Manager of production planning and control Inventory control manager Warehouse manager Accounting department Marketing manager Office administration manager Laboratory manager Materials handling supervisor Traffic manager	Raw materials inventory summary Finished goods inventory summary Balance sheet Physical inventory summary Shrinkage reports Office supplies inventory summaries Obsolescence of merchandise reports
Liquid assets	Manager of finance Manager of accounting Short-term money specialist Controller Purchasing agent Line managers Salesmen Petty cash supervisor	Balance sheet Cash-flow forecasts Flow-of-funds statements Summary of purchases Salesmen's expense accounts Managers' expense accounts
Credit lines	Financial manager Finance Committee: President Treasurer Controller	Balance sheet Debt summary Schedule of bond redemptions Schedule of short-term notes due Debt/equity report Available credit sources Interest rates Funds requirements forecasts

Source: Robert G. Murdick, "MIS for MBO," **Journal of Systems Management,** March 1977.

Figure 4.6 (page 117) shows these five sets of systems. For control purposes, a company must define these systems, establish objectives and plans to achieve such objectives, establish responsibility for control, and provide the MIS required for control. In most companies the responsibility for control of each of the subsystems is either diffused or confused. Yet management realizes vaguely that control is required. We need only to look at the typical MIS reports to deduce this. In Table 6.4 we may observe the possible sharing of responsibility for control of each of the resource subsystems. We also may note the variety of MIS reports that typically are provided for control of a given resource system. It is clear that companies don't, but should, take a systems approach to control.

Human Responses to Control

The processes and effects of control have often baffled managers in the past. As they saw errors and deviations from objectives occur, managers would increase the reporting and control requirements. The more they increased controls, it seemed, the more the employees would resist controls or become so apathetic that the controls were ineffective. Other dysfunctional aspects of measurement and control have included distortion of priorities, conflict between organizational groups, and withholding of information.[2]

The impact of control systems on employee behavior is complex and still being researched. Therefore, only some major concepts relating to MIS will be given here. As the first step, we note that three variables are involved in studying the impact of control on workers and managers:

1. Independent variables such as objectives and tasks, organizational structure, information processes, reward systems, managerial style, and characteristics or "culture" of the people in the organization
2. Intervening variables such as aspirations, group cohesion (morale), and motivation
3. Dependent variables (outputs) such as productivity, efficiency, and worker satisfaction.

Traditionally, control has been exercised by management directives, posted work schedules, and budgets with accompanying feedback of results, reiterating of objectives, and rewards and penalties. The development of the contingency approach to managing and modern theories of motivation have produced a more flexible style of leadership. The emphasis has shifted from control by means of exercise of authority to individual self-control by the worker or manager responsible for performing the task.

[2]See, for example, Chris Argyris, *Personality and Organization: The Conflict Between System and the Individual* (New York: Harper & Row, Pub., 1957); Gene W. Dalton and Paul R. Lawrence, eds., *Motivation and Control in Organizations* (Homewood, Ill.: Richard D. Irwin, 1971); and V. F. Ridgway, "Dysfunctional Consequences of Performance Measurements," *Administrative Science Quarterly*, September 1956; R. Likert, *The Human Organization* (New York: McGraw-Hill, 1967).

The implementation of this decentralization of basic control requires good MIS and operating information systems. The individual worker such as the engineer, salesperson, clerk, or machine operator must be supplied with objectives and prompt feedback of performance variations. In the management structure, the MIS reflects the deviations of the subordinates. However, under a system of *management by exception,* these deviations would be reported only if they were to exceed wider limits than those established at lower levels. The schematic of Fig. 6.9 will make this clearer.

In Fig. 6.9 we see an engineer's responsibility for a $150,000 task over a 12-month period. His budget for the first month is $13,400. The engineer opens a "shop order" or account number to which expenses are charged. The budgeted amount for the first month is $13,400. If the actual expenditures exceed $14,600 or do not reach $12,100, the engineer realizes he must take action by investigating the work charged to the account. He finds this information in a monthly financial report he receives. If expenditures are more than $16,000 or less than $10,000, the section manager receives a variance report and asks the engineer for an explanation. If expenses exceed $25,000 or none are incurred, the engineering department manager will receive an exception report and investigate. Generally, the variance is such that the engineer can take corrective action in the following month without involving higher levels of management.

Figure 6.9
Control limits at three levels for management control by exception

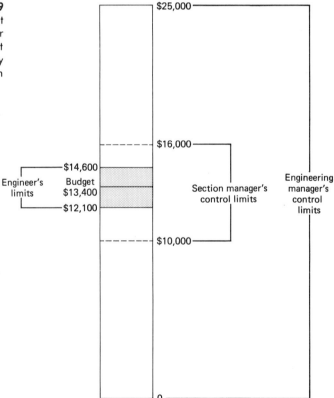

From various studies, we may develop a "before MIS" and "after MIS" picture which explains how the situation just described might come about.[3]

Before the MIS is Installed. The following situation is typical.

1. The organization is departmentalized by function.
2. Communication is primarily up and down the hierarchy with some committees for integration.
3. Management style tends to be autocratic or paternalistic.
4. Leadership is based more on power than on professional competence.
5. The role of the manager is very important because of ambiguity of situations caused by lack of information. The emphasis is on managers who can drive ahead in ignorance using low levels of conceptualization and management sophistication.
6. Nonmanagers are limited in scope of action because of ambiguity of objectives and lack of information about the business system as a whole.
7. Aspirations and motivations of nonmanagers are heavily influenced by goals set for them by their managers.
8. Motivation of nonmanagers is directed more toward filling social needs on the job than toward self-fulfillment through control of one's own work.
9. Group conformity, group norms, and group cohesion are sought above individual job performance.

After the MIS is Installed. Changes occur because of the impact of the MIS on the organization:

1. The organization becomes more sophisticated in structure as a complex cross-functional structure, or a product/investment center/functional/geographical structure.
2. Communication is more formalized into networks represented by the MIS. Emphasis is on getting information *directly to* the individual responsible for a task rather than *through* his or her manager.
3. Management style must become flexible and participative or else it fails.
4. Leadership must be based more on competence than power. Those managers who lack technical competence become very insecure.
5. The old role of the manager changes. Emphasis is on analytical skills and a high level of conceptualization. Many of the pre-MIS managers will become obsolete.

[3]See Chris Argyris, "Management Information Systems: The Challenge to Rationality and Emotionality," *Management Science,* February 1971.

6. Nonmanagers share in developing clear-cut objectives, based on information about the total business system.

7. By setting his or her own goals, the nonmanager develops his or her aspirations and motivations based upon his or her performance and beliefs.

8. Motivation is based on a climate for growth and control over one's own situation.

9. Group cooperation rather than group conformity becomes an objective.

ECONOMICS OF MIS FOR CONTROL

Cost of control with an MIS is determined by three factors. One is the level of detail of data captured, the second is the selection of data captured, and the third is the reporting system. Obviously, the more detailed and the broader in scope the data captured, the higher is the cost. As for reporting, the frequency, the content, and the distribution of the management reports all affect costs.

The value of the MIS is not continuously improved by gathering more and more data or issuing more detailed reports to more managers. Rather, the MIS should deliver an optimum amount of information at needed times and in desired detail. Figure 6.10 shows the nature of control costs. Notice that *no* control may be more cost effective than very high control.

A good guide for design of the MIS for control purposes is the ABC principle. In inventory control, it has been found that about 20% of the raw

Figure 6.10
Economics of
control

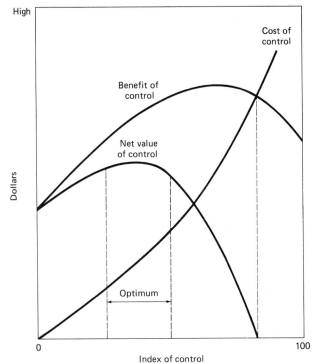

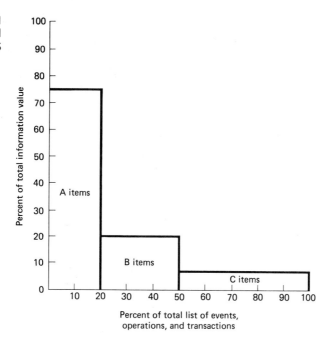

Figure 6.11
ABC control
with MIS

Percent of total information value

Percent of total list of events,
operations, and transactions

material items make up about 75% of the value of the inventory. These so-called "A" items are very closely controlled. Next, about 30% of the items make up about 20% of the value of the inventory. These "B" items must receive some control management. Finally, there are the "C" items, which comprise 50% of the items in inventory but only 5% of the value. The only control exercised over these items is to order them in advance of requirements.

Similarly, the MIS for control purposes should focus on the few operations that have the highest impact upon the success of the firm. Fewer reports and less detail should be supplied to management on the next lower-in-importance category of items. Finally, management need pay no attention to the thousands of minor activities going on continuously throughout the firm. Only when many of these activities affect an important operation (B or A) would management be notified. Figure 6.11 illustrates this ABC control concept.

Another concept of the economics of control may be borrowed from manufacturing quality control. Just as statistical control may be applied to quality of incoming and finished products, statistical control may be applied to quality of information. For example, sampling of accounts overdue or sampling of clerical errors may provide estimates of actual accounts overdue or actual clerical errors. At a much smaller cost, management can obtain a slightly lower quality of information for control. Another measure of quality control of information universally employed is the accounting audit. Much more sophisticated measures for statistical control of decision making may be incorporated in the MIS.[4]

[4]See R. G. Murdick and Emilio J. Gonzales, "CUSUM Charts in Managing by Objectives," *Louisiana Business Review,* March 1973.

Figure 6.12
Reports
relationships

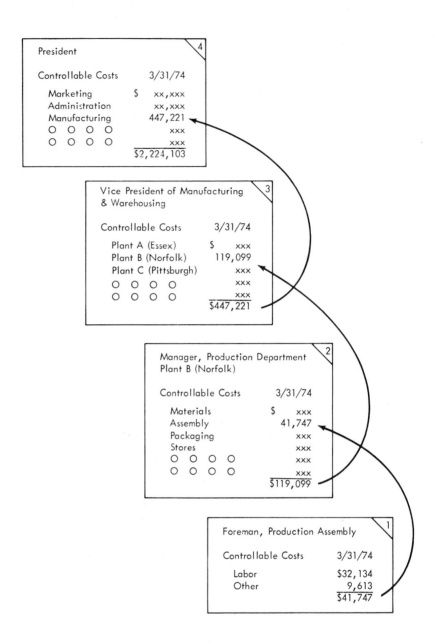

President

Controllable Costs   3/31/74

Marketing $ xx,xxx
Administration   xx,xxx
Manufacturing   447,221
O O O O   xxx
O O O O   xxx
                    $2,224,103

Vice President of Manufacturing
& Warehousing

Controllable Costs   3/31/74

Plant A (Essex) $ xxx
Plant B (Norfolk)   119,099
Plant C (Pittsburgh)   xxx
O O O O   xxx
O O O O   xxx
                     $447,221

Manager, Production Department
Plant B (Norfolk)

Controllable Costs   3/31/74

Materials $ xxx
Assembly   41,747
Packaging   xxx
Stores   xxx
O O O O   xxx
O O O O   xxx
                     $119,099

Foreman, Production Assembly

Controllable Costs   3/31/74

Labor $32,134
Other   9,613
                   $41,747

Note: The design of responsibility
        reports should be tailored by
        the user. The responsible person
        needs to take an active role
        in preparing his own budgets
        and standards.

Source: MSA General Ledger System, Courtesy of Management Science of America, Inc.

Reporting Systems

Feedback on performance is contained in reports of a wide variety. The higher the level of management, the more likely it is that graphic or visual displays are used instead of tables of data. Such graphics permit easy comparison of present performance with past performance. Trends may be observed. Further, it is possible to add bars or curves to show planned values for comparison with actual ones or to show the plan for the future.

The MIS control system should provide a hierarchy of control reports, starting with complete detail at the lowest level. At each higher level, the information becomes more aggregated or summary in nature. As a result, "exception" reports are also required to flag particularly large deviations of performance from plans. Hierarchies of control reports should exist in each of the five dimensions of the firm discussed earlier in connection with Fig. 4.6. An example of aggregation of information up the functional hierarchy is shown in Figure 6.12.

A characteristic of the hierarchy of reports is the associated frequency of reports. At the lowest level of management, weekly or even daily reports are necessary. At the top level, monthly, quarterly, and annual reports are adequate for control purposes. To illustrate this point, Figure 6.13 shows a hospital system of reports. Notice that the weekly reports would be of interest primarily to supervisors. The "pay period," monthly, and less frequent reports are clearly management-oriented.

Pro Forma Earnings Statement and Master Budget

Although the strategic plan provides general control standards for management, the pro forma earnings statement and the master budget are more immediate and specific. The MIS should provide performance results which can be compared to items in these two plans.

The *master budget* consists of a consolidation of an organization's plan for one year plus all backup budgets. The principal, but not the only, components of the master budget are therefore:

1. Operating budget
   a. Sales budget
   b. Production budget (in manufacturing companies)
   c. Cost-of-goods-sold budget (for manufacturing and merchandising companies)
   d. Selling expense budget
   e. Administrative expense budget

2. Financial budget
   a. Cash budget: receipts and disbursements
   b. Budgeted balance sheet
   c. Budgeted statement of sources and applications of funds.

A Reporting Summary

DAILY

ON-DEMAND

Data Control
Automatic Pricing
System Balance
Input Verification
  and Audit
Error Listings
Activity
Interim Census/Bed Control
Final Census
Admissions, Discharges,
  and Transfers
Revenue and Payment
  Analysis
Patient Accounting
Patient Account Status
Charges, Payments,
  Adjustments Detail
Patient Bills,
  Third-Party Bills

Interim Patient Bills
Demand Bills
Third-Party Bills
Charge Master

Patient Information, Billing and Accounts Receivable

Payroll and Labor Management

Financial Reporting and Analysis

Accounts Payable

Medical Records Abstracting and Utilization Review

THE MINICOMPUTER IN
YOUR HOSPITAL IS FOR
DAILY AND SPECIFIC
ON-DEMAND REPORTING.
ALL OTHER REPORTS
ARE PRODUCED BY THE
SHARED COMPUTER.

Figure 6.13 A hospital system of reports

Courtesy of Professional Hospital Services,

*Payroll, payables checks and check registers
 are printed on the minicomputer in the hospital.

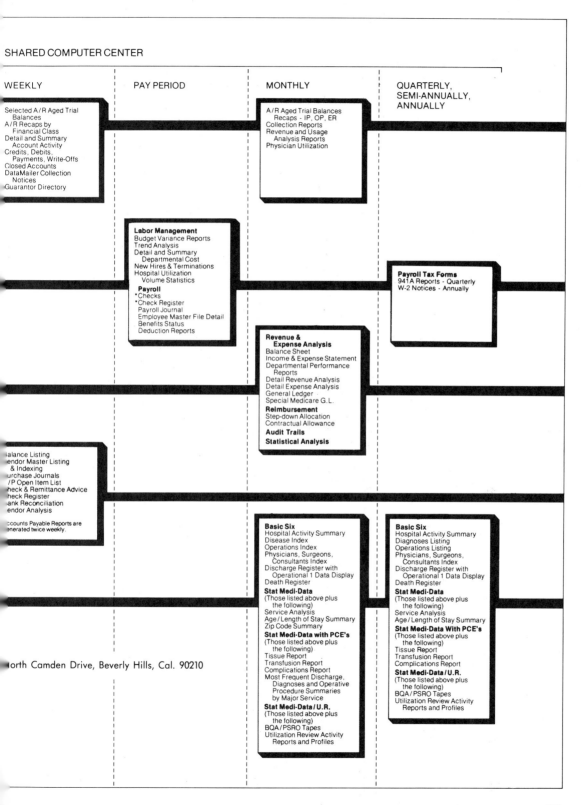

SHARED COMPUTER CENTER

WEEKLY

Selected A/R Aged Trial
   Balances
A/R Recaps by
   Financial Class
Detail and Summary
   Account Activity
Credits, Debits,
   Payments, Write-Offs
Closed Accounts
DataMailer Collection
   Notices
Guarantor Directory

PAY PERIOD

Labor Management
Budget Variance Reports
Trend Analysis
Detail and Summary
   Departmental Cost
New Hires & Terminations
Hospital Utilization
   Volume Statistics
Payroll
*Checks
*Check Register
Payroll Journal
Employee Master File Detail
Benefits Status
Deduction Reports

MONTHLY

A/R Aged Trial Balances
   Recaps - IP, OP, ER
Collection Reports
Revenue and Usage
   Analysis Reports
Physician Utilization

**Revenue &
   Expense Analysis**
Balance Sheet
Income & Expense Statement
Departmental Performance
   Reports
Detail Revenue Analysis
Detail Expense Analysis
General Ledger
Special Medicare G.L.
Reimbursement
Step-down Allocation
Contractual Allowance
Audit Trails
Statistical Analysis

**QUARTERLY,
SEMI-ANNUALLY,
ANNUALLY**

Payroll Tax Forms
941A Reports - Quarterly
W-2 Notices - Annually

alance Listing
endor Master Listing
   & Indexing
urchase Journals
/P Open Item List
heck & Remittance Advice
heck Register
ank Reconciliation
endor Analysis

ccounts Payable Reports are
enerated twice weekly.

Basic Six
Hospital Activity Summary
Disease Index
Operations Index
Physicians, Surgeons,
   Consultants Index
Discharge Register with
   Operational 1 Data Display
Death Register
Stat Medi-Data
(Those listed above plus
   the following)
Service Analysis
Age/Length of Stay Summary
Zip Code Summary
Stat Medi-Data with PCE's
(Those listed above plus
   the following)
Tissue Report
Transfusion Report
Complications Report
Most Frequent Discharge,
   Diagnoses and Operative
   Procedure Summaries
   by Major Service
Stat Medi-Data/U.R.
(Those listed above plus
   the following)
BQA/PSRO Tapes
Utilization Review Activity
   Reports and Profiles

Basic Six
Hospital Activity Summary
Diagnoses Listing
Operations Listing
Physicians, Surgeons,
   Consultants Index
Discharge Register with
   Operational 1 Data Display
Death Register
Stat Medi-Data
(Those listed above plus
   the following)
Service Analysis
Age/Length of Stay Summary
Stat Medi-Data With PCE's
(Those listed above plus
   the following)
Tissue Report
Transfusion Report
Complications Report
Stat Medi-Data/U.R.
(Those listed above plus
   the following)
BQA/PSRO Tapes
Utilization Review Activity
   Reports and Profiles

lorth Camden Drive, Beverly Hills, Cal. 90210

191

The master budget shows budgeted amounts for each month, as well as totals. By means of such devices as three-month rolling forecasts, the budgets are used to track expenditures and potential variances for the year as a whole on a month-to-month basis. Such a three-month rolling forecast shows, each month:

a. Expenditures to date

b. Anticipated monthly expenditures for each of the next three months

c. New estimate of expenditures for the year

d. Variance of estimate from original amount budgeted for the year.

Key Result Areas for Total System Control

Managers tend to become so absorbed in their individual subsystems and daily activities that the firm as a whole is not controlled. That is, certain indexes that measure the health of the whole business are neglected. These indexes relating to so-called *key result areas (KRA's)* are listed in Table 6.5 with typical MIS support information. In most instances the company that developed the KRA concept, General Electric Co., uses other supporting statistical information.

Corporate MIS Room

Despite the efforts of the MIS designers, top management is being buried under an avalanche of statistical data. One way to dig out is the development of

Table 6.5
MIS for control in key result areas

Key Result Area	MIS Information
1. Profitability	Earnings, earnings/share, ROI residual profit, profit trend, profit/sales
2. Market position	Rank, share of market, percent increase in market share
3. Productivity	Sales/employee, production/employee, labor budget/sales, labor costs/capital assets, net change in number of employees/change in sales
4. Product leadership	Number of new company products, number of new company patents. (Considerable judgment is required for this index, so that MIS does not play a big role.)
5. Personnel development	Net change in human resource (accounting) valuation, number of promotions at each level of management, number of employee-hours of training programs
6. Employee attitudes	Analysis of employee attitude surveys, absenteeism and quits, average tenure of employees
7. Public responsibility	Summary of dollar contributions. (Considerable qualitative evaluation is required, so that the MIS plays a minor reporting role,)
8. Balance between short-range and long-range plans	None

Figure 6.14 Corporate MIS room

an executive MIS room or board of directors room with special display facilities connected to the computer. Wall screens or video screens display information immediately upon call from executives. Color is used to make tables and graphs more readable. (See Fig. 6.14.)

Statistical Analyses for Control

The MIS can classify, combine, and summarize masses of data to provide valuable information for control at middle and first-line management levels. One of the most useful types of information is that for control of extreme values of variables. For example, perhaps statistical analysis shows that 10% of the items in inventory represent 70% of the value. Then management will be able to exercise careful procedural control over these items and spend very little on the control of other items.

Another illustration is the distribution of sales according to the dollar value of sales for each item. This information may be presented to the sales manager as in Table 6.6 or to the general manager in chart form as in Fig. 6.15(a). Such information suggests that high-dollar-value accounts should receive careful attention. It also allows management to prune low-value accounts which appear to have no future prospects and cost more to service than they yield in revenue. Other graphs in Fig. 6.15 illustrate other applications of control of extremes of variables.

Figure 6.15 Graphic presentation of statistical data for control of extremes

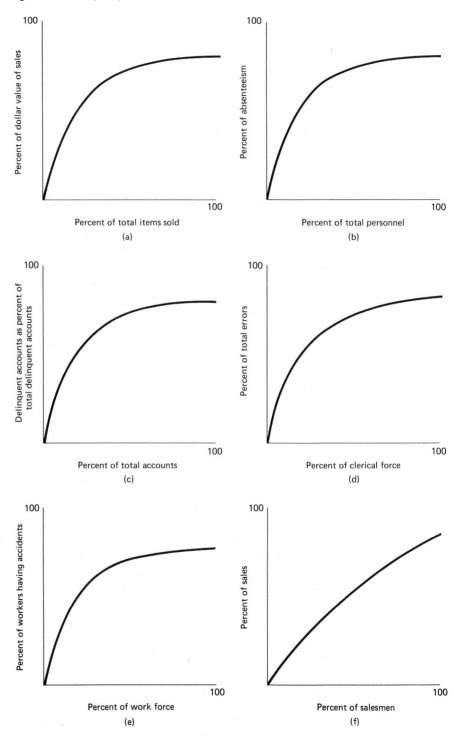

Table 6.6
Distribution-by-
value report

Item No	Cumulative Count		Annual Units	Unit Cost	Annual $ Sales	Cumulative Sales	
	Rank by $ Sales	%				$	%
411045	1	.2	104,578	.966	101,023	101,023	3.8
411118	2	.4	375,959	.246	92,486	193,509	7.3
411063	3	.5	40,602	2.012	81,693	275,202	10.4
411075	4	.7	69,570	1.123	78,128	353,330	13.3
411176	5	.9	133,534	.490	65,432	418,762	15.8
411381	6	1.1	106,651	.510	54,392	473,154	17.8
411368	110	20.0	90,191	.073	6,584	1,886,385	71.0
411425	111	20.2	7,513	.800	6,011	1,892,396	71.2
411263	112	20.4	1,820	3.286	5,983	1,898,379	71.4
411503	113	20.5	10,611	.553	5,868	1,904,247	71.6
411444	545	99.2	813	.145	118	2,657,997	100.0
411465	546	99.4	4,227	.022	93	2,658,090	100.0
411243	547	99.6	90	.715	65	2,658,155	100.0
411516	548	99.8	4	2.916	12	2,658,167	100.0
411541	549	100.0	0	0	0	2,658,167	100.0

PERT/CPM

Program evaluation review technique (PERT) and the critical path method (CPM) are powerful (and essentially the same) methods for controlling large, well-defined projects. In essence, the total project, such as designing a new product, launching a national advertising campaign, or designing and implementing a new MIS, is broken down into a hierarchy of tasks and subtasks. The completion of an activity is called an *event*. Starting with the last event of the project, the preceding required events are arranged in a *network* such as shown in the simple diagram of Fig. 6.16. The times for activities are indicated on the activity arrows. The longest time path through the network, ABCDEG, is called the *critical path*. The MIS reports on any slippage of the critical path so that management can apply more resources to keep the total project on schedule. If an activity not in the critical path falls too far behind schedule, it produces a new critical path to be controlled. Costs associated with each activity are also reported by the MIS for control by management. PERT is discussed in more detail in the chapters dealing with planning and designing the MIS.

Figure 6.16
PERT network

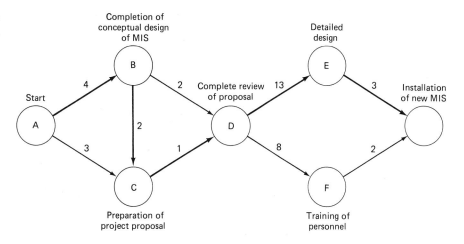

Operations Auditing

A common misunderstanding is that control is aimed at keeping things from happening. The real purpose of control is to make things happen to make the company function better. Operations auditing is a form of control which exemplifies this concept.

Operations auditing is a review and appraisal of the efficiency and effectiveness of operations and operating procedures based upon sampling activities. Every area of the business is investigated for potential improvement.[5] Some experts state that the auditor has the responsibility to recommend courses of action to management, but this is probably too much to expect from sampling. Further, it is management's responsibility to develop courses of action. The relationship of MIS to control through operations auditing is presented in broad terms in Table 6.7.

Table 6.7 Operations auditing for control

Major Purpose	Relation to MIS
1. Verification of the need for data and reports produced by the information system	MIS is the subject of the audit
2. Verification of accuracy of information inputs and outputs	MIS is the subject of the audit
3. Determination of the degree of organizational compliance with policies, procedures, and government regulations	MIS reports on performance are compared with policies, procedures, and government regulations
4. Appraisal of operations of the five sets of subsystems of Fig. 4.6	MIS reports, particularly underlying statistical information, are supplied for analysis
5. Appraisal of supporting processes such as data processing, mail distribution, clerical operations, plant maintenance, and general security	MIS design is compared with actual operations

Accounting Control and Auditing

The most widely accepted source for clarification of accounting terminology is the American Institute of Certified Public Accountants (AICPA). This body issues certain statements on accounting and auditing matters to provide accountants with standardized accounting principles and auditing standards that are generally accepted throughout the profession. In Section 320 of the AICPA's Statement on Auditing Standards No. 1, internal control is defined as a two-part set of controls as follows:

> *Administrative control* includes, but is not limited to, the plan of organization and the procedures and records that are concerned with the decision processes leading

[5]For a lengthy checklist of activities to be investigated, see Roy A. Lindberg and Theodore Cohn, *Operations Auditing* (New York: AMACOM, 1972).

to management's authorization of transactions. Such authorization is a management function directly associated with the responsibility for achieving the objectives of the organization and is the starting point for establishing accounting control of transactions.

Accounting control comprises the plan of organization and the procedures and records that are concerned with the safeguarding of assets and the reliability of financial records and consequently are designed to provide reasonable assurance that:

a. Transactions are executed in accordance with management's general or specific authorization

b. Transactions are recorded as necessary to (1) permit preparation of financial statements in conformity with generally accepted accounting principles or any other criteria applicable to such statements and (2) maintain accountability for assets

c. Access to assets is permitted only in accordance with management's authorization

d. The recorded accountability for assets is compared with the existing assets at reasonable intervals and appropriate action is taken with respect to any differences.

The most notable element of this definition is the emphasis placed on transactions. Previous definitions of internal control have only extended to the safeguarding of assets and reliability of financial records for external reporting purposes. This "transaction-based" definition more clearly demonstrates the integration of internal controls into the management information system. The basic components of business operations are transactions, hence these transactions are the primary subject matter of internal control. As noted earlier, the majority of critical accounting transactions are usually included in the main transaction cycles (purchasing, production, and sales). In each of these cycles, the MIS is concerned with the authorization, execution, and recording of transactions and the accountability for resulting assets. Therefore, it is in these areas of concern that we must integrate the internal controls to insure the reliability of the MIS. Now let us consider how these transactions and transaction cycles of the MIS relate to the two elements of the definition of internal control issued by the AICPA.

The objectives of the internal auditor are to insure that assets are properly safeguarded and transactions are properly authorized, executed, and recorded in the accounts, thereby providing reasonable assurance as to the reliability of the MIS output. To attain these objectives, the internal auditor acts as a "mobile" form of internal control. This function is termed a mobile control because the internal auditor neither verifies each transaction in the system nor determines the proper safeguarding of each asset in the organization. Instead, the internal auditor develops an annual plan to *test* the operation of the MIS. The areas of the MIS that are either loosely controlled or critical to MIS output receive the most audit attention. Other areas of the system are audited to determine that internal controls are operating effectively and output is reliable.

External auditors are usually engaged to certify that the financial statements generated by the MIS are fairly stated in accordance with generally accepted accounting principles. The purpose of this certification is to provide interested outsiders (such as banks, investors, and regulatory agencies) and the owners of the organization with an independent verification of the financial statements.

The objectives of the external auditor are similar to those of the internal auditor. However, the following clearly separate the two functions:

1. The external auditor is concerned with the form and content of the financial statements. The internal audit function usually stops short of this step.

2. The external auditor views the internal auditor as an important internal control to evaluate when planning the audit approach.

3. The external auditor is concerned with the interests of outsiders, where the internal auditor is concerned with determining that transactions are carried out in accordance with management's policies.

SUMMARY

One of the earliest and still important applications of MIS is providing information for control by management. The concept of control has broadened considerably since the management pioneer days. It now recognizes both behavioral control (people) and results control (output). The modern concept also distinguishes among feedback control, steering control, and feedforward control.

Feedback control involves measuring a system's output, comparing it with a standard, feeding back the difference or variance to a controller, and taking corrective action. In steering control, we anticipate the output and we exercise control to prevent the output from deviating from standard. It is similar to driving a car around a curve: we don't wait until we see we are off the road, we steer in anticipation of the curve. Feedforward is also anticipatory control. It depends on making sure the outputs are correct and the system processing is known.

Control may be very simple for simple systems or complex for dynamic systems. Levels of control are (a) fixed setting without any other control, (b) self-regulatory (feedback with a standard output specified), (c) optimal control, whereby the control system adapts itself to optimize results, and (d) adaptive control, whereby the control system adapts itself to the environment.

Control is closely tied to organizational structure. Information flow and decision centers vary according to the organization structure, and the control system will vary correspondingly. Management by objectives (MBO) is also fitted to the organizational structure. Such objectives form a basis for control of the organization. Objectives of a company should be the result of analyzing the subsystems along five dimensions of the company structure:

1. Product systems

2. Area profit or investment centers

3. Functional, or cost, systems

4. Resource systems

5. Major phase systems.

Human responses to control are apt to be dysfunctional. Workers often resent being told how to do things. On the other hand, when an MIS is installed to give workers more opportunity to control their own work, managers may feel insecure.

Control systems should be designed with both costs and benefits in mind. The more detailed the information gathered, the more expensive control becomes and the less is the gain in useful information.

The application of management control with MIS is based upon hierarchical report systems, projected budgets, key result areas, statistical analysis, network planning, operations auditing, and accounting control and auditing.

In conclusion, we may say that the managerial control function is very complex and depends for its functioning upon the MIS.

QUESTIONS AND PROBLEMS

1. Control means bringing or maintaining within prescribed limits:

   a. The performance of an _____ _____ _____ or

   _____.

   b. The characteristics of an _____ _____

   _____ or _____.

   c. The _____ or _____ of a variable.

2. By giving an example for each, complete the following table.

	Item Controlled	Output or Characteristic	Limits	MIS Report
a.	Bank teller			
b.	Hospital A/R			
c.	Hiring costs			
d.	Engineering manager			
e.	Product line			
f.	Variety of models of a product			
g.	Public relations			
h.	Capital expenditures			
i.	Inventory system			
j.	Order processing system			
k.	Training program			
l.	Data			

3. Place the correct letters before the items listed below.

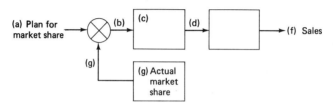

_____ (1) Error signal   _____ (5) Output

_____ (2) Processor   _____ (6) Feedback

_____ (3) Manager   _____ (7) Sensing and measuring

_____ (4) Input   _____ (8) Output of the controller

4. The types of control are: a. _____

                    b. _____

                    c. _____

                    d. _____

                    e. _____

5. The four levels of control complexity are:

    a. _____   c. _____

    b. _____   d. _____

6. For key result areas and MIS, match the following:

    a. Third in sales   (1) Profitability   _____

    b. Training budget of $500,000   (2) Market position   _____

    c. Sued by competitors as a monopoly   (3) Productivity   _____

    d. Leader in contributions to urban renewal   (4) Product leadership   _____

    e. ROI—23%   (5) Personnel development _____

    f. Continuing wildcat strikes   (6) Employee attitudes   _____

    g. 200 cars/employee annually

7. The five dimensions of the firm for planning and control of systems are:

    a. _____   d. _____

    b. _____   e. _____

    c. _____

8. For each of the items listed in Fig. 6.17, give a one-sentence statement of the objective and a specific example to illustrate the activity.

Figure 6.17 Relation of systems control objectives to transaction flow

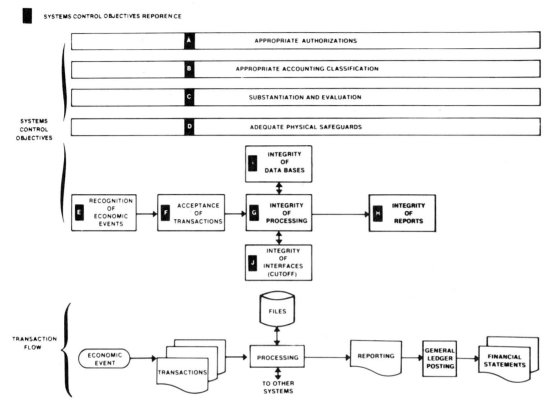

Source: **A Guide for Studying and Evaluating Internal Accounting Controls**
(Chicago: Arthur Andersen & Co., 1978), p. 46.

A. Objective:

   Example:

B. Objective:

   Example:

C. Objective:

   Example:

D. Objective:

   Example:

E. Objective: Economic events should be recognized and submitted for acceptance
            on a timely basis.

   Example:

F. Objective:

   Example:

G. Objective:

　Example:

H. Objective:

　Example:

I. Objective:

　Example:

J. Objective: Events affecting more than one system should result in transactions that are reflected by each system in the same accounting period.
　Example:

9. Define (a) internal control, (b) administrative control, (c) accounting control.

10. Obtain from a company an example of related reports at three to four levels of management similar to Fig. 6.12.

11. Give two illustrations where ABC control might apply other than those in Fig. 6.15.

12. Discuss the impact of tight control systems on the organization.

13. How is control related to organizational structure?

14. A principle of control is segregation of duties. That is, any employee who has access to assets and also access to records of these assets is in a position to embezzle from the firm. Give an example of possible lack of segregation of duties for the following:

   a. The computer operator in a bank
   b. The petty cash clerk
   c. The inventory control clerk
   d. The store managers of government employee stores operated by the General Accounting Office.

15. Obtain a set of appropriate policies for capital expenditures for a particular firm. Prepare a figure similar to Fig. 6.9 to show the discretionary limits at each level of management.

16. Make a list of management reports which the MIS might provide to ensure control throughout for:

   a. A manufacturing company
   b. A bank
   c. A hospital
   d. A chain of department stores.

17. Anthony, CPA, prepared the flow chart in Fig. 6.18 which portrays the raw materials purchasing function of one of Anthony's clients, a medium-sized manufacturing company, from the preparation of initial documents through the vouching of invoices for payment in accounts payable. The flow chart was a portion of the work performed on the audit engagement to evaluate internal control. Identify and explain the systems and control weaknesses evident from the flow chart in Fig. 6.18. Include the internal control weaknesses resulting from activities performed or not performed. All documents are prenumbered.

Figure 6.18 A CPA's flow chart

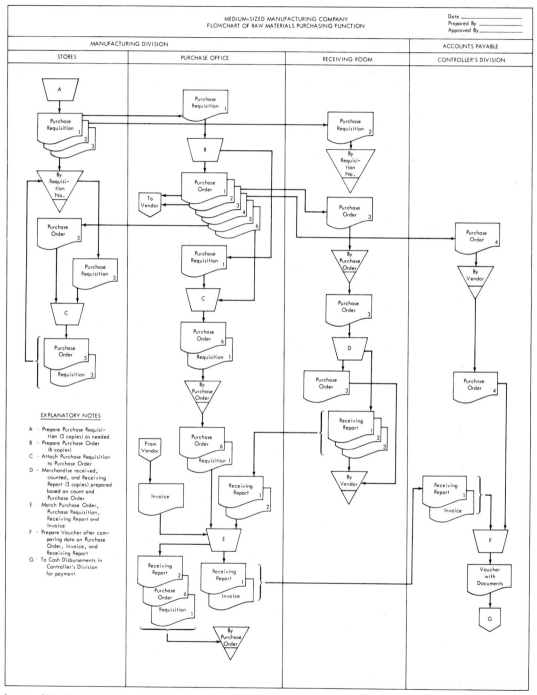

SELECTED REFERENCES

ARTHUR ANDERSEN & CO., *A Guide for Studying and Evaluating Internal Accounting Controls.* Chicago, 1978.

BATESON, ROBERT, *Introduction to Control System Technology.* Columbus, Ohio: Charles E. Merrill, 1973.

"Corporate War Rooms Plug Into the Computer," *Business Week,* August 23, 1976.

DALTON, GENE W., and PAUL R. LAWRENCE, *Motivation and Control in Organizations.* Homewood, Ill.: Richard D. Irwin, 1971.

DRUCKER, PETER F., *Management.* New York: Harper & Row, Pub., 1974.

EMERY, JAMES C., *Organizational Planning and Control Systems.* New York: Macmillan, 1969.

ESTES, RALPH, "Standards for Corporate Social Reporting," *Management Accounting,* November 1976.

GIGLIONI, GIOVANNI B., and ARTHUR G. BEDEIAN, "A Conspectus of Management Control Theory," *Academy of Management Journal,* June 1974.

HERZOG, JOHN P., "Operational Audit," *Journal of Systems Management,* October 1977.

HORNGREN, CHARLES T., *Accounting for Management Control,* 3d ed. Englewood Cliffs, N.J.: Prentice-Hall, 1974.

ISHIKAWA, AKIRA, and CHARLES H. SMITH, "A Feedforward Control System for Organizational Planning and Control," *International Studies of Management and Organization,* Winter 1973–74.

JAGGI, BIKKI, and PETER WEISSENBERG, "Motivational Considerations in Budgeting: An Operant Conditioning Approach," *Managerial Planning,* September/October 1977.

JONES, REGINALD L., and GEORGE H. TRENTIN. *Budgeting: Key to Planning and Control,* rev. ed. New York: American Management Association, 1971.

KOONTZ, HAROLD, and CYRIL O'DONNELL, *Management,* 6th ed. New York: McGraw-Hill, 1976.

LINDBERG, ROY A., and THEODORE COHN, *Operations Auditing.* New York: AMACOM, 1972.

McNEILL, EUGENE. *Financial Accounting: A Decision Information System,* 2d ed. Santa Monica, Cal.: Goodyear, 1974.

MILES, RAYMOND E., and CHARLES C. SNOW, *Organizational Strategy, Structure, and Process.* New York: McGraw-Hill, 1978.

MURDICK, ROBERT G., "Managerial Control: Concepts and Practice," *Advanced Management,* January 1970.

MURDICK, ROBERT G., et al., *Accounting Information Systems.* Englewood Cliffs, N.J.: Prentice-Hall, 1978.

NEWMAN, MAURICE S., *Financial Accounting Estimates Through Statistical Sampling by Computer.* New York: John Wiley, 1976.

NEWMAN, WILLIAM H., *Constructive Control.* Englewood Cliffs, N.J.: Prentice-Hall, 1975.

SAFIUDDIN, MOHAMMED, "Systems Analysis: Applying Control Theory," *Machine Design,* January 25, 1973.

SANTOCKI, J., "Meaning and Scope of Management Audit," *Accounting and Business Research,* Winter 1976.

SCHODERBEK, PETER P., ASTERIOS G. KEFALAS, and CHARLES G. SCHODERBEK, *Management Systems: Conceptual Considerations*. Dallas: Business Publications, 1975.

SEBENIUS, W. G., "Cost Reporting By Exception," *Journal of Systems Management*, May 1975.

WIEST, JEROME D., and FERDINAND K. LEVY, *A Management Guide to PERT/CPM*. Englewood Cliffs, N.J.: Prentice-Hall, 1969.

WILKINSON, JOSEPH W., "The Meaning of Measurements," *Management Accounting*, July 1975.

part 2

PLANNING, DESIGNING, AND IMPLEMENTING THE MIS

chapter 7

Planning for MIS Development

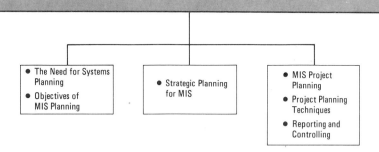

- The Need for Systems Planning
- Objectives of MIS Planning

- Strategic Planning for MIS

- MIS Project Planning
- Project Planning Techniques
- Reporting and Controlling

PURPOSE: To show planning concepts as the first step in MIS development. Both strategic planning and project planning are explained.

There's no substitute for Planning.

SYVERSON

Courtesy of Marsh & McLennan

Planning is difficult especially when it deals with the future.

The MIS development program has been divided into a wide variety of phases by various authorities.[1] For this book we have divided the job into four phases:

1. *Planning and programming.* This first phase, to be covered in this chapter, is concerned with the initial survey, the needs research, the strategic planning, the organizing, and the program planning and control of effort devoted to MIS development.

2. *Conceptual design.* The conceptual design, sometimes referred to as the general design, the gross design, the preliminary design, or the feasibility study, is the specification of the principal subsystems and components, the arrangement and relationships of these subsystems, the general nature of the inputs and outputs, and the anticipated performance of the MIS. It is comparable to the rough sketches and analysis of a product that an engineer makes before developing the detailed design. Its purpose is to evaluate alternate concepts and determine the feasibility of the one that appears best.

[1]For a survey, see Robert G. Murdick, "MIS Development Procedures," *Journal of Systems Management,* December 1970.

3. *Detailed design*. This is a detailed description of the MIS in the form of narrative, charts, tables, and diagrams that is sufficient for someone unfamiliar with the project to implement the proposed MIS. It is mainly an amplification, with necessary modification, of the conceptual design.

4. *Implementation*. Implementation, including testing and debugging, is the conversion of the design specifications into a working system. It covers installation, testing, operation, and maintenance.

In all systems development, phases are overlapping. One reason is that the work is cyclical, because after a subsystem, say, has been designed, it is often necessary to modify it by starting all over. In other words, a portion of design is roughed out and then redesigned. For this reason, the first plan for the MIS development may have to be revised and refined after each phase of the MIS development. If this is true, we should answer the question, "Why plan?"

THE NEED FOR SYSTEMS PLANNING

Little more than lip service has been given to the idea of a total companywide MIS. Instead, we have seen the development of unrelated "islands of mechanization," quick-payoff projects to automate payroll and clerical functions, or perhaps the production of tons of computer data output distributed to managers without regard for needs.

This piecemeal approach to systems development, lacking a unifying framework, has several disadvantages. One of these stems from the unrelated nature of the subsystems developed. Frequently departments and divisions have developed individualistic systems without regard to the way they interface with systems elsewhere in the organization. The result has been communication barriers between systems.

A fairly common example of failure to relate subsystems is the way personnel information is structured. Several departments (sales, production, accounting, personnel) may maintain employee files that overlap with other similar files but do not provide for interface between them. In one instance, critical engineering and labor skills shortages developed in several geographically separated divisions of a multidivision company. Even though these skills were available elsewhere in the company, no identification could be made because of the lack of a common personnel-skills information system.

A second and serious disadvantage of the piecemeal approach is the cost in time, resources, and money. The longer a master plan is put off, the more costly will be the inevitable revisions needed to unify and standardize the approach to integrated systems design. Many companies have invested in the automation of clerical records and subsequently found a complete overhaul of the system necessary in order to integrate it with a larger effort. A popular one-for-one conversion in the past has been the materials inventory *tab* system, which frequently requires complete rework when a production planning and control system is implemented.

The following questions arise: First, why has the piecemeal approach been allowed to develop? And second, what should be done to improve the design situation so that an improved, integrated approach can be taken?

The answer to the first question is complex. The major reason seems to be that managers have failed to realize in the early stages of systems development the scope of the computer and information systems, the investment they would represent, and the impact they would have on the operations of the business. Belatedly, many firms have realized the need for integration through the implementation of a master plan. Evidence seems to indicate that future systems development will be characterized by five favorable trends:

1. MIS development is being recognized as a part of company strategy. It involves the deployment of large amounts of human and financial resources. It affects organization and decision making to a major extent. Also the MIS affects the way in which the company responds to changes in the environment.

2. Recognition of the interrelatedness of decisions throughout the company is leading to increased development of companywide models.

3. The advancement of hardware and software technology is increasing the importance and use of integrated data bases.

4. An increasing fraction of computer system costs will be devoted to system design and software as opposed to mainframe and other hardware.

5. The automation of decision making will accelerate. Increased automation of decision making requires increased systemwide data.

The answer to the second question, what should be done to obtain an integrated approach, is clearly to prepare both strategic and short-range plans. Five major reasons for information systems planning are:

1. To integrate information systems objectives in the strategic and short-range plans

2. To focus on the objectives of the MIS

3. To provide for allocation of resources to MIS development

4. To ensure an efficient and systematic development of information systems

5. To provide the basis for control of information systems projects at all stages

6. To balance MIS benefits and costs.

Information systems objectives should be incorporated in the company plans to ensure that such systems will not be neglected because of the pressure of company operations. Further, by including MIS plans in the strategic and short-range plans, management will be required to define the objectives of future information systems. This is preferable to the common practice of having small organizational units develop information systems piecemeal throughout the company.

By planning for future MIS development, management must allocate resources in advance. This further ensures that MIS development will be carried out as needed. Such advance allocation permits organization and orderly design of the MIS, rather than expedient, unplanned, bottoms-up design and crisis management of MIS.

The cost of designing and implementing an MIS may run as high as several million dollars. Therefore, planning and control of MIS development are essential. Planning provides the technical objectives and budgets which serve as standards for control.

Regardless of how much or how little is spent on MIS development, benefits should exceed costs. Planning requires cost/benefit analysis in advance. Usually there are increasing benefits for the first dollars spent and then diminishing returns as expenditures become very large. Management, by planning, is forced to place a value on such benefits as improved planning and control, improved decision making, and more automated data processing achieved with increased expenditures for MIS. Management is also forced to compare the challenge of competitors who, by developing sophisticated information systems, are able to serve customers better, adapt more quickly to market conditions, and reduce operating costs.

OBJECTIVES OF MIS PLANNING

Planning involves the development and selection from among alternatives of the necessary course of action to achieve an objective. Planning can be useful and commence only when objectives are properly selected. Therefore, systems planning cannot proceed according to a master plan unless the objectives of the information systems plan are detailed and well understood.

We are referring not to specific *objectives* of subsystems but to overall *systems planning objectives*—in other words, to the characteristics of the information systems that should be developed for both the near-term and long-range effort. An excellent framework of objectives for the systems planning function has been developed by Blumenthal:

The systems-planning function must therefore encompass the review of proposed systems in terms of planning criteria designed to minimize the number of systems, to broaden their scope, and to place them in the proper sequence for development. All these requirements can be expressed by the following list of systems-planning objectives:

1. To avoid overlapping development of major systems elements which are widely applicable across organizational lines, when there is no compelling technical or functional reason for difference.

2. To help ensure a uniform basis for determining sequence of development in terms of payoff potential, natural precedence, and probability of success.

3. To minimize the cost of integrating related systems with each other.

4. To reduce the total number of small, isolated systems to be developed, maintained, and operated.

5. To provide adaptability of systems to business change and growth without periodic major overhaul.

6. To provide a foundation for coordinated development of consistent, comprehensive, corporate-wide and interorganizational information systems.

7. To provide guidelines for and direction to continuing systems-development studies and projects.[2]

STRATEGIC PLANNING FOR MIS

The strategic plan for the MIS is obviously part of the company's strategic business plan. When the approach is a passive one, the business plan is developed first and then the MIS plan is developed to fit the resulting needs. This is certainly the easiest approach, if not the best. In the aggressive approach, the MIS influences the organization structure and the decision process. A good MIS is sought in order to achieve a sharper competitive edge, better product planning and marketing, and better utilization of human and capital resources. In this dynamic view, the MIS strategy is developed along with, and integrated with, the total business strategy.

Steps for Developing the MIS Strategic Plan

The development of the MIS strategic plan requires specifying five-year objectives, the milestones to be completed in achieving these objectives, and the resources needed. Strategic planning for the MIS is the responsibility of the Manager—Management Information Systems. He or she must coordinate efforts with the Director—Corporate Planning, line management, and the corporate financial staff. The MIS managers take the following principal steps:

1. Examine the previous long-range plan for the company and determine the nature of the current plan as it is being prepared.

2. Study the business environment and the technological changes anticipated for future information systems.

3. Study the company's strategic posture—that is, its present scope, structure, competitive edge, financial position, risk level of ventures, and policies.

4. Now that the manager has looked both outside and inside the firm, he or she has determined the environment in which the MIS will perform. The MIS manager now investigates information needs of managers

[2]Sherman C. Blumenthal, *Management Information Systems: A Framework for Planning and Development* (Englewood Cliffs, N.J.: Prentice-Hall, 1969), p. 13. By permission.

over the next five years. This cannot be done in detail, of course, but general types of information, frequency of reports, and level of aggregation may be estimated.

5. Define constraints and specify policies to be followed in developing the MIS over the five-year planning horizon.

6. Develop strategic objectives of the MIS. That is, what should the MIS be capable of doing at the end of five years?

7. Block out the current MIS and identify tentatively those subsystems most in need of revision.

8. Identify potential new applications and innovations which may yield high benefits.

9. Develop alternative new concepts for the total MIS. That is, block out possible system arrangements and outline key features such as outputs, hardware and software, organization for operation, and decision-assisting capabilities.

10. Establish criteria and weights for evaluating alternative concepts. Such criteria might be:
   a. Qualitative benefits of the total system
   b. Efficiency of operations
   c. Design and implementation costs
   d. Estimate of dollar equivalent of annual benefits
   e. Annual operating costs in excess of current costs for achieving present results
   f. Present value of annual net benefits over the next five years.

11. Evaluate the alternative concepts by rating the degree to which they meet each criterion. Select a concept using this analysis as a guide.

12. Estimate timing of milestones to be accomplished (priorities) and resources required. With these final pieces of information, the MIS strategic plan can be incorporated in the business plan, subject to (hopefully) minor reconciliation of managers' views.

The MIS strategic planning process is summarized in Figure 7.1 on the following page.

Critical Information Needs

After a study of the firm's environment, operations, and plans, critical information needs for the next five years should be identified. Some information needs may be urgent. For example, in one large bank there was no way that management could find out the asset and liability mixes throughout the year. In another case a retailing chain did not know the value of its inventory, even though it amounted to millions of dollars.

Often, information about technological changes, competitive actions, or government regulations is not getting into the MIS. Models are not being developed which reflect the impact of decisions in one part of the company upon

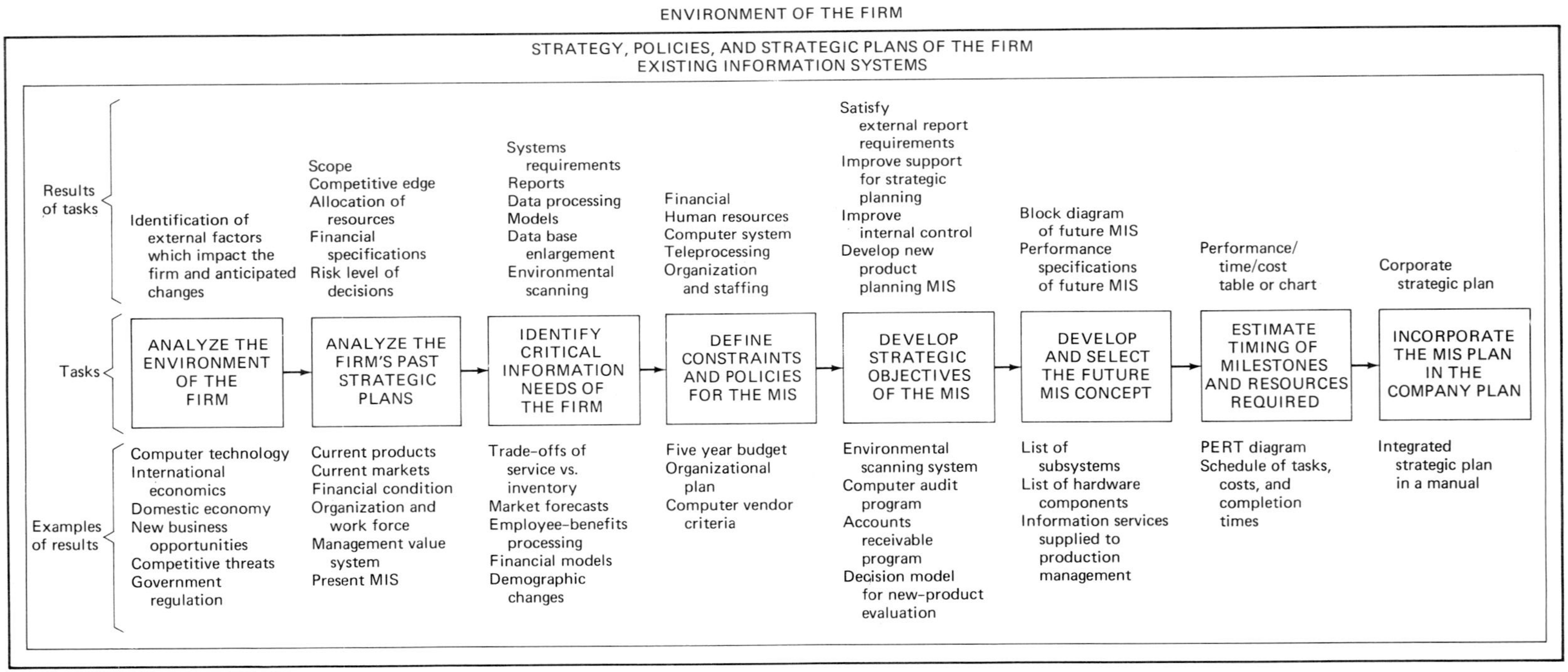

ENVIRONMENT OF THE FIRM

STRATEGY, POLICIES, AND STRATEGIC PLANS OF THE FIRM
EXISTING INFORMATION SYSTEMS

	Results of tasks	Tasks	Examples of results
	Identification of external factors which impact the firm and anticipated changes	ANALYZE THE ENVIRONMENT OF THE FIRM	Computer technology, International economics, Domestic economy, New business opportunities, Competitive threats, Government regulation
	Scope, Competitive edge, Allocation of resources, Financial specifications, Risk level of decisions	ANALYZE THE FIRM'S PAST STRATEGIC PLANS	Current products, Current markets, Financial condition, Organization and work force, Management value system, Present MIS
	Systems requirements, Reports, Data processing, Models, Data base enlargement, Environmental scanning	IDENTIFY CRITICAL INFORMATION NEEDS OF THE FIRM	Trade-offs of service vs. inventory, Market forecasts, Employee-benefits processing, Financial models, Demographic changes
	Financial, Human resources, Computer system, Teleprocessing, Organization and staffing	DEFINE CONSTRAINTS AND POLICIES FOR THE MIS	Five year budget, Organizational plan, Computer vendor criteria
	Satisfy external report requirements, Improve support for strategic planning, Improve internal control, Develop new product planning MIS	DEVELOP STRATEGIC OBJECTIVES OF THE MIS	Environmental scanning system, Computer audit program, Accounts receivable program, Decision model for new-product evaluation
	Block diagram of future MIS, Performance specifications of future MIS	DEVELOP AND SELECT THE FUTURE MIS CONCEPT	List of subsystems, List of hardware components, Information services supplied to production management
	Performance/time/cost table or chart	ESTIMATE TIMING OF MILESTONES AND RESOURCES REQUIRED	PERT diagram, Schedule of tasks, costs, and completion times
	Corporate strategic plan	INCORPORATE THE MIS PLAN IN THE COMPANY PLAN	Integrated strategic plan in a manual

Figure 7.1 Strategic planning for MIS

operations in another part. Analysis of the fringe benefit package for labor negotiations may not be available because computer programs have not been developed. Information may not be produced for management to evaluate and upgrade the firm's human resources. Or capital budgeting decisions may be made at the foreman level because top management lacks information on total company equipment, strategic direction of the firm, and labor/capital trade-offs.

There are many other potential critical areas which the MIS group should attempt to uncover. The potential gains from better information should be estimated so that projects may be ranked in terms of importance.

Constraints and Policies for the MIS

Although MIS needs may be identified and ranked, constraints and policies may limit the plans for the MIS. Almost always funding is the first constraint. The policy or size of the MIS organization may require that the systems work be stretched out over a long period. There may be a policy to use only a particular computer hardware vendor, which reduces flexibility in MIS design. If the policy is to lease computer services, a major constraint exists.

The organization of the company may be decided upon with consideration of systems, information flows, or MIS recommendations. This policy may limit the benefits of the MIS considerably. The policy with regard to the MIS organization itself may be favorable or unfavorable. For example, will MIS work be centralized at headquarters or decentralized to the divisions? If MIS responsibilities are decentralized, will there be a corporate staff director of MIS to integrate division efforts?

Strategic MIS Objectives

Two distinct general strategies exist with respect to MIS. In the first instance, the strategic objective is to increase data processing capabilities by means of more and better hardware and software. In the second, the strategic objective is to model the firm better in order to improve information supplied to management for planning and control. In either case, the previous study of the environment should be utilized to anticipate technological and managerial advances over the duration of the strategic plan. Also, the future organizational structure, product lines, and operational systems should be considered. With this information in hand, MIS objectives bearing upon total system development and priority of specific projects may be established.

Timing and Resources

Milestones are major objectives to be achieved. Therefore, once the MIS strategy is established, long-range plans must be prepared for the accomplishment of the milestones. These plans specify intermediate steps, the timing of all activities to achieve milestones, and resources required for each activity. Since the long-range plan can only approximate the activities of the future, it is foolish to place exact numbers on resources and times. One company with sales of $75 million showed financial data to the nearest dollar for three years in the future!

Incorporate the MIS Plan in the Company Plan

In actual practice, all resource and cost centers of large companies work simultaneously on the strategic plan for about two or three months at the end of the fiscal year. The MIS manager remains in close touch with line management and financial control people during this time. The resulting long-range plan for MIS (see Table 7.1 for a typical table of contents) is fairly well integrated with plans of other organizations when the total strategic plan is first assembled for critical review by top management. Minor changes in some projects or modification of resources or timing may be directed at the review.

While Table 7.1 lists the contents of a strategic MIS plan, Fig. 7.2 offers a more descriptive presentation for further insight into the nature of such a plan.

Table 7.1
Table of contents for an MIS strategic plan

 I. Executive summary
   A. Future information needs
   B. Performance requirements of the MIS
   C. Constraints on MIS development
   D. Systems approach to MIS development
   E. General concept of the MIS
   F. Schedule of MIS development
   G. Resource requirements and schedule
   H. Cost/benefits

 II. Corporate strategy guidelines
   A. Scope: product/market objectives
   B. Financial specifications and budgetary guidelines
   C. Organization structure and size, acquisitions, divestments
   D. Competitive edge
   E. Management information needs

 III. Planning assumptions
   A. Technological projections: hardware and software trends
   B. Legal constraints and requirements
   C. Inflation
   D. MIS human resources availability
   E. Capital budget
   F. Evolution of operating systems

 IV. MIS strategic concept
   A. Objectives of the MIS
   B. General system description of the MIS
   C. Hardware requirements
   D. Modeling development required
   E. Software requirements
   F. Organizational support required

 V. MIS projects and programs for implementation
   A. MIS subsystem projects, priority, timing, resources utilization
   B. Standards development
   C. Model development
   D. Consultation and service support to managers
   E. Training programs
   F. Evaluation of projects and programs: cost/benefits

Figure 7.2 MIS strategic plan

Introduction

- Discuss the purpose of the plan:
  - Establish the goals, objectives, strategies, actions, and responsibilities required to establish a uniform approach to information systems design and development.
  - Provide a vehicle to communicate these plans throughout the business.
  - Improve information handling and management.
  - Establish guidelines to assess the plan's effectiveness.
  - Provide an orderly, economical way of developing the systems needed to meet the increased needs of the business.
  - Ensure that the plan does support overall business planning.
  - Provide a data source to analyze data processing resource utilization.
- Discuss the five major parts of the plan:
  - Section 1 Purpose
  - Section 2 Environment
  - Section 3 Resource Commitment
  - Section 4 Major Project Summaries and Schedules
  - Section 5 Action Synopsis

Environment

- Establish the need for the plan. Point out the demands and problems that underscore the need for improved data processing utilization.

Resource Commitment

- State the objectives of the section: to present the information systems budget, describe how it is committed, and track historical data.
- Summarize the five-year expenditures trend (19___ to 19___) along the following lines:
  - Ways in which current dollars and manpower are being spent to support the business
    - Information systems expense growth
    - Expenditure changes year-to-year
    - Manpower distribution by major function and project
    - Manpower distribution by skills
    - Equipment profile

Major Project Summaries and Schedules

- Write a summary for each major project, including:
  - Purpose and description
  - Schedule (with milestones identified)
  - Resource requirements
  - Definition of testing function
  - Programming standards and education requirements
  - Dependencies
  - Contingency plan

Action Synopsis

OVERALL

- Discuss the necessary activities.
- Define the objectives, goals, strategies, actions, and responsibilities for each of these activities.

INFORMATION SYSTEMS NETWORK

- Discuss each proposed system from the same standpoints (objectives, goals, etc.). Typical objectives may revolve around functional systems, unified systems, data management, and standards development.

INFORMATION SYSTEMS MANAGEMENT

- Discuss management recommendations from the standpoint of architecture, data management, and planning, control, and measurement.
- Recommend the creation of a management function to direct plan development, implementation, and measurement.

Appendices

A   Glossary of Terms
B   Project Schedules by Phases
C   Steps Involved in Project Design and Implementation Phases

Source: IBM, **Business Systems Planning/Information Systems Planning Guide,** GE-20-05271, August 1975. Courtesy of International Business Machines Corp.

The strategic MIS plan outlines long-range directions for MIS development. It serves as a framework for the continuing short-term projects, so that such projects remain part of a larger system. Each project should itself be carefully planned as part of the long-term systems effort.

MIS development is termed a *project* because it is a unique effort with a starting date and ending date, involving a number of tasks related in a complex fashion to achieve a one-time objective. Generally, the flow of work in business is a continuous *process* except for major changes from time to time. Major changes usually result from major innovations (new ideas). The introduction of a new MIS is such an innovation.

Projects such as the design of an MIS differ from programs because they are discrete—they have a beginning and an end, in contrast to company functional operations such as marketing, manufacturing, or accounting. Projects are complex because they require a wide variety of skills. Moreover, they cut across traditional organizational lines and involve a substantial number of interrelated activities. And because each project is a one-time effort, unusual problems arise that call for nontraditional solutions. In addition, projects usually require the development of new techniques and advances in the state-of-the-art while the project is in progress.

Projects are carried out under the leadership of project managers. Because of the complexities and high costs of completing projects, these managers must provide coordination and leadership of an unusual order. Good functional managers may fail miserably as project managers. In particular, when a project manager operates from a staff position, as MIS project managers usually do, the difficulties are greatly compounded. The basic foundations for successful project management are good planning and control systems within the project management cycle. The planning/controlling project cycle is indicated in Fig. 7.3. This chapter covers the method and techniques of project management and how they are used for planning and programming MIS's. In our case, we have included it as a part of the planning phase.

Figure 7.3
The project management cycle

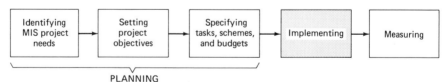

PLANNING

Needs Research

The first stage in the MIS project management cycle is the search for MIS *needs*. If needs of managers are not identified, many thousands of dollars may be lost by developing systems that serve little purpose. Management then finds it necessary to return to the starting point again and again until needs are properly defined. The identification of needs, in terms of MIS's, consists of:

1. The search for planning and operating problems
2. The search for areas of recurring difficult decisions or erroneous decisions
3. The search for company opportunities that depend on expanded information systems
4. Delineation of problems and opportunities (as sought in item 3) so that priorities may be ranked
5. Selection of projects whose payoff in terms of cost and limitations of resources is justified.

Let us amplify some of these concepts. Each company should have an MIS manager or a counterpart whose job is to search continuously for major company problems and opportunities. He must, of course, rely heavily on personal contacts with line managers and top managers as sources. His job is primarily that of gathering together problems, stimulating managers to think about opportunities, and generally getting managers to look beyond their daily jobs, both outside and inside the company. From problems and opportunities thus identified, MIS needs can be recognized in a general way. MIS projects may then be identified by summary descriptions and crude cost estimates, after which they must be evaluated with regard to three basic criteria:

1. How valuable is the solution to the problem or the opportunity (for expansion, market penetration, acquisition program, new production system, reorganization, etc.) to the company?
2. How valuable is the MIS project to the problem solution or the opportunity achievement? What is the net payoff?
3. What is the technology required?

It is evident from these criteria that before any project is undertaken, it should be carefully assessed by asking such questions as

1. What are management's purposes? In what direction is it guiding the company in terms of products, services, market position, and return on investment? In other words, what is the corporate shape intended to be?
2. What possible MIS projects will aid management in planning, controlling, problem solving, and decision making? Is a "total system" feasible, or are the projects so large that only a few may be undertaken at a time?
3. Is the scope of each project defined? Unless descriptions of the project, its contribution, and its required utilization of resources are spelled out, the projects cannot be evaluated and ranked.
4. What are the major assumptions underlying each project? These assumptions relate to the environment, to management's needs, to available resources within the company, to desired goals of managers, and to time.

5. What are the short-term and long-term objectives of the MIS project? Too often MIS systems are proposed and designed to solve today's problems with no consideration for changes in organization, environment, and operations in the next five years.

6. What specific criteria should be used to evaluate and rank projects? The aggressive viewpoint should be taken: "What will the system do to advance the company in the long run?" Criteria are often based erroneously on cost and savings.

7. Is the project technically sound? That is, is it practical in terms of the state-of-the-art of management science, computer science, organizational behavior, and other relevant factors?

8. Are there deadlines or simply desired times for completion of the project?

The needs-research stage is sometimes called the preliminary analysis, or the preproposal stage.

Setting Project Objectives

As opposed to the definition of overall MIS planning objectives discussed earlier, in the planning-programming-control cycle objectives must be in more detailed form for each potential project. Needs research indicates the general nature and scope of MIS projects that are required, but once a project is selected, its purposes must be developed to fulfill the needs. An objective is an end result that is to be accomplished by the execution of the plan.

Objectives of information systems may vary widely in scope and direction. Objectives might be

1. Unify the financial and accounting system of a multidivision company or conglomerate.

2. Develop an environmental scanning system to keep corporate management alerted to new market opportunities and competitive strategic moves.

3. Develop a production and inventory control system that interfaces with the current purchasing and marketing information systems.

4. Develop an on-line information system for companywide materials and finished goods in terms of in-transport and warehouse location.

5. Develop an engineering management information system for control of technical work, costs, and schedules.

6. Develop an MIS for manpower inventory and long-range needs.

7. Update the current MIS for marketing to bring to bear new forecasting techniques and to adapt the system to the new computer being installed.

8. Revise the present financial reporting system to supply more decision-oriented information and to provide it on a weekly basis instead of a quarterly basis.

Besides such major objectives as suggested, each MIS project will have a number of supporting or secondary objectives. It is not enough, as in the first example, to simply specify unification of financial and accounting information. Objectives must be set regarding the nature of reports for each level of the organization, who gets what reports, and how frequently reports are to be issued. Secondary objectives might be enlarging and automating the data master file, relating sales information to production planning, or obtaining measurements of morale through classification of reasons for absenteeism and resignations. A complete list of objectives at the lowest level in the hierarchy of objectives is established subsequently during the planning of specific tasks.

Table 7.2

MIS project
proposal
outline

Introduction
a. A brief, clear statement of the problem or technical requirement.
b. Purposes of the proposed MIS.
c. Conservative estimate of the performance of the proposed system, its limitations, its life, and its cost.
d. Premises and assumptions upon which the MIS is to be developed. These give organizational limitations; special requirements imposed by managers, vendors, or customers; environmental restrictions; or other ground rules.

What Is Offered
a. Description of present method of operation and its weaknesses and problems.
b. Information requirements, present and future. General description of proposed data base.
c. Hardware, present and future, available within the company.
d. Alternative approaches to the information-decision-operational systems. A brief summary of each approach is given and the advantages and disadvantages of each are discussed to show why the proposed system is being offered.
e. A somewhat more detailed description of the proposed MIS is given. The general plan of action, the budget estimate, and the schedule are provided.
f. Management action required for adoption of the proposal and for planning and implementing the MIS are stated.

Method of Approach
An outline of the plan of attack on the gross design, detailed design, and implementation. This demonstrates that the project manager has a practical approach for planning and executing the project.
a. Method of data gathering and analysis.
b. Personnel assignments.
c. Programming techniques to be used for the project.
d. Project reports and review. A description of the type and frequency of reports to keep management abreast of progress on the MIS project.

Conclusion
This is not usually required. If an MIS project looks especially good from a highly technical viewpoint, the conclusion may summarize the strong points to give additional emphasis.

Appendices
Organization charts, schedules, flow charts, quantitative analyses, and other detailed substantiating data of a technical or detailed nature that will aid management or technical staff personnel in evaluating the proposal.

Project Proposal

Two alternative sequences of action are possible for developing project proposals and obtaining management approval. As various projects are identified by needs and objectives, a preliminary definition of the scope of the project work, scheduling, costs, and benefits may be prepared as a *project proposal*. The projects are then evaluated by management and selections made on the basis of criteria discussed previously. Next, detailed plans are prepared and once again reviewed by management.

In the second alternative, an MIS project is singled out. Then the complete and detailed planning, scheduling, and budgeting for the implementation are worked out. At this point a detailed project proposal is presented to management for acceptance or rejection. Because of the cost of preparing such proposals for all known projects, only those likely to be approved are developed in this much detail. Management thus does not have an opportunity to evaluate a broad range of proposals.

The format for the MIS project proposal consists of an introduction, a management summary, a system description, and an estimate of the cost and schedule. The detail given in each section depends on whether a brief proposal is prepared for a large number of projects (alternative 1) or whether a single project is selected on a judgmental informal basis and a proposal developed for management's approval (alternative 2). The nature of information contained in a proposal is outlined in Table 7.2, on the preceding page.

PROJECT PLANNING TECHNIQUES

For very small projects, common-sense techniques for planning and documenting the plans for the MIS project are sufficient. We shall discuss here the more elaborate techniques for planning for larger projects. Most of these techniques and tools have been borrowed from engineering project management theory and practice, where they originated.

The planning techniques rest on some fundamental management premises. The first is that all work can be planned and controlled. The second is that the greater the difficulty in planning the work, the greater the need for such planning. Techniques exist for a rational approach to planning the design and implementation of large systems. The third premise is that the assignment of project management to a project manager with wide responsibilities is an important factor in increasing the probability of success of a project. The project manager must control all funds required for the project. However, the project manager may direct the activities of a program without having direct-line command over all persons involved in the program. He achieves this by means of a clearly defined work breakdown structure for the project.

Work Breakdown Structure

A fundamental concept in project management is the *work breakdown structure (WBS)*. The project work breakdown structure starts with the total end result desired. It is a decomposition of this end result created by a level-by-level definition of tasks. It is a hierarchy of tasks. For example, a possible hierarchy might be:

I. Design of an MIS
   A. Design subsystems making up the MIS
      1. Perform the tasks required to design the subsystem
         a. Perform the subtasks required to complete the tasks
            (1) Complete work packages required to complete the subtasks

The levels of work may vary from top to bottom along different branches of the hierarchy. An illustration of a WBS for the development of a management information system is given in Table 7.3.

Table 7.3
A work breakdown structure for MIS project planning

1.0	Study Phase	
	1.1	Organize for the study
	1.2	Inform organization of nature of the study
	1.3	Study organizational objectives, problems, and decision processes
		1.3.1 Interview managers and specialists
		1.3.2 Study internal documents and their flow
		1.3.3 Perform work-station analyses and process analysis
		1.3.4 Study reports for external users
		1.3.5 Study informational problems
	1.4	Study the company as a framework for MIS
		1.4.1 Review company resources in the strategic plan
		1.4.2 Review environmental assumptions of the strategic plan, threats, and opportunities
		1.4.3 Review market characteristics, product characteristics and competitive plans given in the strategic plan
		1.4.4 Review the strategic plan for MIS
	1.5	Study present computer capabilities and technological forecasts
	1.6	Study present software, applications, and models
	1.7	Prepare a proposal for the most important/urgent project (a trade-off between importance and urgency is required)
2.0	Conceptual Design Phase	
	2.1	Inform the organization of the study
	2.2	Identify required subsystems
		2.2.1 Study system objectives and natural boundaries of skill groupings
		2.2.2 Develop alternative arrangements of subsystems and select one arrangement
		2.2.3 Outline the organization structures for operation of the subsystems
	2.3	Develop information needs
		2.3.1 Develop brief list of responsibilities for each manager in the subsystem
		2.3.2 Develop management information needs
		2.3.3 Identify sources of information for managers
		2.3.4 Outline the list of files (user viewpoint) and general data base structure (data processing viewpoint)

(Continued on next page)

Table 7.3
(Cont'd.)

2.4 Conceptualize hardware and software system
    2.4.1 List principal types of hardware (CPU's, input/output devices, tele-processing equipment, minicomputers, etc.)
    2.4.2 List desired application programs
2.5 Describe the scope of the project based on needs of the company, resources allocated, and time available
2.6 Prepare the Conceptual Design Report

3.0 Detailed Design Phase
  3.1 Inform the organization of the study
  3.2 Form task groups of systems designers, managers, and specialists to deal with appropriate problems
  3.3 Identify dominant and principal trade-off criteria for the MIS design
  3.4 Develop and define the operating and information systems in detail
    3.4.1 Flow-chart the operating systems
    3.4.2 Obtain review of flow charts by specialists and management
    3.4.3 Develop inputs and sources, and outputs of the system
    3.4.4 Flow-chart the information flows
  3.5 Develop hardware and software roles
  3.6 Develop the data base management system
    3.6.1 Develop organization for the DBMS
    3.6.2 List types of files and general contents
    3.6.3 Specify the logical and physical file structure
    3.6.4 Develop the application programs for storage and retrieval
    3.6.5 Identify data sources
    3.6.6 Develop record retention policies
  3.7 Detail the computer architecture
    3.7.1 Develop hardware requirements and locations
    3.7.2 Develop application programs for information systems
  3.8 Establish input and output formats
    3.8.1 Develop input formats and design forms
    3.8.2 Develop output formats including forms
  3.9 Test the system
    3.9.1 Use a checklist to test the design
    3.9.2 Simulate the operation of the system over a range of inputs
  3.10 Propose the formal organization to operate the system
  3.11 Plan the office space requirements and layouts
  3.12 Document the detailed design

4.0 Implementation Phase
  4.1 Staff for implementation
    4.1.1 Hire systems analysts, programmers, operators, etc.
    4.1.2 Continue training programs
  4.2 Obtain and install hardware
    4.2.1 Complete contracts with suppliers
    4.2.2 Prepare the sites for installation
    4.2.3 Install equipment
    4.2.4 Test and debug equipment
  4.3 Develop software
    4.3.1 Purchase software programs
    4.3.2 Prepare new, or modify present, programs
  4.4 Enter data base in secondary storage
  4.5 Order and obtain delivery of forms
  4.6 Prepare manuals and operating instructions
  4.7 Cut over to the new MIS and test
  4.8 Document the MIS as it finally is implemented

Figure 7.4 Functional work package estimate

FUNCTIONAL WORK PACKAGE ESTIMATE

Date ____________

Proposal Time ____________ Proposal No. ____________

Customer ____________ Functional Group ____________

W. P. IDENT. NO.	WORK PACKAGE TITLE	WORK PACKAGE ESTIMATE												
			1	2	3	4	5	6	7	8	9	10	11	12
		Time From Go-Ahead (Months)												
		Manpower (Man Months)												
		Material Costs												
		Other Resources	(Identify and Cost)											
			1	2	3	4	5	6	7	8	9	10	11	12
		Time From Go-Ahead												
		Manpower												
		Material Costs												
		Other Resources												
			1	2	3	4	5	6	7	8	9	10	11	12
		Time From Go-Ahead												
		Manpower												
		Material Costs												
		Other Resources												
			1	2	3	4	5	6	7	8	9	10	11	12
		Time From Go-Ahead												
		Manpower												
		Material Costs												
		Other Resources												

SECTION 3-
FIGURE 7

Estimated By ____________

Approved By ____________

Program Manager Approval ____________

Courtesy of Hamilton Standard Division of United Technologies Corporation

To develop a WBS, we start with a word description of the objective of the entire project. Then we identify the major tasks required to achieve this objective and prepare word descriptions of the objectives of these tasks, and so on. The organizational structure should have no influence on the development of the WBS. On the contrary, project management often requires changes in the organizational structure to fit the work breakdown structure. The primary question at each level is, "What is to be accomplished?" Neither gaps nor overlaps should be allowed, so that the structure interlocks all tasks.

Work Packages

The smallest elements in the work breakdown structure are called *work packages*. They may be at any level of the WBS, because all branches of the WBS do not necessarily get broken down into the same level of detail. *The work package establishes the degree of management visibility and control to be exercised on the project.* It consists of an activity or set of activities that have a common charge account number (or shop order) in the accounting system. In small projects such accounts may be opened for a few hundred dollars, while on large projects the work package account may be established for control of hundreds of thousands of dollars and hundreds of short activities. The financial planning for work packages may be based on a form (see Fig. 7.4, page 227.)

Each work package is assigned to a single manager to provide means for control of the entire project. The work package is of short duration relative to the entire project and has a definite start and completion date. It is identified in all plans and authorization documents. A typical list of items of information contained in a work package form is given in Table 7.4

Table 7.4
Work package
information
checklist

1. Project identification, title, and number
2. Title and number of work package
3. Responsible organization and manager
4. Interface events and dates
5. Start and end date for work package
6. Dollar and labor estimates, projections of dollars and labor on a weekly or monthly basis, and a schedule of actual application of resources maintained as current
7. Contract or funding source identification
8. Account charge number
9. Work order or shop order, to be opened when authorization is obtained to expend a specified amount of money under a particular account number

Sequence Planning and Critical Path Networks

The development of PERT (program evaluation review technique) and CPM (critical path method) produced management powerful tools for project planning and control. The principal difference between the two is that a single time estimate is made for CPM, whereas in PERT three time estimates are made for each activity and used in various analyses. Since we wish to keep our discussion brief, we will use the single time estimate.

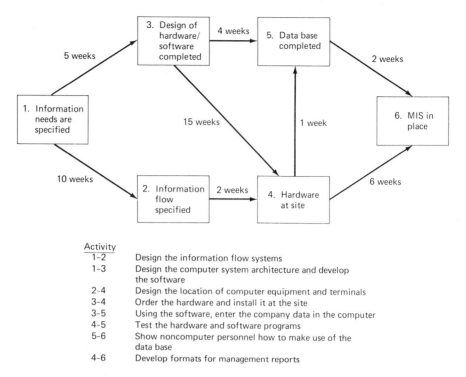

Activity	
1-2	Design the information flow systems
1-3	Design the computer system architecture and develop the software
2-4	Design the location of computer equipment and terminals
3-4	Order the hardware and install it at the site
3-5	Using the software, enter the company data in the computer
4-5	Test the hardware and software programs
5-6	Show noncomputer personnel how to make use of the data base
4-6	Develop formats for management reports

Figure 7.5 Simple precedence network for CPM planning and control

After the tasks (activities) have been defined in the WBS, the *precedence* must be established. That is, for any given activity to be performed, certain other activities must precede it. *Events* are the start or completion of an activity. If we let activities be represented by arrows and events by nodes (circles or boxes where activities are joined), we may represent the precedence relationships among activities by a network (Fig. 7.5).

The precedence relationships must be set by starting at the last event and working backward. In Fig. 7.5, for example, before event 6, the completion of the MIS, can occur, two activities must be performed. These are (5-6) the training of noncomputer personnel and (4-6) the development of computer output formats for management reports. Note next that before event 5, data base loaded, can occur, activities (3-5) the loading of the data and (4-5) testing of the loading programs must take place. By examining each event, we may continue to determine the activities that must immediately precede it and thus develop the network.

The next step is to estimate the time required to perform each activity. This may be taken directly from the work package description. The times are then entered on the arrows in the network, as in Fig. 7.5. Now if we examine all the possible paths from the starting event to the ending event, we find that the longest time path is 1-3-4-6. To complete this sequence of events will require 26 weeks. This *longest* time path is called the *critical path*, because if any activity in this path is extended, the time for completion of the project will be extended. For other paths there may be delays without jeopardizing the completion date of the project. For example, path 1-2-4-6 requires only 18 weeks, and so it has eight weeks of slack before it impacts the critical path time.

Master Program Schedule

The *master program schedule (MPS)* is a management document giving the *calendar* dates for milestones (major tasks and critical path minor tasks), thus providing the control points for management review. The MPS may be in the form of a Gantt chart (Fig. 7.6) for small MIS projects or in machine (computer) printout for large projects whose networks have been programmed for computer analysis and reporting. In the latter case, the MPS is derived from the network schedule by establishing a calendar date for the starting event.

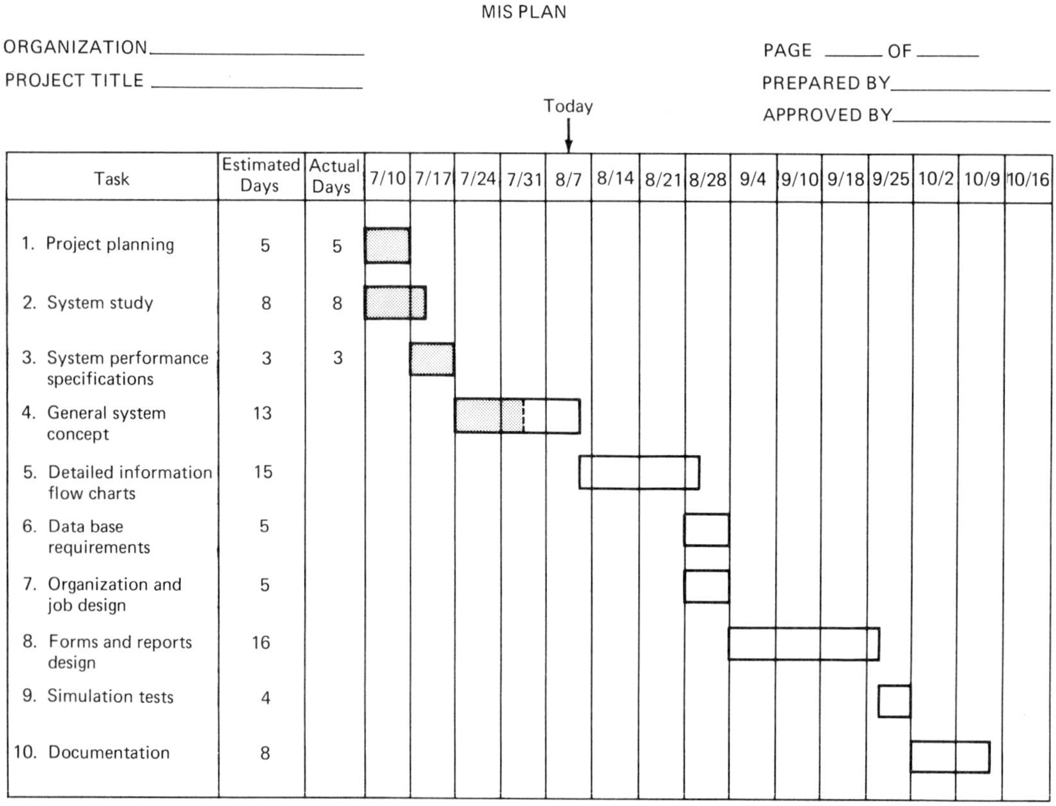

MIS PLAN

ORGANIZATION_____

PROJECT TITLE _____

Today

PAGE _____ OF _____

PREPARED BY_____

APPROVED BY_____

Task	Estimated Days	Actual Days	7/10	7/17	7/24	7/31	8/7	8/14	8/21	8/28	9/4	9/10	9/18	9/25	10/2	10/9	10/16
1. Project planning	5	5															
2. System study	8	8															
3. System performance specifications	3	3															
4. General system concept	13																
5. Detailed information flow charts	15																
6. Data base requirements	5																
7. Organization and job design	5																
8. Forms and reports design	16																
9. Simulation tests	4																
10. Documentation	8																

Figure 7.6 Gantt chart

While the complex methods described above may be used to represent the MIS development plan, a simple plan may often be adequate. For example, a simple list of activities with completion dates is shown below to illustrate such a plan:

Activity	Completion Date
1. Establish MIS objectives	2/6/80
2. Prepare and submit project proposal	3/4/80
3. Conduct a detailed study of present MIS's and information needs of managers	4/24/80
4. Develop the conceptual design	5/29/80
a. MIS conceptual flow chart	5/21/80
b. Centralized information needs	5/19/80
c. List of files needed	5/23/80
d. Extent of model bank needed, if any	5/29/80
e. Scope of computer hardware and software	5/29/80
5. Develop the detailed design	10/11/80
a. Detailed flow charts	8/7/80
b. Data base	8/10/80
c. Computer equipment and software	8/20/80
d. Procedures manual	9/5/80
6. Implement or install the new system	12/11/80
a. Complete training	12/5/80
b. Switch over to new MIS	12/11/80
c. Debug the MIS	12/18/80

Budgeting

The establishment of cost and resource targets for a planned series of periods in advance is project budgeting. Although cost constraints may be applied in a top-down fashion during planning, such constraints must be reconciled with a *bottom-up* approach through the work breakdown structure. The difference that may occur between the total dollar constraint set by top management or the MIS project manager and the requirements developed from adding the costs on all work packages must be eliminated. Reconciliation is accomplished by either (1) allocating more funds or (2) narrowing and reducing the scope of the work and redefining the objectives of the project.

Cost and resource targets must be established for a work package by

1. Performing organization
2. Funding organization
3. Elements of cost: labor, materials, and facilities.

Only direct costs are included in the project budget, because they are the only costs over which the project manager has control.

Cushioning should not be added to the resource costs, because meaningful measures of control depend on realistic goals. However, because experience has shown that project cost overruns are far more common than underruns, a contingency fund should be budgeted to cover unanticipated problems. The project manager's use of the contingency fund is also a measure of his or her performance.

Control of the project means control of performance/cost/time (P/C/T). These elements, P/C/T, must be reported in a way that ties them all together; otherwise the report is meaningless. Consider, for instance, a project in which performance and costs are on target. It is possible for such a project to be behind and in trouble from the time standpoint. On the other hand, a project may show an overrun of costs as of a particular date, yet if the work performance is ahead of schedule, this is good news instead of bad news.

Figure 7.7 Integrated P/C/T chart

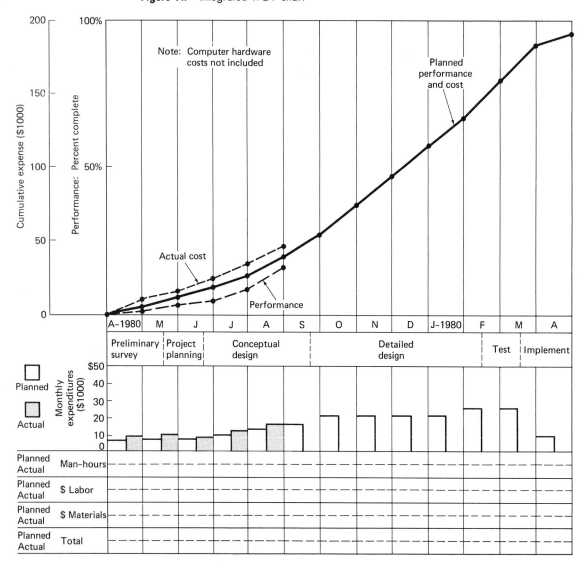

Reporting Techniques

The project management report system is a part of the company's MIS. The types of reports that may be supplied to managers in projects are:

1. Integrated P/C/T charts (an example is shown in Fig. 7.7)
2. PERT or CPM reports
3. Financial schedules showing budgets and variances of expenditures from budgeted amounts
4. Problem analysis and trend charts
5. Progress reports
6. Project control room and computerized graphic systems[3]
7. Design-review meetings and reference designs. A common reference design must provide a formal description of system specifications and goals at any particular time. All designers work on the basis of assumptions about parts of the system other than theirs. If they are not working on the same assumptions, chaos results. The reference design may change with time, and the design review meeting of all key personnel is a good time to make formal changes.

Problems of Reporting

Control is difficult if the only reports are written narratives requiring interpretation by management. At the other extreme, reams of computer data reports are equally poor. Managers prefer graphic displays which reduce large amounts of complex information into easily understood pictorial form. Comparisons and trends of major variables are also effective in communicating. Graphic display must be designed to guard against too gross a level of reporting, however, or else growing problems may be obscured.

Other problems in reporting are the use of complex grammatical structure; high "fog index" of writing; excessive and unexplained abbreviations, codes, and symbols; and too much technical jargon.[4] Projects may fail if the project manager and his technical specialists do not make clear to management what is happening and how the money is being spent.

Control Through Accountability

A manager in a chain of command cannot divest himself of accountability for a task that is delegated to him. Responsibility for a work package may be delegated to the lowest level in the organizational hierarchy, but each manager

---

[3]See, "Corporate 'War Rooms' Plug into the Computer," *Business Week,* August 23, 1976, and Otto P. Kramer, "Management Briefing Room," *Journal of Systems Management,* June 1977.

[4]Robert Gunning, *The Technique of Clear Writing* (New York: McGraw-Hill, 1952). Fog index = 0.4 (average number of words per sentence) + 0.4 (average number of three-syllable words excluding capitalized words and words made up of easy words). Use several samples of about 100 consecutive words.

up the line is evaluated on the basis of completed action on the work package. The worker who has responsibility for a work package should be supplied with adequate reports of P/C/T. As variances are reported to the responsible performer, the burden is on him to take corrective action. His ultimate responsibility is "completed action," the presentation of a completed job to his manager. Only in emergencies and cases of wide variances from planned action should the managers at various levels in the organization step in to reclaim delegated responsibility. The control in a well-run project is essentially self-control, based on a good reporting system.

SUMMARY The design and implementation of an MIS cannot be carried out on an unplanned trial-and-error basis. The complex assemblage of tasks involved and the cost of the design and implementation are such as to constitute a major project. Project management is conducted with special management techniques of its own, techniques related to establishment of project needs and objectives and to planning, scheduling, budgeting, reporting, and controlling.

The outstanding characterisics of these techniques are the breakdown structure, the network approach to defining task relationships, and the integration of performance/cost/time for planning and control. The detailed techniques for implementing these major-project management techniques have provided powerful aids to management. We have summarized the project planning and control cycle in Fig. 7.8.

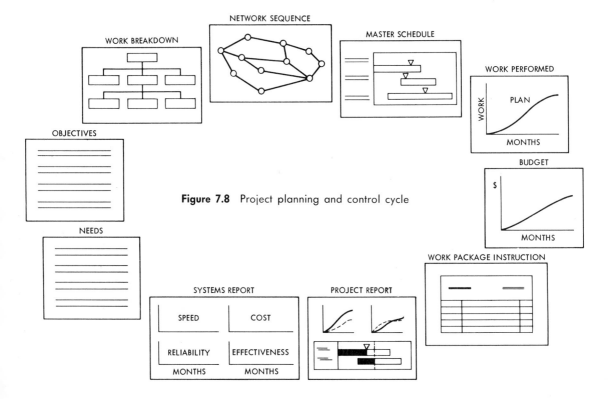

Figure 7.8 Project planning and control cycle

1. The Arat Industries corporation, formed in 1926, produced a wide variety of industrial and building components. Its three divisions had always been Small Machine Tools, Industrial Equipment Parts, and Metal Building Components. As a conservative old-line firm, it had stuck with old markets, old equipment, and manual processing of information well into the 1960s. The controller then introduced a small computer for accounting data processing by experimentation, rather than planning and scheduling the installation.

The president was delighted with the computer and set up a committee to design a production information system that would make use of it. This system was introduced into all three divisions simultaneously. Then he set up another committee to design a marketing MIS.

Within six months it became apparent that the accounting information system no longer gathered the data needed for cost accounting. The production control system was so elaborate that it could not provide information in time to be useful. The small computer was so overloaded that marketing reports and analyses were rarely produced on time, if at all. Necessary software for all systems was still being debugged ten months later.

For each item below, give two examples for the above case:

a. Evidence of a need for total corporate planning

   (1)

   (2)

b. Failure to understand the nature of an MIS

   (1)

   (2)

c. Key information not available to management

   (1)

   (2)

d. Failure to adopt a systems approach

   (1)

   (2)

e. Lack of consideration of interfacing of systems

   (1)

   (2)

f. Lack of planning for hardware and software

   (1)

   (2)

g. Failure to utilize project planning

   (1)

   (2)

h. Failure to develop a strategic plan for MIS

(1)

(2)

2. Show the order of strategic planning steps for the MIS.

a. Identify critical information needs (1) _____

b. Estimate timing of milestones and resources required (2) _____

c. Analyze the environment of the firm (3) _____

d. Develop strategic objectives of the MIS (4) _____

e. Incorporate the MIS plan in the company plan (5) _____

f. Define constraints and policies of the firm (6) _____

g. Develop and select the future MIS concept (7) _____

h. Analyze the firm's past strategic plans (8) _____

3. a. Insert the activity times on the network in the accompanying diagram.

Activity	Description	Time Required: Weeks
1–2	Analyze present system	5
1–3	Identify managers' information needs	10
2–8	Conduct training and development	26
3–4	Determine computer system requirements	6
3–5	Define operating systems	8
4–7	Work computer concepts into the conceptual design	2
5–7	Work the operating systems into the conceptual design	4
5–6	Develop data sources and application	4
6–7	Work the data concepts into the conceptual design	2
7–9	Develop detailed system flow charts	15
7–10	Develop the data-base design	10
7–11	Design the computer system	8
9–12	Design the forms	6
8–13	Dummy	0
12–13	Dummy	0
10–13	Complete the detailed design	4
11–13	Complete the detailed design	12

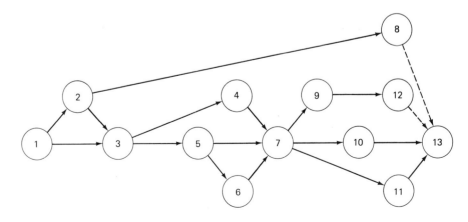

b. The critical path of events is — — — — — — — —

c. The critical path time, in weeks, is _____.

4. a. What three measures could management take to reduce the critical path time of a project?

   b. What effect would these measures have on the cost of the project?

5. A task in a certain MIS development project consists of developing a technological scanning system worldwide. This task is estimated to take about three months if one systems analyst is assigned full time ($16,000/year) and one executive ($30,000/ year) is assigned half time. The technological areas to be monitored are office automation, laser technology, and communications technology. The task is part of the total project named Mercury, code number 1990. The task is to start June 1 and end August 30, 1979. About $350 worth of reports and journals will need to be purchased for study. The manager of MIS is responsible for the project:

   a. Design a simple work package form.

   b. Fill in the form with the data supplied above and any hypothetical data you wish to add.

6. Define *project,* explaining why it is different from programs and functional activities.

7. A bank president has decided it is time for the bank to engage in long-range planning. This will require an expansion of the present MIS, which deals primarily with internal information. Set down the objectives of the MIS project as might be done in planning such a project.

8. Describe a possible budgeting and control system for an MIS project by:

   a. Listing the elements of cost

   b. Listing a method of accumulating such costs by element, by task, and by performing organization

   c. Showing report formats for comparing actual costs with planned costs

   d. Relating costs to performance and time.

9. a. What are the purposes of the MIS project proposal?

   b. What is the difference between a project proposal and a project plan?

10. Prepare a Gantt chart to represent the following plan of activities:

		Start	Finish
(1)	Establish MIS objectives	1/4/80	2/6/76
(2)	Conduct a preliminary study of present operations and MIS	1/10/80	4/25/80
(3)	Prepare a flow chart for the conceptual design of the MIS	4/25/80	5/21/80
(4)	Prepare a list of files needed	5/15/80	5/23/80
(5)	Develop the detailed design of management information and sources	5/21/80	8/26/80
(6)	Develop the data base and subsidiary file specifications	5/21/80	8/2/80
(7)	Develop software programs	5/27/80	8/20/80
(8)	Develop specifications of hardware and software	6/15/80	8/20/80
(9)	Prepare complete detailed design specifications	8/15/80	9/30/80

SELECTED REFERENCES

ANDREWS, WILLIAM C., "The Business System Proposal," *Journal of Systems Management,* February 1978.

BRANDON, DICK H., and MAX GRAY, *Project Control Standards.* Princeton, N.J.: Brandon Systems Press, 1970.

BRYCE, TIM, "Evaluating a Systems Design Methodology—Part 1," *Infosystems,* November 1978.

BUSH, ROBERT L., and K. ERIC KNUTSEN, "Integration of Corporate and MIS Planning: The Impact of Productivity," *Data Base,* Winter 1978.

Business Systems Planning/Information Systems Planning Guide (GE-20-0527-1). White Plains, N.Y.: International Business Machines, 1975.

DAVIS, GORDON B., *Management Information Systems: Conceptual Foundations, Structure, and Development.* New York: McGraw-Hill, 1974.

GUNDERMAN, JAMES R., and FRANK W. McMURRY, "Making Project Management Effective," *Journal of Systems Management,* February 1975.

HEAD, ROBERT V., "Strategic Planning for Information Systems," *Infosystems,* October 1978.

McLEAN, EPHRAIM R., and JOHN V. SODEN, *Strategic Planning for MIS.* New York: John Wiley, 1977.

MURDICK, ROBERT G., and JOEL E. ROSS, *Introduction to Management Information Systems.* Englewood Cliffs, N.J.: Prentice-Hall, 1977.

SCHWARTZ, H. H., "MIS Planning," *Datamation,* September 1970.

SELIG, GAD J., "Planning New Applications of Management Information and Decision Systems," *Industrial Engineering,* June 1972.

STOKES, PAUL M., *A Total Systems Approach to Management Control.* New York: American Management Association, 1968.

WILLOUGHBY, THEODORE C., "Origins of Systems Projects," *Journal of Systems Management,* October 1975.

ZACHMAN, JOHN A., "The Information Systems Management System: A Framework for Planning," *Data Base,* Winter 1978.

chapter 8

Conceptual Design

- Nature of
  Conceptual Design
  of an MIS

- Preparing Members of the
  Organization for Change
- Studying the Characteristics of
  the Company and the Industry
  Problems
- Studying the Company's
  Organization and Decision
  Structure
- Studying the Operating
  Systems
- Determining Information
  Needs
- Identifying System
  Constraints
- Determining Information
  Sources

- Block Diagramming
  the MIS
- Outlining the General
  Information Flow and
  File System
- Hardware and Software
  Configurations
- Making Trade-Off
  Revisions
- Documenting the
  Conceptual Design

PURPOSE: To explain the analysis
and creative work required
to develop the general concept of the MIS

"You've got to admit it's a cost-effective design approach."

If you were trying to invent a new kind of typewriter, you would probably study all the present kinds. Then you would block out various combinations of input modes and printing arrangements. You would next select one as the *conceptual* design. Much more work would have to be done to detail the design.

Similarly, if you were designing your ideal house, you would establish your needs, examine layouts of many homes, and then block out the arrangement and shape of rooms for your house. This would be the *concept* of your house. The detailed design would require setting dimensions more exactly, modifying the shape of rooms, detailing electrical and plumbing systems, and detailing the external features of the house to produce the final total "system."

The conceptual design of the MIS has the same purpose as these conceptual designs. It blocks out the principal components and their relationships within the MIS. If we were to design the MIS in great detail without first conceptualizing the system as a whole, we might discover that our design was very poor. Rearranging major parts of a detailed design would be quite expensive. Therefore, the conceptual design allows us to look at a number of possible designs before selecting one for detailed work.

Conceptual design is a highly creative process. The presentation of all the considerations involved is complex and lengthy. Therefore, we present here only some guidelines with illustrations of some aspects.

NATURE OF CONCEPTUAL DESIGN OF AN MIS

The conceptual design of an MIS is the end result of the design process. It is an outline or sketch of the MIS described by means of narrative, flow charts, layouts, and lists. The conceptual design is a framework within which the detailed design will be developed. It is the general presentation of a system which will fulfill previously established system requirements as described in the project proposal.

General specification of the following components and subsystems comprises the conceptual design:

1. Objectives of the MIS
2. Company organization and list of operating systems
3. Overall operating system of the company
4. List of managers, responsibilities, information received, and information sources
5. List of principal files and records as viewed by users
6. Outline of characteristics of the data base
7. Outline of the computer and communication system
8. Scope of the software requirements.

The report which documents the conceptual design then becomes the basis for expanding the design in detail. It also provides management with a summary of the ultimate detailed MIS design for review and approval. Let us look at the process for developing the conceptual design report.

PREPARING MEMBERS OF THE ORGANIZATION FOR CHANGE

The first step in design is not a technical one, but a behavioral one. The introduction of an MIS involves changes in roles, status, and power of individuals. Unless members of the organization believe that changes are needed and will benefit them, they will resist change (see Chapter 2). The management of change is treated in research and application under the heading of *organizational development*.[1]

Management and systems designers should first be aware of the process of successful change in an organization. One model of this process is shown in Table 8.1. The steps which management must follow are (a) setting objectives, (b) changing social relationships, (c) building self-esteem of organizational members, and (d) providing incentives that motivate change. These steps are carried out by formal educational seminars, information programs, and involvement of all members of the organization in the development of the MIS project. This approach must start concurrently with the setting of objectives for the MIS.

[1] See Gene W. Dalton, Paul R. Lawrence, and Larry E. Greiner, eds., *Organizational Change and Development* (Homewood, Ill.: Richard D. Irwin, 1970), for an overview of recent theory.

Table 8.1 Dalton's model of induced organization change

Processes of Change	PHASES OF CHANGE			
	Tension Experienced within the System	*Intervention of a Prestigious Influencing Agent*	*Individuals Attempt to Implement the Proposed Changes*	*New Behavior and Attitudes Reinforced by Achievement, Social Ties, and Internalized Values— Accompanied by Decreasing Dependence on Influencing Agent*
Setting objectives		Generalized objectives established	Growing specificity of objectives—establishment of subgoals	Achievement and resetting of specific objectives
Altering social ties	Tension within existing social ties	Prior social ties interrupted or attenuated	Formation of new alliances and relationships centering around new activities	New social ties reinforce altered behavior and attitudes
Building self-esteem	Lowered sense of self-esteem	Esteem-building begun on basis of agent's attention and assurance	Esteem-building based on task accomplishment	Heightened sense of self-esteem
Internalized motives for change		External motive for change (new scheme provided)	Improvisation and reality testing	Internalized motive for change

Source: Gene W. Dalton, Paul R. Lawrence, and Larry E. Greiner, eds., **Organizational Change and Development** (Homewood, Ill.: Richard D. Irwin, 1970), p. 8. © 1970 by Richard D. Irwin, Inc.

STUDYING THE CHARACTERISTICS OF THE COMPANY AND THE INDUSTRY

The conceptual design must be based upon the fundamental activities of the company, as shown in Table 4.2. Whether a company is a service company or manufacturing company determines the basic transaction cycles (shown in Fig. 4.19 for a manufacturing company). At a minimum, the MIS must provide information on these transactions for control.

Firms from different industries are concerned with different key variables in the environment and different key indexes within the company. While similarities can always be found, the decisions of bankers, industrialists, and commercial managers relate to quite different types of problems. At the very least, the technical information required for decision making, planning, and control is quite different for diverse industries. Without giving a complete directory, Table 8.2 indicates some differences in emphasis.

In addition, companies within the same industry may be organized differently. With the same apparent organizational relationships, the decentralization of authority may also vary.

One of the first problems of the system designer is to determine exactly what business the company is engaged in and will be engaged in over the next few years. Identification of basic objectives and a unified sense of direction are often lacking. Hence executives may be working toward conflicting ends. In such cases the systems analyst may, by his questioning in interviews, stimulate management to think about such basic questions. If the company has a strategic

Table 8.2 Some key items of information to indicate diversity

Manufacturing	Retailing	Banking	Hospital
Sales in units and dollars/period	Sales in units and dollars/period	Number of depositors/ period	Number of patient-days/period
		Number of loans/period	Billings/period
		Dollar volume of deposits/period	
		Dollar volume of commercial loans/period	
Products, sales by products, share of market	Merchandise, turnover, share of market	Variety of services, market share	Health care services offered, frequency of use of each service/ period
Number of customers and their characteristics	Market identification	Market identification	Geographic area served, constraints on admissions
Plants, warehouses, and offices: locations, size, employment	Stores, warehouses, offices: locations, size, employment	Buildings: locations, size, facilities, employment	Hospital capacity, facilities, access, employment
Key executives	Key executives	Key executives	Department supervisors and top management
Number of vendors, locations, products	Number of vendors, locations, products	Sources of securities	Number of vendors, locations, products
Working capital and cash	Working capital and cash	Working capital and cash	Working capital and cash
Identity of competitors and shares of the market	Identity of competitors and shares of the market	Identity of competitors and shares of the market	Location, services, and prices of nearby health care centers
Telecommunications network used by the company	Telecommunications network used by the company	Telecommunications network used by the company	Monitoring and telecommunications system
Laws relating to manufacturing firms	Laws relating to retailing firms	Laws and regulations related to banks	Laws, regulations, and government transfer payments for hospitals

plan which managers believe in, the systems designer will find his answers there.

It is apparent that if the MIS is to perform effectively, management must take the first step by clarifying the business itself. The description of the business is called the *strategic posture* or *reference business*. It must be referred to, time and again, by all concerned with MIS development to make sure that the MIS serves the objectives of the business.

STUDYING THE COMPANY'S ORGANIZATION AND DECISION STRUCTURE

Since the purpose of the MIS is to serve managers and key decision makers, the systems designer must determine who these people are and what their roles are. He does this by studying the formal and informal structure of the company.

In the ideal situation, systems and information systems would be developed first to solve the company problems. Then the managers of systems would be determined. In real situations, the opposite is true. The MIS designer must usually accept the organization and decision structure as given and then design the MIS to service it. It is possible, also, that during MIS design, obvious changes will be recognized so that some modification organization structure may be brought about.

The organization charts, policy guides, and procedures manuals are the starting points for a study of the organization. If they do not exist, the systems analyst must construct his own on the basis of interviews. From this study, managers may be identified. The responsibilities of managers must be determined, since the MIS is the basis for fulfilling these responsibilities. Position descriptions, if they exist, are helpful. However, the analyst should probe beyond these descriptions to uncover the real power of each executive. Investigation into whose signatures are required for approval of major actions is helpful. Interviews which reveal the degree to which executives have extended their empires beyond their formal charters also help.

IDENTIFYING COMPANY PROBLEMS

Once we have studied the objectives of the company and the structure of the system (business) which exists to achieve these objectives, we next wish to uncover the problems that arise in developing new objectives and achieving them. The problems may be classified into five groups, as shown in Table 8.3. They relate to determining the basic business of the company, formulating strategic objectives, conceiving and designing operating subsystems, making the operating systems function in the complicated environment, and controlling the operating subsystems.

While many problems are common to all companies, some problems are chronic or specific for individual companies. The systems analyst should list continuing problems and anticipated problems over the next few years. Examination of problems provides clues to information needs of managers.

Table 8.3 Classes of problems

Problems	Examples
1. What should be the basic type of business we will engage in?	Genesco is engaged in the manufacture and retail distribution of men's apparel
	Lubrizol manufactures and sells oil additives
	Rockwell International engages in the manufacture and sales of aerospace and automotive components, industrial goods, electronic and consumer products
	Control Data Corp. manufactures, sells, and leases computer equipment, provides insurance services, and provides commercial credit services
2. What should our strategic objective be?	The scope for International Paper Co. includes exploration and development of oil, gas, and minerals; the management of renewable wood fiber resources, production of solid wood products and pulp, paper, and paperboard
	The development of resources at IPC will include a $3 million project in Arkansas paper mill
	At Honeywell, one of the competitive edges is its focus on energy conservation and control, and relating the company and its products to social concerns
	At International Harvester (1978) an objective will be to trim expenses drastically, restructure the company, and eliminate duplication of activities. Deployment of resources will include a tremendous modernization program for existing plants
	Oil companies opt for high risks in bidding for leases in the Baltimore Canyon (1978)
3. What operating systems are needed to conduct our business?	See Chapter 4
4. How do we make the operating systems function?	Overcoming a problem of high inventory costs
	Overcoming a problem of a machine breakdown
	Developing good managers
	Overcoming a problem of loss of market share in New York
	For a bank, overcoming a loss of deposits to higher-interest-bearing securities
	For a retail store, overcoming shoplifting
5. Controlling the operating systems	Measuring sales performance to permit control
	Controlling productivity of professionals
	Controlling quality of finished goods
	Controlling labor costs
	Controlling the company image

STUDYING THE OPERATING SYSTEMS

The operating systems represent management's view of the means of reaching company objectives. If flow charts and procedures manuals are lacking, the analyst may well spend time sketching the operating systems, identifying decision points, and studying reports to management.

The previous study steps have all been directed toward the heart of the MIS, the information needs of managers. The analyst who has studied the industry and company, familiarized himself with the structure, searched for the problems of the company, and studied the operating systems is now in a position to meet with managers to uncover their information needs.

A clear statement of the information needs of each manager is fundamental to good MIS design. Companies mistakenly spend large sums on computer hardware and software to perpetuate existing systems, build sophisticated models, or simply speed up data processing. What is really needed is availability of information that can increase the perceptions of managers in critical areas such as problem identification, alternative solutions, opportunities and threats, and planning and controlling.

The MIS design will be only as effective as the specification of managers' information needs. The manager-user must be able to spell out his or her objectives and the information most valuable to him or her under the probing of the systems analyst. Failure to be specific on these two items probably accounts for the downfall of more design efforts than any other factor. If the manager is unable or unwilling to clarify objectives and information needs, it is likely that the analyst or technician will substitute *his* perceptions of objectives and information needs.

It is not easy for managers to describe the specific information requirements of their jobs. They tend to view each problem and decision as unique without observing commonalities of information required. Both the manager and the analyst may feel frustrated in this search, as indicated by the following typical interchange:

Analyst:	We wish to supply you promptly with information vital to your job. Could you tell me what the basic objectives of this field engineering system are?
Manager of Field Engineering:	Sure. To get equipment working for customers. You know, to keep the customers happy. Well, we also get test information this way. I suppose that we try to keep the customer happy.
Analyst:	Yes, I understand. Let me put it another way. What are your specific responsibilities as you see them?
Manager:	Whatta ya mean? I'm responsible for the startup and repair of equipment out there.
Analyst:	I see, but could you list and rank responsibilities for which you are measured by your manager?
Manager:	I guess I could, but that would take a little time. Why don't you come back?
Analyst:	That would certainly allow you to give some careful thought to your list. Would you at the same time list items of information you need to carry out each responsibility? That way we could save your time when we meet again. Could we get together a week from today?

This hypothetical conversation reflects the difficulty of getting managers to be specific about their objectives and information needs. One approach, sometimes used by consultants, is to have top management decree that subordinate managers prepare in writing a statement containing (1) five to ten major responsibilities for which each manager believes he is held accountable, and (2) about five to ten specific items of information that are required to carry out these responsibilities. These statements could be prepared in table format and amplified to give (a) objectives of the position, (b) major responsibilities, (c) major types of problems, (d) typical decisions, (e) current information supplied, and (f) information actually needed. The idea is to stimulate the manager to think in terms of information needs.

Another approach is avoidance of the direct question, "What information do you need?" Instead, the designer requests that the user describe what occurs in the decision-making process; then the designer concerns himself with the identification of the questions that are to be resolved in the activity for which the system is being designed. This approach is also a good one for the manager-user, because he is intimately familiar with his operation and presumably with the difficult decision operations in it.

One way of determining what managers do *not* need in the way of information is to cease issuing selected periodic reports or reduce their circulation list. If a manager really uses a report, he will complain, and his name may be restored to the circulation list.

A manager needs information for a variety of reasons concerned with the management process. His needs at various times and for various purposes depend largely on two factors that we shall examine briefly: the personal managerial attributes of the individual manager, and the organizational environment in which decisions are made.

Personal Attributes

Knowledge of information systems

If the manager is aware of what computer-based systems can do, his information requests will probably be more sophisticated and more specific. His knowledge of capabilities and costs places him in a much better position to aid in the design of a good system.

Managerial style

A manager's technical background, his leadership style, and his decision-making ability all affect the kind and amount of information he requires. Some prefer a great amount of detail; others like to decide with a minimum of detail and prefer personal consultation with subordinates.

Manager's perception of information needs

"You tell me what I need to know" and "Get me all the facts" represent two opposite perceptions of information needs. This dichotomy is due partly to the fact that many managers are ignorant of what information they need. Another dimension of the problem is the widely differing views of managers regarding their obligation to disseminate information to subordinates and to groups outside the firm. The manager who cannot or will not delegate authority is likely to keep information closely held.

In Table 8.4 we have shown a format for collecting and listing basic information needs of managers as the managers perceive them. To help the managers focus on their needs, rather than on information actually received, they were first asked to give the basic objectives of their positions.

Table 8.4
Information needs of several managers in a manufacturing company at the gross design level

Manager	Function or Objectives	Principal Information Needs
President	Short- and long-run profitability, expansion, stability of earnings	Summary reports: 1. Financial 2. Sales 3. Marketing 4. Public relations 5. Consumer division 6. Industrial division 7. International operations 8. Engineering/research 9. Forecasts of the future Exception reports: Major problems affecting company operations and deviations from plans, competitive actions posing a threat, government activities of major significance
Vice president and treasurer	Directs all financial matters for the company and is responsible for all financial reports, budgets, and their analysis	Revenue and costs Cash flow Tax liabilities Gross insurance budgets Capital structure factors such as bond rates, cost of floating new equity, and trends in financial markets
Senior VP, marketing and sales	Directs all marketing functions and public relations	Summarized sales forecast Summarized market research reports on 1. Attitudes and buying habits of customers 2. Analysis of past marketing strategies 3. Competitors and their products Exception reports on sales signficantly above or below plans, by product, region, or sales group
Manager, national sales training	Conducts training seminars in the field to strengthen the sales force and its supervision	Number and location of new sales and new salesmen Areas of weakness in sales improvement Training needs

Traffic manager	Directs traffic activities for incoming and outgoing materials	Location of warehouses Location of supplies Train, truck, water, and air rates Differences in quality of service provided by various carriers
Data processing manager	Is responsible for the equipment and staffing of the data processing center; provides data processing service to all managers, particularly the financial, MIS, marketing, and engineering organizations	Forecasts of services required from each organization New equipment coming on the market Forecasts of growth of services required Format of reports and media of reports desired by users Data-base specifications Sources of input data

Organizational Environment

The organizational environment in which decisions are made in the case of a particular manager are the level of management and the organizational design.

Level of management

We discussed in Chapter 5 the levels of management: corporate, division, middle, and first-line management. Each level requires a different kind of information and in different detail. Top levels of management need the one-time reports, the exception reports, and summaries. The middle and first-line management require the frequent periodic reports, the exception reports, and the detailed analyses. Managers at *all* levels also have changing needs for specific information in addition to what they regularly receive.

Organizational design

Although we have highlighted the personal attributes of managers as affecting their information needs, the total nature of the organizational design relates these managers to their environment. That is, organizational structure, tasks, decision processes, and individuals making up the organization will affect the style of managers and their information needs. Jay R. Galbraith has integrated research studies to represent the variables determining organizational design in Fig. 8.1. This figure suggests check questions for the MIS designer when gathering information needs of managers:

1. Are stated needs appropriate to the structure, or is the manager asking for information completely unrelated to his or her unit?
2. Is all information related to decision processes expressed?
3. Is information appropriate and in adequate depth for the tasks assigned?
4. Is information adequate for the development and appraisal of subordinates?
5. Is information adequate for the development and maintenance of the reward system?

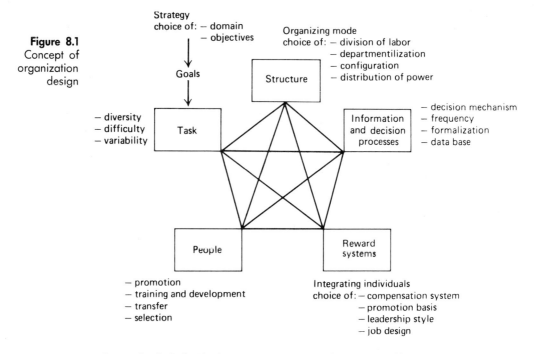

Figure 8.1
Concept of organization design

Strategy
choice of: — domain
— objectives

↓

Goals

Organizing mode
choice of: — division of labor
— departmentilization
— configuration
— distribution of power

Structure

— diversity
— difficulty
— variability

Task

Information
and decision
processes

— decision mechanism
— frequency
— formalization
— data base

People

Reward
systems

— promotion
— training and development
— transfer
— selection

Integrating individuals
choice of: — compensation system
— promotion basis
— leadership style
— job design

Source: Jay R. Galbraith, **Organization Design** (Reading, Mass.: Addison-Wesley, 1977), p. 31.

IDENTIFYING SYSTEM CONSTRAINTS

Constraints are the limitations imposed upon the design of the MIS. They may limit resources or time available, for example, or they may impose a requirement that the MIS must meet. In particular, all the system requirements (performance specifications) represent constraints. (See Fig. 8.2.)

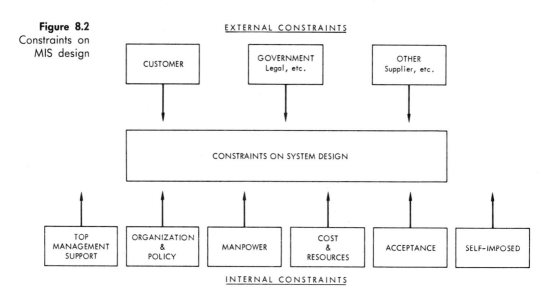

Figure 8.2
Constraints on MIS design

EXTERNAL CONSTRAINTS

CUSTOMER

GOVERNMENT
Legal, etc.

OTHER
Supplier, etc.

CONSTRAINTS ON SYSTEM DESIGN

TOP MANAGEMENT SUPPORT

ORGANIZATION & POLICY

MANPOWER

COST & RESOURCES

ACCEPTANCE

SELF-IMPOSED

INTERNAL CONSTRAINTS

If *top-management support* is not obtained for the systems concept and for the notion that computer-based information systems are vital for management planning and control, the type of design effort discussed in these chapters cannot be implemented. A good environment for information systems must be set, and one essential ingredient is the approval and support of top management. This constraint definitely influences the kind of system the manager-user may design.

Organizational and policy considerations frequently set limits on objectives and modify an intended approach to design of a system. The organizational structure and the managers occupying various positions influence information flow and use of system outputs. In a decentralized multiplant organization with a wide product line, the design of common systems in cost accounting or production control is obviously less acceptable than in a more centralized organization with fewer products. An additional organizational difficulty is related to the turnover of managers. More than one head of computer operations has stated that his major difficulty is the abandonment or redesign of systems due to the turnover among manager-users. Also, company policies frequently define or limit the approach to systems design. Among these policies are those concerned with product and service, research and development, production, marketing, finance, and personnel. For example, a "promote from within" personnel policy would have an impact on the type of system design to build a skills inventory. Other important considerations in design are those concerning audits.

Manpower needs and *personnel availability* are a major limiting factor in both the design and utilization of information systems. Computer and systems skills are among the most critical in the nation; rare indeed is the manager who admits to having sufficient personnel to design, implement, and operate the systems he desires. Additional considerations concern the nature of the work force and the skill mix of users. Elaborate and sophisticated systems are of little value if they cannot be put to use.

Perhaps the most significant constraint of all is the one concerning *people*. "People problems" is probably the factor most often mentioned where failure to achieve expected results is concerned. Here we have the difficulties associated with the natural human reaction to change, the antagonism, and the lack of interest and support frequently met in systems design and operation. Automation, computer systems, and systems design often call for the realignment of people and facilities, organizational changes, and individual job changes. Therefore, these reactions are to be expected and should be anticipated in designing systems to achieve the objective.

Cost is a major *resource* limitation. The cost to achieve the objective should be compared with the benefits to be derived. You do not want to spend $20,000 to save $10,000. Although a cost-benefit analysis is frequently difficult, some approach to priority setting must be undertaken. Considerations similar to those surrounding cost apply also to the use of other resources. *Computer capacity* and other facilities relating to operation of data processing systems should be utilized in an optimum way.

Self-imposed restrictions are those placed on the design by the manager or the designer. In designing the system to achieve the objective, he may have to scale down several requirements in order to make the system fit with other outputs, equipment, or constraints. Usually, he will also restrict the amount of time and effort devoted to investigation. For example, he may want to design a pilot or test system around one product, one plant, or one portion of an operation before making it generally applicable elsewhere. Functional requirements also define constraints placed on the system by its users. The data requirements, the data volumes, and the rate of processing are constraints imposed by the immediate users. More remote users impose constraints by the need to integrate with related systems.

External Constraints

Foremost among the considerations surrounding the external environment are those concerning the *customer*. Order entry, billing, and other systems that interface with systems of the customer must be designed with his needs in mind. If certain outputs from the system are not acceptable to the customer, a definite limitation must be faced up to. He may require that bills be submitted in a form that provides input to his system of accounts payable. For example, standard progress reporting and billing procedures are among the requirements imposed for processing data under many military procurement programs.

A variety of additional external constraints should be considered in addition to the customer. The *government* (federal, state, local) imposes certain restrictions on the processing data. Among these are the need to maintain the security of certain classes of information (e.g., personnel) in order to comply with law and regulation in the conduct of business (e.g., taxes, reporting) and to meet certain procedures regarding record keeping and reporting to stockholders (e.g., outside audit). *Unions* can and do affect the operation of systems involving members in matters such as compensation, grievances, and working conditions. *Suppliers* are also an important group to be considered when designing

Table 8.5 External constraints	Subsystem	Statement of Constraint
	Inventory	Regardless of reorder points and reorder quantities, the supplier will not accept orders for less than carload lots for raw materials 7 and 12
	Accounts payable	The individual who prepares the check for payment of invoices must not be the same individual who approves payment
	Purchasing	It is not necessary to negotiate purchases in amounts under $500
	Production control	System output for shop control will be identified by department only and not by the individual worker or foreman
	Project control	We are required to report weekly to the U.S. Department of Defense any slippages in time or cost exceeding 10% of any event in the project control critical path

information systems because these systems frequently interface with that group.

In summary, it is important to recognize the constraints that have an impact on systems design. Having recognized them and made appropriate allowance in the design function, the manager will then be in a position to complete the remaining steps toward the design of an operating system that will achieve the objective he has previously determined.

The nature of constraints is illustrated here by stating a hypothetical constraint for each of our selected functional subsystems (Table 8.5).

Redefining the MIS Objectives

The MIS objectives have been set initially in the plan. Certainly the main thrust of the project has been established. Now we can more specifically define or redefine some objectives. Objectives must be set in measurable terms.

Table 8.6
Examples of
MIS objectives

Type	MIS Objective	Related Company Objective
1. Early warning signals	(a) Prevent a long-term gap between average plant capacity and demand for the firm's product	Minimize production costs with expansion of plant capacity
	(b) Prevent surprises due to technological break-throughs affecting the firm's products	Avoid crash development programs or loss of market share
	(c) Maintain awareness of top management succession problems	Plan for orderly change of top managers over the next ten years
2. Decision-assisting information	(a) Supply financial trends and ratios to management	Make good cash and capital investment decisions
	(b) Provide a model and computer hardware and software that will answer managers' "What if . . . ?" questions on profits for combinations of products	Achieve a profitable product mix within company constraints
3. Programmed decision making	(a) Assignment of orders to machines and scheduling of orders	Lower production costs
	(b) Allocating advertising expenditures among selected magazines	Provide economical and broad support for salesmen
4. Automation of routine clerical operations	(a) Automation of payroll computations	Timely and accurate pay of employees at minimum cost
	(b) Automation of inventory status and reports	Up-to-date accurate records of inventory to serve customers without delays

It would be nice to set the objective of the MIS as supplying each manager with all the information he needs when he needs it. This is not very practical, however. First, the information may not be available within the company when it is needed. Second, the cost of storing all information that could possibly be used would be prohibitive. Third, the cost of obtaining certain items of information about the environment is prohibitive.

Effectiveness is the degree to which an individual achieves system objectives. Each manager must define his MIS objectives with the view toward increasing his or her own effectiveness in achieving company objectives. This will take into account the benefits and costs of the MIS service to him or her. Too often managers seek an MIS which places efficiency ahead of effectiveness, so that they accomplish the wrong things at low cost. Managerial effectiveness may be increased by (1) early warning signals from the MIS about the environment and (2) decision-assisting information. Efficiency may be increased by (1) programmed decision making and (2) automation of clerical or other routine activities. Thus specific objectives of the MIS are usually established in these four areas for the MIS tasks given in the MIS plan. An example of each is illustrated in Table 8.6. Each objective is, of course, derived from some objective of the company.

DETERMINING INFORMATION SOURCES

After we have identified the principal information needs of managers and established the organization and operations structures, we must next determine sources for the information supplied. Managers receive information from both formal MIS sources and random informal sources. Further, information received is generated by external sources or internal sources. Table 8.7 illustrates these classifications by means of examples.

If managers are to receive the internal information they need, then data must be captured and converted to information. Let us illustrate with an example

Table 8.7 Managers' sources of information		*Formal MIS*	*Informal, Random*
	Internal	Higher-level management directives and reports	Conferences
		Reports from managers on the same level	Coffee breaks
		Reports from subordinates	Socializing with other employees outside of work
		Regular computer-generated reports	
		Interaction with the computer	
		Regularly scheduled staff meetings	
	External	Marketing research	News media
		Environmental scanning organization	Acquaintances
		Customer surveys	Customers and vendors
		Government mailings	Trade shows
		Business periodical subscriptions	Continuing education programs
		Commercial information services	
		Industry reports	

the case where information is needed but the basic data were not captured. In this example a company has a system for aiding management to make capital budgeting decisions. The system gathers recommendations from marketing, production, engineering, and corporate management. These recommendations are tabulated and ranked by a committee. A total capital budget constraint is then imposed by top management, and a final selection of investments is made. At one of these annual reviews, a conversation starts:

Engineering Manager: Our unit manufacturing costs seem to be creeping up. Why do we have so many rejects?

Production Manager: Our equipment is aging, Jim. You know I've tried to get some new numerical controlled modern lathes and drill presses in the budget for the last five years.

Marketing Manager: That's true, Bill, but when is a machine old or obsolete? And what is the average age of each class of machines that you have?

Production Manager: I don't know. We'd have to research that, Sam.

This shows that the capital resource subsystem was not designed to produce information that managers need. In fact, if the records on the purchase date of the equipment were not kept for a period of 10 to 15 years, it might be very difficult to determine the average age of classes of equipment. The subsystem needs to be redesigned to furnish such information at capital budgeting time.

How to Locate Sources of Information That Managers Need

We have previously determined information needs, but what is the source of the information or original data in each case? There are two possibilities. The source may be tracked down to a particular system. That is, an existing system captures the transaction data or an environmental scanning process picks it up. Alternatively, there may be no source because the data are not generated or captured. This will require a modification of functional operating systems in the company. The conversation in the section above dealing with the average age of machinery was just such an example.

Procedures for locating sources of information are as follows:

1. Examining current *internal records* and *external documents received.* Internal records may consist of forms, document files, microfiche, secondary computer memory (tapes, disks), or reports. External data may be located in government documents (especially in the company library), government reports and regulations (usually found in an individual's office), trade publications, economic and competitive statistics (often found in the marketing research files), and computer tape files purchased from firms providing special services.

2. *Interviewing managers and operating personnel* to uncover data produced by systems, stored, and possibly not currently used or forgotten.

Figure 8.3 Input/output chart for customer order processing

	Invoices	Shipping papers	Shipping labels	Quantity shipped	Back orders	Net price	Shipping terms	Stock ledgers	Stock report	Billing & cost dist.	Tax reports	Unfilled orders ($)	Orders entered ($)	Statistical analysis
Customer order no.	X	X	X											
Cust. ident. no.	X	X	X		X	X	X					X	X	X
Item ident. no.	X	X		X	X	X	X	X	X	X	X	X	X	X
Quantity ordered	X	X		X	X	X		X	X	X	X	X	X	X
Net price	X													X
Receipts	X	X		X	X			X	X	X	X	X	X	X

3. *Sampling and estimating* to obtain sources of information where the basic data are available but uneconomical to study completely. For instance, work sampling provides information about how people spend their time. Statistical quality control provides information about defects in production. Sampling of transactions provides information about the number and kinds of errors made in operating systems.

4. *Input/output analysis* of data *to* systems and *from* systems. Two forms of input/output charts are shown in Figs. 8.3 and 8.4. In Fig. 8.3, output data are related to input for a particular system, the order processing system. Figure 8.4 essentially lists systems and provides both inputs and outputs for each system.

5. *Multidimensional flow charting* to organize information sources or depict the existing design of a subsystem. A flow chart can be constructed to trace the routing or flow of information from origin to destination and to arrange this flow in a chronological sequence that shows the progression of information through the organization. Although they are not specifically required for identification of information sources, the factors of frequency, volume, time, cost, and physical distance can also be shown on such a chart.

Matching Users with Information Sources

We have now assured ourselves that information needed by managers can be derived from some source within the company. We should now investigate whether we are capturing data or generating information that serves no need. We therefore prepare a list of data sources matched to needs. If some need is highly unlikely to occur, then we should consider the cost of capturing the basic data vs. the loss if it is not available because we did not capture it.

Figure 8.4 Data classes-to-systems matrix (university)

Data Classes (columns):

1. Student
2. Demographic & Biographic
3. Previous Education
4. Recruiting/Admittance
5. Current Term Data
6. Course Data
7. Financial Status
8. Program/Degree Status
9. Facilities & Capital Equip.
10. Facilities
11. Capital Equipment
12. Rental Equipment/Services
13. Expendable Inventory
14. Project Control
15. Alumni/Development
16. General
17. Alumni
18. Development
19. Finance
20. General
21. Income Related
22. Expense Related
23. Extra-Institutional
24. Institutional Affiliations
25. Census/Demographic
26. Economic
27. Inter-University Comparative
28. Gov. Regulations & Reqmnts.
29. Budget
30. Manpower
31. Demographic/Biographic
32. Experience/Skills/Educ.
33. Appointment/Employment
34. Assignment
35. Faculty Activity
36. Curriculum & Instruction
37. Course Attributes
38. Section Attributes
39. Section Resume
40. Program/Degree

Legend: o = used; I = created; ⊘ = cell split diagonally (created and used).

Systems	1	2	3	4	5	6	7	8	9	10	11	12	13	14	15	16	17	18	19	20	21	22	23	24	25	26	27	28	29	30	31	32	33	34	35	36	37	38	39	40
Student																																								
Admissions	⊘	I	⊘	I		⊘											I			o	⊘	o		⊘			⊘										o			o
Registration	I	I		⊘	⊘	⊘		⊘		⊘										o	⊘	o		⊘			⊘										o	o		o
Financial Aid	o	o	o	o	o	⊘	o											o		o	⊘	o		⊘							o		o	o						o
Evaluation				o	o		o													o	o	o															o	o	o	o
Status Reporting	o	o	o	o	o	o	o	o		o										o	o	o																		
Student Flow	o	o	o	o	o	o	o	o																			o										o	o	o	o
Facilities & Cap. Equip.																																								
Library Ordering & Circ.																																								
Order Control													⊘							o	o	o																		
Project Control														⊘						o	o	o																		
Space Management			o							⊘										o	o	o											o	o			o	o	o	
Capital Equip. Mgmt.											⊘									o	o	o											o	o			o		o	
Supplies Management													⊘							o	o	o																	o	
Food Services																																							o	
Alumni/Development																																								
Grant/Donation Status																⊘	⊘			o	⊘																			
Alumni/Donor Contact	o															⊘	⊘			o	o																	o		
Alumni Profile	o															⊘	⊘																							
Gift & Grant Tracking																⊘		⊘		o	⊘																			
Financial																																								
Receivables			o					⊘		o						⊘	⊘			⊘	⊘																			
Payables								⊘												⊘	⊘	⊘																		
Payroll																				⊘		⊘											⊘							
Portfolio Mgmt.																				⊘	⊘																			
Accounting										⊘	⊘	⊘	⊘	⊘						⊘	⊘	⊘																		
Planning & Control																																								
Records Maintenance																								I	I	I	I	I												
Models	o	o	o	o	o					o	o	o	o	o		o	o	o		o	o	o		o	o	o	o						o	o	o		o	o	o	o
Budget Prep./Tracking										o	o	o	o	o		o	o	o		⊘	⊘	⊘											o	o	o		o	o		
Manpower																																								
Salary & Benefits Admin.																				⊘		⊘									o		o	⊘	o					
Personnel Eval./Tracking			o																	o		o									⊘	I	⊘	⊘	⊘		o	o		
Manpower Track./Forecast													o							o	o	o											o	o	o					
Curriculum/Instruction																																								
Course Offering/Reqmnts.		o	o	o						o										o	o	o			o		o						o	o	o		⊘	⊘	⊘	
Degree Programs																					o				o		o						o		o					⊘
Trends/Statistics Anal.		o	o	o	o					o												o			o		o										o	o	o	o
Course/Section Schedules										⊘	⊘	⊘																									o	⊘	o	

Source: **Business Systems Planning,** GE-20-0527-1 (White Plains, N.Y.: IBM, 1975) (Courtesy of International Business Machines Corp.)

Data sources may be analyzed by means of a listing, or by system tables, such as Table 8.8, or by a matrix, such as that of Fig. 8.5. Intermediate sources of information may also be related to managers' needs by a matrix such as shown in Fig. 8.6.

Figure 8.5 City of Pompano Beach data source matrix

INFORMATION NEEDED/RECEIVED

DEPARTMENT MANAGER	Monthly Water Consumption	Council Minutes	Daily Cash Register Receipt	Monthly Budget Report	Cash Report and Statement Disbursement	Weekly Trial Balance	Weekly Expenditure Approval List	Monthly Balance Sheet	Monthly Detail Budget List	Monthly Accounts Payable Vendor List	Special Assessments	Purchase Orders	Attendance Reports	Citizen Attitude Surveys	Monthly Planning	Weekly Crime Report	Weekly Fire Report	Vehicle Maintenance	Accident Report	Building Maintenance	Property Ownership Change	Energy Consumption	Annual Budget Worksheet Revenue	Annual Expenditure Report	Annual Budget Worksheet Expenditures	Accounts Recorded List	Employee Update
Finance	×	×	×	×	×	×	×	×	×	×	×	×										×	×	×	×		
Community Development			×	×								×	×				×			×		×	×	×			
Engineering and Utilities	×		×	×				×				×		×							×	×	×	×	×		
Airpark		×	×	×						×		×					×						×	×			
Personnel			×					×				×					×					×	×	×	×	×	
City Clerk		×	×	×				×				×								×		×	×	×	×		
Public Works			×	×				×				×							×		×	×	×	×	×		
Legal								×				×					×			×			×	×			
Golf			×	×				×	×			×										×	×	×			
Recreation			×	×				×				×	×				×						×	×	×		
Transportation and Traffic Engineering				×				×				×					×						×	×	×		
Fire			×	×				×				×				×	×					×	×	×	×		
Police			×	×				×				×			×			×				×	×	×	×		
Library		×	×	×				×				×										×	×	×	×		

258

MANAGER-USER \ FILE	Customer	Accounts Payable	Accounts Receivable	Orders—Completed	Orders—In Process	Sales	Manufacturing Costs	Market Costs	Purchasing Costs	Shipping Costs	Competitor Operations	Engineering	Inventory	Payroll	Authorized Personnel	Employees	Job Schedule
Order Department	X			X	X	X				X							X
Controller	X	X	X			X	X	X					X				
Accounting	X	X	X			X				X			X				
Payroll						X								X		X	
Roof Truss Fabrication				X			X					X	X				X
Saw Department				X									X				X
Table Leaders																	X
Shipping Roof Truss										X							X
Connector Plate Fabrication				X			X					X	X				X
Plate Fabrication													X				X
Plate Application													X				X
Steel Department				X									X				X
Tool and Die				X								X					X
Shipping and Receiving	X			X						X							X
Parts Department																	
Support Operations	X			X	X				X				X				X
Duplication Services							X										
Mailroom	X									X							
Purchasing				X				X	X	X		X	X				X
Security															X	X	
Sales	X			X	X	X	X			X	X	X					X
Chief Engineer			X	X			X	X	X			X	X				X
Drafting and Engineering				X	X							X	X				X
Research				X	X								X				
Development												X	X				
Computer Operations	X	X	X	X	X	X	X	X	X	X			X	X	X	X	
New Product Testing											X	X					X

Figure 8.6 Partial list of users and file sources

Table 8.8	Subsystem	Information Sources	
Information sources for subsystems	Inventory	Need:	Items falling below minimum inventory level
		Source:	Stock-level determination subsystem compares current balance against minimum inventory level
	Accounts payable	Need:	Code invoices "days to due date"
		Source:	Coded upon entry into accounts payable subsystem
	Purchasing	Need:	Performance of individual buyers
		Source:	Purchasing system compares outgoing purchase prices against predetermined standards
	Production control	Need:	Cost variances over or under 5%
		Source:	Integration of costing with manufacturing applications: shop control, stores requisitioning, labor distribution, etc.
	Project control	Need:	Progress against plan for events in critical path
		Source:	Project control subsystem

BLOCK-DIAGRAMMING THE MIS

When need and sources of information are known, the flow of data and information may be described by means of block diagrams or matrixes. Information received by a manager comes from other managed groups within the company, directly from outside agencies such as the government, business services, competitors, and vendors, or from computer-produced reports. The purpose of the block diagram is to present an overall picture of the MIS information flow. The difficulty is that such diagrams get more complex as they get more detailed. Figure 8.7 attempts to present the essentials of information flow using codes and supporting code tables. An alternative, which allows the presentation of more detail and permits easy analysis, is the individualized chart in Fig. 8.8. A set of these figures has the drawback that the overall view cannot be seen at a glance. Another alternative is to prepare a matrix with a list of all managers, outside sources, and the computer in the vertical margin. These headings, except for outside sources, are repeated again across the top of the matrix. Within each cell, information originating from the source at the left and received by the receptor at the top is written out or listed by code. Such a matrix is most useful, although of wall size, if codes are avoided. Wall-size charts have been used for PERT diagrams for years, so that such size should not be considered an unusual feature for such a matrix chart.

OUTLINING THE GENERAL INFORMATION FLOW AND FILE SYSTEM

Flow Charts of Subsystems

At this point we develop the conceptual design of the subsystems which make up the MIS. Generally, we try to link inputs, files, reports, and computer role. Figure 8.9 shows how this might be done for an accounts receivable system of a hospital.

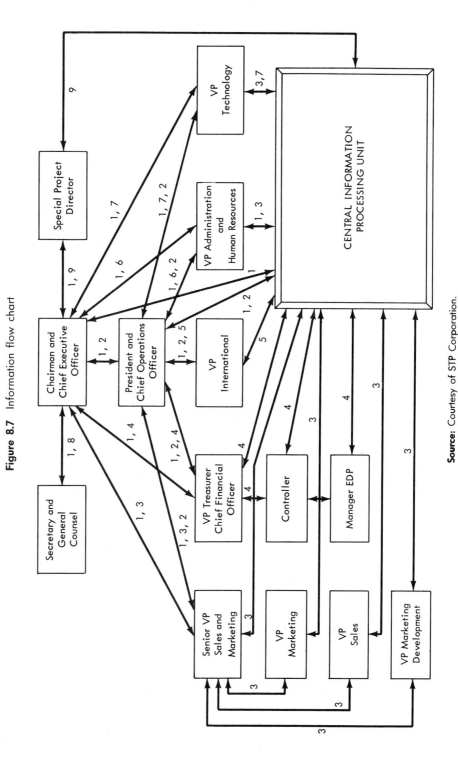

Figure 8.7 Information flow chart

Source: Courtesy of STP Corporation.

261

Figure 8.7 (continued) Code for Information Flow Chart

1. *General Operational Information and Reports*
   Profit center performance reports
   Variance analysis
   Profitability by product life
   Long-range & annual profit plans
   Overhead budget reports
   Financial position
   Market & economic trends
   Advertising & advertising quality
   Sales & sales promotion
   Long-term supplies agreements
   Personnel requirements
   Relevant issues
   General aspects of business

2. *Specific Operational Reports and Information*
   Inventory status
   Work-in-process backlog summary
   Cash position
   Orders awaiting shipment
   Pricing information
   Sales data
   Warehouse stock

3. *Marketing and Sales Information and Reports*
   Daily summary of selling (broken down by product and task)
   Budget performance forecast
   General administration information
   Sales & marketing status reports
   Sales trend analysis
   Share of market report
   Results of special promotions
   Reports on capital projects
   Revised forecast & variations
   Outstanding purchase commitments
   Marketing personnel analysis
   Advertising strategy & expenditure reports
   Marketing cost & deviation reports
   Life cycle analysis
   Promotional allowances
   Customer lists & new accounts
   Sales recapitulation report
   Buyer price analysis report
   Sales audit reports

4. *Financial Information and Reports*
   Budget & periodic reports on performance against budget
   Accounting control
   Payroll by hourly & salaried groups
   Payroll distribution reports
   Inventories of products
   Aged trial balance
   Customer credit information
   Accounting reports
   Order & customer profile reports
   Unfilled & back order information

Sales reports
Warehouse shipments information
Anticipated stockouts
Work-in-process backlog summary
Expediting information
Purchase orders & receiving data
Open purchase order status
Vendor delivery performance reports

5. *International Information and Reports*
   Share of market report
   Sales trend analysis
   Revised forecast & variations
   Overhead budget reports
   Financial position
   Profitability by product line
   Item performance
   Profit center performance reports
   Variance analysis
   Market & economic trends
   Shipment reports

6. *Administration and Human Resources Information and Reports*
   Personnel management reports
   Manpower requirement reports
   Personnel performance reports
   Salary information
   Labor distribution
   Personnel requirement forecasts
   Operating plans
   Personnel training data
   Personnel history

7. *Technology Information and Reports*
   New product status reports
   Schedules
   Equipment inventories
   Cost information
   Research & development information
   Item performance reports
   Quality control reports
   Market & economic trends
   End-product requirements

8. *Legal Counsel Information and Reports*
   Legal documents
   Contracts
   Patent rights information
   Pension plans
   Government control information

9. *Special Product Director Information and Reports*
   Item performance
   Raw materials forecasts
   Overhead budget reports
   Financial position
   Variance analysis
   Profitability by product line reports

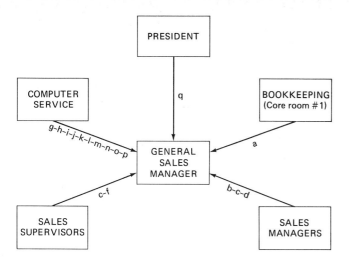

a. Daily sales inventory report
b. Sales performance report
c. Sales authorizations from chain stores
d. Dales forecast report
e. Post-off information (data on competing firms)
f. Supervisors report
g. Monthly sales report
h. Chain store reports
i. Key accounts by brands
j. Nonbuying accounts
k. Classification analysis report
l. Route master file
m. Customer master file
n. Draft sales weekly postings
o. Package sales weekly postings
p. Batch balance (verification report)
q. Legal constraint data

Figure 8.8 General sales manager: information flows

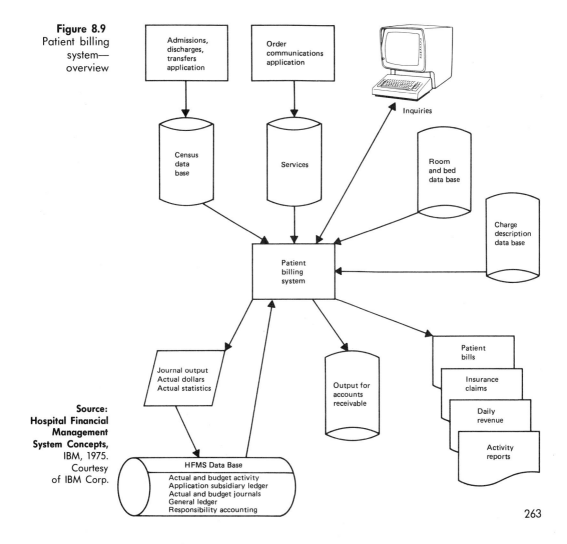

Figure 8.9 Patient billing system—overview

Source: Hospital Financial Management System Concepts, IBM, 1975. Courtesy of IBM Corp.

263

List of Files

When all of such subsystems have been conceptualized, a list of files may be prepared. (The records and elements of these files will be developed in the detailed design.) Files may be simply listed (Table 8.9) or they may be prepared in pictorial form as in Fig. 8.10. Finally, a matrix may be prepared which relates the files to usage in subsystems.

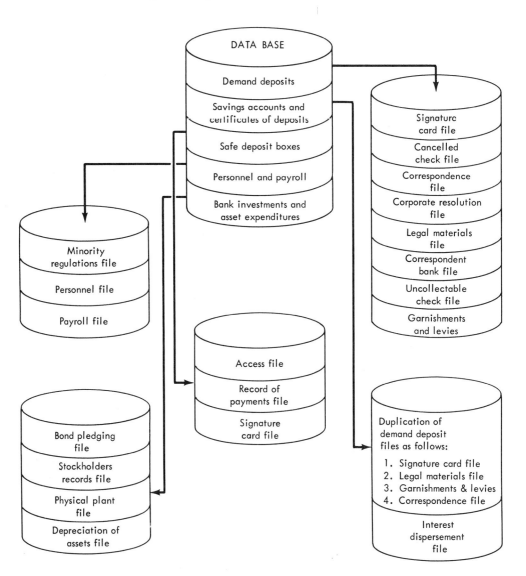

Figure 8.10 Operational area data base

Table 8.9 List of files and maintenance update periods

	Periodically	Annually	Monthly	Daily	Biweekly
City Manager					
Activity reports		X	X	X	
Financial reports		X	X		
Projects reports		X	X	X	
City programs		X	X	X	
Plats and maps	X				
Annual budget		X			
Administrative code	X				
Job descriptions and specifications		X			
Training programs	X				
Resolutions	X				
Ordinances	X				
Citizen complaints				X	
Finance Department					
City programs	X				
Taxes		X	X		
Liens			X		
Government programs	X				
Financial reports		X	X		
Revenue sharing programs		X	X		
Community development	X				
Instruments and investment funds			X		
Employee retirement information					X
Accounting information			X		
Employee payroll information (T&A report)					X
Master data file on every employee					X
Leave information				X	X
Employee insurance					X
Vehicle maintenance system			X		
Revenues and expenditures		X	X		
Travel expense statements			X		
Batch total record reports					X
Administrative code	X				
Bills and invoices				X	
City Clerk					
City Commission minutes					X
City ordinances	X				
Zoning ordinance	X				
Resolutions	X				
Information pertaining to city licenses				X	
City charter	X				
Administrative Code	X				
Oaths of office on all city officials	X				
Surety bonds on city employees	X				
Plats and maps of city	X				
Election budget of candidates for City Commission	X				
All city contracts	X				
Improve districts			X		
Annual budget		X			
Requests from citizens				X	

Table 8.9 (Cont'd.)

	Periodically	Annually	Monthly	Daily	Biweekly
Public Works Director					
Building regulations and codes	X				
Permits from governmental regulatory agencies	X				
Improvement projects			X	X	
Subdivision regulations	X				
Sanitary assessment programs			X		
Budget information		X			
City code	X				
Citizen complaints				X	
City building maintenance records			X	X	
Refuse collection contracts		X			
Animal control ordinances	X				
Vehicle maintenance records			X		
Construction programs			X	X	
Equipment inventory			X		
City maps and plats	X				
Zoning ordinances	X				
Rate studies		X			
Plan specifications		X	X	X	
Inspection reports				X	
All federal, state, and county ordinances dealing with engineering	X				
Utilities Authority reimbursements to general funds			X		
Personnel Director					
Application for employment				X	
Test scores of applicants				X	
Employee grievances	X				
Training programs	X				
Salary information				X	X
Employee file maintenance			X	X	
Job descriptions and specifications			X		
Leave request				X	
Batch total record reports					X
Time and attendance records					X
Budget information			X		
Personnel action forms				X	
Vacancy notices	X				
Affirmative action information	X				
Labor market information	X				
Labor relations information	X				
Administrative code	X				
Building and Zoning Department					
Improvement projects		X	X	X	
Contractor applications				X	
Building permits				X	
Certificates of contractors' building competence	X				
Sewer and gas connections				X	
Board of Adjustments and Appeals applications			X		
Notification of code violations and action taken				X	
Zoning maps	X				
Minutes of Board of Adjustments and Planning Board					X
Zoning	X				

Note: All codes of ordinances are updated as changes arise.

Table 8.9   (Cont'd.) List of Files

1. Accounting Files
   A. Budget systems
   B. Cash flow analysis
   C. Budget evaluation reports
   D. Financial reports
   E. General ledger
   F. Annual information
   G. Journal vouchers
   H. Bank reconciliations
   I. Accounts payable
   J. Accounts receivable
   K. Budget of expense
   L. Construction accounting

2. Order Entry and Billing Files
   A. Order allocation
   B. Order standard costing
   C. Order entry
   D. Billing and invoicing
   E. Order writing

3. Corporate Support Files
   A. Shareholder analysis reports
   B. Stock dividend
   C. Mortgage and real estate
   D. Leasing reports
   E. Automated mailing
   F. Insurance
   G. Stock option
   H. Stock transfer

4. Data Processing Files
   A. Design callouts
   B. Documentation systems
   C. MIS system
   D. Table update and maintenance
   E. Data processing—regional center
   F. MIS systems reports
   G. Special studies—MIS director and staff
   H. DOS-OS Conversion

5. Experimental—Research Files
   A. Research
   B. Paper testing

6. Forecasting—Marketing Files
   A. Forecasting—annual
   B. Forecasting—monthly
   C. Marketing reports
   D. Market research
   E. Forecasting—weekly

7. Logistics—Inventory and Purchasing Files
   A. Fixed assets
   B. Production inventories
   C. Log accounting
   D. Lands and minerals
   E. Purchase order systems
   F. Raw materials inventories

G. Stores inventories
H. Work-in process inventory
I. Construction stores

8. Modeling Functions Files
   A. Matrix generator
   B. Scheduling network (PPS IV)
   C. Model solution retrieval
   D. Model solution (linear programming)

9. A. Production analysis
   B. Cost report
   C. Production cost estimating
   D. PIC network—ship/production/inventory
   E. Plant maintenance
   F. Planning improvement
   G. Production reports
   H. Production scheduling
   I. Trim
   J. Pulpwood supply report

10. Personnel Resources Files
    A. Salary administration
    B. Payroll distribution
    C. Pension checks
    D. Industrial relations
    E. Mill and plant payrolls
    F. Pension reports
    G. Salary payroll
    H. Maintenance labor
    I. Payroll taxes
    J. Construction payroll

11. Sales Function Files
    A. Sales analysis
    B. Sales costs
    C. Sales network
    D. Sales report

12. Transportation Files
    A. Transportation system
    B. Automobile and heavy equipment leasing
    C. Packer rentals
    D. Outside rentals

13. Teleprocessing and Communications Files
    A. CICS or analogous monitor
    B. On-line programming system
    C. Communications reports
    D. OSCAP or slow-speed network
    E. ATMS or text processors

14. Operating System and Installation Maintenance Files
    A. Systems backup
    B. OS/VS system generation
    C. OS/VS system maintenance
    D. OS utility routines

Source: Courtesy of St. Regis Paper Co.

System Outputs

System outputs are of two types. The first consists of information relating one system to another so that routine or cyclical work may be continued. The other is produced for management planning and control. In the latter case, we are interested in relating such information to manager-users. For each system, a schematic (Fig. 8.11) is helpful.

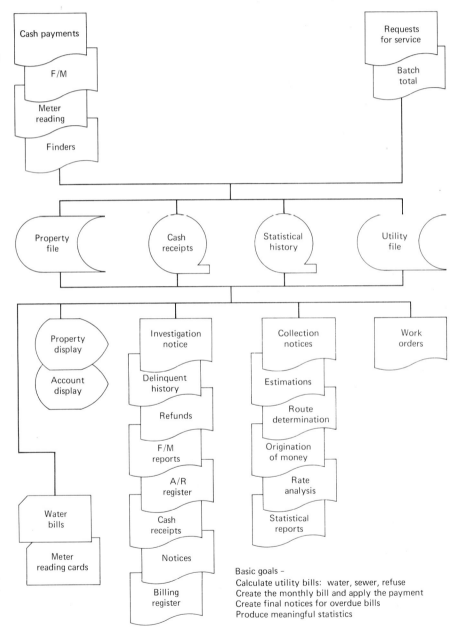

Figure 8.11
Utilities operating system and outputs

Basic goals –
Calculate utility bills: water, sewer, refuse
Create the monthly bill and apply the payment
Create final notices for overdue bills
Produce meaningful statistics

From the technical standpoint, output-data definition includes the specification of destination—i.e., where data go, what form they take, and who is responsible for receiving them. Included in the specifications are the distribution of output (who gets what, how many copies, and by what means), the frequency with which output will be called for and its timing, and the form the output will take (tape, hard copy, data terminal, etc.). Questions that the designer will ask in the process of developing output specifications include:

1. What form are the output reports to take? On-line or off-line?
2. Should the information be detailed, summary, or exception?
3. What can I do with the output data that will be reused at a later time?
4. What kind of hard copy output will be required? How many copies?
5. Are reports generated on demand? By exception? On schedule? At what frequency?

Despite the need to answer these details of output specification, the manager is concerned primarily with getting his or her information needs as previously determined in some type of output format. In other words, the consideration is how to *present the information to the eye or the ear of the manager*. The answer lies in the content and form design of the output. The form design is a direct function of information needs. Care should be taken not to ask for *too much* information *too frequently*. "Management by exception" and "information by summary" should be the guiding principles.

HARDWARE AND SOFTWARE CONFIGURATIONS

The general nature of the hardware should be developed for the conceptual design. Many possible combinations of equipment may be appropriate for a particular MIS. User needs; locations of users; type of data, files, and information involved; quantity of data; currency and frequency of information desired; and security are all primary considerations. Trade-offs must then be made against initial costs, operating and service costs, and flexibility for future changes. However, one or two possible concepts of computer system "architecture" should be established for further consideration and selection in the detailed design stage.

From Chapter 3 we recall that basic components of a computer system are:

1. Central processor unit
2. Primary storage
3. Input/output devices
4. Secondary storage
5. Teleprocessing equipment

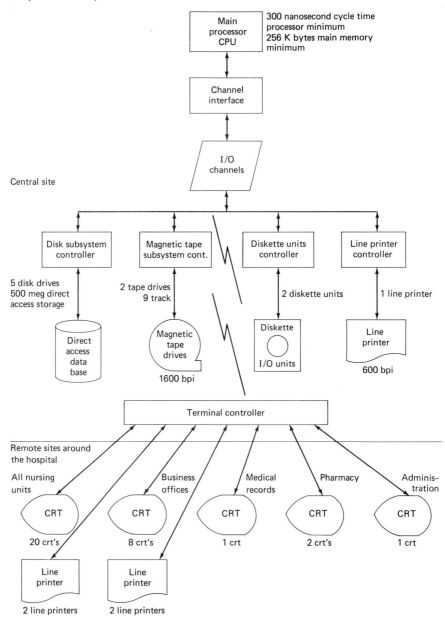

Computer hardware specifications for MIS

Figure 8.12 Computer architecture for Bethesda Memorial Hospital MIS

Sketches may be developed to indicate the nature and location of processing equipment, terminals, and teleprocessing lines (Fig. 8.12). A general description or a tentative listing may suffice, however. An example for a bank holding company is as follows:

1 main frame	1 card punch
1 operator console	3 tape drives
2 drum controllers	1 I/O controller
4 disk drives	7 modems
1 drum	31 character display terminals
1 card reader	7 leased telephone lines
2 printers	1 minicomputer terminal controller

Some estimate may be made of the total software requirements for the general type of computer architecture selected. This may be developed by listing desirable models, data-base management system, off-the-shelf programs, and applications to be developed in-house.

MAKING TRADE-OFF REVISIONS

Management continually makes decisions in the face of conflicting objectives and conflicting demands for resources. An MIS objective might be to keep all managers informed of all phases of the business. A conflicting objective is to make managers as productive as possible within their own areas of work. That is, time spent on their learning about other areas reduces time spent on their own jobs. Yet, the more a manager knows about the business as a whole, the better his decisions in his own area may be.

The basic characteristic of a trade-off is that more of one thing gives us less of another. The objective we seek is to make trade-offs among subsystems which will maximize total system performance. A basic trade-off, to start with, is the allocation of resources to MIS. If all of the company's resources were devoted to MIS, we would have a great MIS but no company (total system) output. On the other hand, if zero resources were devoted to MIS, total system performance might lead to disaster. Therefore, there must be a trade-off of resources among MIS and other activities to seek the optimum total system performance.

It is up to the managers, not the MIS designer or the technician, to decide upon trade-offs to be made in MIS design. The MIS design analyst provides the analysis of advantages and disadvantages to aid the managers in these decisions.

When the conceptual design is first completed, management should review possible alternative arrangements of people, equipment, and information flows, asking: what changes can we make that will provide more benefits in terms of costs?

DOCUMENTING THE CONCEPTUAL DESIGN

Although working papers are prepared as the MIS conceptual design progresses, these are not sufficient for recording the design. A formal report should be prepared, including such subjects as:

1. Background and need for the MIS
2. Objectives of the MIS

3. Constraints

4. Conceptual design
   a. List of managers, responsibilities, and information requirements
   b. Information flow charts
   c. Subsystems: inputs and outputs
   d. General description of the data base and list of files
   e. General description of the report system
   f. General description of the computer system
   g. Proposed organization
   h. Cost estimate for detailed design and implementation

SUMMARY The conceptual design of the MIS is a preliminary general description of the MIS elements and structural relationships. It is the most important phase for management because it determines the general performance of the eventual MIS. Management decisions on trade-offs throughout the conceptual design also establish costs and cost/benefit outcomes.

The conceptual design depends upon first making a study of the total system (the business or organization), identifying needs and constraints, establishing objectives of the MIS, and finally designing, approximately, the major components of the MIS. Cost, performance, and project schedules restrict the final design.

QUESTIONS AND PROBLEMS

1. In the blocks in the accompanying flow chart, fill in the steps in the conceptual design from the list below.

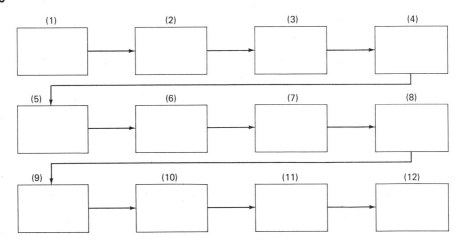

a. Document the design
b. Identify company problems
c. Determine information needs
d. Study the organization's division structure
e. Determine information sources
f. Scope the hardware and software

g. Prepare the organization for change
h. Block-diagram the MIS
i. Study the competition and industry
j. Make trade-off revisions

k. Identify system constraints
l. Study the operating systems

2. Indicate the information flow on the chart for a mass distributor of furniture.

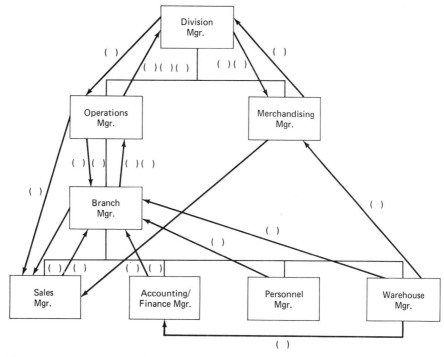

(1) Pricing policies
(2) Sales report
(3) Sales forecast
(4) Distribution costs
(5) Financial plan
(6) Purchasing budget
(7) Warehouse utilization
(8) Delivery schedule
(9) Supervisory expense
(10) Shipping schedule
(11) Government regulations
(12) Overhead cost budget
(13) Direct labor standards
(14) Buyer performance report
(15) Accounts payable
(16) Inventory control report

3. Indicate the frequency with which the managers should receive the indicated reports by checking the appropriate column in the following table:

	Daily	Weekly	Monthly	Quarterly	Annually

Merchandising Manager
a. Product performance
b. Price report
c. ROI report
d. Turnover rate
e. Market analysis
f. Sales forecast
g. Inventory status
h. Purchase-order log

Personnel Manager
i. Employee turnover rates
j. Employee efficiency
k. Wage/salary summary
l. Position openings
m. Absenteeism/tardiness

4. Sam Kane has been newly hired as MIS manager for a manufacturing company employing 1800 people. The company has depended upon reports that were developed as needed in the past. It has no computer system.

    a. Kane wants to study the organization structure, identify the important decisions, and identify who makes these decisions. How should he proceed?

    b. The company has 2300 regular customers throughout the United States and processes about 70 orders per day. It has a product mix that generally requires short runs on different machines. It also currently maintains a large inventory of finished goods in a warehouse adjacent to its plant. It employs 100 branch sales managers throughout the country. Discuss the general nature of a computer system that might be suitable for this firm.

5. Discuss reasons that different individuals might require different kinds of information if each were assigned to the same position at different times.

6. What is a basic source of all internal information?

7. Discuss the role of the accounting information system as part of the management information system.

8. Give an example of a decision involving a trade-off between:

    a. Customer service and writeoff of damaged goods
    b. Credit to customers and financial loss
    c. Promptness and accuracy in reporting
    d. Reliability and usefulness of information
    e. Managers' needs for information and cost of the MIS.

9. Obtain a position description of a manager. From this document, deduce the information that the manager would require to fulfill his responsibilities.

10. *Case Study: The Artcraft Company.* The Artcraft Company was formed in 1924 to service sign painters with supplies required by their trade. The company began simply as a jobber; sales were made through a simple 24-page catalog directed to sign painters and to stores dealing in such supplies.

    In 1928, Mr. E. C. Parsons, Artcraft's owner, developed a lettering device suitable for use by draftsmen, advertising art studios, sign painters, and others. At first, Artcraft had the parts made on the outside and then assembled and packaged the item. Subsequently, they undertook manufacture of a number of the component parts.

    The lettering device filled a particular market need; it was successful on its own and also was responsible for attracting business to the company's general line of supplies. Although the general economy deteriorated following 1928, Artcraft's sales went from $750,000 to $1.8 million by 1935.

    Following World War II, popular interest in painting escalated, and Artcraft's sales increased greatly, particularly with art supply stores. By 1960, their sales were nearly $10 million, of which $6 million was in items they manufactured—paints, brushes, palettes, and related items. The balance was imported or purchased domestically and packaged under Artcraft's name.

    In 1962, E. C. Parsons II entered the business after his graduation from business school. From the outset it was clear that he was both alert and aggressive. He concluded rather quickly that the company had been the fortunate victim of circumstances, that it had been carried along by the tides of a generally improved economy and the growing popularity of art as a hobby. In line with his belief that the company was far from having reached its potential, he proposed that the product line be increased, by amplifying the art supplies offerings and by extension into engineering and drafting supplies, and that a sales force be added to reinforce the catalog.

In 1964, the elder Parsons died. Young Parsons took over and immediately set the wheels in motion to move the company onto higher ground. He decided it would be too much of a financial strain on the company to both increase manufacturing activity and develop a sales force, and so it was decided to increase the line by jobbing rather than manufacturing additional items and to concentrate on sales force development.

By 1970, company sales had reached $18 million. Company strategy had taken hold. There were now 300 employees, handing 100,000 orders annually from distributors, art supply and drafting supply stores, hardware and paint stores, college book stores, advertising agencies' art departments, and industrial and research firms. In all, Artcraft had 18,000 customers, of whom 500 had annual purchases of $15,000 or more, and a line of nearly 12,000 items. Further increases in the range of 10% per year were expected.

Artcraft's accounting and information systems, which relied on manual and mechanical methods, were under the direction of Ed Simpson, who had been with the company for 20 years. Recently a number of problems had arisen. Although none were critical, in the aggregate they suggested that with further growth, present methods were likely to prove inadequate. The situation was reflected in comments by various company executives and workers:

George Saunders, sales vice president: "Our catalog is vital, both for mail orders and to support our salesmen. Considering the thousands of items we carry, a salesman could not function without it. Our problem here is our inability to get a catalog out on time even once a year. Even then it is filled with items that should have been dropped, and new items are often omitted. Under pressure of getting it out, we do not change prices to reflect cost changes. Actually, we should produce two catalogs a year, with supplements quarterly."

Al Beven, production vice president: "I'm spending too much time putting out fires. Most of our production problems are a matter of deciding between Urgent, Very Urgent, and Extra Very Urgent. This business was built on service to the customer. We still think this is the most important thing. Consequently, we make one short run after another just to have something in stock. The high cost of short runs takes a back seat to customer service."

Joe Dean, purchasing agent: "We now have many low-value, low-volume items on which we can't afford to keep unit inventory records. The warehouse is supposed to notify us when items reach reorder quantities. They don't; they either forget or don't care. You know, there is a lot of turnover in help there. In any event, most of my buyers spend half their day on the phone expediting shipment. They should be shopping for prices and new items and helping me with the catalog."

Al Parker, credit manager: "We have a lot of small accounts that I believe should be written off if they do not pay after a couple of reminders. Understand, I'm not sure our collection costs exceed our collections for small accounts, but it is my educated guess they do. Actually, just going through customer-account ledger cards to flag delinquent accounts costs us a fortune. On top of this, half the reminders that go out should never have been sent; during busy seasons it takes three days or more between receiving a collection and getting it onto the customer's records."

Mitch Webber, warehouse supervisor: "We keep feeding the order-editing department lists of items going out of stock and to be taken off back order status. It doesn't seem to make any difference. Practically every order we get lists out-of-stock items, and this means retyping and refiguring these invoices. Even worse, they are back-ordering items we have presently in stock. By the time they release the back orders, the items will be out again."

Artcraft's sales are firm; they are making money. In fact, they are having the best year in their history by a considerable margin.

Notes in the file of Al Beven, Production VP of Artcraft:

No. of Units in a Production Run	No. of Runs
1–99	13,510
100–500	18,050
600–900	3,100
1000 and over	220

Major Product Line*	Units of Sales/Product Line	Sales in Dollars
A	220,000	$ 3,000,000
B	191,000	5,200,000
C	165,000	2,900,000
D	160,000	1,981,000
E	98,000	3,800,000
F	40,000	520,000
G	25,000	310,000
H	4,000	30,000
I	4,000	19,000
J	1,000	400,000
		$18,160,000

*A product line may have between 1 and 180 items in the line to yield the 12,000 items Artcraft produces.

Notes in the file of George Saunders, Sales VP:

Year	Artcraft Sales (millions)	U.S. Disposable Personal Income (billions)
1935	1.81	58.5
1940	2.10	75.7
1945	2.90	150
1950	4.83	—
1955	6.95	—
1965	13.9	469
1975	24.4	—

Notes in the file of Al Parker, Credit Manager (industry data):

Bad-Debt Accounts	Approximate Debt/Equity	Years Business Has Been in Existence
12	0.85	1.5–2.0
25	0.75	1.0–2.0
30	0.75	0.5–1.0
10	0.50	0.5–1.0
3	0.85	3.0–5.0

a. List the management problems.
b. List management's information needs.
c. Draw a **conceptual** design flow chart showing flow of information to managers.

SELECTED REFERENCES

BARIFF, M. L., and E. J. LUSK, "Cognitive and Personality Tests for the Design of Management Information Systems," *Management Science,* April 1977.

BLUMENTHAL, SHERMAN C., *Management Information Systems: A Framework for Planning and Development.* Englewood Cliffs, N.J.: Prentice-Hall, 1969.

Business Systems Planning (GE-20-0527-1). White Plains, N.Y.: IBM, 1975.

CHASE, WILTON P., *Management of Systems Engineering.* New York: John Wiley, 1974.

Communications Oriented Production Information and Control System, Vols. I through VIII. White Plains, N.Y.: IBM, 1972.

DALTON, GENE W., PAUL R. LAWRENCE, and LARRY E. GREINER, eds., *Organizational Change and Development.* Homewood, Ill.: Richard D. Irwin, 1970.

DEBRABANDER, BERT, and ANDERS EDSTROM, "Successful Information Systems Development," *Management Science,* October 1977.

HERSHAUER, JAMES C., "What's Wrong with Our Systems Design Methods? It's Our Assumptions!" *Journal of Systems Management,* April 1978.

MEISTER, DAVID, *Behavioral Foundations of System Development.* New York: John Wiley, 1976.

MUNRO, MALCOLM C., "Determining the Manager's Information Needs," *Journal of Systems Management,* June 1978.

MURDICK, ROBERT G., "MIS Development Procedures," *Journal of Systems Management,* December 1970.

SRINIVASAN, C. A., and H. M. SCHOENFELD, "Some Problems and Prospects in Design and Development of Corporate-Wide Information Systems," *Management International Review,* February 1978.

WILKINSON, JOSEPH W., "Specifying Management's Information Needs," *Cost and Management,* September–October 1974.

ZALTMAN, GERALD, ROBERT DUNCAN, and JONNY HOLBEK, *Innovations and Organizations.* New York: John Wiley, 1973.

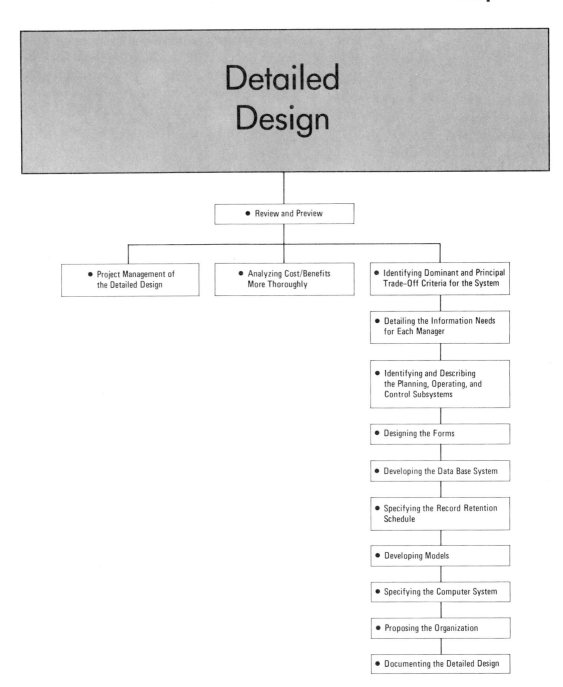

chapter 9

Detailed
Design

- Review and Preview

- Project Management of the Detailed Design
- Analyzing Cost/Benefits More Thoroughly
- Identifying Dominant and Principal Trade-Off Criteria for the System

- Detailing the Information Needs for Each Manager

- Identifying and Describing the Planning, Operating, and Control Subsystems

- Designing the Forms

- Developing the Data Base System

- Specifying the Record Retention Schedule

- Developing Models

- Specifying the Computer System

- Proposing the Organization

- Documenting the Detailed Design

PURPOSE: To present the steps required in the detailed design of the MIS and give a brief discussion of each

The primary objectives of all dedicated systems analysts should be to analyze thoroughly all systems, anticipate all problems, have answers to all problems, and move swiftly to fulfill management's changing MIS needs. However . . . when you're up to your neck in alligators, it is difficult to remind yourself that your initial objective was to drain the swamp.

The detailed design of the MIS consists of specifying everything about the MIS. Such specifications should be so complete that people unfamiliar with the project could implement the design.

A step-by-step explanation of how to develop the detailed design is not possible because:

1. Designing a system requires many simultaneous activities interacting with each other. A textbook description can follow only one sequence at a time.

2. There is no clear separation between the end of conceptual design and the start of the detailed design. The conceptual design is generally considered complete when the framework for the detailed design is established. This framework may include some detailed design, however.

3. Different designers will assume different states of the art. That is, one designer may design the MIS on present technology. A bolder designer may design on changes in technology anticipated for the implementation phase.

4. It is not possible to anticipate and describe the organizational reactions that may occur in given circumstances. Therefore, we may present only the technical approach for the general situation. In practice, modifications would be required as the detailed design developed.

5. Presenting all the details of the procedure and illustrations of specifications of the detailed design would obscure the main ideas. Digressions to explain techniques and tools would further confuse the main issues. On the other hand, if we present only generalizations, the reader gains no real understanding of the specifics of detailed design.

Within the limits imposed by these considerations, we shall attempt to present the main ideas of detailed design in this chapter. After the next chapter, which covers implementation, we shall take up a number of specialized topics that would be digressions were we to consider them in the designing and implementing chapters.

REVIEW AND PREVIEW

In a sense we are at the midpoint of MIS development. We have covered planning and the conceptual design. We now look forward to detailing and implementing the design. We have identified performance, cost, and time as factors interacting constantly with design and implementation. These factors provide constraints, requirements, and trade-off opportunities. Figure 9.1 presents a systems view of the design process as both a review and a preview.

PROJECT MANAGEMENT OF THE DETAILED DESIGN

Although the planning may have been simple for the conceptual design, it is apt to be more complex for the detailed design. There are many more steps to be taken, and costs rise rapidly if some people in the project are held up because of delays in other parts of the project. *Planning* and *control* are essential. The key steps are recapitulated here.

Project Planning

1. Establish the project objectives. This involves a review, subdivision, and refinement of the performance objectives established by the gross design.

2. Define the project tasks. The definition identifies a hierarchical structure of tasks to be performed in the design of the MIS and may be documented by work package instructions for large projects.

3. Plan the logical development of sequential and concurrent tasks and task activities. This usually requires a network diagram of events and activities.

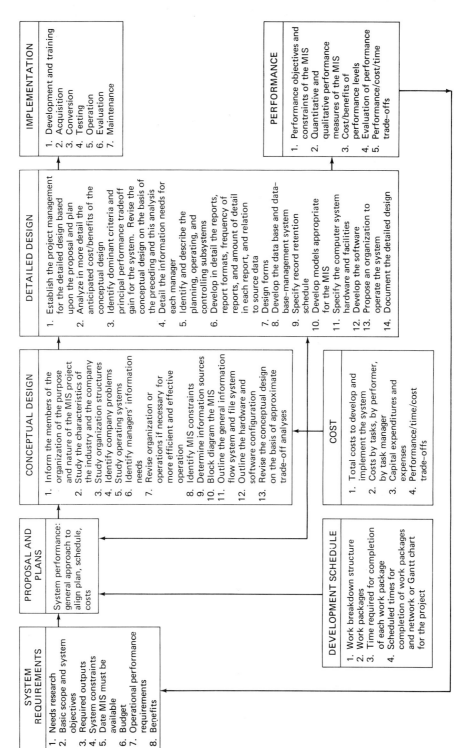

Figure 9.1 MIS development

4. Schedule the work as required by management-established end date and activity-network constraints. Essentially, the work and schedule are tied together by completion of the PERT (program evaluation and review technique) diagram.

5. Estimate labor, equipment, and other costs for the project.

6. Establish a budget for the project by allocating funds to each task and expenditures month by month over the life of the project.

7. Plan the staffing of the project organization over its life.

Project Control

1. Determine whether project objectives are being met as the project progresses.

2. Maintain control over schedule by changing work loads and emphasis as required by delays in critical activities.

3. Evaluate expenditure of funds in terms of both work accomplished and time. Revise the budget as required to reflect changes in work definition.

4. Evaluate manpower utilization and individual work progress, and make adjustments as required.

5. Evaluate time, cost, and work performance in terms of schedules, budgets, and technical plans to identify interaction problems.

ANALYZING COST/BENEFITS MORE THOROUGHLY

In the conceptual design report, the cost and benefits of the MIS are included. Before proceeding with the detailed design, a further analysis should be made based upon the more detailed plan. A search should be made for possible not-so-obvious costs. If specific problems occur in design *and* implementation, their cost should be estimated. Benefits should be questioned, but the value of better, more timely, information for managers should be explored thoroughly. Some possible benefits are indicated in Table 9.1. Allocating costs is even more difficult than estimating benefits. Some costs such as model building, software, and computer time can serve as a start. Data gathering and some overhead costs are difficult to estimate, however.

IDENTIFYING DOMINANT AND PRINCIPAL
TRADE-OFF PERFORMANCE CRITERIA FOR THE SYSTEM

Dominant criteria for a system are those that make an activity so important that it overrides all other activities. For example, a dominant criterion might be that the system operates so that there is never a stockout. This overrides the criterion of minimizing inventory cost. Such a criterion might hold for a company selling

Table 9.1
Estimating
benefits

MIS Output	Manager-User	Benefit	Estimated Annual Value
Market share	Mgr.—marketing	Can initiate promotional response immediately	$750,000
Engineering budget variances within three days after end-of-month	Mgr.—engineering	Can relocate resources and control costs	$52,000
Forecast of sales under differing assumptions of product mix, price, and economic conditions	Top management	Can adjust long and short range plans to increase profits	$2,700,000
Employee profile summary table	All managers	Top management can plan for replacement of key managers. All managers can hire and promote from within the company. Increased employee morale	$300,000

human blood, life-preserving drugs, or electric power. It might even hold for a company selling a consumer product in a situation where loss of a customer is permanent and all competitors have a no-stockout policy.

Examples of other dominant criteria might be one-day customer service, zero-defect product, specified price range for products, maintenance of multiple sources of supply for all materials and components purchased, or conformity of all research and engineering to long-range corporate plans. It is obvious that identification of the dominant criteria is necessary before subsequent design steps can proceed.

Trade-off criteria are those in which the criterion for performance of an activity may be reduced to increase performance of another activity. For example, the criterion of low manufacturing costs might be balanced against that of long-range public image of the firm achieved by reduction in environmental pollution. Again, the criterion of producing styles or models for many segments of the market might be balanced against that of maintaining low manufacturing and service costs.

The reason for identifying dominant and trade-off criteria is that as the detailed design is developed, decision centers (managers or computers) must be identified to achieve such criteria or to permit trade-offs. Further, the conceptual design should be reviewed at this point to determine whether changes must be made before proceeding.

In the development of the conceptual design, the first rough cut was made to uncover information needs of each manager. Once the concept of the MIS has been established, a careful and detailed determination of these needs must be made. The needs should be classified as:

1. Information important enough or used frequently enough to be provided by the MIS
2. Information so rarely used that it is less expensive to search for it when it is needed than to store it.

The information needs of a manager may be developed in detail by starting with an analysis of the position description, the objectives of the systems for which the manager is responsible, and types of environmental changes which impact these systems. Planning and controlling responsibilities should then be amplified. At this point, the manager and the systems analyst should meet to discuss typical problems and decisions that the manager faces throughout the year. As the manager describes his or her style of problem solving, the type of information desired will become more apparent. A review of reports that the manager currently receives and the degree to which the manager uses them will be helpful in this analysis.

Generally, the analyst should encourage the manager to control by exception and summary, so that volumes of detailed reports will not have to be sent to lie useless on the desk. For planning purposes, broader and more detailed information may be desirable. Environmental changes are apt to need more emphasis than historical data. Managers should not receive reports unless they are needed for their job at some particular time. Management information needs relative to information received will likely follow the pattern of Fig. 9.2. The objective of MIS design is to reduce data in the upper left and lower right quadrants.

The final step in identifying the manager's information needs is to prepare a detailed description of each item by specifying the following:

Information needed

Purpose of the information

Level of detail or aggregation

Frequency of reporting

Media (written, display, oral, etc.)

Format (organization of the information)

Time (monthly reports, for example, could be issued on the first or the fifteenth of the month)

Currency (how up-to-date is the information in the report when it is issued?)

Acceptable levels of reliability and precision.

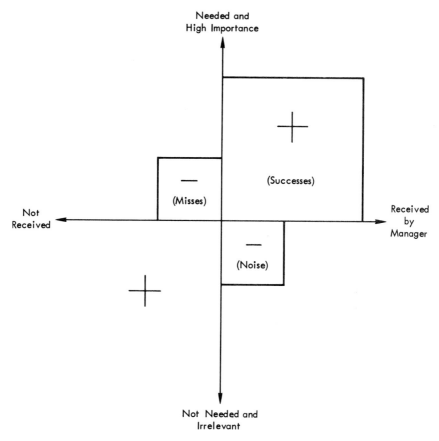

Figure 9.2
Measure of
information
need
satisfaction

Needed and
High Importance

(Successes)

(Misses)

Not
Received

Received
by
Manager

(Noise)

Not Needed and
Irrelevant

IDENTIFYING AND DESCRIBING THE PLANNING, OPERATING, AND CONTROL SUBSYSTEMS

In Chapters 4, 5, and 6 we covered flow-chart descriptions of planning, operating, and control systems. The detailed design for a system consists of the following:

1. System objectives
2. System flow charts
3. System narratives detailing each function of the system in nonjargon language
4. Record layouts
5. Source data for every program used by the system
6. Programs used
7. Procedures manual with easy-to-follow operating instructions
8. Output reports, formats, distribution, and retention.

Selected examples of the above will indicate the nature of detailed design. A complete detailed design of a single system is too extensive for our text. First, in Fig. 9.3, we show a statement of objectives for a General Ledger System. In this case, subsystems objectives are included.

Figure 9.3
Objectives of a
general ledger
system

PURPOSE AND SCOPE

Objectives

The objectives of a fully implemented General Ledger System can be summarized briefly as follows:

- To provide control over the company's financial books.
- To report, for management use and stockholder satisfaction, information showing the financial position of the company.
- To reduce peak workloads and the attendant expenses caused by the preparation of financial statements at month, quarter and year-end.
- To provide information that aids in evaluating an individual manager's performance with regard to meeting the financial and production goals of the company.
- To produce the information needed to analyze the profitability of each product and service of the company.

Subsystems

In order to meet the specific requirements of a company, MSA's General Ledger System has been subdivided into **five subsystems**. These are:

- General Ledger Accounting
- Budgeting
- Responsibility Reporting
- Cost Allocation
- Profitability Reporting

The first subsystem is **General Ledger Accounting**. This subsystem is responsible for performing several major functions:

- To capture, and maintain in detail, the financial and statistical data required by the other subsystems to report on profitability and performance.
- To produce the reports needed to evaluate the financial position of the company and the position of certain segments within it (such as subsidiaries, divisions, regions, products, or projects).
- To allocate, at point of entry, those income and expense items that can be directly associated with a product or project.

An effective and timely method of evaluating performance is a vital necessity in today's dynamic business environment. Performance can only be evaluated in relationship to a standard or plan. The second subsystem of MSA's General Ledger System, the **Budgeting Module,** helps management accomplish this objective. The Budgeting subsystem enables management to establish both historical (complete fiscal year) plans as well as variable budgets—short-range goals that are directly responsive to current sales and production requirements.

Figure 9.3
(Cont'd.)

The third module, the **Responsibility Reporting** subsystem, compares income and expense items, as well as any assets, liabilities, equity accounts and statistics, with the approved plan or budget, noting any variances. It also summarizes these individual reports to other levels of management within the hierarchy of the organization—a process traditionally referred to as the pyramiding of reports. One of the key features of MSA's General Ledger System is the fact that the Responsibility Reporting module draws its information from the data base aggregated by the General Ledger Accounting Subsystem. This integration of systems provides information that is credible and consistent.

Cost Allocation is the fourth subsystem. It differs from the preceding segments in that its primary purpose is not to account for data as it is entering the system, but rather to re-distribute or allocate financial information captured by and maintained in the General Ledger Accounting data base. Cost Allocation performs several diverse functions:

- It allocates administrative and service center costs (those responsibility or cost centers not responsible for profit) to cost centers or operating departments responsible for profit, products or both.
- It allocates the cost of a group of specified accounts for an administrative or service center to centers responsible for profit, products or both.
- It allocates the costs of a specific account from a designated support center to centers responsible for profit, products or both.
- It allocates either profit centers, or income and expenses not directly identifiable with products at point of entry, to products or services.

The fifth and last subsystem of MSA's General Ledger System is **Profitability Reporting.** Profitability reports allow management to bring together, for purposes of analysis, those incomes and expenses **directly incurred** (historical) by a profit center or product as well as any **indirect** (allocated) revenues or expenses. Profitability reports, thereby, permit an objective appraisal of a profit center's or product's net contribution. Both types of revenue and cost may be compared with an approved plan, and variances noted.

Source: MSA's General Ledger System, 1976. Courtesy of Management Science America, Inc.—The Financial Software Company.

An example of a detailed system flow chart is given in Fig. 9.4.

An abbreviated example of a system narrative for a Bill of Material Processing Subsystem is as follows:

The Bill of Material Processing Subsystem constructs the product structure file using the material file, product configurations, and parts usage data.

This subsystem provides the means for establishing relationships among material items and for making changes to these relationships as required. As part of establishing and maintaining the product structure, the subsystem also maintains the hierarchy of product structure level numbers.

This subsystem automatically creates and maintains level numbers of all material items. The level number contained in the data base is bottom-justified. All items that have no components are, by definition, the lowest level in the file. Level numbers refer to an internally generated low level code used to control the explosion process and product structure integrity.

The level number of any other item in the file is then computed as one more than the highest level number of its own components. Thus the end products have the highest level number in any product structure.

The raw materials and purchased parts of all structures are at level one. A material item appears only once in the file and therefore has only one level number.

Creation of a product structure involves the relating of material items to product subassemblies, assemblies, and end items. Each relationship is established by means of two pointers: a component pointer attached to the higher level item and a where-used pointer attached to the lower level item.

Any number of product structure relationships can be established by entering component transactions for each desired relationship, while material items are recorded only once.

Figure 9.4
Payroll system

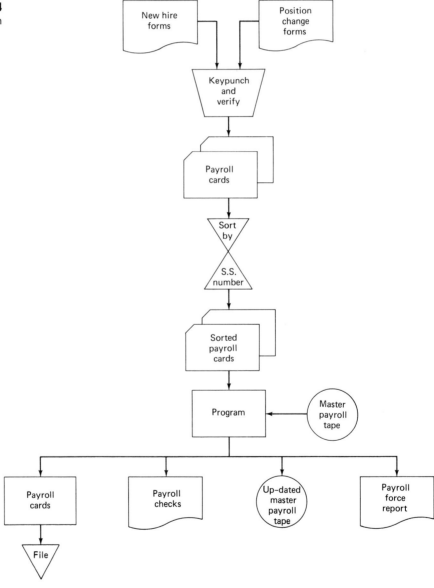

The component and where-used pointers are automatically generated by the subsystem on the basis of the relationship entered on the component transaction.

Apart from building and maintaining the product structure, the subsystem also provides single, multiple, and last level product structure inquiries. These capabilities use EXPLOSION and IMPLOSION techniques, which can also be implemented in user-developed applications, interfacing with the bill of material file.

The subsystem accepts a full range of transactions to maintain structure relationships.[1]

Record layouts may be in simple table form as portrayed in Table 9.2 or in special tabular form such as that shown in Fig. 9.5.

Table 9.2
Personnel master file: application record

Card	Card–Column	Field
1	1–3	Inquiry code
	4–12	Social security number
	13–14	Branch
	15–34	Last name
	35–44	First name
	45	Middle initial
	46–55	Telephone number
	56–60	Job code
	61–65	Primary position desired
	66–70	Second position sought
	71–75	Salary level
	76–80	Start date D/M
2	1–3	Shift priority
	4–9	Date of birth M/D/YR
	10–11	Age
	12	Handicap code
	13	Marital status
	14–33	Address
	34–48	City, state
	49–53	Zip code
	54–55	Years of education
	56–58	Degree received
	59–63	Area of major
	64–67	Military status
	68–69	Total years of industry experience
	70–71	Years of experience in field
3	1–5	Position available
	6–10	Branch I.D. of position available
	11–15	Position available
	16–20	Branch I.D. of position available
	21–25	Position available

Source: Courtesy of Levitz Furniture Corp.

[1]Adapted from *Factor Inventory Management System/2000 Summary Description, 1974.* Courtesy of Honeywell Information Systems.

Figure 9.5 Record layout

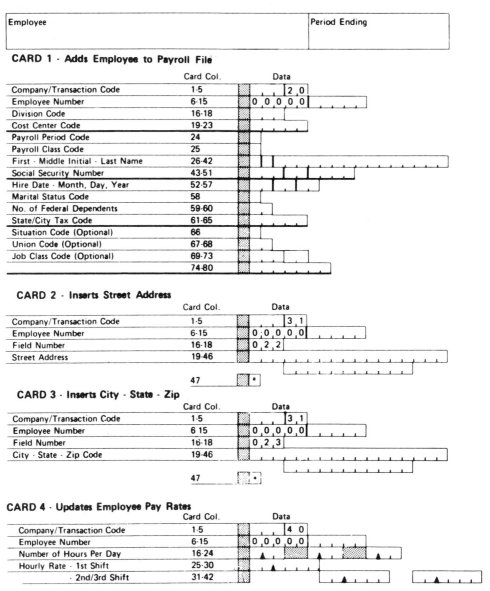

NEW EMPLOYEE DATA

Employee	Period Ending

CARD 1 - Adds Employee to Payroll File

	Card Col.	Data
Company/Transaction Code	1-5	2 0
Employee Number	6-15	0 0 0 0 0
Division Code	16-18	
Cost Center Code	19-23	
Payroll Period Code	24	
Payroll Class Code	25	
First - Middle Initial - Last Name	26-42	
Social Security Number	43-51	
Hire Date - Month, Day, Year	52-57	
Marital Status Code	58	
No. of Federal Dependents	59-60	
State/City Tax Code	61-65	
Situation Code (Optional)	66	
Union Code (Optional)	67-68	
Job Class Code (Optional)	69-73	
	74-80	

CARD 2 - Inserts Street Address

	Card Col.	Data
Company/Transaction Code	1-5	3 1
Employee Number	6-15	0 0 0 0 0
Field Number	16-18	0 2 2
Street Address	19-46	
	47	•

CARD 3 - Inserts City - State - Zip

	Card Col.	Data
Company/Transaction Code	1-5	3 1
Employee Number	6 15	0 0 0 0 0
Field Number	16-18	0 2 3
City - State - Zip Code	19-46	
	47	•

CARD 4 - Updates Employee Pay Rates

	Card Col.	Data
Company/Transaction Code	1-5	4 0
Employee Number	6-15	0 0 0 0 0
Number of Hours Per Day	16-24	
Hourly Rate - 1st Shift	25-30	
- 2nd/3rd Shift	31-42	
Fixed Pay Each Pay Period	43-49	

Source: PAY-RYTE Specification Manual. Courtesy of Condata

Source data may be tabulated by describing the source records employed by the system. Programs may be listed with code number for identification. The procedures manual should include the information or operation which triggers the procedure of the system, a list of work stations, a clear explanation of each operation in the procedure, the documents used in the procedure, and the act or information which terminates the procedure. Finally, output reports for operations within the system as well as outputs reports of the system as a whole should be described, including the format of the report, time of distribution, distribution, and retention of the report.

DESIGNING THE FORMS

In the systems sense, *any standardized communication that is an essential link in an operating procedure is the equivalent of a form.* Forms may appear as:

1. Preprinted forms on paper or cardboard
2. Formats stored for such computer outputs as printouts or video images
3. Punched tickets used for product and price coding in retailing
4. Edge-punched forms such as McBee Keysort
5. OCR (optical character recognition) forms for optical scanning and input to computers
6. MICR (magnetic ink character recognition) forms commonly used for banking checks
7. Microfilm and microfiche as media for standardized recording
8. Standard formats for regular periodic narrative reports to managements
9. Wall charts and video displays in corporate management "war rooms."

In the MIS, forms appear as inputs and outputs to systems as well as intermediate links. The detailed design of the MIS is concerned with the number of forms, the format, the physical media used, and the inventory.

Poor forms design may lead to costly operations and costly errors. Some major features of forms design and control are covered in Chapter 11.

DEVELOPING THE DATA-BASE SYSTEM

The manager-user desires information of good quality, when he needs it and at a cost as low as is consistent with his needs and the value of the information. He or she is generally not concerned with *how* the information is captured, stored, or retrieved. Two managers are exceptions: the MIS manager and the computer systems manager. In particular, the computer systems manager views the problem as one of data management, leading eventually to production of reports requested by management.

Let us look at the old days (which still exist for small companies). Each manager had several four-drawer file cabinets in his or her office. The manager's data base was this set of file cabinets, which gave access to information most frequently used. A set of folders bearing upon a single subject represented a file. Each folder contained a record consisting of a related set of elements of information. *From the user's viewpoint* these same concepts still exist and are defined as follows:

Data base—the aggregate of files required to meet the user's need. This aggregate, in a computerized MIS, is a collection of interrelated data stored with controlled redundancy to serve one or more applications. Thus there may be only one computerized data base to serve the whole company.

File—a related set of records.

Record—a collection of data elements related to a common identifier, such as a person, machine, place, or operation

Data element (sometimes called a *field*)—the lowest level of the data structure which conveys meaning and to which a specific value may be attached. For example, age, part number, expense, department, and name are data elements.

On one side of the coin we have the problem of determining what information, and hence what data, are of interest to the managers. On the other side we have the problem of developing computer hardware and software which will store and retrieve the data. The detailed design requires that we develop both these concepts fully. The computer aspect requires considerable technical amplification, however, so that it is covered in this book (in Chapter 14) only in principle.

The development of files and records for the detailed design is a continuation of the approach used in the conceptual design. The steps are as follows:

1. Develop information needs more fully.
2. Determine the data required as a basis for the information.
3. Relate, by means of tables or matrixes:

    a. Data to systems inputs and outputs.
    b. Data to information to managers.
    c. Data to organizational components.
    d. Data to files and records.
    e. Data to forms.
    f. Data to reports.

4. Analyze the data in item 3 in terms of economics and completeness. Record all needed data items on a form such as that in Fig. 9.6 for use by the data-base manager in the computer organization.
5. Summarize the file characteristics in terms of volatility, activity, size, and expandability (Fig. 9.7).

Figure 9.6
Data element
form

DATA ELEMENT DESCRIPTION

File Name _____

File Number _____ Date _____

Date Element _____

Field Element _____ Group Label _____

Form _____ Source _____

Maximum Length (Characters/Item Group) _____

Retention Characteristics _____

_____

Update Procedure _____

_____

_____

Initial Value _____

Units _____

Figure 9.7 File characteristics

	Volatility*	Activity*	Record Retention Period	File Size (Records)	Expandability (Records)
Customer File	M	H	Perm.	12000	15000
Vendor File	M	M	Perm.	1000	3000
Customer Order File	H	H	4 yr.	3000	5000
Purchase Order File	H	H	3 yr.	774	3000
Sales Data File	H	H	Temp.	9000	12000
Product File	L	H	20 yr.	75	125
Plant Master Schedule	H	H	Perm.	3000	5000
Master Parts List	L	L	Perm.	75000	150000
Inventory File	L	M	7 yr.	250	500
Operations File	H	H	Perm.	100	250
Engineering Design File	L	L	Perm.	25	125
Price Lists	H	H	Perm.	500	1000
Accounts Receivable File	H	H	10 yr.	10000	20000
Accounts Payable File	H	H	Perm.	2000	3000
Payroll File	L	H	3 yr.	125	250
General Ledger	L	H	Perm.	5000	15000

*H = high, M = medium, L = low

SPECIFYING THE RECORD RETENTION SCHEDULE

The volume of data to be stored in the data base is a function both of the data entered and the specified retention time for each record. Record retention is a critical design feature often overlooked until the MIS has been operating for some years. By that time, the files have expanded to the crisis state.

Every company must develop retention periods for its own unique files. Some sources for guides are:

Fair Labor Standards Act
Armed Services Procurement Regulation
Interstate Commerce Commission
Industrial Security Manual (attachment to DD Form 441)
Prentice-Hall's *Payroll Guide*
Corporate tax department audit requirements
Corporate legal department
Internal Revenue Code
Corporate Records Retention (requirements of state governments)
Federal Register—Guide to Record Retention
Federal Insurance Compensation Act
Federal Reserve Operating Circular No. 20
Walsh-Healey Act
Revenue Ruling 71-20

Figure 9.8 provides more specific suggestions for business records. Bankers Box, a Division of Fellowes Manufacturing Company, has also prepared a suggested schedule for bank records.

Figure 9.8 Suggested Retention Schedule for Business Records

The Retention Schedule shown below was determined by a nationwide survey of record retention schedules recommended by leading authorities on records storage and by the practices of businesses with established procedures. This schedule reflects current business thinking.

A word of caution: Although much study has gone into the preparation of this schedule, the retention periods shown are not offered as final authority, but as guideposts against which to check your company needs. Statutes of limitations for your State, as well as regulations of government agencies pertaining to your business must be considered. Also, there may be very good reasons to keep records longer than legally required, for historical or reference purposes.

To be sure that you establish retention periods that are both legal and practical for your own company, follow the procedure outlined on pages 6 to 10 of this Handbook.

For retention requirements established by Federal laws and regulations, see the current "Guide to Record Retention Requirements" published annually in the Federal Register which can be obtained at nominal cost from the Superintendent of Documents, U.S. Government Printing Office, Washington, D.C. 20402.

KEY:

"P" means Permanently, "O" stands for Optional, otherwise the figures represent the suggested number of years for retaining the records.

Figure 9.8 (Cont'd.)

Accounting and Fiscal

Accounts, charged off	7
Accounts payable ledger	P
Accounts receivable	10
Accounts receivable ledger	10
Balance sheets	P
Bank deposit record	7
Bank reconcilement papers	7
Bank statements	7
Bills collectible	7
Bills of sale of registered bonds	3
Bill stubs	7
Bonds cancelled	3
Bonds registered	P
Bonds, sales or transfer	P
Budget work sheets	2
Capital stock bills of sales	P
Capital stock certificates	P
Captial stock ledger	P
Captial stock transfer records	P
Cash books	P
Cash receipts & disbursement records	P
Cash sales slips	3
Cash slips	3
Charge slips	10
Check records	7
Check register	P
Checks, dividend	6
Checks, expense	9
Checks, paid & cancelled	9
Checks, payroll	7
Checks, voucher	6
Checks, warrants	P
Correspondence, accounting	5
Correspondence, credit & collection	7
Cost account records	7
Customer ledger	P
Donations	7
Drafts paid	8
Earnings register	3
Entertainment, gifts & gratuities	3
Estimates, projections	7
Expense reports, departmental	5
Expense reports, employee	7
Financial statements, certified	P
Financial statements, periodic	P
Fixed capital records	P
General cash book	P
General journal	P
General journal supporting papers	P
General ledger	P
Notes, cancelled	10
Note ledgers	P
Payroll register	7
Petty cash records	4
Plant ledger	P
Profit and loss statements	P
Property asset summary	10
Royalty ledger	P
Salesman commission reports	6
Stock ledger	P
Tabulating cards & magnetic tape	1
Traveling auditor reports	15
Trial balance, accounts receivable	3
Trial balance sheets	P
Uncollectible accounts	7
Work papers, rough	2

Administrative

Audit reports, internal	6
Audit reports, public & government	P
Audit work papers, internal	6
Classified documents: control, inventories, reports	5
Correspondence, accounting	5
Correspondence, advertising	3
Correspondence, credit & collection	7
Correspondence, engineering & technical	10
Correspondence, general	3
Correspondence, personal	6
Correspondence, production	3
Correspondence, purchase	5
Correspondence, sales & service	3
Correspondence, tax	P
Correspondence, traffic	5
Forms control	P
Inventory cards	3
Inventory, plant records	P
Organized charts	P
Requisitions	3
Research reports	P
System & procedure records	P
Telegram & cable copies	4
Telephone records	P

Advertising

Activity reports, media schedules	5
Contracts	P
Correspondence	3
Drawings & artwork	5
Estimates	2
House organs	P
Market data & surveys	5
Samples, displays, labels, etc.	P
Tear sheets	3

Corporate

Annual reports	P
Authority to issue securities	P
Authorization & appropriations for expenditures	3
Bonds, surety	7
Capital stock certificates	P
Capital stock ledger	P
Capital stock transfer records	P
Charters, constitution, bylaws & amendments	P
Contracts, advertising	7
Contracts, employee	P
Contracts, government	P
Contracts, labor union	P
Contract, vendor	P
Dividend checks	6
Dividend register	P
Easements	20

Figure 9.8 (Cont'd.)

Election ballots	20
Election records, corporate	P
General cashbooks, treasurers' and auditors'	P
Incorporation records & certificates	P
Licenses, federal, state, local	P
Permits to do business	P
Records of mergers, consolidations, acquisitions, dissolutions & reorganizations	P
Reports to Securities & Exchange Commission	P
Securities: documents of issuance, listing, & registration	P
Stock applications for issuance	P
Stock certificates, cancelled	P
Stock, stock transfer & stockholders records	P
Stockholder minute books, resolutions	P
Stockholder proxies	10
Stockholder reports	P
Voter proxies	15

Executive

Correspondence	P
Policy statements, directives	P
Projects, ideas, notes	P
Research reports	P
Speeches, publications	P

Insurance

Accident reports	P
Appraisals	P
Claims, automobile	10
Claims, group life & hospital	10
Claims, loss or damage in transit	5
Claims, plant	P
Claims, workmen's compensation	10
Expired policy, accident	8
Expired policy, fidelity	8

Expired policy, fire	7
Expired policy, group	P
Expired policy, hospital	7
Expired policy, inspection certificates	7
Expired policy, liability	8
Expired policy, life	8
Expired policy, marine	7
Expired policy, property	8
Expired policy, surety	10
Expired policy, workmen's compensation	10

Legal

Affidavits	10
Charters	P
Claims & litigation of torts & breach of contract	P
Copyrights	P
Mortgages	P
Patents & related data	P
Trademarks	P

Manufacturing

Authorities for sale of scrap	3
Bills of material	3
Blueprints	P
Correspondence, engineering & technical	10
Correspondence, production	3
Credit memoranda	5
Credit ratings & classifications	7
Drafting records	P
Drawings & tracings, original	P
Inspection records	2
Inventory records	7
Invoice copies	6
Invoices, received	7
Job records	P
Journals	P
Ledgers	P
Operating reports	P
Order register	P
Production reports	3
Quality control reports	5
Receipts, delivery	3
Reliability records	P

Specifications, customer	P
Stores issue records	3
Time & motion studies	P
Tool control	3
Work orders	5

Personnel

Accident reports, injury claims, settlements	P
Applications, changes, terminations	P
Attendance records	7
Clock records	5
Correspondence	6
Daily time reports	5
Disability & sick benefits records	6
Earnings records	P
Employee service records	P
Employee contracts	P
Fidelity bonds	3
File, individual employee, after separation	5
Garnishments	5
Health & safety bulletins	P
Injury frequency charts	P
Insurance records: group, employee	11
Medical folders, employee	5
Paychecks	7
Payroll records, after termination	10
Pension plan	P
Pension plan, applications	P
Pension plan, claims	P
Pension plan, correspondence	P
Rating cards	3
Salary and rate changes	8
Salesmen auto records	2
Salesmen performance records	P
Salesmen expense accounts	2
Time cards	5
Time tickets	5
Time tickets, receipted	P
Training manuals	P
Union (collective bargaining) agreements after termination	3

Figure 9.8 (Cont'd.)

Withholding, exemption certificates	10	Receiving reports	5	Dividend register	P
Workmen's compensation reports	10	Receiving slips	4	Employee withholding certificates	10
		Vendor contracts	7	Exemption status	P
Plant and Property				Excise reports	P
		Sales and Marketing		Inventory reports	P
Appraisals	P	Claims (loss or damage)	2	Real estate	P
Damage reports	7	Complaints	7	Sales & use	P
Deeds, titles	P	Contract progress reports	3	Social security	P
Depreciation schedules	P	Contracts, customers	3	Tax bills & statements	P
Inventory records	P	Contracts, representatives, agents, distributors, etc.	3	Tax returns & working papers	P
Leases	P	Correspondence	3		
Maintenance & repair, buildings	10	Discount rates	P	**Traffic**	
Maintenance & repair, machinery	5	Guarantees, warrantees	P	Aircraft operating & maintenance	P
Plans & specifications	P	Invoices, copies	6	Bills of lading	2
Plant account cards, equipment records, historical folders	P	Invoices received	7	Delivery reports	3
		Mailing & prospect lists	P	Employee travel	1
Purchase, lease records	P	Market research studies & analysis	P	Export declarations	4
Sales	P	Market surveys	P	Freight bills	5
Space allocation records	2	Orders acknowledgment	4	Freight claims	5
Taxes	P	Orders filled	6	Leases	P
Water rights	P	Price lists	P	Manifests	3
		Shipping notices & reports	3	Receiving documents	3
Purchasing		Tax—exempt sales	P	Routing records	1
Acknowledgements	3			Shipping instructions	5
Bids, awards	3	**Taxation**		Shipping tickets	6
Contracts	3	Agent's reports	P	Title papers	P
Correspondence	5	Annuity or deferred payment plan	P	Tonnage summaries	P
Exception notices	6	Correspondence	P	Tracer reports	P
Purchase orders	3	Depreciation schedules	P	Vehicle operation & maintenance	2
Purchase requisitions	3				
Quotations	3				

Source: Courtesy of Bankers Box Records Storage Systems, Division of Fellowes Manufacturing Company

DEVELOPING MODELS

Models are abstractions or representations of reality. Symbolic models are those which are expressed in alphabetical and numerical symbols, such as equations and inequations. The purpose of a model may be to (a) suggest an optimum solution to a problem, or (b) provide information to assist a manager in decision making. To computer technicians, a model which is programmed is called an "application."

Modeling is an ongoing process in companies. However, during the development of the MIS, a number of basic models which the company feels it must have should be developed. These models are often developed by operations research personnel (management scientists).

SPECIFYING THE COMPUTER SYSTEM

The computer system is specified in the detailed design. Such a specification would include such items as the hardware components, the location of components, the complete architecture of the hardware system, the basic software programs, the organization required to operate and maintain the system, the facilities required, and the training programs. Proposals for the computer system are prepared by the manager of the computer systems center. Selection and other decisions should be made by top management.

PROPOSING THE ORGANIZATION

The MIS will very likely require new positions and abolishment of old positions. Workers as well as managers will be doing things differently and doing new things. The system approach which leads to a new MIS will likely require modifications of the organization. Therefore, the MIS team should propose a new organization to match the new MIS.

DOCUMENTING THE DETAILED DESIGN

Documentation is not a new concept or practice. It has, however, become increasingly important as systems have grown more complex and more costly. Documentation is one of the most important steps in MIS development and the one least adequately performed.

Documentation is the physical record, generally in written or printed form, of the following:

1. Policies and standards relating to MIS development, implementation, operation, and maintenance
2. The design of the MIS
3. Procedures for installing the MIS
4. Procedures for operating the MIS
5. Procedures for maintaining (revising) the MIS.

It provides descriptions of the system in general or summary form and then in the finest detail. *The MIS has not been completely designed until the documentation has been completed.*

Purposes of Documentation

Documentation of the MIS may save a company hundreds of thousands of dollars. Some companies have depended on a key individual who has kept the information flows and programs in his head, only to have him leave the company. The company's only choice was then to restudy the entire system and document it or design a new system. Some of the reasons, then, that *good* documentation is important are:

1. Turnover of key personnel. If the MIS designer failed to document the system or did an inadequate or piecemeal job, his successor must restudy the system to solve problems or make modifications.

2. The MIS will require modification, either for improvement or because of changing conditions. Even if there is no personnel turnover, it is very unlikely that systems analysts can retain all details of the MIS in their heads over a period of time.

3. The increasing complexity of the fourth- and fifth-generation computer systems and data transmission systems will require documentation so that the original systems designers will not have to keep refamiliarizing themselves with equipment as the MIS design progresses.

4. Equipment conversion will require new flow charts and new programs. Good documentation will make this much easier to carry out.

5. Documentation will reveal poor design features and lack of standards so that corrective action may be taken.

Specification and Standardization

Specification

Specification means a clear, sufficiently detailed description. At the beginning of the MIS design process, *performance* specifications are prepared that describe objectives of the system. During the detailed design process, *design* specifications should be prepared that describe the systems. Then *operating* specifications should be prepared that describe the functions and activities of personnel who run the system. Finally, *test* specifications describe the tests and their conduct for checking out the system.

Standardization

The use of standardized procedures and documentation provides a basis for clear, rapid communication, for less costly training of analysts, for reduced filing costs, and for assessing performance of the analysts and the MIS.

Standardization means that standard symbols are used in all flow charts, that procedures manuals are prepared to prescribe standardized MIS and operating procedures, and that standardized forms are used for documentation.

Sources of standards are:

1. American National Standards Institute (ANSI) and International Standards Organization (ISO)

2. Industry users

3. Manufacturers

4. Published articles and books

5. Internal company staff organizations.

Maintenance of standards is achieved by publication of a manual of standards and proper training and control.

Documentation Manual

Documentation of the MIS should be combined into a *documentation manual*. Table 9.3 suggests the possible contents of such a manual.

The reasons for poor documentation stem from the attitude of management. When management constantly presses for new developments and new jobs, documentation receives a low priority. Documentation is a tedious, detailed job at best, and systems designers are only too glad to turn to new, more exciting work. If management wants good documentation, it must rate the documentation manual as the completion event of design. Until the manual has been published, the MIS project manager must retain responsibility for an unfinished project.

Table 9.3 Documentation manual

Topic	Purpose	Forms	Tables	Diagrams	Narrative
I. General Concept of the MIS	Gives a general overview for management				
A. Strategic MIS objectives	Shows long-range direction of the MIS		X	X	X
B. MIS policies/constraints	Defines limitations on MIS development				X
C. Current MIS objectives	Defines the scope of current MIS projects		X		X
D. Performance specifications	States the required performance characteristics of currently planned MIS, preferably in quantitative terms		X	X	X
E. Concept of operating systems	Shows the relationship of activities among the operating systems			X	X
F. MIS information flow	Shows the flow of principal elements of information to each manager			X	X
G. Data-base outline	Lists the principal files		X		X
H. Outline of computer system	Indicates scope of computer operations		X	X	X
I. Major organizational changes	Indicates major changes in operations		X		X
II. Detailed Design	Provides the specifications for the MIS in detail for implementation				
A. Detailed specification of managers' information needs	Basis for entire design	X	X		X
B. Detailed description of the planning, operating, and controlling subsystems	Basis for capturing data and reporting information to ensure information needs will be met	X	X	X	X
C. Forms	Specifies in detail the design of all forms used in systems inputs, operations, and outputs	X			

Table 9.3 (Cont'd)

Topic	Purpose	Forms	Tables	Diagrams	Narrative
D. Reports	Specifies design of all reports required for decision making, planning, and controlling to ensure completeness and minimize redundancy		X		X
E. Record retention schedule	Limits storage of completed forms and reports		X		
F. Models	Abstracts of models. (Complete models may be documented in a separate volume)			X	X
G. Data base	Specifies files and records, data elements, and data relationships	X	X	X	X
H. Detailed design of the computer system	Shows hardware, computer architecture, facilities, and organization	X	X	X	X
I. Software	Lists software applications and purposes. (Complete software programs may be documented in separate volumes.) Special language			X	X
J. Detailed organizational changes	Shows new manpower requirements, new position changes, and new relationships			X	X
III. Operation	Shows how the MIS operates				
A. Sequence of steps performed to operate the subsystems	Documents the operating steps in relation to the design		X	X	X
B. Work stations responsible for each step	Shows who is responsible for each aspect of the MIS		X		X
C. Management inquiry procedures	Shows active mode of management as opposed to passive reception of information		X		X

SUMMARY   When the general framework of the MIS has been established by the conceptual design report, the detailed specification of every feature of the MIS follows. The detailed design requires many man-hours of work, so that a review of the project plan should be made at this time.

Figure 9.1 summarizes the steps in detailed design. The major phases are:

1. Factor the cost, time, and performance into trade-offs which will optimize the general design of the MIS.
2. Develop in detail the information needs of each manager.
3. Develop the subsystems in detail.
4. Develop the data-base system.

5. Develop the hardware and software requirements.

6. Revise the organization as necessary to match the proposed subsystems and MIS.

In theory, MIS development may seem to be a straightforward process. In practice, the problems of integrating human, technical, economic, time, and priority factors have sunk many a project. The cost of failure is not a negligible one, as evidenced by Table 9.4.

Table 9.4 Prototypal MIS development failures

Industry	Application	Original Development Cost Estimate ($ MM)	Original Payback Period Estimate (Years)	Development Cost Incurred at Abandonment ($ MM)	Development Cost Estimate at Abandonment ($ MM)	Payback Period Estimate at Abandonment (Years)
Utility	Customer information	2.5	4	7.0	15.0	15
Consumer goods	Order processing	0.9	3	2.5	5.5	Net cost increase
Banking	Integrated loan	1.5	—	1.3	2.5	Net cost increase
Petroleum	Well information	1.0	—	0.9	—	Net cost increase
Insurance	Customer accounting	1.3	4	1.9	4.0	12

Source: John V. Soden, "Understanding MIS Failures," **Data Management,** July 1975, p. 31.

QUESTIONS AND PROBLEMS

1. In the table that follows, suggest the principal manager-user of the MIS output, a possible benefit, and whether the benefit is roughly measurable in terms of dollars (Yes or No).

MIS Output	Manager-Users	Benefit of the Information	Roughly Measurable in Dollars
a. Cash flow projection			
b. Cancellation of a large order by a long-time customer			
c. Technological breakthrough in a new product of the company's			

MIS Output	Manager-Users	Benefit of the Information	Roughly Measurable in Dollars

d. Average age of equipment exceeds seven years

e. Productivity declining in one division while increasing in others

f. Salaries not keeping pace with inflation

2. Use the following code to evaluate information relative to the managers listed below.

NHR—needed and of high importance, received by the manager
NHN—needed and of high importance, *not* received by the manager
NNN—not needed and *not* received
NNR—not needed and received

Manager of marketing

_____ a. Receives information on an engineering test

_____ b. Does not receive information about a new competitive product

_____ c. Does not receive a report of cash flow

_____ d. Receives sales forecast from marketing research

_____ e. Receives shop loading schedule

Manager of manufacturing

_____ f. Receives a report of sales by area and salesperson

_____ g. Receives a raw materials status report

_____ h. Does not receive a report of an issue of securities

_____ i. Receives report of large labor variance

Complete with an example:

President

NHR j.

NHN k.

NNN l.

NNR m.

3. For the loan system of a bank, indicate the process by placing the appropriate letter code in each charting symbol.

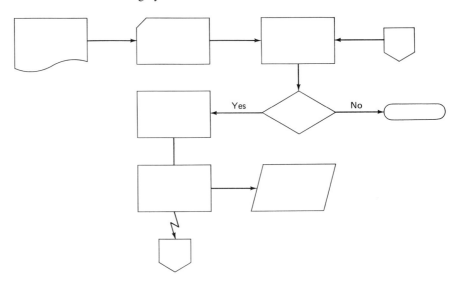

(a) Print reports
(b) Edit loan transactions
(c) Loan files via telecommunications
(d) Update files
(e) New accounts, delinquent accounts, alterations

(f) Key-punch cards from input sheets
(g) Edit good?
(h) Alterations made from terminals
(i) Process input
(j) Transmit loans via telecommunications

4. Explain by narrative the operations and transactions in the system diagram on the next page.

5. How are company policies related to dominant criteria for the design of the MIS?

6. Differentiate between performance specifications and design specifications.

7. An MIS could periodically produce one complete report that would include all information required by all managers. Alternatively, several hundred special reports could be issued at varying periods, each tailored to a particular manager. The reporting system of companies lies between these two extremes. What considerations go into designing the number of reports, content, and publication frequency?

8. How would a system of checklists help a systems analyst in MIS design? What topics would you include in such a checklist?

9. If you were developing a new total MIS, what reasons would you have to develop the accounting information system first?

10. Prepare a narrative for the objectives (purpose and scope) of:

    a. A materials control information system.
    b. A bank's mortgage loan information system.
    c. A hospital patient-admission information system.
    d. A department store's merchandising information system.

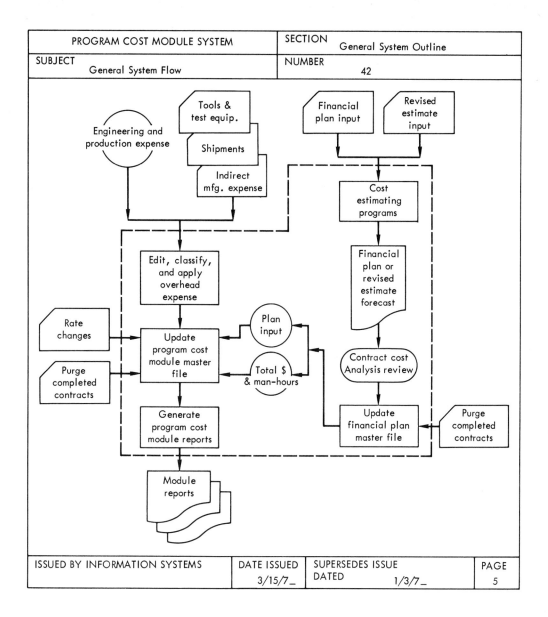

PROGRAM COST MODULE SYSTEM	SECTION General System Outline
SUBJECT General System Flow	NUMBER 42

Tools & test equip.

Engineering and production expense

Shipments

Indirect mfg. expense

Financial plan input

Revised estimate input

Cost estimating programs

Edit, classify, and apply overhead expense

Financial plan or revised estimate forecast

Rate changes

Plan input

Update program cost module master file

Contract cost Analysis review

Purge completed contracts

Total $ & man-hours

Generate program cost module reports

Update financial plan master file

Purge completed contracts

Module reports

ISSUED BY INFORMATION SYSTEMS	DATE ISSUED 3/15/7_	SUPERSEDES ISSUE DATED 1/3/7_	PAGE 5

SELECTED REFERENCES

BINGHAM, J. E., and G. W. P. DAVIES, *Handbook of Systems Analysis.* New York: Halsted Press (Wiley), 1972.

BURCH, JOHN G., JR., FELIX R. STRATER, JR., and GARY GRUDNITSKI, *Information Systems: Theory and Practice,* 2d ed. New York: John Wiley, 1979.

"Corporate 'War Rooms' Plug Into the Computer," *Business Week,* August 23, 1976.

CUSHING, BARRY, E. *Accounting Information Systems and Business Organizations,* 2d ed. Reading, Mass.: Addison-Wesley, 1978.

DAVIS, GORDON B., *Management Information Systems: Conceptual Foundations, Structure, and Development.* New York: McGraw-Hill, 1974.

HARTMAN, W., H. MATHES, and A. PROEME. *Management Information Systems Handbook.* New York: McGraw-Hill, 1968.

How Order Information Serves Apparel Management. Arlington, Va.: American Apparel Manufacturer's Association, 1974.

MARTIN, JAMES, *Principles of Data Base Management.* Englewood Cliffs, N.J.: Prentice-Hall, 1976.

MENKUS, BELDEN, "Defining Adequate Systems Documentation," *Journal of Systems Management,* December 1970.

MITCHELL, WILLIAM E., "Records Retention Schedules," *Journal of Systems Management,* August 1977.

MURDICK, ROBERT G., et al., *Accounting Information Systems.* Englewood Cliffs, N.J.: Prentice-Hall, 1978.

PALMER, IAN, *Data Base Systems: A Practical Reference,* 2d ed. Wellesley, Mass.: QED Information Sciences, Inc., 1975.

Records Retention Timetable. Electric Wastebasket Corp., 145 West 45th St., New York, N.Y. 10036.

RUBIN, MARTIN L., *Introduction to the System Life Cycle.* Princeton, N.J.: Brandon/Systems Press, 1970.

SIMON, CHARLES K., and DONALD L. GERBER, "Fully Automated Records Management," *Journal of Systems Management,* May 1978.

VOICH, DAN, JR., HOMER J. MOTTICE, and WILLIAM A. SCHRODE, *Information Systems for Operation and Management.* Cincinnati: South-Western Publishing Co., 1975.

WEAVER, BARBARA N., and WILEY L. BISHOP, *The Corporate Memory.* New York: John Wiley, 1974.

chapter 10

Implementation

- Organizing for Implementation
- Planning the Implementation
- Organization Development and Training
- Acquisition

- Conversion
- Testing
- Operation
- Evaluation
- Maintenance

PURPOSE: To show how to convert the MIS design into an operating MIS. Testing, operation, evaluation, and maintenance are included to complete the operational objective

Effective management of computer resources requires attention to more than the formal devices and tasks and ongoing operations in a steady state. The MIS manager and senior management must conceive of this job as managing a resource that is a *change agent*. As such, attention must be paid to an analysis of *informal and behavioral forces* that emerge as sources of resistance or support when change is contemplated, and to the opportunities for modification of organizational structure and control devices as means to achieve change goals.[1]

Designing an MIS may be an expensive and lengthy project. Converting the design concepts into a working system may be even more difficult. This conversion is usually called *implementation* of the design.

Implementation consists of organizational change and technical change. The significant problems of organizational change are often overlooked so that technical implementation fails. *Technical implementation* consists of acquiring facilities, equipment, and personnel; training and transferring personnel; conversion from the old to the new MIS; testing the new MIS; operating the MIS; evaluating the MIS project; and maintaining the system.

The relative cost of implementation may be high compared to design cost. The reason is the cost of software packages, training, equipment and supplies, debugging, and preparing operating manuals. Figure 10.1 indicates the nature of cumulative expenditures in MIS development.

[1]Cyrus F. Gibson and Richard L. Nolan, "Organizational Issues in the Stages of EDP Growth," *Data Base,* Nos. 2, 3, 4, 1973 (emphasis added).

Figure 10.1
MIS cost vs. time

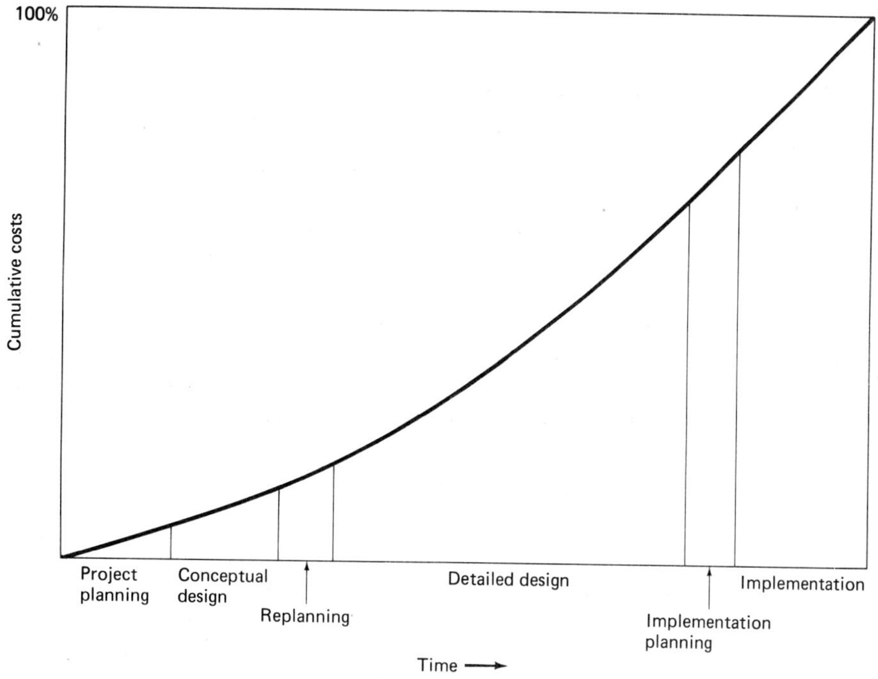

Chart axes and labels: 100% at top of vertical axis labeled "Cumulative costs"; horizontal axis labeled "Time →". Along the curve the phases are marked: Project planning, Conceptual design, Replanning, Detailed design, Implementation planning, Implementation.

ORGANIZING FOR IMPLEMENTATION

Once the implementation tasks have been defined in the planning phase, management usually assigns a project manager to guide the implementation. A manager of management information systems may assume this responsibility by virtue of his permanent assignment. In smaller companies someone from the finance/accounting department, or even the computer center manager, may be placed in charge. A project manager, responsible for the entire MIS development and implementation, as described in Chapter 7, usually works best.

The role of line managers must be made clear. Because the purpose of the MIS is to increase the amount and quality of their contributions, the system is really *their* system. Top management must take explicit steps to make the middle managers aware of this and of the necessity for their involvement in implementation. Essentially, the system specialists are there to *assist* management with the implementation; they are assigned to the project as needed for this purpose.

Besides assigning responsibilities to line managers, systems specialists, and computer programmers, top management should make sure that line functional personnel have active parts in the implementation. These people who will operate the system must feel that it is *their* system.

Proper organization by assignment of specific leadership and by diffusion of task responsibility widely throughout the organization can prevent the moans and wails so often heard after a new MIS is installed and fails. Mature people respond to work assignments that call forth their full talents. They resist the control implied when they are simply handed a system installed by specialists and told exactly how to operate it. But when they have a hand in shaping and constructing the system they must operate, employees react favorably. Without such acceptance, management finds that new systems fail because of inertia, apathy, resistance to change, and employee feelings of insecurity.

PLANNING THE IMPLEMENTATION

Each phase of MIS development should start with a review or reformulation of a plan. Too many interrelated activities are involved to direct on a day-to-day basis. Many of these activities may be carried on in parallel, and yet they must mesh. Further, line management is responsible for implementation, and the plan is the means for expressing the important decisions on implementation. Implementation is a major project, and the project management techniques of Chapter 7 should be applied.

Identifying the Implementation Tasks

Major implementation tasks usually consist of

1. Acquiring personnel
2. Training personnel
3. Changing attitudes, behavior patterns, and interrelationships
4. Acquiring and laying out facilities and offices
5. Acquiring the hardware
6. Acquiring the software
7. Acquiring forms and other supplies
8. Generating the files
9. Developing test procedures
10. Testing the system
11. Operating the system
12. Evaluating the new MIS
13. Providing system maintenance
14. Documenting the working system.

A number of subtasks associated with each of the above may constitute significant work packages. These should also be identified at this time.

Establishing Relationships among Tasks

For small projects, the order of performance may simply be described in text form. Even in small projects, however, a Gantt chart or network diagram makes visualization of the plan and schedule much clearer. In large projects, many concurrent and sequential activities are interrelated so that a network diagram must be employed in any good plan. Figure 10.2 shows a Gantt chart, and Figure 10.3 shows a network diagram (condensed) for illustrating task relationships.

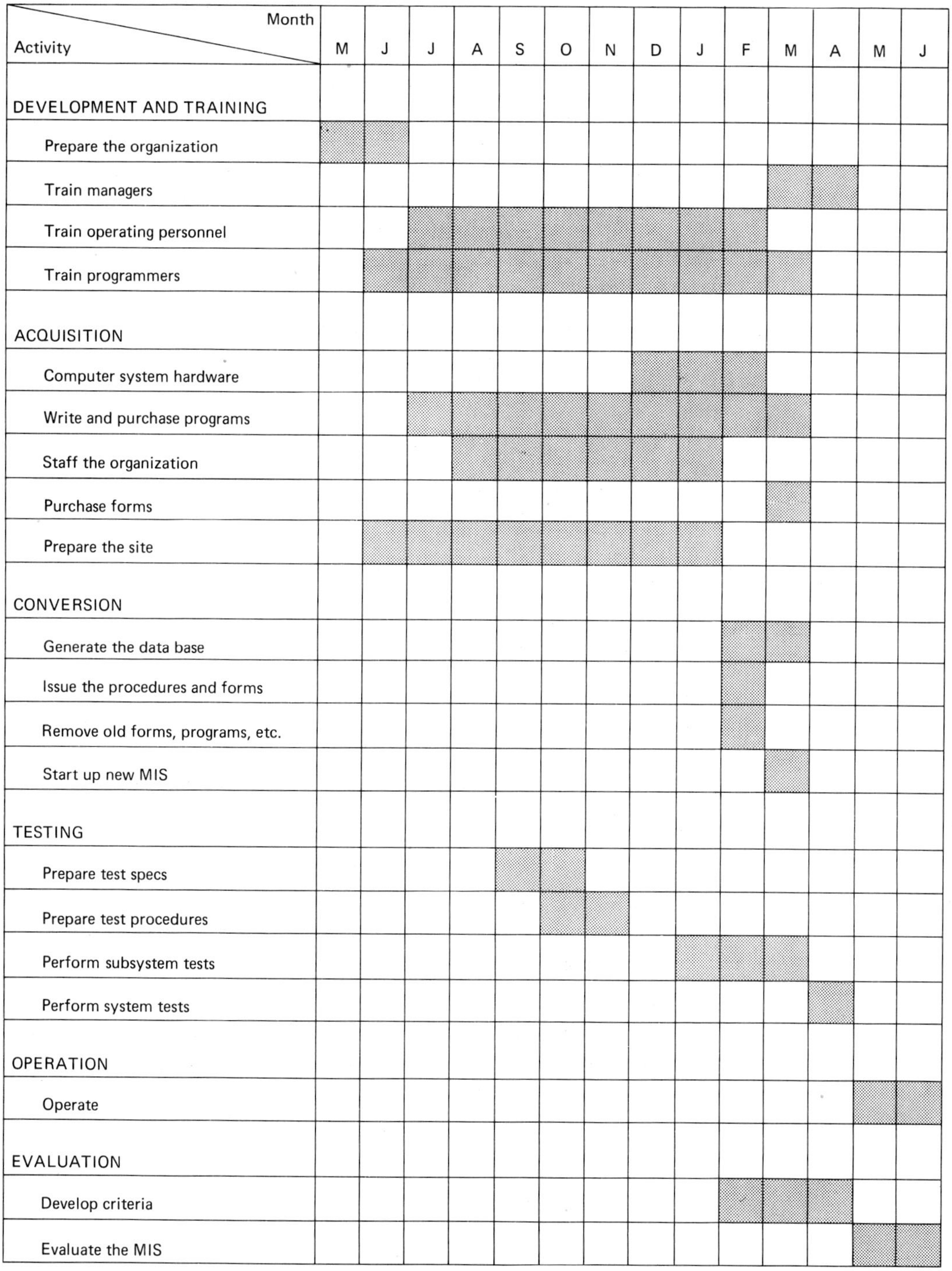

Activity \ Month	M	J	J	A	S	O	N	D	J	F	M	A	M	J
DEVELOPMENT AND TRAINING														
Prepare the organization	░	░												
Train managers											░	░		
Train operating personnel			░	░	░	░	░	░	░	░	░			
Train programmers		░	░	░	░	░	░	░						
ACQUISITION														
Computer system hardware							░	░						
Write and purchase programs			░	░	░	░	░	░	░					
Staff the organization				░	░	░	░	░						
Purchase forms										░				
Prepare the site		░	░	░	░	░	░	░						
CONVERSION														
Generate the data base										░	░			
Issue the procedures and forms										░				
Remove old forms, programs, etc.										░				
Start up new MIS										░				
TESTING														
Prepare test specs				░	░									
Prepare test procedures					░	░								
Perform subsystem tests								░	░					
Perform system tests												░		
OPERATION														
Operate													░	░
EVALUATION														
Develop criteria										░	░			
Evaluate the MIS													░	░

Figure 10.2 Gantt chart for implementation

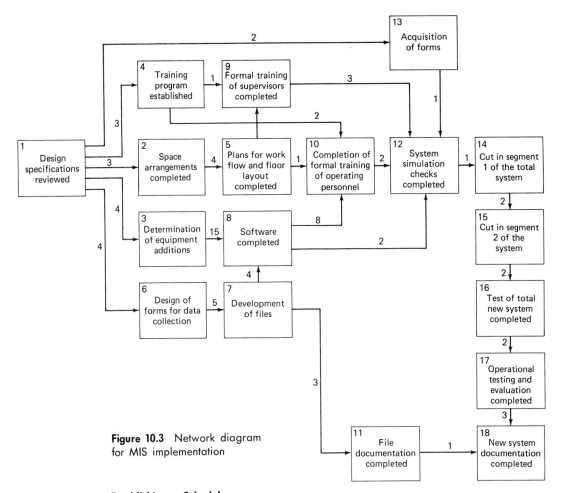

Figure 10.3 Network diagram for MIS implementation

Establishing a Schedule

The Gantt chart or the network shows estimated times of each activity. The total time for the project may be read directly from the Gantt chart by looking at the completion of the last activity. In the network diagram, the critical path must be computed. In Fig. 10.2 the time for the project is 31 months. In Fig. 10.3 the critical path is 39 months. Management may then establish start and end dates for implementation. If the end date is not soon enough, some activity times in the critical path may be shortened by applying more resources or restructuring the network to conduct some tasks in the critical path in parallel. This usually results in some waste of resources.

For each task, a starting and completion date should then be set. These become part of the work package for the task.

Preparing a Cost Schedule Tied to Tasks and Time

The total labor and material costs should be established and a monthly budget prepared for each task. (See Chapter 7.)

Establishing a Reporting and Control System

A temporary MIS for project control should be formally established. Reporting and control may be achieved by regular weekly meetings of the key people involved. Brief written reports of progress and problems should be prepared for management. The financial department should make certain that report formats allow them to show cost and performance progress as well as cost and time relationships. When a large number of people throughout the company are involved part-time on a systems project, communication and coordination are difficult. The purpose of the control system is to minimize confusion, delays, and cost overruns.

ORGANIZATION DEVELOPMENT AND TRAINING

Modifying the Organization

Although development and training are directed toward implementation, many of these activities may be carried out in the latter stages of the detailed design. Organization development (OD) consists of preparing the members of the organization for change. In Chapter 2 we discussed why people resist change. We will discuss briefly how management may change attitudes through a series of steps.

Organization development requires data gathering about the organization, diagnosis of the problems involved in change, and data feedback and discussion. In essence, someone outside the organization, such as an external consultant or a corporate staff consultant, is brought in as a change agent. Because the consultant is supposedly unbiased, it is easier to build trust between the consultant and personnel within the affected organization.

Figure 10.4 Organizational development for implementing the new MIS

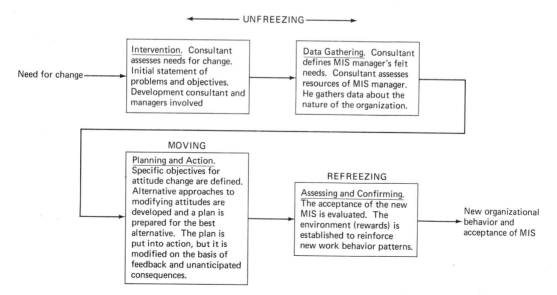

According to the Kurt Lewin model, there is an "unfreezing" stage of readying the organization for change. The organization is made aware of the problems and the need for a new MIS. The second stage involves actually changing (moving) old behaviors by discussion and experimentation. "Refreezing" consists of reinforcement activities to strengthen the new behavior in operating and using the MIS. In Fig. 10.4 the unfreezing, moving, and refreezing stages are described by activity blocks. The bibliography provides references to three other models of change: Larry Greiner's, David A. Kolb and Alan L. Frohman's, and Jay R. Galbraith's.

Training

Training operating personnel and management also results in modifying the organization. It is therefore a special aspect of OD. However, because training is directed toward very specific objectives and skills, it is more readily understood and applied.

The training program may be considered to be divided into four parts:

1. Management orientation
2. Management use of the MIS
3. Operating personnel's use of the system
4. Programmer training.

Particular attention should be paid to the training of first-line supervisors. They must have a thorough understanding of what the new MIS is like and what it is supposed to do. Because, in essence, they oversee the operation of the system, they must learn how it will operate. They are faced with many changes in their work, and they must obtain acceptance of changes by their subordinates. Supervisors will therefore have an intense interest in the answers to the following questions:

1. What new skills must we and our people learn?
2. How many people do we gain or lose?
3. What changes in procedures do we make?
4. What are the new forms? Are there more or fewer?
5. What jobs will be upgraded or downgraded?
6. How will our performance be measured?

Certain professional support personnel—such as computer center personnel, marketing researchers, production planners, and accounting personnel who provide input to the MIS or are concerned with processing data and information—should also attend one or several orientation meetings. Because these people will be working with only a small part of the MIS, the seminars should be designed to give them an understanding of the complete system. This will furnish direction for their own jobs and give them a perspective that may reduce the likelihood of blunders.

Finally, longer and more formal training programs should be established for people who perform the daily operational tasks of the MIS. These are the clerks, the computer operators, the input and output machine operators, file maintenance personnel, and printing production and graphic arts personnel.

In most medium and large companies a training specialist arranges such programs. The specialist schedules classes, arranges for facilities, and assists the technical people (in this case, the systems analysts) in developing course content and notes for distribution. In small companies the MIS manager will probably have to develop the training program.

The most common training approach is likely to be the seminar. One or several short sessions are adequate for users of the system. Written procedures for operating personnel are used to supplement the seminars. Programmers may require more intensive training in company operations in order to understand company models and communicate with functional specialists and managers.

ACQUISITION

Acquisition consists of bringing on the site

1. Computer system hardware
2. Software
3. Personnel
4. Materials
5. Facilities and equipment.

Hardware

The acquisition of computer system equipment is a complex subject more suitable for a specialized book. Basically, the design of the computer system and the architecture available from vendors are closely tied together. Once a choice of CPU and peripheral equipment has been made, a major decision is whether to buy or lease. Capital expenditure analysis is only one of many factors involved in this decision. Others are prestige, usage, anticipated replacement schedule, and vendor's options.

An alternative used by smaller companies is simply to lease computer time from a service bureau.

Software

Today many software packages are commercially available. Therefore, for small companies all software might be purchased. In large companies with specialized forecasting, planning, operating, and control models, most software must be developed internally or under contract. In either case, the software development must take into account the nature of the hardware.

Purchase of software packages has a pitfall. Often, so much modification of the software is required to fit the company that it would have been cheaper to develop the entire software internally.

Figure 10.5 MIS organization chart

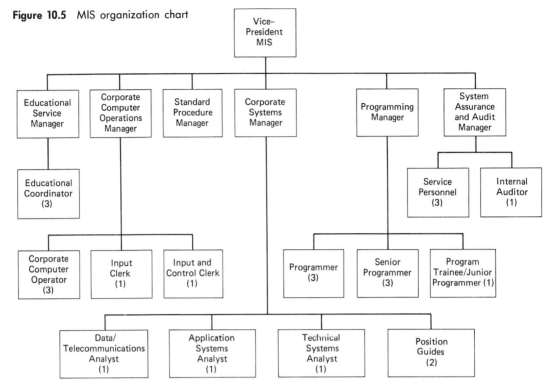

Courtesy of Levitz Furniture Corporation

Personnel

Implementation of an MIS offers the company an opportunity to upgrade and promote personnel after training. Jobs may be restructured at higher levels by using the computer to handle routine procedures which were traditionally handled by people.

A personnel planning chart should be prepared showing the number of individuals required in terms of skill, the source (internal or external), and the time they will be required to report for work. An organization chart with the numbers of required personnel may be used for such planning, as shown by Levitz' MIS chart, Figure 10.5.

Materials

Forms and manuals are the principal materials to be ordered for the MIS. The demand for these must be estimated so that an adequate number may be ordered. The economic order size may be calculated to set the order size and minimize system costs.

Computer supplies such as cards, tapes, printout paper, and storage cabinets should be checked and orders placed if necessary.

Facilities

Rearrangement of current facilities and acquisition of additional space for staff and equipment will probably be necessary. Space requirements should be calculated for

1. All operating personnel directly affected by the MIS
2. The manager and employees of the computer center
3. The library rooms for storing magnetic tapes, disk packs, and cards
4. Storage space for office supplies, printing paper, and forms
5. The computer room and its equipment
6. Remote terminals and teleprocessing equipment.

Other facilities to be acquired may be special power supplies, power outlets, lighting, air conditioning, and humidity and dust control equipment. A large investment in good working conditions will be repaid many times over. It is shortsighted and costly to scrimp on facilities and working environment when a major renovation for a new system is undertaken.

CONVERSION

Conversion consists of building up the new system, changing to the new procedures, changing to the new equipment, and relocating personnel to their new work stations. Complications at such a time can be overwhelming unless careful planning and execution are enforced.

There are six methods for conversion:

1. Introducing the MIS on a specified date, if a new company is just starting.
2. Cutting off the old MIS and starting up the new MIS. This introduces a time gap during which no system is in operation. The interim is feasible for small companies where installation may require only one or two days. For large companies, the conversion might be made during a vacation shutdown or over an extended weekend.
3. Cutting over system by system, or phasing in the new MIS. If this method is possible, some probing questions should be asked about the new system. Is it really just automation of isolated groups of clerical activities? Generally, new systems are substitutable piece by piece for previous *nonsystems*. Substitution for a piece of a system implies that there are no boundary problems, such as incompatible intersystem forms and reports.
4. Cutting over location by location. This ensures that a particular work group and terminal area will function properly. It entails the same problems as method 3.

5. Operating in parallel and then cutting over. The new system is installed and operated in parallel with the current system until it has been checked out; then the current system is cut out. This method is expensive because of the extra personnel and related costs. However, it is required in certain essential systems, such as payroll or customer billing. Its big advantage is that the system is fairly well debugged when it becomes the essential information system of the company.

6. Converting to the new MIS as the design progresses. This piecemeal approach involves users in a sort of implementation/test/redesign process. It provides operational testing of the design on a continuous basis, but it limits consideration of major design alternatives. It is a trial-and-error process. Completion of conceptual and analytical design in advance of equipment installation offers many advantages besides cost.

Conversion must be carefully controlled. Written procedures and personal supervision are essential. A major problem is to prevent loss of data during the changeover. Another is the generation of new files. For example, consider an inventory file of 5000 items, each having 200 characters of descriptive information. This means that 1,000,000 characters must be entered in magnetic storage. This data must first be prepared for key punching. If a key-punch operator can average 8000 strokes per hour (including corrections), it will take 125 hours or 3.1 weeks for one person to enter the data on cards or tape.

Several more problems should be specifically mentioned. Late delivery of hardware components may delay the startup. Debugging of the computer may not proceed smoothly. Office rearrangements may be delayed for any number of reasons.

TESTING

Testing the new MIS consists of (1) testing each program independently, (2) testing all programs by processing test problems through the whole system (simulating inputs), (3) testing procedures, (4) testing forms and reports, and (4) testing controls.

Testing occurs both *before* cutover or conversion and *after*. For example, computer programs may be checked out before the MIS is installed. On the other hand, the same program may be tested after the MIS is installed—either by itself, or in a "string" of several programs, or in use with a simulated total system problem.

If the testing is properly planned, test specifications and test procedures will be prepared. Test specs express the objectives of the tests and the acceptable results. Test procedures define the steps in carrying out the tests. Test specifications will specify inputs and outputs in terms of accuracy, reliability, range, frequency of inputs, common operating conditions, and "human factor" characteristics. Formal test reports should be prepared. Difficulties during testing may lead to design changes which may bring great benefits when the MIS is finally operating normally.

One point difficult to cover in a general discussion is a very important and *practical* one: How are the new pieces of equipment, new forms, new procedures, and so on being tested in an organization where daily operations must be maintained? This is particularly relevant where components cannot be substituted, but the entire new system must be installed, operated in parallel, and then cut in on a given day. It is a test of the ingenuity of the MIS project manager in preventing utter chaos. One possible approach is to plan for new equipment to be in different locations from old equipment. Sometimes operating personnel, using a few files and tables fitted into the room, can handle both old procedures and the testing of the new components from their regular work stations. In other cases, adjacent available office space may be used for testing, and the physical substitution of the new for the old system may take place in overtime on the night before cutover. Removal of partitions may permit temporary, crowded, side-by-side arrangements until the acceptance testing is complete.

As more components are installed, subsystems may be tested. There is a considerable difference between the testing of a component and the testing of a system. System tests require verification of multiple inputs, complex logic systems, interaction of humans and widely varied equipment, interfacing of systems, and timing aspects of the many parts. If, for example, the programming for the computer fails to work in the system test, costly delays may take place. Minor difficulties cropping up often require redesign of forms, procedures, work flow, or organizational changes. The training program itself is being tested, because, if the supervisors and operators lose confidence in the system at this point, they may in overt or subtle ways resist further implementation of the new system.

Although complete parallel testing before a target-day cutover is perhaps the most difficult to implement, it is sometimes necessary. Consider a bank that must collect and process millions of dollars in checks before shipment to various points for collection. A delay of a day, or even of several hours, can be very expensive in terms of interest forgone. Order processing, payroll operations, project management control, retail operations management, and airline reservation service are other functions in which a break in system operation is extremely undesirable.

OPERATION

When all tests have been performed and the total MIS has been checked out, normal operating procedures take effect. Operations should be monitored for several months, since unexpected problems may arise despite previous testing. Application of forms, procedures, software, hardware, and control systems are observed to make sure they are working in the manner specified.

Once operations are going smoothly, the documentation of the MIS design and the operations procedure manual should be revised to describe the system as it is actually functioning.

EVALUATION

An evaluation committee of company executives should be established to provide as impartial an evaluation of the MIS as possible. Alternatively, the operational audit department of the company or outside consultants may be called upon to perform the evaluation.

Evaluation requires that we (a) identify objectives, (b) establish criteria for measuring achievement of these objectives, and (c) measure performance in terms of the criteria. Basically, we wish to measure the effectiveness and efficiency of total MIS performance. *Effectiveness* is the degree to which we achieve system objectives. *Efficiency* is the degree to which we minimize utilization of resources to achieve an objective. We could be very efficient by achieving the *wrong* goals at low cost. It is better to be effective but inefficient than to be highly efficient in reaching the wrong objectives.

Figure 10.6 Evaluation of system objective

SYSTEM CONCEPTS AND OBJECTIVES

	Existing Problems — Accounts Payable System	Improvement Priority		
		Top	Med	Low
PRIMARY	The accounts payable cycle, from the receipt of the invoice, to the issuance of the payment requires 3-4 weeks. This is deemed to be excessive by 1 to 2 weeks. The existing processing method and resources cannot operate at an increased rate to reduce the time taken by the cycle.	X		
OTHERS	Excessive transcription of information — from invoice, to voucher and to subsidiary ledgers.		X	
	Excessive verification of clerical work (such as invoice extension).		X	
	Loss of discounts available for prompt payment.			X
	High volume of "rush" cheques due to complaints by suppliers.		X	

Desired System Objectives	Acceptable Score – 70%	Objectives Satisfied By	Measurement of Results Reported By
PRIMARY	Issue payments to suppliers within 2 weeks of receipt of invoice, while maintaining at least a 98% accuracy and not more than 2 man weeks of backlog.	Savings of 1½ weeks of processing through; — Automation of A/P System to verify and pay supplier's invoices; — reduction of clerical processing; — simplification of payment authorization procedure; — automation of cheque preparation.	Payment Analysis Report

320

Figure 10.6 (Cont'd.)

Desired System Objectives	Acceptable Score – 70%	Objectives Satisfied By	Measurement of Results Reported By
S E C O N D A R Y	*Service/Volume* 1) Processing priority accorded to invoice with cash discount terms. 2) Backlog from 1-2 man weeks maximum. 3) Payment priority to 50 key suppliers. QUALITY Error rate — volume 2% — value + – ½% invoice value	1) Priority programmed, manual procedures developed to comply. 2) Duplication of clerical effort elimination of unnecessary verifications and other improvements listed below. 3) As in 1) above. 1) Supervisory quality control cheque of work sample. 2) Computer edit; 100% key-verification.	1) Check Register 2) Payment Analysis Report (No. AH4) 3) Supervisory Check 1) Supervisor's Report 2) Edit Report (EDP) 3) Supplier complaint
O T H E R S	*Costs/Savings* One time implementation costs not to exceed $35,000 including programming, forms and training. Reduce clerical workload from 4 to 2 clerks. *Feasibility of implementation* With 3 months of start, parallel operations must cease.	Costs estimated at $38-45,000 1) Replacement of 100% clerical work verification with 95% confidence level random sample results in the saving of ½ clerk. 2) Elimination of manual posting of subsidiary ledgers result in the saving of 1 clerk. 3) Conversion of voucher and cheque typing to computer processing results in the saving of ½ clerk. System is planned to be fully implemented within 2 months after conversion.	Project Control System Transfer of an A/P Verifier clerk planned for 1 month after implementation and upon reorganization of jobs, 2nd clerk will be transferred (no later than 3 months after implementation).

Source: John P. Herzog, "System Evaluation Technique for Users," **Journal of Systems Management,** May 1975.

In evaluating an MIS we must determine what objectives to relate to and what criteria to measure against. Should we focus on total system objectives, processes to achieve total system objectives, or a collection of subsystem objectives? Should we reduce all criteria to dollars of benefits per dollar of costs? The answers are not easy to come by. An example of evaluation of system objectives was shown in Figure 10.6 on pages 320 and 321.

Hierarchy of Criteria

The fundamental purpose of the MIS is to bring the company closer toward achieving its primary objectives more efficiently. Profit and return on investment are generally accepted objectives. Service to society and workers' satisfactions are others. The problem in measuring the contribution to these objectives is that so many other factors act upon the company at the same time.

We might consider, then, isolating the contribution of MIS to revenues and isolating the cost of the MIS to the company. Both are difficult to do. We could next consider revenues and costs to be the result of planning and control; we might be able to develop some measures of the impact of MIS on these functions.

Table 10.1 shows a continuing breakdown of factors that might serve as criteria for evaluating the MIS. Examples of variables to be measured to evaluate each factor are also shown. Although measuring many of the variables poses difficulties, this hierarchy can be used for crude evaluations.

Evaluation of Improvement of MIS Functions

G. B. Davis divides the MIS into functional subsystems:

Strategic planning information system
Managerial control information system
Operations information system
Transaction processing system

Evaluation of the MIS could be based upon criteria established for each of these four systems. For example, borrowing from S. Stimler, the transaction system could be in terms of

1. Throughput—total transactions processed over the evaluation period
2. Throughput rate—amount of work processed per unit of time
3. Throughput rate capability—the maximum throughput rate possible for the system.

Unfortunately, measuring the MIS contribution to the other three systems presents the same difficulties as in the hierarchical approach. Measures of effectiveness (MOE's) closely corresponding to the MIS activities listed by Davis, have been developed by W. A. Smith, Jr. These are shown in Table 10.2.

	Hierarchy in the MIS	Change that Is Measured
Level 1	Company profit, return on investment	Dollars
Level 2	Company costs, revenues	Dollars
Level 3	Planning	Specificity, quantification, degree to which plans are achieved, time required to produce plans, number of alternative plans made available for consideration, cost.
	Control	Degree of control by exception, selection of activities to be controlled, forewarning of activities going beyond acceptable limits, managerial time required for control, automation of control of repetitive situations, cost.
Level 4	Decisions	Quality of decisions, frequency of reversal of decisions by superiors in the organization, number of alternatives examined in arriving at decisions, sophistication of "What if . . . ?" questions permitted, time required for decisions, automation of repetitive decision situations, cost.
Level 5	Information	Validity, accuracy, clarity, distribution, frequency, appropriateness of detail for each level of management, timeliness, format, availability on demand, selectivity of content, disposition method, retention time, cost.
Level 6	System characteristics	Number of people required, equipment and facilities, response time, frequency of breakdowns, inputs, outputs, number of forms, number of operations, number of storages, sizes and quality of data bank, size and quality of model bank, flexibility, simplicity, degree of automation, scope of business components that are related by the MIS, user satisfaction, error rates, persistent problem areas, ease of maintenance and modification, unplanned-for impact on company performance, savings, cost, etc.

Table 10.1 Measurement hierarchy

Cost/Benefit Analysis

Another approach to evaluation is to determine the life-cycle cost of the system and estimate the benefits over the same period. Design, conversion, and testing costs can be estimated fairly well under a project system with account numbers for all labor times to be charged. Hardware and software costs, in particular, are readily determined. Initial operating costs may also be estimated by adding (or subtracting) incremental costs from the previous operating costs.

Table 10.2 Characteristic performance indicators

Activity		Dominant Issues	Example MOE's (Measures of Effectiveness)
Clerical	Function:	cost displacement, task execution	Units per labor hour, backlog
	System:	efficiency, speed of operation, economy	Throughput, capacity utilization, data preparation cost per unit
	Information:	accuracy	Percent error transactions
Operational	Function:	monitoring and control over activity and resources	Inventory level, yield rate, messages delivered/received, missed shipping dates
	System:	maintainability, sustainability, availability, sensitivity	Percent down time, time between failures, frequency of service, percent requests with special handling
	Information:	timeliness, reliability	Response time
Tactical	Function:	decision quality, functional objectives	Return on investment, volume orders per district, unit cost, overtime/regular hours, percent returned product, delivery time
	System:	auditability, compatibility, flexibility, security, scope	Actual users vs. intended users, percent service of total cost, reports returned vs. delivered
	Information:	sufficiency, conciseness, discovery	Percent file used when appropriate, volume of inquiries
Strategic	Function:	organizational mission, planning, outcome of decisions	Share of market, new products, earnings/share, change in risk, percent R&D of total expense
	System:	user satisfaction[a]	Number of accesses per inquiry, time to formulate inquiry, percent compliments vs. complaints
	Information:	relevance	Percent responses appropriate

[a] Access ease, available period, dependable source, suitability to purpose, personal convenience.
Source: W. A. Smith, Jr., **Effectiveness of Information Systems** (Bethlehem, Pa.: Lehigh University, Dept. of I.E., June 1972) (AD744027), National Technical Information Service.

Projecting future operating costs is more difficult because of the impact of the experience curve on the one hand and modifications of the MIS on the other. The result of such an analysis is expressed in units of dollars.

Benefits, unfortunately, are not so easily converted to dollars. Broad benefits may include

1. Improved management understanding of the business
2. Improved effectiveness in the functioning of the operating systems
3. Improved inter- and intraorganizational relationships
4. Greater work satisfaction for more employees
5. More timely and better quality information for managers, both external and internal

6. Reduction in errors because of greater standardization and better procedures and policies

7. Freeing of managerial time for higher-level contributions

8. Better historical record systems.

A somewhat opposite approach to evaluating benefits is to prepare a "laundry list" of all *specific* measurable benefits from the new MIS. This list might run into hundreds of items. A few examples will indicate its nature:

1. Decrease in product design life cycle

2. Improved customer repair service

3. Managerial time spent in committee meetings

4. Preparation-time improvement for the capital budget

5. Decrease in absenteeism

6. Shorter delivery time

7. Reduced loss of orders from stockouts

8. Decrease in management time spent on preparing the strategic plans

9. Better use of salesmen's time

10. Lower recruiting costs because of a new personnel profile system and more promotions from within.

The general format of a cost/benefit analysis, without the detail involved in an actual one, is shown in Figure 10.7. A more detailed list of costs and benefits is given in Table 10.3.

Table 10.3
Proposed list of costs and benefits for information systems evaluation

Possible Information System Costs
Procurement costs
Consulting costs
Actual equipment purchase or lease costs
Equipment installation costs
Costs for modifying the equipment site (air conditioning, security, etc.)
Cost of capital
Cost of management and staff dealing with procurement
Start-up costs
Cost of operating system software
Cost of communications equipment installation (telephone lines, data lines, etc.)
Cost of start-up personnel
Cost of personnel searches and hiring activities
Cost of disruption to the rest of the organization
Cost of management required to direct start-up activity
Project-related costs
Cost of applications software purchased
Cost of software modifications to fit local systems
Cost of personnel, overhead, etc., from in-house application development
Cost for interacting with users during development
Cost for training user personnel in application use
Cost of data collection and installing data collection procedures
Cost of preparing documentation
Cost of development management

Table 10.3
(Cont'd.)

Possible Information System Costs

Ongoing costs
    System maintenance costs (hardware, software, and facilities)
    Rental costs (electricity, telephones, etc.)
    Depreciation costs on hardware
    Cost of staff involved in information systems management, operation, and planning
      activities

Possible Information System Benefits[a]

Benefits from contributions of calculating and printing tasks
    Reduction in per-unit costs of calculating and printing (CR)
    Improved accuracy in calculating tasks (ER)
    Ability to quickly change variables and values in calculation programs (IF)
    Greatly increased speed in calculating and printing (IS)
Benefits from contributions to record-keeping tasks
    Ability to "automatically" collect and store data for records (CR, IS, ER)
    More complete and systematic keeping of records (CR, ER)
    Increased capacity for recordkeeping in terms of space and cost (CR)
    Standardization of recordkeeping (CR, IS)
    Increase in amount of data that can be stored per record (CR, IS)
    Improved security in records storage (ER, CR, MC)
    Improved portability of records (IF, CR, IS)
Benefits from contributions to record searching tasks
    Faster retrieval of records (IS)
    Improved ability to access records from large databases (IF)
    Improved ability to change records in databases (IF, CR)
    Ability to link sites that need search capability through telecommunications (IF, IS)
    Improved ability to create records of records accessed and by whom (ER, MC)
    Ability to audit and analyze record searching activity (MC, ER)
Benefits from contributions to system restructuring capability
    Ability to simultaneously change entire classes of records (IS, IF, CR)
    Ability to move large files of data about (IS, IF)
    Ability to create new files by merging aspects of other files (IS, IF)
Benefits from contributions of analysis and simulation capability
    Ability to perform complex, simultaneous calculations quickly (IS, IF, ER)
    Ability to create simulations of complex phenomena in order to answer "what if?"
      questions (MC, IF)
    Ability to aggregate large amounts of data in various ways useful for planning and
      decision making (MC, IF)
Benefits from contributions to process and resource control
    Reduction of need for manpower in process and resource control (CR)
    Improved ability to "fine tune" processes such as assembly lines (CR, MC, IS, ER)
    Improved ability to maintain continuous monitoring of processes and available re-
      sources (MC, ER, IF)

[a]CR = Cost reduction or avoidance; ER = Error reduction; IF = Increased flexibility; IS = Increased speed of activity; MC = Improvement in management planning or control. The classification of tasks is adapted from K. L. Kraemer, W. H. Dutton and J. R. Mathews, "Municipal Computers: Growth, Usage, and Management," **Urban Data Service Reports** 7, 11 (1975), 8.

Source: John Leslie King and Edward L. Schrems, "Cost Benefit Analysis of Information Systems Development and Operation," **ACM Computing Surveys,** March 1978. Copyright © 1978, Association for Computing Machinery, Inc., reprinted by permission.

Figure 10.7
MIS evaluation
form

			PAGE _____ DATE _____
MIS PROJECT NAME _____			NO. _____

Initial Costs	1974	1975	1976	TOTAL
1. Project planning	$5,000			$ 5,000
2. Gross design	1,000	$ 2,000		3,000
3. Detailed design		10,000	$ 23,000	33,000
4. Implementation			7,000	7,000
5. Testing			4,800	4,800
6. Special			600	600
TOTAL INITIAL COSTS	$6,000	$12,000	$ 35,400	$ 53,400

Capital Costs				
7. Computer center hardware		$10,300	$ 33,000	$ 43,300
8. Facilities		5,000	13,000	18,000
TOTAL CAPITAL COSTS		$15,300	$ 46,000	$ 61,300

Annual Operating Costs				
9. Computer and equipment lease		$ 5,000	$ 24,000	$ 29,000
10. Personnel		47,000	200,000	247,000
11. Overhead and supplies		10,000	20,000	30,000
TOTAL ANNUAL OPERATING COSTS		$62,000	$244,000	$306,000

Benefits				
12. Reduced salary and labor costs			$ 2,000	$ 2,000
13. Reduced inventory costs			97,000	97,000
14. Better strategic decisions (estimated impact)		$50,000	320,000	370,000
15. Freeing up of managerial time (estimated)		5,000	60,000	65,000
TOTAL BENEFITS		$55,000	$479,000	$534,000

Evaluating Outputs and Procedures

If a system is designed properly, its outputs will increase the effectiveness of the system. One approach, therefore, to evaluating an MIS is to compare the outputs before and after. That is, what are the benefits of output reports and improved physical output? Although one-to-one comparison for the old and new system is not likely to be possible, the aggregate of outputs from each may be compared.

Improved procedures also yield benefits, such as speed, accuracy, worker satisfaction, greater standardization of work, and decreased training requirements. These benefits may be measured, even though the units are different. A narrative description or table of such benefits may be reviewed in terms of the cost of the MIS.

MAINTENANCE

Maintenance is that ongoing activity which keeps the MIS at the highest levels of effectiveness and efficiency within cost constraints. In other words, maintenance of the MIS is directed toward reducing errors due to design, reducing errors due to environmental changes, and improving the system's scope and services. These activities are sometimes classified as (a) emergency maintenance, (b) routine maintenance, (c) requests for special (one-time) reports, and (4) systems improvements.

Maintenance may be applied to the following entities or activities:

1. Changes in policy statements
2. Changes in reports received by a manager who replaces an outgoing manager
3. Changes in forms
4. Changes in operating systems
5. Changes in procedures
6. Changes in hardware or hardware configuration
7. Software modification or addition
8. System controls and security needs
9. Changes in inputs from the environment.

Item 9 requires some amplification. If changes in the environment are not monitored closely, a constant stream of errors may run rampant throughout the MIS. The maintenance team may lose many hours tracking them to their source. Let us look at some areas of change in the environment.

Environmental Change

Government policies, regulations, and legislation

Most large companies require specialists or lawyers to keep management apprised of the numerous changes in reporting requirements, compliance requirements, and pressures for change. For example, banks must be aware of new regulations, maximum interest rates, interest rates established through Federal Reserve activities, minimum downpayments required on loans and mortgages, and mortgage acceptance rules. Manufacturing companies must be aware of changes in pension rules, financial disclosure, and so on. Health care facilities must be aware of legislation and rulings with regard to state and federal government payments for the elderly, indigent, and so on. In other words, there is a continual flow of rules from government that requires constant updating of the AIS in a company.

Economic conditions

Changes in general economic conditions play a major role in defining financial information systems. If the system is properly designed, it should meet the needs of all users, not just the accounting and finance departments. General economic conditions dictate corporate policy in several areas, and the ability to internalize these changes is an important part of good systems design. As these changes are only partly predictable, the system should be evaluated periodically to ensure both proper inclusion and measurement of new conditions. Changes in the unemployment rate, both nationally and locally, could affect the direct labor cost and could also affect the time-frame for completion of planned projects. Changes in inflation and interest rates have even more far-reaching impacts. A rise in interest rates may hinder customers' attempting to obtain short-term credit to purchase a company's product. The same rise in interest rates may stop a company from expanding plant capacity, stockpiling inventories, or replacing and updating fixed assets. This list is not all-inclusive, but it should be noted that periodic systems evaluations will help ensure that these and similar items are included.

Industry and competitive conditions

Changes in industry conditions should be treated in the same manner as changes in economic conditions; however, the timing of reactions to these changes may be more important. The expansion or collapse of a market for a company's products is of such importance that failure to react on a timely basis may mean failure of the business as a whole. Competitive strategies, price policy, hiring, and capital budgeting are but a few of the areas affected by changes in business conditions. New technology, either in production of products or in the creation of alternative products, may affect even the basic concepts that form the corporate objectives.

New standards for measurement such as package sizes or the metric system may have great financial impact. Industry innovations in reporting or gathering data, such as point-of-purchase data collection in retailing and video responses to stock-price information in brokerage houses, are other examples. These and the above changes require anything from routine to major changes in the MIS.

New technology

The development of computer technology, applications programs, and management techniques has progressed at such a rate as to make farcical the articles of only a few years ago suggesting that total information systems would always be myths. Data communication systems, interactive systems with video displays, tremendous storage capacities, and higher-speed computers are staggering to old-line managers. This new technology is being introduced and used by the flood of accounting and business graduates entering organizations each year. The aggressiveness of computer and software companies in promoting entire systems has also been a major factor. Thus, technological change alone requires continual system maintenance.

Internal Problems Related to MIS Maintenance

The National Association for State Information Systems, in its 1976–77 annual report on information systems technology in state government, ranked the order of problems in data processing beyond the control of the EDP manager. The results (shown in Table 10.4) are very likely applicable to all organizations; they indicate the most important areas where maintenance may be required. No other problem has shown such a reversal of importance as has recruitment of personnel. Since 1971, it has moved from last to first place as the most serious external problem.

Table 10.4
Ranking of problems in data processing

Problem Category	1974	1975	1976	1977	1978
Management understanding	1	1	1	1	2
Lack of definitive plan	2	3	2	3	3
Management commitment	3	2	3	2	4
Management interest	7	5	4	6	6
Resistance to consolidation	5	4	5	4	5
User unfamiliarity with information system	4	7	6	8	7
User agency cooperation	6	8	7	7	8
Recruitment of qualified personnel	8	6	8	5	1
Inadequate financing	11	9	9	10	10
Lack of standards	10	10	10	9	9
Need for documentation	12	11	11	11	10
Need for common data base	9	12	12	12	12

Source: National Association for State Information Systems, 1978-79 **Annual Report on Information Systems Technology in State Government.**

Responsibility for Maintenance

Specific responsibility for maintenance should be assigned to a supervisor and team of MIS analysts, programmers, and forms specialists. Fragmentation of responsibility to MIS analysts, the EDP section, and the forms coordinator, without at least a unifying committee, can lead to compounding of MIS maintenance problems. Although many view MIS maintenance as primarily computer program maintenance, it is not. The most important maintenance activities may precede, or not even include, program maintenance.

Initiation of Maintenance Projects

Maintenance activity may be initiated by error reports, a user's change request, a member of the maintenance team, or company management. Usually, specially designed forms for error reports and for change requests must be completed. A barrier to soliciting information on errors or for changes is the detail required in the form. It may be more useful to have a very simple form that calls for only the requested correction or change and a brief statement of the need. Once a maintenance analyst receives such a form, he may fill out more detailed documentation after an interview.

Planning

Maintenance cannot be performed on a haphazard, informal basis or on a first-come, first-served basis. Four steps are necessary for a good maintenance program:

1. Log all requests for change. Only written requests should be accepted and included in the log.
2. Assign priorities to all requests. These will be determined by urgency of the project for the MIS, long-range benefits, time and resources required, and, in some cases, management dictum.
3. Prepare annual and short-range (usually monthly) plans.
4. Document maintenance as it occurs. When a project is completed, revise the MIS design manual.

SUMMARY   The implementation state of MIS development is the conversion of the design to an operating system. It is the equivalent of the manufacture of a product from the engineering design drawings. Implementation is usually a complex project which requires careful planning and control of resources.

The steps in implementation are:

1. Organization development and training
2. Acquisition
3. Conversion
4. Testing
5. Operation
6. Evaluation
7. Maintenance.

Organization development (OD) means preparing the organization for change. New attitudes may be required. Employees must desire change rather than resist it. Training is an extension of OD designed to increase technical as well as interpersonal skills.

Acquisition refers to acquiring all components of the MIS, including such items as the computer hardware, software, and manpower.

Conversion is the switching over from the old to the new system. The various methods are (a) install a system in a new company, (b) cut off the old and start up the new MIS, (c) phase in the new MIS one system at a time, (d) phase in location after location, (3) operate the old and new MIS in parallel, cutting over when the MIS is working satisfactorily, and (f) convert to the new MIS as the design progresses.

After, if not before, conversion, the components of the system should be tested. After conversion, various tests may be performed to check out the total MIS. When testing is completed, the system is put into regular operation.

After the system has been operating smoothly for a short time, it should be evaluated to determine (a) whether it meets performance specifications, (b) the extent of the benefits relative to the costs, and (c) whether changes have been made in the design. Evaluation of the MIS is difficult, but an attempt should be made along the lines suggested in the text.

Maintenance is the ongoing activity of revising, correcting, and upgrading the MIS. Responsibility should be assigned to one person or committee rather than to individuals without coordination. Maintenance continues to the end of the life cycle of the MIS. When organizational, technological, or environmental changes accumulate, maintenance may not be adequate. At this point an entire new MIS will need to be developed, and the life cycle starts again.

QUESTIONS AND PROBLEMS

1. Group the individual tasks in list B into the work breakdown structure for implementation by placing the numbers under the correct milestone tasks in structure A.

A. WORK BREAKDOWN STRUCTURE

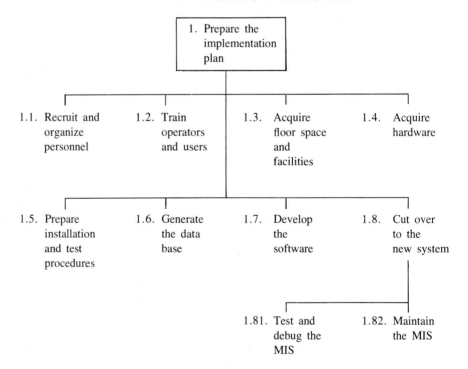

B. INDIVIDUAL TASKS

1. Prepare new position guides
2. Develop a list of training courses
3. Determine floor area for equipment
4. Prepare detailed layout plans
5. Write test procedures for hardware
6. List data on data element forms
7. Brief personnel on the implementation plan
8. Determine application programs to be written
9. Remove old equipment and forms
10. Connect data communication system components
11. Estimate time for each task
12. Assign data files to hardware components
13. Write application programs
14. Monitor MIS procedures
15. Prepare software for planning and decision models
16. Select instructors
17. Set up a procedure for transfer of personnel
18. Key-punch data on tapes or cards
19. Identify training needs for operators
20. Perform tests of the MIS
21. Estimate cost of each task
22. Accept delivery of hardware components
23. Assign a project manager for implementation
24. Prepare operating test procedures for the MIS
25. Enter data in storage
26. Shift personnel and desks
27. Operate the new system and test it
28. Order CPU's
29. Prepare rough layouts and estimates of floor area
30. Hire specialists not available in the company
31. Schedule training sessions
32. Estimate power requirements
33. Have staff review all tests
34. Debug the MIS
35. Define human resource needs by skill
36. Estimate floor area for personnel
37. Introduce the new forms
38. Revise the MIS
39. Review manufacturers' installations and tests
40. Order disk and tape drives
41. List implementation milestones
42. Monitor all models in the MIS
43. Monitor inputs to the MIS
44. Obtain approval of the plan
45. Analyze operation of the MIS
46. Hold seminars for manager-users
47. Connect up the hardware
48. Write test procedures for MIS modules
49. Plan the cutover method and schedule
50. Analyze the error reports
51. Set up the input/output terminals
52. Write test procedures for application programs

2. Draw the network diagram for the implementation plan by labeling the events 1 through 8 and drawing arrows connecting the events to show the activities listed below. Draw heavy lines over the critical path and compute the time for it.

Activity	Description	Time Required
1–2	Review personnel needs	1
1–4	Set up the training program	4
1–5	Order hardware	6
2–3	Hire new personnel	4
3–4	Conduct the training program	4
4–6	Determine office space requirements	4
5–6	Determine equipment space requirements	3
3–7	Purchase software	10
7–8	Test software	2
6–8	Cut over to the new system	1

3. Check the appropriate column to indicate whether the activity is a planning, design, or implementation activity.

Activity	Planning	Design	Implementation
a. Lay out a form	⎯⎯	⎯⎯	⎯⎯
b. Prepare a WBS	⎯⎯	⎯⎯	⎯⎯
c. Bring the CPU on the site	⎯⎯	⎯⎯	⎯⎯
d. Purchase the software for a hospital financial system	⎯⎯	⎯⎯	⎯⎯
e. Flowchart the marketing MIS	⎯⎯	⎯⎯	⎯⎯
f. Set MIS objectives	⎯⎯	⎯⎯	⎯⎯
g. Arrange work stations	⎯⎯	⎯⎯	⎯⎯
h. Describe the computer configuration	⎯⎯	⎯⎯	⎯⎯
i. Document the actual MIS	⎯⎯	⎯⎯	⎯⎯
j. Run the new MIS in parallel with the old	⎯⎯	⎯⎯	⎯⎯

4. The general manager is receiving the monthly engineering report two weeks after the end of the month instead of one week after, as the new MIS specified. The engineering report consists of project reports contributed by project managers and gathered by a technical editor, who checks for clarity, edits for readability, and then supervises a typist in preparing the engineering report. On the basis of this test of real input to the MIS, what suggestions would you make for achieving the MIS design objectives?

5. Compare the organizational impact of MIS design with that of MIS implementation. Discuss how management should deal with each.

6. In an organization of 1500 people, a new MIS is ready to be implemented. Estimate the cost of implementation (very roughly) on the basis of the following data.

a. About 1000 employees will receive an average of five hours of training each.
b. Eight new people will have to be recruited at a cost of $1200 each.
c. Office rearrangement will cost about $50,000.
d. New computer hardware will cost $320,000.
e. Software development will require six man-years.
f. Printing of forms will cost $2500.
g. Creating the files will require four man-months.
h. Testing of the system will require three man-months.
i. Documenting the system will require four man-months.

7. Bill Maxwell is manager of business systems development in a large, decentralized corporation with a diversified product line. The executive vice president one day said to him, "Bill, we would like to find out if our management information system for the whole company is really helping management cope with significant problem areas. We are not interested in procedural audits or efficiency of computer operations in this connection, but rather in decisions relating to project priorities. We want to know whether systems projects are related to long-range plans that have measurable, consistent objectives." Bill replied, "We have been preparing just such a postimplementation study this past month, sir. Here is an outline of the key action items we are examining."

Question: Develop an outline of key action items that Bill might have prepared.

8. The basic organization of the Bank and Trust Co. is diagrammed below.

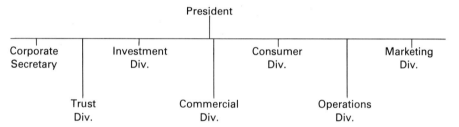

The bank has assets of $158 million at the main office and about $40 million at each of two branches. The data base consists of a common central file and specialized files as shown below:

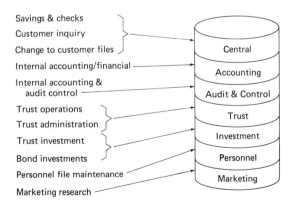

The computer system design is shown in the schematic which follows.

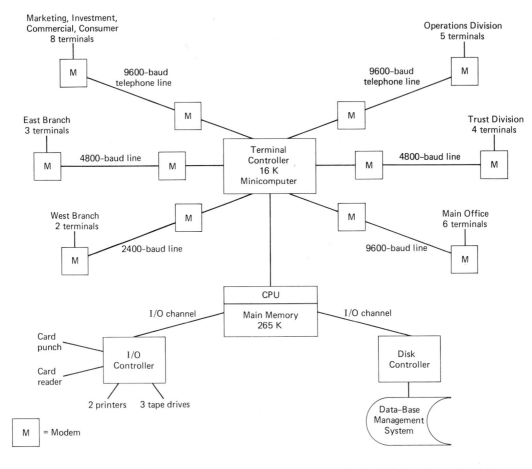

a. Develop a brief plan for implementation of this MIS for the bank, which now has essentially a manual system.

b. Describe the cutover process you would recommend, and give your reasons.

c. List some tests you would perform to check out the new system.

SELECTED REFERENCES

Business Systems Planning, GE-20-0527-1. White Plains, N.Y.: IBM, 1975.

CHENEY, PAUL H., "Measuring MIS Project Success," *Proceedings, 9th Annual Conference, American Institute for Decision Sciences*, Chicago, October 19, 1975, 1977.

CUSHING, BARRY E. *Accounting Information Systems and Business Organizations*, 2d ed. Reading, Mass.: Addison-Wesley, 1978.

DALTON, GENE W., PAUL R. LAWRENCE, and LARRY E. GREINER, eds., *Organizational Change and Development*. Homewood, Ill.: Richard D. Irwin, 1970.

GALBRAITH, JAY R., *Organization Design*. Reading, Mass.: Addison-Wesley, 1977.

GIBSON, CYRUS F., and RICHARD L. NOLAN, "Organizational Issues in the Stages of EDP Growth," *Data Base,* Nos. 2, 3, 4, 1973.

GINSBERG, MICHAEL J., *A Detailed Look at Implementation Research,* Report CISR-4, Sloan WP 753-14. Cambridge, Mass.: M.I.T., 1974.

————, *Implementation as a Process of Change: A Framework and Empirical Study,* Report CISR-13, Sloan WP 797-75. Cambridge, Mass.: Center for Information Systems Research, M.I.T., 1975.

GLANS, THOMAS B., et al., *Management Systems.* New York: Holt, Rinehart and Winston, 1968.

HARTMAN, W., H. MATTHES, and A. PROEME, *Management Information Systems Handbook.* New York: McGraw-Hill, 1968.

HERZOG, JOHN P., "System Evaluation Technique, Selected References for Users," *Journal of Systems Management,* May 1975.

KANTER, JEROME, *Management Guide to Computer System Selection and Use.* Englewood Cliffs, N.J.: Prentice-Hall, 1970.

KHAN, JAFAR, "How to Tackle the Systems Maintenance Dilemma," *Canadian Datasystems,* March 1975.

KING, JOHN LESLIE, and EDWARD L. SCHREMS, "Cost Benefit Analysis of Information Systems Development and Operation," *ACM Computing Surveys,* March 1978.

KLATT, LAWRENCE A., ROBERT G. MURDICK, and FRED E. SCHUSTER, *Human Resources Management.* Homewood, Ill.: Richard D. Irwin, 1978.

KOLB, DAVID A., and ALAN L. FROHMAN, "An Organizational Development Approach to Consulting," *Sloan Management Review*, Fall 1970.

MOCK, THEODORE J., and HUGH D. GROVE. *Measurement, Accounting, and Organizational Information.* New York: John Wiley, 1979.

PRICE WATERHOUSE & Co., *Management Controls for Data Processing*, 2d ed. White Plains, N.Y.: IBM, 1976.

RADFORD, K. J., *Information Systems in Management.* Reston, Va.: Reston, 1973.

SMITH, WILLIAM A., JR., and ALAN M. WOLF, *Guide for Evaluation of Information Systems.* Atlanta: American Institute of Industrial Engineers, 1973.

STIMLER, SAUL, *Data Processing Systems: Their Performance, Evaluation, Measurement, and Improvement.* Trenton, N.J.: Motivational Learning Programs, 1974.

VALLOROSI, JOSEPH, "Cost Effectiveness of People," paper, Consolidated Edison Company, New York, September 11, 1975.

chapter 11

Techniques and Tools for System Development

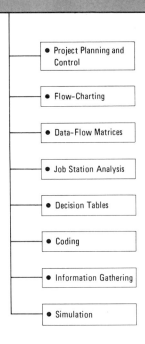

- Project Planning and Control
- Flow-Charting
- Data-Flow Matrices
- Job Station Analysis
- Decision Tables
- Coding
- Information Gathering
- Simulation

PURPOSE: To detail the use of a variety of special tools and techniques for MIS design

Civilization can be measured by the development of its tools. Systems development requires the application of specialized techniques and tools suitable for most practitioners.

PROJECT PLANNING AND CONTROL

Without the serious application of project planning and control techniques, actual costs and time for projects have ballooned to three or four times their original estimates. *Planning and control are critical to the success of a project.*

A project is a unique, well-defined effort to produce specified results at a particular point in time. Good project planning is required, therefore, to

1. Provide a basis for control of time, cost, and performance
2. Make sure that objectives are established
3. Make sure that key tasks are identified
4. Establish precedence relationships among tasks
5. Establish costs and prepare budgets related to time and performance of tasks
6. Organize and assign personnel to ensure that tasks will be performed.

Figure 11.1 shows the planning and control cycle for the MIS project. Before engaging in design work, we should first determine the most pressing needs of the organization. Then, as we see in this figure, the objectives of the project are established. These are sometimes called the *performance specifications,* because they tell us what the MIS should do when it is designed and installed. The planning continues with the establishment of a work breakdown structure. This is the hierarchy of tasks required to achieve project objectives, as discussed in the previous chapter.

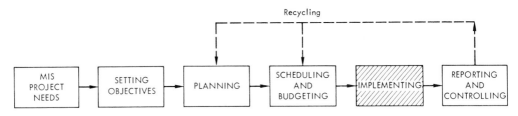

Figure 11.1 The planning-controlling cycle for project management

A commonly used technique, PERT (program evaluation review technique) or CPM (critical path method) is employed to relate the timing of tasks to each other and to the project finish date. These techniques have evolved until they are essentially the same. Generally, they are referred to as critical path network methods. The bare-bones idea of critical path network will be shown here in a series of tables. The reader should refer to entire books devoted to the fine points for further information.

Basic Network Concepts and the Critical Path

PERT requires the selection of specific identifiable *events*. An event is essentially the completion of an *activity*. The events are sequenced relative to each other. Estimates of times required to carry out an activity are prepared.

Let us take the A/R project with the necessary activities shown in Figure 11.2. The network is constructed by identifying the end event, completion of the A/R design, and then determining the last tasks that *must* be done to finish the design. Three such tasks or activities are shown in Figure 11.2. These are 3–5, 4–5, and 2–5. For each event immediately preceding event 5, the same process is repeated. We determine that event 2 and event 3 must occur before event 4 can occur. And event 3 cannot occur until event 2 has occurred. Finally, event 2 cannot occur until event 1, start the project, has occurred. By this method, we set up precedence relationships shown by the *network* diagram of Figure 11.2.

Note that no "activity" is associated with the arrow from event 3 to 4. The dotted arrow means that event 4 cannot occur until after activities 2–3 and 2–4 have been completed. Since two arrows joining the same two events are not allowed by PERT, activity 3–4 is a "dummy" activity required to establish that event 3 must precede event 4.

Next look at Figure 11.3. We have shown the expected time required to carry out each activity and placed it on the corresponding arrow in the network.

Figure 11.2
Precedence
network

PROJECT: Design a new A/R System

ACTIVITIES: Specify the requirements
Design the information flow
Establish the organization and equipment
Develop the forms
Specify the data base
Design the management reports

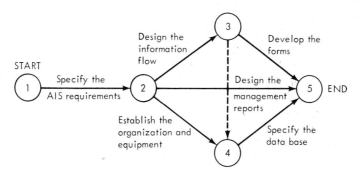

Note that the following chains of events exist from start to finish:

1–2–3–5	12 weeks
1–2–3–4–5	7 weeks
1–2–5	6 weeks
1–2–4–5	8 weeks

In three of the paths, time slippages could occur and the paths could still be carried out in less than 12 weeks. In the 12-week path, any time slippage means the end event will occur later. This *longest time path* is called the *critical path*.

Figure 11.3
Critical
time path
development

ACTIVITIES	TIME DURATION (WEEKS)
1—2	2
2—3	4
2—4	3
3—4	0
3—5	6
2—5	4
4—5	3

The MIS project manager must therefore monitor and control the chain of activities in this path very closely.

The difference between the time for any complete path and the critical path is called the *slack time*. The slack for the critical path is obviously zero. By means of routine calculation, the slack time for completion of intermediate events may be calculated. Since standard computer programs exist for these calculation methods, we refer the interested reader to specialized books on PERT.

The length of time to complete an activity is difficult to judge. Variability is produced by random unforeseen causes and by the experience, optimism, or pessimism of the person making the estimate. For these reasons, the estimated time to complete an activity is assumed to be a variable following a probability distribution.

The person responsible for completing a task estimates the minimum time for the activity, the maximum time the task will take if bad breaks occur, and the *most likely time*. These times are designated *a, b,* and *m,* respectively (see Fig. 11.4). The expected times shown in Fig. 11.4 were based on estimates,

$$t_e = \frac{a + 4m + b}{6} :$$

a	m	b	t_e
1.0	1.95	3.2	2 weeks
3.0	3.75	6.0	4 weeks
2.5	1.90	4.0	3 weeks
4.4	5.85	8.2	6 weeks
2.6	4.10	5.0	4 weeks
1.0	3.25	4.0	3 weeks

Figure 11.4
Estimating
expected time
for an activity

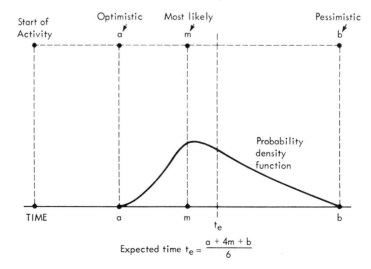

A typical computer output report for a large-scale project using PERT is shown in Figure 11.5.

Figure 11.5 PERT network printout

EVENT Pre-ceding	EVENT Fol-lowing	ACTIVITY	Est. Time Weeks	DATES PL	ES	EF	LS	LF	SE	FLOATS TF	FFE	FFL	IF
1	2	Define site	2	0	0	2	30	32	2	30	0	30	0
* 1	4	Employ manager	6	0	0	6	0	6	6	0	0	0	0
1	17	Select computer	4	0	0	4	3	7	4	3	0	3	0
2	3	Prepare site	10	32	2	12	32	42	12	30	0	0	0
3	20	Dummy	0	42	12	12	42	42	42	30	30	0	0
* 4	5	Employ programmers	4	6	6	10	6	10	10	0	0	0	0
4	10	Employ analysts	6	6	6	12	17	23	12	11	0	11	0
4	12	Employ operators	3	6	6	9	25	28	17	19	8	19	8
* 5	6	Train programmers	6	10	10	16	10	16	16	0	0	0	0
* 6	7	Write programs	16	16	16	32	16	32	32	0	0	0	0
* 7	8	Develop test data	4	32	32	36	32	36	36	0	0	0	0
8	9	Complete documentation	4	36	36	40	38	42	40	2	0	2	0
* 8	14	Dummy	0	36	36	36	36	36	36	0	0	0	0
9	20	Dummy	0	42	40	40	42	42	42	2	2	0	0
10	11	Write detailed procedures	5	23	12	17	23	28	17	11	0	0	0
11	12	Dummy	0	28	17	17	28	28	17	11	0	0	0
11	15	Design forms	4	28	17	21	30	34	21	13	0	2	0
12	13	Train operators	4	28	17	21	28	32	21	11	0	0	0
13	14	Convert files	4	32	21	25	32	36	36	11	11	0	0
*14	20	Test and debug programs	6	36	36	42	36	42	42	0	0	0	0
15	16	Order forms	2	34	21	23	34	36	23	13	0	0	0
16	20	Await forms	6	36	23	29	36	42	42	13	13	0	0
17	18	Order computer	4	7	4	8	7	11	8	3	0	0	0
18	19	Await delivery	30	11	8	38	11	41	38	3	0	0	0
19	20	Install computer	1	41	38	39	41	42	42	3	3	0	0
*20	21	Run parallel	8	42	42	50	42	50	50	0	0	0	0

Legend:
PL — latest date of preceding event
ES — earliest starting date
EF — earliest finishing date
LS — latest starting date
LF — latest finishing date
SE — earliest date of succeeding event
* — critical path

TF — total float
FFE — free float early
FFL — free float late
IF — independent float

LF — ES — A
SE — ES — A
LF — PL — A
SE — PL — A

Output in sequence by preceding event and following event.

Source: Alton R. Kindred, **Data Systems and Management,** © 1973, p. 229. Reprinted by permission of Prentice-Hall, Inc.

FLOW CHARTING

Flow charts are diagrams consisting of pictorial symbols connected by directed line segments to show the sequencing of activities, operations, logic flow, materials flow, data/information flow, or authority flow in organizations. (We are not concerned here with technical engineering flow charts.) We have presented flow charts earlier in the text because they are easy to read without explanation.

However, the systems designer who must construct flow charts needs a good understanding of their characteristics and applications.

Flow charts are useful to the systems designer because they aid in (1) problem definition, (2) problem presentation and review, (3) solution of problems, and (4) documentation of systems design.

The basic system and program flow chart symbols are:

Two additional symbols that permit connecting a flow chart from one page to the next are:

Additional and specialized symbols are shown in Figure 11.6. These are adequate for the MIS designer. The important point is that *standardization within the company is essential.*

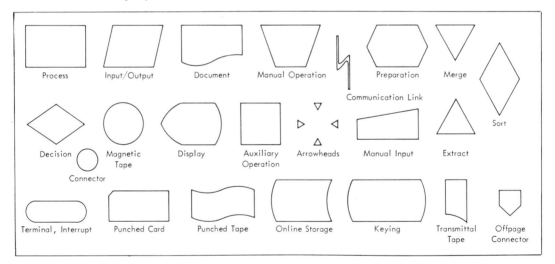

Figure 11.6 Program and system flow-chart symbols

Guidelines to Flow-Charting

The expert systems analyst will develop his own approach to creating flow charts. Flow charting is indeed a creative problem-solving process, so no method can be completely prescribed. Some guidelines that may help the novice are:

1. Specify the objective of the flow chart.

2. Establish the level at which you are going to flow-chart.

3. If a completely new system is being developed, start with a high level of aggregation and block out major subsystems.

4. Proceed from the known to the unknown. That is, identify subsystems that you know must appear and develop the subsystems that must relate to them.

5. Use standardized symbols and a template, a plastic device with symbols cut out. Templates are available from computer vendors or office equipment stores.

6. Chart the main line of data flow in the system or program first.

7. Begin flow-charting at the top of each page. The charts should run from top to bottom or left to right.

8. Each page should have a heading or caption that clearly identifies the project, the chart, the date (of revision, if any), the author, and the page number.

9. Write within the symbols, using as few words as possible. Use the annotation symbol to describe data more fully.

10. Collect incoming flows so that the flow lines shown actually entering a symbol are kept to a minimum. Similarly for outgoing flow lines.

11. Leave blank space around major nonconvergent flows.

12. When flow lines are numerous on complex charts, use connectors to reduce their number.

13. Avoid intersecting (crossover) flow lines.

14. Be neat. Put yourself in the place of the reader and ask if the diagram can be quickly and clearly read.

Types of Flow Charts

There is a lack of standardization in flow-charting because practitioners have drawn charts in any way that served their purposes. "Structured programming," to be discussed later, is an exception and has proven very valuable. Examination of numerous flow charts developed in companies leads to the classification below.

1. *Block diagrams of general system relations.* This type of diagram is used early in the design process to define the problems, or it is used as a summary after the design is completed to give an overall view of the system.

2. *Block diagrams combining both operations sequences and information flow.*

3. *Process charts.* These charts show the sequence of steps required to complete a defined operation. Such a chart may take the usual block-diagram form or the special format shown in Figure 11.7.

Figure 11.7
Flow process

FLOW PROCESS CHART

No. 765B

Page 1 of 1

	Present		Proposed		Difference	
	No	Time	No	Time	No	Time
Operations	4		2		2	
Transportations	4		2		2	
Inspections	2		1		1	
Delays	6		3		3	
Storages	0		0		0	
Distance Travelled	1560'		1525'		35'	

Job Complete Expense Acct.

Man ☐ Mat'l ☒ Form

Chart begins _____

Chart ends _____

Charted by ____ B. Davis

Date ____ 7/27

	OPER TRANS STORE INSP DELAY	Dist.	Time	~~(PRESENT)~~ Details of (PROPOSED) Method
1	○⇨△☐D			Expense account form written (4 copies) by employee
2	○⇨△☐D			In basket awaiting interoffice mail pickup
3	○⇨△☐D	1500'		To accounting office
4	○⇨△☐D			Waiting on accounting officer's desk
5	○⇨△☐D			Examined by accounting officer
6	○⇨△☐D			Approved by accounting officer
7	○⇨△☐D	25'		To accounting clerk's desk
8	○⇨△☐D			On desk waiting for preparation of check
9	○⇨△☐D			
10	○⇨△☐D			
11	○⇨△☐D			
12	○⇨△☐D			
13	○⇨△☐D			
14	○⇨△☐D			
15	○⇨△☐D			
16	○⇨△☐D			
17	○⇨△☐D			
18	○⇨△☐D			

COMMENTS:

Source: Arthur C. Laufer, **Operations Management** (Cincinnati: South-Western Publishing Company, 1975), p. 306.

4. *Detailed system flow chart.* This more complex chart is useful in the detailed design phase. An example is shown in Figure 11.8.

5. *Forms flow chart.* This chart shows the flow of forms and the distribution of copies of forms (Figure 11.9).

6. *Data-base flow charts.* A wide variety of such charts are possible. Figure 11.10 shows inputs and outputs for user files.

Figure 11.8 University student system

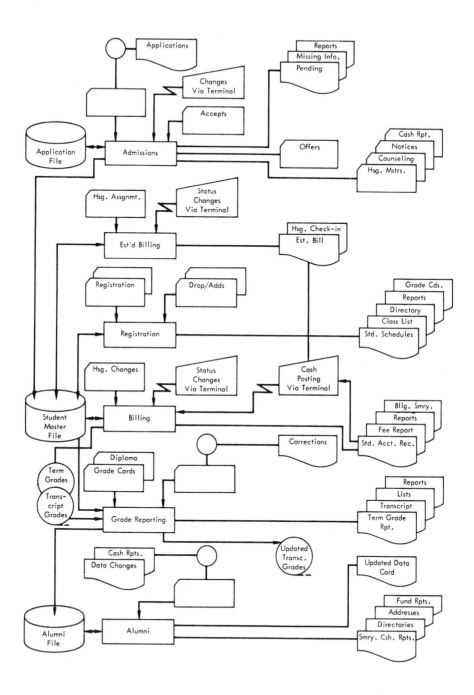

Source: Alton R. Kindred, **Data Systems and Management,** © 1973. Reprinted by permission of Prentice-Hall, Inc.

Figure 11.9 Forms distribution flow chart

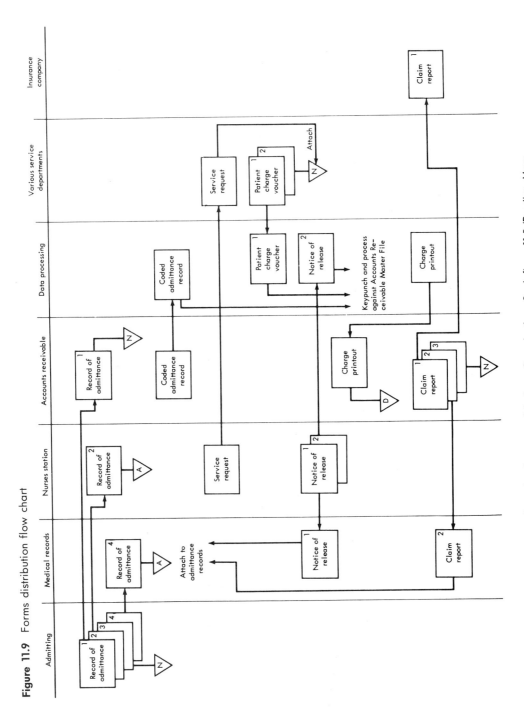

Source: Barry E. Cushing, **Accounting Information Systems and Business Organizations,** 2 ed. figure 11.5 (Reading, Mass.: Addison-Wesley, 1978.) © 1978. Reprinted with permission.

Figure 11.10 Schematic of input, files and output

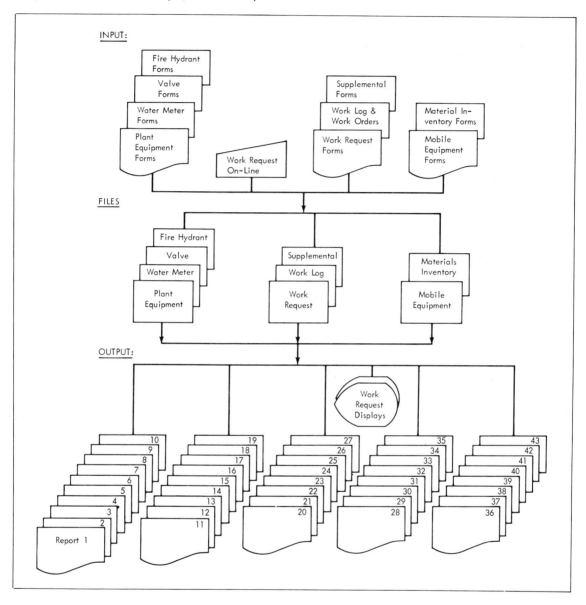

7. *Detailed computer flow charts.* With structured programming, detailed program charts may be prepared using three basic control structures. The purpose of the structured approach is to eliminate complexity and errors caused by program steps that jump around with GO TO instructions rather than proceeding serially. Figure 11.11 shows the basic flow charts. The subject of structured programming, while very important to programmers, is beyond the scope of this book.

Figure 11.11
Structured
programming:
basic flow
charts

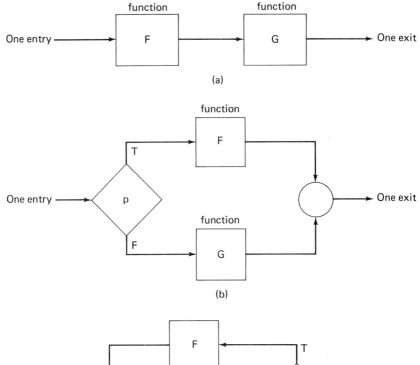

(a)

(b)

(c)

(a) Simple sequence: Statements are executed in the order in
which they appear.
(b) IFTHENELSE: Predicate (condition) p is tested. If p is
true, function F is executed and G is skipped. If p does not
hold, then F is skipped and G is executed.
(c) DOWHILE: Condition p is tested. If p is true, the statement F
is executed; otherwise F is skipped and control passes to the
next statement.

DATA-FLOW MATRICES

Matrices (tables) showing various relationships between data and sources, desti-
nations, files, users, and other system components are very helpful in systems
analysis and documentation. Such tables often serve as a good substitute for
some types of flow diagrams. They are valuable in gathering information during
interviews with managers and operating personnel. They also provide an integrated view of some aspects of the MIS.

Data matrices are listed below, and some examples are cited:

1. Managers vs. information needed or received
2. Reports vs. data sources
3. Reports vs. user
4. Subsystems vs. data input
5. Subsystems vs. data output
6. Documents vs. user
7. Information user vs. information transmitter
8. File vs. data source
9. File vs. user
10. Reports vs. files
11. Computer application program vs. departmental user

JOB-STATION ANALYSIS

Job-station analysis is a technique for uncovering problems, evaluating control, measuring errors, measuring work output, and reviewing transactions and document/report flow at the "nodes" of the information system. It consists of a study of a position from the systems view. The steps in job-station analysis are outlined in the following sections.

Figure 11.12
Position
description for
an individual
worker

Data Processing Control Clerk

Reports to: Operations and Systems Supervisor

Department: Data Processing

Job responsibilities are as follows:

1. Receives input data from various departments and users; reviews input for acceptability; maintains log of all input activity.
2. Distributes input to keypunch and/or computer operations.
3. Sees that work is punched on cards and checked for proper format.
4. Controls work flow and schedule from keypunch to computer operations.
5. Supervises the keypunch operators in the absence of the Keypunch Supervisor and/or Lead Keypunch Operator.
6. Reviews output for acceptability.
7. Balances reports to control totals.
8. Checks for obvious errors; reports all suspected discrepancies and possible causes.
9. Maintains list of departments and individuals for receipt of input from and output to.
10. Responsible for the distribution of reports to the various departments—and/or individuals.
11. Maintains log of output distributed.
12. Notifies supervisor of schedule delays and all inadequacies.

Obtain the Title and Position Description

The first step in job-station analysis is to study the present objectives of the position. Every position should have a title and a position description. If it does not, a position description should be prepared based upon a detailed analysis of activities. A good job description contains (1) job title and reporting relationship, (2) summary of objectives and functions, and (3) a full list of responsibilities. Figure 11.12 shows actual examples which are not as elaborate as many job descriptions.

List of Operations, Filings, and Transports

A list of operations actually performed at the work stations is prepared. Interviews and observation may be used as cross-checks. This list may be checked further against the position description.

In addition to performing operations, the incumbent may file, and remove from file, documents as part of the job. The incumbent may also transport records or documents from one work station to another. The process chart mentioned earlier is a useful tool in this phase of work-station analysis.

Inputs and Outputs

Inputs of all forms (documents, verbal, video, and so on) and outputs from the work station should be tabulated for analysis. Content, format, frequency, source, and destination should be considered.

Equipment Used

Equipment used at accounting work stations may consist of desk computers, computer video terminals, typewriters, file tubs, special telephones, reproduction machines, and mechanical stamping devices. Any design of a work station must take into account not only the process but the equipment.

Work Relationships with Other Work Stations

By means of flow charts or matrices, the interactions among work stations should be described. Frequency of contact and physical distance between stations are important considerations for office layout.

Although the stopwatch time study in the office is certainly a rarity, methods for performing routine or repetitive operations are applicable. The basic work principles, such as placing materials close to their point of usage, and the principles of finger, hand, and arm motions from industrial engineering are equally valid in the office. Predetermined time standards for motions may be used to establish a standard time for each task. If tasks are not repetitive, average time for a complete process (even involving several work stations) may be determined on the basis of a series of measurements of the entire process time.

Work Measurement

If some work stations are bottlenecks, or if the systems analyst believes that the number of work stations can be reduced, the analyst may call for a methods analysis and a work measurement study. Such a study will reveal the standard time required to perform certain operations. Standard time may be compared with actual time for efficiency measurement; it is also used to redesign the station work load. Figure 11.13 shows methods for determining the standard time for an operation.

The normal time for an operation may vary from worker to worker. Therefore, when a particular worker is being studied, the elemental time must be multiplied by an arbitrary leveling factor appropriate for the individual. For example, for a fast worker the leveling factor might be 1.10, while for a slow worker the leveling time might be 0.96. In the case of predetermined time standards, available tables will supply normal times directly.

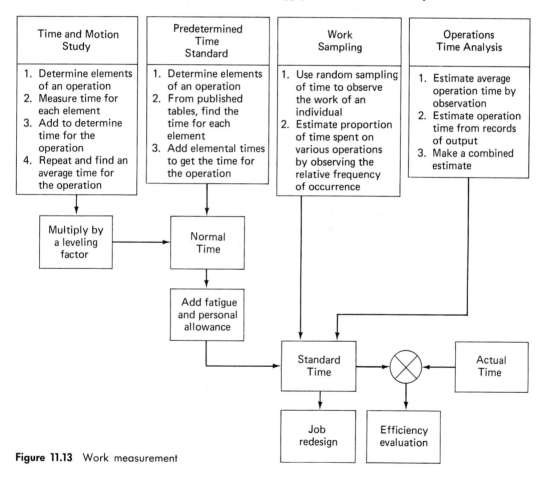

Figure 11.13 Work measurement

A decision table (DT) is a visual means for showing how a rule (or set of rules) applies to repetitive situations. Table 11.1 demonstrates a simple example of a rule. An order for the company's product is received by a clerk, who examines the order and finds that the order comes from someone with whom the company has never done business. The order is therefore sent to the credit department. (If the order had come from a regular customer, it would have been sent to the shipping department.) The decision table shows the two possible conditions as statements. The two columns on the right each represent a rule. A rule says, "If conditions A, B, C, . . . exist, then take Action 1." In essence, the rule when applied to a specific case yields a *decision* on action to be taken.

One purpose of the MIS is to relieve managers from routine decision making. Quite complex decision rules may be structured by the use of decision tables. *If a decision table can be formulated, the decision can be programmed for the computer to make!*

Another purpose of the DT is to force the decision-maker to clarify the basis of his decisions on objective rather than subjective grounds. Once this has been done, *consistency* of decision making will result, even though several different people deal with the repetitive situations. In fact, if it is economical, the decision making may again be turned over to the computer.

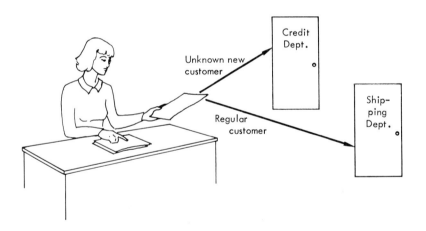

Table 11.1
Decision rule

	Conditions	Rules	
		1	2
C1	Order from new customer	Yes	No
C2	Order from regular customer	No	Yes
A1	Action: Send to Credit Dept.	Yes	—
A2	Action: Send to Shipping Dept.	—	Yes

Table 11.2
Components of
a decision
table

Header		
		Rule identifiers
Action condition identifiers	Condition statements	Condition entries
	Action statements	Action entries
Notes		

A further use of the DT is to facilitate communication between the manager and the systems analyst or programmer. The logic flow chart of the programmer can be converted to DT for the manager. On the other hand, the manager can represent his decision process through DT to the systems analyst in a form that can be readily converted to flow diagrams for computer programming.

Finally, the DT is a method of documentation in MIS that is easily prepared, changed, and updated.

Definitions

Decision tables are visual representations of a decision situation consisting of

1. *Conditions*—factors to consider in making a decision
2. *Actions*—steps to be taken when a certain combination of conditions exists
3. *Rules*—specific combinations of conditions and the actions to be taken under those conditions.

In Table 11.1, C1 refers to Condition 1, C2 to Condition 2, A1 to Action 1, and A2 to Action 2. The parts that make up this decision table are shown in Table 11.2 as consisting of

1. *Condition statements*—statements that introduce one or more conditions
2. *Condition entries*—entries that complete the condition statements
3. *Action statements*—statements that introduce one or more conditions
4. *Action entries*—entries that complete the action statements
5. *Rules*—unique combinations of conditions and the actions to be taken under those conditions
6. *Header*—a title and/or code identifying the table
7. *Rule identifiers*—codes uniquely identifying each rule within a table
8. *Condition identifiers*—codes uniquely identifying each condition statement/entry

9. *Action identifiers*—codes uniquely identifying each action statement/entry

10. *Notes*—comments concerning the contents of the tables. Notes are not required, but might be used to clarify some items recorded in the table.

Types of Decision Tables

There are three types of decision tables: limited entry, extended entry, and mixed entry. Table 11.1 is a limited entry table because the entries give simple "yes" and "no" answers to condition and action statements.

In an extended entry table, the wording of all statements carries over into the condition and action entries. Table 11.3 gives us an example. The third type of table, mixed entry, is one in which there are some limited entries and some extended entries.

Open tables are those wherein the last action of each rule tells you to go to another table and gives the name and number of this next table.

Closed tables are those which don't tell you where to go when the table is completed. Control remains with the original table, which sends you to a closed table. When the closed table has been executed, you return to the original table.

Table 11.3 Extended decision table for personnel recruiter: Hiring procedure

		R1	*R2*	*R3*	*R4*	*R5*
C1	Education	High-school degree	High-school degree	College degree	College degree	College degree
C2	Age	21–35	Over 30	21–30	21–30	Over 30
C3	Experience	Some	Government service only	None	Significant	Managerial experience
A1		Refer to Mgr.—Administrative services for interview	—	—	—	—
A2		—	Place name in file	—	—	—
A3		—	—	Recruit for training program	—	—
A4		—	—	—	Refer to appropriate functional manager for interview	—
A5		—	—	—	—	Refer to General Manager

Table 11.4
Single-rule
action table

Morning Routine		
		R1
C1	Enter	Y
A1	Check sales report	X
A2	Call shipping on delayed sales	X
A3	Make scheduled sales calls	X

Guidelines for Constructing a DT

When beginners start to make decision tables, they tend to make them too large. Often several small tables are better than one large table because the decision may be made in the first small table, or at worst, by the use of two small tables. The size that best facilitates communication should be sought.

Some rules for constructing a DT are:

Rule 1—Define specific boundaries for the decision problem.

a. Define the objective. For example, a firm may have the option of answering a sales inquiry by personal telephone call, sending out a salesman, writing a letter, or ignoring it. The objective of the decision table would be to provide a decision for the order-inquiry dispatcher.

b. Identify the variables. In our example, customer characteristics, size of order, and timing might be the variables that affect the decision.

c. Set limits and ranges on the variables. Thus, orders between $2000 and $5000 might be a range that would influence the decision heavily toward making a personal telephone call. Orders over $5000 might be the limit set to trigger off sending a salesman, *provided* some other condition statements such as credit rating were favorable.

Rule 2—Enumerate individual elementary decisions. Rarely are real-world decisions simply "yes" or "no." Often, decisions call for further steps and decisions.

Rule 3—Define all alternative outcomes

Rule 4—Develop the set of value states (conditions) that yield each outcome.

Rule 5—Assign a decision to each outcome.

CODING

A code is a set of symbols, a visual arrangement, a physical pattern, or an electrical or magnetic arrangement which represents information, a data element, or a character of a data element. The purposes of codes are to

1. Identify classes of information or data

2. Identify individuals and their characteristics

3. Permit easier and more rapid handling of data (because codes are generally shorter than the information they represent; also, most codes are numeric, so that they are readily handled by computers)

4. Provide security access to data, assets, and locations

5. Prevent errors and identify errors that do occur

Coding is obviously a necessary and important aspect of the detailed design of the MIS. The selection of good codes will not only facilitate data handling but also provide better information. Some examples of the nature and applications of codes are shown in Table 11.5.

Two very common types of coding are sequential and block. A sequential or serial code is a simple one-for-one serial numbering as used for journal entries, purchase orders, sales orders, and payroll checks. In a block code, groups of the numbers or letters are designated to provide special information. For example, the five-digit ZIP code consists of a one-digit block followed by

Table 11.5 Examples of codes

Application	Nature of Code
1. Punched cards	Arrangement of holes representing characters (computer cards), product data (retail merchandise tickets), or data classes (McBee card system)
2. Chart of accounts and shop orders	Numeric codes to represent a classification of accounts in which financial data are accumulated
3. Policy guides	Numeric or alphanumeric codes to classify policies of a firm
4. Parts and stock numbers	Numeric and alphanumeric codes to identify, classify, and relate parts and products
5. Standard Industrial Classification Code (SIC)	Alphanumeric code for identifying industries. Usually a two-digit or a four-digit classification abbreviated from the full seven-digit classification
6. Individual, area, company, etc. identification codes, such as codes for ZIP, telephone areas, telephone numbers, social security identification, street addresses, airports, firms listed on the stock exchange, and individuals who are permitted access to certain areas of a plant or to certain computer programs	Alpha, alphanumeric, and numeric
7. Universal Product Code	A series of parallel lines representing ten characters placed on grocery items for optical scanning at point of sale
8. Detection of errors in coding or transmitting codes	An extra digit is appended to a code which, by means of mathematical combination with the code numbers, indicates whether an error has been made. The Modulus 11 check method developed by Friden, Inc., is one such example

two two-digit blocks to identify major region, sectional sorting center, and local post office. The block code includes the very important hierarchical code. One example of the hierarchical code is the work breakdown structure discussed in Chapter 7.

In summary, codes provide means for expediting the classification and for handling, interpretation, and security of data and assets. Every modern MIS depends heavily upon the structure of its codes.

INFORMATION GATHERING

The more the analyst knows about the company or other institution, the better the systems job he or she will be able to do. Under the pressure of time in actual situations, the analyst must often proceed without a full investigation. We will cover briefly here the kind of information, the sources of information, and some techniques for collecting information for MIS development. Information gathering is a complex process. It does not consist of simply asking questions and receiving expertly formulated and complete answers. Rather, it consists of using a variety of techniques, considerable tenacity, and patience in order to piece together system views.

At the beginning of a project, the analyst will be trying to learn

1. What is being done
2. Why it is being done
3. How it is being done
4. Who is doing it
5. Major problems associated with what is being done.

For most major systems, the analyst will gather data at the following levels:

1. Environment of the industry and the company
2. The industry
3. The company and top management
4. Middle management
5. First-line management and operating systems.

For small projects, the analyst will focus only on the lower levels of the company.

More specifically, we recall that managers make strategic decisions, tactical decisions, and implementation decisions. Under these headings we seek information that will assist managers in

1. Identifying opportunities for the company in the marketplace
2. Describing the long-range goals and strategies of the company

3. Evaluating goals and strategies

4. Developing marketing, manufacturing, financial, and other systems within the company which are related to the company's total operational system

5. Developing standards of performance, methods of measurement, and methods of control over long-range and operational activities

6. Achieving greater effectiveness (reaching goals) and greater efficiency (decreasing costs)

7. Preventing disasters.

Methods of Data Gathering

The methods of data gathering may yield information at only one or several levels. In many cases, useful information may be obtained. In other cases, the raw data must be organized and interpreted by the analyst before it is useful. The methods are as follows:

1. Search for organization charts, organization missions (Figure 11.14 for an example), policy manuals at different levels, product catalogs, and strategic plans.

2. Search for any documentation of the present MIS. If the MIS is not documented, try to find people who developed it and get it sketched from interviews.

3. Examine physical-layout plans for offices and plants.

4. Make work-station analyses as described earlier in this chapter.

5. Obtain a list and samples of all forms for the organization relevant to the current project.

6. By means of statistical sampling, determine the number of transactions per day of each type involved in the MIS. For example, a count of the transactions per hour over a period of a month may be made for a random sample of 20 hourly periods. The average for the sample will be an estimate of the hourly volume; levels of precision and reliability of the estimate may also be computed.

   Inputs, outputs, or status may also be sampled. For example, we might want to take a sample of number of sales orders, customers, complaints, machine downtime, inspection reports, or employee grievances to determine averages. We might also wish to study the sample to obtain an idea of the nature of problems.

   Records of ages of machines, computer center backlog, back orders, or contents of scrap containers might be sampled. Further opinions of operating employees, when sampled, may be valuable. Statistical sampling allows fairly rigorous conclusions to be drawn about needs or problems from a relatively small number of cases.

7. Use questionnaires to obtain from managers (or samples of operating employees) their information needs, problems they see, and decisions

Figure 11.14
Corporate data
systems charter

THE CONTINENTAL GROUP

A. MISSION

1. Corporate Data Systems (CDS), as a corporate staff department of the Financial Group of The Continental Group, Inc., has a dual mission.

   a. *Consultive Support*
   Initiate, design, plan, guide, monitor and evaluate systems, data processing, telecommunications and information resources management (IRM) functions and facilities on a world-wide basis to assist the Company in fulfilling its short-range objectives and long-range goals on a cost-effective basis.

   b. *Design and Management of Facilities and Services*
   Provide cost-effective systems, data processing, and telecommunication facilities and services to the corporate staff, and to operating companies requesting similar services. Design, implement and manage shared-telecommunications networks serving world-wide requirements.

2. To this end, CDS will serve various levels of the Company as follows:

   a. *Corporate Executive Office*
   Provide approval-support evaluations of major EDP and telecommunication P.E.A.'s according to Company policy. Keep the Executive Office informed of major systems and technology trends, effectivity measures, costs, etc. Perform studies as requested.

   b. *Corporate Staff Departments*
   Provide consulting, planning, development and maintenance services for EDP systems, telecommunications, IRM, and administrative publications and forms. Operate the Corporate Data Center and provide data processing and technical services to corporate staff departments on a direct-charge basis. Design and manage shared information distribution networks.

   c. *Operating Company Executive Management*
   Provide objective systems-management reviews, guidelines for managing systems functions, concurrence reviews; and, upon request, systems, tele-communications, and IRM consulting assignments.

   d. *Operating Company and Business Units Systems-and-Telecommunications Management*
   Provide a full range of systems, telecommunications and IRM services similar to those provided to Corporate Staff Departments, upon request and on a service-charge basis.

3. The terminology used in this charter is defined as follows:

   a. *Systems*
   The term "systems" refers to the information and data resources and networks used by an organization to instruct, inform, guide and provide effective planning and control of its operations. It includes administrative methods, procedures, forms, Company instructions, communications systems, data systems, computers, terminals, data processing and data communications equipment, and all related hardware, software, and facilities to meet stated management short-term and long-range objectives.

   b. *Information Resources Management (IRM)*
   The term "information resources management (IRM)" refers to the employment of computers, telecommunications, and other technologies to facilitate the paperless office of the future. It includes such applications as word processing, electronic funds transfer, electronic mail, copying, filing, document retrieval, text processing, and teleconferencing.

Figure 11.14
(Cont'd.)

THE CONTINENTAL GROUP

c. *Operating Companies*
The term "operating companies" refers to such entities as Continental Can Company; Continental Forest Industries; Continental Diversified Industries; and The Continental Group of Canada, Limited.

d. *Business Units*
The term "business units" refers to the divisions or subsidiaries of The Continental Group, normally under the jurisdiction of an operating company.

B. BASIC RESPONSIBILITIES

To fulfill its mission, CDS has the following basic responsibilities:

1. *EDP and Telecommunications Services* — This area of responsibility covers:

    a. *Corporate Staff*
    Initiate, design and plan EDP and telecommunications systems; provide consultive analysis; perform feasibility studies; develop and maintain systems; and operate the Corporate Data Center. Design, develop, and manage shared-information distribution networks.

    b. *Operating Companies*
    The same as for the Corporate Staff, when requested and on a service-charge basis.

2. *Planning (Global)* — This responsibility is primarily long-range systems, telecommunications and IRM planning. It involves developing corporate goals and strategies, external and internal assumptions and planning guidelines for operating companies and their business units, assisting and guiding the decentralized business units with their plans, and long-range EDP and telecommunications resource management of people, hardware, software, data, and applications. It also includes reviewing operating company EDP, telecommunications and IRM systems-plans for compatability with corporate long-range goals. Included is support and participation in the EDP Systems Planning Task Force.

3. *Monitoring and Consulting (Global)* — This involves monitoring the plans, progress versus plans, major project concurrence reviews, and EDP program management reviews for corporate and operating company executive management. Included are consulting studies and periodic reviews, both on request and on CDS initiative. Also involved are annual review of Company information systems and telecommunications costs of business units, and the reporting to corporate and operating management of trends, comparisons, out-of-line conditions, etc. with remedial recommendations. Finally, there will be efforts to cross-pollinate technology and successful EDP, telecommunications and IRM.

4. *Research (Global)* — This area covers systems, telecommunications and IRM research and development. It includes studies, introduction of new technology, guidance, leadership, "seed money" and stimulation to keep systems, telecommunications and IRM programs current and competitive.

5. *Management Development and Source of EDP and Telecommunications Management Personnel (Global)* — This involves recruiting, training and developing EDP and telecommunications management personnel who will be available to operating companies and their business units. It includes developing career paths, position analyses, and maintaining level-symmetry within systems and telecommunications throughout Company. It also includes the education and orientation of non-EDP and non-telecommunications management (executive seminars).

APPROVED: 5/3/77
EDP Systems Planning Task Force

Courtesy of the Continental Group, Inc.

Figure 11.15
General
questionnaire

Position Title: Date:

1. What are the major problems you anticipate facing over the next two years?
2. What major decisions do you make during a year? (List about ten to twenty.)
3. What information would you like to have to help you solve such problems, that is not available to you under present circumstances?
4. What repetitive problems do you face that you feel could be resolved by the development of a set of rules (decision table) or model (mathematical relationship) to yield the "best" answer?
5. What reports do you receive that you don't have time to read at all?
6. What reports do you receive so frequently that you read one only once in a while?
7. What reports do you receive that are much more detailed than you need?
8. If you had more time, what operations or systems for which you are responsible do you feel could be significantly improved?

Figure 11.16
Structured
questionnaire

Position Title: MARKETING MANAGER   Date:

1. What information would you like to have to help you estimate market potential and forecast sales?
2. Would you like information on structural change of our industry such as mergers, new competitors, etc., besides what you are now getting?
3. What information would help you with pricing decisions?
4. What additional information about customers do you desire?
5. What additional information would help you to find, evaluate, and select new products for your company?
6. What additional information do you need to make product decisions on mix, lines of products, warranties, price/quality combination, etc.?
7. What additional information do you need to control sales operations?
8. What type of information would help you in making major promotional decisions?
9. Are you obtaining adequate information on new technological developments? Government and legal actions?
10. Do you need more information on channels of distribution? Physical distribution?

that they make. The proper preparation of such questionnaires requires considerable knowledge and skill. Questionnaires may be loosely structured, as shown in Figure 11.15, asking broad questions about problems, decisions, types of information the decision makers would like to receive, and its detail and frequency. On the other hand, in a particular situation and company, the systems designer may gain more valuable information from a detailed questionnaire tailored to each individual (see Figure 11.16 for an example).

Elaboration of Interview Techniques

The MIS designer will interview managers and others of higher status in the organization than his or her own. In order to gain consideration and the desired information, the designer should try to save the manager's time as much as possible. This requires careful preparation before the interview.

First, the analyst should try to learn as much as possible about the manager's operation by the other techniques listed above. Second, the analyst should learn as much as the time constraints allow about the manager and his or her style. Third, the analyst should mentally assume the manager's position to see what the manager's reaction to the interview might be.

The manager is usually interviewed briefly at the beginning of the project to get his or her ideas, during the project to allow the manager to monitor the project, and at the end of the project to obtain the manager's approval before the implementation proposal is made.

Schedule

The interviewer should establish an overall schedule for interviews and then juggle the interviews to meet the schedules of the managers. Once the final schedule is made up, it should be adhered to. No interviews should be proposed, in general, just before lunch, late in the afternoon, Monday morning, or Friday afternoon. Monday is usually a "get-started" day for managers. Late in the afternoon the manager may be tired or wish to get away early. The MIS analyst should remind the manager's secretary of the appointment several days in advance of the interview.

Approval

The analyst requires the approval of a manager before interviewing the manager's subordinates or seeking information by the other techniques. A letter of request by the analyst or the analyst's manager stating the purpose of the study and the amount of time operating employees will be giving up may be necessary in large companies.

Selling a service

Outside investigators coming into a department are usually viewed with suspicion and distrust. In the initial interview, the systems analyst must gain the trust and confidence of the respondent. To do this, he must present his role as a *service* to the respondent. He must not come on strong as an efficiency expert. An informal manner and a sincere desire to uncover problems he can help with through the MIS are important. The first interview should be short; the objectives of the study and the involvement of all personnel in the study should be brought out. Broad questions may be raised so that both parties will think about their elaboration before subsequent meetings.

Conducting the interview

The systems analyst should try to obtain a location where there will be no distractions. He or she should attempt to keep the interview on the subject to make the most of the time the manager has allocated. Questions that can be answered "yes" or "no" should be avoided because they may elicit snap judgments or easy agreements. In fact, the interviewer should encourage "thinking time" before answers.

The systems analyst is at the interview to learn. Any intimation of criticism should be avoided. Rather he should encourage the idea that every healthy organization constantly seeks new ideas and ways to improve.

The systems analyst must be interested and show interest in what the respondent is saying at all times. He should never contradict or express disagreement with the interviewee; he is there to *get* information, not give it or stifle it.

The analyst should be a good listener, which means he or she should stop talking so the person interviewed can talk freely. Don't interrupt; ask questions after the interviewee has run down. Look at the other person to show you are giving total attention. Don't assume; if you don't understand something, ask questions. Don't argue mentally, evaluate, or analyze at the interview; your objective at this time is simply to gather data for further confirmation and analyses.

Note-taking may slow down the interview and make it difficult for the systems analyst to probe more deeply into problems. If possible, a tape recorder should be used. This requires agreement with the interviewee in advance as to how tape will be used.

Interviews should be brought to a close when the respondent shows signs of fatigue or restlessness. The interview should not be terminated abruptly, however. A review of key ideas, followed by a brief interval or pause, may cause an important idea to surface at this time.

Investigation questions

Investigation questions for managers may deal with such topics as suggested below or as appropriate for the problem at hand. Possible questions are:

1. What are your principal responsibilities, goals, and problems, as *you* see them?
2. What programs are you now administering?
3. What are your sources of information?
   a. What reports or documents do you receive—how frequently, and how timely?
   b. What action do you take with the documents?
   c. What information do you find it necessary to request because it is not supplied to you routinely?
   d. What other information do you receive periodically or by request through other modes (telecommunications, video, staff meetings, etc.)?
   e. What documents or formal transmittals of information do you prepare, and to whom do these go?
4. What information do you receive that is unnecessary for your job?
5. What information would you like to receive to aid you with planning, implementing, and controlling?
6. What files do you maintain in your office?
7. What information in your files is also stored in other files?

8. What suggestions do you have for rearranging responsibilities, relationships, and work systems to form an integrated system for your department and all components to which your department relates?

9. Describe how you feel toward the computer center as providing a systems type of service for the company.

10. How do you feel about using a computer terminal in your office to ask "What if . . . ?" questions for planning?

11. How do you feel about all managers' becoming familiar with the use of computer terminals through short workshop programs?

SIMULATION

Simulation means to "make like" the real system in process, in the context of MIS. Simulation will not provide optimization except by trial and error. It will provide comparisons of alternative systems or show how a particular system works under specified conditions. It requires a representation of the system or its inputs or both. Thus we can

1. Use the actual MIS and introduce the kind of job mixes and timings that we think will occur in actual practice. Representative job mixes are called *bench marks*.

2. Use the actual job mixes and timings and run them through a simplified version of the system, a portion of the system, or a computerized model of the system.

3. Use the kind of job mixes and timings we think will occur and run them through a computerized model.

4. Use extreme values of the job mix and run them through a computerized model.

In real life we find that work (input) usually arrives in a random fashion. For example, invoices reach a clerk's desk or customer orders by the day. (An exception, of course, is the paced mass production line.) When it arrives at a desk or work station it must wait its turn in line to be serviced. Also, the length of time it takes a person or "work station" to service a work unit (such as preparing a customer's order or a purchase order, assembling a component, starting a computer run, or preparing a report) varies randomly. The complexity of many random arrivals and random transactions (servicings) in a system and the complex relationships with the system can be handled economically only with a computer.

Components of Simulation

Simulation depends on four basic concepts: probability distributions of arrivals of units to be serviced, probability of service times, a model that represents the flow of work and/or information, and a computer.

Example

Now that we have told you how complex it is to simulate a system, we shall show you several simulations of a very simple system as done with pencil and paper. In practice, the computer may perform hundreds or thousands of simulations to obtain probability distributions of the output rate.

Parts (a) and (c) of Figure 11.17 in our case are based on historical relative frequencies or estimates by the system designer. Parts (b) and (d) are the corresponding cumulative probability distributions.

Probability for Number of Arrivals in a Time Period

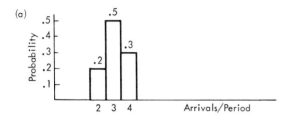

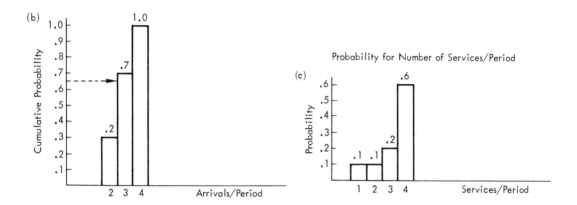

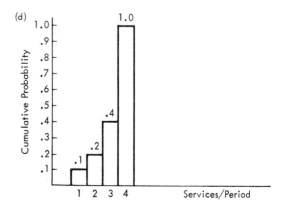

Figure 11.17 Probabilities for a system simulation

Figure 11.18
Simulation of
customer order
processing for
three weeks

Period	RN	Units Arriving During the Period	RN	Units Serviced During the Period*	Units in Line Waiting to Be Serviced at End of Period
1	—	0	—	0	0
2	.63	3	.17	2	1
3	.87	4	.03	1	4
4	.11	2	.42	3	3

*These would proceed to the next station.

In our example, we assume that nothing happens in the first period as the employee sets up his work. The simulation procedure is as follows:

1. Set up table headings to represent the time and position characteristics of each item in the system as in Figure 11.18.

2. Obtain a table of random numbers (found in most statistic texts or math tables). A portion of a table of such unrelated numbers is shown in Figure 11.19.

3. Select a row and columns, *and then* proceed to the RN table. We selected the first and second column to start and decided to read *down*. Enter the RN in the table representing the system. The number was 0.63 for the second column and 0.17 for the fourth column.

4. Go to the first cumulative probability chart (b); find 0.63 on the vertical scale. Draw a horizontal line to the bar it first meets. This is the three arrivals per period bar. Enter 3 in the table in the appropriate column.

5. Go to the second cumulative probability chart and find 0.17 on the vertical scale. Draw a horizontal line to the bar it first meets. This is the two units serviced per period bar. Enter 2 in the appropriate column in the table.

6. Units arriving minus units serviced in the period gives a surplus of one waiting to be serviced in the next period.

7. Repeat steps 3 through 5, keeping track of units left over to be serviced in each following period, *if any*.

Note that no matter how complex the system may be, simulation consists of examining the inputs, waiting lines, services, and output at one particular time period. Then the "clock" is moved up one time period, and the system is examined again. After hundreds of simulations, breakdowns in the system may be noted or average waiting periods or average total service times through many different transactions may be found, or idle times may be noted.

Figure 11.19
Portion of a
table of
random
numbers

5497	6317	5736	9468
0234	8703	2454	6094
9821	1142	6650	2749
9681	5613	9971	0081

Besides statistically varying inputs, systems designers like to know how the system will respond to sudden surges in the quantity of inputs (step functions), steady and more gradual increases in input (ramp functions), or oscillating inputs. Simulation may provide answers in all cases.

When inputs consist of representative job mixes, the simulation is called *bench-mark simulation.*

Simulation Advantages and Disadvantages

The advantages of simulation are

1. When a model has been constructed, it may be used over and over to analyze all kinds of different situations.
2. Simulation allows modeling of systems whose solutions are too complex to express by one or several grand mathematical relationships.
3. Simulation requires a much lower level of mathematical skill than do analytical (mathematical) models.
4. Simulation is usually cheaper than building the actual system and testing it in operation.

The disadvantages are

1. Simulation models may be very costly to construct and program for the computer.
2. Running a simulation program often requires hundreds of simulations and consequently much computer time. This may be very costly.
3. Because it is so easy to carry out the steps of developing a simulation model, people tend to employ simulation when analytic (mathematical modeling) techniques are better and more economical.

Simulation Languages

If a simulation of a system were to be programmed in FORTRAN, inclusion of all the detail would require a great deal of effort, much of it repetitive. Therefore, simulation languages have been developed that allow the system designer to write down *characteristics* of the system components so that the built-in computer program will take over from this description. Programming of elemental time steps is not required.

We present here only enough to give the reader the flavor of two of these languages. Knowledge that they exist is enough to send you to your local computer programmer.

GPSS

In GPSS (general-purpose systems simulation), a system is described by terms of four types of entities:

1. Dynamic

2. Statistical

3. Equipment

4. Operational.

Each entity is described by its own standard numerical attributes (SNA). For example, suppose a series of invoices arrive at the accounting department for processing and payment. These *dynamic* entities are described by *transit time* (accumulated time in the system waiting and being processed) and priority relative to others in the system. The accounting department is an *equipment* entity and is called a *facility*.

A simple queueing system is represented by the block diagram in Figure 11.20. The first block indicates that the computer program will generate the arrival of invoices according to a uniform (equal) probability distribution with

Figure 11.20
GPSS flow chart of the system for processing an invoice

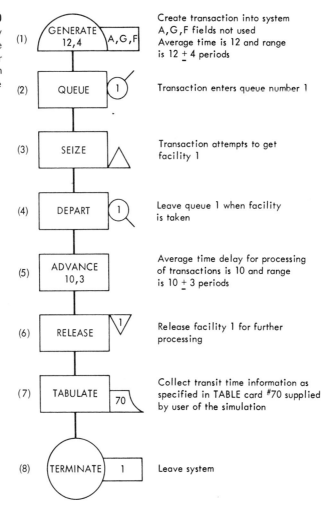

(1) GENERATE 12,4 A,G,F — Create transaction into system. A,G,F fields not used. Average time is 12 and range is 12 ± 4 periods

(2) QUEUE 1 — Transaction enters queue number 1

(3) SEIZE — Transaction attempts to get facility 1

(4) DEPART 1 — Leave queue 1 when facility is taken

(5) ADVANCE 10,3 — Average time delay for processing of transactions is 10 and range is 10 ± 3 periods

(6) RELEASE 1 — Release facility 1 for further processing

(7) TABULATE 70 — Collect transit time information as specified in TABLE card #70 supplied by user of the simulation

(8) TERMINATE 1 — Leave system

mean of 12 time periods and range of 12 ± 4 periods. Equally spaced arrival times or other probability functions may be specified in GPSS. In the second block, the invoice is told to enter waiting line 1. Block 3 tells the invoice to attempt to be serviced in FACILITY 1. When FACILITY 1 is available, the invoice departs from the waiting line as instructed by Block 4 and enters the FACILITY. Block 5, ADVANCE, provides the random time interval for servicing the invoice. Block 6 releases the FACILITY for further processing. Block 7 says to tabulate certain information that the user of the simulation desires and has previously specified on card 70. Finally, the transaction (invoice) is TERMINATED and leaves the system.

This example shows only a few of 43 specific block types available in GPSS.

SIMSCRIPT II

Simscript II is a language that is divided into essentially five levels. Level 1 is a very basic programming language for teaching programming concepts. The highest, level 5, introduces the simulation features such as time-advance routines, event and activity processing, process generation, and accumulation and analysis of statistical information.

The concepts used in Simscript are

Entities: things that exist in the simulated world
>Temporary: such as a job that passes through for processing and then leaves the system
>Permanent: receipt times of a service facility, types of machines, types of personnel, etc.

Attributes: characteristics of entities such as number of each type of machine, age of each type of machine, number of each type of personnel

Sets: sets to which entities belong or are made up of

Events { *Exogenus* events that arise from outside the simulation process such as the addition of new machines into the system
Endogenous events, which are caused by prior occurrences in the simulation.

SIMULA

A SIMULA program describes a sequence of events over time rather than a set of permanent relationships. In permanent relationships such as the service counter system, customers are passive entities acted upon by the service clerk. The disadvantage of this viewpoint is that passive entities cannot be studied. For example, what happens when the impatient customer leaves the line?

The format of an ALGOL block is used to define the components of a physical system. Then for the SIMULA system, there are five basic components: activities, processes, elements, sets, and the sequencing set.

1. Indicate the primary order of the phases in the project management cycle.

(1) _____   a. Scheduling and budgeting

(2) _____   b. Setting objectives

(3) _____   c. Reporting and controlling

(4) _____   d. Implementing

(5) _____   e. MIS project needs

(6) _____   f. Planning

2.

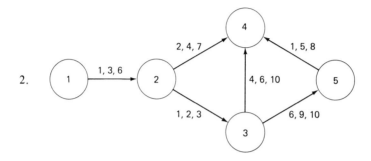

a. Give the expected times of the activities:

(1,2) _____   (3,4) _____

(2,4) _____   (4,5) _____

(2,3) _____   (3,5) _____

b. Circle the critical path:

1–2–4–5   1–2–3–5

1–2–3–4–5   1–5

3. Match the following:

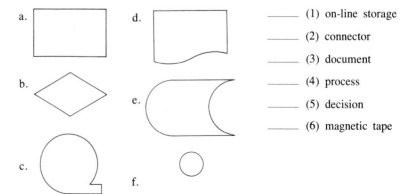

_____ (1) on-line storage

_____ (2) connector

_____ (3) document

_____ (4) process

_____ (5) decision

_____ (6) magnetic tape

4. Match the purposes in the left-hand column with the items on the right.

a. Aid in problem definition and solution _____ (1) decision table

b. Find standard time for an operation
_____ (2) data flow matrix
c. Make programmed selection of action

d. Aid in information and data analysis _____ (3) data flow matrix

e. Determine longest time to completion
_____ (4) flow chart

_____ (5) PERT

_____ (6) work measurement

5. Check the cells to indicate the information the various managers of a retail department store chain should receive.

Information \ Managers	General	Operations	Personnel	Display	Merchandising VP
a. Merchandise report					
b. Sales reports					
c. Inventory reports					
d. Hours and dollars sales report					
e. Buyer reports					
f. Display plans					
g. Promotional plans					
h. Shipping schedules					
i. Industry-average reports					
j. Warehouse information					
k. Security reports					
l. Company policies					
m. Training-program information					
n. Employee turnover					
o. Budget information					
p. Audit information					

6. Check the level of information for the following:

Information	Environment	Industry	Company	Middle Management	First-line Management
a. New company enters the market with a competing product					
b. New plant layout is required					

Information	Environment	Industry	Company	Middle Management	First-line Management
c. Sales forecast indicates a downturn					
d. Technological breakthrough in bubble memory					
e. New marketing research proposal					
f. Hostile merger move is made by another company					
g. Department's absenteeism is increasing					
h. U.S. population is aging					

7. Develop a decision table for the purpose of screening out least likely new-product proposals.

8. a. Construct a PERT network of about 15 to 25 events with estimated activity times for the design of an MIS for
   (1) A bank
   (2) A hospital
   (3) A single-plant manufacturing company with about 800 employees (state assumptions about the nature of this hypothetical company, such as organization chart).
   b. Use the computer to obtain a PERT network printout similar to that of Fig. 11.5.

9. Seek out the cooperation of a local company and perform a job-station analysis on a manager's position.

10. Show an accounting classification with codes for the following; if possible, obtain industry-recommended codings:
    a. A manufacturing company
    b. A hospital
    c. A retail department store
    d. A bank.

11. Develop an interview guide for interviewing
    a. The president of a company (specify the type of company)
    b. Manager of accounting
    c. Manager of manufacturing
    d. Manager of engineering
    e. Manager of personnel
    f. Manager of production planning and control.

12. Show a simple information-flow system, perhaps with as few as three or four operations, and discuss how you would simulate its operation.

13. Develop a file description sheet for the personnel file. Include such items as record length, file number, volatility, activity, retention period, inputs, outputs, storage, and organization of the file.

SELECTED REFERENCES

Project Planning and Control

ARCHIBALD, RUSSELL D., *Managing High-Technology Programs and Projects.* New York: John Wiley, 1976.

ARCHIBALD, RUSSELL D., and RICHARD L. VILLORIA, *Network-based Management Systems.* New York: John Wiley, 1967.

BRANDON, DICK H., and MAX GRAY, *Project Control Standards.* Princeton, N.J.: Auerbach Publishers, Inc., 1970.

GUNDERMAN, JAMES R., and FRANK W. McMURRY, "Making Project Management Effective," *Journal of Systems Management,* February 1975.

INGRASSIA, FRANK S., "Combating the '90% Complete' Syndrome," *Datamation,* January 1978.

LISTON, DAVID M., JR., and MARY L. SCHOENE, "A Systems Approach to the Design of Information Systems," *Journal of the American Society for Information Science,* March–April 1973.

METZGER, PHILIP W., *Managing a Programming Project.* Englewood Cliffs, N.J.: Prentice-Hall, 1973.

MODER, JOSEPH J., and CECIL R. PHILLIPS, *Project Management with CPM and PERT,* 2d ed. New York: Van Nostrand Reinhold, 1970.

SHAW, JOHN C., and WILLIAM AKINS, *Managing Computer System Projects.* New York: McGraw-Hill, 1970.

WIEST, JEROME K., and FERDINAND R. LEVY. *A Management Guide to PERT/CPM.* Englewood Cliffs, N.J.: Prentice-Hall, 1969.

WILLOUGHBY, THEODORE C., "Origins of Systems Projects," *Journal of Systems Management,* October 1975.

Flow Charting

BOHL, MARILYN, *A Guide for Programmers.* Englewood Cliffs. N.J.: Prentice-Hall, Inc., 1978.

BURCH, JOHN G., JR., FELIX R. STRATER, Jr. and GARY GRUDNITSKI, *Information Systems: Theory and Practice,* 2d ed. New York: John Wiley, 1979.

GANE, CHRIS, and JIM KAIN, "Structured Analysis Tools Please Users—Cut Effort," *Infosystems,* June 1978.

JENKINS, A. MILTON, and JOHN V. CARLIS. *Control Flowcharting for Data Driven Systems.* Working Paper, MI SRC-WP-76-02, Management Information Systems Research Center, U. of Minnesota, November 1975.

MURDICK, ROBERT G., and JOEL E. ROSS, *Introduction to Management Information Systems.* Englewood Cliffs, N.J.: Prentice-Hall, 1977.

MURDICK, ROBERT G., et al., *Accounting Information Systems.* Englewood Cliffs, N.J.: Prentice-Hall, 1978.

Structured Programming (SR20-7149-0). Poughkeepsie, N.Y.: IBM, 1974.

Data-Flow Matrices

Business Systems Planning (GE-20-0527-1). White Plains, N.Y.: IBM, 1975.

CHEN, HUI-CHUAN, and RUSSELL C. KICK, JR., "A Computer-Based Financial Management System for Small Business," *Management Adviser,* November–December 1973.

How Order Information Serves Apparel Management. Arlington, Va.: American Apparel Manufacturers' Association, 1974.

MURDICK, ROBERT G., and JOEL E. ROSS, *Introduction to Management Information Systems.* Englewood Cliffs, N.J.: Prentice-Hall, 1977.

"Small Business," *Management Adviser,* November–December 1973.

STULTS, FRED C., "Data Information, and Decision Making," *Journal of Systems Management,* June 1971.

Job-Station Analysis

BUFFA, ELWOOD D., *Basic Production Management.* New York: John Wiley, 1971. (See Chapter 11, "Design of Jobs and Work Methods.")

MAYNARD, H. B., ed., *Handbook of Business Administration.* New York: McGraw Hill, 1967. (See Chapter 6, "Office Work Measurement.")

NEUNER, JOHN J. W., B. LEWIS KEELING, and NORMAN F. KALLAUS, *Administrative Office Management.* Cincinnati: South-Western Publishing Company, 1972. (See Chapter 18, "Analyzing Office Jobs.")

SCHATZ, HARVEY E., "The Uses of Work Management," *Management Services,* November–December 1969.

Decision Tables

GILDERSLEEVE, THOMAS R., *Decision Tables and Their Practical Application in Data Processing.* Englewood Cliffs, N.J.: Prentice-Hall, 1970.

HUGHES, MARION L., RICHARD M. SHANK, and ELINOR S. STEIN, *Decision Tables.* Wayne, Pa.: Information Industries, Inc., 1968.

McDANIEL, HERMAN, ed., *Applications of Decision Tables.* Princeton, N.J.: Auerbach Publishers, Inc., 1970.

Coding

BURCH, JOHN G., JR., and FELIX R. STRATER, JR., *Information: Systems Theory and Practice.* Santa Barbara, Cal.: Hamilton Publishing Co., 1974.

Coding Methods. White Plains, N.Y.: IBM (undated).

CUSHING, BARRY. *Accounting Information Systems and Business Organizations,* 2d ed. Reading, Mass.: Addison-Wesley Publishing Co., 1978.

DAVIS, GORDON B., *Management Information Systems: Conceptual Foundations Structure and Development.* New York: McGraw-Hill, 1974.

Information Gathering

BRAMSON, ROBERT, and NICHOLAS PARLETTE, "Methods of Data Collection for Decision Making," *Personnel Journal,* May 1978.

BURGSTALLER, HEINZ A., and JOHN D. FORSYTH, "The Key-Result Approach to Designing Information Systems," *Management Adviser,* May–June 1973.

COLLARD, ALBERT F., "Sharpening Interviewing Skills," *Journal of Systems Management,* December 1975.

GROSS, PAUL, and ROBERT D. SMITH, *Systems Analysis and Design for Management.* New York: Dun-Donnelley, 1976. (See pp. 222–241.)

HARTMAN, W., H. MATHES, and A. PROEME, *Management Information Systems Handbook.* New York: McGraw-Hill, 1968. (See Section 6-3, "Data Gathering.")

KOUDREY, HERBERT J., "Techniques of Interviewing," *Journal of Systems Management,* May 1972.

MURDICK, ROBERT G., *Business Research: Concept and Practice.* New York: Dun-Donnelley, 1969.

RUBIN, MARTIN L. *Introduction to the System Life Cycle.* Princeton, N.J.: Auerbach Publishers, Inc., 1970. (See pp. 62–66.)

SEMPREVIVO, PHILIP C. *Systems Analysis: Definition, Process, and Design.* Chicago: Science Research Associates, Inc., 1976.

TAGGERT, WILLIAM M., JR., "A Survey of Information Requirements Analysis Techniques," *Computing Surveys,* 9:4 (December 1977).

TALIS, TERRY, "Question Your Way to Success," *Journal of Systems Management,* September 1978.

Documentation

BINGHAM, J. E., and G. W. P. DAVIES, *A Handbook of Systems Analysis.* New York: John Wiley, 1972.

JINKS, DANIEL W., "Systems Documentation," *Journal of Systems Management,* June 1977.

MENKUS, BELDEN, "Defining Adequate Systems Documentation," *Journal of Systems Management,* December 1970, pp. 16–21

MILLER, FLOYD G., "Managing Forms," *Journal of Systems Management,* August 1972, pp. 27–29.

MURDICK, ROBERT G., JOEL E. ROSS, and JACK E. WESTMORELAND, "Linear Organization Chart Clears Away Confusion," *Journal of Systems Management,* August 1971, pp. 23–25.

RUBIN, MARTIN L., *Introduction to the System Life Cycle.* Princeton, N.J.: Auerbach Publishers, Inc., 1970.

Simulation

GORDON, GEOFFREY, *System Simulation.* Englewood Cliffs, N.J.: Prentice-Hall, 1969.

KIVIAT, P. J., R. VILLANUEVA, and H. M. MARKOWITZ, *The Simscript II Programming Language.* Englewood Cliffs, N.J.: Prentice-Hall, 1969.

SCHMIDT, J. W., and R. E. TAYLOR, *Simulation and Analysis of Industrial Systems.* Homewood, Ill.: Richard D. Irwin, 1970.

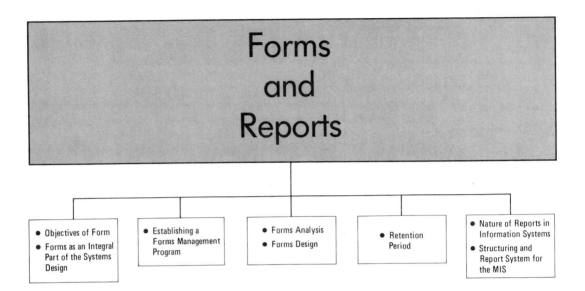

chapter 12

Forms
and
Reports

Objectives of Form	Establishing a Forms Management Program	Forms Analysis	Retention Period	Nature of Reports in Information Systems
Forms as an Integral Part of the Systems Design		Forms Design		Structuring and Report System for the MIS

PURPOSE To develop the modern concept of forms for the capture of data and presentation of information. The principles of forms management, forms analysis, forms design, and retention are also developed

The more work they do, the more reports they must write.
The more reports that are written, the more reports they must read.
The more reports they must read, the less work they can do.
The less work they do, the fewer reports they write.
Oh wow! Where will all this end?

It may at first seem strange to combine the topics of forms and reports in one chapter. We will show, however, by a careful definition of each, that *every form is a report, and most reports are forms!* Further, both forms and reports serve as both inputs and outputs of systems. In a computerized MIS, the forms and the reports are the interfaces between the computer and people as well as among people. On the one hand, forms and reports make the operation of our modern businesses possible. On the other hand, overwhelming demand, external and internal, for forms and reports is stifling thousands of businesses.

The concept of an information system implies communication by means of formal reports and forms. The selection of the medium for reports and forms, the methods of storage, the format, and the content are critical to the information system. No matter how many millions of transactions per minute a computer may perform, if the input is slow and inaccurate, and if the output is disorganized, then the information system is not producing information.

Forms and reports existed long before the electronic computer. Forms have been the basis of recording and communicating information in business for so long that it is difficult to imagine business being conducted without them.

OBJECTIVES OF FORMS

In a modern, broad, and systems sense, *any standardized communication that is an essential link in an operating procedure is the equivalent of a form.* One of the most important objectives of forms is to serve as the means for recording transactions or events at the time of occurrence. If the data are not recorded at this time, their recapture later may be much more costly and the possibility of errors and inaccuracies will be greatly increased.

Other objectives for using forms are to facilitate the flow, processing, and analysis of data by (a) arranging data, (b) minimizing recording time by elimination of constant data, and (c) providing control of operations. Arrangement of data in a standardized form makes them easier to enter, easier to read, and easier to check. The use of constant information positions data, identifies variable data, and allows shortcuts in entering data by such means as checking or circling items. Control of operation is provided by having copies of the same form go to different people or different types of forms brought to one person for comparison. (The computer, of course, may be the "controller" in some procedures.)

A detailed classification of functions is given as follows:

1. Acknowledge	11. Certify	21. Lay out	31. Request
2. Agree	12. Claim	22. List	32. Research
3. Apply for	13. Classify	23. Notify	33. Route
4. Approve	14. Control	24. Offer	34. Schedule
5. Assign	15. Estimate	25. Order	35. Terminate
6. Attest	16. Expedite	26. Pay	36. Transfer
7. Authorize	17. Explain	27. Purge	37. Transmit
8. Bill	18. Follow up	28. Record	38. Verify
9. Cancel	19. Identify	29. Release	
10. Change	20. Instruct	30. Report	

FORMS AS AN INTEGRAL PART OF THE SYSTEMS DESIGN

The relationship between a particular procedure for a system and the communication processes utilizing forms is that they are inseparable. Both procedure and form must be designed as an integral unit. In essence, when data are generated or communicated, the decision must be made as to how to record and transmit the data. Figure 12-1 shows this basic procedure/recording module.

Forms may be designed as inputs to a particular information system, outputs from the same system, or intermediate records that remain within the system. The purpose of the form and the needs of users of the forms in these three cases obviously have important impact on the design of the form.

In summary, and for emphasis, we state that forms must be related to the design of both the operations and information systems. Forms and systems design must be an integrated process.

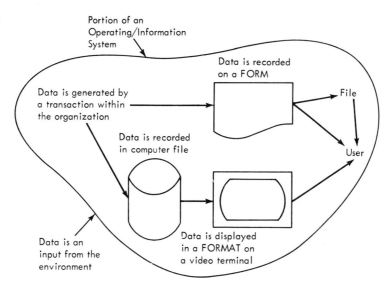

Figure 12.1 Forms as communications devices in information systems

Portion of an Operating/Information System

Data is recorded on a FORM

Data is generated by a transaction within the organization

Data is recorded in computer file

File

User

Data is an input from the environment

Data is displayed in a FORMAT on a video terminal

ESTABLISHING A FORMS MANAGEMENT PROGRAM

Need for Forms Management

The development of forms is part of systems *design* and systems *maintenance*. Responsibility for this activity must be centralized in one group or individual. Without such centralization, would-be Leonardo da Vinci's of forms design would be creating their masterpieces throughout the organization at great cost and confusion to the company. Even when responsibility has been clearly established, the systems manager must be alert for "home-grown" forms throughout the organization.

Organization

The person responsible for forms management may be called a "forms specialist," a "forms controller," a "records manager," or a "systems manager." The position may be located within the controller's organization, the systems organization, or the company's management services (administration division). An example of a position guide is given in Figure 12.2.

In some companies a forms committee made up of members from each functional organization reviews all proposed requests for new forms.

A possible organizational approach to forms management is shown in Figure 12.3. As our previous discussion indicated, we feel that the responsibility for forms management should belong to the manager of systems development. A good argument, however, may be made for placing it with the controller.

Policies and Procedures

Once the position responsibility has been established, a policy (for the policy manual) should be prepared to clearly define this responsibility. Related to

Figure 12.2
Position guide
for a forms
controller

FORMS TECHNICIAN

Responsible to Director of Systems for development and implementation of the forms control and design function of the company.

Responsibility and Authority

A. Operational

1. Forms Design
   a. Set specifications for all company forms.
   b. Design all new company forms.
   c. Review and redesign all forms at reprint time as necessary.

2. Forms Control
   a. Combine and eliminate forms as possible.
   b. Establish and maintain a criteria of basis to determine need for new forms.
   c. Identify changed API's and manuals and update them or cause them to be updated as a result of forms work.
   d. Set standards for consistency and uniformity in forms and maintain and implement these standards.
   e. Establish necessary records.

3. Reporting
   a. Report on plans, programs and progress as required.

B. Organizational

None.

Relationships

A. Within Company

1. Direct contact with all supervisory and subordinate personnel as necessary to complete assignments. Particular emphasis should be placed on relations with Office Services personnel.

B. Outside Company

1. Attend meetings and seminars as required.

Source: John Woychick, "Defining and Assigning the Forms Control Design Responsibility," Computer and Business Equipment Manufacturers' Association, **New Techniques in Office Operations,** (Elmhurst, Ill.: The Business Press, 1968), p. 56 (Out of Print).

this, the procedure for initiating or revising a form should also be prepared and distributed to all managers. The actual policies and procedures will, of course, vary widely from company to company.

Policies may also be developed on such topics as numbering and classification of forms, procurement and inventory of forms, issuance of forms, retention of forms, and maintenance of files of forms.

Stock Control of Forms

It is obviously not wise to order a ten-year supply of forms or to order new supplies of each form daily. In the first instance, money and storage space will be tied up over a long period. Equally important, the forms may quickly become obsolete and have to be destroyed. In the second instance, the cost of ordering small amounts daily would be too expensive and time consuming.

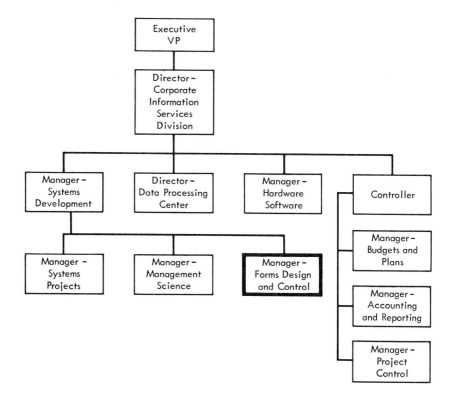

Figure 12.3
Organization
for forms
management

In Figure 12.4, we know or estimate the usage rate for a particular form as D units/month. We also know how long it takes to get delivery after we order as time T. When the inventory reaches a level that will be used up during the delivery period, we place our order. Therefore, reorder level is

$$L = DT$$

Figure 12.4 Inventory model

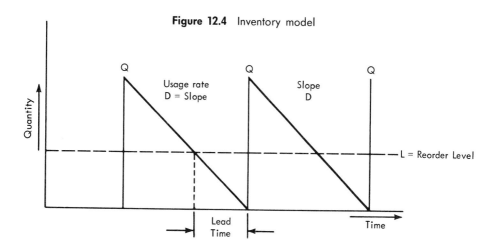

383

The next problem is to find how many units, Q, to order each time. To do this, we find the total cost for the inventory system and then find the value of Q that will minimize this cost. The system cost is:

Total system cost per month = cost of the forms purchased per month
+ cost of processing purchases per month
+ cost of storing forms for the month

$$TC = C_i D + C_p D/Q + C_h Q/2$$

where
C_i = cost of one unit of forms
C_p = cost of processing a single purchase
C_h = cost of stocking a unit of forms for one month
$Q/2$ = average inventory for a month
TC = total system cost per month

By setting the derivative of TC with respect to Q equal to zero and solving for Q, we find a simple formula for the "economic order quantity" to be:[1]

$$Q = \sqrt{\frac{2C_p D}{C_h}}$$

As an example, suppose that a box of forms, C_i, costs $80, the cost of placing an order, C_p, is $15, the cost of holding a box in inventory for one month is $0.30, and demand, D, for the forms is three boxes per month. Then

$$Q = \sqrt{\frac{2 \times \$15 \times 3}{\$.30}} = 17 \text{ boxes}$$

If it takes two months from the time the order is initiated until the forms arrive at the stock room, the reorder level is

$$L = DT = 3 \times 2 = 6 \text{ boxes}$$

As a safety precaution, a buffer stock of three boxes may be kept in reserve so that if shipment is delayed, a month will elapse before the company faces the prospect of stockout.

Forms Files and Forms Classifications

The first step in effective control of forms is to gather copies of every printed document and every standard format displayed on computer peripheral equipment. Usually several copies are required, one for a numerical file, one for a form-title file, and one for either a subject, department, or function file, and in some cases, a file by media. The purpose is to permit a study of current forms,

[1]See W. J. Fabrycky and Paul E. Torgersen, *Operations Economy* (Englewood Cliffs, N.J.: Prentice-Hall, 1966), pp. 264–265, for a good exposition and derivation.

overlapping of forms, and obstacles to easy access of data. As an aid to studying current operations, such files are very valuable.

The numerical file is based upon an identification number assigned to each form. This number may be assigned in sequence in the order that forms arrive at forms control. For example, 215–77 may indicate that this is the 215th form to be issued and the year of issue was 1977. Alternatively, a block of numbers and the department or operations number may be assigned. Suppose that the marketing department has been assigned the account number 350 by the accounting department in order to accumulate costs. This number might also be used to identify forms originated and used by the marketing department. A block of numbers may also be made available to marketing to identify forms in sequence of their creation or to identify subsystems within marketing. As an illustration, form number 350-13-21 might indicate marketing, advertising, and form 21 as used by the advertising department.

The forms title file, if the titles are properly chosen, organizes the forms to some extent by procedure, operation, or subject. Thus this file serves a double purpose.

The classification of forms on the basis of department is usually one of the first methods tried to organize forms. One expert, at least, believes that this never works. Too many forms are used and needed by too many departments to permit such classification. A more useful classification is by function. A code number for each function may be printed on each form as part of the identification number, as well. We have listed earlier 38 functions which forms may serve as the basis for this file.

Table 12.1 Examples of classification codes

Index of Forms by Medium		Frequency Index	
0	Purchased outside the company	1	Daily
1	Printed by the company, up to 8½ × 13 inches, paper	2	Weekly
2	Printed by the company, over 8½ × 13 inches, paper	3	Biweekly
3	Cardboard	4	Monthly
4	Multilith printed forms	5	Quarterly
5	Mimeograph printed forms	6	Semiannually
6	Hecto printed forms	7	Annually
7	Envelopes	8	Five years
8	Tags	A	Four-week rolling report
9	Labels	B	Three-month rolling report
10	Edge punched cards	C	Six-month rolling report
11	Punched cards	D	Five-year rolling report
12	Microfilm		
13	Microfiche		
14	Format stored in the computer		
A	Single sheet		
B	Multicarbon copy		
C	Multicopy, no carbon required		
D	Continuous strip		
E	Pad		

The classification of forms according to media is sometimes useful. In Table 12.1 (page 385) we show a possible list of media and a coding. With paper being replaced by video displays more and more, such an index may become very important for forms analysis.

In the case of forms used for reports, report frequency codes are also helpful for analysis. A typical coding might be as shown in Table 12.1.

A rolling report means that one period is dropped off and another added, each reporting period. For example, a three-month rolling budget report made monthly covers a three-month period. Each month, the report is issued for the next three months, so that an old month is dropped as a new one is added.

FORMS ANALYSIS

Forms analysis overlaps both forms control and forms design. It has four objectives:

1. Determining the necessity of information
2. Preparing the information
3. Presenting the information
4. Storing the data

Forms in use should be analyzed to determine whether different data, fewer data, or more data are appropriate. The only data on the form should be those that are absolutely necessary. Too often, data that appear interesting are gathered without view to cost or use. In addition, the entire form may be eliminated or consolidated with another form.

Analysis of the preparation of the material is concerned with finding the easiest and most economical way of getting the data. This requires a study of the entire operating and information system. Data may be collected in real time as transactions are performed, in batches after the transactions have been completed, or, in some cases, from forms prepared for other purposes. The systems specialist must take into account those people who fill in the data, those who handle the forms, and those who use the forms.

Data become information when somebody uses them to make decisions or take action. The information must be presented in a form that is clear, easy to understand, and current for the decision maker. Cluttered forms, complex report formats, or computer printouts loaded with irrelevant data should be identified. With modern computerized data banks, well-designed formats may permit instant reporting to managers upon inquiry. Emphasis on information presented should not take precedence over the need to present the information in a form easily interpreted.

A study of the files and records is also a part of forms analysis. What forms are retained? How long has each form been retained? Have forms been converted to other media such as microfilm or computer tapes for storage? What is the condition of the stored data? In one instance, a tax accountant using a no-carbon-required form lost his entire file when the writing faded to a blank.

Forms analysis leads to form design or redesign. We will summarize the main points to consider in designing forms. The accountant who is knowledgeable about design may be of great assistance to the forms designer.

General Considerations in Forms Design

From the forms analysis, the need for specific data in accounting and management information systems has first been established. That is, we must first identify:

1. The function of a form;
2. When the form is used;
3. How many copies are used in a single cycle for the transaction, transmission, and storage;
4. Who fills out the forms and who uses the form;
5. How many units of the form are required per year.

Principles of Forms Design

There are a number of specific factors that should be considered in forms design. These are presented below in the form of a check list:

1. After all of the following factors have been considered, the form should be attractive and easy to read.
2. Most forms should have a title. Examples of those that do not may be checks, labels, tags, and video displays. The title should be specific enough so that the function of the form may be determined, in most cases, without seeing the form. Figure 12.5 shows a reorder notification for a form.
3. Forms should have an identification number with the date of issuance. For example, the Pitney Bowes service call form shown in Fig. 12.6 shows a form number 103-Y4/7-74 in the lower left corner. Note that this form does not have a title.
4. Group information into related areas on the form. Use a box design with captions printed in small, distinct type in the upper left-hand corner of the boxes.
5. Arrange the items so that there is a logical flow from left to right and top to bottom in filling out the form. Reporting forms usually have summaries in the right columns and bottom rows. Shading may also be used to make report forms more readable.
6. The use of box items to be checked or coded improves the readability of the design. When extreme emphasis is on accuracy, large boxes, heavily blocked sections, and lots of open space help, as shown in Fig. 12.7.

Figure 12.5 Reorder notification for a form

FORMS REORDER NOTIFICATION

DATE

TO ▶

FROM

PHONE EXT.
☐ 2991   ☐ 2992

The attached form _____ has reached a reorder position.

Your reorder approval is required <u>within one (1) week</u> from the above notification date.

IF YOUR REPLY IS NOT RECEIVED WITHIN THIS PERIOD, WE WILL AUTOMATICALLY PROCEED WITH THE REORDERING (AS-IS) OF THIS FORM IN ORDER TO MAINTAIN AN ADEQUATE SUPPLY OF FORMS.

PLEASE COMPLETE THE FOLLOWING:

CHECK ONE

☐ REPRINT (AS-IS – NO CHANGES)   ☐ REVISE (AS INDICATED ON ATTACHED SAMPLE)

If Form Requires a Revision, Please Complete the Following: ▶

DISPOSITION OF EXISTING STOCK
☐ DESTROY   ☐ USE BEFORE ISSUING REVISED FORM

SUGGESTED REORDER QUANTITY

ACCOUNT CODE NUMBER TO BE CHARGED FOR COST OF FORMS

If You Feel Above Suggested Reorder Quantity Is Incorrect, Please Contact Me.

If Above Account Code No. Is Not Valid, Please Indicate Correct Account Code No.: ▶

CORRECTED ACCOUNT CODE NO.

REORDER APPROVAL ▶

SIGNATURE

DATE

COMMENTS

FORM 35-39 REV. 10/72

©JOHNSON & JOHNSON·RARITAN, N.J. 1972

PLEASE RETURN THIS FORM TO – FORMS CONTROL, MANAGEMENT INFORMATION CENTER, RARITAN, N.J. ANY QUESTIONS REGARDING THIS NOTIFICATION SHOULD BE DIRECTED TO ABOVE MENTIONED PERSON.

Courtesy of Chicopee, a wholly owned subsidiary of Johnson and Johnson.

7. Provide sufficient space for entering data and do not bleed lines off the sides of the forms. If the horizontal lines stop short of the edge of the sheets, it is less likely that variable data will run off the edge.

8. Consider colored ink for captions to make variable data stand out. Colored ink may also be used for serial identification numbers.

9. "Boiler plate" or standard contract information is often on the back of forms such as purchase orders. Alternatively, detailed instructions on how to fill out the form may be printed on the back.

10. Routing instructions for each copy may be indicated by using a different color of paper for each copy and printing routing instructions on the margin.

11. Type faces, the use of heavy and light lines, shaded areas, and color should be combined to provide an aesthetic form that makes the variable data stand out.

12. Standard form sizes should be used. These range from label sizes and shapes to the usual $8\frac{1}{2} \times 11''$ forms to $11 \times 17''$ foldouts. If forms are kept small, they may be cramped in appearance, difficult to handle, and awkward to file. On the other hand, cost savings may be

Figure 12.6
Service call
form

DO NOT WRITE IN BLUE AREA
NUMERALS **MUST** BE SHAPED LIKE THESE ▶ 1234567890

PEEDISET® MOORE BUSINESS FORMS, INC., T

☐ G C A

Pitney Bowes

FT. LAUDERDALE, FLA. ☐ OUT OF TERR

PRINT NAME

BR/DIST. NO.

1 2 5

MONTH | DAY | YEAR

7

ADDRESS

CITY-STATE-ZIP

EMPLOYEE NO.

UNIT VALUE	DATE OF PROOF	C A N				PROGRAM 1 2
ASC. REG.			ASC. REG. ▶			
DESC. REG.			METER PCN & SN			
TOTAL READ			MACH. PCN & SN.			
TOTAL SET						

INSPECT-CLEAN-OIL-ADJUST-TEST	TYPE CALL	PRIMARY SERVICE	TRAVEL TIME HRS	QTRS	TIMEonPREM HRS	QTRS	RESERVE	CHG. STATUS TIME	PARTS	TOTAL PARTS $ EXCEPT CS/P 5&O
☐ METER ☐ MACHINE										

PART NO	QUAN	DESCRIPTION	UNIT PRICE	AMOUNT

☐ A M ☐ P M IN : OUT : TIME ON PREMISES : TOTAL PARTS

LESS : METER INSP. = SERVICE TIME : TIME CHARGE

TOTAL TRAVEL TIME : CHARGEABLE TRAVEL TIME : TAX

ZONE MILES TOTAL CHARGEABLE TIME : EXPENSES

SIGN HERE ▶ SIGNED FOR CUSTOMER BY **TOTAL CHARGE**

PB FORM 103-Y4 7-74 SERVICE REPRESENTATIVE CUSTOMER'S ORDER NO.

HOME OFFICE COPY INVOICE NO. INVOICE DATE

Courtesy of Pitney Bowes, Stamford, Conn.

389

Figure 12.7
Use of boxes, blocks, and open space

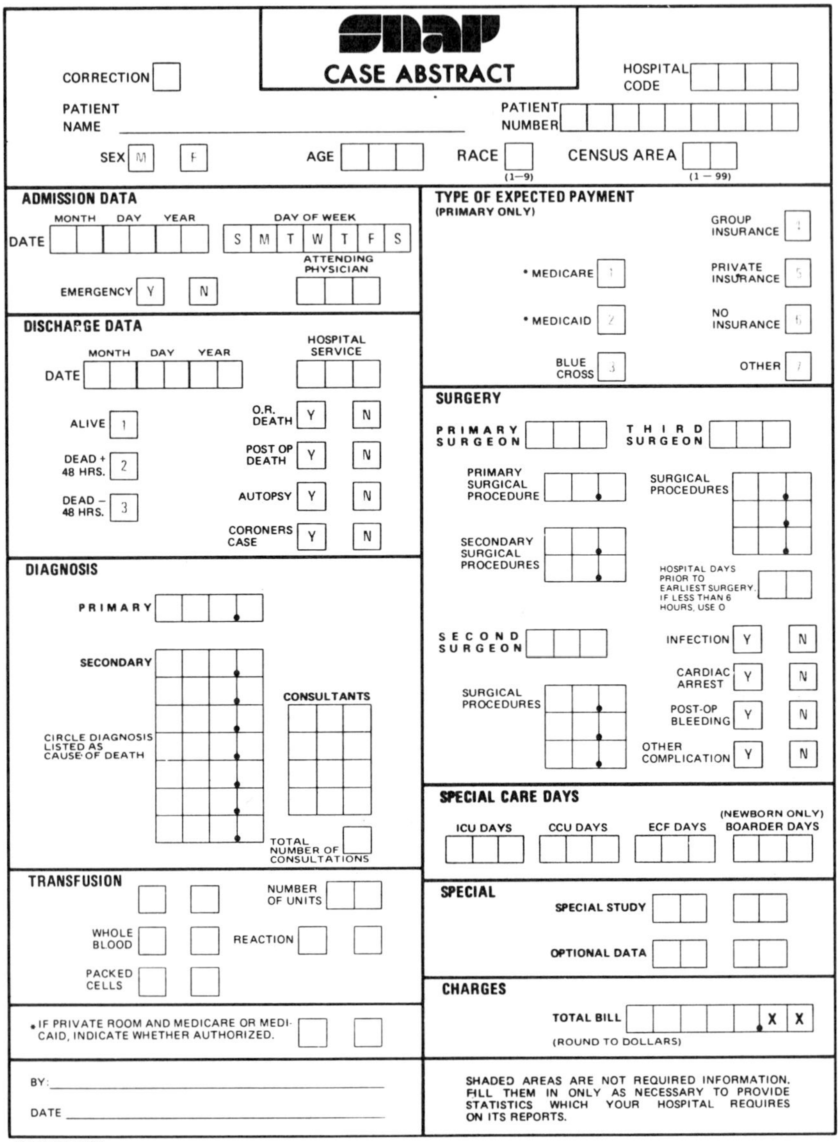
snap
CASE ABSTRACT

CORRECTION

HOSPITAL CODE

PATIENT NAME

PATIENT NUMBER

SEX M F AGE RACE (1–9) CENSUS AREA (1 – 99)

ADMISSION DATA

DATE MONTH DAY YEAR DAY OF WEEK S M T W T F S

EMERGENCY Y N ATTENDING PHYSICIAN

DISCHARGE DATA

DATE MONTH DAY YEAR HOSPITAL SERVICE

ALIVE 1 O.R. DEATH Y N

DEAD + 48 HRS. 2 POST OP DEATH Y N

DEAD – 48 HRS. 3 AUTOPSY Y N

CORONERS CASE Y N

DIAGNOSIS

PRIMARY

SECONDARY

CONSULTANTS

CIRCLE DIAGNOSIS LISTED AS CAUSE OF DEATH

TOTAL NUMBER OF CONSULTATIONS

TRANSFUSION

NUMBER OF UNITS

WHOLE BLOOD REACTION

PACKED CELLS

• IF PRIVATE ROOM AND MEDICARE OR MEDICAID, INDICATE WHETHER AUTHORIZED.

BY:

DATE

TYPE OF EXPECTED PAYMENT (PRIMARY ONLY)

GROUP INSURANCE 4

• MEDICARE 1 PRIVATE INSURANCE 5

• MEDICAID 2 NO INSURANCE 6

BLUE CROSS 3 OTHER 7

SURGERY

PRIMARY SURGEON THIRD SURGEON

PRIMARY SURGICAL PROCEDURE SURGICAL PROCEDURES

SECONDARY SURGICAL PROCEDURES

HOSPITAL DAYS PRIOR TO EARLIEST SURGERY. IF LESS THAN 6 HOURS, USE 0

SECOND SURGEON INFECTION Y N

CARDIAC ARREST Y N

SURGICAL PROCEDURES POST-OP BLEEDING Y N

OTHER COMPLICATION Y N

SPECIAL CARE DAYS

ICU DAYS CCU DAYS ECF DAYS (NEWBORN ONLY) BOARDER DAYS

SPECIAL

SPECIAL STUDY

OPTIONAL DATA

CHARGES

TOTAL BILL X X

(ROUND TO DOLLARS)

SHADED AREAS ARE NOT REQUIRED INFORMATION. FILL THEM IN ONLY AS NECESSARY TO PROVIDE STATISTICS WHICH YOUR HOSPITAL REQUIRES ON ITS REPORTS.

FORM NO. 1050

Courtesy of Medical Dimensions, Inc., Houston, Texas

realized, since less paper or cardboard is required. Size is also related to the standard equipment available to process the forms—for example, sorters for checks in banks.

13. If the form is to be placed in a binder, leave adequate blank space at the top or sides.
14. If forms and envelopes are designed to match, the location of the address shown on the form must show through the envelope window with normal folding.

15. When multiple copies of a form are desired, they may be obtained in several ways. Multiple sheets may have carbon interleaves, or special no-carbon-required paper may be used. The form may be a ditto master from which, after the variable data have been added, copies may be run off. (This is appropriate for five or more copies.) Finally, a single copy of the form may be completed and then copies run off on an office copier.

16. Formats to be shown on video terminals should separate blocks of information adequately. If too many data are attempted in one display, they will be difficult to read. It is no problem to show a series of formats for clear presentation (see Figure 12.8).

Figure 12.8
Formats on
video terminals

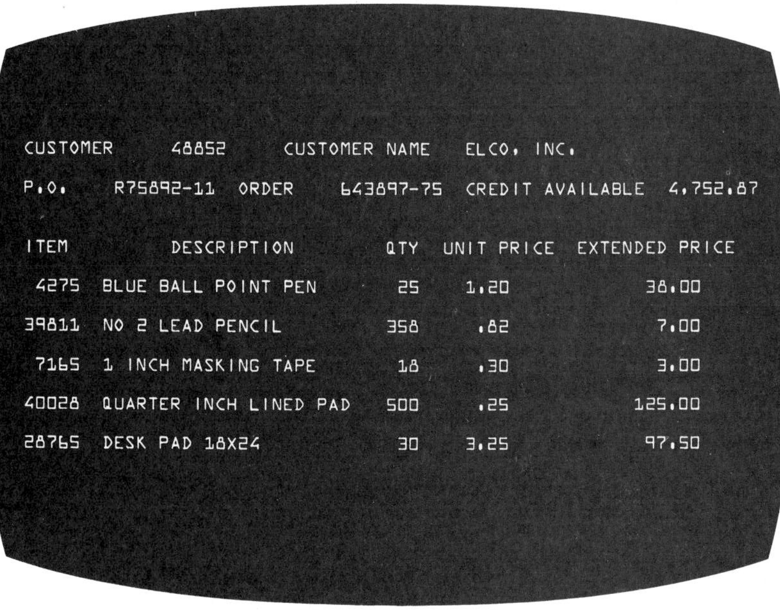

Source: IBM, **Communications Oriented Production Information and Control Systems,** Volume VII, 1972, p. 8. Courtesy of International Business Machines Corporation

RETENTION PERIOD

One of the most difficult and frustrating operating problems that a firm faces is the maintenance of records. Records obviously cannot be kept indefinitely. Different types of records must be retained for varying amounts of time, depending upon internal needs and external requirements. With the complexity and hazards of today's legal environment, the development of specific retention periods is essential. A number of sources to serve as guides to the system designer is listed on the following page.

Fair Labor Standards Act

Armed Services Procurement Regulation

Interstate Commerce Commission

Industrial Security Manual (attachment to DD Form 441)

Prentice-Hall's *Payroll Guide*

Corporate tax department audit requirements

Corporate legal department

Internal Revenue Code

Corporate Records Retention (Requirements of State Governments)

Federal Register—Guide to Record Retention

Federal Insurance Compensation Act

Federal Reserve Operating Circular No. 20

Walsh-Healey Act

Revenue Ruling 71-20

The designer may reduce the task by first dividing the total list of forms and records into two classes: intermediate forms or records, and input/output forms. The "intermediate" forms are those used simply to accomplish daily tasks and lead to formal or summary output records.

NATURE OF REPORTS IN INFORMATION SYSTEMS

Although reports may vary from gossip around the coffee machine to certified audit reports to the president of the company, we will discuss here only reports in information systems. Since information systems are formal systems, *reports in information systems are planned and formal records of information transmitted to individuals for their application to planning, inplementing, controlling, and decision problems.* Reports are transmitted to, and used by, nonmanagers as well as managers.

By this definition, all forms are reports. Forms used even at the lowest level of operations contain data, which, when received by the user for action, become information.

Not all reports are forms, however. The similarity of reports to forms lies in the standardized format and headings of many reports. Most reports in business are produced periodically, each covering the same subject matter as its predecessor. The table of contents tends to be standardized, and the headings throughout the report may also be standardized. It is this fixed-information characteristic which makes most reports forms.

In many cases, reports are made on much more obvious forms. A foreman's report of an accident, for example, or a grievance report contains considerable fixed information. The monthly cost vs. budget report contains fixed information such as column headings and a listing of account codes in the left column.

Special reports, which generally are not periodic, have few or no characteristics of forms. A market research report prepared as a response to a management inquiry is an example. Investigations of major operating crises, such as violation of the integrity of the data base or an explosion in the chemistry laboratory, would likely produce unique types of reports.

Reports, then, may be periodic with varying cycles, they may be produced irregularly (accident reports), or they may be one of a kind (response to a particular inquiry).

For the MIS designer, the question of the amount of fixed information to establish for a report is not a trivial one. The more fixed information in a report, the more quickly it can be prepared and read by the user. However, there is a loss involved. Even if room is supplied for comments on the report form, many implications and subtleties of the situation may be omitted. One way to overcome this problem is to require an unstructured narrative report every so often in the midst of the series of periodic form reports.

STRUCTURING A REPORT SYSTEM FOR THE MIS

Report "systems" for most companies are not really systems; they are a hodgepodge result of additions and subtractions. This approach overlooks such failings of reports as excessive variety, excessive frequency, redundancy of contents among reports, excessive distribution lists, delays and resistance to adding new reports or dropping obsolete reports, and nonrecognition of needed reports. What is needed is a systems approach to report structuring. Responsibility for the report structure should be made a continuing responsibility of someone in the MIS organization.

In the systems approach to report structuring, a single direction of analysis does not suffice. Rather, many needs must be analyzed before the system may be synthesized. We will discuss the design concepts listed below:

1. Managers' information needs
2. Information requirements for management of organizational subsystems
3. Performance and incident reports
4. Progress reports
5. Future-oriented reports: planning and decision making
6. Requested research reports
7. Computerized data-base query systems
8. Hierarchy of reports
9. External reporting requirements
10. Distribution and restrictions.

Figure 12.9 portrays this systems approach. The synthesis of the report structures developed for each of the ten requirements above is indeed a complex task for each situation. We can only describe approaches to developing the alternative structures before they are integrated into the final structure.

Managers' Information Needs

The development of a structure of reports should be started with research into the information needs of managers. Analysis of job responsibilities as discussed earlier, is supplemented with questionnaires and personal interviews by the systems analyst.

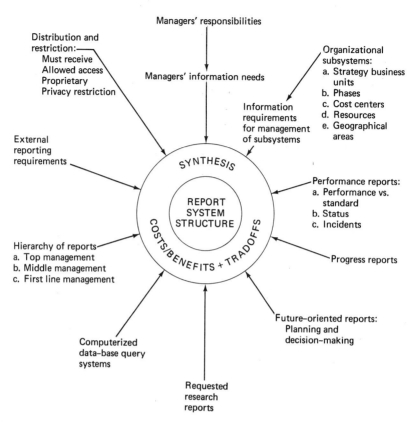

Figure 12.9
Structuring a
report system
for the MIS

Managers' responsibilities

Distribution and
restriction:
  Must receive
  Allowed access
  Proprietary
  Privacy restriction

Managers' information needs

Organizational
subsystems:
a. Strategy business
   units
b. Phases
c. Cost centers
d. Resources
e. Geographical
   areas

Information
requirements
for management
of subsystems

External
reporting
requirements

SYNTHESIS

REPORT
SYSTEM
STRUCTURE

COSTS/BENEFITS + TRADOFFS

Performance reports:
a. Performance vs.
   standard
b. Status
c. Incidents

Hierarchy of reports
a. Top management
b. Middle management
c. First line management

Progress reports

Future–oriented reports:
Planning and
decision-making

Computerized
data–base query
systems

Requested
research
reports

Analysis of job responsibilities starts with the organization chart and identification of managers and their roles. The second step is to obtain the position guide (or position description) for each manager and prepare a table listing his or her responsibilities. A column is included for information the manager presently *receives*. The next two columns should indicate the frequency with which the information is received and the (approximate) level of detail of each item of information. The next three columns deal with information that the manager *needs* for performing his or her job, the frequency with which the information is needed, and the detail needed. With the first part of the table in hand, the manager is in a better position to develop the second part dealing with his or her needs.

The system analyst next may prepare three tables as shown in (a), (b), and (c) of Table 12.2. Their preparation depends upon analysis, judgment, and just plain trial and error. The purpose is to construct a minimum set of reports with minimum redundancy and with minimum irrelevant data (noninformation) for each manager. For example, a single report could serve all managers in the company, but each manager would use only a portion of it. Alternatively, a set of specialized reports could be prepared for each manager, but this would be very costly. Somewhere between these extremes the desired number of reports and their contents are determined by trade-offs to minimize total system costs and satisfy management needs.

Table 12.2 Construction of a report structure from information-needs analysis

(a)

INFORMATION ITEMS	MANAGERS			
	M1	M2	M3	etc.
I1				
I2				
I3				
etc.				

(b)

INFORMATION ITEMS	REPORTS			
	R1	R2	R3	etc.
I1				
I2				
I3				
etc.				

(c)

REPORTS	MANAGERS			
	M1	M2	M3	etc.
R1				
R2				
R3				
R4				
etc.				

Table 12.3 Construction of a report structure from systems-management analysis

(a)

INFORMATION ITEMS	SYSTEMS			
	S1	S2	S3	etc.
I1				
I2				
I3				
etc.				

(b)

INFORMATION ITEMS	REPORTS			
	R1	R2	R3	etc.
I1				
I2				
I3				
etc.				

(c)

REPORTS	SYSTEMS			
	S1	S2	S3	etc.
R1				
R2				
R3				
etc.				

In Chapter 4 we showed that organization may be viewed from five different perspectives. From each perspective we could see the organization composed of a set of systems. These five perspectives (or dimensions) of the business are (1) strategic business units, (2) phases, (3) cost centers, (4) resource systems, and (5) geographical area systems (see Fig. 4.5).

For each subsystem in each of the dimensions listed, there should be a responsible individual, committee, or task force. A report structure should be established which serves the needs of such system managers. The procedure is similar to that of the previous section except that focus is on systems management. (See Table 12.3 on the previous page)

Performance Reports

Performance reports are reports for the responsible head of each organizational unit. They are periodic, of short time span, and focus on variances from budgets and plans. Basically, they should relate performance, costs, and time to plans and budgets. In practice they cover only costs vs. budgeted costs and rate of expenditures vs. planned rate of expenditures. Performance reports parallel the organizational hierarchy with greater detail in reports at each lower level (refer back to Figure 6.13).

The establishment of a hierarchy of performance reports starts with first-line supervisors and managers in all functional areas. At the next higher level of management, the performance report for a manager aggregates the performance of all subordinate managers into a report for his or her entire organization, and so on up the organization. When significant variances occur, the manager identifies the source from his or her report and takes corrective action.[2]

Besides the well-known hierarchy of responsibility reports covering all types of expenses, revenues, asset changes, and liability changes, there is a class of required nonperiodic or incident reports. These are performance reports which show unexpected performances, such as reports on safety, accident incidence, employee complaints, lawsuits filed against the company, or field failure of a product category. Many of these irregular reports are made on standard company forms.

In many cases, the report structure developed by analyzing managers' information needs will be reasonably close to the performance report structure, except that progress reports and future-oriented reports must be added to performance reports.

Progress Reports

Progress reports are usually a monthly characteristic of long-term projects and programs. One report usually covers all tasks of the project. Progress on

[2]For additional reading see Glenn A. Welsch, *Budgeting: Profit Planning and Control* (Englewood Cliffs, N.J.: Prentice-Hall, 1976), Chapter 15, "Performance Reports for Management Control."

each task is described by giving the objective of the task, current status, present problems, and evaluation of the progress.

Future-oriented Reports

Future-oriented reports deal with the output of research, judgment, and speculation about the future. Long-range plans, annual profit plans, and economic, technological, and sales forecasts are common in business. In large businesses we might find forecasts of world resources and world demographic shifts, among others.

Requested Research Reports

Although not every special research report that management will request can be identified in advance, the need for certain types of information can be projected. Regardless, the MIS design should propose the organizational structure to carry out such research. Essentially, research reports supply information that is too costly to prepare for regular periodic reports or is a response to unexpected problems.

Computerized Data-Base Query Systems

Written reports may be reduced by the design of computerized data-base query systems into the report structure. Suppose that a number of managers require a certain type of information only a few times a year. Rather than supplying them with written monthly reports containing this information, we could store it in the data base. The storage of such data and the program for retrieving it in useful format would be considered part of the report structure.

Hierarchy of Reports

Although performance reports form a hierarchy, the focus of that structure is performance, cost, and time. In using the hierarchy approach, we must first interpret the organization in terms of specific levels of hierarchies. The level of detail and the *breadth* of the reports are defined at each level. The top-down or bottom-up approach may be taken to develop the report structure.

If the top-down approach is used, the reports which go to the president are specified. The system of reports at the next lower level of the hierarchy must cover in more detail all the topics of the president's reports. Further, reports must be appropriate for the responsibilities of each manager at this lower level. When this level of reports is structured, reports for the next lower level are structured similarly.

The bottoms-up approach establishes all the reports required by first-line supervisors. Appropriate reports are combined, including more summary and less detail, to construct reports for the next higher level. The weakness of the approach is that new, external, information is required as we go up the organization.

EXTERNAL REPORTING REQUIREMENTS

Many external reports are required by federal and state law and regulatory agencies. The type of report, its frequency, specific content, recipients, and back-up records are a function of the nature of the company (public or privately owned), the number of employees, and the nature of the business or industry the company is in.

For example, publicly owned companies under the jurisdiction of the Securities and Exchange Commission must produce audited financial reports annually and quarterly, Form 10-K reports annually, Form 10-Q reports quarterly (if applicable), Form 8-K reports of unusual events, and Form S-1 and Form 10 reports for the issuance of securities.

The Equal Employment Opportunity Act requires employers of 100 or more employees to file Form EED-1 annually. If the employer conducts apprenticeship programs, he must file Form EED-2-E annually. The Employee Retirement Income Security Act requires reports to plan participants, beneficiaries, and the government. These are primarily annual reports.

Utilities, depending upon their scope, are required to issue regular reports to state and federal agencies.[3]

DISTRIBUTION AND RESTRICTIONS

The structure of the report system and the internal distribution are interdependent. The broader a report's scope, the more managers it is likely to serve. The more summaries that detailed reports contain, the more levels of management they may serve.

Distribution of reports to external users may be chosen by the company in some cases and required by law in others. At the same time, the company may restrict distribution of certain internal reports to protect proprietary secrets. It may also be required to restrict distribution of some reports because of laws regulating privacy.

Synthesis

The research described above may be synthesized by setting up a table that lists the different report structures for comparison. We should take into account the restrictions imposed by distribution, privacy, proprietary, and cost factors. The contents of the reports will doubtless require some shifting as the structure is developed.

Such a structure, once developed, requires constant review, and modifications should be anticipated at least yearly.

---

[3]For somewhat more detail on required reports, see R. G. Murdick, et al., *Accounting Information Systems* (Englewood Cliffs, N.J.: Prentice-Hall, Inc., 1978), and Laurence R. Miller, "Law and Information Systems," *Journal of Systems Management,* January 1977.

SUMMARY   As a user of information, every manager is concerned with the design of forms. The manager is concerned also as the person responsible for the efficient functioning of systems within his or her area of responsibility, since the specification of forms affects efficient functioning. The manager should be able to distinguish between good and poor forms and should be familiar with the broader aspects of forms management.

In this chapter we have discussed the elements of forms management on the basis of a broad definition of forms and formats, taking into account the role of the computer in data processing.

The development of the forms-management program, forms control, forms analysis, and forms design have been discussed. Examples of forms in this chapter and throughout the text serve to illustrate the points made.

The problem of developing an optimal structure for a system of reports has, in general, not been given much attention. When we consider that in most companies managers receive reports that include information irrelevant to their responsibilities and that omit information that is relevant, the need for a good system of reports is apparent.

With a systems approach, a report structure may be developed which takes into account the individual manager's needs, the information required to manage all subsystems, reports of past, present, and future activities, and internal and external requirements.

QUESTIONS AND PROBLEMS

1. Match the following:

＿＿＿ (1) Purchase order	a. Report
＿＿＿ (2) Quality control form	b. Certify
＿＿＿ (3) Tool requisition form	c. Apply for
＿＿＿ (4) Patient admission form	d. Authorize
＿＿＿ (5) Inventory status form	e. Instruct
＿＿＿ (6) Job application form	f. Release
＿＿＿ (7) Capital expenditure proposal form	g. Cancel
＿＿＿ (8) Sales receipt	h. Record
＿＿＿ (9) Credit application form	i. Request
＿＿＿ (10) Work order form	j. Bill
＿＿＿ (11) Shop release order	k. Route
＿＿＿ (12) Report dissemination list	l. Research

2. Complete the following table by inserting one of the 38 functions and checking the correct answer in each of the last two columns:

Form	Function	Initiator	Recipient or User
a. Job ticket		( ) Salesman ( ) Foreman ( ) Engineer	( ) Shop worker ( ) Customer ( ) Draftsman
b. Bank check		( ) Accounts receivable ( ) Sales manager ( ) Controller	( ) President ( ) Bank ( ) Personnel
c. Employee termination form		( ) Manager ( ) Personnel ( ) Employee	( ) Employee ( ) Payroll ( ) Scheduling
d. Time card		( ) President ( ) Accounts receivable ( ) Mail clerk	( ) Payroll ( ) Sales ( ) Employees
e. Monthly budget variance report		( ) Personnel ( ) Accounting ( ) Treasurer	( ) Shopworkers ( ) Management ( ) Board of Directors
f. Engineering progress report		( ) Project manager ( ) Data processing ( ) MIS	( ) Executive Committee ( ) Data processing ( ) Engineering

3. Indicate the retention schedule for the following, where P = permanent, Y = years, M = months.

a. Cash sales slip	_____ P	_____ 6M	_____ 3Y
b. Payroll checks	_____ P	_____ 7Y	_____ 10Y
c. Inventory cards	_____ 1M	_____ 3Y	_____ 1Y
d. Requisitions	_____ 3Y	_____ 3M	_____ P
e. Contracts	_____ P	_____ 7Y	_____ 3Y
f. Insurance accident reports	_____ 10Y	_____ P	_____ 7Y
g. Invoice copies	_____ P	_____ 6M	_____ 6Y
h. Work orders	_____ 10Y	_____ 5M	_____ 5Y
i. Invoices	_____ 6Y	_____ 3M	_____ P
j. Plant equipment records	_____ 6M	_____ 1Y	_____ P
k. Damage claims	_____ P	_____ 10Y	_____ 2Y
l. Employee travel report	_____ 1Y	_____ 6M	_____ 3Y

4. Identify errors and poor forms design in Figure 12.10, shown as originally sketched by the forms designer.

Figure 12.10

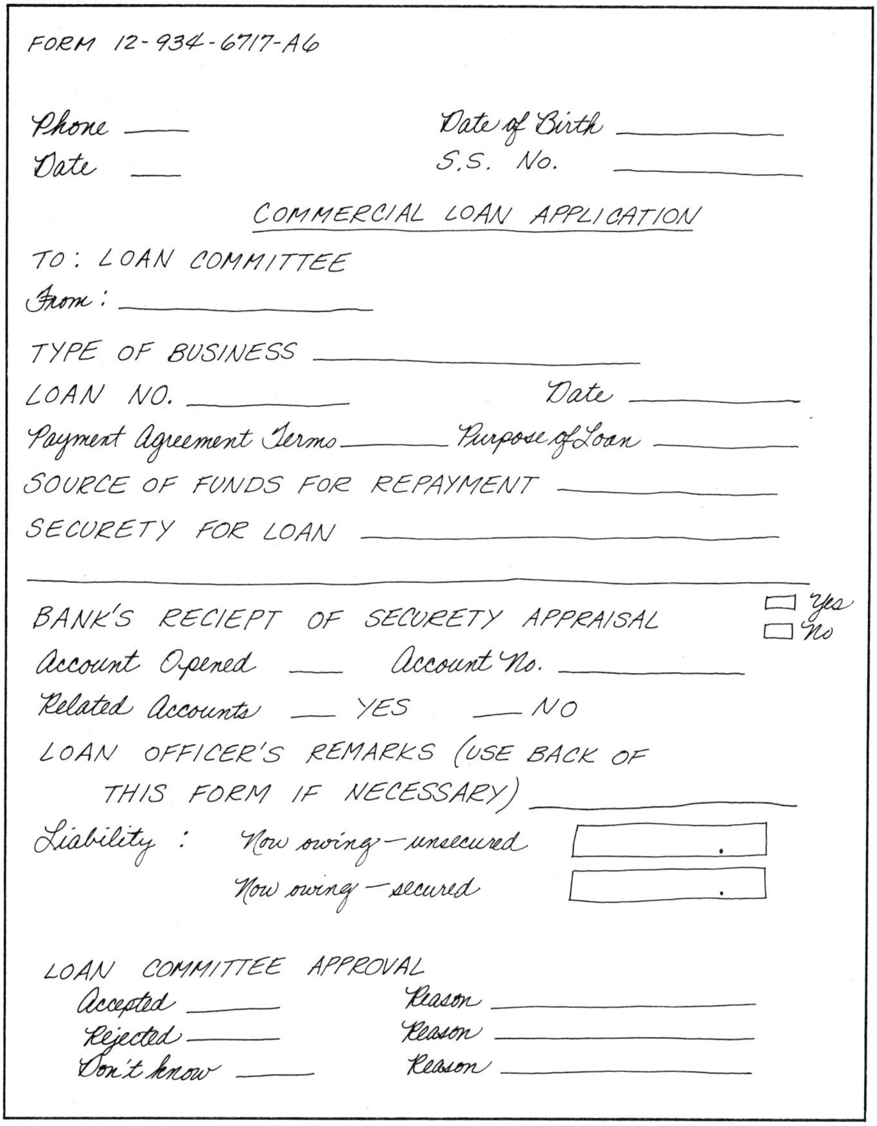

FORM 12-934-6717-A6

Phone ——   Date of Birth ————
Date ——   S.S. No. ————

COMMERCIAL LOAN APPLICATION

TO: LOAN COMMITTEE
From : ————————

TYPE OF BUSINESS ————————

LOAN NO. ————   Date ————
Payment Agreement Terms ———— Purpose of Loan ————
SOURCE OF FUNDS FOR REPAYMENT ————
SECURETY FOR LOAN ————————

BANK'S RECIEPT OF SECURETY APPRAISAL   ☐ Yes
                                           ☐ No
Account Opened ——   Account No. ————
Related Accounts —— YES   —— NO
LOAN OFFICER'S REMARKS (USE BACK OF
    THIS FORM IF NECESSARY) ————
Liability :   Now owing—unsecured   [.]
              Now owing—secured   [.]

LOAN COMMITTEE APPROVAL
    Accepted ————   Reason ————————
    Rejected ————   Reason ————————
    Don't know ————   Reason ————————

5. a. Find the economic order quantity for forms if the cost of processing an order for the forms is $5, the cost of stocking one box of forms for one month is $0.05, and the demand for the forms within the company is 30 boxes/month.
   b. If the lead time for placing an order is ten days, what is the reorder level?

6. a. List or describe briefly three forms which have two or more functions; specify the functions.
   b. Identify a form which has three or more functions; specify the functions.

7. Discuss the differences in design principles for a CRT format and hard-copy forms.

8. Identify three forms that do not have titles besides those given in the text.

9. Discuss the impact of the computer on management reports.

10. As a field project, select a business or nonprofit organization and obtain a complete list of regularly issued reports. Discuss the structure of this system of reports.

SELECTED REFERENCES

CLARK, FRANK J., RONALD GALE, and ROBERT GRAY, *Business Systems and Data Processing Procedures*. Englewood Cliffs, N.J.: Prentice-Hall, 1972.

General Ledger and Financial Reporting System. Andover, Mass.: Software International, 1976.

JONES, REGINALD L., and H. GEORGE TRENTIN, *Budgeting: Key to Planning and Control*, 2d ed. New York: American Management Associations, 1971.

KAISER, JULIUS B., *Forms Design and Control*. New York: American Management Associations, 1968.

KISH, JOSEPH L., JR., *Business Forms: Design and Control*. New York: The Ronald Press, 1971.

KNOX, FRANK M., *The Knox Standard Guide to Design and Control of Business*, New York: McGraw-Hill, 1965.

LAZZARO, VICTOR, ed., *Systems and Procedures*, 2d ed. Englewood Cliffs, N.J.: Prentice-Hall, 1968.

LITTLEFIELD, C. L., FRANK M. RACHEL, and DONALD I. GARUTH, *Office and Administrative Management*, 3d ed. Englewood Cliffs, N.J.: Prentice-Hall, 1970.

McDONALD, ALAN, "Intelligent Terminal 'Soft Copy' Forms Eliminate Paper Chase," *Data Management*, June 1977.

MILLER, LAWRENCE R., "Law and Information Systems," *Journal of Systems Management*, November 1976.

MITCHELL, WILLIAM E., "Records Retention Schedule," *Journal of Systems Management*, August 1977.

MSA General Ledger System, 9th ed. Atlanta: Management Science America, Inc., 1976.

MYERS, GIBBS, "Forms Management, Part 1: Why Forms Management?" *Journal of Systems Management*, September 1976.

———, "Forms Management, Part 2: How to Design Business Forms," *Journal of Systems Management*, October 1976.

VARDAMAN, PATRICIA BLACK, *Forms for Better Communication*. New York: Van Nostrand Reinhold, 1971.

WEAVER, BARBARA N., and WILEY L. BISHOP, *The Corporate Memory*. New York: John Wiley, 1974.

WELSCH, GLENN A., *Budgeting: Profit Planning and Control*, 4th ed. Englewood Cliffs, N.J.: Prentice-Hall, 1976.

WILKINSON, JOSEPH, "Effective Reporting Structures," *Journal of Systems Management*, November 1976.

part 3

ADVANCED CONCEPTS FOR MIS

chapter 13

Problem Solving
and
Decision Making

- Nature of Problems
- Formulation of the Problem
- The Problem-Solving Process

- The Decision Process
- Models of the Decision Process
- Simplifying the Decision Process
- Decision Making and MIS

PURPOSE: To show how problems are identified,
formulated, and solved,
how alternative solutions are evaluated
and a decision made,
and how the MIS plays a role
in problem solving and decision making

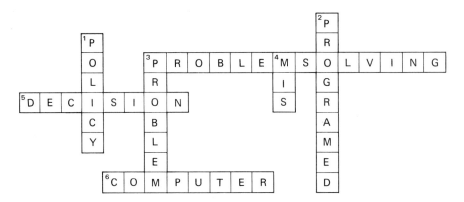

ACROSS

3. Action taken when information is so incomplete the answer is not obvious
5. What a manager makes when he can't form a committee
6. The problem or the solution?

DOWN

1. Precooked decision
2. Robot's decision
3. If well formulated, it is half solved
4. Decision supporting

Problems and decisions seem to plague us at work and at home throughout our lives. Yet how do we know when we have a problem? How are decisions related to problems? What kind of information and techniques will help us solve problems and make decisions? These are complex questions which the MIS analyst must attempt to answer in order to design a useful system.

Many writers confuse problem solutions with decisions, and problem solving with decision making, which makes these processes even more difficult. Problems arise when we are dissatisfied, when something bothers us to the extent that we feel we must take action. The problem-solving activity is the seeking of solutions, or courses of action, that will reduce our dissatisfaction.

Usually there are numerous solutions to a problem, some better than others. The choosing among these solutions or courses of action is decision making. Important decisions also are made throughout the problem-solving process, often without being recognized. For example, we decide

1. Objectives to be sought by the problem-solving process
2. Criteria to be met by the solutions
3. Constraints imposed upon the situation
4. Basic assumptions and value inputs
5. Time and money to be expended on the problem and decision
6. Data to be accepted as relevant, accurate, and reliable, and data to be rejected

7. Range of input and output variables for the problem solution
8. Whom we should call upon for help
9. Alternatives to be chosen in the means-ends chains of activities for each solution.

NATURE OF PROBLEMS

Managers spend much of their time solving problems. The important question is: Are they solving the right problems? To answer this question, the manager must understand the concept of "problem" and then must establish a priority among problems. It is unlikely that a manager can work on all problems that fall within his domain of responsibility.

Definition of "Problem"

Although many problems—the crises—are obvious, other problems may not have been identified. The major types of present or impending problems may be described as follows:

1. Performance is *presently* not meeting present objectives.
2. It is *anticipated* that at some future time performance will not continue to achieve present objectives.
3. Objectives of the present *are going to be changed* and *present* operating procedures will not result in the achievement of the *new*, future objectives.
4. Objectives of the present are *going to be changed* and anticipated new operations will not achieve the new objectives.

A problem is therefore a deviation between a desire and an actual or anticipated situation. Table 13.1 illustrates the four conditions described above.

Table 13.1
Illustrations of basic types of problems

OBJECTIVE	PERFORMANCE	
	Present	*Anticipated Future*
Present	Sales of $1.8 million/ month —— Sales of $2 million/ month	Sales growth to $4 million —— Sales growth to $5 million
Future	Rank fourth in industry sales —— Rank second in industry sales	Rank second in industry sales —— Rank first in industry sales

Let us examine the meaning of the lower right cell. This cell shows that our future objective will be to rank first in sales for our industry, whereas at present our objective is to rank second. Next, after we have examined our plans and the anticipated behavior of competitors, we conclude that we will rank only second at the specified time in the future. This calls for a change in plans and operations or a revision of objective to solve the problem.

Sources of Problems

Problems arise because of *change*. The dynamic nature of organizations and their environment results in changes in

1. The environment
2. Objectives and desires of managers
3. The functioning of the business and its subsystems
4. Role relationships
5. Interpersonal relationships.

Table 13.2 indicates how the MIS makes managers aware that a problem is arising in the first four areas above. Problems in interpersonal relationships—personality conflicts—do not appear in MIS reports; they are usually observed by members of the organization. The MIS may indirectly indicate such conflicts by reports showing decline in performance.

Table 13.2 How the MIS may detect changes that produce problems

Factor	Management Objective	Change in the Factor	MIS Reports Indicating Change
1. Environment	To be the technological leader	A competitor develops an advanced process protected as a proprietary secret	Environmental scan detects the new process. Marketing research shows that competitor's product has become superior to ours
2. Objectives of managers	To franchise all fast-food stores in our chain	Management wishes to own most fast-food stores in our chain	Long-range plan shows present posture and the new desired objective of management
3. Performance of a business subsystem	To hold manufacturing costs to 40% of present selling price	Manufacturing costs have crept up slowly to 45% of selling price	Cost-of-production reports and key-variable reports
4. Role relationships	To have no overlapping responsiblities among managers	New managers are hired and new position guides are prepared as the organization is restructured	Linear organization chart reports on responsibilities of all managers and shows overlapping as well as undelegated responsibilities

Table 13.3 The problem-structure continuum

Problem Structure	Methods for Solving	Data	Anticipated Nature of Solution	Example
1. Very well-structured	Known and specific	Known, available, and accurate	Specific form of solution is known	Breakeven analysis for a single-product firm
2. Well-structured	Known, but alternative methods may be considered	Mostly known accurately, but some key data have a possible small error	Known, or alternatives known	Evaluation of capital equipment alternatives. Present value or discounted rate of return are alternative methods. Cost of capital and future operating costs are subject to error
3. Somewhat ill-structured	Methods for solving are known, but management judgment must use the technical solution only as an aid	Data known but quite imprecise or approximate	Not anticipated well	Plant layout for a multi-product firm using a variety of processes in production. Heuristic and trial-and-error approaches provide alternative solutions
4. Ill-structured	Problem is limited in scope but difficult to formulate	Approximate, not complete, somewhat unreliable	Nature of the solution is only generally known	Development of a marketing program by a firm that has been losing market share for years because of poor marketing management
5. Very ill-structured	Specific techniques or models not known. Only a general problem-solving approach is available	Approximate, incomplete, unreliable	Nature of the solution is not known	A firm is beset by a multitude of problems such as dwindling sources of raw materials, entrenched incompetent management, obsolete equipment, new aggressive competitors, shrinking credit, and massive inventory problem

409

Problems occur continuously in the management of human systems, and businesses are no exception. The importance of the MIS for detecting problems when they are just starting and for anticipating future problems cannot be overstated. In addition, a good MIS will identify problems in terms of impact on the business as a whole. Managers can deal with only a limited number of problems at a time. Temporary and trivial problems must often be neglected.

Structure of Problems

The structure of problems varies along a conceptual continuum from well-structured to ill-structured. In well-structured problems, the objective to be achieved is clearly defined, the variables and parameters are clearly identified, the procedure for solution is known, and all required data are available.

Ill-structured problems are so complex that they are not even defined. The problem solver must first define the problem amid a complex of symptoms and objectives. Data may be missing, inaccurate, or unreliable. Each problem solver may define the problem—usually a cluster of related problems—differently. Finally, a specific procedure or algorithm for solving the problem is not known; only a generalized method is available as a guide.

Table 13.3 indicates the nature of the problem-structure continuum.

FORMULATION OF THE PROBLEM

Careful thought must be given to the formulation of a problem. We must not too readily accept a set of "facts" or the statement of the problem by others. For example, the MIS may show an increasing cost trend for the manufacture of Product A. This appears to be a manufacturing operating problem. Further investigation shows, however, that because of a management policy to phase out another product, overhead had to be shifted to the cost of Product A.

Whether we are defining a well-structured or ill-structured problem, we must define the problem subsystem and its relationship to the total system (if the problem is not a total-system problem). Let us consider a company that has dominated the hand-size calculator market by being first in technology and first on the market. It charges a high price for its unique product. Suddenly sales fall off, as many competitors enter the field with low-priced calculators. The problem could be formulated as follows:

Elements
1. Company objectives
2. Company product characteristics and costs
3. Competitive products and their characteristics
4. Company technology
5. Pricing policies of the company and competitors
6. Present and forecasted demand for the product
7. Company production, technological, and marketing resources

8. The participants in the problem-solving process
9. Time as a factor.

Present State
1. The company has had rapid profit growth for the product until the last two years
2. Sales have dropped 10% and 30% in the last two years
3. The company has decreased R & D slightly over the past five years
4. Five well-financed high-technology companies have entered the market in the past three years.

Desired State (conflicting objectives may appear)
1. To be a technological leader
2. To market a unique high-quality product with a high markup
3. To be the dominant factor in the market (a condition that adds to item 2)
4. Steadily increasing sales and profits
5. To reduce manufacturing costs
6. To have a clear identification of the market.

Constraints
1. Growth to be accomplished internally rather than through merger
2. Increased R & D expenditures are limited to 6% of sales
3. Problem solution must be found and action taken within three months
4. Present marketing channels must be maintained
5. Resistance to major shifts in policy and operations.

Criteria for the Solution
1. Image of high-quality unique products must be maintained
2. Anticipated market share must be 45%
3. Manufacturing costs must be reduced by 20% through new designs and increased efficiencies
4. Minimum company reorganization required
5. The solution must include means to protect the company against future surprises of this nature; that is, the solution must have fairly wide generality.

In practice, the analysis of the problem would be longer than the version given above. The greater the degree to which actual numbers may be specified in the analysis, the clearer will be the resulting problem formulation. As solutions are developed, they may be modeled and stored in the computer system as part of the MIS. Management can then change any of the factors in the problem formulation, except those listed under "Present State," and determine the effect on the solutions.

Problem formulation for complex, ill-structured problems may be started by the use of narratives. A narrative should list all symptoms of problems together with all apparent problems, then attempt to identify a central problem. At this point it should be possible to proceed to a more highly structured formulation, such as we have given for our simple case.

Problem formulation for well-structured problem types may start with descriptions of objectives and inputs. Then statements of relationships between input and output variables are constructed. Finally, these statements are translated into mathematical notation.

THE PROBLEM-SOLVING PROCESS

Basic Concepts

Problem solving for very simple problems is a one-person, one-step process of creating one or more acceptable solutions. For complex problems a series of alternate solutions, each followed by a decision, leads to the ultimate solution. Many people may be involved at each step. The design of an MIS illustrates this process. After needs research and data gathering provide a base, the objectives of the proposed design are established. Creativity is required to "induct" objectives, and decision making is required to rank and select from among the objectives. Next, several conceptual designs must be "created." A decision follows to select the design to be detailed. The detailed design consists of many small problems involving many decisions.

A Pragmatic Approach

Skilled problem solvers depend upon rapid access to information stored in their heads. As a secondary resource, information quickly available from a data base also is valuable. That is, the executive who bases his solutions on "gut feeling" is drawing from experience. The new MBA often reaches the same solutions as the executive, based on acquired academic knowledge.

In practice, the first step in solving a problem is to gain a thorough understanding of the situation. The second step is to formulate (or define) the problem. If solving the problem appears to require considerable time and effort, then an expert within the company should be consulted. The expert may produce a solution, suggest an approach, or recommend a search of specific literature to see if someone has previously solved the same or a similar problem.

If these approaches don't work, then we must develop solutions ourselves or take action to avoid the problem. We may seek solutions by using several basic approaches:

1. *Free association.* In one version of this approach, called brainstorming, a group of people suggest ideas freely without analysis or criticism. The ideas are subsequently analyzed and the good ones considered further.

2. *Forced relationships.* A checklist of possibilities is developed.

3. *Analytical*. In morphological analysis, for example, the problem is broken into parts and alternative solutions for each part are developed. Then integrated alternative solutions are developed.

For complex problems in business where the resources and outcomes are considered significant, the problem solver develops several alternative solutions. If the problems are sufficiently large, a team, task force, or organizational unit may be assigned to the problem, which often is designated as a project. Brief statements of alternative solutions to three problems are shown in Table 13.4 on the next page.

A Systems Approach for Solving Ill-Structured Problems

Werner Ulrich says, "Problem solving, from a systems point of view, is to be considered as a complex cognitive-affective process of formation and reorganization of conceptual systems. . . . From a systems point of view it is useful to consider problem solving as a process of *systems design*."[1] The term "cognitive-affective" refers to the close association of thought processes with emotions and motives. Ulrich developed a taxonomy of problem-solving levels to help the systems designer conceptualize his or her task. The basic taxonomy, rather than Ulrich's extended taxonomy, is shown in Figure 13.1.

The three main levels of problem solving are those of the information system, the action system, and the value system. The basic design questions at these levels are (1) the *methodological* question (how to produce information) for the information system, (2) the *pragmatic* question (how to use information) for the action system, and (3) the *ethical* question (what is the information to be used for?) for the value system.

In order to attack ill-structured problems, we must first study and analyze the system in which the problems exist. Next we step outside the system to ask, "What are management's problems in making this system work?" And then we formulate the research whose outcome will provide the solutions to management's problems. This problem formulation we call Phase I. Phase II is the attempt at solution. It requires searches for data, relationships, and alternative solutions. Let us detail these phases.

Phase I, the formulation process

A. Analyze the functions of the system, its components, its operation, and the information system that controls it. This step clarifies the structure in which the problem is imbedded.

  1. Identify and trace each channel of communication that links components (humans, machines, facilities) in the system.

  2. Identify each transformation of data in the system.

  3. Identify each operation performed in the system.

[1] Werner Ulrich, "The Design of Problem Solving Systems," *Management Science,* June 1977.

Table 13.4 Characteristic problems of the prospector type of firm

Entrepreneurial Problem	Engineering Problem	Administrative Problem
Problem: How to locate and exploit new product and market opportunities	*Problem:* How to avoid long-term commitments to a single technological process	*Problem:* How to facilitate and coordinate numerous and diverse operations
Solutions: 1. Broad and continuously developing domain 2. Monitors wide range of environmental conditions and events 3. Creates change in the industry 4. Growth through product and market development 5. Growth may occur in spurts	*Solutions:* 1. Flexible, prototypical technologies 2. Multiple technologies 3. Low degree of routinization and mechanization; technology embedded in people	*Solutions:* 1. Marketing and research and development experts most powerful members of the dominant coalition 2. Dominant coalition is large, diverse, and transitory; may include an inner circle 3. Tenure of dominant coalition not always lengthy; key managers may be hired from outside as well as promoted from within 4. Planning is comprehensive, problem oriented, and cannot be finalized before action is taken 5. Tendency toward product structure with low division of labor and low degree of formalization 6. Decentralized control and short-looped horizontal information systems 7. Complex coordination mechanisms and conflict resolved through integrators 8. Organizational performance measured against important competitors; reward system favors marketing and research and development.
Costs and Benefits: Product and market innovation protect the organization from a changing environment, but the organization runs the risk of low profitability and overextension of its resources	*Costs and Benefits:* Technological flexibility permits a rapid response to a changing domain, but the organization cannot develop maximum efficiency in its production and distribution system because of multiple technologies	*Costs and Benefits:* Administrative system is ideally suited to maintain flexibility and effectiveness but may underutilize and misutilize resources

Source: Raymond E. Miles and Charles C. Snow, **Organizational Strategy, Structure, and Process** (New York: McGraw-Hill, 1978).

Figure 13.1
Basic
taxonomy of
complementary
problem-
solving levels

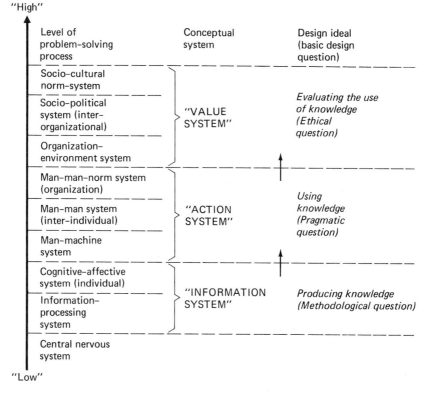

"High"

Level of problem-solving process	Conceptual system	Design ideal (basic design question)
Socio-cultural norm-system		
Socio-political system (inter-organizational)	"VALUE SYSTEM"	*Evaluating the use of knowledge (Ethical question)*
Organization-environment system		
Man-man-norm system (organization)		
Man-man system (inter-individual)	"ACTION SYSTEM"	*Using knowledge (Pragmatic question)*
Man-machine system		
Cognitive-affective system (individual)		
Information-processing system	"INFORMATION SYSTEM"	*Producing knowledge (Methodological question)*
Central nervous system		

"Low"

Source: Werner Ulrich, "The Design of Problem-Solving Systems," **Management Science,** June 1977.

4. Locate control (decision) points in the system. Generally, a control point is associated with either a manager or a checkpoint that controls on a routine basis (such as an individual operator or a machine).

5. Drop from consideration each operation or transaction that has no effect on the objectives of the system.

6. Group together the operations performed between every pair of control points.

7. Prepare a flowchart showing:
   a. Control points and kind of decisions made at each control point.
   b. Information that flows between every connected pair of control points.
   c. Materials, if any, that flow between every connected pair of control points.
   d. Times required for flow of information and flow of materials in (b) and (c).

B. Formulate management's problems.

1. Identify decision makers and the decision-making procedure.

2. Determine the decision makers' relevant objectives.

3. Identify other participants and the channels of their influence on a solution.

4. Determine objectives of the other participants.

5. Determine alternative courses of action available to decision makers.

6. Determine counteractions available to other participants.

7. Establish criteria for evaluation of solutions.

C. Formulate the research problems that are most likely to lead to a solution of management's problems.

1. Edit and condense the relevant objectives.

2. Edit and condense the relevant courses of action.

3. Define the measure of effectiveness to be used.[2]

Phase II, the search process

The search process consists of uncovering data and transformations that bring the problem solver closer to his final goal. If the final goal is undefined in the problem formulation, the search also involves the development of trial goals along with alternative chains of means-ends.

The construction of all possible alternative paths that link the present state of affairs with the desired state of affairs is usually impossible. Even if many alternatives could be constructed, evaluating all of them to find the best is too difficult. Therefore, general, heuristic rules, either objectively framed or so complex that they are internalized in his mind, guide the problem solver in a sequential series of steps or among major strategies. The following steps can only crudely represent this search process.

A. Gather data that seem relevant to the specific research problem to be solved. Find conditions imposed on the problem. Look for trends in data.

B. Classify the data. Draw charts, diagrams, and tables if they will help to organize the data. Look for conflicting data.

C. Devise a plan of attack.

1. Hypothesize complete broad solutions to be detailed subsequently.

2. Devise an incremental approach whereby a small part of the problem is solved first, the remainder is studied, and another small part is solved. This way we arrive at a solution by a step-by-step or means-end approach.

3. Design research to answer specific questions that, when answered, will make a set of solutions evident to the decision maker.

[2]See C. West Churchman, Russell L. Ackoff, and E. Leonard Arnoff, *Introduction to Operations Research* (New York: John Wiley, 1957), p. 132.

D. Carry out the plan of attack by employing reflective processes and systematic questioning.

1. Find relationships among the variables of the problem.

2. Draw upon experience and creative reflection to develop hypotheses (trial solutions) to be tested.

3. Search for analogies, differences, inversions, substitutions, and similar past problems that may produce hypotheses for solutions.

4. Start with the desired state of affairs and work backward to determine what is required to achieve the goals.

5. Develop tests, if possible, to check out parts of the tentative solution or the entire solution. At this stage, models or simulation may be helpful.

6. Evaluate test results and iterate the first five steps to the extent that modification is indicated.

7. Evaluate the alternative solutions in terms of criteria established in the formulation of the management problem.

Organizational and Individual Problem Solving

Observation of problem solving in large institutions such as business corporations reveals that there is a spectrum of problem situations and problem solving. At one end of the spectrum is the individual who solves a problem completely independently and implements the solution. At the other end is the solving of the organizational problem of viability, to which everyone contributes

Table 13.5
Problem-
solving:
individuals and
groups

	Individuals	Groups
Goal setting	A. Task demands	A. Task demands
	B. Personality	B. Group vs. individual conflicts
	C. Establish operational hypothesis	C. Establish operational plan to problem
Search	A. Invoke basic strategy	A. Development—seek discussions
	B. Recall and manipulate information	B. Summarizing—seek discussions
	C. Consider information in light of the hypothesis	C. Consider supporting and opposing discussions
Hypothesis testing (proposed solution)	A. Suggest solution as "correct"	A. Agree to solutions as "correct"
	B. If no solution, use feedback to develop another hypothesis	B. If not, try different planning of problem on feedback basis
	C. Repeat, if necessary	C. Repeat, if necessary
	D. If (A) is correct, problem solved	D. If (A) is correct, problem solved

Source: Marcus Alexis and Charles Z. Wilson, **Organizational Decision Making** (Englewood Cliffs, N.J.: Prentice-Hall, 1967), p. 75.

on a continuous basis. It is likely that the janitor solves more problems independently than does the president of a large corporation. The president deals with problems of such breadth that he must seek guidance, counsel, and evaluation at every step of the problem-solving process. Although he may make some lonely major decisions, the development of alternatives that offer him a decision situation is a shared process.

Organizational problem solving is affected by conflicting values and interests of organizational members. Conflict and compromise are mixed with rationality. A comparison of individual and organizational problem-solving activities in greatly abbreviated form is shown in Table 13.5 on the previous page.

THE DECISION PROCESS

In one dimension we must study two approaches to decision making. The *normative* approach deals with how to make rational decisions and achieve organizational acceptance. The *descriptive* approach deals with how decisions are actually made. In a second dimension we study decision making by an individual and by a group.

Decision making is the *cutting off* of further consideration. It consists of two parts: *evaluating* alternative courses of action and *selecting* a course of action. Although decisions may be made with almost no information, managers today require considerable selected information for decision making.

The Decision Makers

All people within an organization make decisions. A complete study of the decision process would require us to consider decisions made by (1) an individual, (2) a small group, and (3) large complex organizations. Although an individual may make decisions, the unseen influence of the environment, particularly that of the organization, weighs heavily upon him.

In large complex organizations, the number of people who may participate in a decision would astound the inexperienced student. Consider an aircraft company that wishes to buy jet engines for an advanced airplane it is developing. It must choose among several proposals put forth by jet engine companies. The decision as to which proposal to accept will depend upon engineering approval, manufacturing approval, legal reviews, top management approval, and very often customer approval. Within the jet engine company we may find as many as seventeen persons and groups who influence design decisions. Table 13.6 shows the relative influence of decision makers in each stage of the design.

Factors That Shape the Decision Process

The most important factors that shape the decision process—the actual evaluation and choosing—are

1. Time
2. Cost

Table 13.6 Rank order of importance of decision influencers in commercial jet engine development across all design and development stages

RANK ORDER (ALL DESIGN AND DEVELOPMENT STAGES)	DECISION INFLUENCER	RANK IN DESIGN AND DEVELOPMENT STAGES			
		Preliminary Design	Exploratory Development	Advanced Development	Engineering Development
1	Chief, Engineering*	8	1	1	1
2	Airlines	1	5	2	2
3	Airframe Manufacturers	2	5	2	3
4	Executive Officer*	3	5	5	4
5	Manager, Preliminary Design and Development*	10	2	2	6
6	Board of Directors*	6	5	10	6
6	Finance Director*	6	5	10	6
8	Marketing Director*	4	11	10	6
9	Project Director*	11	10	6	5
10	Strategic Planning Director*	4	11	14	11
11	Legal Director*	9	11	13	11
11	Department of Defense	13	2	7	11
11	NASA	13	2	7	11
14	FAA/EPA	12	11	7	10
15	Department of Commerce	13	11	14	11
15	Department of State	13	11	14	11
15	Manager, Manufacturing Services*	13	11	14	11

*Jet Engine Manufacturer

Source: J. Douglas Hill and Richard Ollila, "Complex Decisionmaking Processes," **IEEE Transactions on Systems, Man, and Cybernetics,** March 1978.

3. Technical analysis
4. Psychological characteristics (style) of the decision maker
5. Social (organizational) influences
6. Cultural influences.

Limitations of *time* often preclude the examination of all possible alternatives or the consideration in great depth of even a few. In the same way, limitations of *cost* prevent the development of the "optimum" or best decision.

Technical analysis is "rational" evaluation and choice, such as provided by economics or management science. It usually is devoid of behavioral assumptions and neglects the impact of decisions on the organization and its publics. Nevertheless, technical analysis is valuable to the decision maker. The more limited the problem, the more helpful a technical optimization method can be. For complex, broad problems, however, technical analysis may lead to the rejection of viable alternatives.

Psychological characteristics involve the decision maker's personality, experience, capabilities, perceptions, values, and aspirations.[3] There is, of course, considerable overlap among psychological, social, and cultural influences, because individuals cannot stand apart from society and culture. *Social influences* require that decisions be acceptable to the organization; therefore the decision maker, unless he or she is completely autocratic, will make choices that are likely to be implemented. Participative decision making is often employed to reach a decision that will be accepted by the group.

Cultural influences extend beyond the present society or the organizational unit. Culture is a set of values, attitudes, and symbols passed down from generation to generation to govern the behavior of members of the group or society. Culture produces learned patterns of behavior acceptable to the cultural group. For business organizations in the United States three cultural influences predominate: those of the particular firm, of the geographical region in which it is located, and of the American people.

Let us give an example of a cultural influence from each of these classes. The learned behavior in an R&D-oriented firm is one of innovation, aggressive change, and search for new ideas, whereas in the United States shipbuilding industry, there is resistance to technological changes and a desire to retain old ways. Regional cultural differences are most evident to those who have worked in the frenetic, competitive pace of New York City and then in firms in the South where activity is more moderate.

National cultural differences are great. In the United States the workday differs from that of many countries; some countries have a long siesta period and the workday ends later. In the United States there is a greater opportunity for young men to exercise a voice in corporate affairs, whereas in many countries, firms are dominated by single families and elderly leaders. In U.S. firms, continuing education is a strong cultural characteristic rarely found in other countries. Many other differences could be listed that distinguish the culture of U.S. firms from those in other particular countries.

Besides the more obvious cultural differences in firms in different countries, there are some that most of us are not aware of. These are internalized and rarely verbalized differences in values and thought processes. For example, we behave as if youth were the most valuable attribute of people, whereas in some countries the elders are held in high esteem. We believe that Americans have the best management, the most advanced technology, and the greatest "know-how," and this unspoken assumption is often reflected in our dealings with businessmen from other countries and in our decisions. We believe our system of ethics is superior to that of others, and yet we often engage in business practices abroad that we would not condone in the United States. Our decisions are influenced by the reasoning processes we have learned in our schools. Without our realizing it, our approach to problem solving and decision making is quite different from that of people in other cultures.

---

[3]See, for example, Walter McGhee, Michael D. Shields, and Jacob G. Birnbert, "The Effects of Personality on a Subject's Information Processing," *The Accounting Review,* July 1978.

Many writers distinguish between normative models (what we should do) and descriptive models (what we actually do). The difference may be that normative models do not, or cannot, include (1) the multiple objectives of the decision makers, and (2) all the principal factors which necessitate complex trade-offs in real situations.

Paul C. Nutt classified decision models as follows:

1. Bureaucratic model
2. Normative decision theory
3. Behavioral decision theory
4. Group decision making
5. Conflict-equilibrium model
6. Open system model.[4]

These models are summarized in Table 13.7 which appears on the following pages.

The *bureaucratic model* has been described by Max Weber. *Normative decision theory* includes both probabilistic and deterministic optimization models. *Behavioral decision theory* is descriptive. Nobel Prize winner Herbert Simon stated that decision makers satisfice (satisfy + suffice). That is, they look for a course of action that is good enough, rather than continuing a long search for the optimal. People cannot handle masses of information or anticipate the future well. Therefore, they simplify decision making by using a small number of criteria and by generating just a few alternatives. Alternatives are tested as they are developed until one just meets the simple criteria established. This model is illustrated by Figure 13.2. The elements of the process are:

1. Objectives of the decision maker
2. Decision criteria and decision rules
3. Possible states of nature (that is, possible real-world situations, or possible values representing "states" or conditions of a key variable)
4. Research outcomes predicting the likelihood that various states of nature will occur
5. Alternative actions that may be taken.

The remaining models are also descriptive. Of special interest is the "muddling-through" concept of Model 6 as proposed by C. E. Lindblom.[5] Lindblom believes that most decisions are made to incorporate small changes in the system rather than making complete or major changes in design. A problem is solved by deciding upon a series of small changes, one at a time, so that the decision maker can test for improvement each time.

---

[4]Paul C. Nutt, "Models for Decision Making in Organizations and Some Contextual Variables which Stipulate Optimal Use," *The Academy of Management Review,* April 1976.

[5]D. Bray and C. E. Lindblom, *A Strategy of Decision* (New York: The Free Press, 1963), and C. E. Lindblom, "The Science of Muddling Through," *Public Administration Review,* 1959, 19.

Table 13.7 Comparison of organizational decision-making models

Models of Organizational Decision Making	Decision Criteria	Key Ingredients	Key Assumptions
Model 1: Bureaucratic model	Maximum efficiency	1. Define decision maker's jurisdiction 2. Appoint experts to office and invest power in office holder 3. Rules, procedures, and precedents depict decision premises 4. Refer decisions "up" hierarchy 5. Rewards based on adherence to master plan	1. Goals known 2. Master plan to judge action is a given 3. Tasks repetitive or predictable 4. Environment does not influence choices 5. Resources adequate
Model 2: Normative decision theory (e.g., operation research theorists)	Maximum subjective expected utility	1. States of nature (S_i) 2. Alternatives (A_i) 3. Probability distribution for S_i 4. Utilities for each A_i-S_i intersection based on how the S_i affects A_i 5. Criteria to determine the intrinsic value of A_i—measured by the properties of A_i and the normative importance of each criterion to the decision maker	1. Goals known 2. Needed information obtainable 3. Adequate resources available 4. Prediction feasible 5. Criteria to judge effects and cause-effect relations are known
Model 3: Behavioral decision theory	Satisficing	1. Identify acceptable S_i and generate A_i until acceptable A_i is found, using normative decision theory model 2. Sequential generation of information concerning A_i 3. Processes: searching, learning, choosing 4. Satisficing replaces optimizing in decision processes	1. Goals can be inferred through domain decisions 2. Environment will not fully disclose all A_i and/or can justify search costs for all A_i 3. Consequences of A_i cannot be fully predicted but some predictions can be made 4. Resources interact with decision processes
Model 4: Group decision making	Satisficing on objectives set by participants	1. *Forming* (membership criteria, information needs and political consideration) for groups composed of clients, content experts, and/or resource controllers 2. *Coalescing* (structure of group process, decision rules, power-influence, interpersonal relations, type of interaction)	1. Goals consistent with organizations will be used by group to guide choices 2. Interdisciplinary synthesis feasible and multidisciplinary choices acceptable 3. Implementation likelihood enhanced via participation 4. Needed resources and information made available through cooptation

Table 13.7 (Cont'd.)

Models of Organizational Decision Making	Decision Criteria	Key Ingredients	Key Assumptions
		3. *Processes* (estimate-discuss-estimate, interacting group techniques, other group processes) 4. *Control* (mechanisms to elicit information; group and individual rewards and penalties)	
Model 5: Conflict-equilibrium	Resolution of conflict by consensus	1. The properties of alternatives (when A_i's are uncomparable, unacceptable, or uncertain) cause conflict 2. Both group and individual conflict can occur 3. Processes: bargaining, politicking, persuasion and problem solving for conflict resolution 4. Lockian compromise (consensus sought) 5. Contextual factors (e.g., perceptions, rewards, dependencies, cost of search, level of aspiration, coalition formation, and side payments) have a strong influence on choice among A_i's	1. Goals and arena must be defined 2. Organizations seek to reduce conflict 3. Conflict and time pressure will cause the adoption of conspicuous alternatives 4. Further evaluation of existing alternatives will precede the search for new ideas (new A_i's) 5. Level of aspiration changes vis-a-vis results of search, which modifies decision premises
Model 6: Open system	Survival (agency's view) and acceptability (client's view)	1. Partisans with a problem provide stimulus 2. Processes: Politics and bargaining generate adaptive incremental responses to problems 3. Constraints: Decision maker not free to choose; must involve clients and other third parties in decision process 4. Control: Use of sentiments, cliques, social norms expressed through a variety of agents to test quality of decisions made through feedback from clients	1. Goals unknown and unknowable in an arena that is unknown or unmanaged 2. Abstractions (models) not precise enough to make decisions 3. Pressures from informal norms greater than formal norms 4. Strong interaction of environment and decisions 5. Reacting better than planning

Source: Adapted from Paul C. Nutt, "Models for Decision Making in Organizations and Some Contextual Variables which Stipulate Optimal Use," **The Academy of Management Review,** April 1976.

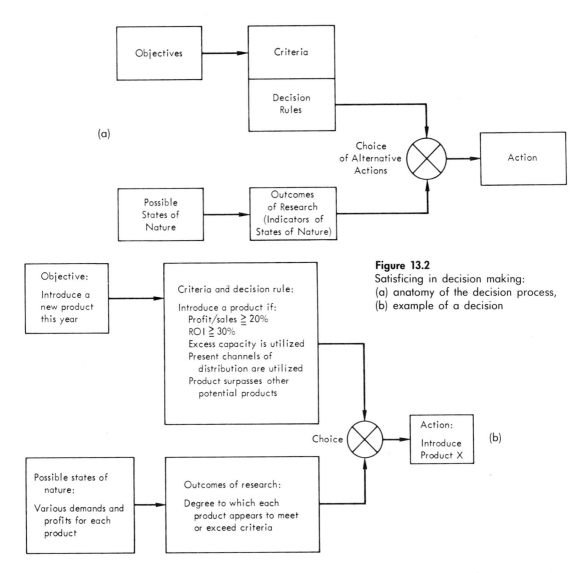

(a)

Figure 13.2
Satisficing in decision making:
(a) anatomy of the decision process,
(b) example of a decision

(b)

Research on decision style has been extensive. Michael J. Driver and Theodore J. Mock have summarized four styles: decisive, flexible, hierarchic, and integrative in terms of values, planning, goals, organization, and communication. The decisive and the flexible decision makers are minimal data users who satisfice with respect to information search. The hierarchic and integrative style decision makers are maximal data users. They are not satisfied until all data which may be relevant are gathered and massaged to yield several excellent decisions.[6] Table 13.8 summarizes the characteristics of the above decision styles.

[6]Michael J. Driver and Theodore J. Mock, "Human Information Processing, Decision Style Theory, and Accounting Information Systems," *Accounting Review,* July 1975.

Table 13.8 Summary decision style chart

| | MINIMAL DATA USER (SATISFICER) | | MAXIMAL DATA USER (OPTIMIZER) | |
	Decisive	*Flexible*	*Hierarchic*	*Integrative*
Values	Efficiency Speed Consistency	Adaptability Speed Variety	Quality Rigorous method System	Information Creativity
Planning	Low data base Short-range Tight control for results	Low data base Intuitive	High data base Long-range Tight control of method and results	High data base Long-range Adaptive
Goals	Few; organization focus	Many; self-focus	Few; self-focus	Many; self- and organization- focus
Organization	Short span of control Rules Classic organization	Control by confusion Loose	Wide span of control Elaborate procedures Automation	Team process Matrix organization
Communication	Short summary format Results focus on one solution	Short, summary format Variety; several solutions	Long, elaborate reports Problem, methods, data, give "best conclusion"	Long, elaborate Problem analysis from many views; Multiple solution

Source: Michael J. Driver and Theodore J. Mock, "Human Information Processing, Decision Style Theory, and Accounting Information Systems," **Accounting Review,** July 1975.

SIMPLIFYING THE DECISION PROCESS

The complexity of our environment is such that the abstraction of management science models removes too much of reality. The decision maker must find some way of selecting important elements and evaluating them to reach a decision. Some of the ways in which complexity is handled are suggested by William T. Morris.[7]

1. Rules of thumb based on past experience are employed to narrow the search for alternatives. Examples: Three-year payback for capital investment. Hire only experienced salesmen. Keep 30 days of inventory on hand. Allow an annual increase in payroll of only 6%.
   Often these rules are poor guides to choice, and their only merit is that they lead to a choice in a short time.

[7]William T. Morris, *Management Science, A Bayesian Approach* (Englewood Cliffs, N.J.: Prentice-Hall, 1968), p. 15.

2. Categorization of guidelines provides general guidance and rules. Company operating and policy guides, standard operating instructions, procedures manuals, and administrative memos and circulars circumscribe behavior to limit choice to a great degree.

3. Suppression of intangible values such as employee morale, customer goodwill, ethical considerations, public welfare, and industry relationships simplifies the choice process greatly. The focus is on economic units, profits, costs, number of employees, and efficiency.

4. Adoption of a short-range view is common. It is much easier to make a choice if the ramifications of the act beyond today, next week, next year, or the next five years are not taken into consideration.

5. Suppression of risk or a rough estimation of the total risk has sufficed in the past. Deterministic estimates of sales, costs, and new-product profits are still common. Management science and the computer have steadily introduced more and more subjective risk estimates into the choice process in recent years.

6. Quasi-resolution of conflict has simplified organizational decision making. Goals of different departments are treated as independent constraints. Problems are broken into parts and treated separately. Different goals and aspirations of individuals are treated at different times in order to reduce conflict. Compromises and "satisficing" are employed to find mutually agreeable decisions.

7. An indifference approach is taken to making small decisions. Where two choices are apparent and the import of the action is obviously not significant, a snap judgment is made to eliminate the time-consuming effort of evaluating all the tangible and intangible aspects of each choice.

8. "Muddling through," according to C. E. Lindblom, is a common approach in public administration and policy formation. This approach avoids clear-cut decisions on long-range objectives and plans.

DECISION MAKING AND MIS

The MIS performs two functions with respect to decision making. First, it helps managers make decisions by supplying needed information and solving optimization problems for guidance. Second, the MIS makes repetitive types of decisions where the decision process remains constant but the input varies (decision tables and models).

The quality of information is an important factor for the MIS. Quality may be measured by such factors as uncertainty, timeliness, rate, conciseness, clarity, level of detail, relevance, currency, accuracy, precision, and completeness. The objective of the MIS is to provide information according to trade-offs between cost, benefits, and objectives established for these factors for quality.

The most valuable contribution of MIS is the information it supplies in support of decisions. Steven Alter studied 56 decision support systems to develop a descriptive taxonomy. He found that the systems ranged from extremely data-oriented to extremely model-oriented as follows:

1. Retrieving a single item of information
2. Providing a means for ad hoc analysis
3. Providing prespecified aggregations of data as reports
4. Estimating the consequences of proposed decisions
5. Proposing decisions
6. Making decisions.[8]

On this basis Alter identified seven reasonably distinct types of decision systems:

1. File-drawer systems, which allow immediate access to data items
2. Data-analysis systems, which allow manipulation of the data
3. Analysis information systems, which provide access to data bases and small models
4. Accounting information systems, which calculate the consequences of planned actions based on accounting definitions
5. Representational models, which estimate the consequences of actions based on models which are nondefinitional
6. Optimization models, which provide guidelines for action by giving optimal solutions
7. Suggestion models, which perform mechanical work leading to a specific suggested decision for a fairly well-structured task.

The relationships among these decision support systems are further developed in Figure 13.3.

[8]Steven Alter, "A Taxonomy of Decision Support Systems," *Sloan Management Review*, Fall 1977.

Figure 13.3
Data-oriented
vs. model-
oriented types
of decision
support systems

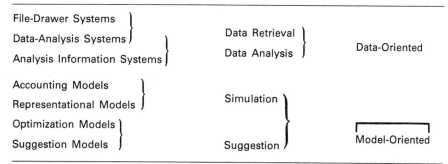

Source: Steven Alter, "A Taxonomy of Decision Support Systems," **Sloan Management Review**, Fall 1977, p. 42.

SUMMARY *Problem Solving*

Problem solving is a creative process directed toward resolving an unsatisfactory situation. A problem can be recognized when a desired condition does not match an existing or anticipated condition. There are usually many solutions to a problem. By developing several alternatives, management increases its chances of finding a good solution.

The source of problems is change. Change either in management's objectives or in the environment may produce a problem. Some problems are well structured in that the problem is well defined, the procedure for solving it is established, and the necessary data are available in good form. Other problems range from well structured to ill structured. When a problem is ill-structured, it is not defined, the specific procedure to obtain a solution is not available, multiple and conflicting objectives exist, and the data may not be complete, accurate, or reliable.

An approach to formulating a problem is to define the elements of the problem situation; describe the present status; define the desired status; specify constraints that may exist in seeking a solution; and define criteria that the solution must fulfill.

The pragmatic approach to problem solving is to seek expert help, find similar problems solved in the past, or avoid the problem. If these steps fail, we must solve the problem ourselves.

The systems approach to problem solving may be conceptualized in terms of three levels: how we produce information; how we use the information; and what we use the information for. In application, the process consists of formulating the systems problem, formulating management's problems, formulating the research problems, and searching for solutions according to the "scientific method."

Problems in large organizations may be solved by individuals or organizational groups. The effect of the organizational approach is to bring together conflicting objectives and values and achieve solutions through conflict, compromise, or integration.

The solving of a complex business problem consists of solving many small problems involving many decisions at each step. From a systems view, problem solving consists of determining how to produce information, how to use information, and what the information is to be used for.

Decision Making

Decision making terminates the consideration of alternative courses of action by the making of a choice. Decisions are made by individual contributors, managers, and groups, but the organization exerts its influence in many ways. The factors which shape the decision process are (1) time, (2) cost, (3) technical analysis, (4) psychological characteristics of the decision maker, (5) organizational behavior influences, and (6) cultural influences.

Models of the decision process may be classified as (1) bureaucratic, (2) normative decision theory, (3) behavioral decision theory, (4) group decision making, (5) conflict-equilibrium, and (6) open system.

Because of the complexity of the real world and human limitations, people limit their considerations of alternatives in a number of ways. Thus, true rationality—the collection of complete information and the evaluation of all alternatives—is not achieved in practice. Rather, we select a few likely alternatives and use shortcuts for evaluating them.

The role of the MIS in decision making varies from data-oriented analysis to making routine decisions to providing model-oriented information for the support of management decisions. The difficulty of problem solving and decision making in modern business generates the need for the MIS. The information supplied must be designed to meet the requirements of modern management.

1. _____ (1) Problem

   _____ (2) Decision

   _____ (3) Source of problems

   _____ (4) Well-structured problem

   _____ (5) Ill-structured problem

   _____ (6) Problem formulation

   _____ (7) Systems view of problem solving

   _____ (8) Decision makers

   _____ (9) Shapes the decision process

   _____ (10) Model of the decision process

a. Linear programming
b. Elements, present and desired states, constraints and criteria
c. Cognitive-affective process
d. Industrial, small group, large organization
e. Choosing a course of action
f. Technical analysis and social influence
g. Change
h. Conflict-equilbrium
i. A question with multiple answers
j. Mission of the firm

2. Changes occur in (1) the environment, (2) objectives and desires of managers, (3) functioning of the business, (4) role relationships, and (5) interpersonal relationships. Using these numbers as codes, relate the following problems to likely causes.

   _____ a. Because Jones and Viking have contrasting value systems, they have difficulty in working smoothly on joint problems.

   _____ b. Equipment in the factory breaks down more frequently as it ages.

   _____ c. Two competitors merge.

   _____ d. A new law upgrades pollution control requirements.

   _____ e. Among "equal" vice presidents, one manages to dominate the others.

   _____ f. Marketing is not aggressive and salespeople are not motivated.

   _____ g. The president's secretary is biased against some executives and makes it difficult for them to see the president.

   _____ h. The chairman of the board and the president disagree on the program of acquisition of companies.

3. A company is evaluating three computer systems prior to purchasing one. It sets up the following table.

CRITERION FACTOR	Weight	EVALUATION		
		System 1	System 2	System 3
Cost of equipment	9	5	4	4
Cost to operate	7	4	5	4
Time to implement	3	2	5	2
Improvement in operations	8	4	4	5
Improvement in managing	10	4	5	4
Total points				

a. Multiply the weight by each evaluation and enter in the appropriate cell.
b. The total points for each system are

(1) _____ (2) _____ (3) _____ and system _____ is best.

4. Explain how the decision-making processes for *satisficing* and for *optimizing* differ in the following situations:

a. Deciding on the level of customer service
b. Selecting a new product for development among several hundred tentative ideas
c. Locating a new plant site
d. Making a layout or arrangement of departments in a process-oriented production plant
e. Selecting a candidate to hire for a highly technical position.

5. Identify a problem of your own or of some company with which you are very familiar. List the elements of the problem. Describe the present state of the situation and the desired state. List the constraints. Develop criteria for solutions. Suggest several possible solutions.

6. Outspoken executives have admitted that they are lucky if they make correct decisions 50% of the time. Would structuring a decision problem to provide an analytical decision, or even flipping a coin, be more economical than paying over $200,000 a year for the decision making of top executives? Discuss.

7. List the problems you have faced over the past week. Select the ones that are somewhat repetitive. Develop a programming logic for solving several of these problems.

8. Look up in a textbook on management science the method of developing a utility curve by means of the "standard gamble." Develop your utility curve for money.

9. Joe and Bill Turnip have developed the Turnip Nursery in Florida into a $500,000

annual business. The business has boomed, along with the rapid population growth of the state. About 30% of revenue comes from sales of plants, 20% from lawn maintenance. Bill, Jr., has been attending a business school in upper New York State and working summers at the nursery. As he has grown familiar with the business, he has been asking questions of the partners about the future of the firm—questions such as: "What are your plans for the company for five years from now?" "What are the objectives of the company, in terms of growth, services supplied, geographic area to be served, and ROI?" "You are growing at a rate of 15% a year; how will you be able to operate from this limited, hemmed-in site three years from now?" "Why don't we have inventory records of shrubs?" "Why don't we forecast sales?" Because the nursery has always operated very profitably from the beginning, the partners have responded somewhat grumpily because they don't have the answers, but they are beginning to wonder if they have problems without realizing it.

Student: List the problems faced, the information needed, and how the information could be obtained.

10. The Caterpillar Tractor Co. has been producing diesel engines for 48 years, but since 1972 it has spent over $1 billion on development and on quadrupling capacity for manufacturing. The company estimates its diesel sales will amount to $1.6 billion annually and represent over 20% of sales by 1981.

   Diesels are 45% more fuel-efficient than gasoline engines. As a result, production valued at $1.9 billion in 1971 has grown to $5.5 billion in 1979. It is expected to grow at 15% per year over the next decade. Recent additions to U.S. plant capacity in the industry have outrun sales of 600,000 units annually by 300,000 units. Diesel engines are used mainly for highway trucks, drilling rigs, boats, and stand-by generators. One fly in the soup is that a diesel engine emits up to 90 times as much particulate matter as a comparable gasoline engine, and the EPA is announcing new emission standards to take effect early in 1983.

   Competitors of Caterpillar are:

Cummins Engine Co. (1978 diesel sales, $1.4 billion)	Deere and Co.
	Klockner-Humboldt-Dentz
Detroit Diesel (1978 diesel sales, $1.4 billion)	Renault
	Volvo
International Harvester	

   Cummins, in trying to serve the traditional heavy truck industry, left the medium truck market open. Caterpillar jumped in and obtained 50% of that market. Now all competitors are spending heavily on technology to compete in the total diesel market.

   a. Five sources of problems are discussed in the text. Which of these are sources of Caterpillar's problem and why?
   b. Describe the Caterpillar problem in terms of elements, present state, desired state, possible constraints, and possible criteria for a solution.
   c. Describe generally the approach that you would take to solving this problem if you were CEO of Caterpillar.
   d. What are several major alternatives Caterpillar could follow?
   e. How could an MIS help management monitor what will probably be a continuing problem situation?

   (The reader may wish to refer to "A Revved-up Market for Diesel Engine Makers," *Business Week,* February 5, 1979, pp. 76–79.)

SELECTED REFERENCES

ALTER, STEVEN, "A Taxonomy of Decision Support Systems," *Sloan Management Review,* Fall 1977.

BAUER, RAYMOND A., and KENNETH J. GERGEN, eds., *The Study of Policy Formation.* New York: The Free Press, 1968.

DAVIS, GORDON B., *Management Information Systems: Conceptual Foundations, Structure and Development.* New York: McGraw-Hill, 1974.

DUNCAN, W. JACK, *Decision Making and Social Issues.* Hinsdale, Ill.: Dryden Press, 1973.

EASTON, ALLAN, *Complex Managerial Decisions Involving Multiple Objectives.* New York: John Wiley, 1973.

EILON, SAMUEL, "What is a Decision?" *Management Science,* December 1969.

ESTES, W. K., "A Descriptive Approach to the Dynamics of Choice Behavior," *Behavioral Science,* July 1961.

HARRISON, E. FRANK, *The Managerial Decision Making Process.* Boston: Houghton Mifflin, 1975.

HELLER, FRANK A., *Managerial Decision-making.* New York: Barnes & Noble, distributors, 1971.

HILL, J. DOUGLAS, "Analysis of Complex Decision Making Processes," *IEEE Transactions on Systems, Man, and Cybernetics,* March 1978.

KELLEY, GEORGE, "Seducing the Elites: The Politics of Decision Making and Innovation in Organizational Networks," *Academy of Management Review,* July 1976.

MORRIS, WILLIAM T. *Decision Analysis.* Columbus, Ohio: Grid, Inc., 1977.

MURDICK, ROBERT G., and JOEL E. ROSS, *Information Systems for Modern Management,* 2d ed. Englewood Cliffs, N.J.: Prentice-Hall, 1975.

NUTT, PAUL C., "Models for Decision Making in Organizations and Some Conceptual Variables Which Stipulate Optimal Use," *Academy of Management Review,* April 1976.

PAINE, FRANK T., and WILLIAM NAUMES, *Organizational Strategy and Policy,* 2d ed. Philadelphia: Saunders, 1978.

POLYA, G., *How to Solve It,* 2d ed. New York: Doubleday Anchor Books, 1957.

RADFORD, K. J., *Complex Decision Problems: An Integrated Strategy for Resolution.* Reston, Va.: Reston, 1977.

SIMON, HERBERT, *Human Problem Solving.* Englewood Cliffs, N.J.: Prentice-Hall, 1972.

SUMMERS, IRVIN, and DAVID E. WHITE, "Creativity Techniques: Toward Improvement of the Decision Process," *Academy of Management Review,* April 1976.

TROWBRIDGE, MARTIN, "Managing in Crisis Situations," *International Management,* September 1972.

ULRICH, WERNER, "The Design of Problem-Solving Systems," *Management Science,* June 1977.

VASARHELYI, MIKLOS ANTAL, "Man-machine Planning Systems: A Cognitive Style Examination of Interactive Decision Making," *Journal of Accounting Research,* Spring 1977.

WEBBER, ROSS A., *Culture and Management.* Homewood, Ill.: Richard D. Irwin, 1969.

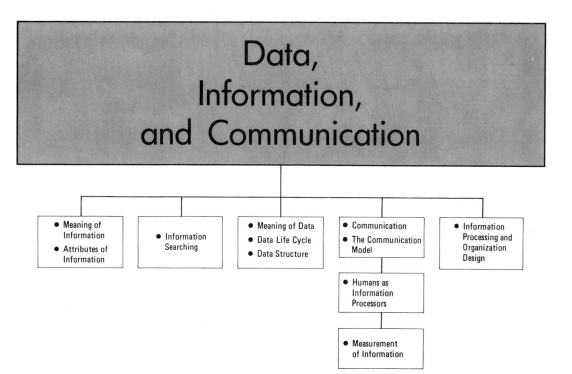

chapter 14

Data, Information, and Communication

PURPOSE: To provide advanced concepts of information, data, and communication which will help the MIS designer make more acceptable, more sophisticated management information systems

The methodological reason for needing to study information and data as distinct, related concepts is that to design an information system we must tackle both the problems: (a) to find out *what* information the users want and to describe this in a way that the users can understand and verify, and (b) to give the data system designers freedom to design the data structures and processes most suitable for meeting the needs or desires of the users by specifying to the designers *what* data are required but *not how* one should produce them.[1]

Our definition of a system requires two or more elements acting together to achieve some common objectives. Communication is the enabling process of such a system. Organized activity of people would not be possible without communication.

In order to design effective communication systems such as the MIS, we should understand the basic concepts of data, information, and communication. This will take us into the study of human information processing and the characteristics of humans as information processors. It will also require a look at the organization as a data and information processor.

MEANING OF INFORMATION

Information is behavior-initiating stimuli in the form of signs. Data consist of symbols and experience-stimuli which are not relevant to behavior at a given point in time.

[1]Borje Langefors and Bo Sundgren, *Information Systems Architecture* (New York: Petrocelli/Charter, 1975), pp. 21–22.

The distinction between information and data is important for two reasons: first, so that we may separately establish the information needs of managers and the requirements for data-base design, and second, so that we may provide managers with information and not data.

Information, from the behavioral view, predisposes a person to act in a certain way based upon his or her processing of signs received. Charles Morris describes two kinds of signs.[2] One is a signal that originates from an actual experience. For instance, a manager observes a machine broken down in the factory and work backed up. This is a meaningful direct signal. The other type of sign is a symbol which is a synonymous substitute for an experience-act or for another sign. Examples are a report of absenteeism and a report of a machine breakdown. Thus information may be in the form of language signs, behavior signs, phenomenological signs (the warehouse in flames), other sensory signs, or other forms, signals and symbols.

We define information in terms of signs that affect behavior because we are concerned in business with problems and with action to solve problems. Information is the matching of elements of a problem with signs stored in our memory or signs from the environment. Our knowledge of the real world is limited; we do not have complete information about aspects of the world which are of concern to us. "Information is any input that changes probabilities (or certainties) in any way. An input that *increases* uncertainty could then be information."[3]

The MIS designer is concerned with (a) the forms of information input, (b) the communication of information to managers, and (c) the human processing of information. We have discussed the nature of information in terms of signs. These signs, externally produced, affect the senses of seeing, hearing, feeling, smelling, and tasting. A manager may read a report or listen to a report; a merchandising manager may feel the texture of cloth; a chef in charge of cooks may smell or taste food for quality control purposes.

By far the most common form of information input to managers is language, written and spoken. Language provides an organization of visual and aural signs to convey information. The two sciences concerned with language are semiotic (the science of signs) and linguistics (the study of human speech). Figure 14.1 shows the subdivisions of these sciences and their overlap. The subdivisions relevant to information theory, in the boxes, are semantics, syntax, and pragmatics.

Although semiotic is concerned with all signs, it is not concerned with physiological and psychophysiological aspects of signs. These topics are generally covered in the field of psychology, which deals with human processing of information.

[2]See Charles Morris, *Signs, Language, and Behavior* (New York: George Braziller, 1955), pp. 24–25.

[3]Harold M. Schroder, Michael J. Driver, and Siegfried Streufert, *Human Information Processing* (New York: Holt, Rinehart and Winston, 1967), p. 95.

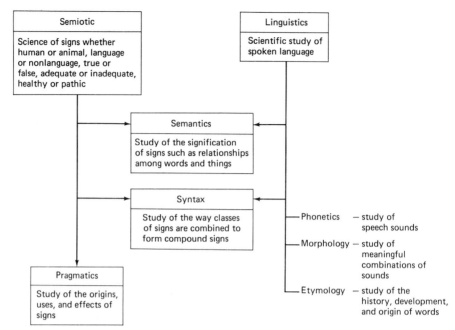

Figure 14.1
Scientific study of signs as information inputs to humans

| Semiotic |
| Science of signs whether human or animal, language or nonlanguage, true or false, adequate or inadequate, healthy or pathic |

| Linguistics |
| Scientific study of spoken language |

| Semantics |
| Study of the signification of signs such as relationships among words and things |

| Syntax |
| Study of the way classes of signs are combined to form compound signs |

| Pragmatics |
| Study of the origins, uses, and effects of signs |

— Phonetics — study of speech sounds

— Morphology — study of meaningful combinations of sounds

— Etymology — study of the history, development, and origin of words

ATTRIBUTES OF INFORMATION

The design of an MIS requires consideration of some important attributes of information. Attributes for machine systems extend beyond those for human systems.

Information Attributes for Humans and Machines

1. Purpose

Information must have purpose at the time it is transmitted to a person or machine, otherwise it is simply data or noise. Information communicated to people has a wide diversity of purposes because of the variety of activities of people in organizations and systems. The basic purposes of information are to inform, evaluate, persuade, or organize other information. Creating new concepts, identifying problems, solving problems, decision making, planning, initiating, controlling, and searching are just some of the purposes to which information is directed for human activity in business organizations. The purpose of supplying information (not data) to machines is to provide instructions or to provide information for stored instructions to act upon.

2. Mode and format

The modes for communicating information to humans are sensory (through sight, hearing, taste, touch, and smell), but mainly visual and aural in business organizations. Machines are capable of receiving information in a wide variety of modes that include the equivalent of human sensory perceptions and also extend to electrical, chemical, and other means.

The format is also a common characteristic of information for man or machine. Humans receive most of their information in the formats of verbal material or documents. Machines receive information in the format of energy patterns, tapes, cards, or even written form.

3. Redundancy/efficiency

Redundancy is, roughly, the excess of information carried per unit of data. Redundancy is a safeguard against errors in the communication process. One of the simplest and most common examples of redundancy is in correspondence or contracts that spell out a number (three) and follow it by the numerical character in parentheses (3). The redundancy concept is very important in systems design. Where the cost of error, misinterpretation of instructions, or failure of a portion of a system is critical, considerable redundancy may be built into the system. It may appear in the form of parallel design, whereby two parts of the system perform the same operation and the results are reconciled before the next step. Redundancy occurs in every organization by supervisory checkups on workers.

The efficiency of the data language is the complement of the redundancy:

$$\text{Efficiency} = 1 - \text{Redundancy}$$

Numerical calculations indicate that English has a redundancy of about 22%.[4]

4. Rate

The rate of transmission reception of information may be represented by the time required to understand a particular situation, such as a major foul-up in the factory. Generally, in MIS, the human component is easily overloaded at low rates of transmission.

5. Frequency

The frequency with which information is transmitted or received affects its value. Financial reports prepared weekly may show so little change that they have small value, whereas monthly reports may indicate changes big enough to show problems or trends. Further, information that appears too frequently tends to act as interference, noise, or distraction and to overload the receiver.

6. Deterministic or probabilistic

Information may be known with certainty, as is usually the case with historical information. Information concerning the future must always have an element of doubt, yet often it is considered deterministic in the sense that a single value is assumed to exist. The computation of inventory, of return on investment, of next month's sales, or of the P&L statement is often performed to yield a single value, the deterministic solution of a problem.

---

[4]From *A Methodology for Systems Engineering,* by Arthur D. Hall, copyright © 1962 by Litton Educational Publishing, Inc., by permission of Van Nostrand Reinhold Company.

If information is probabilistic, a range or set of possible outcomes and their associated probabilities are given. In simulating the operation of a firm, the model may be so constructed (with Monte Carlo techniques) that return on investment appears stochastically as:

ROI	Probability
5%	.1
10%	.4
15%	.3
20%	.2

A major consideration in the design of MIS is the utilization of probabilistic as well as deterministic information for decision making. As we show in Chapter 13, both deterministic and probabilistic techniques of management science are concerned with the development of decision aids.

7. Cost

Cost is a limiting factor in obtaining information. A small, nonscientific sample for determining market potential costs far less, generally, than a probability-sample survey or test-marketing a new product. Even internal information from company records may be extremely costly because of the necessity to gather, store, process, and retrieve it. Both the systems designer and manager must contantly evaluate or trade off the value of the information against its cost.

8. Value

What is the value of a specific piece of information? This may be too complex and expensive a question to answer in a going business. Management may have to evaluate by judgment the possible gain from the information or the possible loss from its absence. Because many pieces of information are employed in making a decision, the difficulty of evaluating any one of them is evident. However, the systems designer may be in a better position to evaluate the total value of a certain subsystem. For many programmed decisions, the "expected value" of perfect information may be computed and the cost of uncertainty determined. In conclusion, it may be said that the measurement of the value (both qualitative and quantitative) of information is a fertile area for designer ingenuity. The value is highly dependent on other characterisics, such as mode, rate, frequency, deterministic/stochastic features, reliability, and validity.[5]

9. Reliability and precision

When statistical estimates of parameters are made, the actual value of the parameter will fall within a certain range according to a certain probability.

---

[5]For a good discussion of this subject, see Rudolph E. Hirsch, "The Value of Information," *The Journal of Accountancy,* June 1968.

Suppose that we obtain a random sample of incomes of households in a city. The mean of the sample turns out to be $8300. We may relate the precision of the estimate (calculated as ±$560) with a reliability of 90%. In other words, the mean of *all* incomes will fall in the range of $8300 ± 570 with a probability of .90. If we were to reduce the precision to ±$1000, we would find that the reliability of our estimate of $8300 ± 1000 increased.

It is more expensive to obtain both high precision and high reliability than low values of each. Therefore, a cost and precision/reliability trade-off is possible.

10. Accuracy

Accuracy measures the closeness of a number to what it should truly be. In sampling, it represents the degree of bias in an estimating procedure. As an example, it is the difference between the mean of all sample means and the true value of the mean of the population.

11. Validity

The validity of information is a measure of the degree to which the information represents what it purports to represent. Suppose we develop an index that we say represents the efficiency (output/input) of a system. We may then find out that the index is also influenced somewhat by cost and some external economic factor. The fact that the index actually measures (and is influenced by) factors other than what we want to measure will lower its validity.

12. Currency

Currency refers to the age of the information. If a manager receives a report at the end of a quarter, the information in it may be as recent as the previous week or in some cases as old as the previous quarter. Computer-based information systems have upgraded the currency of reports tremendously in the past 20 years.

13. Compactness

Compactness is the "information density" of a report or message. Long, rambling, redundant reports obviously have a low compactness of information. Tables and graphs often present the greatest amount of information in the shortest message form.

Information Attributes Primarily for Machines

14. Steady state or dynamic

Characteristics of information especially related to machines are derived from the difference in types of "sensing" by machines and in the response purposes of machines. Although machines may sense information in many ways, electrical, mechanical, and optical are by far the most common. Electrical inputs from card or tape sources, variations in power, switching circuits, and mechanical keys and levers are examples of methods for providing information inputs. A characteristic of such information is that it may be steady state or dynamic. Information that does not vary with time is called steady state. A numerical control machine may receive information from a tape that tells it to cut ⅛ inch off a unit for one unit in process after another. This is a steady-state situation.

Now consider a real-time warehouse and factory inventory system. Information on the number of units in each warehouse, forecasts of demand, and factory production rate is supplied to a computer for determination of future production rate and shipments to warehouse. Both inputs to and outputs from the computer vary with time and so represent information with dynamic characteristics.

15. Linear or nonlinear

When information inputs are linear functions of some variable, the information is linear, as opposed to nonlinear. Much information that management uses is linear, mainly because it is easy to comprehend and because no better information is available. Some example of *nonlinear* information are: (a) double-declining-balance method of depreciation, (b) forecast of sales as increasing at the *rate* of 5% per year, and (c) compound-interest value of money in evaluating capital budget items on a discounted cash-flow basis.

16. Continuous or discrete

The information may represent a continuous variable and hence be a continuous input, or it may be discrete in form. Most information is discrete. That is, managers receive reports on sales, production, personnel problems, crises in the plant, or financial data at separated periods of time. Real-time information systems supply information continuously as a function of time (a continuous variable), but managers obviously do not make decisions by monitoring such information. Continuous, real-time information is used for managerial decision making when reorganized into batches. Continuous information is also suited for input to machines requiring such information for uninterrupted operation.

INFORMATION SEARCHING

In organizational systems and man-machine systems, decision-making elements are not usually supplied automatically and gratuitously with data; the data must be selectively retrieved or obtained from any or all of three sources:

1. The environment
2. The storage system developed for the operating system
3. Actualized situations (laboratory or similarly controlled operation)

Methods of obtaining information from each of these sources for the operation of a system may be extremely difficult.

The problem of searching for information in the *environment* is difficult because often we do not know what will represent information and what will be irrelevant data. Even when we do know generally what we are looking for, the source and form may be completely unsuspected. F. J. Aguilar defines four modes of scanning the environment:

1. *Undirected observation.* The searcher has no specific object in mind except to scan for items that may be useful to him now or in the future. The manager accomplishes this by reading newspapers and trade journals, listening to shop talk at social gatherings, attending industry meetings, and generally staying alert to word of anything that may bear upon his company.

2. *Conditioned viewing.* The observer directs his attention to a more or less clearly identified area without making an active search. If a signal of some kind appears, he is ready to evaluate it. The manager is apt to follow closely the activities of his company's competitors or read the financial news for significant changes.

3. *Informal search.* This is active, directed, but relatively unstructured search for specific information. Often an investigation into the possible market for potential new products follows this informal type of search. Recruiting of personnel or a search for new product ideas are other examples.

4. *Formal search.* This is a systematic method following a preestablished plan to obtain specific information or information relating to a specific problem. Carefully developed, scientifically planned sample survey designs, some types of industrial intelligence search, or the recruiting of a new president for the company typify this search pattern.[6]

The storage system within the company is, of course, the data base. The problems of relating data in the data base so that data elements may be retrieved and combined as information are covered in Chapter 15.

When data must be stored in precombined form, such as documents and reports, the storage and retrieval problem becomes more difficult. Let us look briefly at this problem.

Consider an organization which maintains a document library of both external and internal reports covering all areas of the business. A manager wishes to determine a standard for turnover in his or her department. The manager wishes to have a search made of all reports touching on turnover. Such information might appear in company general reports, trade association reports, personnel reports, special study reports, or productivity reports. The manager's chances of obtaining the desired information obviously depend upon how reports and their contents were classified when the reports were stored.

[6]Francis Joseph Aguilar, *Scanning the Business Environment* (New York: Macmillan, 1967), p. 19.

When large amounts of data are to be put in storage for later retrieval, the data must be classified in some way so that particular items can be withdrawn. Classification consists of arranging subject matter into batches on the basis of *differences* and *similarities*. Classification is commonly by hierarchy or by attribute. For example, a hierarchical arrangement of marketing data would be:

Marketing
 Selling
  Sales expense
   Telephone expense
    John Smith's telephone expense

Finally, statements or index terms are usually coded to save space and time. Codes are shorthand representations of words or statements. Thus the Dewey Decimal System uses codes as representations of content descriptors. In a hierarchical system, a letter might designate a major area of information, and numbers might be used for subclasses. Decimals are sometimes employed to aid in establishing subclass level. Three examples of "alphanumeric" code terms are: M 9232, A 1.200.28, HB/128/5.

Company policy manuals and many business systems attempt to provide memory aids in their codes: for example, ADM may stand for administrative, LEG for legal, and PER for personnel. This makes coding and decoding easier. It is important to note that the more refined the index and the code classification, the more expensive the storage of data. However, the more refined the index and classification system, the lower the cost of retrieval, because relevant data may be pinpointed better. Costs for classifying information and for writing retrieval specifications rise rapidly with complexity in either. It is therefore important for the system designer to develop an optimum storage and retrieval system by trade-off between indexing and retrieval requirements. The system itself is expensive to design and usually even more expensive to revise if it fails to meet future needs.

Although the mechanics of storage and retrieval of data represent some of the most complex aspects of MIS, there are other aspects of importance. A summary overview of the total problem is given below.

1. *Identification of the users and their needs.* The user of information is certainly the principal figure in the MIS. The success of any system depends on how effectively and efficiently it serves the user's needs.

2. *Selection of data* for storage and retrieval. The user's needs must be well defined and the relative importance of these needs must be established. Only the user can do this, and therefore the specification of type of data to be stored and to be made available is the responsibility of the user. In other words, *the manager must actively take part in the design of the MIS*.

3. *Maintaining "interest profiles"* of users. The MIS must include a means for recording current and changing needs of users. As new data flow

into the company or are generated, the MIS must compare the data with the requirements of the user profiles so that timely information is automatically sent to the managers.

4. *Method of classifying and indexing.* Service and economics are critical to classifying and indexing in MIS design. Further, it is not only today's needs that must be considered. The system should be able to encompass changing and increasing demands upon it so that it will not have to be redesigned and reconstructed repeatedly, a very costly undertaking.

5. *Procedures for retrieval.* Procedures need to be established for the manager, the information specialist, and the computer operation group to function in the search process. The information specialist is an interpreter who links the manager and the computer by his knowledge of the information classification and coding system.

6. *Type or types of storage.* Although the computer disks and chips are usually considered to be the mass storage units, data are stored in other places and forms in an MIS. Reference and document libraries, file cabinets, reports (including computer printouts), microfilm, microfiche, aperture cards, engineering drawing files, and manual card-sort systems are examples of types of storage that may all be present. The selection of such types of storage is often based upon tradition rather than on economics, modern technology, and MIS considerations.

7. *Dissemination of information.* Although managers may call for information as they need it, there are many formats for presenting it to them. Verbal, visual, and hard copy are the most common means of dissemination. Another aspect of dissemination is related to the "interest profile." Procedures must be established so that relevant information that the managers may not even know is existent or available may be disseminated in a timely and useful form.

8. *Updating of storage files.* Unless a completely mechanical procedure can be employed, removing obsolete material from storage files as new data are added is a major problem. Managers simply do not have time to review complete files periodically. Most companies either continue adding data to a file until it collapses or they remove data from an accessible file like a computer system to some remote storage space where it is practically inaccessible on an economic basis. Again, this illustrates the need for professional information specialists in the design of these systems.

In the final analysis, the information storage and retrieval system must be measured by its efficiency and effectiveness.

The development of computer-based search systems for searching specialized fields outside and within the company has received little attention. Table 14.1 lists some illustrations of specialized search services. The table source provides summary descriptions of each.

I. Strategic Planning: Extraorganizational Information
(1) SDC Search Service (ORBIT®)
(2) DIALOG™
(3) New York Times Information Bank
(4) INTERFILE
(5) DISCLOSURE®
(6) National Automated Accounting Research System (NAARS)
(7) WESTLAW
(8) LEXIS
(9) FLITE

II. Strategic Planning: Intraorganizational Information
(No illustrations)

III. Management Control: Intraorganizational Information
(10) Construction Project Management System
(11) Intelligence Information System
(12) ACDMS (Automated Control of a Document Management System)
(13) CDMAN (Computer-Based System for Control and Dissemination)

IV. Operational Control: Intraorganization Information
(14) CUBE Registration System
(15) CADM (Configuration and Data Management)
(16) Engineering Drawing System

V. Office Communications
(17) DAISY (Decision Aiding Information System)
(18) Augmented Knowledge Workshop (AKW)
(19) Paperless Office Project
(20) WILTEK
(21) Electronic Information Exchange System (ELES)
(22) Management Work Stations (MWS)

Source: E. Burton Swanson and Mary J. Culnan, "Document-Based Systems for Management Planning and Control," Information Systems Working Paper 9-77, Center for Information Studies, Graduate School of Management, University of California at Los Angeles, September 1977.

MEANING OF DATA

Information affects behavior while data do not, either because of their format or because of their location relative to a potential user at a particular time. Data are symbols that describe some object, condition, or situation.[7] "Data is the set of basic facts about a person, thing, or transaction. It includes such things as date, size, quantity, description, amount, rate, name or place."[8] Data management systems are concerned with the capture, storage, retrieval, and assembly of data in forms related to product information.

[7]See William D. Haseman and Andrew B. Whinston, *Introduction to Data Management* (Homewood, Ill.: Richard D. Irwin, 1977), p. 412.

[8]Alton R. Kindred, *Data Systems and Management* (Englewood Cliffs, N.J.: Prentice-Hall, 1973), p. 9.

444

DATA LIFE CYCLE

Data within an MIS have their own life cycle. Three aspects of this life cycle are particularly important in the development, design, and operation of systems. First, we need to know how data are *generated,* i.e., how they are born. Second, we need to know what *manipulation* or processing of data is carried out. Finally, we need to know *how* certain types of information processing are carried out, particularly the *transmission of data* (and *communication of information*) and *storing/retrieving* of data. The reproduction of data may occur at various points in the life cycle, and therefore it is not shown on the life-cycle diagram of Figure 14.2.

The generation and capture of data, indicated by the left block of the figure, may occur because of an internal transaction or an event external to the company. Further processing after initial generation and capture consists of

1. *Storage or destruction.* The birth of data is the result of some phenomenon in the environment or in the company that is observed and recorded. Experiments, transactions, and operations represent planned generation of data. Data captured are then usually stored in documents or the computer data base. If the data appear to be worthless, perhaps because of an error in their generation, they are destroyed instead of stored.

2. *Transportation.* Data are repeatedly transported over the life cycle from one process to another.

3. *Retrieving.* Retrieving data from data-base management systems is no longer a great problem. In Chapter 15, various methods for relating and retrieving data are discussed.

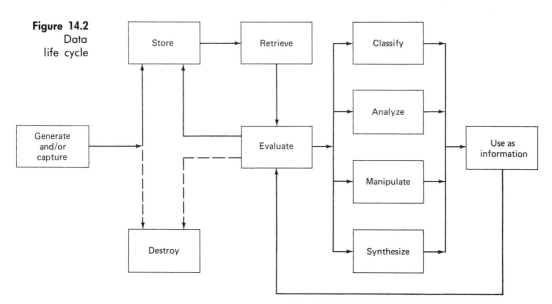

Figure 14.2
Data
life cycle

445

4. *Reproduction*. Data as stored in computer memory media or in records are not in a convenient form for management use. They must be reproduced, reorganized or manipulated, and reproduced again. Even data in usable form may have to be reproduced in multiple copies for multiple users.

5. *Evaluation*. When data are retrieved, they usually have to be evaluated to determine whether they should be further processed, returned to storage, or destroyed. After the data are developed into information and used, they are evaluated again. Some data have a one-time purpose only and are destroyed; other data are returned to storage.

   The quantity of data stored is limited by storage costs. Therefore data files should be continually monitored and evaluated to eliminate and remove useless or low-priority data, making room for more useful or higher-priority data.

6. *Classification*. Data are often accumulated at random and must be sorted to be useful. Even data that have been sorted and classified may be needed in a differently ordered form. In marketing, sales data may be stored on the basis of salesman; sorting on the basis of product and customer may then be needed.

7. *Analysis*. Data may be analyzed before use by identification of areas of interest, trends, and unusual occurrences, and by interpretation.

8. *Manipulation*. Quantitative data must often be operated upon—by adding, subtracting, and so on—to change their form or to develop their meaning through formulas or equations. For example, statistical methods may be used for estimating sales potential or for sales forecasting and computation of financial ratios.

9. *Synthesis*. Aggregation of many data is often required to structure a meaningful whole or complete report. Examples are individual salesmen's reports, the collection of all factory costs, or the summarizing of marketing intelligence data on a particular competitor.

10. *Utilization*. When transformed into meaningful form for use by members of the organization, the data become information. After use, the information reverts to data, which are evaluated for storage in their original or new form.

11. *Destruction*. After evaluation, data may be destroyed (removed from the system). For example, data regading meeting times and places for an in-house company seminar, or plans for an annual company picnic, have no value after the event.

DATA STRUCTURE

The structure of data in the information system serves as a basis for developing and measuring information. Two aspects of data structure will be touched upon here: data structure in a data base, and the semantic role structure of data.

The smallest data element we are concerned with here, commonly called a field, consists of a string of related characters which represent a predicate. For example, a person's income, a geographical area, or the unit of money constitute a data element. Such elements are stored in the data base in such a way that related elements can be found and retrieved. The most common data structures established for this purpose are

1. *Linked list for serial searching.* All data elements or sets of data are tied together in order, so that a search requires going through the whole list.
2. *Keyed-list structure.* Each data set has a key number (pointer field) associated with it, and pointer fields establish the structure of the data by taking us through the data in some order.
3. *Tree or hierarchical structure.* The data elements are divided and subdivided into finer classes, much as subjects are subdivided in a library. For example, a product may be subdivided into subassemblies. Each subassembly is then divided into sub-subassemblies, and so on until the smallest components are reached. The search starts at the top and goes down the tree.
4. *Network structures.* Data elements are linked in a network fashion. A data element may be searched for through a number of paths.

Obviously, the development of various structures for data is an important concept for storage and retrieval of large masses of data. In the next chapter we will discuss such structuring for data bases.

The relationship of data in the data base to information is obtained through concepts of language and semantics. A single word does not, in general, supply information except in the context of a particular situation. On the other hand, a very simple sentence may contain two or more elementary messages. For example, "Cynthia sells 100 shares of AT&T" breaks down into three elementary messages:

1. Cynthia sells shares.
2. The quantity sold is 100.
3. The kind sold is AT&T.[9]

Figure 14.3 shows the construction of data from characters (signs), the building of words from characters, and the development of sentence statements from words. Words or data in context are stored in the data base so that they may be retrieved in context as information. Table 14.2 defines the terms. (See following pages.)

[9]For a thorough development of the relationship of data to information, see Borje Langefors and Bo Sundgren, *Information Systems Architecture* (New York: Petrocelli/Charter, 1975), Chapter 1.

Figure 14.3
Terminological
precedence
relationships,
showing
defined terms
in boxes

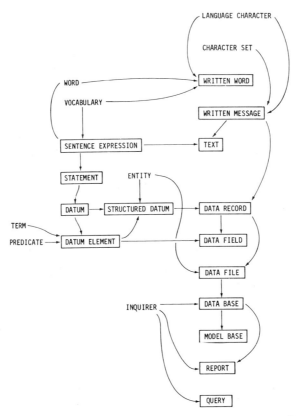

Source: E. Burton Swanson, "On the Nature of a Data Base and Its Use in Inquiry," **Information and Management,** 1, 1978, p. 96.

Table 14.2
Forms of data

	A. Natural Linguistic Forms
1. Word (logical)	A configuration of one or more language characters representing a word in an established vocabulary.
2. Sentence expression	An ordered selection of words from an established vocabulary, formulated and expressed so as to communicate as a whole. A sentence states a complete thought usually by means of a subject, a verb, and a predicate.
3. Written message	An ordered selection of language characters from an established character set configured so as to communicate to the receiver.
4. Text	Messages representing a sequence of sentence expressions which communicate a whole idea.
5. Document	Documents generally consist of one or more physical pages, comprise an ordered set of recorded visual images, and are constructed so as to communicate a whole idea. They may be based on text or on other linguistic form. Examples of documents include an article, a book, a motion picture film, a musical score and an engineering drawing. (See Swanson and Culnan, 1977.)

Table 14.2
(Cont'd.)

B. *Forms with "Truth" Value*

6. Statement — A sentence expression admitting of evaluation as "true" or "false" within an established community of information producers and receivers.

7. Datum — A statement given or taken as "true" for the purpose of facilitating inquiry.

8. Datum element — A term representing a predicate included within a datum. For example, the identification of a property or of a unit of time may constitute a datum element.

9. Structured datum — A representation of a datum, composed of a conjunction of datum elements, identifying and describing a single object or event observed. A typical structured datum contains a conjunctive predicate which (a) identifies an object or event, (b) specifies properties (or attributes) of the object or event together with measures of the extent to which it possesses the property, and (c) indicates a point in time. The general form is, "Object, O, had property, P, at time, t." O is a *key* (or identifier). P and t are *values* (or descriptors). A complex structured datum contains additional O's, P's, and t's and relationships among them. The structured datum form is used widely in fields with formal languages such as accounting, scientific research, management information systems, etc.

10. Data record — Structured data associated with a given object or event, formulated as a written message, encoded and recorded as required for storage, retrieval, transmission, or further processing. For example, an accounts receivable data record contains all of the data elements relating to a particular entity which has received goods on credit from an organization.

11. Data file — A configuration of data records associated with the members of a particular class of objects and events observed. For example, the accounts receivable file contains accounts receivable records for all people to whom credit was extended.

12. Data base — A configuration of data files which together represent some state-of-the-world relevant to the receiver (or inquirer). For example, the accounts receivable and sales data files might be part of an organization's data base.

13. Report — Data, retrieved and/or computed from a data base, arranged and presented so as to inform a receiver (or inquirer) about a particular class of events, objects, or descriptors. For example, an accounts receivable statement (bill) and an aged analysis of accounts receivable records are reports.

14. Query — A written message, formulated by an inquirer, accepted and processed by the producing unit, and used to generate a report from a data base.

Source: Richard O. Mason, "Measures of Information Output," Information Systems Working Paper 12-77, Graduate School of Management, UCLA, December 1977, and E. Burton Swanson, "On the Nature of a Data Base and Its Use in Inquiry," **Information and Management,** 1, 1978, p. 96.

COMMUNICATION

The exchange of information takes place at three levels:

1. *The statistical level.* This treats information in terms of "surprise." Claude E. Shannon, who developed the mathematical theory of communication, wrote, "The fundamental problem of communication is that of reproducing at one point either exactly or approximately a message selected at another point."

2. *The semantic level.* When symbols are transmitted, does the receiver decode the signals to get the same meaning intended by the sender?

3. *The pragmatic level.* Does the message produce the behavior by the receiver that the sender intended?

We note that the semantic and the pragmatic objectives depend upon the accurate transmission of signals—the statistical objective. In this section we discuss some features of mathematical theory of communication. Such theory provides a basis for measuring information and therefore has a direct application to MIS design. In the next section we look briefly at the semantic level by examining human information processing. The pragmatic level is related to motivation and leadership, which were discussed in Chapter 2.

THE COMMUNICATION MODEL

The basic communication model (Figure 14.4) consists of:

1. *Source.* This is the sender and contains a population of possible messages (signs). Examples are a human voice, a book, or a scene.

2. *Encoder.* The encoder operates on messages from the source to convert them to signals that the channel will accept. For example, a microphone converts sound waves to electrical signals.

3. *Signal channel.* Many forms of channels carry signals. Examples are air waves, wires, electromagnetic waves, and light waves.

4. *Decoder.* The decoder operates on received signals and tries to extract the message in a form usable to the receiver.

5. *Receiver.* The receiver receives the message as it is extracted by the decoder.

6. *Noise source.* External events introduce interfering signals into the communication system. Examples are atmospheric static, environmental sounds, and cross talk.

A message is a sign or sequence of signs from a repertory of signs common to both sender and receiver. The repertory of signs available to a source or receiver is called an alphabet. From an information systems point of view, an

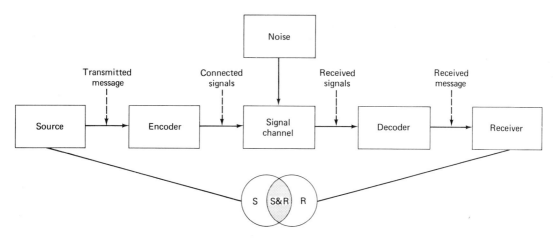

Figure 14.4 Model of the communication system

important management objective is to enlarge the stock of signs common to all members of the organization.

A. D. Hall raises the major questions that we like answered in the analysis of communications in a system and points out the very narrow limitations of mathematical information theory for MIS design:

> Suppose that in trying to understand how some system behaves, a systems engineer stands astride a path carrying messages from one place in the system to another. Among the many questions he might raise about the messages are:
>
> a. How much information is flowing?
> b. How many different kinds of messages are there?
> c. What is the meaning of each message to the recipient?
> d. How valuable are the messages?
> e. How frequently does each kind of message pass by, and is the passage of one kind correlated to the passage of another kind?
>
> The answers to these questions might be quite relevant to the design of some new system. However, information theory is not even concerned with *c* and *d*. It is concerned with questions *a, b,* and *e,* but the measure of information the theory provides is very special—much narrower than that required for the engineering of practical systems.[10]

Despite the narrowness of application, the principal concepts developed in mathematical data transmission theory as listed below *suggest a structure* for some aspects of MIS:

1. Definition of a unit of "information"

[10]A. D. Hall, *A Methodology for Systems Engineering* (New York: Van Nostrand Reinhold, 1962), pp. 384–385.

2. Noiseless systems
   a. Discrete sources
      (1) Average "information" transmitted
      (2) Channel capacity
      (3) Redundancy of "message" symbols
   b. Continuous sources
      (1) Average information transmitted
      (2) Channel capacity
3. Noisy systems (same subtopics as for item 2)

Information Content of Sources, Signs, and Messages

Suppose that we hear a person make a statement. If we *expected* this statement, we have not received any information. The information content of a message is determined by its unexpectedness. We can express this in terms of the following function, which increases as likelihood of a message decreases:

$$I = \log_2 \left(\frac{1}{p_i} \right),$$

where p_i is the probability that the ith sign is transmitted and I is the information carried by the sign.

The average information transmitted by a source or sender is the weighted mean of all possible signs:

$$h = \sum^{n} p_i \log_2 (1/p_i) = -\sum p_i \log_2 p_i$$

where n is the number of signs. Thus if a source has an alphabet of two equally likely signs,

$$h = \sum_{i=1}^{2} \tfrac{1}{2} \log_2 (1/.5) = \log_2 = 1$$

This amount of information is called a *bit,* shortened from binary digit.

The function h is the *entropy* of the source. It is a measure of disorder or randomness of signals that are transmitted. The maximum entropy for a source occurs if the probabilities of all signals are equal. For example, the entropy for a binary source is maximum for $p = .5$, as shown in Figure 14.5.

For the letters of the English alphabet, the maximum entropy is 4.701 bits per character. This assumes that each character is transmitted with a probability of $1/26$. Figure 14.6 shows the information content in terms of probability for single characters.

As A. D. Hall points out, the relative frequencies of appearance of letters in English differ. Hall calculates the average information per character as $h = 4.14$ bits. The efficiency of the English alphabet, then, is

$$E = \frac{\text{entropy of sources}}{\text{maximum possible entropy}} = \frac{4.14}{4.70} = 0.88$$

Although the treatment of communication only in terms of transmission of signals may seem remote from MIS, it offers some definite benefits. First, it provides us with a view of information in terms of surprise or unexpectedness. Second, it brings out the idea of limitations on the repertoire of senders and receivers. Third, it provides a measure of information. And finally, this treatment draws our attention to efficiency of signs.

Figure 14.5
The entropy for a binary source for different relative frequencies of the two signals

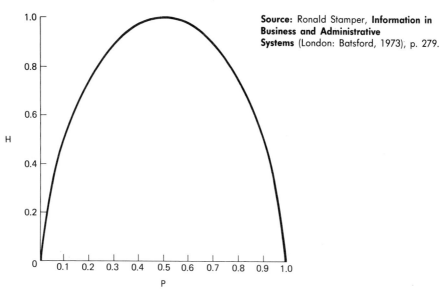

Source: Ronald Stamper, **Information in Business and Administrative Systems** (London: Batsford, 1973), p. 279.

Figure 14.6
Information content of an element or event with probability *p*

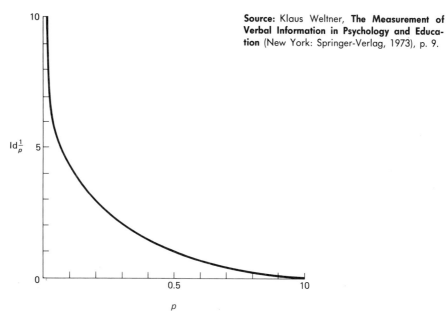

Source: Klaus Weltner, **The Measurement of Verbal Information in Psychology and Education** (New York: Springer-Verlag, 1973), p. 9.

Interest in humans as information processors has increased enormously in recent years because of interest in learning and decision making.[11] Certainly the developments in psychology are important to MIS designers if they can be applied. M. J. Driver and T. J. Mock would like to apply a "differential approach" to cognitive decision theory, whereby general principles from psychology can be modified for different categories of people with similar thought processes.

Our purpose here will be to present some general concepts of how humans process information. This should make the MIS designer more sensitive to the nature of managers' information needs. We will study human processing of information by examining certain variables:

1. Sensing
2. Pattern recognition
3. Syntax, semantics, and context of language
4. Memory
5. Processing and organizational structure.

Sensing

The starting point for human information processing is the reception from the environment of energy that affects neural activity. Information flows to the eyes at a tremendous rate, about 10^6 bits/sec. Considerable research deals with the minimum amount of energy required for a person to become aware of its existence. It has been found that the eye is so sensitive that a single quantum of light received can lead to a response. Response varies according to level, fluctuations, and color of light received. At normal reading levels, discrimination between levels of light perceived follows *Weber's law*:

$$\frac{\Delta I}{I} = k,$$

where I is the intensity of the light, ΔI is the incremental change, and k is a constant. Thus, for a high intensity, a greater *change* in intensity is required before we notice it.

Similar studies of hearing deal with threshold levels, saturation curves, and discrimination. Weber's law applies also to hearing. The information flow to the ears is of the order of 10^4 bits/sec.

We should note here that sensing involves complex constructive processes at high cognitive levels. That is, the mind is involved in abstracting and interpreting sensory perceptions; sensing is not simply a mechanical process.

[11]See Michael J. Driver and Theodore J. Mock, "Human Information Processing, Decision Style Theory, and Accounting Information Systems, *Accounting Review,* July 1975, for a summary of literature related to this subject.

Pattern Recognition

Humans are able to construct a variety of patterns from the same environmental input. Some factors which affect pattern recognition, visual or auditory, are the type of stimulus, duration of stimulus, delay between two stimulus presentations, processing after the stimulus is stopped, learning and memory, context of the stimulus, and attention.

Pattern-recognition research is of direct benefit to MIS designers. For example, the layout of forms, the development of characters to be read by optical scanners and also by people, and graphical displays in reports depend upon humans' pattern recognition. The goal of enabling people to talk to computers depends upon our developing better pattern-recognition theory.

A general model of the pattern-recognition system, developed by David E. Rumelhart, is shown in Figure 14.7. The physical stimulus is received and stored temporarily in the sensory system. Critical features are extracted but are affected by memory, by semantic, syntactic, and contextual information, and by other constraints. An abstract image is constructed and stored in memory. Resources of attention must be allocated among inputs. Thus, if a manager is trying to read a report, answer a phone call, and converse with a subordinate in the office, there is a trade-off between depth and breadth of attention in processing. In short, humans have fairly limited processing capacity by comparison with computers.

Figure 14.7 Diagram illustrating the interactions among environment, sensory system, pattern-recognition system, and memory system

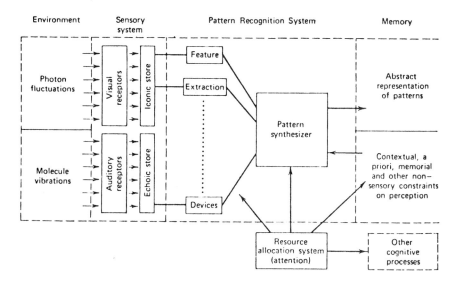

Source: David E. Rumelhart, **Introduction to Human Information Processing** (New York: John Wiley, 1977), p. 100.

Syntax, Semantics, and Context

Syntax is our knowledge about *form* of a language. Strings of words are meaningless to us unless arranged in a form determined by our complex knowledge of sentence structure, tenses, and word meanings. For MIS, this implies that language in reports and on forms must be in sentences or phrases which can be understood in the context of the situation. Conversation by computers depends upon our being able to construct syntax rules.

We can readily construct sentences in correct syntax that have no meaning. "The desk ate itself," for example, is a syntactically correct sentence without meaning. In other sentences of correct syntax the meaning may be ambiguous. Words themselves are abstractions of reality at the lowest level. Thus, when a person refers to a "worker," his or her understanding of the word may differ from that of the listener. When we label dissimilar objects or people with a single word or phrase, such as "blue collar worker," we disregard the wide variation among individuals. Further, our language often forces us into two-valued logic. Something is either black or white, right or wrong, good or evil, sweet or sour. We have many prefixes which provide us with words of opposite meaning (clear, unclear). Alfred Korzybski's writings deal extensively with the effects of semantics on our behavior.

The problems of semantics become even more complicated when we try to label constructs that have no physical referents. Anxiety, capitalism, and ego are examples of such constructs. As another example, an engineer wrote in a progress report that "14 units out of 22 failed a life test." In the final report, this was changed to read, "Eight of 22 units passed the life test." From the MIS view, the purpose of some reports may not be achieved because their meaning is obscure.

Definitions and meanings are aided by cognitive processes which place words and images in meaningful relationships to each other and to the situation. When we attempt to be too explicit and specify context in detail, we get the kind of writing that appears in government regulations or on the back of insurance policies.

Memory

Memory is essential for processing information because processing requires time, however brief. By analogy, the computer must store items in short-term

Figure 14.8 Simplified model of transmission and storage of information in human processing of information

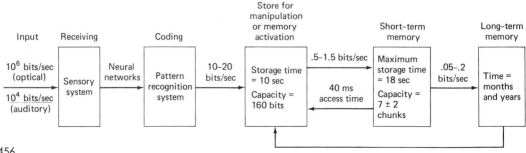

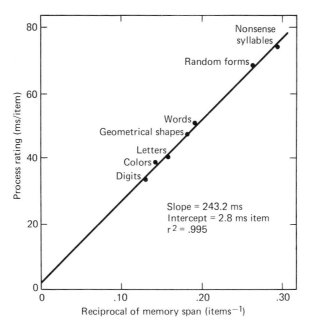

Figure 14.9
The relation between short-term memory processing rate and the reciprocal of the memory span for seven classes of stimuli

Source: J. P. Cavanaugh, "Relation Between Immediate Memory Span and Memory Search Rate," **Psychological Review,** 79 (1972), 525–530. Reprinted by permission.

and long-term memory in order to operate on them. In Figure 14.7 we saw a model of sensing and pattern recognition in humans. Memory was indicated as a support and a constraint. Now let us view memory in terms of capacity and information flow rates.

Figure 14.8 shows the memory system of humans as composed of short-term (primary) memory and long-term (secondary) memory. The inputs, or perceptions of the environment, are received at a very rapid rate. These data are coded and reduced by several orders of magnitude in being processed by neural networks and lines.[12] The consciousness accepts the coded information and activates the short-term memory. This store may manipulate patterns (for example, rotate an image) and simplify to eliminate interference.

Short-term memory is extremely limited. Results of many research experiments show that we can only hold 7 ± 2 items in memory. Originally, these items were believed to be characters or words. However, information may be coded into "chunks," as George A. Miller called them, to extend the memory span. When a chunk is recalled, it may then be broken down into its parts.[13] There is some variation of memory span for different types of chunks, as indicated in Figure 14.9.

[12]See K. Weltner, *The Measurement of Verbal Information in Psychology and Education* (New York: Springer-Verlag, 1973), p. 104.

[13]George A. Miller, "The Magic Number Seven, Plus or Minus Two," *The Psychological Review,* March 1956.

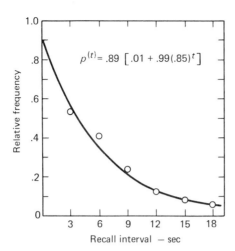

Figure 14.10
Percentage correct recalls as a function of recall delay interval

$$p^{(t)} = .89 \left[.01 + .99(.85)^t \right]$$

Relative frequency

Recall interval — sec

Source: L. R. Peterson and M. J. Peterson, "Short Term Retention of Individual Items," **Journal of Experimental Psychology,** 58 (1959), 193–198. Reprinted by permission.

Another important constraint on primary memory is a rapid decline in ability to recall after short delays. Figure 14.10 shows the result of an experiment by L. R. and M. J. Peterson. There is an obvious decline after a three-second delay. After 12 to 18 seconds the probability of a correct response to verbal stimuli is close to zero.

The search of primary memory to recall an item is serial and exhaustive. This compares with serial processing of magnetic tape in computer systems. Although access appears to be instantaneous, it requires 38 to 40 msec for each item.

The secondary memory of humans is very large. It consists of two types of information: (1) specific events that we have experienced or been told about, and (2) general information about objects and events. The first is called *episodic* memory and the second, *semantic* memory. Semantic memory is achieved through structuring of relationships, associations, networks, and spatial representations.

Processing

Information processing for human problem solving and decision making has been receiving considerable attention in recent years, owing to the work of Herbert Simon and Allen Newell. Although a review of this field is beyond the scope of this book, the concept of input information overload as a related topic is singled out here for the MIS designer.[14]

It is believed that as information input (environmental load) increases, people process more and more up to a point of "overload." After the overload, they select information from the input and process less input, as shown in Figure 14.11. Input, or environmental load, is the aggregate effect of information complexity, negative feeling produced by the input, and positive feeling pro-

[14]See Harold M. Schroder, Michael J. Driver, and Siegfried Streufert, *Human Information Processing* (New York: Holt, Rinehart and Winston, 1967).

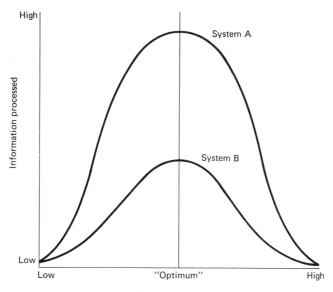

Figure 14.11 Relation of information used to environmental load

Source: Michael J. Driver and Theodore J. Mock, "Human Information Processing, Decision Style Theory, and Accounting Information Systems," **Accounting Review**, July 1975, p. 496.

duced by the input. As an example, a large cost overrun would produce negative feelings, and a sales increase would produce positive feelings.

"System A" in Figure 14.11 represents maximal data users. Such an individual or group will analyze all relevant data until the best solution to a problem appears to be found. System B represents minimal data users. They will satisfice to save time, using just enough data to achieve an adequate solution or decision.

MEASUREMENT OF INFORMATION

Measurement of the information in a message is important to the design of MIS reports. The busy executive would like as much information per page as he or she can process. Too much compression of information, however, may actually increase the time required for human processing. This would occur, for example, if many tables of data were reduced to fine print and squeezed onto a page without any text to guide the user.

Let us look now at some approaches to the measurement and evaluation of information in messages.

Statistical Value of Information

We have discussed Shannon's approach to the measurement of characters, messages, and information sources. This approach neglects semantic content, context, and related memory of the receiver. It does, however, suggest the idea of surprise as a measure of information in the more general sense.

Subjective Information

K. Weltner, referring to the information in a given text, considers information to be a measure of the relationship between text and recipient. Subjective information is a measure of the recipient's uncertainty regarding a field of events. The greater the uncertainty about the next letter, word, or idea in the text, the greater the subjective value of the next part of the message. The more a receiver knows about the subject and the more intelligent he or she is, the less information is conveyed. Weltner provides a procedure for quantitative measurement of this concept of information called "digitized prediction by means of branching diagrams."

On a more pragmatic level, we may ask a manager to state a subjective probability as to the truth of a statement or the occurrence of a future event. We then give the manager a message and measure the change in subjective probability. This change represents the amount of information in the message.[15]

Bayesian analysis illustrates this concept in more rigorous form. For example, suppose that a plant manager estimates machine downtime as 30 hours per month. A probability sample of machines is selected and their downtime for a month is measured and found to be 38 hours. If the variances of both estimates have also been estimated, then the revised downtime may be calculated. The manager will likely change his subjective probability that a machine will break down during a month.

Expected Value of Perfect Information

One measure of the value of information is to evaluate the expected profit for the best decision under uncertainty and subtract this profit from what would be obtained if we were certain of the future. A simple numerical case will clarify this concept.

Suppose that we manufacture seasonal goods such as ladies dresses. A new line is produced every quarter, and items are worthless if not sold at the end of the quarter. From historical sales records, we find the relative frequency with which we sold 8000, 9000, 10,000, or 11,000 dresses. These relative frequencies are represented in Table 14.3(a) as probabilities. The cost of a dress is $6 and the selling price $8, so the profit is $2. Table 14.3(a) shows the profit for various demands and profits weighted by the relative frequency of occurrence. In other words, if we know exactly when a demand for 8000 dresses will occur, we have perfect information. Such a demand occurs 20% of the time, so that we multiply $16,000 (the profit on 8000 dresses) by .20 to obtain the expected value, $3,200. Similarly, we weight the profits for the other demands, then add all the expected values to obtain the expected value under certainty.

Table 14.3(b) assumes that we do not know when a particular demand will occur. Therefore, we calculate the profits for various production runs vs. various demands.

---

[15]See Ronald Stamper, *Information in Business and Administrative Systems* (London: B. T. Batsford, 1973), p. 330. Also, see William R. King and Barry Jay Epstein, "Assessing the Value of Information," *Management Datamatics,* 5:4 (1976), 173.

Table 14.3
Computation of
expected value
of perfect
information

(a) Expected Value Under Certainty
(Units and dollars in 1000's)

Demand	Probability	Profit	EV
8	.20	$16	$ 3.2
9	.40	18	7.2
10	.30	20	6.0
11	.10	27	2.2
		Expected value under certainty =	$18.6

(b) Conditional Profits Under Uncertainty

	Production			
Demand	8	9	10	11
8	$16	$16−6	$16−12	$16−18
9	16	18	18−6	18−12
10	16	18	20	20−6
11	16	18	20	22

(c) *Expected Value of Best Decision Under Uncertainty

		Production Decision							
		8		9		10		11	
Demand	Proba-bility	CV	EV	CV	EV	CV	EV	CV	EV
8	.20	16	3.2	10	2.0	4	.8	−6	−1.2
9	.40	16	6.4	18	7.2	12	4.8	6	2.4
10	.30	16	4.8	18	5.4	20	6.0	14	4.2
11	.10	16	1.6	18	1.8	20	2.0	22	2.2
			16.0		16.4*		13.6		7.6

Table 14.3(c) computes the expected value for each production decision. The conditional profits (CV) from Table 14.3b are weighted by the appropriate probabilities to obtain the expected values (EV). The decision to produce 9000 units yields the highest total expected value of profits.

The expected value of perfect information is

$$EVPI = \$18{,}600 - \$16{,}400 = \$2{,}200$$

Evaluation of Characteristics of Information

Various authors have listed characteristics of information which are important to the manager. These characteristics may be roughly evaluated and the evaluations combined into a summary. The American Accounting Association lists four basic standards: relevance, verifiability, freedom from bias, and quantifiability. Earlier in this chapter we gave a longer list of characteristics.

The contingency approach to organizational design has pointed out variables which affect the functioning of the organization. What has been lacking is an integration of research on design of structures in different situations. M. L. Tushman and D. A. Nadler build on the view of *organizations as information-processing systems facing uncertainty* to develop a conceptual model for organizational structuring.[16] The highlights of their model are presented on these pages because it suggests the relationship of an MIS to effective functioning of an organization.

Briefly, the authors assume that

1. Organizations are open social systems which must deal with work-related uncertainty.
2. Organizations can be viewed as information-processing systems.
3. Organizations are composed of subunits differentiated by specialized skills.

The model, based upon analysis of the research literature, is described by means of Figure 14.12 and five explanatory propositions:

P1 The tasks of organizational subunits vary in their degree of uncertainty.

P2 As work-related uncertainty increases, so does the need for increased amounts of information, and thus the need for increased information-processing capacity.

P3 Different organizational structures have different capacities for effective information processing.

P4 Organizations will be more effective when there is a match between the information-processing requirements facing the organization and the information-processing capacity of the organization's structure.

P4A Owing to the alternative modes of achieving integration, the choice of coordinating and control mechanisms will not be deterministic.

P5 If organizations (or subunits) face different conditions over time, more effective units will adapt their structures to meet the changed information-processing requirements.

One implication of this model is that organizations must select structures which deal most effectively with their information needs. Another implication is that the MIS should provide information which matches information needs of the organization; that is, the information should be neither excessive nor deficient.

[16]Michael L. Tushman and David A. Nadler, "Information Processing as an Integrating Concept in Organizational Design," *Academy of Management Review,* July 1978.

Figure 14.12 The information-processing model

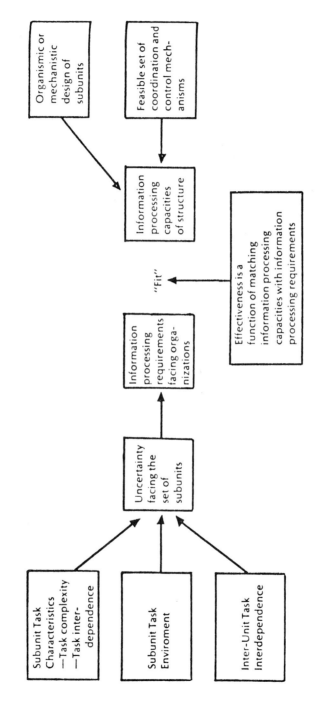

Source: Michael L. Tushman and David A. Nadler, "Information Processing as an Integrating Concept in Organizational Design," **Academy of Management Review**, July 1978.

SUMMARY Communication is a necessary process in a system. An MIS designer must distinguish between data and information in communication. Data are signals which do *not* affect behavior, whereas information consists of signs which *do* affect behavior.

Information possesses certain attributes: purpose, mode and format, redundancy, rate, frequency, deterministic/probabilistic, cost, value, reliability and precision, accuracy, validity, currency, compactness, steady-state or dynamic, linear or nonlinear, and continuous or discrete.

Information is obtained for an organization by searching the environment or by converting internal data into information. The problem of searching for information involves consideration of users' needs; selection of data stored; interest profiles of users; methods for classifying, indexing, and retrieving data; types of storage; methods of dissemination; and updating of storage files.

Data within an MIS have their own life cycle, in which they are generated, manipulated, transmitted, stored, and destroyed. The structure of data in the MIS serves as a basis for developing information from them. The most common data-base structures are linked-list, keyed-list, hierarchical, and network. Single words stored in the data base do not, in general, equate to information. Rather, words must be put in context or combined with other words in statement form to have meaning.

Communication, the exchange of information, takes place at three levels: statistical, semantic, and pragmatic. The basic communication model consists of a source, encoder, signal channel, decoder, receiver, and a noise source. Communication theory has been developed by Claude Shannon from a statistical point of view, neglecting semantic content. One result is the definition of a "bit" of information, which may be used to measure "information" received. One important and useful concept of this theory is that information received is related to its surprise value or unexpectedness.

Humans are elements in the MIS, and therefore their characteristics as information processors are important. Variables which affect human processing of information are sensing; pattern recognition; syntax, semantics, and context of language; memory; and processing related to organizational structure.

For the MIS, measurement and evaluation of information received by users is important in communications and report preparation. An important aspect is to avoid overloading the user while supplying him or her with as much information as can be used.

The problem of measuring the amount of information in a message is a difficult one. Shannon's statistical method of measuring in "bits" omits the essential element of meaning. Another approach makes use of before-and-after estimates of subjective probabilities of an event. The degree to which the message recipient revises his subjective probability estimate is a measure of the information received. The expected value of perfect information serves as a good measure in certain special situations. A more general approach consists of evaluating the characteristics of information, as described at the beginning of this chapter.

In conclusion, this chapter is devoted to a more rigorous study of information, data, and communication than is usually presented to the systems analyst. As MIS design becomes more sophisticated, the MIS designer will require a better understanding of the conceptual underpinnings of MIS theory.

1. Place a check in either or both columns to indicate whether the listed items refer to data or information

Data   Information

   a. Symbols

   b. Behavior-initiating stimuli

   c. Reports in a file

   d. Decreases or increases uncertainty

   e. Meaningless signals

2. Match the following

   a. unity minus efficiency
   b. the way words are put together to form phrases
   c. age of information
   d. passive directed scanning
   e. searching for classes of information
   f. science of signs
   g. not discrete
   h. users' profiles

   i. meaning of words and their relationships
   j. tables and graphs
   k. systematic, scientific observation
   l. relations between signs and their users
   m. sensory
   n. single-valued
   o. study of spoken language

_____ (1) Semiotic

_____ (2) linguistics

_____ (3) semantics

_____ (4) syntax

_____ (5) pragmatics

_____ (6) redundancy

_____ (7) deterministic

_____ (8) currency

_____ (9) mode of information perception

_____ (10) continuous

_____ (11) conditioned viewing

_____ (12) formal search

_____ (13) theory of sets

_____ (14) dissemination of information

_____ (15) compactness

3. Insert the code letters in the data life cycle diagram below.

   a. At the end of the month, reports on our competitor are taken from the files.
   b. Observation of a new safety feature on our competitor's electric knife is re-corded.
   c. Market research finds that our competitor's electric knife has a new safety feature.
   d. A study indicates that our competitor may take 15% of the market share from us with his new feature. Cost analysis shows such a feature will add only 17¢ to production costs.
   e. The report of management's decision with respect to the safety feature is placed in a file.
   f. Management reviews the analysis and decides that engineering should develop a similar safety feature.
   g. Information about a safety feature on our competitor's electric knife is decided to be important to management.
   h. The analysis and management's decision are documented and evaluated for retention purposes.

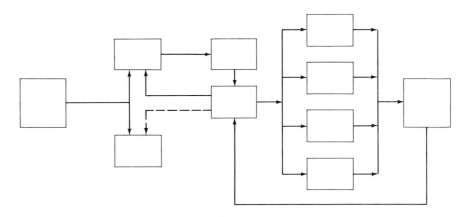

4. Give the precedence relationship for the structure of data that make up a report.

   a. report   1. _____
   b. data record   2. _____
   c. language character 3. _____
   d. data file   4. _____
   e. written message   5. _____
   f. data base   6. _____

5. a. Exchange of information takes place at 3 levels:

      (1) _____

      (2) _____

      (3) _____

b. The basic communication model consists of:

(1) _____ (3) _____ (5) _____

(2) _____ (4) _____ (6) _____

c. A source sends 10 digits with equal probability. The information carried by one digit is _____ bits.

d. A meter reading at a manager's desk shows 10 foot-candles. She barely notices the difference in illumination when it is increased by one foot-candle. A brighter light is installed to give 16 foot-candles. A difference of how many foot-candles is required for her to notice the difference now? _____

6. Place the code letters in blocks for the model of human processing of information below.

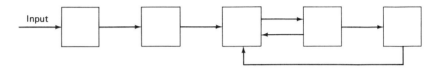

a. Short-term memory
b. Receiving, sensory system
c. Long-term memory
d. Memory activation store
e. Coding, pattern recognition system

7. Discuss the following definition of information. "Information, on the other hand, is data interpreted within some problem context or view-of-the-world. Information exists at the semantic and pragmatic level. The ultimate purpose of any information producing unit is to convert data to information." (From Richard O. Mason, "Measures of Information Output," Information Systems Working Paper 12-77, Graduate School of Management, University of California at Los Angeles, December 1977.)

8. What is the significance to the MIS user of distinguishing between information and data?

9. The marketing manager sends a monthly report of sales activities, marketing research results, and a probability distribution of forecasted sales for the following quarter. In the report, the market share for the most recent month was estimated at 28% ± 3% with 90% reliability. The report is distributed within 3 days after the end of the month and costs about $800 to prepare. Sales have been about $100,000 per month higher since the report has been in effect.
    Discuss this report in terms of the attributes of information.

10. Trace the life cycle on a block diagram of the following data:

    a. Sales of each salesperson in the field are recorded on order forms
    b. Labor time and rates are recorded on job tickets of units in manufacturing

11. Give an illustration of 4 types of data structures.

12. A manager, in a conversation, requests a subordinate to carry out a certain task. Sketch the block diagram of the communication model for this request.

13. Discuss possible approaches to answering the 5 questions about the analysis of communications raised by A. D. Hall.

14. Discuss the importance of sensing, pattern recognition, syntax/semantics/context, memory, and processing of information by managers in terms of the design of an MIS.

15. You have just been appointed to the general manager's staff as an MIS consultant. You are asked to review the formal reports of the company. You find that there are 32 periodic reports with some overlapping among many of the reports. You wish to measure, also, the value of information in each report. Discuss how you would approach your review of the reports.

16. Give an example to illustrate each proposition of the Tushman and Nadler model of information processing and organizational design.

SELECTED REFERENCES

AGUILAR, FRANCIS J., *Scanning the Business Environment*. New York: Macmillan, 1967.

BELZER, JACK, "Information Theory as a Measure of Information Content," *Journal of the Society for Information Science*, July–August 1973.

DAVIS, GORDON B., *Management Information Systems: Conceptual Foundations, Structure, and Development*. New York: McGraw-Hill, 1974.

FELTHAM, GERALD A., "The Value of Information," *Accounting Review*, October 1968.

FELTHAM, GERALD A., *Information Evaluation*. Sarasota, Fla.: *American Accounting Association*, 1972.

FELTHAM, G. A., and J. S. DEMSKI, "The Use of Models in Information Evaluation," *Accounting Review*, October 1970.

FLORES, IVAN, *Data Structure and Management*. Englewood Cliffs, N.J.: Prentice-Hall, 1970.

GARNER, WENDELL R., *The Processing of Information and Structure*. New York: John Wiley, 1974.

GRINGRAS, LIN, "The Psychology of Users and Designers of Information Systems," Working Paper 14-75, Center for Information Studies, Graduate School of Management, University of California at Los Angeles, June 1975.

HALL, ARTHUR D., *A Methodology for Systems Engineering*. New York: Van Nostrand Reinhold, 1962.

KANTOWITZ, BARRY H., ed., *Human Information Processing: Tutorials in Performance and Cognition*. New York: John Wiley, 1974.

KING, WILLIAM R., and BARRY J. EPSTEIN, "Assessing the Value of Information," *Management Datamatics*, 5:4 (1976).

KUHN, ALFRED, *The Study of Society: A Unified Approach*. Homewood, Ill.: Richard D. Irwin, 1963. See Part II, "Communications."

LANGEFORS, BÖRJE, and BO SUNDGREN, *Information Systems Architecture*. New York: Petrocelli/Charter, 1975.

MASON, RICHARD O., "Measures of Information Output," Working Paper, December 1977, Center for Information Studies, Graduate School of Management, University of California, Los Angeles.

MINTZBERG, HENRY, *Impediments to the Use of Management Information*. New York: National Association of Accountants, 1975.

MORRIS, WILLIAM T., *Management Science: A Bayesian Approach*. Englewood Cliffs, N.J.: Prentice-Hall, 1968. See "The Value of Information" in Chapter 5.

MORRIS, CHARLES, *Signs, Language and Behavior*. New York: George Braziller, 1955.

NEWELL, ALLEN, and HERBERT SIMON, *Human Problem Solving*. Englewood Cliffs, N.J.: Prentice-Hall, 1972.

ROGERS, EVERETT M., and REKHA AGARWALA-ROGERS, *Communications in Organizations*. New York: The Free Press, 1976.

RUMELHART, DAVID E., *Introduction to Human Information Processing*. New York: John Wiley, 1977.

SCHEWE, CHARLES D., "The Management Information System User: An Exploratory Behavioral Analysis," *Academy of Management Journal*, December 1976.

SCHRODER, HAROLD M., MICHAEL J. DRIVER, and SIEGFRIED STREUFERT, *Human Information Processing*. New York: Holt, Rinehart and Winston, 1967.

STAMPER, RONALD, *Information in Business and Administrative Systems*. London: Batsford, 1973.

SWANSON, E. BURTON, and MARY J. CULNAN, "Document-Based Systems for Management Planning and Control," Working Paper 9-77, Center for Information Studies, Graduate School of Management, University of California at Los Angeles, September 1977.

TUSHMAN, MICHAEL L., and DAVID A. NADLER, "Information Processing as an Integrating Concept in Organizational Design," *Academy of Management Review*, July 1978.

WELTNER, KLAUS, *The Measurement of Verbal Information in Psychology and Education*. New York: Springer-Verlag, 1973.

WILKINSON, JOSEPH W., "Specifying Management's Information Needs," *Cost and Management*, October 1974.

chapter 15

Data-Base Management

- The Management
  Viewpoint

- Definition of a
  Data-Base
  Management
  System
- Objectives of a
  DBMS

- Data Aggregates
- The Programmer
- Data Files

- The Computer
  Program
- Structured
  Records
- The Data Base

- Data-Base
  Administrator

- Security and
  Privacy

- The Librarian

- Data-Base
  System Model

PURPOSE: To present the basic concepts
underlying data-base management in an MIS

"Whatever happened to ol' Fred after that
little problem with the master file?"

Courtesy of UCC, Dallas, Texas (Adapted)

Information is not always born as information. It more frequently is developed from data. Companies gather and store *data* for conversion to information at appropriate times. The integrated collection of logically organized data of an organization, when centrally controlled, is called a *data base*. The data base is a very valuable resource. If we were suddenly to wipe out a company's data base, so that customer records, transaction data, and accounting data vanished, the company would be paralyzed. Less drastically, if stored data cannot be retrieved, as frequently occurred in manual systems, business operations are hampered. The managing of data is therefore of great concern to top executives.

THE MANAGEMENT VIEWPOINT

Previously, with manual systems, data were stored throughout the company in various types of physical files, such as file cabinets, tub files, and key-sort cards. There was tremendous duplication of data in such files.

Computer hardware and software have greatly reduced the redundancy of data. The data base may now be considered *conceptually* as one collection, regardless of any physical dispersal or configuration of equipment. That is, the computer system might make available to the manager almost instantaneously any data in the data base.

Management is concerned with performance and economics in the development of a data base. It must seek answers, in terms of cost, to such questions as:

1. How large is the data base?
2. How long should data be stored in the data base?
3. How rapidly is retrieval of data desired and in what form?
4. What equipment and software should be selected?
5. How should the company organize for data resource management?

In order to come to grips with such problems, managers must become familiar with the logical concepts of data-base systems, the physical configurations possible, and the nature of data-management software. Logical concepts are the most important for our purpose. The physical configurations are developed after the logical concepts are specified. Further, the rapidly changing offerings of hardware, data transmission alternatives, and data system software require that management review the most recent equipment when the decision is made. For these reasons, we will focus on the concepts of the data-base management system rather than attempting to review the many possible physical configurations.

Definition of a Data-Base Management System

"A data-base management system (DBMS) is any computer-based system that will define, create, retrieve, update, revise, and maintain the integrity of the system," according to Dr. Gordon C. Everest of the University of Minnesota. Companies selling software and some authorities, such as Dr. Eugene E. Payne and Dr. Gordon B. Davis, consider that "DBMS is a software package that assists the user in the managing of the computerized data base." We will work with the broader definition implied by Dr. Everest. On this premise, the data-base management system has seven fundamental components (see Fig. 15.1):

1. The *data-base administrator,* who is responsible for the data-base schema
2. The *schema,* which describes the nature of logical and physical relationships among records in the data base
3. The *data-management program,* which creates all physical records in the data base and controls all subsequent record input and output activities of the data base
4. *Query-language programs,* which permit managers to ask questions and receive answers by querying the data base in ordinary language
5. The *data base,* which contains the physical records
6. The *programmer,* who serves as a user interface to the data-base system
7. *Data-base programs,* which the programmer uses to derive information from data in the data base. These are "application programs."

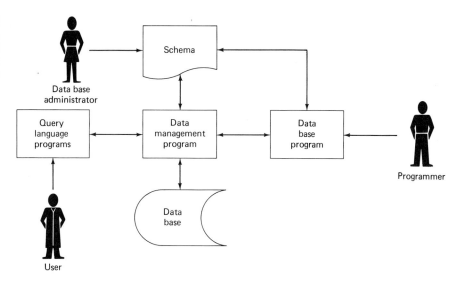

Figure 15.1
Data-base
management
system
components

OBJECTIVES OF A DBMS

The essential objectives of a data-base management system, as derived from the CODASYL group[1] and IBM's COPICS (Vol. VIII), are to

1. Provide instant system access to latest transactions related to an information system
2. Eliminate redundancy by data structuring suitable for all applications
3. Allow multiple concurrent updatings and retrievals
4. Provide a system that offers evolutionary growth by addition of data and programs
5. Provide a description of the data base not tied to any particular processing language
6. Reduce application program maintenance and provide on-line maintenance of data bases
7. Provide protection against unauthorized use and invasion of privacy of specified files.

Are these objectives achieved in practice? A recent study of 27 sites measured the perceived degree of change subsequent to installation of a DBMS. Table 15.1 shows the results, which may be readily related to the above objectives. Generally, we may conclude that objectives are being achieved only to a moderate degree.

[1]CODASYL, Conference on Data Systems Languages, is a voluntary group of people, supported by their respective organizations, who are interested in the development of the data-base techniques and language.

Table 15.1 Degree of change after installing DBMS for 27 sites (on a scale of 1 to 5)

Advantage realized	Gain or (Reduction)
Data independence	3.2
Data integrity	2.5
Centralized control	2.3
Ease and flexibility in restructuring and maintaining data	2.8
Data redundancy	(1.5)
Integrated vs. independent applications	2.3
Quick handling of unanticipated requests	2.0
Programmers not having to know physical structure	2.0
Security and privacy	1.2
Other change:	
Maintenance costs	(0.7)
Cost of adding applications	(1.7)
Ability to back up and recover	2.2
Number of characters stored	0.8
Timeliness of information	2.6
Usefulness of information	2.5

Note: Some changes realized with the installation of a data-base management system are actually not directly related to it. Many users claimed, for instance, that backup and recovery was made more difficult by the installation of DBMS; the gain in recoverability actually came from their being forced into developing better procedures to make the DBMS applications work.

Source: Gabrielle K. and John J. Wiorkowski, "Does a Data Base Management System Pay Off?" **Datamation,** April 1978.

DATA AGGREGATES

The first step in developing the DBMS may be considered to be the specification of the data base. Two perspectives exist. The first is that of the user, who desires information based upon specified data. The second is that of the data processing designer, who is concerned with logical and physical structure as well as data processing economics.

The user thinks in terms of information files and records. The data processor thinks in terms of data, groups, records, and blocks. Before we discuss these concepts in detail, we need some approximate definitions to relate these terms:

Data base: aggregate of files to meet MIS requirements

  File: related records or blocks

   Block: two or more records retained in a particular storage medium such as a file cabinet or computer tape

    Record: a collection of data elements related to a common identifier such as a person, machine, place, or operation.

     Group: two or more data elements that are logically related and must appear together to form a complete unit of meaning (street number and name, first and last name of a person)

Data element: (sometimes called *words, fields,* or *data items*): the lowest level of the data structure and the only one with which a specific value may be associated. For example, age, part number, or department number are data elements, as are names or descriptions.

Data Fields (Elements)

All a computer can do is read one character at a time. Similarly, it can print one character at a time. It is the responsibility of someone else to insure that characters are logically grouped and presented to a computer in a sensible fashion. When characters are grouped together in this fashion, they constitute a data aggregate called a *field*.

Fields are usually composed of a fixed number of characters. For example, a field might be established to contain a telephone number (with an area code), making this field ten characters long. The fact that fields are usually a fixed length or contain a fixed number of characters raises a very important point. If a field were not composed of a fixed number of characters, then it would have to carry a special character as its beginning and at its end, called a delimiter, which would serve to tell the computer where the field began and where it ended. Further, the user program in the computer which was reading these characters would have to examine each character as it arrived to see if it was a delimiter. This process creates extra work for the computer which is not directly productive in solving a user problem. Computer time invested in this manner is called *overhead*.

In addition to a length property, a field also has an attribute dimension. That is, only a certain type of character may be put in a particular field. Consider a field set aside to contain social security numbers. It should be long enough to contain the full nine characters of a social security number. There will never be letters or even special characters in this field; it will only have numbers in it—hence it is called a *numeric* field. On the other hand, it may be useful to set up a field containing only letters—an *alphabetic* field. If the field can contain either alphabetic or numeric characters, it is called *alphanumeric*. These are but three types of fields. As our discussion progresses, we will see the need for other types of fields.

As it turns out, there is actually another attribute dimension to the concept of fields. Exactly two types of characters may be put in any field: correct ones and incorrect ones. There are two ways in which incorrect characters may be put in fields. To return to the example of the field containing social security numbers, it occasionally happens that well-intentioned computer users put dashes as characters between the third and fourth digits and the sixth and seventh digits of their social security numbers in what should have been a strictly numeric field. This constitutes an error in type and should be trapped as part of the input edit function. Another error, which ultimately causes greater anguish to data processing people, is logical error. In this case the user records the wrong social security number. This is a very costly error because it cannot be so readily diagnosed. Typically, it will be found only when Mr. 123456789 does not receive his monthly social security check because it has been sent to Mr. 123456788. Errors of this kind create a very special type of grief in data-base systems, as will become apparent below.

Data Records

Fields may be grouped together to constitute the next type of data aggregate, which is a *record*. A record is simply a collection of related fields. Clearly, the fields must be ordered in some fashion such that a given field may always be found in the same place in each record. The physical organization of a record is called a *record layout*. A typical record layout for a time card application may be seen in Table 15.2. From this example we can see that a record is composed of three fields: the social security field of numeric characters, the name field of alphabetic characters, and the hours-worked field, which in turn is composed of five subfields for each day of the week. It is the programmer's function to prepare such a record layout for each type of record with which he will be working. For the programmer's purposes this will be called a *logical record*.

Extremely important with respect to understanding data-base concepts is the notion that a programmer is doing much more than simply listing fields when hs is preparing a record layout. He is forming a logical association among the fields of the record. This process is called *binding*. Thus, a programmer creates the fields SS-NO, NAME, and HOURS-WORKED, orders them, and thus binds them together into a larger data aggregate called a record. This record is given a name, probably PAYROLL, which will later serve to identify a set of employee records, all of type PAYROLL.

The record layout of Table 15.2 serves to describe a logical record of type PAYROLL. Sooner or later, there will have to be a physical representation of this record which the computer can read. Next the programmer will have to choose the appropriate medium for this type of record. He may choose to place these records on magnetic tape, on disk, on drum, and even on computer cards. When the appropriate choice has been made, the logical record description is transformed into a physical record description. Let us suppose that the programmer wishes to place these records on data cards. He must take a description of the card in terms of its physical composition (a computer card is 80 characters long) and transform the record layout to the physical layout. An example of this physical record layout for the record PAYROLL can be seen in Figure 15.2.

Table 15.2
Payroll
record

Field Name	Field Format
SS-NO	9-character numeric
NAME	40-character alphabetic
HOURS-WORKED	
MON	3-character numeric
TUES	3-character numeric
WED	3-character numeric
THUR	3-character numeric
FRI	3-character numeric

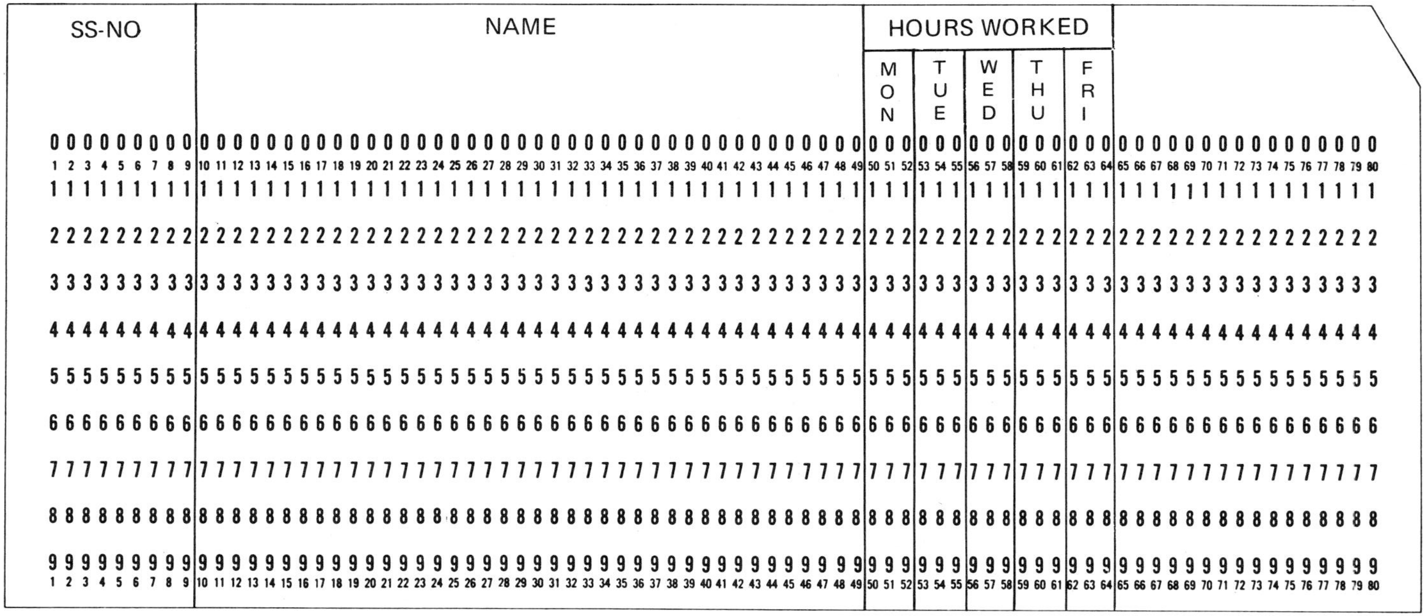

Figure 15.2 Physical Payroll record

477

Thus we find that there are two types of records. First, there is the logical record, which describes the fields of the record and their relationship one to another. Second, there is the physical record, which shows how the logical record will be represented, depending on the particular medium chosen to store that kind of record. In the case of a logical record of type PAYROLL, it can be seen that the total record length is 64 characters. On the other hand, the physical record will be 80 characters long.

In the special case of records of type PAYROLL, there is a one-to-one correspondence between logical records and physical records. Sometimes more than one card per physical record is required. In this case the logical record is said to be a *spanned record*. On the other hand, more than one logical record may be grouped in one physical record. (Clearly this would not be possible with the example above, because the PAYROLL record is 64 characters long and a card is only 80 characters long.) Logical records grouped in this manner are said to be *blocked*. Where there is a one-to-one correspondence between the logical and the physical records, the logical records are said to be *unblocked*.

THE PROGRAMMER

In terms of our present discussion of records, we can now summarize the function of a programmer. The programmer must

1. Establish fields and the necessary attributes for each
2. Bind these fields into groups called records and order the fields within them
3. Choose the appropriate medium for the records to be represented on
4. Decide how the records must be blocked
5. Select the appropriate file access method for each file.

In the last analysis, the programmer will have very little choice in these matters. There is always a *best* or an optimal way to represent records. Suboptimal solutions can be extremely expensive to financially ruinous. A bad decision by the programmer can be catastrophic.

Let us note that the records described above contain only user data. This will not always be the case.

DATA FILES

After the computer programmer has created the concept of a record, he then sets about to construct a computer program which will read a record organized according to the designated record layout. Presumably, there will be more than one record of the type specified in the record layout. That is, the programmer will write the program in such a fashion as to read a group of cards of the type PAYROLL from a card reader. This group of cards will be stacked one on top of another, placed into the card reader, and read one at a time by the card reader under control of the computer program. These cards will be presented to the computer program in a strictly sequential order.

This ordered collection of records is called a *sequential file*. Thus, a file is a group of records having the same format. In the case of the PAYROLL records, they are stored on the card medium. As such, they constitute a *card file*. These records could just as easily have been stored on magnetic tape or on disk. It is possible to construct sequential files on both magnetic tape and disk.

One of the principal virtues of files constructed on disk units is that the records do not have to be placed in them in a strictly sequential order. Rather, records may be placed in disk files in a random order. This type of file would be called a random access file. Each record in a random access file has associated with it a relative index number. Whenever a record is to be read from a random access file, a computer program must produce a relative index number for this record in order to locate the record in the file. One of the principal virtues of a file organized this way is that, to obtain record number 100, we merely produce the number and use it directly to read the necessary record. Hence the term *direct access file* is sometimes used interchangeably with the term random access file.

Consider now the problem of reading record number 100 from a file which has a sequential organization. We must read record number 1, read record number 2, read record number 3, and so forth until the necessary record is obtained. Thus to obtain one record we must read 100 records. This would seem to suggest that we immediately abandon all magnetic tape files, card files, and sequential disk files in favor of a clearly superior random access file organization. This would be an extremely expensive suggestion. Disk storage is one of the most expensive storage media available. Magnetic tape, on the other hand, is relatively inexpensive. Large volumes of data can be stored on sequential files on magnetic tape at the least possible cost.

This direct cost associated with storing records on disk files is not the entire problem associated with their use. With the introduction of third-generation computer hardware and software, the task of writing computer programs to be read directly from the various I/O devices associated with this new generation of computers becomes far too complex for even the more sophisticated programmers to manage. Consequently, most computer vendors supply a set of programs to people who purchase their machines which handle all of the input and output activities for each type of computer peripheral. When a programmer wishes to either read or write a record to an I/O device, his computer program will format the request in a particular manner and present it to the appropriate program supplied by the vendor. The vendor's program then performs the action indicated by the user's program.

The set of programs provided by a computer manufacturer defines a set of *access methods* which serve to define the way in which records will be written or read from peripheral devices. The typical program provided by the vendor to perform a *sequential file access* is fairly simple and uncomplicated. The typical program provided by the vendor to perform a *random file access* is fairly complex and lengthy. Thus, if a file is organized as a random access file, every attempt to read from or write into this file causes the execution of a rather lengthy program. While the computer is executing this access program it is not directly performing useful work for the user. Thus the user has increased the *overhead* associated with a given program activity by using random access file methods. This overhead might at first glance lead us to the conclusion that we should forego the use of direct access methods and disk files.

Data Files: An Example

In order to understand the circumstances which would force the use of direct access file methodology, let us invent a commercial bank. This bank has a small computer system complete with two magnetic tape transports and an MICR reader, which will allow the computer to read the special magnetic ink characters recorded on the bottom of each check or deposit slip. The bank is a small one. At the end of each business day, the bank employees will sort each of the day's checks and deposit slips into ascending order by account order. These employees will then turn on the power to the computer and put a magnetic tape on each of the tape units. One of these magnetic tapes contains a sequential file of records. Each record on this tape contains a field for account number, account balance, and a field for each transaction against this account number. The records are arranged in this file in ascending order by account number. The bank employees now cause a computer program to be loaded into computer memory. This program will read an MICR record, which will be either a deposit or withdrawal. It will then read a record from the magnetic tape which contains current account information. As each account is updated, it is written into a sequential tape file on the other tape unit. This new file will become the current account file for tomorrow. When the last account has been updated, the employees turn the computer off, put the tapes in the vault, and leave. If this bank were to replace its magnetic tape units and files with disk units and random access files, its costs would probably double because of the additional expense of the disk units and the overhead created by the random access files.

As long as the bank managers are happy with this approach, they probably have the best possible system. As business prospers, however, the number of accounts increases, the total check volume begins to rise, and the employees have to stay later each day to sort and process the checks. Finally it is decided that it would probably be better to equip each of the tellers with a terminal connected directly to the computer and process each transaction as it occurs. Now consider the problems involved with the use of sequential file methodology. A customer will approach a teller with a check to be cashed. The teller will key the number of the customer's account into the terminal, and the computer program will find the corresponding account on the magnetic tape, inform the teller as to the account balance, and process the transaction. Let us assume that the bank at this point in time has over a thousand such accounts and that the customer who just approached the teller has the fortune to have the highest account number yet assigned by the bank. Every single record on the magnetic tape will have to be read individually to check the account number to see if it matches the one sought by the teller. Clearly this is a waste. The customer will probably leave in disgust long before the necessary record is found.

The point here is that this unnecessary record processing dictated by the sequential method file processing is in itself a form of overhead. For this application, the trade-off between sequential magnetic tape file and the expense and overhead induced by disk random access files is in favor of the disk files. Had disk files organized in random access fashion been used in the teller application above, the customer's account number could probably have been used directly to obtain the customer's account information without any unnecessary I/O. In this case a savings, at least in goodwill, will be realized through the use of expensive and high-overhead file access methods.

Many more different types of file access methods are available to a programmer. Without loss of generality, these are but variants of the basic sequential and direct access methods. Each of these methods is tailored to a specific application. Thus we see an application of the fifth function of the programmer. Just as for the other functions, a bad decision by the programmer can be extremely costly.

THE LIBRARIAN

Most computer installations have a very large number of computer programs and files on magnetic tape and disk. These files constitute a centralized collection of data supporting a firm's business needs. As indicated above, this collection of files is not a data base. It is a very large collection of files which is in desperate need of management. As a result, a person is generally found in computer installations whose sole responsibility is to physically manage the collection of magnetic tapes. He or she is called a *librarian*.

The librarian's function is very similar to that of a librarian in a regular library: to classify the materials he or she is responsible for, know what these materials contain, and insure that they can be found or retrieved when requested. In addition to managing the physical magnetic tape reels, this librarian typically maintains a description of the record layout of each major type of file. The librarian is also responsible for maintaining listings and documentation of all programs which process his files. For example, in the case of the PAYROLL file, the librarian would be responsible for all magnetic tapes containing the PAYROLL file, would have a description of the record layout for records of type PAYROLL, and would have documentation on programs which create the PAYROLL record, maintain them, or simply create reports from them. Specifically, then, the duties of a librarian are as follows:

1. Maintain the physical storage media containing the various files of a computer installation
2. Control the access to these files to prevent unauthorized use of the information or the accidental destruction of data contained on them

3. Maintain a description of the record layout or record layouts of a file

4. Maintain a description of the file access method used to build the file

5. Maintain the documentation of all programs which process these files.

As can be seen, the librarian's function is strictly one of maintenance. This maintenance function may be much more than any one person can handle for a big computer shop. Thus, in a larger computer installation we would expect to find a librarian whose function is to manage other librarians. These subordinate librarians would each manage a subset of library functions. There would be a tape librarian, a program librarian, and so forth. The number of librarians would depend directly on the size of the installation.

There is a very definite communication interface between the librarian and the programmer. As programs are modified or created, the programmer must keep the librarian informed. Also, should the record layout or access methodology of a file be altered by a programmer, the librarian must be informed. This is so because the librarian is the central source of information on data files. This timely interchange of information between the programmer and the librarian is also necessary from another standpoint. The average tenure of a programmer at any one computer installation is approximately two years. A programmer's exit is usually rather rapid. He or she will often leave without doing any extra documentation. Thus, if programmer modifications to record formats and program are not captured immediately, whole files may be lost because they can't be processed.

THE COMPUTER PROGRAM

Previously we have looked upon computer programs as a sequence of simple operations. From a data-base concept, a program does more than just cause the computer to perform operations. *The computer program is the initiating device which causes the contents of two or more files to be associated at some point in time.* It forms logical relationships among records. To understand this concept of *binding,* consider the following example.

Tables 15.3, 15.4, and 15.5 describe three separate record layouts. We could write a computer program which would simply read SALARY records and extract from each SALARY record the EMPLOYEE-NO from that record. We could write a program which would read the employee number from the SALARY file and use that employee number to obtain a matching record from the WEEKLY file. This program would form a logical association between the SALARY file and the WEEKLY file.

Consider now the number of unique data fields (EMPLOYEE-NO occurs in all three record types). Even for this simple example, a program can be written to form logical associations among the various fields of records of these three files. It is important to note that whenever a new association is needed, a computer program must be written to make it. Assume that we would like a report which listed by job classification the social security number, name, and

Table 15.3 Salary record	Field Name	Field Format
	EMPLOYEE-NO	5-character alphanumeric
	OFFICE-NO	3-character alphanumeric
	WK-SALARY	5-character alphanumeric
	NO-DEDUCT	2-character alphanumeric
	JOB-CLASSIFICATION	3-character alphanumeric

Table 15.4 Weekly record	Field Name	Field Format
	EMPLOYEE-NO	5-character alphanumeric
	SS-NO	9-character numeric
	ANNUAL-LEAVE	3-character numeric
	SICK-DAYS	3-character numeric
	CREDIT-UNION	5-character numeric
	FICA-TO-DATE	6-character numeric

Table 15.5 Employee record	Field Name	Field Format
	EMPLOYEE-NO	5-character alphanumeric
	NAME	40-character alphabetic
	SEX	1-character alphabetic
	BIRTHDAY	6-character numeric
	ADDRESS	40-character alphanumeric
	MARITAL-ST	1-character numeric

sex of everyone occupying that job classification. A computer program would have to be written to produce that report. Writing a computer program is a very tedious and expensive process. Every time it is necessary to form a new logical relationship among files, a new program must be written to form it.

STRUCTURED RECORDS

In order to avoid writing new programs to structure records, we may incorporate the necessary logical relations into the programs themselves. There are four common methods of structuring records: linked-list, keyed-list, hierarchical, and network structures.

Linked-list Structure

We will use the records of the type SALARY from Table 15.3 to illustrate the linked-list structure. We will assume that each of these records is in a direct access file. In order to process this file as it is, we will have to write a program which will systematically produce relatively record numbers so that the appropriate access method can secure the appropriate record for us. Every time the program processes the file, it will have to produce the relative record number in precisely the same sequence. To relieve the program and the programmer of this

Table 15.6
Linked salary
record

Field Name	Field Format
EMPLOYEE-NO	5-character alphanumeric
OFFICE-NO	3-character alphanumeric
WK-SALARY	5-character alphanumeric
NO-DEDUCT	2-character alphanumeric
JOB-CLASSIFICATION	3-character numeric
NEXT-RECORD	5-character numeric

function, let us create a new file with the record layout described in Table 15.6. The principal difference between the record SALARY in Table 15.3 and the new record SALARY of Table 15.6 is that the new record contains an additional field called NEXT-RECORD. In this field will be stored the relative record number of the next record. To process this file we will simply need to read the first record. From this first record we can obtain the next logical record from the field NEXT-RECORD. Hence, the logical or sequential relationship among the records of this file is built into the file structure. Records organized in this manner are said to form a *linked list*.

Figure 15.3(a) gives a graphical representation of records in a linked list. Figure 15.3(b) shows how the records would be organized if the order were to be based upon EMPLOYEE-NO.

The linked list with its serial searching for retrieval of data has an advantage over other methods. Suppose we have a list of records which are linked by names of individuals in alphabetical order. Now assume that a query comes in asking if we have a record on Moore. We search the file serially until we come to Moore or until we come to a name that would follow Moore. In the latter case, we know that Moore is not in the file. In other record structures, we would have to search the entire file before we could be sure that Moore was not there.

Figure 15.3
Linked list
of records

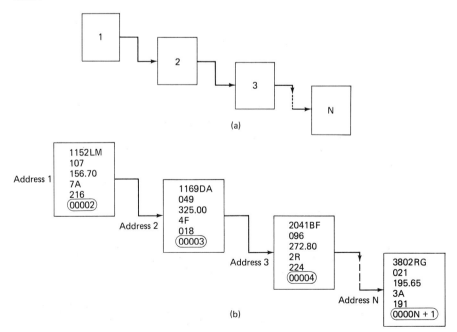

(a)

(b)

Keyed-list Structure

Let us now suppose that we wish to read the SALARY file of records such as in Table 15.3 and print a report in the order of the JOB-CLASSIFICATION field. To do this we cannot use the linked structure by NEXT-RECORD, because it would present the records to us in order of EMPLOYEE-NO. Consequently, we would have to write a program to sort these records and present them in order of JOB-CLASSIFICATION. It is possible, assuming that the job classification order will occur rather frequently, for us to add yet another field to records of type SALARY. Let us call this new record field NEXT-JOB. The new record layout will be seen in Table 15.7.

Field Name	Field Format
EMPLOYEE-NO	5-character alphanumeric
•	•
•	•
•	•
NEXT-RECORD	5-character numeric
NEXT-JOB	5-character numeric

After reading the first record of this new type SALARY, we can get the next record by employee number by using the field NEXT-RECORD, or we can get the next record by job classification by using the contents of the field NEXT-JOB. A graphical representation of this new record structure can be seen in Fig. 15.4. This new structure of records is called a *keyed list*.

These new fields do not contain any data that directly relate to the employees whose record they occupy. Rather they serve to locate or point to the *next* record where "next" is a logical relationship established when the record was created. These new fields are called *pointer fields*. It is the function of these pointer fields to allow us to order in some logical fashion the records of a file without having to use a computer program or computer programmer to do this ordering function.

The use of pointer fields considerably reduces the programming overhead, but it also increases the total amount of computer storage required to store each occurrence of records of type SALARY. In a sense, we have traded off between programming and computer processing overhead for an increase in data overhead.

If we are willing to pay the price there are many different ways that records can be joined together. Another very useful linkage for a programmer to create would be to link records of different files together. To return to the record layouts of Tables 15.3, 15.4, and 15.5, we might want to link, for each employee, records of type SALARY to the corresponding record WEEKLY, which would in turn be linked to a record of type EMPLOYEE. That is, for each employee number we would form a linked list *across* files associating those records with the same number. With this arrangement of pointer fields, we could simply identify an employee in the SALARY file, and, having secured the

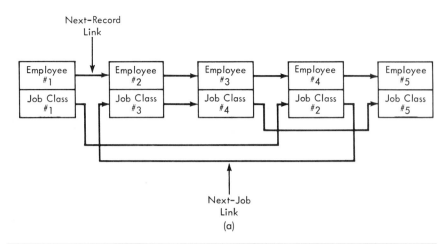

Figure 15.4
List of records linked with different keys: (a) two keys, (b) three keys

Next-Record Link

Employee #1	Employee #2	Employee #3	Employee #4	Employee #5
Job Class #1	Job Class #3	Job Class #4	Job Class #2	Job Class #5

Next-Job Link

(a)

	KEY			KEYS	
Record address	Employee Number			Job Class	Annual Leave
1	Employee number	Job class	Annual leave	3	1
2	Employee number	Job class	Annual leave	7	3
3	Employee number	Job class	Annual leave	1	2
4	Employee number	Job class	Annual leave	5	6
5	Employee number	Job class	Annual leave	4	7
6	Employee number	Job class	Annual leave	2	4
7	Employee number	Job class	Annual leave	6	5

(b)

record, we would have a pointer to his or her WEEKLY record. This would in turn have a pointer to the employee record. Normally, without the use of this linked structure, it would be the purpose of a computer program to perform this binding of all three record types. Through the use of pointer fields, however, we have preestablished the logical relationships of these different record types.

Tree and Network Structured Records

The number of possibilities of different types of record structures is limited only by the creativity of the computer programmer. Some of these data structures are more important to this discussion of data-base systems than are others. Two of particular note are shown in Figs. 15.5 and 15.6. Figure 15.5(a) is a *tree* structure or *hierarchical* data structure. In this type of data arrangement, data records are organized into *echelons* or levels. To obtain a particular record from, say, the third echelon, we would first identify the appropriate *parent* or *owner* record at the second echelon, which would in turn be identified by the choice of

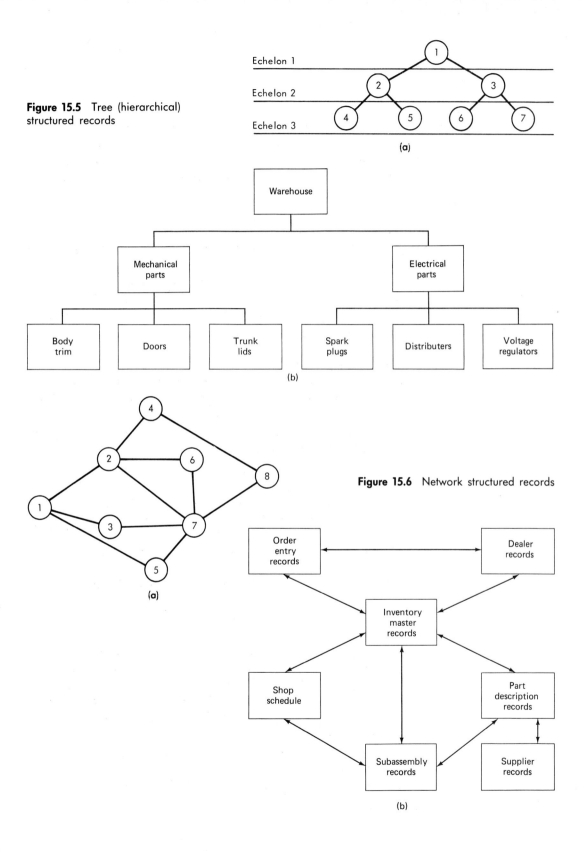

Figure 15.5 Tree (hierarchical) structured records

Figure 15.6 Network structured records

a particular pointer from echelon 1. For example, Fig. 15.5(b) shows a tree structure for an inventory system file. If we wish to search records of trunk lids to find a particular year and model, we must first specify the warehouse. Then we search "mechanical parts" until we reach "trunk lids." Finally, we search the "trunk lid" file.

Figure 15.6(a) is a representation of records associated in a *network* or *plex* fashion. In a network, complex associations can be formed among the related groups of records. Figure 15.6(b) illustrates a network structure for an inventory system. Suppose that an order entry clerk wishes to know the parts list for a specified subassembly on an order. He will request a search of the inventory master records to find the pointer which will locate the subassembly description in the subassembly records. Once the subassembly is located here, the parts list can be read out of the record.

In a more complicated case, if the order entry clerk wished to obtain information about a supplier, he would have to proceed from the inventory master records to the Part Description records to the supplier records. Or he could proceed to the supplier records through any connected set of records.

THE DATA BASE

We have discussed how records may be related. An organized collection of all records is the data base. Unlike records in a file-oriented data processing system, the logical relationships among records in a data base are not formed by programs or programmers. Rather, records in a data base are related one to another in an exceedingly complex fashion in advance of their creation. The description of the logical relationships is not characterized by the programs which process these records, nor are the physical descriptions of the records necessarily formed in programs. Instead, a *schema* is created. This schema describes the logical and the physical relationships among the records in the data base in a formal manner. It is like a giant map showing all record types in the data base together with the name of the record and the fields it contains. These links between the nodes of the map are the logical record relationships, and the nodes themselves are the records.

The exact set of rules used to form associations among the various records in the system will determine the type of the data base. There are three major types of data-base systems: relational data bases, network or plex data bases, and hierarchical data bases. Hierarchical data bases are composed of records organized in a tree structure as in Fig. 15.5. Network data bases have records organized as a system of networks as in Fig. 15.6. Relational data bases, on the other hand, work entirely with *flat* files—files which have been structured into tables as opposed to lists or trees. In this system, a file is said to be a relation, and fields within the files or relations define domains of *tuples*. On the whole, relational approaches are rather more primitive with respect to the structure of the data. They depend heavily on a data management program to form logical associations.

Data-Management Program

The actual input/output operations in a data-base system are far too complex for any individual to comprehend, let along control. Thus, another fundamental constituent of a data-base management system is the *data-management program*. This data-management program will control all access to and from the data base. Typically this program is the nucleus of a data-base system and is provided by the computer manufacturer or a vendor of computer software as part of the total data-base management system.

DATA-BASE ADMINISTRATOR

A very important part of the total data-base management system is a person and not a set of computer software. This person is called a *data-base administrator*. The data-base administrator performs a role very similar to that of an accountant. That is, he or she specifies the exact relationships among data records, classifying and placing these types of records according to established sets of rules. By the very nature of the way in which record relationships are made, the data-base administrator can make the data-base system extremely responsive to the data needs of his firm or can let the various sources of overhead grow in an uncontrolled manner until the data-base management system is consuming the entire profit potential of a business.

As part of the overall system, the data-base administrator is needed to provide standardization, organization, maintenance, and resolution of conflicts among users of the system. The administrator performs such specific functions as

1. Determining data needs of all users
2. Determining the trade-offs between data overhead and computer processing-programming overhead
3. Publishing a directory of proposed data structures for review with potential users of the system
4. Publishing data dictionaries containing basic information about the data stored in the data base (data field definition, format, editing rules, security considerations, etc.)
5. Resolving with all users special-purpose variations to the data base
6. Setting up generalized methods for retrieval and a library of data-base access programs
7. Maintaining the data base, its integrity and completeness
8. Providing and assigning privacy locks and security measures and monitoring for breaches of these.

As can be seen, this data-base administrator has assumed a significant amount of the programmers' and the librarians' duties and responsibilities. Through the data-base administrator, we have *central control* on and access to information in the data base. The programmer in a data-base environment still prepares programs in the usual manner. However, these programs will obtain the necessary record description information from the data-base schema, and all access these programs make to the data base will be through the data management program. Both of these activities occur under the auspices of the data-base administrator.

The alliance of the data-base administrator and the accountant is a critical one in future business enterprises. Their functions within the business are totally interrelated and remarkably similar in terms of functions and responsibilities. By virtue of their roles in data organization, both serve to provide an important information base to assist a decision maker for management decisions.

DATA-BASE SYSTEM MODEL

Let us now examine a model of a working data-base system. Such a model may be seen in Fig. 15.7. On a regular basis, events occur which will influence the nature of the data in the data base. These events are called transactions. A typical transaction would be the arrival of a purchase order.

To process this transaction, we must submit the transaction to some type of *transaction interface program* which will check for errors in the various elementary fields, a process called editing. Once a transaction has been edited and approved, the change indicated by the transaction type is made to the data base and the edited transaction is recorded on a *transaction history file*. All edited transactions are recorded to provide backup for the data-base system.

Figure 15.7
Data-base
system with
support systems

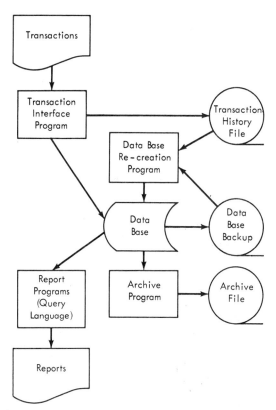

The entire data base is periodically copied in its entirety onto a series of backup files. Should the data base be destroyed accidentally, it can be entirely recreated by restoring the most recent copy of the *data-base save file* and reprocessing the transactions from the date of the last data-base backup from the transaction history file. This very simple process provides almost complete data security. Also the transaction history serves as a built-in audit trail.

Because information in a data base is never destroyed, data bases grow predictably over a period of time. Standards must be set which determine the useful life of all of the various types of data records in a data base. Once these standards have been set, a program called an *archival program* will be run against the data base. This program will selectively, according to the established age criteria, remove records from the data base. These records will be placed in an *archive file*. Thus, we see that there are three principal repositories of data in a data-base system: the transaction history file, the data base proper, and the archive files.

SECURITY AND PRIVACY

To impress his employer with the need for additional security, a programmer designed an undetectable program to automatically write payroll checks for several of his relatives, including a two-year-old girl. He ran the system for 3 months, keeping the checks in their unopened envelopes, then he dropped the entire collection of 30 checks on the security director's desk. He is now in charge of DP security.[2]

In historical times people went to great lengths to protect their gold. In modern civilization, more companies are concerned with protecting their data. No system can be made 100% secure. The function of design and maintenance is to keep searching for ways to make the company's system and data base more secure. Since resources for this purpose, as for all others, are limited, a rule of thumb is to keep expenditures below 10% of total expenditures for design and maintenance.

The subjects of security and privacy have been so thoroughly treated from so many similar perspectives by others that we can only report on some of the basic concepts here.

Definitions of Security and Privacy

Data security means protection of data against

1. Accidental destruction or modification by forces of nature (such as flood, fire, and lightning) or by people
2. Intentional destruction or modification by unauthorized people
3. Accidental or intentional disclosure to unauthorized people.

---

[2]"Computer Security . . . the Imperative Nuisance," *Infosystems*, February 1974, p. 27.

Privacy means that organizations or people have the right to restrict dissemination of information about themselves.

For data within a company, security and privacy are closely related. We will focus on this environment rather than on the large problem of privacy in a society with computerized data bases in many private and public agencies.

System Threats

There are numerous risks to the security of a data base. A number of possible breaches of security and privacy are shown in Table 15.8.

Clark Weissman has structured a classification of system threats as follows:

Table 15.8 Types of data-base security exposure

Type of Exposure	Inability to Process	Loss of an Entire File	Loss of Single Records	Modification of Records	Unauthorized Reading or Copying
Acts of God					
Fire	√	√			
Flood	√	√			
Other catastrophe	√	√			
Mechanical failure					
Computer outage	√				
File unit damages disk track			√		
Tape unit damages part of tape			√		
Disk, or other volume, unreadable		√			
Hardware/software error damages file		√	√	√	
Data transmission error not detected			√	√	
Card (or other input) chewed up by machine			√	√	
Error in application program damages record			√	√	
Human carelessness					
Keypunch error			√	√	
Terminal operator input error			√	√	
Computer operator error		√	√	√	
Wrong volume mounted and updated		√		√	
Wrong version of program used		√		√	
Accident during program testing		√	√	√	
Mislaid tape or disk		√			
Physical damage to tape or disk		√	√		
Malicious damage					
Looting	√	√			
Violent sabotage	√	√			
Nonviolent sabotage (e.g., tape erasure)	√	√	√	√	

Accidental threats

1. Some user, employee, or outsider accidentally stumbles upon a loophole which makes the system or its data base accessible. Such loopholes are sometimes called "trapdoors."

2. Component failure invalidates a safeguard which protects the system from intrusion.

3. An error in application of the communication system leaks information improperly.

4. A component failure reveals or leaves vulnerable critical protection mechanisms. This differs from item 2 in that the protection mechanism must still be overcome.

Table 15.8   (Cont'd.)

Type of Exposure	Inability to Process	Loss of an Entire File	Loss of Single Records	Modification of Records	Unauthorized Reading or Copying
Malicious computer operator		✓	✓	✓	
Malicious programmer		✓	✓	✓	
Malicious tape librarian		✓			
Malicious terminal operator		✓	✓	✓	
Malicious user (e.g., user who punches holes in returnable card)			✓	✓	
Playful malignancy (e.g., misusing terminal for fun)		✓	✓	✓	✓
Crime					
Embezzlement			✓	✓	✓
Industrial espionage					✓
Employees selling commercial secrets					✓
Employees selling data for mailing lists					✓
Data bank information used for bribery or extortion					✓
Invasion of privacy					
Casual curiosity (e.g., looking up employee salaries)					✓
Looking up data of a competing corporation					✓
Obtaining personal information for political or legal reasons					✓
Nondeliberate revealing of private information					✓
Malicious invasion of privacy					✓

Source: James Martin, **Principles of Data Base Management** (Englewood Cliffs, N.J.: Prentice-Hall, 1976). Reprinted by permission.

Passive threats

5. Electromagnetic pickup of system radiations such as those of microwave transmission.

6. Wire tapping of the communication subsystem of transmission by wire or coaxial cable.

7. Exposure of critical system data to unauthorized persons. In a classic case, a college student retrieved guides, procedures, operating instructions, and forms in the trash cans outside the Pacific Telephone and Telegraph supply office. He learned enough to cut into the purchasing and invoice system and take away thousands of dollars worth of equipment.

Active threats

8. Employees, users, or computer operators may browse through system files for sensitive (unauthorized) data.

9. An employee or outsider impersonates an authorized user. A knowledgeable outsider may call the computer center and ask that an entry code be used. He or she may then call back later using the new code as identification. There are a number of ways that access identification codes may be obtained.

10. "Between lines" entry. The system is used by an intruder when the user is on the system but inactive.

11. "Piggy-backing." An intruder intercepts the communication and substitutes for the original-user/system dialog.

12. Corrupt knowledgeable systems people. In the Equity Funding Corp. scandal (1973) over $120 million in nonexistent assets were created by computers and about $2 billion in phony life insurance policies were sold to reinsurers.

13. Active search for and entry through trapdoors.

14. Data acquired from residual memory. When a program run has been completed, data may be left in memory (unless a special program clears it). Such data may be sensitive and readily available to any user.

15. The system, in the hands of a skilled programmer, may be used to ferret out its own weaknesses.[3]

Protection of the MIS

There are a number of ways of developing the security of computerized information systems. One approach starts with the design of the system itself. We must find ways in both design and maintenance to minimize the probability

[3]Adapted from Clark Weissman, "Tradeoff Considerations in Security System Design," *Data Management,* April 1972.

that a breach can occur. We must design into the system the ability to audit data after the fact to detect and track violations. We would also like to deter people from attempting to breach the system. Finally, after all these means have made the risk of violating the system small, we may want to shift this risk to a third party.

Clark Weissman has identified successful protection strategies used in modern society as:

1. *Isolate*. Protection is gained by isolating the valuable commodity and controlling access to it. History is filled with examples: the fortress, the jail, the bank vault, and the military shielded computer room (isolated from electromagnetic radiation). Most aspects of physical security embody this strategy.

2. *Confound*. Protection is gained by isolation (but not controlled access), based upon obfuscation. Valuables are hidden by removing them from view (e.g., buried dog bone), or by camouflage and disguise to confound and confuse search. Cryptography is the ultimate example of this strategy.

3. *Deter*. Deterrence protects by making pilferage unprofitable. The profit/ loss (gain/risk) equation is foremost. When gain is high and risk low, deterrence fails, and thievery is encouraged. To dissuade the interloper, risk or punishment must be high and always visible (legally or physically). Department of Defense security regulations and military and industrial espionage laws exploit this strategy.

4. *Wager*. As with deterrence, the profit/loss equation is again foremost; however, here it applies to the owner. Protection is in the form of a wager. Because the probability of loss is low, it is a good investment to hedge against loss by betting that such a loss *will* occur. If loss occurs, the owner wins the wager, which is usually adequate to replace the valuables lost. If the loss never occurs, as is most likely, the small premiums are less costly than other forms of protection or replacement. All in all, the wager is a better investment than other forms of purchased protection. The insurance industry is founded on this strategy. I predict that we shall see major use of this strategy to protect information as information systems become more pervasive in our society.

5. *Delegate*. Protection is achieved by shifting protection responsibility and liability to a second party, such as bank trusts, escrow agents, baby sitters, and police and fire departments. The strategy is most useful when the limited resources of many can be concentrated for the protection of the group. The second party protects by adopting one of the other strategies. One of the significant dampening factors in the current information utility boom is the failure of government and business to delegate protection of their "corporate data base" to the utility because of their lack of confidence in the privacy and security technology being

Table 15.9 Protection of programs and master files

COMPUTER SYSTEM ELEMENTS	HAZARDS		
	Loss	*Defects*	*Disclosure*
Hardware	• Conscientious preventive maintenance.		• Hardware encoding of key information. • Protection against electronic eavesdropping or intrusion into remote access systems.
Software	• Careful program design, testing and maintenance to: 1. Ensure appropriate response to hardware malfunctions. 2. Limit entry of erroneous input data. 3. Detect and eliminate program bugs. 4. Minimize operator errors.		• Passwords, etc., to prevent outside access to programs and files of remote access systems. • Passwords, etc., to limit access to critical programs and files by in-house personnel. • Software encoding or other concealment of key information.
Personnel	• Proper training and qualification of personnel for key job positions.		• Pre-employment screening of personnel.
Procedures	• Adequate supervision and scheduling of work assignments. • Systematic copying of program and master files. • Controls over storage and use of programs and master files. • Separation of programming, data control, computer operation, and librarian functions. • Complete contingency plan, including loss prevention measures and provision for back-up facilities.	• Controls over data input and output, programs and master files. • Controls over program changes.	• Limited access to key areas. • Special supervision of key processing. • Careful disposal of printout, cards, tape, etc. • Good internal access control and supervision of personal belongings. • Controls over access to and use of programs, master files, and the computer.
Facilities	• Design and location of building to minimize exposure to fire, flooding, smoke, structural collapse, riot, sabotage, and vandalism. Safe storage facilities for programs, master files and documentation. • Off-site storage facilities.	• Good control of environment—air-conditioned room for prime power, and freedom from dirt contamination—to minimize hardware errors.	• Building design to permit adequate access control, and to minimize opportunities for intrusion.

Source: Robert V. Jacobson, "Providing Data Security," **Automation,** June 1970, p. 88.

employed. This factor is a distorting influence and has encouraged the proliferation and growth of private, dedicated, in-house systems.[4]

Another approach to protecting the system is to examine hazards and preventative measures for each element of the system. These elements are hardware, software, personnel, procedures, and facilities. Table 15.9 summarizes this approach to security.

SUMMARY Every organization stores data. If the organization has a modern MIS, it will likely have a data base which is centrally controlled. The management of data within the company is an important responsibility of company executives.

The data-base management system is defined here as more than simply data-base management software. The seven components of the DBMS are:

1. Data-base administrator
2. Schema or relationships of records
3. Data-management program
4. Query-language programs
5. Data base
6. Programmer
7. Data-base programs

The objective of DBMS are primarily to eliminate redundancy in storage of data and to make access to the data base quick and economical.

Data bases are designed first to suit the needs of users and second to suit the viewpoint of the data processing specialist. In both cases, the logical concept of the data base is the overriding concern.

Previously we have viewed software as directing the computer to perform a sequence of operations. From a data-base perspective, a computer program causes the contents of two or more files to be associated at the same point in time through formation of "logical" relationships. These relationships are:

1. Linked-list structure
2. Keyed-list structure
3. Tree (hierarchical) structure
4. Network structure

The data base is an organized collection of records. These records are not linked by programs (as in file-oriented data processing systems), but rather they are related to each other in their logical design.

The data-base administrator is a very important part of the DBMS. Essentially, the administrator oversees the creation, operation, maintenance, and security of the DBMS.

---

[4]*Ibid.,* p. 16.

A model of a data-base system (which is part of the DBMS) is presented in the text. This model shows how the data are entered into the data base from transactions. It also shows the various files which may be used to reconstruct the data base in case data are lost.

Security of data in the data base and protection of data on individuals or organizations from unauthorized persons has become a very serious problem. System threats have been classified as accidental, passive, and active. The data as an economic asset may be protected through isolating the system, confounding potential violators, deterrence, insurance, and shifting responsibility for protection to others.

1. Place the identifying descriptions in the accompanying International Data Base Systems, Inc., schematic of a DBMS.

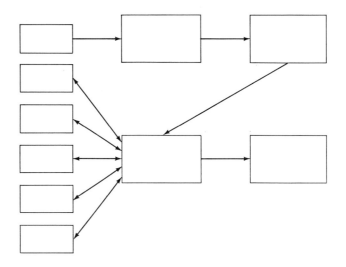

a. Data base
b. Data-base manager
c. User program
d. File data descriptions
e. Query processor

f. Dictionary or schema
g. Report generator
h. Update processor
i. User program
j. File description processor

2. Complete each entry in the table below by giving an example.

Objective of DBMS	Subsystem	Example
a. Instant access to latest transactions	Accounting	
b. Eliminate redundancy	Production/ Engineering/ Marketing	
c. Allow multiple concurrent updatings and retrievals	Personnel	

d. Offer evolutionary growth by addition of   Marketing
   data and programs

e. Provide protection against unauthorized   Personnel
   use

3. Match the following:

_____ (1) Query-language program   a. Describes logical relationships among
                                             records
_____ (2) Record   b. Records follow each in order
_____ (3) Programmer   c. Controls access to files
                                          d. Associates contents of two or more
_____ (4) Sequential file   files at the same time
_____ (5) Direct access file   e. Selects the appropriate file access
                                             method
_____ (6) DBMS schema   f. Managers can talk to data base
_____ (7) Librarian   g. Determines needs of DB users
                                          h. Pointer fields
_____ (8) Computer program   i. Records randomly distributed in data
                                             base
_____ (9) Keyed list   j. Collection of related data elements
_____ (10) Data-base administrator

4. A manufacturing company is operating with file cabinets of records and a small
    computer for payroll records. The company has long outgrown this distributed
    manual file system. Give a step-by-step approach to the development and implemen-
    tation of a DBMS for the company.

5. Define (a) field, (b) record, (c) file, (d) data base, (e) DBMS.

6. Develop a personnel record for an employee, showing field names and field formats.

7. Develop a record for a product, where product records form a linked-list.

8. In project management, tasks and subtasks form a work breakdown structure. The
    project itself is considered the first level, tasks are second level, and subtasks are
    third level. The data contained in a task record are identification number, name,
    objective, budget, start date, and end date for the task. Draw a schematic of this
    tree structure, showing the fields in the records at each level as you envision them.

9. A large automobile dealer wishes to use a relational data base to keep track of past
    customers and potential buyers who have contacted the agency. Demonstrate the
    nature of this data by means of a table with rows as "tuples" and columns as
    attributes (or "domains"). Such attributes as name, age, sex, and occupation, should
    be considered. Three rows, or tuples, will be adequate for this demonstration table.

10. The FBI arrested a 32-year-old computer expert on November 6, 1978, in California
    on charges that he masterminded a sophisticated theft of $10.2 million from Security
    Pacific Bank and then used the money to buy diamonds from the Soviet government.
    It was alleged that the suspect used a complex scheme involving computers and
    secret codes which he stole while working as a computer subcontractor for the bank.
    Discuss the precautions the bank might have taken to prevent such a theft. Does a
    set of precautions exist which could have prevented it?

SELECTED REFERENCES

APPLETON, DANIEL S., "What Data Base Isn't," *Datamation,* January 1977.

CHOW, JOHN V., "What You Need to Know About DBMS," Parts 1 and 2, *Journal of Systems Management,* May and June 1975.

CUSHING, BARRY, *Accounting Information Systems and Business Organizations,* 2d ed. Reading, Mass.: Addison-Wesley, 1978.

HAMILTON, PETER, *Computer Security.* Philadelphia: Auerbach Publishers, 1972.

HOFFMAN, LANCE J., *Security and Privacy in Computer Systems.* Los Angeles: Melville Publishing Company, 1973.

KRAUSS, LEONARD I., and AILEEN MACGAHAN. *Computer Fraud and Countermeasures.* Englewood Cliffs, N.J.: Prentice-Hall, 1979.

KROENKE, DAVID, *Database Processing.* Chicago: Science Research Associates, 1977.

MARTIN, JAMES, *Principles of Data-Base Management.* Englewood Cliffs, N.J.: Prentice-Hall, 1976.

MILLER, FREDERICK W., "Data Security—A 'Common Sense' Approach Pays Off," *Infosystems,* August 1978.

MILLER, LAWRENCE R., "Law and Information Systems," *Journal of Systems Management,* January 1977.

MITCHELL, WILLIAM E., "Records Retention Schedules," *Journal of Systems Management,* August 1977.

MITCHELL, WILLIAM E., *Records Retention,* 2d ed. Evansville, Ind.: Ellsworth Publishing Co., 1976.

MOHAN, C., "An Overview of Recent Data Base Research," *Data Base,* Fall 1978.

PALMER, IAN R., *Data Base Systems: A Practical Reference.* Wellesley, Mass.: Q.E.D. Information Sciences, 1975.

POWERS, VICTOR, "Implementing Generalized Data Base Management Systems," *Data Management,* May 1975.

SCHANSTRA, CARLA, "Diminishing the DBMS Mystique," *Infosystems,* September 1978.

SMEJDA, HELLENA, "Build Controls into System for EDP Security," *Hospital Financial Management,* March 1977.

TURN, REIN, "Cost Implications of Privacy Protection in Databank Systems," *Data Base,* Spring 1975.

WEAVER, BARBARA N., and WILEY L. BISHOP, *The Corporate Memory.* New York: John Wiley, 1974.

WINSKI, DONALD T., "Distributed Systems—Is Your Organization Ready?" *Infosystems,* September 1978.

WIORKOWSKI, GABRIELLE K., and WIORKOWSKI, JOHN J., "Does a Data Base Management System Pay Off?" *Datamation,* April 1978.

VAN TASSEL, DENNIS, *Computer Security Management.* Englewood Cliffs, N.J.: Prentice-Hall, 1972.

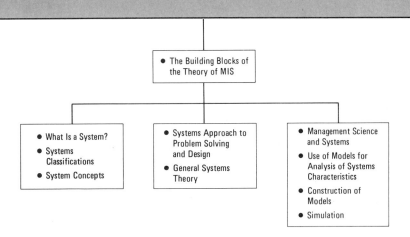

chapter 16

Systems Concepts
and Management Science

- The Building Blocks of
  the Theory of MIS

- What Is a System?
- Systems
  Classifications
- System Concepts

- Systems Approach to
  Problem Solving
  and Design
- General Systems
  Theory

- Management Science
  and Systems
- Use of Models for
  Analysis of Systems
  Characteristics
- Construction of
  Models
- Simulation

PURPOSE: To study the nature of systems
in greater depth and to show how management science
incorporates the systems approach
to problem solving and design

Management information systems are both subsystems of a larger class of systems, namely, organization systems, and members of a set consisting of *all* systems. General theory of systems provides us with a better approach to the analysis and design of MIS. Management science provides the specifics of methodology and tools to carry out the systems approach.

THE BUILDING BLOCKS OF THE THEORY OF MIS

Our focus in this chapter will be on a particular class of systems, the MIS, as we develop the general nature of systems and management science. In order to keep this central theme in mind, let us list the building blocks of MIS theory so that this, and previous, chapters may be related to MIS theory. These building blocks are:

Topic	Contribution to Systems Theory and MIS
Systems definition, classifications, and concepts	Classifies systems to aid in description and analyses
	Clarifies description and operation of systems
Control and communications	Identifies type of control: feedback, feedforward, steering
	Develops theory of feedback and control of organizations
Organizations	Develops theory of organization design and functioning
	Relates role of information to organizational problem solving
Decision making	Relates information role to decision making
	Leads to better structuring of decisions and programmed decision making

Management science	Modeling aids in defining and analyzing systems
	Models provide decision-supporting information as well as programmed decisions
Systems design	Provides a systems approach to MIS design to achieve, as much as possible, optimum system performance
Computers	Tremendous speed and storage capacity for data processing permits the development and application of numerous complex models
	Places at hand a wide variety of information within a brief period

Of all these topics, we have covered aspects of control, organization theory, decision making, systems design, and computers in earlier chapters. In this chapter we cover the remaining topics of systems and management science.

WHAT IS A SYSTEM?

A system is a set of tangible elements seeking some common goal or goals by operating on data and/or information and/or energy and/or matter and/or organisms in a time reference to produce information and/or energy and/or matter and/or organisms as outputs.

Some specific cases illustrate the somewhat abstract definition:

1. *Manufacturing system.* A group of people, machines, and facilities (*a set of elements*) work to produce a specified number and type of products (*seek a common goal*) by operating on product specifications, schedules, raw materials, subassemblies, and electrical power converted to mechanical power (*operate on data, matter, and energy*) to yield the specified products and information by the date the customer wants them (*yield matter in a time reference*).

2. *Management information system.* A group of people, a set of manuals, and data processing equipment (*a set of elements*) select, store, process, and retrieve data (*operate on data and matter*) to reduce the uncertainty in decision making (*seek a common goal*) by yielding information for managers at a time they can most efficiently use it (*yield information* in a time reference).

3. *Business organization system.* A group of people (*set of elements*) gather and process material and informational resources (*form an activity*) toward a set of multiple common goals including an economic profit for the business (*seek common goals*) by performing financing, design, production, and marketing (*operate on data, energy, and matter*) to achieve finished products and their sale at a specified minimum cost per year (*yield matter in a time reference*).

System concepts developed rapidly after World War II. The surge in complexity of defense systems and equipment led to a whole new perspective on management and engineering design. The difficulties experienced in managing our economy, our society, and individual global companies have forced the adoption of a systems approach.

We will limit our discussion of system in this book to empirical open systems. Such systems are made up of real-world entities and interact with their environments. This does not prevent us from using closed-system analysis, however. This limitation excludes mathematics, logic, or other philosophical disciplines as systems.

SYSTEMS CLASSIFICATIONS

A system may be classified in a number of ways which help us understand its nature. The following classifications are important for a study of business and information systems.[1]

Natural and Man-Made

Natural systems abound in nature. The entire ecology of life is a natural system, and each organism is a unique natural system of its own. The water system of the world, at least before man affected it, was a natural system. Our own solar system is a natural system.

Man-made systems appear in infinite variety all about us, extending from the manufacturing system of a company to the system of space exploration. Their objectives likewise vary tremendously. One system may be concerned with national defense; another may be a transportation system. A business organization is a system with many smaller systems included—production, accounting, and so on—as well as others such as communication systems and office layout systems overlaid upon the main economic organization of people.

Systems may fall in a range from purely natural to purely man-made. The U.S. Inland Waterway is composed of lakes, rivers, and man-made canals and water modifications; thus it is partly natural and partly man-made.

Social, Man-Machine, and Machine

Systems made up of people may be viewed purely as *social* systems, apart from other systems objectives and processes. Business organizations, government agencies, political parties, social clubs, and technical societies are examples of systems that may be so studied. Admittedly, all of these employ objects and artifacts that form physical systems, yet the most relevant aspects may be considered to be organizational structure and human behavior.

Most empirical systems fall in the category of *man-machine* systems. Today, most people all over the world use equipment of some kind in their organized endeavors.

[1]Stanford L. Optner, *Systems Analysis for Business and Industrial Problem Solving* (Englewood Cliffs, N.J.: Prentice-Hall, 1965), Chapter 2.

Pure *machine* systems would have to obtain their own inputs and maintain themselves. The development of a self-healing machine system would bring these systems closer to simulation of living organisms. Such systems would need to adapt to their environment. Although some electrical power generating systems approach self-sufficiency, self-repairing and completely self-sufficient machine systems are still in the category of science fiction.

Open and Closed

An *open* system is one that interacts with its environment. All systems containing living organisms are open, because they are affected by what is sensed by the organisms. In a more important sense, organizations are usually systems operating within larger systems and are therefore open. For example, a company's marketing organization is a system that is a part of the larger system, the entire company. The company in turn is a system within the larger industry system.

The fact that a company interacts with its environment—a larger system— makes that individual company an open system. The open system may be further identified by its individually small influence on its environment and inadequate feedback of information from the environment. As business managers will readily agree, they must somehow manage their companies in great ignorance about the future impact of environmental conditions. The environmental system with which they can best contend is the particular industry system of which they are a part.

Continuing in this direction, then, we note that the industry is part of the national economic system, which in turn is a system within our society. Our society is a system within the world system; the world system is a part of the solar system; and so on into the unknown.

The question of what constitutes a *closed* system is more difficult. A closed system is one that does not interact with its environment. Whatever environment surrounds the closed system does not change, or if it does, a barrier exists between the environment and the system to prevent the system from being affected. Although it is doubtful that closed systems really exist, the concept has important implications. We attempt in research to develop models that are essentially closed systems. When we set up experiments in the laboratory for the study of human behavior, we are attempting to establish a closed system temporarily. The scientist who devises a laboratory system to measure the elasticity of a metal is assuming a closed system such that environmental changes that would affect his results are avoided. Problems in business are sometimes resolved as if a closed system existed in order to simplify the situation enough so that at least a first approximation can be obtained.

Technically, a system is either open or it is closed. Some writers, however, refer to degrees of openness. That is, a system that interacts very little with its environment is called "partially open." Some authors distinguish further between open systems that are simply influenced passively by the environment and those that react and adapt to the environment. These subclasses are designated as *nonadaptive* and *adaptive* systems.

Permanent and Temporary

Relatively few, if any, man-made systems are *permanent*. However, for practical purposes, systems enduring considerably longer than the operations of humans in them may be said to be "permanent." Our economic system, which is gradually changing, is essentially permanent for our plans for the future. At another extreme, the policies of a business organization are "permanent" as far as year-to-year operations are concerned. It is true that major policy changes may be made, but these will then last an indefinite and "long" time relative to the daily activities of employees.

Truly *temporary* systems are designed to last a specified period and then dissolve. The television system set up to record and transmit the proceedings of a national political convention is only a temporary system. A small group-research project in the laboratory is a temporary system. Some systems that are temporary are not so by design. A company that is formed and quickly goes bankrupt is an example. Temporary systems are important for the accomplishment of specific tasks in business and for research in science.

Stationary and Nonstationary

A *stationary* system is one whose properties and operations either do not vary significantly or else vary only in repetitive cycles. The automatic factory, the government agency that processes social security payments, the supermarket store operation, the high school, and the ferry system are examples of stationary systems.

An advertising organization, a continental defense system, a research and development laboratory, and a human being are examples of *nonstationary* systems.

Let us compare the stationary system—the automatic factory—with the nonstationary continental defense system. In the automatic factory, system quantities may change with time and operating levels may vary within certain limits. However, there is a manufacturing cycle that is repeated with relatively little change. Such a system may be very complex and its cost of failure high. Failure is not necessarily permanent, though, because the factory could be modified to operate properly. In the case of the continental defense system, the cost is likewise very large. One major difference is that initial failure is apt to rule out the opportunity to revise the system. In nonrepetitive systems, failure in one case does not always lead to successful modification for different cases in the future.

Subsystems and Supersystems

From the preceding discussions, it has become apparent that each system is nested in a larger system. The system in the hierarchy that we are most interested in studying or controlling is usually called "the system." The business firm is viewed as "the system" or "the total system" when focus is on production, distribution of goods, and sources of profit and income. As Stanford L. Optner says, "The total system consists of all the objects, attributes, and relationships necessary to accomplish an objective, given a number of constraints. The term *system* is most frequently employed in the sense of total system. The objective of the total system defines the purpose for which all the system objects, attributes, and relationships have been organized."[2]

Smaller systems within the system are called *subsystems*. This distinction has important implications in practice with regard to optimization and the "systems approach," as we shall see later.

Supersystem is not usually used in antithesis to subsystem; it denotes extremely large and complex systems. *Supersystem* may refer to any system which includes the system under consideration. The economy may be considered a supersystem relative to a business firm.

Adaptive and Nonadaptive

Another range or spectrum of possibilities for a system runs from adaptive to nonadaptive.

A system that reacts with its environment in such a way as to improve its functioning, achievement, or probability of survival is called an adaptive system. High-level living organisms such as animals and man use adaptation in meeting threats of changes in the physical environment or changes in their societies. Evolutional theory is based heavily on the concept of an adaptive system. We note that successful businesses are those which adapt to changes in the environment, while many failures are attributed to businesses that failed to respond in time to external change.

Finally, we may associate energy source, learning, and self-modification with adaptation. For example, if computers could attach themselves to a long-term source of energy, "learn" how to modify and heal themselves, and then actually do so, they would become adaptive systems.

Classification of Organizational Systems and MIS

We may examine both organizational systems and MIS in the light of the above classifications.

Organizational systems

1. Natural, if we are discussing man as part of the ecology of life on earth; man-made, if we discuss any other organization of man.
2. Social. All man-made groupings of people are social systems, whose behavior has been subjected to considerable research. Chapter 2 offered some insights into the social system of business organizations.
3. Open. Every social organization is open, because it reacts with its environment. In particular, organizational units within a company interact with each other.

[2]*Ibid.*, Chapter 2, p. 35.

4. There is no way to determine whether any organization will be permanent. Some organizations, such as well-established countries or Lloyd's of London or General Motors, may be treated as "permanent" because they apparently will exist in the indefinite future. Within a business, we must treat some organizational systems as permanent for current planning. Some organizations are known to be temporary, and we plan accordingly.

5. Nonstationary, in general. Organizational systems tend to change to adapt to a changing environment in the long run. In the short run, we may treat some of those listed earlier as stationary for convenience in studying them.

6. Subsystems, systems, and supersystems. Organizational systems range from the smallest units of two people to the largest groups on earth. The "system" of interest at a particular time is the focal point along this range.

7. Adaptive, in general. Organizations strive to perpetuate their own existence. To do this, they must adapt to their environment. Companies with built-in rigidities, such as incompetent top managements, do not adapt and go out of business. Often, a company adapts because new management is brought in.

Management information systems

1. Man-made. Human information systems are devised by men and are not simply "born."

2. Social *and* man-machine. MIS may be viewed purely from the human, social aspect, which includes communication and decision making. The MIS in its most sophisticated form includes equipment such as electronic computers and is therefore a man-machine system.

3. Open. Each segment or subsystem of the MIS requires inputs from other subsystems, so that each is an open system. The total MIS depends upon inputs from the business operations and from the environment so that it, too, is an open system.

4. Temporary. MIS's are constantly being revised, both formally and informally.

5. Stationary. Once designed, the MIS is supposed to handle certain types of problems on a more or less routine basis and supply information to management according to a specified program.

6. Systems and subsystems. The MIS may be a businesswide system or may be a subsystem, such as the financial or production MIS.

7. Adaptive. Because people make up part of the MIS, the MIS will adapt itself to some degree by means of small changes. If the MIS has been poorly designed, however, it is likely that only a complete redesign can make it work effectively.

It is the approach of science to ask, "What are the parts?" It is a requirement for design that we ask, "What are systems composed of?" Here we take a conceptual view of systems to answer this question, because the answer has already been given: empirical systems are composed of real-life things. Identification of concepts will be important in the development of system theory, in the design of systems, and in the evaluation of systems. System concepts also provide an introduction to models of systems.

To help explain these concepts, we will refer to the simple marketing information system shown in Figure 16.1.

Variables

Every system is a processor, according to the definition given earlier. Inputs to the system may take on different values and are therefore system variables. Outputs of the system also vary in magnitude and are also system variables.

In MARIS, shown in Fig. 16.1, we see that there is an imput from operations, the variable unit sales. Another input variable is monthly industry sales, obtained from a newsletter to which the company subscribes. Output variables are product sales, salesmen's sales, regional sales, and various forecasts of sales.

Figure 16.1 Marketing information system (MARIS)

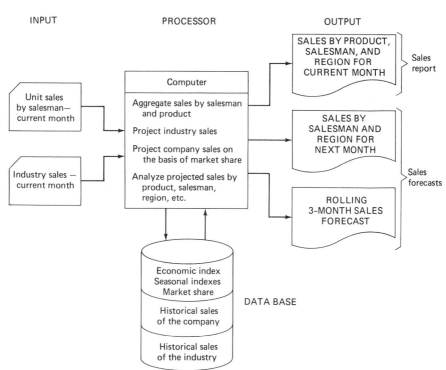

509

System Parameters

Many quantities that enter into the relationships among the input variables and the output variables are considered constant for a specific period of time or system operational style. In essence, for a fixed set of these values, the system is said to be in a specified "state." These quantities, which determine the state of the system, are called *parameters*. Not entirely jokingly, we might call these parameters "variable constants."

In the MARIS example, the economic index is an estimate of general economic conditions for the year. This would be constant for the year, say 1.15 for a boom year and 0.96 for a depressed year. Each company establishes a different value for this parameter. Adjustments for seasonal ups and downs are established by a seasonal parameter, which is established for each quarter of a year.

Components

A system's components are simply the various identifiable parts of the system. If a system is large enough so that it is composed of subsystems, and each subsystem is composed of subsystems, eventually we reach some parts that individually are not subsystems. In other words, in a hierarchy of subsystems, the components exist at the lowest level.

In our MARIS system, there are two subsystems: the sales reporting system and the sales forecasting system. The components of the system are telecommunication devices, people, an electric computer, procedure manuals, and reports. These components, except for some of the people, are shared by both systems.

Attributes of Components

Components, because they are objects or people, possess properties or characteristics. These characteristics affect the operation of the system in speed, accuracy, reliability, capacity, and many other ways. Choices must be made in systems design between the use of humans and the use of machines, and between various kinds of machines, on the basis of attributes and cost.

Humans, for example, have very limited capacity to absorb information per unit of time compared with machines. However, humans are better than machines in analyzing poorly structured problems. It has been said that man is the most effective control component that can be mass-produced by inexperienced labor.

An example of a choice between machines might be the selection of an output device from among a cathode-ray tube, an audio system, a mechanical printer, or a plotting device. In the MARIS, the characteristics of the output component are not high speed, but clarity, economy, and relative permanence. Therefore a printer, auxiliary to the computer, is chosen and the format of the output is a "printed" report, sent to management once a month.

Structure

The structure of a system is the set of relationships among objects and attributes of the objects in a system. The degree to which the elements of the system work together to achieve total objectives also helps define the structure. Although we tend to think of systems in which all elements are working 100% for common system goals, few, if any, systems actually function this way. Elements of a system work together to different degrees.

1. Dysfunctional relationships may exist because of natural phenomena, conflicting attributes, or organizational conflicts. For example, the manufacturing and marketing organizations may disagree about production schedules, product inventories, or customer service.

2. Symbiotic relationships may exist between dissimilar organisms or organizations that serve each other's needs. For example, the cowbird that lives on the cow to eat ticks, which serves the need of the cow to have them removed. Again, a company and its vendors need each other and work together in a symbiotic relationship.

3. Synergistic relationships may exist in which subsystems and elements reinforce each other in working toward common objectives.

4. Optimized relationships may exist, in which trade-offs of resources and trade-offs among objectives of subsystems remain in dynamic balance to optimize the total system output continuously over time. This is probably an ideal system, whereas the synergistic system striving for optimization is representative of real-world systems.

The functional relationships among the people and the equipment form the structure of the MARIS. The organizational hierarchy, the lateral relationships among the people in the system, and the relationship between the computer and the people could be set forth in a block diagram representing the structure of the system.

Dysfunctional relationships among people may be present because of poor system design or personality conflicts among the people. There may be dysfunctional relationships between people and the computer due to humans' inability to perform monotonous, repetitive operations connected with the outputs or inputs of the computer. On the other hand, the computer may fail to operate properly because of rough or careless treatment of punched cards or equipment by humans.

Symbiosis in the MARIS is the necessary relationship between the computer and humans. Each needs the other to accomplish system objectives.

Synergistic effects in the social group making up the system may be achieved by different individuals supplementing each other so that total output is greater than the simple addition of each individual's work.

Process

The total process of a system is the net result of all ongoing activities in converting inputs to outputs. When management and systems designers have established the data that will be available as inputs to an MIS and the information desired for the output, the systems designers have the major project of designing the conversion process.

The total process is actually made up of many small processes. A parallel between a material-processing system and an MIS may help clarify the meaning of a single process. In a certain factory, a worker receives a square of sheet metal, places it in a punch press, and operates the press to produce a formed and perforated piece of metal. This is a single process in the entire production process.

In our marketing information system, the computer flow chart shows the aggregation, by the process of addition, of individual sales reports into total sales. This is a single process among many in the system. The functional relationship between an input and output of a process is called the *transfer function*. This term is commonly used in the design and evaluation of feedback systems.

Boundaries

The concept of a system boundary makes it possible to focus on a particular system within a hierarchy of systems. The boundary of a system may exist either physically or conceptually. The operational definition of a system in terms of its boundary is:

1. List all components that are to make up the system and circumscribe them. Everything within the circumscribed space is called the system, and everything outside is called the environment.
2. List all flows across the boundary. Flows from the environment into the system are inputs; flows from inside the boundary to outside are called outputs.
3. Identify all elements that contribute to the specific goals of the system and include these within the boundary if they are not already included.

We will substitute nested political systems for our marketing information system because the boundaries are easily recognized. Let us start with the city as the smallest system and consider it as part of the county system, which is part of the state system, which in turn is part of the national governmental system.

The boundaries of the city are physical, informational, and legal. The physical boundaries are identified on a map, and all physical components of the city system are simply circumscribed on the map. Flows across the physical boundary are inputs from the environment and include flows of people, vehicles, or even animals. Water supply, electrical power, and weather movements are more esoteric examples of inputs. The outputs are of the same type.

The city is an open system that reacts with its environment on the basis of information crossing the boundaries in either direction. The information is usually recorded in newspapers—within the city if it is input or outside the city if it is output. Television, radio, and word of mouth also provide information flow across the boundaries.

The legal boundaries of the city circumscribe all legal or political actions the city may take. The city is limited to action over its inhabitants, its physical system, and people or companies that operate or pass upon its physical system. However, further restrictions limit the legal actions (or components of the legal system) and reserve them for the state or federal systems.

The city is thus composed of several major systems, each of which has fairly well defined boundaries. What has been said about the city boundaries may be translated to the county system and then to the state as a system.

Interfaces

An interface is the connection between two systems, the region of contact. The interface between humans and computers is the output of the humans which matches the input of the computer. This might be the preparation of punched cards or the computer terminal. The computer interfaces with its electric power system at the wall plug. For an information system, the output of one system must be in a form acceptable to the system it interfaces. The interface is the common link between the two systems, perhaps a completed form, a punched card, or an electrical signal.

In our example of MARIS, the interface between MARIS and the production system is the sales forecasts. These must be in a format acceptable to the production organization so that production can schedule operations.

Table 16.1
Characteristics
of man-
machine
systems

1. Performance of basic and subsidiary functions
2. Accuracy of performance
3. Speed of performance
4. Cost
5. Reliability
6. Environmental adaptability
7. Maintainability
8. Replaceability by successive models
9. Safety and fail-safe features
10. Producibility (feasibility of manufacture)
11. Optimum materials and process for size of manufacturing run
12. Simplification, standardization, and preferred sizes
13. Weight
14. Size and shape
15. Styling and packaging
16. Compatibility with other systems or auxiliary equipment
17. Modular design
18. Ease of operation (human engineering)
19. Balanced design through trade-offs
20. Ease of transporting and installing
21. Legality
22. Social aspects

Characteristics of Systems

For the solution of a given problem there are good systems and poor ones. The poor systems have characteristics that do not fit the requirements of the problem or of the decision makers. Our marketing information system may be a poor system if its sales forecasts are monthly and manufacturing requires weekly forecasts for planning. It may be a poor system if some salesmen's reports are not included from time to time because of lack of control over reporting.

Many characteristics of systems are important for design, production, diagnosis, and evaluation. Man-machine systems have a large spectrum of such characteristics, as shown in Table 16.1 on the previous page.

Table 16.1 is useful because it can serve as a checklist for the designer. Each characteristic must be considered in terms of its degree of importance for the system under scrutiny.

SYSTEMS APPROACH TO PROBLEM SOLVING AND DESIGN

Now that we are aware of the complexity of systems, we might ask, "How do you go about designing such a structure of interrelated functioning parts?" In fact, most complex problems we face pose the same question, because they require design of a system. The answer is that we adopt a *systems view* of the problem from the outset.

Characteristics of the Systems Approach

The systems approach is a combination of philosophy and general methodology. The philosophical aspects may be described by the following characteristics of the systems approach. The approach is:

1. *Interdisciplinary*. The approach to problem solving and systems design is not bounded by a single discipline, but rather all relevant disciplines are brought to bear upon the design of a solution.

2. *Both qualitative and quantitative*. The systems approach uses an eclectic approach in that the designer is not bound by any particular tools. The systems solution may be described entirely qualitatively, entirely quantitatively, or in combination—whichever is most appropriate.

3. *Organized*. The systems approach is a means for solving large, amorphous problems whose solutions involve the application of large amounts of resources in an organized fashion. Usually a team of skilled professional generalists (systems designers) and specialists (technique and component experts) examine the problem domain for a specified period in order to formulate the problem. The problem formulation is critical to the entire design project because the objectives of the system are derived from the problem statement on needs. Management plays a large part in the identification and formulation of problems. Although the development of the system in later stages may not provide the best component design, the system may still function to provide an adequate solution.

If the problem is incorrectly diagnosed, however, and incorrect objectives are established, the system fails, regardless of how well the detailed design is carried out.

The organized approach requires that the systems team members, despite diverse specialized backgrounds, understand the systems approach. The language of systems design is the basis for their communicating.

4. *Creative*. Despite the generalized procedures developed for systems design, the systems approach must be a creative one that focuses on goals first and methods second. The ultimate system depends greatly on the originality and creativeness of the individuals contributing to its design.

The systems approach must be creative because

a. The problems are so complex and ill-structured that there is no unique formulation or solution.

b. Many of the available data are so incomplete, uncertain, or ambiguous that imagination of a high order must be used to form a theoretical framework for the problem.

c. Alternative solutions must be generated for subsystem problems, and from among many solutions, selections must be made that yield an approximation of an optimal total system.

d. Traditional functional and disciplinary barriers must be subordinated to the synthesis of the solution.

5. *Theoretical*. Underlying the systems approach are the methods of science. Science provides theoretical structures (their validation increasing with time) upon which we can construct practical solutions to problems. The structure is the skeleton, and the data provide the flesh that fills out the form. Different data may yield different forms, but the theory provides the mold. Relevant theory for the systems approach may be drawn from any discipline as required, and systems theory itself is based on many disciplines.

6. *Empirical*. The search for empirical data is an essential part of the approach. Relevant data must be distinguished from irrelevant, and true data from false. Pertinent data generally include not only facts on the technical aspects but also facts on the practices, functions, interactions, attitudes, and other characteristics of organization in man-machine systems.

7. *Pragmatic*. For empirical or real systems, a crucial characteristic of the systems approach is that it yields an action-oriented result. The system must be feasible, producible, and operable. Systems activities are directed toward fulfilling a set of actual purposes or of real needs. The systems designers must therefore gain a good understanding of the organization for which the work is being done. Further, the personnel of the organization must become involved in the process of diagnosis, development, and design.[3]

[3]The author is indebted to Professor Ronald Zoll for providing the basis of the discussion of these ideas.

General Methodology for the Systems Approach

The systems approach focuses on total system objectives at all times. For this reason it is important to define the objectives of the system first and to continually examine and perhaps redefine them as the design progresses.

Once the objectives have been defined, as many data as *appear* economical to gather are assembled. These data include inputs, outputs, criteria and constraints, and the general structure of the system.

The next step requires considerable creativity. The system is blocked out in terms of major elements and relationships. Alternatives and modifications are created and examined. Analogies from various disciplines are considered. This step is the first one in the conceptual design.

Analysis enters in when the designer attempts to refine the system by improving the components and subsystems. As trade-offs are made among subsystem outputs, the designer continually focuses on total system objectives. Criteria and constraints are also evaluated and perhaps revised at this stage.

GENERAL SYSTEMS THEORY

We have noted that there are many types of systems, although our main interest has been in management, organizational, and information systems. We have also discussed a "systems approach" that appears to apply to the design of any system. Is there, then, a general theory for all systems that could be applied to the design of MIS?

As early as the 1920s the "father of general systems theory," Ludwig von Bertalanffy, saw the need for unifying principles in the natural and social sciences. He and a group of diverse scientists founded the Society for General Systems Research in 1954. Since then books and articles on general systems theory have proliferated.

One problem that appears to pose a semantic barrier for writers is the phrase "general systems theory." Some interpret this as "theory of general systems." Others say that there is no such empirical entity as a general system; they interpret the phrase as meaning a general theory applicable to all systems.

The classification of systems and the characteristics of system structure and behavior have received most attention from mathematicians. For this reason the language of the theory is not familiar to everyone.[4]

MANAGEMENT SCIENCE AND SYSTEMS

Management science is a scientific approach to solving systems problems in the field of management. It includes the systems approach and a variety of quantitative techniques that have been developed to solve generic and recurring problems in management. It provides management with *decision aids* and *decision rules* derived from:

[4]One exception is a book by John W. Sutherland, *Systems Analysis, Administration, and Architecture* (New York: Van Nostrand Reinhold, 1975).

1. A total systems orientation
2. Scientific and eclectic methods of investigation
3. Models, preferably based on quantitative measurements and techniques.

The application of management science to MIS represents a tremendous advance over the disorganized collection of information and management by experience based on "feel." Management science requires the manager to define his problems and assumptions carefully, usually in terms that may be quantified and measured, so that he may achieve better problem definition. When it is applied to the design of organizational and operating systems for problem solving, management science uses a considerable volume of man's knowledge of many related sciences. Therefore, problem-solving systems may be designed that are more effective and more efficient for the organization as a whole.

The techniques of management science are also incorporated *in* the system. Basically, these techniques, employed in conjunction with modern computers, provide "programmed" decision making for the solution of many subproblems in the system. Optimum solutions to such subproblems may be obtained in minutes. This contrasts with rule-of-thumb, intuitive, and approximate solutions that decision makers were forced to rely on in the past. Without the computational power of the computer, management science techniques usually could not be applied within the time span of realistic operational requirements. Thus the computer and management science combine to free humans from repetitive decision making, so that they may concentrate on more complex, novel, and ill-constructed problems as well as on "nonprogrammed" decision making.

The dysfunctional aspects of the increased application of management science are twofold. The first is the failure of the systems designer to recognize that his models of systems and problems will always be abstractions of the real world. Qualitative factors and human judgments must find a place in all higher-level decisions. Mathematically derived solutions must be checked against intuition, and variances must be accounted for. Failure to do this may result in absurd and costly decisions. The second drawback to the introduction of management science techniques is organizational resistance to change. This resistance is further complicated when the management scientist fails to communicate with manager-users in terms that the manager understands.

The generally accepted styles of management science parallel the steps in problem solving as follows:

Management Science	Problem Solving
1. Search for problems	1. Observation
2. Statement of a problem	2. Statement of a problem
3. Collection of data	3. Collection of data
4. Development and testing of a model representing the problem solution	4. Development of hypotheses for solution of the problem
5. Manipulation of the model to determine the outcomes of various input conditions	5. Evaluation of the alternative hypotheses

The problem-solving process of developing feasible alternatives is followed by the decision process, in which the parallelism continues:

Management Science	Decision Making and Action
1. Selection of the best course of action	1. Selection of best alternative
2. Implementation of the solution	2. Implementation of best alternative
3. Control of the model by maintaining a check on its validity as time goes by	3. Review of results

We now look at the third characteristic of management science—modeling. Since the time when cave men drew symbols and pictures on the walls of caves, man has used "models" to represent aspects of his environment. It is only recently that scientists in many disciplines have discovered that the term *model* applies to what they have been doing all along. It now appears that most scientific conversations start with a mention of a model. The field of MIS is no exception; models are a necessity for both study and design of MIS. Because models are so important, we need to know what they are, what their characteristics are, and how they help us.

What Are Models?

We can solve both simple and complex problems of the practical world if we concentrate on some *portion* or some *key features* instead of on every detail of real life. This approximation or *abstraction* of reality, which we may construct in various forms, is called a *model*. Models do not, and cannot, represent every aspect of reality because of the innumerable and changing characteristics of the real world to be represented. If we wished to study the flow of material through a factory, we might construct a scaled diagram on paper showing the factory floor, position of equipment, tools, and men. It would not be necessary to give such details as the color of the machines, the heights of the men, or the temperature of the building. In other words, models deal with the relevant variables, and often only the relevant variables that have a major impact on the decision situation.

Many forms of models exist, and the particular form selected depends upon the purpose. Generally, models may be used to define or describe something such as an MIS; to assist with analysis of a system; to specify relationships and processes; or to present a situation in symbolic terms that may be manipulated to derive predictions. This last purpose—to provide a prediction system that can be manipulated to aid a decision maker—is perhaps the most important attribute of models.

Models provide two very important benefits that are closely related but distinct. The first is economy in representation and inquiry. It is cheaper, for instance, to represent a factory layout or an MIS visually in a diagram than to construct either one. It is also cheaper to try out modifications of such systems by rearrangements on paper. Second, models permit us to analyze and experiment with complex situations to a degree that would be impossible by constructing the actual system and its environment. For example, the experimental firing of an Apollo lunar vehicle may cost tens of millions of dollars and require months of preparation. If the lunar flight and the systems are simulated by a model, the application of large computers permits the simulation of many flights under various conditions. By simulation, information may be obtained in a few minutes that could not be obtained in generations of time or with billions of dollars of expenditure if the life-size system alone were used for experimentation.

Kinds of Models

Models may be divided into five different classes. The characteristics of a particular model may then be represented by a term from each class. Thus a manager might ask a management scientist in his marketing organization to construct a model for the selling and logistics system of a new shoe-cleaning product. The management scientist might then ask, "Shall we make that a symbolic, dynamic, probabilistic, and general model, or should we try to keep costs under $10,000 and construct an iconic, static, deterministic, and specialized model?" When put as a single question, this may seem facetious; in practice the answer to this question must be evolved in the discussion.

It is apparent that a few terms must be defined to describe classes of models, simply for economy of expression. It is also desirable to know what options exist when we are about to embark upon the construction of models. Models may be classified in five ways:

Class I—function

Type	Characteristics	Examples
1. Descriptive	Descriptive models simply provide a "picture" of a situation and do not predict or recommend.	(a) Organization chart (b) Plant layout diagram (c) Block diagram representing the structure of each chapter of this book
2. Predictive	Predictive models indicate that "if *this* occurs, then *that* will follow." They relate dependent and independent variables and permit trying out "what if" questions.	(a) $BE = F/(1 - v)$, which says that if fixed costs (F) are given, and variable costs as a fraction of sales (v) are known, then breakeven sales (BE) are predicted (deterministically) (b) $S(t) = aS(t - 1) + (1 - a)S(t - 2)$, which says that predicted sales for period t depend on sales for the previous two periods
3. Normative	Normative models are those that provide the "best" answer to a problem. They provide recommended courses of action.	(a) Advertising-budget model (b) Economic-lot-size model (c) Marketing-mix model

Class II—structure

Type	Characteristics	Examples
1. Iconic	Iconic models retain some of the physical characteristics of the things they represent.	(a) Scaled three-dimensional mockup of a factory layout (b) Blueprints of a warehouse (c) Scale model of next year's automobile
2. Analog	Analog models are those for which there is a substitution of components or processes to provide a parallel with what is being modeled.	An analog computer in which components and circuits parallel marketing institutions and facilities and processes so that by varying electrical inputs, the electrical outputs provide an analog simulation of the marketing system outputs
3. Symbolic	Symbolic models use symbols to describe the real world.	(a) $R = a\,[\ln(A)] + b$, which says in symbols that sales response (R) equals a constant times the natural log of advertising expenditure (A), plus another constant (b) $TC = PC + CC + IC$, which says in symbols that total inventory cost (TC) equals purchase cost (PC) plus carrying cost (CC) plus item cost (IC)

Class III—time reference

Type	Characteristics	Examples
1. Static	Static models do not account for changes over time.	(a) Organization chart (b) $E = P_1 S_1 + P_2 S_2$, which states that the expected profit (E) equals the probability (P_1) of the occurrence of payoff (S_1) multiplied by the value of the payoff (S_1), plus the probability (P_2) of payoff (S_2) multiplied by the value of (S_2)
2. Dynamic	Dynamic models have time as an independent variable.	$dS/dt = rA(t)\,(m - S)/M - \lambda S$, which gives the change in sales rate as a function of a response constant r, advertising rate as a function of time $A(t)$, sales saturation (M), sales rate (S), and sales decay constant (λ)

Class IV—uncertainty reference

Type	Characteristics	Examples
1. Deterministic	For a specific set of input values, there is a uniquely determined output that represents the solution of a model under conditions of *certainty*.	Profit = revenue minus costs
2. Probabilistic	Probabilistic models involve probability distributions for inputs or processes and provide a range of values of at least one output variable with a probability associated with each value. These models assist with decisions made under conditions of *risk*.	(a) Actuarial tables that give the probability of death as a function of age (b) Return on investment is simulated by using a probability distribution for each of the various costs and revenues with values selected by the Monte Carlo (random) technique. ROI appears in graph form as return in dollars vs. probability of the various dollar returns.
3. Game	Game-theory models attempt to develop optimum solutions in the face of complete ignorance or *uncertainty*. Games against nature and games of competition are subclassifications.	Two gasoline stations are next to each other. One owner wonders: "Shall I raise or lower my price? If I raise mine, my competitor may raise or lower his. If I lower mine, he may raise or lower his. I know the gain or loss in any situation, but once each of us sets the price, we must keep it for the week. We can't collude."

Class V—generality

Type	Characteristics	Examples
1. General	General models for business are models that have applications in several functional areas of business.	(a) Linear-programming algorithm for all functional areas (b) Waiting-line model. Applications appear in production, marketing, and personnel
2. Specialized	Specialized models are those that have application to a unique problem only.	(a) Sales response as a function of advertising may be based on a unique set of equations. (b) The probabilistic bidding model has a single application to one functional area.

The foregoing classification provides a structure for the understanding of models; specific descriptions of elementary forms of general models will shed more light on their use in business applications. In Fig. 16.2, therefore, we show the objectives of some selected models, usually in a specific application. It is necessary to introduce definitions of terms in Fig. 16.2 so that a pictorial description of the situation and the mathematical representation may be made meaningful, to some degree at least. We admit that only an impression of the nature of models is given by the figure; only through the detailed derivation of a model can the student gain a complete insight.

What does all of the preceding mean to the student of MIS? First, information systems should solve as many problems as possible on a routine basis. The computer and the application of models make possible much routine problem solving to relieve management. Second, the solutions from models may supply valuable information to aid managers in solving problems. Managers must evaluate the amount of aid that a particular type of model can supply, as well as the associated cost. A probabilistic dynamic prediction model may be very helpful, but it may cost $100,000 to develop and use for a year. On the other hand, a deterministic model may be reasonably helpful and cost only $10,000 to develop and process on the computer for a year. In some instances, development of a complex model of a firm's operations may be necessary for survival because of modeling being carried out by competitors. Modeling has become an extremely potent tool in the hands of those who know how to use it in MIS.

USE OF MODELS FOR ANALYSIS OF SYSTEM CHARACTERISTICS

The applications of flow-chart models, simulation models, and feedback control theory are very helpful in evaluating the MIS design and locating problem areas. They help us measure the efficiency of the MIS, the response to inputs, and the stability of the system under sudden large changes in input.

Block-Diagram Models and the "Black-Box" Concept

A block-diagram model of a system consists of a network of blocks, each block representing an activity or operation (Fig. 16.3). Lines with arrowheads represent the flow of information. The inverse or dual model shows the information in blocks and represents the processing by the directed lines.

In the block-diagram flow chart, all basic modules have the same characteristics if we treat the operation as a "black box." The black-box concept says that we don't know exactly what goes on in a process, but we can determine how outputs change with inputs. The black-box model is illustrated in Figure 16.4. The inputs are information and resources. These are acted upon by the processor (black box) to produce information and other outputs.

Figure 16.2 Illustrations of models

Model	Objective	Nomenclature for Relevant Variables	Pictorial Representation	Mathematical Representation of the System
Inventory Model	Find Economic Order Quantity by trade-off of carrying costs and ordering costs so as to minimize the system cost.	Q = size of order K = carrying costs S = ordering costs D = estimated annual demand TC = total system cost	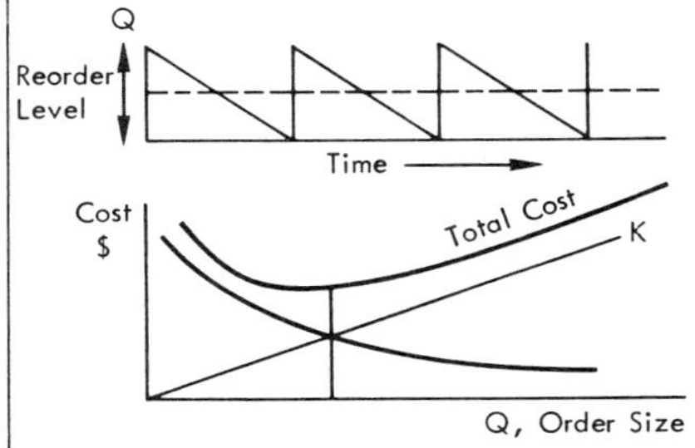	$TC = (Q/2) \cdot K + (D/Q) \cdot S$
Progress Model	Find time, cost, or price per unit after declines due to experience gained.	K = cost of first unit produced N = N-th unit produced ϕ = fraction of initial cost required to produce a unit after any doubling of production C_N = cost to produce N-th unit	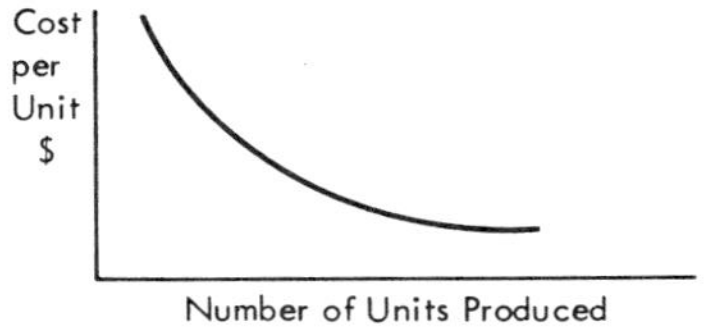	$C_n = KN^{(\log \phi/\log 2)}$
Waiting-Line Model	Find the average length of a waiting line, the average waiting time, or the optimum number of service facilities.	Poisson arrival rate with exponentially distributed service times for a single service facility. λ = average number of arrivals/period μ = average number of service completions/period C_w = cost per period for a person or unit waiting C_f = service facility cost for one unit TC = total system cost	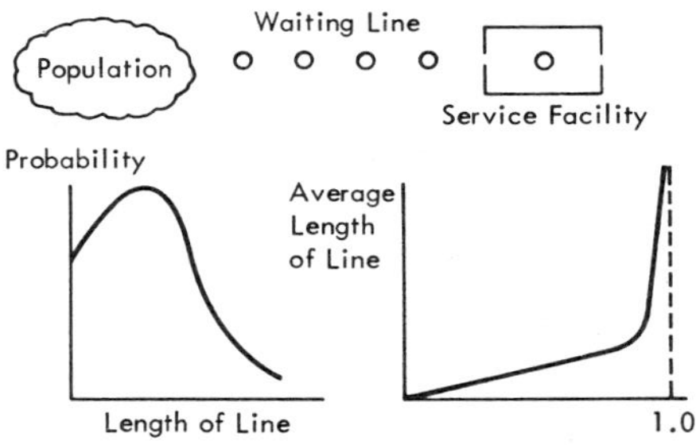	Average number of units in system $= \lambda/(\mu - \lambda)$ Average time a unit waits in the system $= 1/(\mu - \lambda)$ Service rate for minimum cost, min $= \lambda + \sqrt{\lambda\, C_w/C_f}$

Figure 16.2 (Cont'd.)

Model	Objective	Nomenclature for Relevant Variables	Pictorial Representation	Mathematical Representation of the System
Markov Process Model	Find the share of the market held by each company if the probabilities of brand switching by the customers can be estimated.	S_{11} = share of market for brand 1 in period 1 S_{21} = share of market for brand 2 in period 1 S_{12}, S_{22}, similarly P_{11} = probability that a customer who bought brand 1 in period 1 will buy brand 1 in the next period P_{12} = probability of switch from brand 1 to brand 2 P_{21}, P_{22}, similarly	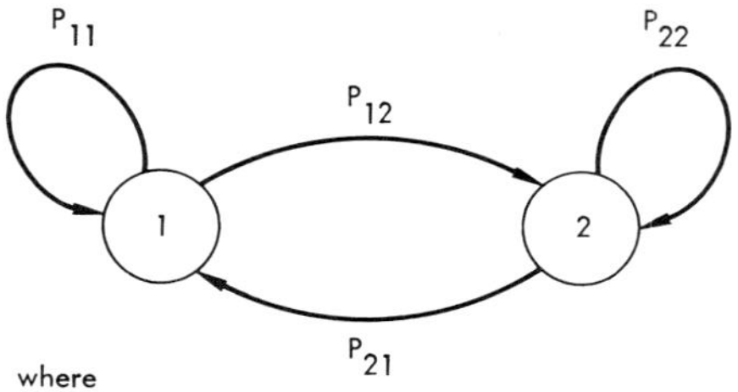 P_{11}, P_{12}, P_{21}, P_{22} (state diagram with states 1 and 2) where $P_{11} + P_{12} = 1$ $P_{21} + P_{22} = 1$	$$(S_{12}\;\; S_{22}) = (S_{11}\;\; S_{21})\begin{pmatrix} P_{11} & P_{12} \\ P_{21} & P_{22} \end{pmatrix}$$ $$= (S_{11}P_{11} + S_{21}P_{21} \quad S_{11}P_{12} + S_{21}P_{22})$$
Expected-Value Model	Determine the course of action that will yield the greatest expected gain.	☐ Decision point ◯ Random event in the world P_i = probability that a particular event occurs a_i = gain or loss resulting from outcome of random event EV = expected value of a course of action	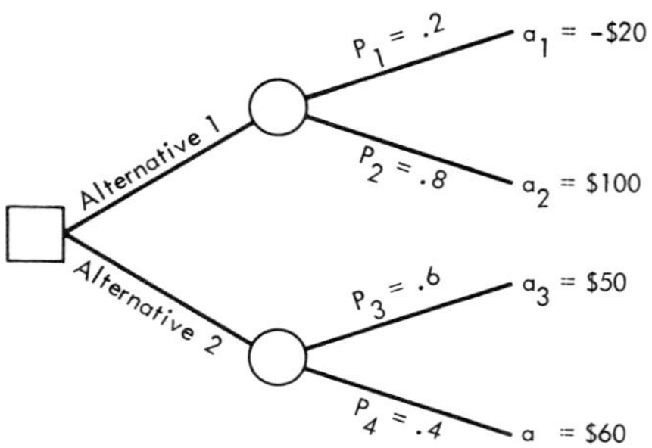 Decision tree: Alternative 1: $P_1 = .2$, $a_1 = -\$20$; $P_2 = .8$, $a_2 = \$100$ Alternative 2: $P_3 = .6$, $a_3 = \$50$; $P_4 = .4$, $a_4 = \$60$	EV (alternative 1) = $P_1 a_1 + P_2 a_2 = .2(-20) + .8(100)$ EV (alternative 2) = $P_3 a_3 + P_4 a_4 = .6(50) + .4(60)$

Figure 16.2 (Cont'd.)

Model	Objective	Nomenclature for Relevant Variables	Pictorial Representation	Mathematical Representation of the System
Forecasting Model	Estimate short-term demand by a smoothing of past data and extrapolating.	A = arbitrary smoothing weight S_t = actual sales during period t $\bar{S}_{t-1}$ = former forecast of sales for period t $\bar{S}_t$ = forecast of sales		$\bar{S}_t = A S_t + (1-A)\bar{S}_{t-1}$ $0 < A < 1$
Linear Programming Model	Optimize a linear function with linear constraints. In particular, maximize profit from production of two products when a limited number of hours, per period of time, is available on each of two machines used.	 **Profit/ Hours Required** Product — unit — Machine 1 — Machine 2 P_1 — \$8 — 4 — 3 P_2 — \$7 — 2 — 4 Machine hours available — 40 — 48 Z = profit x = number of units of P_1 y = number of units of P_2		Maximize $Z = \$8\,x + \$7\,y$ subject to $4x + 3y = 40$ $2x + 5y = 30$
Games-of-Conflict Model	For two competitors each of whom adopts his own set of strategies and knows the payoff for any pair of one of his strategies and one of his competitor's, find the strategy each should adopt.	A = firm A B = firm B i = one of A's strategies j = one of B's strategies a_{ij} = amount B pays A for the pair of strategies i and j		Given $\|a_{ij}\|$ find a payoff, if it exists, as determined by $\max_i \left(\min_j a_{ij}\right) = \min_j \left(\max_i a_{ij}\right)$ (Find a number that is lowest in its row and highest in its column)

For the Linear Programming Model nomenclature:

Product	Profit/ unit	Hours Required Machine 1	Machine 2
P_1	\$8	4	3
P_2	\$7	2	4
Machine hours available		40	48

For the Games-of-Conflict Model pictorial (B pays A):

Strategy	$j=1$	$j=2$	$j=3$
$i=1$	3	-5	0
$i=2$	5	4	2
$i=3$	-4	-2	1

A wins from B

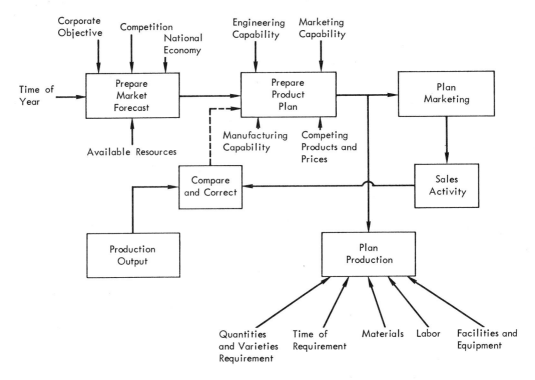

Figure 16.3 Flow chart with operations as blocks

Figure 16.4 Black-box model

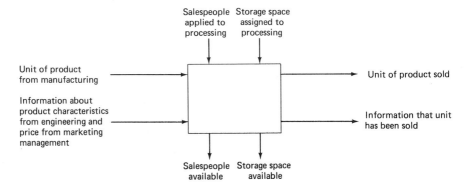

Figure 16.5 Black-box model of sales activity

Let us apply the black-box model to the sales activity in Fig. 16.3. The model is shown in Fig. 16.5 with inputs that are processed—products and information—and outputs of product sales and information supplied to the customer. The principal resources that go into the black-box processor are the labor of salespeople and storage space. The salespeople and storage are available after processing to go into processing again.

The application of the black-box model to an MIS flow chart reveals (1) whether we have all the desired outputs from an activity, (2) whether we have provided the proper information and resources to the activity, (3) whether we have provided a *source* for the information needed.

Feedback Control Models

If, instead of a black-box model, we are able to define the function that relates output to input for each block (operation) in a block-diagram model, we may design the proper amount of feed required to keep the system operating smoothly. This means that the system will respond well to sudden or unexpected changes in input.

The general model of a system with a single feedback loop is shown in Figure 16.6(a). Figure 16.6(b) provides an illustration; here the reference input is the profit plan which is established by the reference elements, the top managers. The signal which goes to the system controllers, the middle managers, is an error signal, resulting from a comparison of desired profit with the actual profit value as fed back from the system output. On the basis of the error in profit,

Figure 16.6
Simple
feedback
model

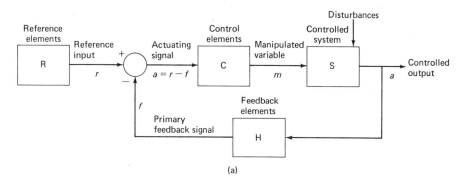

(a)

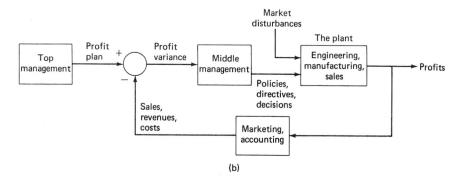

(b)

middle management issues policies and directives and decides on needed action relative to resources and procedures. The implementation of management's output is carried out by the individual contributors in the plant, such as engineers, shop workers, and salespeople. The rapidity, degree, and accuracy of response are limited by the peformance of marketing and accounting. These activities are therefore of as great importance as middle management.

The advanced student may wish to model a more complex and realistic system to determine the time-dependent response of the output to input changes. Generally, the time-dependent input/output function for each block must first be determined. By methods discussed in control-system theory, the Laplace transforms of these functions are next determined in order to reduce the total system problem to the algebraic level. Rules for combining these transfer functions for the blocks are available. Finally, the transfer function for the entire system is determined, and the inverse Laplace transformation is made to relate output to input.

CONSTRUCTION OF MODELS

The construction of models often depends upon recognizing a problem and then finding a matching technique for its solution. The danger in this method is that the analyst may find himself looking for problems to match his techniques instead of vice versa. A general procedure for constructing a model, especially in complex situations, is as follows:

1. Identify and formulate the manager's decision problem in writing.
2. Identify the constants, parameters, and variables involved. Define them verbally and then introduce symbols to represent each one.
3. Select the variables that appear to be most influential so that the model may be kept as simple as possible. Distinguish between those that are controllable by the manager and those that are not.
4. State verbal relationships among the variables, based upon known principles, specially gathered data, intuition, and reflection. Make assumptions or predictions concerning the behavior of the noncontrollable variables.
5. Construct the model by combining all relationships into a system of symbolic relationships.
6. Perform symbolic manipulations (such as solving systems of equations, differentiating, or making statistical analyses).
7. Derive solutions from the model.
8. Test the model by making predictions from it and checking against real-world data.
9. Revise the model as necessary.[5]

[5]See also William T. Morris, "On the Art of Modeling," *Management Science*, August 1967.

Let us see how we might develop a useful seasonal style-goods sales forecasting model by applying the foregoing steps. In the Jantzen Company, management faced the problem of determining when to phase out production on their seasonal products.[6] If too many units were produced, they would have to be dumped at discounted values at the end of the season. If too few were produced, the company would lose the opportunity for additional profits. The decision problem was: How many units should be produced?

The data consisted of initial orders from each customer for previous years, initial orders/week in previous years, attrition rate (number of accounts lost per year), and reorders as a percentage of initial orders. Current-year initial orders were also known on a week-to-week basis.

The important variable appeared to be sales to date in the current year for each week throughout the season.

Verbally, we could construct the following relationships:

Forecast of initial orders for the season might be estimated by scaling up or down last year's initial orders. A logical scaling factor might be the ratio of initial orders to date divided by last year's initial orders for the same number of weeks. However, we should include only those customers common to both periods, because our objective is to determine if the same customers will order more or less this year than last year.

Some customers will be lost, so we need to multiply our forecast by an attrition factor. Also, we will gain some new accounts, so we should scale up last year's total dollar value of new accounts by a ratio that depends on new accounts to date compared to the same period last year. We will add the value of these new accounts to our forecast.

Finally, we will have some reorders toward the end of our season. These amount to only 5% to 10% of initial orders in dollar volume, so we will just add on a percentage of initial orders to complete our forecast.

We are now ready to convert our verbal model into shorthand, using symbols as follows.

First Approximation to the Forecast of Initial Orders

As a first approximation of the season's sales, we use last season's initial order sales and multiply by the ratio of initial orders received to initial orders from the same customers last season:

$$I = I' \frac{I_s}{I'_s} \tag{1}$$

where I = forecast of total initial orders from all stores

I' = actual total initial orders received in previous season

I_s = initial orders received to date; S is the set of customers who ordered to date

I'_s = initial orders received last season from the set of customers, S

[6]Carl Vreeland, "The Jantzen Method of Short-Range Forecasting," *Journal of Marketing,* April 1963. See also Robert G. Murdick, *Mathematical Models in Marketing* (Scranton, Pa.: Intext, 1971).

Second Approximation to Forecast of Initial Orders

Unfortunately, all old accounts don't come back for the current season. If for the moment we assume no new accounts, then we must reduce our forecast by an attrition factor A, where $A < 1.00$.

$$I = AI' \left(\frac{I_s}{I'_s} \right) \tag{2}$$

Final Estimate of Forecast of Initial Orders

We must now forecast the season's sales contributed by initial orders from new accounts. We use a ratio to scale up or down the total initial orders from new accounts. Consider the initial orders from new accounts that we have received so far this season. Compare this with initial orders received from any new accounts for the same period of time last season to form a ratio. Then

$$I = AI' \left(\frac{I'_s}{I_s} \right) + I'_N \left(\frac{N}{N'} \right) \tag{3}$$

where I'_N = total of initial orders received from last year's new accounts

$\quad N$ = new-account initial orders received so far this season

$\quad N'$ = new-account initial orders received at the same point in time last season

Total Sales Forecast

The total sales forecast is the sum of the forecast of initial orders plus the forecast of reorders. Because reorders are a small portion of total sales, the forecast of reorders is assumed to be a fraction of initial orders, the fraction based on a historical average:

$$F = I \, (1 + \bar{R}/\bar{I}) \tag{4}$$

where $\bar{R}$ = average reorders for past years, dollars

$\quad \bar{I}$ = average initial orders for past years, dollars

$\quad F$ = final forecast for the season, dollars

The averages of reorders and initial orders should be taken for the same number of years, and preferably a number of recent years such as five.

SIMULATION

Another powerful application of modeling is the numerical simulation of a system process. A simulation is carried out by specifying a set of starting conditions and a set of rules for the system action. Numerical values are then calculated for the change in the system due to a random input of the exogenous

Figure 16.7
Simulation

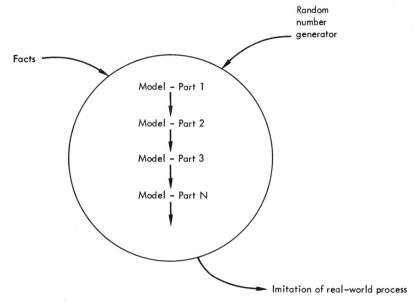

variables. The new state of the system becomes the starting point for another "pass." Simulation is a very valuable technique because (1) it provides for testing of explicit models, those that can be stated in a complete "formula" fashion, and (2) it makes possible the solution of implicit or "chain" types of models whose analytic solution may not even be possible. Figure 16.7 shows the latter case. The model is composed of parts, each depending on the results of the previous part.

We will attempt to explain a simulation of an inventory system without lengthy development of many details. The purpose is to give the reader the flavor of the technique rather than a treatise on how to do it.

The following "facts" are given:

1. The objective is to study an inventory system to determine probability distributions for the size of the inventory and for the size of shortages (stockouts), to aid management in evaluating inventory policies.
2. The procurement level is 4 units. This is a parameter, because it is held constant for this simulation, but it could be changed for another simulation of the system. It is also under the control of management. Thus, when inventory drops to 4 units, an order is placed.
3. The size of the order placed each time, the procurement quantity, is 12 units. This is also a parameter under the control of management.
4. There are two exogenous input variables, variables not under the control of management. These are demand and lead time. The demand is simply the number of units to be withdrawn from inventory in a time period, and this obviously fluctuates. The lead time is the number of periods of time from placing an order to receiving the goods that replenish the inventory; this also obviously fluctuates.

5. A cumulative probability function or graph links probability values to demand values; this may be constructed from historical data or from a theoretical basis. A cumulative probability function or graph links probability values to lead time values; this may be constructed similarly to that for demand.

6. A cycle consists of the number of periods from placing an order to the placing of the next order and is determined therefore by the time it takes the inventory level to drop to 4 units.

7. Assume that the initial stock is 4 units.

Now we set up a table, Fig. 16.8, to represent the system. Because initial stock is 4 units, we must place an order for 12 more units, according to management policy given under "facts" 2 and 3 above. In order to find the lead time, we use a table of random numbers to give us a number from 0 to 100 and convert it to a probability index by dividing by 100. Suppose the number drawn were 72; this becomes a probability of .72. Corresponding to this probability, we obtain from the graph mentioned in "fact" 5 a value of the lead time as 4. This is entered in column (D) of Fig. 16.8.

Figure 16.8 Inventory system simulation	(A) Cycle	(B) Period	(C) Initial Stock	(D) Lead Time	(E) Demand	(F) Final Stock	(G) Units On Hand	(H) Units Short
	1	1	4	4	0	4	4	0
		2	4		2	2	2	0
		3	2		1	1	1	0
		4	1		0	13	1	0
		5	13		5	8	13	0
		6	8		2	6	8	0
		7	6		3	3	6	0
	2	1	3	2	0	3	3	0
		2	3		4	0	3	1
	3	1	0	5	1	10	0	1
		2	10		2	8	10	0
		3	8		2	6	8	0 etc.

We now obtain a value of demand by the same process, and this value turns out to be zero. We enter this in column (E). Because no units were demanded in this period and no units arrived, final stock remains at 4, the number of units on hand for the period is 4, and there is no shortage.

The simulation is continued in this manner until Period 4, when 12 units arrive at the end of the period. Figure 16.8 shows the computations into a portion of the third cycle. In practice, *several hundred cycles* would be carried out. The necessity for an electronic computer in such work is apparent. The results in columns (G) and (H) permit management to determine average inventories, average stockouts, and costs associated with each. Probability distributions for inventory size and shortage amounts may also be obtained.

This simulation is of only a small subsystem; many companies are developing models and simulating entire product ventures. Du Pont developed a model for its now-defunct Corfam® product. General Electric has been simulating the development of venture models at the department (business profit center) level. The Boise Cascade Corporation has experimented with a computerized model of the Timber and Wood Products Division, which has almost 8000 equations and 15,000 variables.[7] The Sun Oil Company has developed a complex, computerized, corporate financial model that uses simulation to improve budgeting, operational control, and planning.[8]

SUMMARY The concept of a system is developed more rigorously in this chapter, although not as rigorously as has been done by mathematical systems writers. The building blocks of theory for MIS are listed as: systems definitions, classification, and concepts; control and communication theory; organization theory; decision making; management science; system design; and computers.

Empirical systems may be classified as natural/man-made; social/man-machine; open or closed; permanent or temporary; stationary or nonstationary; subsystem/system/ supersystem; and adaptive/nonadaptive.

System concepts are required to analyze and design systems. These system concepts are variables such as inputs and outputs; system parameters which establish the state of the system; components or objects which make up the system; attributes or properties of components; structure of the system or relationships among components; process performed by the system on its inputs; boundaries which separate the system from its environment; interfaces which represent the connections between two systems or a system and its environment; and system characteristics or performance as seen from an environmental view.

Once the concept of a system has been clarified, we may develop the *systems approach* to the design of systems and solution of problems. The systems approach implies that all possible knowledge without regard for narrow bias of a single discipline is brought to bear on the problem. The systems approach requires both analysis (deduction) and creativity (synthesis). The general systems approach starts with data and system objectives. The system is then sketched vaguely. In one cycle after another, the system is refined, employing subsystem trade-offs along the way to attempt to optimize total system performance.

Scientists have been working at a primitive level to develop a general theory for systems. Such a theory would describe common characteristics and propositions of most systems.

[7] "The New Management Finally Takes Over," *Business Week,* August 23, 1969, p. 58.

[8] George W. Gershefski, "Building a Corporate Financial Model," *Harvard Business Review,* July–August 1969. For further discussion of systems modeling, see A. F. Moravec, "Using Simulation to Design a Management Information System," *Management Services,* May–June 1966; and Albert N. Schrieber, ed., *Corporate Simulation Models* (Seattle: Graduate School of Business Administration, University of Washington, 1970).

Management Science and Systems

Management science, in many respects, represents a somewhat quantitative or mainly quantitative systems approach. The characteristic of management science is the construction of models to represent systems. Models are *abstractions of reality* and thus can never completely represent reality.

One very general type of model for representing a system is the block-diagram or flow-chart model of processes. Management science includes many models suitable for analyzing subsystems. Some of these are linear programming, inventory, and waiting-line models. Another very general model which may employ these specialized models is a simulation model. Such models deal with systems in numerical terms for analysis at many close intervals of time.

Conclusion

Systems theory and management science are powerful tools for the design and evaluation of MIS. Time and cost are two barriers to their more frequent use. Managers' lack of ability to understand and communicate in the language of mathematics is another obstacle. At the same time, more practical-minded systems and management scientists are needed to convert esoteric concepts into the language of management.

QUESTIONS AND PROBLEMS

1. Match the following right column items with the building blocks of MIS theory.

——— (1) Systems definition, classification, concept

——— (2) Control and communications

——— (3) Organizations

——— (4) Decision making

——— (5) Management science

——— (6) Systems design

——— (7) Computer

   a. Entropy
   b. Task structure
   c. Modeling
   d. Adaptive system
   e. Holistic perspective
   f. Multiprocessing
   g. Satisficing

2. For each system below, place a check if the characteristic in the left column applies.

	Human being	MIS	Sears, Roebuck	Automobile in operation	Marketing Department	Universe
Natural						
Man–made						
Natural and man–made						
Social						
Man—Machine						
Open						
Closed						
Stationary						
Nonstationary						
Adaptive						
Nonadaptive						

3. For the following system, fill in the blanks below.

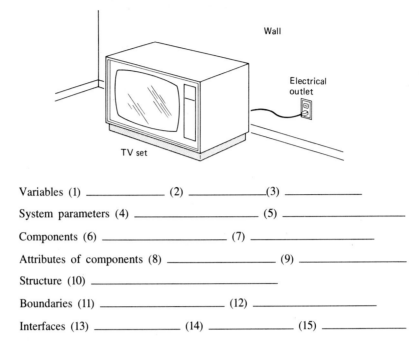

Wall

Electrical
outlet

TV set

Variables (1) ——————— (2) ——————(3) ———————

System parameters (4) ————————————— (5) —————————

Components (6) ————————————— (7) ———————————

Attributes of components (8) ————————————— (9) ——————————

Structure (10) —————————————————————

Boundaries (11) ————————————— (12) ———————————

Interfaces (13) ——————— (14) ——————— (15) ———————

4. Check the following characteristics of the model listed.

Model	Descrip-tive	Predic-tive	Norma-tive	Dynamic	Deter-ministic	Proba-bilistic
a. Probability of escaping ruin $\cong 1 - (q/p)^C$ where p = probability of ruin after each transaction, $q = 1 - p$, and C = initial capital						
b. Decision table						
c. Percentage of branch sales which is a transfer from the main store = $\frac{100\,(1 - e^{-s})}{(1 - e^{-1})}$, where s = share of the trading area presently held by the parent store						
d. PERT network						
e. Present value of future revenue = $\sum\limits_{t\,=\,1}^{n} \frac{R_t}{(1 + i)^t}$ where i = interest rate and R_t = revenue at end of the t-th year						

Model	Descriptive	Predictive	Normative	Dynamic	Deterministic	Probabilistic

f. $Y_x = Y_1 x^b$, where Y_x = time required to produce the x-th unit
$b = (\log \emptyset)/(\log 2)$
$\emptyset$ = rate of decline of time with doubling of production

g. In a rectifying inspection system with defectives discarded from each lot, the average inspection is
$I = n + (1 - P_a)(N - n)$
where N = lot size, n = sample size, and P_a = probability that a lot will be accepted

5. Label the following block diagram for the control system of a person reaching for an object.

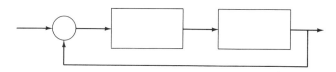

a. BRAIN   d. +   g. Object position
b. Hand position   e. −   h. Plant
c. HAND   f. Controller   i. Eyes

6. For the following block diagram of a company, complete the description by writing the code letters in the proper places on the diagram.

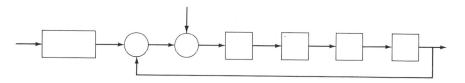

a. +   e. Manufacturing   i. Warehouse activities
b. −   f. Customer   j. Inventory policy
c. Delivery   g. Incoming orders   k. Production planning
d. Order processing   h. Sales forecast

7. Represent an order processing system by means of a block diagram with feedback control.

8. What are the advantages of the concept of a "module" in systems design?

9. Identify a system that is small in physical size but very complex.

10. Show by means of a diagram how a particular business is a subsystem of its industry.

11. Look in the library for other definitions of a system, compare with the one in the text, and try to develop a better definition.

12. Identify common characteristics of an organizational system, an MIS, and the economic system of the country. Discuss how general systems theory might be useful (if it were available) in designing such systems.

13. Table 15.1 gives characteristics of man–machine systems. Set up a table to show which of these characteristics apply to an organization, an MIS, a commercial aircraft, and an electric toaster.

14. A large retail chain sells a variety of powered tools and garden equipment. It is fairly common for a customer to purchase such equipment, use it once, and then return it as unsatisfactory. Show how you would use the systems approach, step-by-step, to design a system for accepting (or not accepting) such returns and method of disposing of returns. To show the systems approach, you should evolve a system design as your solution.

15. Describe briefly how management science might be applied to

    a. Conceptual design of an MIS
    b. MIS evaluation
    c. Detailed design of an MIS
    d. Economics of MIS design

16. Robin Industries produces commercial and consumer products based upon small computing units or integrated circuits. This is a small firm with annual sales of about $10 million. Ms. Fermi, Manager of New Product Development, says, "We obtain new ideas from customers, vendors, from scanning technical publications, and from our own engineering and marketing people. Our problem has been to develop a screening procedure that is fast and reliable. We need to incorporate a product life-cycle concept in our projections for sales, also."

    Develop a detailed systems approach to this problem and narrative descriptions of models (or quantitative models) to help Ms. Fermi solve this problem.

17. Top management of a large chemical company has studied long-range technological and social trends. It foresees continuing rapid growth for the industry and its own sales over a ten-year period. It faces a major strategic decision with regard to plant expansion. It can expand only in multiples of the $50,000 vats it uses to produce its products. That is, it could expend $50,000, say, for one vat every year, or it could expend $500,000 for one large vat right now. The larger vat is far more efficient than ten small vats, but the utilization rate will be low at first and considerable capital will be tied up.

    a. Make assumptions with regard to sales growth and develop a model that will guide management as to times and amounts to invest in expansion. (A simplifying assumption may be made that the same number of vats are added each time or that equal time intervals between additions will be established. Another simplifying assumption is that capacity must always be greater than, or equal to, demand. Remember that time-value of money and working capital are important factors.)
    b. Specify the information that top management would desire to make a really good decision in such circumstances.

SELECTED
REFERENCES

"A Framework for Management Information Systems," *Sloan Management Review,* Fall 1971.

ACKOFF, RUSSELL L., and MAURICE W. SASIENI, *Fundamentals of Operations Research.* New York: John Wiley, 1968. See p. 6 for a definition of operations research.

ELLIS, DAVID O., and FRED J. LUDWIG, *Systems Philosophy.* Englewood Cliffs, N.J.: Prentice-Hall, 1962.

FOWLER, PETER H., "System Pathology," *IEEE Transactions on Reliability,* September 1968.

GORRY, G. ANTHONY, and MICHAEL S. SCOTT MORTON, "A Framework for Management Information Systems," *Sloan Management Review,* Fall 1971.

HALL, ARTHUR D., *A Methodology for Systems Engineering.* New York: Van Nostrand Reinhold, 1962.

HARE, VAN COURT, JR., *Systems Analysis: A Diagnostic Approach.* New York: Harcourt Brace Jovanovich, 1967.

HARTNETT, WILLIAM E., *Systems: Approaches, Theories, and Applications.* Dordrecht, Holland: D. Reidel Publishing Co., 1977.

HOPKINS, R. C., "A Systematic Procedure for Systems Development," *IRE Transactions on Engineering Management,* June 1961.

International Journal of Systems Management (Quarterly).

KLIR, GEORGE J., *An Approach to General Systems Theory.* New York: Van Nostrand Reinhold, 1969.

LASZLO, ERVIN, "The Meaning and Significance of General System Theory," *Behavioral Science,* Vol. 20 (1975).

LEE, ALEC M., *Systems Analysis Frameworks.* New York: Macmillan, 1970.

MELDMAN, JEFFREY A., "A New Technique for Modeling the Behavior of Man-Machine Information Systems," *Sloan Management Review,* Spring 1977.

RUBIN, MILTON D., ed., *Man in Systems.* New York: Gordon and Breach Science Publishers, 1971.

SUTHERLAND, JOHN W., *Systems Analysis, Administration, and Architecture.* New York: Van Nostrand Reinhold, 1975.

TRAPPLE, ROBERT, and F. DE P. HANIKA, eds., *Progress in Cybernetics and Systems Research,* Vol. II. New York: John Wiley, 1975.

TRAPPLE, ROBERT, ed., *Trends in General Systems Theory.* New York: John Wiley, 1972.

WAGNER, HARVEY M., *Principles of Operations Research.* New York: McGraw-Hill, 1959. See especially pp. 3–4.

WEINBERG, GERALD M., *An Introduction to General Systems Thinking.* New York: John Wiley, 1975.

CASES

Wagner Electric Corporation*

COMPANY BACKGROUND

Wagner Electric Corporation is a subsidiary of Studebaker-Worthington, Inc. Studebaker-Worthington is a large, diversified company, organized in two operating groups, the Process Equipment Group and the Consumer and Industrial Products Group, each of which accounted for 50% of consolidated sales in 1977. Studebaker-Worthington, through its subsidiaries, provides equipment and services for raw materials processing and energy industries throughout the world. It manufactures consumer and industrial products, including automotive products, generators, engines, industrial cleaning equipment, garden tractors, and chain saws, mainly for domestic markets.

As a leader in the automotive brake and lighting field, Wagner Electric Corporation achieved record sales and earnings in 1977. The company attributed this success to the highest North American vehicle demand in history and to improvements in the control of its operations. A comparison of 1976 and 1977 financial data is as follows:

	1977	1976†	1976–1977 % Change
Sales (millions)	$290.3	$248.7	+ 16.7%

†Restated to reflect operations discontinued in 1977.

*This case was prepared by Dr. Robert E. Markland, Academic Program Director and Professor— Management Science, College of Business Administration, University of South Carolina, Columbia, S.C., and Dr. L. Douglas Smith, Associate Professor—Management Science, School of Business Administration, University of Missouri, St. Louis.

In 1977, Wagner Electric Corporation also completed its planned transition to a company focusing on the automotive market. As a result, virtually all of its 1977 sales were in the automotive market, with slightly more than one-half going to the original-equipment market (OEM) and the balance going to the replacement market. About one-third of its current OEM sales are for passenger cars; the remaining two-thirds are for trucks, trailers, and off-highway equipment. It currently produces air and hydraulic brake systems, brake fluid, electronic skid-control systems, sealed-beam headlamps, miniature lamps, flashers, electroswitch devices, auto cigarette lighters, power supplies; and digital readout devices. These products are manufactured at ten domestic, one Canadian, and five foreign plants. It maintains 13 branch sales offices and warehouse locations.

BACKGROUND OF THE PROBLEM

In early 1977, management of Wagner Electric Corporation began to consider the development and implementation of a comprehensive sales and marketing information system. Its computer facility consisted of an IBM 370/158 central processing unit, operating under DOS, with a four-phase telecommunications system linking domestic plants and branch warehouses to the central computing facility. Over the years it had developed and implemented a number of computer applications, including:

Accounting reports
Order entry (polled nightly by host computer)
    Inventory status
    Customer verification
    Parts verification
    Production of sorted picking lists
    Back orders
Order billing
Payroll reports
Data-base inquiries through IBM Customer Information Control System
    Software
Salesmen's activity log
Manufacturing
    Bill of material maintained by IBM Communications Oriented Production Information and Control System Software (COPICS)
    Perpetual inventory status
Procurement
    Message switching for accounts payables
    Message switching for interwarehouse transfers

Through the origination and implementation of these and other applications, the company had developed a first-rate data processing facility with well-qualified and highly motivated systems and data processing personnel.

In considering the possibility of developing and implementing a comprehensive sales and marketing information system, company management had decided to use an outside consulting team to develop a project proposal. This decision was made for two reasons. First, the systems and data processing staff of the company was already heavily committed to several other important projects. Second, the company management wanted an independent and objective appraisal of the company's needs for a comprehensive sales and marketing information system. Consequently, in the fall of 1977, a three-man consulting team was hired from the business school of a local university. One member of this consulting team was a marketing professor; the other two members were management science/information systems professors. All three members had considerable previous consulting experience. They were given the responsibility of developing a detailed proposal for the development and implementation of a sales and marketing information system for Wagner Electric Corporation, including a consideration of the following:

1. Scope of the project
2. Managerial functions to be supported by the information system
3. System software and reports to be produced
4. Proposed activities of the consulting team, working in conjunction with Wagner Electric Corporation systems personnel
5. A PERT network plan for systems development and implementation, indicating time and resources required for each activity
6. Summaries of estimated costs and anticipated benefits associated with each module of the system.

DEVELOPING THE PROPOSAL

During the latter months of 1977 and the early months of 1978 the consulting team conducted extensive interviews with key management personnel of the Wagner Electric Corporation. The following interviews were arranged and coordinated by the sales and marketing department:

1. Dec. 14, 1977 – Administrative Sales Manager—Aftermarket
Administrative Sales Manager—OEM
Sales Systems Coordinator
2. Dec. 22, 1977 – Corporate Director of Marketing
Marketing Controller
3. Dec. 28, 1977 – Corporate Director of Marketing
Corporate Budget Manager
Director of OEM Marketing
Project Leader, order entry system
Analyst, order entry system
4. Jan. 3, 1978 – Director of Retailer Marketing
Manager of Product Distribution

5. Jan. 4, 1978   – Director of Data Processing
                             Manager of Programming
                             Manager of Systems

6. Jan. 9, 1978   – Vice President of OEM Sales
                             Manager—Zone Warehouse Operations

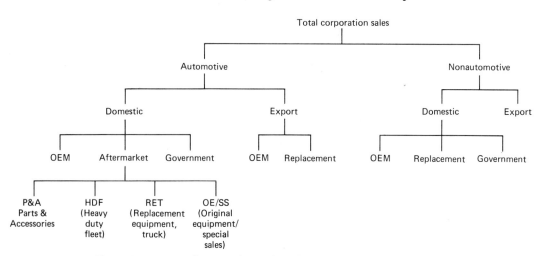

Figure 1 Wagner Electric sales and marketing environment

These interviews were very fruitful and instructive in familiarizing the consulting team with the sales and marketing environment (see Fig. 1) and with the systems environment of the company. During the interviewing process the consulting team confirmed that the company's present information system lacked the capability of providing timely answers to basic sales and marketing questions of the following nature:

1. Which customers generate the highest sales volumes?
2. Which customers generate the greatest contributions to profit for Wagner Electric?
3. Has the product mix changed for a particular account?
4. Is Wagner Electric obtaining an acceptable market share in a certain sales area?
5. What is an appropriate sales quota for a particular zone?
6. What would be the impact on profits of raising prices on a certain product line?

The consulting team structured their review and analysis from a "top-down" information systems perspective in three major steps:

1. A review of business processes and general environmental factors affecting Wagner Electric Corporation.
2. A review and definition of responsibilities and functions of the marketing and sales personnel.
3. A *preliminary* appraisal of the informational requirements for achieving the missions of the sales and marketing areas of the company. Particular concern was devoted to methods of improving the planning process. Historically, concern had been primarily focused upon provision of information which documented previous sales and marketing efforts.

In early February, 1978, having completed the interviewing process and thoroughly reviewed the information and data obtained, the consulting team prepared its proposal.

PRECIS OF THE PROPOSAL FOR DEVELOPING A SALES AND MARKETING INFORMATION SYSTEM

Introduction

Given the overall objective of developing and implementing a comprehensive sales and marketing information system, it is first necessary to consider those areas of sales and marketing decision making that lend themselves to improvement through such a system. Based on the consulting team's observation and analysis, three broad information system applications should be considered within the sales and marketing environment of Wagner Electric Corporation. These applications, with selected examples of potential information systems outputs, are as follows:

Application	*Potential Output*
1. *Market Research*	
Pricing policy	Pricing policy based on historical analysis of past or simulated conditions
Promotional strategy	Promotional strategy based on analysis of market segments
2. *Market Planning*	
Forecasting	Materials, parts, production requirements, end product demands
Credit and billing management	Automated credit and billing decisions
3. *Market Control*	
Marketing costs	Tracking of deviations from standards or trend analysis
4. *Sales performance*	
Market segments	Timely reporting of sales performance by market segments and on a geographical basis
Geographical	

In considering these four broad application areas, three major types of systems, each potentially having many subsystems or modules, would evolve. The major systems required would be

1. *Marketing Research.* Information systems designed to predict and test the consequences of various actions taken with respect to pricing, promotions, channels of distribution, packaging, product design, etc.

2. *Marketing Planning.* Information systems designed to facilitate both the long-term and short-term planning of the sales and marketing efforts.

3. *Marketing Control.* Information systems developed to provide a timely and continuous monitoring of performance against plan, highlighting deviations from planned or forecasted performance, and identifying both favorable and unfavorable trends.

In making these suggestions with respect to the types of information systems that should be developed in the sales and marketing areas, several important points should be made. First, as management information systems have evolved, marketing information has typically been overlooked as accounting or financial information requirements have been emphasized. Thus, it is quite common to find that much of the decision making in the sales and marketing area relies heavily on experience and intuition. Consequently, the systems suggested for development in this proposal are oriented toward increasing objectivity in the decision process.

Second, there has been a tendency to maintain information only about sales records and orders and shipments. We propose a more complicated set of interacting systems which will give sales and marketing managers specific and timely information. This will allow them to make improved decisions concerning pricing, promotion, sales force effort, and product lines. Sales or order history is an important part of decision making in these areas, but the historical reporting of data is an inadequate basis for the design of a comprehensive and useful sales and marketing information system.

Third, the systems development will have a complex set of interactions throughout the organization. This must be emphasized at the outset, because information concerning sales and marketing necessarily has a profound impact on decision making in other areas of the organization. Thus, development of a marketing information system should be accompanied by an openness to make complementary efforts in modifying or developing systems which serve other functional areas—particularly production, distribution, and financial planning.

SYSTEMS OUTLINE

To organize the project from a systems perspective, the first step was to determine the managerial functions which the system is to support. Next, appropriate computer software and reports were tentatively defined. Finally, consideration was given to the data base required by the computer software modules. Our systems outline addresses each of these three aspects individually.

Managerial Functions to Be Supported by
the Sales and Marketing Information System

Fundamental in structuring the project was a review of the managerial functions which the sytem is to support. Note that a function may be performed in a department with a different name, e.g., product distribution versus sales management. Indeed, there can be some realignment of responsibilities motivated by the availability of a computer-based information system. Some of our suggestions may, therefore, be of interest to, and subject to the review of, managers outside sales and marketing per se.

Sales management

There are five general functions we have categorized under sales management. These functions are presented below with an elaboration which includes the suggested software support.

Forecasting and Tracking Sales. Sales forecasting at this level would be in terms of dollars by product line. Statistical forecasting models would be used to project past sales history, making adjustments to reflect seasonality, economic conditions, and other measurable influences which can usefully be incorporated into a forecasting model. These forecasts could be used to establish general activity levels for aggregate planning and to scale unit forecasts required for production and distribution. Provision will be explicitly included for altering forecasts to reflect human judgment.

Sales Reporting. Sales reports would depict sales in a form amenable to analysis and to initiate action. Reports would contain sales summaries in dollars, units, and contribution to gross margin (calculated at standard production cost). Comparisons would be made against previous periods, forecasts, and quotas. OEM and aftermarket would tend to have sales broken out differently from each other because their sales activity would be subject to different types of review and control. Reports would be produced to analyze sales routinely by sales territory, by salesperson, by customer, and by other criteria useful for management.

Administrative Functions. Support would be provided to reduce the manual activity associated with maintenance of a centralized billing price file and notification of price changes. This should enable much faster processing of price changes and reduce processing errors.

Justification of Price Increases in the OEM. Documenting reasons for price increases on products for OEM would be greatly facilitated by rapid retrieval of relevant data from computer files structured with this application in mind. A more complete and accurate accounting would be possible.

Analysis of Promotional Activities. A promotional data file would be structured to allow analysis of the effects of different promotional activities. Actual experiments could be performed to identify the promotions to which sales are most responsive, and the impact of various promotions upon profits could be analyzed.

Ad Hoc Analysis. Other types of analysis would be supported by the data base. For example, one might analyze the design of the sales and distribution territories to see whether costs could be reduced by altering boundaries. One might also investigate the impact of varying service levels at branch warehouses or field warehouses. These types of nonroutine studies usually yield significant benefits.

Marketing management

The marketing function is divided into strategic planning and marketing control. The former involves planning for the future; the latter involves reviewing current and past performance.

Strategic Planning. The activities in connection with strategic planning entail historical profit analysis and pro-forma estimation of profits under alternative assumptions about factors such as economic conditions, product prices, promotional activity, and market sales. A simulation model would be constructed to enable asking a series of "What if?" questions about future activities.

Marketing Control. Sales would be compared against forecasts and quotas. Variance analyses would be undertaken to explain deviations of actual sales from expected sales. Attention would be directed to areas needing improvement and to areas where marketing has been particularly successful.

Production

Sales and marketing generate the orders which eventually become planned requirements for the MRP system. The detailed unit forecasts for production, e.g., those produced by exponential smoothing for inventory management, can be scaled to reflect additional information available to sales and marketing personnel. Leading indicators should be identified and monitored to enable updating planned requirements when sales activity deviates significantly from expected levels.

Finance

The sales and marketing strategic planning simulator could be designed to project working capital requirements under alternative assumptions about the future.

Having outlined the general functions to be supported by the sales and marketing information system, we are able to suggest computer software and reports needed to make the system operational. The next section addresses this aspect.

Suggested Software Modules

The sales and marketing management information system will be developed modularly to facilitate management of the project and maintenance of the software. A modular approach also enables the higher-priority applications to be implemented early, so that Wagner may realize benefits from the project as early as possible.

It is premature to impose a great deal of structure upon the components of the information system before completing a comprehensive review and analysis of the decision-making process in sales and marketing. Considering our conversations to date, however, we are able to suggest software modules which would likely be produced for the system. Extensive consideration of managerial decision-making processes at Wagner and detailed systems analysis will, of course, be required to produce a complete set of specifications for the software modules and data base. Preliminary impressions are frequently subject to major revisions when considering the integration of a sales and marketing system with other systems such as purchasing, distribution, and production. The software modules to support analysis and decision making for sales and marketing are tentatively outlined in Figures 2 through 16.

Each of the modules outlined in the figures does, of course, require access to relevant data. Discussion of issues in the construction and maintenance of a comprehensive data base follows.

Data-Base Considerations

It is apparent that much of the information required for sales and marketing management is used by other areas but in a different form. Capability must be provided to enable managers from different functional areas to view data organized in the form which supports the specific decisions for which they are responsible. Similarly, the software modules for the sales and marketing subsystem share the same data but for different uses. To eliminate redundancy in the collection and maintenance of data and to maintain its integrity, Wagner Electric will be using "data-base management software," structuring the data base, and giving access to different users in such a way that responsibility for various components can be assigned to specific individuals. In designing the data base, Wagner Electric systems personnel will have to perform an intensive study of the access required to specific data items by every user, the frequency of access by each user, modes of data collection, updating procedures, and the need to have different items of data available simultaneously for particular applications. This study will extend to systems beyond sales and marketing. The order-entry system, for example, provides many of the data vital to sales and marketing management. Sales forecasting, another example, has much in common with purchasing, distribution, and production.

To give an indication of the wide variety of data required by the sales and marketing information system, several components of the data base to be constructed are identified on page 555.

Figure 2

Module: Aggregate Sales Forecasting

Purpose: To produce price-level-adjusted and seasonally adjusted sales forecasts by product line for aggregate planning, i.e., projection of levels of activity in manufacturing and distribution to assess needs for capital resources, manpower, and supplies

Components:
1. OEM Forecasting Models
   a. Combinations (as appropriate) of Box-Jenkins time-series extrapolations and explanatory multiple regression models using leading indicators (economy, automotive industry forecasts, etc.) to operate in interactive mode
   b. Disaggregative estimating procedures for market potential, market share, and sales by product line
   c. Interactive review and adjustments to enable an analyst to superimpose management's qualitative judgment upon the statistical forecasts
2. Aftermarket Forecasting Models. Similar methodology to OEM but using different explanatory variables (vehicle registrations, equipment failure rates, historical sales, etc.)
3. H/D Fleet Forecasting Models. Similar methodology to OEM but using different explanatory variables (age of equipment on the road, driving conditions, historical sales, etc.)

Figure 3

Module: Aggregate Sales Tracking

Purpose: To monitor actual sales versus forecasted sales and draw attention to significant deviations; to initiate investigation to determine cause of deviations, prescribe remedial action, and update previous aggregate forecasts

Components:
1. Forecasting Review Component. Comparison of actual sales versus forecasted sales. "Filter" to highlight deviations not attributable to randomness
2. Component for removing influence of unexpected events (e.g., competitor's strike) before using data for statistical forecasts
3. Forecasting Adjustment Component. Capability of updating forecasts by scaling factor which reflects recent forecasting error and qualitative influences

Figure 4

Module: Detailed sales forecasting

Purpose: To produce planned requirements for the MRP system, enabling preliminary estimates of requirements to be given to major suppliers so they might reserve capacity for Wagner

Components:
1. Adaptive Exponential Smoothing Models with Seasonal Adjustor for Extrapolation of Basic Unit Sales (including tracking signal to alter smoothing constant values in response to pattern of forecasting errors)
2. Product Grouping Component to group items whose sales are interdependent, forecast sales for the group, and then break out sales for individual items according to historical percentages

Figure 5

Module: Detailed sales tracking

Purpose: To monitor actual unit sales versus forecasted sales, initiate remedial action, and update previous unit forecasts

Components:
1. "Filter" to identify forecasts with errors large enough to be attributable to nonrandom causes
2. Forecasting Auditor to ensure the appropriate forecasting model is being employed (e.g., model including trend to be used only for items with significant trend)
3. Updating Component to enable scale revision of forecasts to reflect recent errors and influence of qualitative factors

---

Figure 6

Module: Aftermarket Sales Reporting

Purpose: To monitor aftermarket sales versus historical and forecasted sales for the various products by sales territory and customer, etc.; to draw attention to significant deviations, and to initiate inquiries to determine reasons behind discrepancies

Components:
1. Sales report in dollar terms and unit terms for product groups and individual items
   a. Sales this period and year-to-date
   b. Comparisons versus forecasts
   c. Comparisons versus same period previous year and year-to-date previous year
   e. Significant changes highlighted
2. Ranking of product groups and individual products by dollar sales and contribution to gross margin at standard costs
3. Ranking of sales territories by dollar sales and contribution to gross margin at standard costs
4. Ranking of customers by dollar sales and contribution to gross margin at standard costs

---

Figure 7

Module: OEM Sales Reporting

Purpose: To monitor original equipment sales versus historical and forecasted sales for the various products by customers to draw attention to significant deviations, and to initiate inquiries to determine reasons behind discrepancies

Components:
1. Sales Report in dollar terms and unit terms for product groups and individual items
   a. Sales this period and year-to-date
   b. Comparisons versus forecasts
   c. Comparisons versus same period previous year and year-to-date previous year
   d. Significant changes highlighted
2. Ranking of product groups and individual products by dollar sales
3. Ranking of product groups and individual products by contribution to gross margin calculated at standard costs
4. Ranking of customers by dollar sales and by contribution to gross margin calculated at standard costs

Figure 8

> *Module:* Maintenance of Centralized Billing Price File
>
> *Purpose:* To eliminate the laborious, time-consuming activities of maintaining the billing price files and to generate notification of price changes in an accurate and timely manner
>
> *Components:*
> 1. Updating Component to change prices and/or pricing structures
> 2. Report Generator for notification of price changes

Figure 9

> *Module:* OEM Pricing
>
> *Purpose:* To demonstrate the impact of changes in costs of productive resources (labor, supplies, raw materials) upon the cost of finished products. This module would be used to justify price changes and to project the impact of alternative pricing/cost structures upon contribution to company profits.
>
> *Components:*
> 1. Augmentation of bill of material to include labor inputs in product structure
> 2. Integrator of sales forecasts with augmented bills of material to determine impact of changes in prices of products and costs of productive resources and/or raw materials upon profit contribution

Figure 10

> *Module:* Promotional Review
>
> *Purpose:* To predict and analyze the effects of various marketing strategies and sales promotions upon company sales and company profitability
>
> *Components:*
> 1. Statistical Description of promotions and changes in market strategy (type, duration, costs, etc.)
> 2. Component for adjusting sales forecasts to reflect estimates of additional sales to occur in response to nonregular promotions. Adjustments will be allowed in either incremental percentages or incremental quantities during different stages of promotional period
> 3. General Multiple Regression Model for statistically estimating impact of changes in promotional mix upon company sales. This would be an augmented version of the aggregate sales forecasting model, which includes indicator variables describing changes in promotional strategy.
> 4. Report Generator to compare predicted promotional effects versus forecasted promotional effects

Figure 11

Module: Reporting Unusual Sales Activity

Purpose: To focus immediate attention upon significant sales transactions which deviate significantly from expectations and alert senior management to their occurrence

Compo-
nent: Exception Report Generator which summarizes major transactions

Figure 12

Module: Sales Query

Purpose: To enable individuals, upon their own initiative, to extract information (relevant to their sphere of responsibilities) from the data base and to perform various ad hoc analyses

Components:
1. Inquiry for summaries of sales by customer and comparisons versus historical and forecasted sales
2. Inquiry for summaries of sales by product group or individual product and comparisons versus historical and forecasted sales
3. Inquiry for summaries of sales by salesman and comparison versus historical sales and sales quotas
4. Inquiry for summaries of sales by territory and comparison versus historical and forecasted sales
5. Inquiry for recent sales transactions by customer (probably to be integrated with the order-entry system)

Figure 13

Module: Sales Personnel Management

Purpose: To help establish quotas for sales territories and individual salesmen; to aid in reviewing the performance of sales personnel; to monitor field activity and review its effectiveness

Components:
1. Estimator of regional market potential and company sales potential for product groups and individual products. Model to consider factors such as registered vehicles, economic conditions, historical sales and market share, geographical features, and type of driving
2. Salesmen's Activity Reports: call frequency for various customers, travel time
3. Salesmen's Accounts Gained and Lost
4. Ranking of salesmen in terms of dollar sales and gross contribution at standard costs
5. Ranking of salesmen by sales versus quotas in terms of dollar sales and contribution to profit calculated at standard cost
6. Changes in product sales mix by salesmen
7. Comparison of salesmen's sales versus quota, and sales versus previous year same period and previous year-to-date

Figure 14

Module: Strategic Planning for Marketing

Purpose: To examine effects of hypothetical changes in market potential, market share, prices of product lines, distribution costs, etc., upon company profitability

Components:
1. Deterministic Simulation Model designed to operate in interactive mode to help answer "What if?" questions in the development of marketing strategy
   a. Analysis would be performed incrementally from the aggregate sales forecast for a base marketing plan.
   b. Considered would be such factors as responsiveness of sales to different promotional efforts, changes in product cost structures, effects of sales of some products upon others (cross-elasticities of demand).
2. Depending upon the degree of sophistication and specificity desired, an extension could be developed to include finance, purchasing, production, distribution, and manpower management for overall organizational planning and control.

Figure 15

Module: Projecting Working Capital Requirements

Purpose: To convert output of the strategic planning simulator into working capital requirements for financial management

Components:
1. Indicators of inventories of raw materials, finished goods, and different levels of organizational activity
2. Link to output of strategic planning module to convert aggregate performance into working capital requirements

Figure 16

Module: Analyzing Efficiency of Sales and Distribution System and Adjusting Territorial Boundaries

Purpose: To ensure that sales and distribution territories are designed to yield the best service at a given cost or to achieve lowest costs for a given service level. This analysis could be undertaken on an annual basis.

Components:
1. Simulator to analyze the effects of altering stocking policies (service levels) from regional warehouses to zone warehouses and from zone warehouses to final customers. This would enable a series of experiments to minimize total costs of distribution and carrying inventory to achieve a given level of service to final customers.
2. Optimizing Procedure to assign warehouses and salesmen to serve specific customers considering production capacity, distribution costs, warehouse capacity, possible joint shipment, etc.

Identifying specific items to be included in the data base and designing its structure will require considerable time and effort. These activities will coincide with the development of detailed specifications for computer software. Samples from anticipated components of the data base are presented below as a reminder of the extent of integration required with systems that serve other functional areas.

Data-base components

1. *Historical sales*
   Product line
   Product code
   Product number
   Geographical location
   Customer
   Salesman
   Promotion
   Price
   Method of shipment
   Warehouse utilized
2. *Historical Forecasts*
   Seasonal factors
   Error-tracking signal
   Type of forecasting model used
   Product group
3. *Promotional Data*
   Timing and duration
   Nature of promotion
   Expected sales results
   Actual sales results
4. *Supplier Costs*
   Raw material costs (current)
   Raw material costs (projected)
5. *Production Inputs*
   Labor component of products
   Bills of material (accessible
      through MRP system)
   Supplies
6. *Market Indicators*
   Economic time series
   Leading indicators for Wagner
      Electric activity

Leading indicators for automotive industry
Current production data for industry
Automotive industry sales
Automotive industry inventories
7. *Major Events Affecting Sales*
   Governmental action
   Major strikes
   Labor contracts pending
8. *Competitive Indicators*
   Advertising by primary
      competitors
   Advertising by industry
   Advertising by Wagner Electric
   Price index for primary
      competitors
   Price index for industry
   Price index for Wagner Electric
9. *Sales Personnel*
   Expected sales
   Quotas
   Accounts for whom each salesman has responsibility
   Salesmen's activities
10. *Distribution Information*
    Geographical routings
    Modes of distribution
    Distribution costs
11. *Billing/Price Data*
    Prices and terms of billing for
       various customers
    Account status descriptors

It should finally be acknowledged that design and construction of the data base will not be undertaken without regard to existing systems in the company.

Good data-base management software will help insulate existing applications from structural changes in the methods of storing and managing data, yet give considerable flexibility in the development of new applications.

1. What is your appraisal of the consulting team's proposal, as contained in the "Systems Outline" section of the case?

2. What other areas should have been considered by the consulting team?

3. What difficulties do you foresee in attempting to implement such a proposed information system?

4. Should the consulting team have a role in the implementation of the proposed information system, and if so, what should that role be?

5. How should the project be organized and managed?

6. How do you obtain the commitment and cooperation needed for undertaking such a massive project affecting so many people?

7. How would you expect individual managers to react to the proposal?

8. Lay out the format for a *management* report resulting from the data made available by the modules, i.e., one report associated with each software module.

9. What data structure would you recommend for the data base, and why?

10. Draw a block diagram or flow chart to illustrate the strategic planning system as it relates to the marketing information system.

11. Draw a flow chart for the order procsessing system on the assumption that orders for all lines are received initially at one point within the company.

12. Show, in outline form, a hierarchy of reports covering the sales forecasts. That is, show the general format and some hypothetical figures for the report that goes to each level of marketing management.

13. Propose sales forecasting models that Wagner Electric might find suitable for forecasting sales of the following:

   a. OEM sales for passenger cars
   b. Industrial cleaning equipment
   c. Garden tractors.

   In answering this question, describe in more detail (in narrative form, if desired) *your* proposed forecasting procedures *or* the procedures mentioned in the Aggregate Sales Forecasting Module.

Community Hospital, Inc.*

The soaring cost of hospital care has received national attention. Administrators say that employee salaries are by far the largest factor in operating costs, running from 55% to 65% of total outlays.

Longer-range problems of hospitals are steadily increasing or steadily decreasing demands for patient care accompanied by fluctuations that frequently disguise such change. Hospital administrators should be preparing long-range plans for (1) financing, (2) accommodating increased and changing population, (3) increasing level and diversity of health care, (4) rapid advances and changes in equipment and procedures, and (5) appearance of new competing hospitals, nursing homes, out-patient care institutions, etc.[1]

COMMUNITY HOSPITAL

The Community Hospital (CH) is located in Florida on the outskirts of a large metropolitan area. It was built on a 20-acre site and consists of a four-story building and a small office building housing the personnel department and a systems group. There are both a large out-patient clinic and an emergency department. The former has about 2000 and the latter about 4000 visits per month. With 346 beds, the average census for the hospital is 292 patients daily and is increasing at about 4% per year.

---

*This case represents a collection of individual problems which have been found by examining a wide variety of hospital operations. It does not represent any single hospital.

[1]See, for example, Raymond D. Garrett, *Hospitals: A Systems Approach* (Philadelphia: Auerback Publishers, 1973).

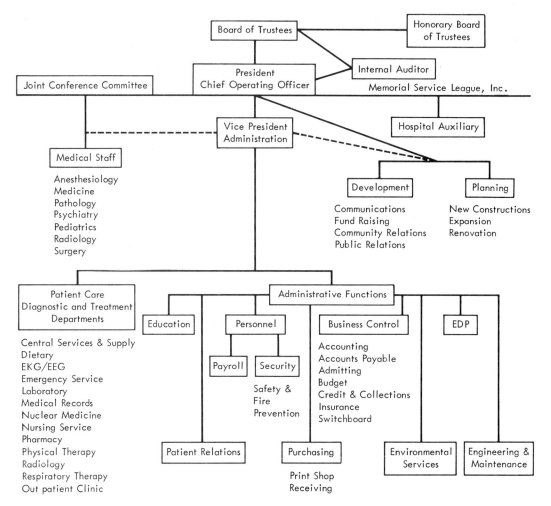

Figure 1 Table of organization, Community Hospital, Inc.

The organization of CH is shown in Fig. 1. CH has a miscellaneous group of manual, semiautomated, and automated systems for administrative and patient control. It also has followed the chart of accounts for hospitals as shown in Table 1.

THE SYSTEMS TEAM

A systems engineer, A. Star, was hired by CH in January 1980 and given one staff assistant, R. G. Gordon. A hospital staff executive with previous systems experience at the Metropolitan Life Insurance Company, Matt Blood, was included with these two to form a systems team. This team was charged with the development and implementation of improved systems to be related and integrated as time went on.

The team was wary of introducing a "total system" at one time. It also noted a report to the effect that (1) a new computer system should be virtually invisible, and (2) it should eliminate unnecessary duplication of procedures by different departments. The reasons are that most medical personnel do not see any need to change their present methods, and the interdepartmental links are weak or nonexistent.[2]

[2]Hari Anand, "A Computer-Based Hospital Information System," *Hospital Administration*, September 1971.

Table 1 General plan for the chart of accounts for hospitals

A. Overall Numbering System

110–199 Assets

110–114	Operating Fund
120–122	Specific Purpose Fund
130–132	Endowment Fund
140–146	Plant Fund
150–155	Construction Fund
160–199	Other Funds

217–299 Liabilities

217	Operating Fund
227	Specific Purpose Fund
237–238	Endowment Fund
247–248	Plant Fund
257–258	Construction Fund
267–299	Other Funds

219–299 Capital Accounts

219	Operating Fund
229	Special Purpose Fund
239	Endowment Fund
249	Plant Fund
259	Construction Fund
269–299	Other Funds

310–599 Revenue Accounts

313–359	Revenue from Patient Services
360–399	Revenue from Other Nursing Services
402–499	Revenue from Other Services
500–539	Deductions from Revenue
540–599	Other Revenue

600–999 Expense Accounts

600–699	Patient Services
700–799	Other Professional Services
800–899	Other Services
900–979	Fiscal and Administrative Services
980–999	Unassigned Expenses

B. Further Subclassification of Revenue

310–359 Revenue from Patient Services

310–339	Medical, Surgical, and Pediatric
340–342	Intensive Care
343–345	Psychiatric
346–349	Newborn and Premature Nurseries

360–399 Revenue from Other Nursing Services

360–364	Operating Rooms
365–369	Recovery Rooms
370–374	Delivery and Labor Rooms
375–376	Central Services and Supply
377	Intravenous Therapy
378–379	Emergency
380–389	Other

402–499 Revenue from Other Services

402–409	Laboratory
410	Blood Bank
411	Whole Blood
412–413	Electrocardiograph
414	Electroencephalograph
421–429	Radiology
430–434	Pharmacy
435	Anesthesiology
436	Inhalation Therapy
437	Physical Therapy
438	Occupational Therapy
440–469	Other (e.g. Recreational Therapy, Home Health Care, Service)
480–489	Clinics

The systems team initiated a preliminary study of problems, procedures, and information needs at CH. They gathered the following data:

In 1978, CH had a number of manual systems that each department had developed independently. Each department faced delays in getting information from other departments, and the information received was not usually complete or in the form desired. In addition, typical problems that occurred because of delay or lack of information follow:

1. Invoices were frequently paid more than once. Of 350 invoices paid per month, about 3% were paid twice in error. This necessitated considerable correspondence and additional clerical work.

2. Patient charges varied among patients because only a partial list of charge rates was kept and frequent changes were made.

3. About 17 patients' accounts were lost per month.

4. Inventories of medical supplies and drugs were maintained, but shortages of medical supply items frequently occurred.

5. The hospital dietician was supplied with incomplete records, often late, of classes of patients and diet requirements. As a result, it was very difficult to order food and prepare menus. It was often necessary to supply patients with incomplete meals or improper meal items because a "house diet" was sent to such patients. Part of the difficulty was caused when a patient was transferred to a different room and missed out on checking his desires on the daily menu form (see Figures 2 and 3).

6. Delays in releasing patients occurred because of billing delays. Approximately 1400 charges to patients' accounts were made daily (with delays and errors) and about 36 patients were discharged daily.

7. Personnel records were skimpy and not updated on a regular basis. No evaluation of training needs existed, and there was no educational

Figure 2

```
DIET REQUISITION FORM D3


DATE OF ADMISSION _____ DIAGNOSIS _____.
NEW DIET _____ CHANGE OF DIET _____ DISCHARGE _____
ROOM TRANS. FROM _____ TO _____ TIME TO BEGIN _____
BR. _____ LUNCH _____ DIN.. _____ DIET REQ. & INSTRUCTION _____
_____
_____

DATE:                    SIGNATURE                         R.N.
```

Figure 3

DIET ORDER

INSTRUCTIONS	
	1. PRINT ALL DIET ORDERS 2. LIST THE PATIENT'S LAST NAME FIRST 3. USE THE PROPER SECTION FOR EACH DIET ORDER 4. PREPARE IN DUPLICATE ORIGINAL-DIETARY, CARBON-NURSING

Floor ______________

Date ______________

Meal ______________

Prepared By ______________

DISCHARGES:

ROOM	NAME

TRANSFERS:

FROM	TO	NAME	DIET ORDER

NEW ADMISSIONS:

ROOM	NAME	DIET ORDER

SPECIAL REQUESTS (Visitation, Diet Instruction, Special Orders, etc.)

ROOM	NAME	REQUEST

CHANGE OF DIET:

ROOM	NAME	DIET ORDER

HOLD AND DELAYED MEALS:

ROOM	NAME	HOLD OR DELAY

NPO (SURGERY, NPO):

ROOM	NAME	REASON

policy or program. Information on absentee employees was not available.

8. The daily census of patients was prepared by the admitting office and circulated to all departments at midnight. This report was sometimes as much as six hours late and contained about 0.5% errors because it was compiled manually. Empty beds were reported by each nursing station at the end of the day shift. Some fragmentary records indicated bed occupancy in 1978 was distributed as shown in Table 2.

Table 2
Estimated
patient stay
in 1979

Number of Days	Percent
1-3	3
4-7	31
8-10	22
11-13	15
14-19	14
20-30	9
31-40	3
41-50	1
51-60	2
	100

9. Clinic scheduling involving patients, physicians, nursing services, and out-patients was notoriously poor.

10. One patient, a consultant in a hospital management consulting firm, wrote the hospital president after his release that a good scheduling system for laboratory, X-ray, and other ancillary services could shorten the average patient's stay by two days at CH.

11. Patient monitoring errors sometimes occurred. A current specific problem being given attention was duplication of blood-test requests. The nurse would read the patient's bed chart and order a blood test; the physician sometimes unwittingly filed a duplicate test. Another source of duplication involved nurses on two different shifts.

12. Analysis of the billing cycle showed the results in Table 3.

Table 3
Billing cycle

	Average No. of Days after Discharge That First Billing Was Submitted	Average No. of Days from First Billing to Receipt of First Payment
Medicare	17.9	36.1
Blue Cross	17.5	18.7
Commercial insurance	16.2	45.2
Self-pay	6	46.6

The preliminary analysis indicated that a computerized hospital information system (HIS) could assist decision making with respect to the following functions or processes:

1. *Lab data processing*. EKG analysis. Computer-assisted analysis of test results. Lab reporting at nursing stations. Posting of lab reports to patients' medical records and billing accounts.
2. *Registering*. Maintenance of files by medical subject such as psychiatric, stroke, heart, tumor, etc. Blood donor register. Poison data bank (manner, toxic effects, treatments, etc.). Drug bank (information on drugs).
3. *Administrative controls*. Patient transfer. Service scheduling printout of work to be done in and by each department for each work shift. Maintenance scheduling. Dietary planning and control (daily printout of each patient's menu and summary report for meal production planning). Inventory control for consumable and nonconsumable items. Census function and bed availability.
4. *Patient care records and control*. Although a form was currently used to maintain medical records of each patient manually, the study team was interested in storing such data for computerized analysis and aggregation for reports. Three of several typical input forms which the team had gathered are shown in Figures 4, 5, and 6. The essential data for each patient account are listed in Table 4 on page 566.

The team decided that eight subsystems could be developed and linked together by means of a single data bank. The systems were:

1. Patient diagnosis and treatment system
2. Patient record system
3. Patient scheduling and order system
4. Patient accounting system
5. Expenditure and general accounting system
6. Personnel system
7. General supportive services system
8. Management control system.

On the basis of these systems, it would appear that the *data file/function* matrix would be of the form shown in Figure 7 on page 567.

OTTAWA CIVIC HOSPITAL   **MEDICAL RECORD CODING SOURCE DOCUMENT**

1 2	ADMISSION NO.	8 9	10 SOCIAL INSURANCE NO. 18	19-20	AGE CODE:	1-HOURS	4-YEARS	21	22 AGE 23
C.C.						2-DAYS	5-100 PLUS		
1					0-NEW BORN	3-MONTH	6-UNKNOWN		

SEX AND MARTIAL STATUS CODE

0-MALE - SINGLE	5-FEMALE - SINGLE	24	25 30	31 36	37 40
1- MARRIED	6- MARRIED		ADMISSION DATE	DISCHARGE DATE	ADM. TIME
2- SEPARATED	7- SEPARATED				
3- DIVORCED	8- DIVORCED				
4- WIDOWED	9- WIDOWED				

ADMISSION STATUS

01-EMERGENCY	06-EMERG. SHORT STAY		43 48	ACCOMMODATION/PREV. ADM.
02-ELECTIVE	07-ELECTIVE SHORT STAY	41-42	FLOORS	1-PRIV. YES 5-ST. PAY YES	49
03-URGENT	08-URGENT SHORT STAY			2- NO 6- NO
04-SHORT STAY	09-EMERG. MATERNITY			3-S.P. YES 7-ST.W. YES
05-MATERNITY	10-ELECTIVE MATERNITY			4- NO 8- NO
	11-URGENT MATERNITY			

COND. ON DISCHARGE		AUTOPSY		— DEATH STATUS —				
1-ALIVE WITH APPROVAL	50	REQUESTED	51	UNDER 48 HOURS	OVER 48 HOURS	UNDER 48 HOURS IN O.R.	UNDER 48 HOURS POST OP	OVER 48 HOURS POST OP UNDER 11 DAYS	52
2-ALIVE AGAINST ADVICE		1-YES		0-AUTOPSY	2-AUTOPSY	4-AUTOPSY	6-AUTOPSY	8-AUTOPSY
3-ALIVE TRANSFERRED		2-NO		1-NO AUTOPSY	3-NO AUTOPSY	5-NO AUTOPSY	7-NO AUTOPSY	9-NO AUTOPSY
4-DEAD		3-UNKNOWN						

53	FINAL DIAGNOSIS	62	63	CAUSE OF DEATH	72	73 SERVICES 76	77	NOTE: ENTER 9 IN COL. 80 IF
	SNOP			SNOP				SECOND SHEET OR CARD
								IS USED

1		10 11 12	14 15	17 18	20 21	23 24	26 27	29 30	32 33	35 36	38 39	41 42	44 80
C.C.	PHYSICIANS NO PHY												
2													

1	CON-	10 11 12	14 15	17 18	20 21	23 24	26 27	29 30	32 33	35 36	38 39	41 42	44 80
C.C.	SULTANTS NO PHY												
3													

1		10	SNOP	20 21	SNOP	31 32	SNOP	42
C.C.	ASSOCIATE	43		53 54		64 65		75 80
4	DIAGNOSIS							

1		10	15 16	21 22	27 28	33 34	39	80
C.C.	COMPLICATIONS							
5								

1		10	15 16	21 22	27 28	33 34	39	80
C.C.	INFECTIONS							
6								

1		10	TISSUE CODE	DAY MO. YR.	25 26 SURGEON	TISSUE CODE	DAY MO. YR.	41 SURGEON
C.C.	OPERATIONS	42			57 58			73 80
7								

1		10	25 26	41
C.C.	OPERATIONS	42	57 58	73 80
7				

M.R. 74794 (REV. 10.69)

Figure 4

Figure 5

TOXICOLOGY

G 00762

PATIENT'S NAME

CHART COPY

040 TOXICOLOGY | DONE BY | DATE DONE

ACID PHOSPHATASE (SPERMINE)
ALCOHOL
AMPHETAMINE
ARSENIC
BARBITURATE
BROMIDE
CARBON MONOXIDE
CHLORAL HYDRATE
CHOLINESTERASE
CYANIDE
DARVON
DILANTIN
DILAUDID
DORIDEN
DRUG SCREENING
ELAVIL
HALLUCINATING DRUGS
HEAVY METALS SCREEN
LEAD
LIBRIUM
MEPROBAMATE
MERCURY
METHEMOGLOBIN
MORPHINE/HEROIN
PESTICIDES
PHENOTHIAZINES
PLACYDIL
POISON SURVEY
QUININE/QUINIDINE
SALICYLATE
SOLID DOSAGE ID
STRYCHNINE
THIN LAYER CHROM.

NAME · ADMIT NO. · ROOM NO. · AGE-SEX · DOC-TOR · NO.

SPECIMEN — BLOOD · URINE · GASTRIC · TISSUE · FOMITE · OTHER

TIME OUT

G00762

ROUTINE □ · STAT. □ · DATE ORDERED · WRITTEN BY

RESULTS

COMMUNITY HOSPITAL

Figure 6

| 421 | X-RAY SPECIALS BRCH NO. 481-4 | DONE BY | DATE DONE |

COMMUNITY HOSPITAL

MAMMOGRAM BILATERAL
MAMMOGRAM UNILATERAL
MYELOGRAM CERVICAL
MYELOGRAM COMPLETE
MYELOGRAM LUMBAR
MYELOGRAM THORACIC
PACEMAKER INSERTION
PELVIC ARTERIO SELECT-SUBSELEC
PERCUTANEOUS CHOLANGIOGRAM
POST REDUCTION FILMS-SURGERY
PULMONARY ANGIO BILAT SELECT
PULMONARY ANGIO UNILAT SELECT
RENAL ARTERIO UNILAT SELECT
RENAL VEIN BLOOD SAMPLING
RENAL VENOGRAM BILAT SELECT
RENAL VENOGRAM UNILAT SELECT
SALPINGOGRAM/HYSTEROSALPINGOGM
SEL BILAT EXTN ARTER-CEREBRAL
SELECT CAROTID ARTERIO UNILAT
SEL-CEREBL CAROTID ARTER BILAT
SELECT VERTEBRAL ANGIOGRAM
SIALOGRAPHY
SPENOPORTOGRAM
THORACIC AORTOGRAM
VENOGRAPHY INFERIOR VENA CAVA
VENOGRAPHY SUPERIOR VENA CAVA
* VISCERAL ARTERIO SUBSELECTIVE
VOIDING CYSTOURETHROGRAM

EXAM REQ. BY · PREVIOUS X-RAY NO. · X-RAY NO. · DATE ORDERED · DATE REPORTED

□ PRE-OP. □ ROUTINE · □ TODAY □ STAT.

X-RAY
SPECIALS
FILE COPY

565

Table 4 Essential data for each patient account

Identification Data	Service, Charge, and Payment Data
Room Number	Accommodations
Hospital Number	Intensive Care
Name	Self-Care
Address	Operating Room
Sex	Anesthesia
Date of Birth	Blood Administration
Bill to (Name and Address)	Pharmacy
Admission Date	Radiology
Time	Laboratory
Doctor	Medical, Surgical, and Central Supplies
Blue Cross Number	Physical Therapy
Social Security Number	Occupational Therapy
Other Insurance Company	Speech Therapy
Policy Date	Inhalation Therapy
Receivable Classification	Other
Previous Admission Year	

Medical Data:

Admitting Diagnosis
Discharge Date
Discharge or Current Diagnosis
Surgical Procedures

Insurance Data:

This section will vary depending on the type of insurance the patient carries. For Blue Cross and most commercial insurance, coverage codes are available. The computer can refer to the codes in the drum storage and compute the payment due from each party. Unique cases must be computed separately by the cashier at discharge. Medicare patients must be handled differently. The data that must be in storage for Medicare are listed below:

Medicare Insurance Data:

Effective Date—Hospital Insurance
Effective Date—Medical Insurance
Hospital Days Remaining—Full
Hospital Days Remaining—Coinsurance
Lifetime Reserve Days Remaining
Medical Plan Deductible—Met or Not Met
Remaining Inpatient Deductible
Pints Remaining Blood Deductible
Extended Care Facility Days Remaining—Full
Extended Care Facility Days Remaining—Coinsurance
Three Days Hospital Stay Requirement—Met or Not Met
14 Days Transfer Requirement—Met or Not Met
Home Health Representative Visits Remaining—Hospital Insurance
Home Health Representative Visits Remaining—Medical Insurance
Psychiatric Days Remaining

Source: Belverd Needles, Jr., "A Single Information Flow System for Hospital Data Processing," **Management Services,** September—October 1969.

Figure 7
Hospital information system, file/function interaction matrix

MAJOR SYSTEMS AND SUBSYSTEMS	Patient billing	Patient master	Utilization	Bed reservation	Clinic appointment schedule	Physician availability	Nurse availability	Pharmacy inventory	Central service disposable	Central service reusable	Pricing	Professional services	Payroll	Personnel	Cost center	Accounts receivable	Accounts payable	Dietary	Data processing management
Patient diagnosis and treatment																			
Patient records																			
Patient scheduling and ordering																			
Inpatient census																			
Clinic appointment																			
Patient ordering																			
Patient accounting																			
General accounting																			
Budget																			
Payroll and labor reporting																			
General ledger																			
Commodity and nonpatient related service accounting																			
Equipment control																			
Cost accounting																			
Production analysis and report																			
Personnel																			
General support																			
Dietary																			
Data processing management																			
Management information																			

THE DESIGN

As the first step in the conceptual design, the team decided to make a list of major reports which the hospital administration could use in making planning and control decisions. Second, it would list detailed reports which the medical staff and services departments could use for operations. Then general subsystem flow diagrams would be prepared based in the data file/function matrix and the decision/information needs. The team felt that computer hardware and software requirements could then be established.

1. Identify five major problems that exist in Community Hospital and arrange them in the order in which they should be solved.

2. Prepare a general systems-design flow chart that links or integrates the eight subsystems that are identified by the systems team.

3. Prepare a data file/function matrix by completing the format in Fig. 7.

4. Prepare a diagram to show the concept for a computerized patient billing system. (Essentially, show inputs and outputs of the systems.) Discuss objectives of such a system for CH.

5. Draw a detailed flow chart for one of the eight subsystems identified by the systems team.

6. Identify one or more alternative computer configurations that Community Hospital might use.

7. Provide a rough estimate of the design and installation costs.

8. For the eight subsystems identified by the systems team, list the management benefits expected in terms of improved planning, decision making, and control.

9. Discuss why you agree or disagree with the team's idea of introducing the systems one at a time instead of all at once.

10. Discuss the support or lack of support to top management planning provided by the proposed "MIS."

SUGGESTED READINGS FOR THE COMMUNITY HOSPITAL CASE

BALL, M. J., "An Overview of Total Medical Information Systems," *Methods of Information in Medicine,* April 1971.

BOLDT, BEN I., JR., "Financial Modeling: A Must for Today's Hospital Management," *Hospital Cost Management,* Summer 1979.

DALTON, EDWARD F., JOHN S. MORRISON, and ROBERT E. DIGGS, *Hospital Financial Management Concepts,* GE20-0466-0. White Plains, N.Y.: IBM, 1975.

HANCOCK, SIDNEY, "An Approach to Hospital Data Processing Development," *Management Accounting,* March 1978.

HANSEN, JAMES V., "Progress in Health Care Systems," *Journal of Systems Management,* April 1975.

"Hospitals Trim off their Staffing Fat," *Business Week,* May 16, 1977.

MICHELA, WILLIAM, "Defining and Analyzing Costs—A Statistical Approach," *Hospital Financial Management,* January 1975.

PEARSON, DAVE, "Payment Patterns," *Hospital Financial Management,* February 1978.

Hospital Financial Management Concepts, GE20-0466-0. White Plains, N.Y.: IBM, 1975.

TAYLOR, JAMES D., "Control System Ensures Documentation of Care," *Medical Records,* December 1, 1976.

Strategic Planning for MIS at GTE Sylvania Incorporated*

GTE Sylvania Incorporated is owned by GTE Products Corporation, a wholly owned subsidiary of General Telephone & Electronics Corporation. The Western Division of Sylvania's Electronic Systems Group, located in Mountain View, Cal., employed about 1700 people in 1974. It designs, manufactures, and sells electronic product lines such as

Information processing systems
Radio-frequency equipment
Receiving systems
Security systems
Lasers

The organization chart for ESG-WD in 1974 is shown in Figure 1 on the following page.

*Data for this case were supplied by Gene Giannotti, Manager, Computer Services, GTE Sylvania Incorporated, Electronic Systems Group Western Division, and edited by the author to give recognition to Mr. Giannotti's role in strategic planning for MIS.

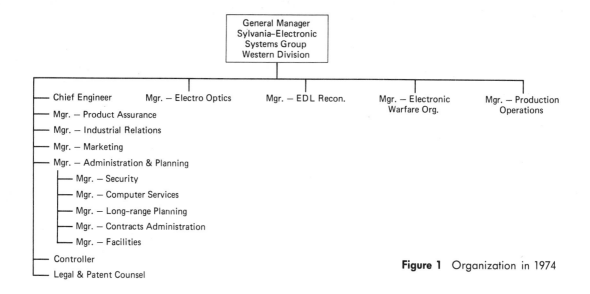

Figure 1 Organization in 1974

BUSINESS SYSTEMS ENVIRONMENT

In the early 1970s, the usual course of development for management information systems was to add hardware and data processing staff whenever new computer applications appeared desirable. Strategic planning for MIS was unheard of. ESG-WD was no exception.

As Gene Giannotti, Manager, Computer Services, for ESG-WD put it in September, 1974:

> Business systems for ESG-WD evolved over the years in providing comprehensive service in the following areas:
>
>> Cost Accumulations (labor, material and other charges)
>> Cost History
>> Commitments
>> Cost Estimating
>> Bid & Proposal Management
>> Technical Data Control
>> Personnel Administration
>> Purchasing & Sub-contracts Administration
>> Inventory Control
>> Purchased Material Quality Assurance
>> Electronic Instrumentation & Control
>> Classified Material Control
>> Library Document Control
>
> To support the maintenance of these systems, the current staffing level is 4 Analysts (and 1 open requisition), 5 Programmers, 1 Programming Aide and 1 Data Base Administrator. While a significant portion of the business data is already captured and reported by automated systems, a number of areas remain untouched.

Furthermore, external influences (such as the demand for contracts supported by C/SCSC reporting) require that significant developments to our portfolio of systems be made in the near future.

EMERGING PROBLEMS

The rapid growth in size and complexity of operations at ESG-WD put considerable pressure on management in planning and decision making. The lack of information, information delays, and information errors were increasing because of the ad hoc approach to adding data processing equipment and applications. Table 1 lists major problems which were evident at the time.

These problems led to

User dissatisfaction

Error-prone systems

Gaps in data flow

Late and inadequate reports

Manual backup to computer systems

High level of maintenance on existing systems

CONCEPT OF LONG-RANGE MIS PLAN

Although the concept of corporate strategic planning had developed rapidly since the 1950s, this concept had apparently by-passed data processing and computer acquisition.[1] Mr. Giannotti, however, early recognized that the investment in

[1]The first two books on this subject were Paul Siegle, *Strategic Planning of Management Information Systems* (New York: Petrocelli, 1975), and Ephraim R. McLean and John V. Soden, eds., *Strategic Planning for MIS* (New York: John Wiley, 1977).

Table 1 Information systems problems, 1973

Problems	Example or Evidence of Problem
Information systems development plans are not always consistent with the division's business plans.	Plans for manufacturing system while business was essentially research and development
Lack of integrated systems	Finance system did not know of commitments generated by purchasing system.
Lack of visibility as to where we are going (can go or should go) with information systems	A quarterly budget was the only MIS planning activity.
Inadequate system for setting priorities and applying Computer Services resources	Each major user had his own priorities. There was no mechanization for resolving conflicts.
Lack of management-level information from systems which were designed for operational functions	Top-level management reports were manually prepared from detailed computer data.
Inadequate use of new technology and capability in computer systems	Most systems were batch oriented. Even database systems lacked on-line update capability.

MIS resources should be approached the same as any other strategic decision. Therefore, in 1974, with the blessing of the general manager, his staff conducted interviews with key line and staff managers to obtain their perspectives. The people from the following offices were interviewed:

Chief engineer	EOO
Controller	EDL
Industrial relations	EWO
Administration and planning	Product assurance
Marketing	Production operations

The outcome of this study was the 100-page proposed long-range plan for MIS of 1974. The Table of Contents of this report is shown in Figure 2. This plan listed 56 present and proposed information systems in the format shown in Table 2 and Figures 3 and 4. It concluded with an analysis of costs, benefits, and cost avoidance for each major group of information systems. The response is indicated in a memo by D. A. Wolf, Mgr., Production Operations: "I think you have made a great start towards putting together a coherent long term plan and I would like to applaud the efforts."

Figure 2 Table of Contents

COMPUTER SERVICES DEPARTMENT

1974 Long Range Plan for Information Systems Development

		Contents	Page
PART I.		Plan Description	
		Purpose	1
Chapter			
	1.	Introduction	2
	2.	Systems Concepts	4
	3.	Criteria for Selection of Applications	10
	4.	Criteria for Selection of Systems Development Priorities	21
	5.	Development Plan	22
PART II.		Supporting Schedules	
Exhibit			
	A.	Environment Analysis	29
	B.	Application Descriptions and Functional Relationships	36
	C.	System Benefits	88
	D.	Development Costs	95
	E.	Persons Interviewed	96
	F.	Development Groups	98
	G.	Schedule	102

Table 2 List of existing and potential applications

GROUP 6. – MANUFACTURING APPLICATIONS

Application	Prime User	New/Existing	Description/Comments
Product Data System	Manufacturing Quality Assurance Tech Data & Controls	New	This system provides storage and retrieval of all manufacturing, quality, and procurement data for make and buy components.
			For make components: Routing Time Standards Work Centers Alternate Routine & Work Centers Manufacturing Lead Times Commodity Class Quality Requirements —Inspection Routing —Inspection Characteristics
			For buy components: Recommended Vendors Inspection Requirements Method of Purchase Data Requirements
Material Requirements Planning	Manufacturing	New	Using the Master Schedule as a base, Material Requirements Planning develops time-phased requirements for each assembly, sub-assembly, and component. The Tech Data System is used for explosion of the end-item to its component parts. Where a Bill of Material does not exist, the quasi-bill of material generated at proposal time is used for a "rough" pass.
Detailed Schedule Planning	Manufacturing	New	Makes the requirements schedules of Material Requirements Planning a reality by planning the capacity level (manpower & equipment) necessary to meet them. Generates shop load [support function load (e.g., drafting) if required], and determines start dates, calculates priorities and develops order release dates.

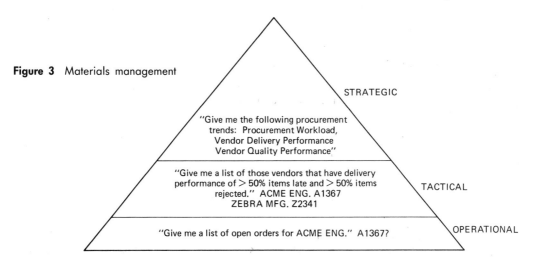

Figure 3 Materials management

STRATEGIC

"Give me the following procurement trends: Procurement Workload, Vendor Delivery Performance Vendor Quality Performance"

"Give me a list of those vendors that have delivery performance of > 50% items late and > 50% items rejected." ACME ENG. A1367 ZEBRA MFG. Z2341

TACTICAL

"Give me a list of open orders for ACME ENG." A1367?

OPERATIONAL

Figure 4

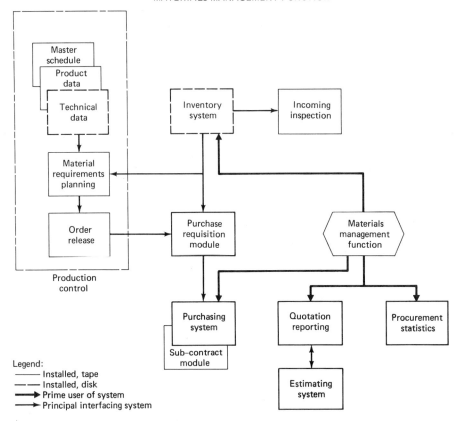

THE AD HOC COMMITTEE
ON MANAGEMENT INFORMATION SYSTEMS

As a result of the 1974 proposed strategic plan for MIS at the Western Division, D. O. Kiser, the General Manager, decided that it was time to put his weight behind this type of planning. R. M. Silver, Manager of Administration and Planning, stated in a memo of April 16, 1975, to Kiser: "The key is to obtain general management acceptance and commitment to whatever the plan is so that it is not misconstrued as being a computer services plan." Selected key managers would have to become involved in, and held responsible for, the long-range decisions. Such decisions would have to be made in the light of the total long-range plan for the Western Division.

Kiser, in a letter of July 7, 1975, appointed a committee of *full-time members* as follows:

Phil Gugliotta, Proposal Center Manager, Chairman
Bill Maryeski, Engineering Manager, EDL Reconnaissance
Jim Alsup, Manufacturing Systems, Production Operations
Bob Burke, Cost Control Manager, Finance

In his letter, which was widely distributed throughout the organization, Kiser concluded, "The amount of money being spent by the Division for management information systems is substantial, and it is essential that we receive maximum value. I know I can rely on your support and cooperation in working with the committee toward achieving that objective."

By September 5, 1975, the Ad Hoc Committee had completed its research and deliberations and issued its final report. Basically, this report identified three major systems: (1) Manufacturing and material, (2) product assurance, and (3) financial and administrative. These were broken down into a total of 30 management information subsystems, as shown in Table 3 (page 576) and Figure 5.

The bulk of the report contained an analysis and proposal (essentially a work package) for each of the 30 systems. An example of such a subsystem proposal is given in Figure 6.

In addition, a schedule for implementation of the plan for the years 1976 and 1977 was presented. The report concluded with a number of specific recommendations for a permanent steering committee to evaluate progress and changing priorities. "The present system of accommodating 'squeaking wheels' can be disadvantageous to our total Division requirements," the report stated. One final area for investigation was the number of reports produced and distributed.

Figure 5

MANAGEMENT INFORMATION SYSTEMS
ARCHITECTURAL DEPENDENCIES

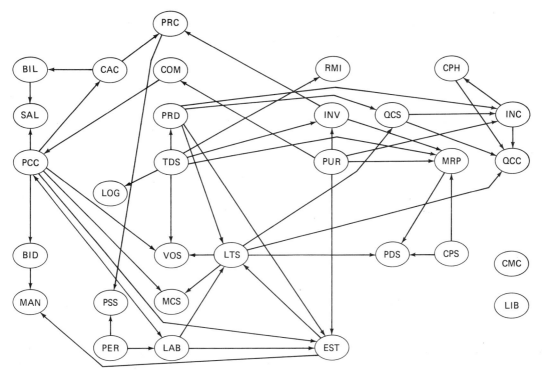

Table 3 The thirty MIS subsystems

	Management Information Systems	
BID	— Bid and Proposal (1)	MCS — Management Control System (3)
BIL	— Billing System (1)	MRP — Material Requirements Planning (5)
CAC	— Contract Administration Closeout (5)	PCC — Project Cost Control (1)
CMC	— Classified Material Control (4)	PDS — Production Detailed Schedule (5)
COM	— Commitments (1)	PER — Personnel Management (1)
CPH	— Component Performance History (5)	PRC — Property Control (5)
CPS	— Consolidated Projects Schedule (5)	PRD — Product Data (5)
EST	— Estimating (1)	PSS — Property Services System (1)
INC	— Incoming Inspection System (5)	PUR — Purchasing (1)
INV	— Inventory (2)	QCC — Quality Costs (5)
LAB	— Labor System (1)	QCS — QC Statistics (5)
LIB	— Library (4)	RMI — Reliability/Maintainability Interface (5)
LOG	— Logistics (1)	SAL — Sales (1)
LTS	— Labor Tracking System (1)	TDS — Technical Data (2)
MAN	— Manpower Forecasting (5)	VOS — Value of Shipments Reporting (5)

Notes: (1) Existing system (tape)—requires rework.
(2) Existing system (disk)—requires modification.
(3) Existing system (disk)—can be absorbed in the data base as is.
(4) Existing system—essentially free-standing and not a data-base candidate.
(5) New system—data-base candidate.

Figure 6
Plan and work package for an MIS subsystem

QUALITY COST SYSTEM (QCC)

Synopsis

QCC system would provide management with analysis of quality costs (labor and material) expended versus resultant product quality. Its purpose is to identify, measure, control, and minimize quality costs to achieve product quality objectives at optimum costs. The system would achieve these objectives within the framework of MIL-Q-9858A, a contractual requirement.

Features
    Analyzes and reports product quality costs
    Provides means of optimizing quality costs

Prerequisites
    Component Performance History
    Incoming Inspection
    Quality Control Statistics
    Labor Tracking System

Development Costs

User	2 man-months	
Systems Analysis	3 man-months	$ 6,750
Programming	6 man-months	13,500
Computer		8,000
Total		$28,250

Estimated Annual Cost Savings

	Soft	Hard
Reduced quality costs	$30,000	
Reduced manual reporting	4,000	
Total	$34,000	-0-

Figure 7 Management information systems implementation

SYSTEM	DEVELOPMENT COSTS	"HARD" COST SAVINGS	"SOFT" COST SAVINGS
1. INV – Inventory	25K	29K	16K
1. PUR – Purchasing	57	47	52
1. TDS – Technical Data	60	20	3
2. MCS – Mgmt Control	41	0	0
3. COM – Commitments	17	0	36
3. LAB – Labor System	28	8	30
3. PCC – Project Cost Control	91	62	276
4. CPS – Con. Proj. Schedule	58	20	150
5. CPH – Comp.Perf.History	41	85	15
5. INC – Incoming Inspection	31	0	41
5. QCS – QC Statistics	19	25	5
6. MRP – Mat'l Req.Planning	59	42	25
6. PRD – Product Data	44	40	0
7. PDS – Prod.Detailed Sch.	50	45	45
8. LTS – Labor Tracking	28	0	35
9. EST – Estimating	42	82	0
10. BID – Bid and Proposal	22	0	30
11. PRC – Property Control	25	30	8
12. PSS – Prop. Services	0	0	0
12. QCC – Quality Costs	28	0	34
12. RMI – Rel/Main Interface	20	90	0
13. MAN – Manpower Forecast	42	0	50
13. SAL – Sales	38	0	15
14. LOG – Logistics	37	0	35
15. BIL – Billing	18	0	15
15. CAC – Con.Admin.C/O	9	0	2
16. PER – Personnel Mgmt	41	0	4
17. CMC – Class.Mat'l Control	18	0	2
17. LIB – Library	38	0	7
17. VOS – Value of Ship.Rptg.	30	0	10
TOTAL	**1,057K**	**625K**	**941K**

Schedule columns span 1975 (4Q), 1976, 1977, 1978 (quarterly), and 1979, 1980, 1981. For 1979–1981: FIRM PLANS NOT YET ESTABLISHED.

Staffing (by quarter):

	1975 4Q	1976 1Q	2Q	3Q	4Q	1977 1Q	2Q	3Q	4Q
DATA-BASE ADMINISTRATOR									
SYSTEMS ANALYSTS	2	3	3	3	3	3	3	3	3
PROGRAMMERS	3	3	5	5	5	5	5	5	5
(ANALYSTS/PROGRAMMERS)	3	3	4	6	10	6	6	3	3
ISSR's AND MAINTENANCE	5	5	5	5	10	5	5	5	5
TOTAL									

The 1974 plan was quite specific in terms of objectives, systems, and schedule, and the Ad Hoc Committee Report elaborated further on plans and criteria for priorities. The general manager directed the Computer Services Department to issue an updated plan which followed the contents of the previous plans. The updated plan was completed in March, 1976.

The work packages and cost estimates in the 1976 plan remained the same as for the Ad Hoc Committee Report. The schedule, however, had shifted from completion of projects in 1976–77 to the schedule shown in Figure 7.

1. ESG-WD started incorporating long-range MIS in the division plan only in 1974. Although the concept of strategic planning has received emphasis since the 1950s, few companies even today prepare a strategic plan for MIS. Why does this condition exist?

2. Discuss the relationship between the ESG-WD organization and the 30 information systems.

3. Are the problems of information deficiencies at ESG-WD to which the long-range plan is addressed much different from those at other companies? Why or why not?

4. Relate the long-range MIS plan to the five components of strategy discussed in Chapter 5.

5. Why do you think that the plan which appeared in 1976 was so similar to the 1974 plan and the Ad Hoc Committee plan? What was the principal difference? Why do you believe that this difference arose?

6. Add the subsystems identifiers to the three major systems shown below, using Table 3 and Fig. 5 as your sources. Dashed circles represent support systems.

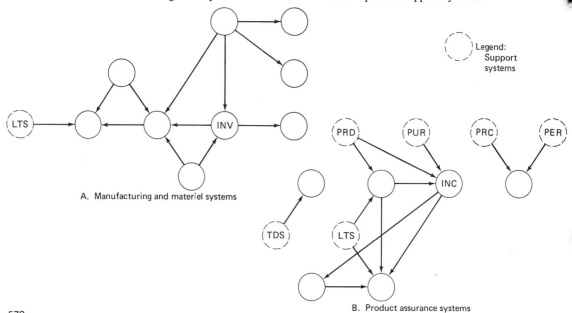

A. Manufacturing and materiel systems

B. Product assurance systems

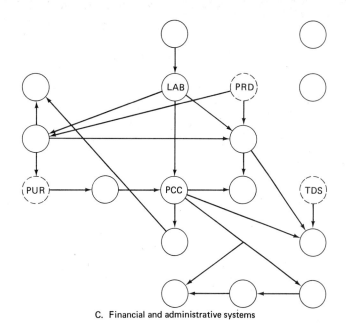

C. Financial and administrative systems

7. Redraw the triangle on a full page and place each item of information listed below in the correct section.

a. Capital expenditures
b. Gross factory requirements
c. Business area cash needs
d. Forecast of revenue for business area
e. Gross facility requirements for business area
f. Marginal contributors
g. Task cost data
h. Division P&L
i. Business area P&L
j. Cost to complete

k. Forecast of revenue for division
l. Return on investment
m. Account data
n. Item cost data
o. Business area return on investment
p. Division cash needs
q. Cost YTD
r. Utilization of capacity
s. Forecast of division revenue
t. Business area capital expenditures
u. Business area utilization

8. Assess the development of long-range planning for MIS at the Western Division. Appraise the nature of the plan as best you can from the limited material given in this case.

Van Dam, Inc.

SCENE 1. *Brooks Van Dam, President and General Manager, in conference with Vite Gonzalez, Marketing Manager*

Brooks Van Dam, tall, white-haired, and distinguished, rose from behind his desk facing Vite. Dressed in his navy blue Bill Blass blazer, gray houndstooth trousers, and royal blue Gucci shoes, he turned slowly and walked to the floor-to-wall window overlooking the grounds and pond below. Hands clasped behind his back, as he watched the ducks swimming single file, he said, "Vite, I like to keep all my ducks in a row. Our sales have grown 15% in the past year, and that's great. This year we seem to be in a state of confusion. More orders are coming in, but more orders are being cancelled. Grimes (Manager of Manufacturing) has been telling me that he can't make up good production schedules because sales forecasts and booked orders come in too late and erratically. He also says he has to override his production schedules several times a month with rush orders your department insists on. Is this true?"

Vite swallowed, a lump in his throat and perspiration beading his forehead. He recalled that his predecessor had been given two hours to clean out his desk after "resigning."

"Well, sir," he said, "this sudden expansion *has* posed some problems of information. We don't have the staff or time to prepare our sales forecasts as well as we'd like. Our order processing is being done manually still, and I think that we should put the computer to work on it."

"Vite," said BVD, "your saying that you need better information confirms my belief. In fact, last week I hired a woman for a new position of Manager of Management Information Systems. She'll be with us next week and will be around to see you."

"Whooee, it sure is dark in here!" Hans exclaimed. "Now, what is it you wanted to talk about, Jim?"

"Hans, I think we've got a real problem at the plant. Hans . . . Hans . . . did you hear what I said?"

"Oh yeah, Jim," Hans replied, turning his gaze from the gyrations of the performers on the small stage. "What's up?"

"What's up is that we've been having a lot of orders cancelled because of time and cost overruns," Grimes went on. "I realize that Vite's lousy forecasts are part of the problem, but on engineered products your gang seems to be looking for perfection in eternity. I'm not exactly innocent either. We have so many orders, overrides, and parts not available that we can't get a good materials system going. I can't help but wonder if, with Fuller (Manager of Accounting) tying up the computer all the time, we shouldn't get another computer to help us out.

"Jim, we ought to work on that. I can't get information on the 150 projects going on in time to keep them under control. And if we could get more computer time for computations besides, we could get design specs to you on time. By the way, Vite told me yesterday that the old man hired an MIS manager, Delphi Jones."

BACKGROUND OF VAN DAM, INC.

Van Dam, Inc., was founded in 1947 by the grandfather of the current owner and president. VDI started making some simple aircraft instruments in a garage in Ft. Lauderdale, Florida. As the company grew over the years, it found it necessary to relocate, and it built its own plant on land that was then very cheap (1950).

At the time we are concerned with, the firm manufactured three classes of closely related products:

Products	1979 Sales (millions of dollars)
1. Electrical and electronic instruments, stock items	4.8
2. Instrumentation systems, custom engineered	8.3
3. Electronic testing devices and systems, custom engineered	7.1
	$20.2

VDI employed about 1650 people. The organization chart is shown in Fig. 1. No functional or position descriptions existed. Three years earlier 1300 people were employed, generating, on the average, $13,100 per employee. Sales of stock items generally followed the fluctuations of general business conditions.

Figure 1 Organization of Van Dam, Inc.

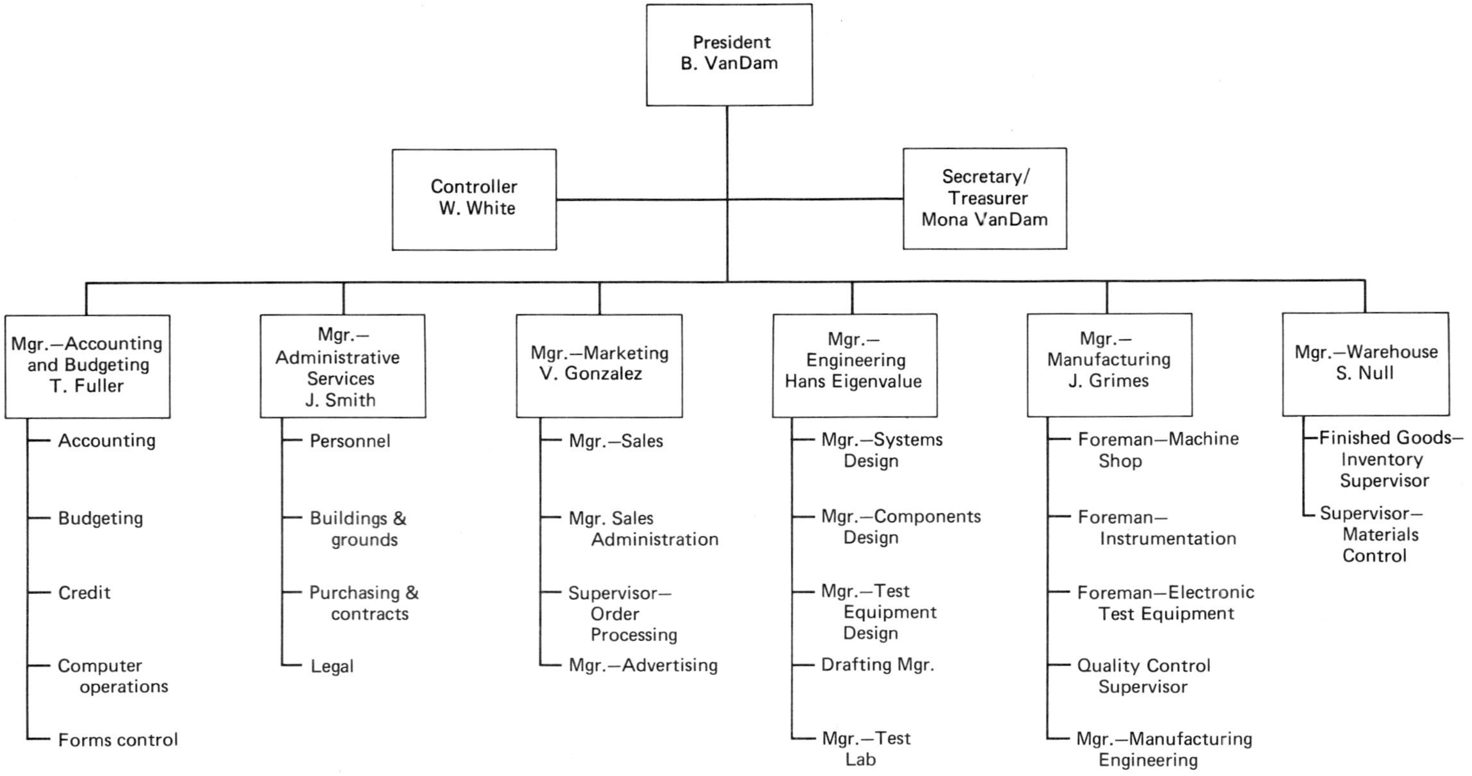

Sales of engineered items did not follow any particular pattern that Gonzalez could determine, but the orders were usually large ($30,000 to $200,000) and placed a heavy burden on engineering and manufacturing. The company usually had a backlog of six months of orders.

Brooks Van Dam, a Yale graduate with an English major, was an aloof, formal, courteous person who depended upon his key managers to get things done. He rarely interfered with their work, but those who let things slip were quickly replaced. Some managers were now the subjects of such thoughts.

DELPHI JONES

Delphi Jones, 28, had obtained a degree in general engineering. With the encouragement of D. W. Karger, who was then Dean of the School of Management at Rensselaer Polytechnic Institute, she applied for and received a scholarship for the management engineering program. She obtained her master's degree with a straight-A record. Subsequently she obtained a position as project planning manager in a high-technology firm near Boston. At one point she was assigned to a special team to develop an MIS for the company. Van Dam heard of her through a management consultant and hired her for $33,000 per year plus the company's usual executive bonus.

She spent her first two weeks at VDI studying the company and meeting various people in the organization. Jones then arranged to interview key managers to explore their problems and needs. She also made arrangements for a secretary and technician as part of her staff. Some highlights of her interviews follow.

Temporarily she reported to Brooks Van Dam. When her study ended she was to make a recommendation for her organization and reporting relationships.

BILL BUFFUN (PERSONNEL)

Delphi arranged, through the manager of administrative services, an interview with Bill Buffun, the personnel manager. Buffun, 60, a former accountant and military supply officer, had 15 years of experience as the dean of a small college of business at a state university. He had been with VDI for the past ten years. He saw his job primarily as that of keeping the factory workers happy.

When Jones asked if he had established any procedures for hiring, transfers, or promotions, he replied, "No, we are one big family here, and we just work things out as they come along. It sure saves a lot of paperwork." Jones than asked if he had ever considered putting worker profiles in a computer base for use in filling openings and promoting. "No, we don't believe you can computerize people. Accounting uses the computer for payroll and keeping track of employee benefits. This is how the modern companies use the computer." Delphi learned further that manpower forecasts were not prepared except by individual managers for their operating plans. That is, there was no comprehensive integrated forecast of the work force by job classification.

VITE GONZALEZ (MARKETING)

When Delphi met with Vite and explained her purpose as that of helping him develop a better information system, Vite was enthusiastic.

"You're just what we've needed here. I don't have the time or staff to develop a good scanning and forecasting group," he exclaimed. "Also, our order processing and inventory systems are a mess. We've been growing so rapidly in the last few years that we don't have time to overhaul them. Nobody knows anything about computers except Don Ali, head of computer operations. I think accounting is holding him incommunicado. We're still using forms and procedures designed over ten years ago."

"I see," answered Delphi, when Vite appeared to run down. "What kind of information would you like to have to help you with planning, as well as control?"

"Well, I think an analysis of product trends, identification of potential customer groups, and analysis of sales would help a lot. Also, we would like to be able to price better on engineered products by getting better estimates of engineering costs and manufacturing costs earlier. Right now, we quote high to be safe and lose a lot of business."

With regard to control, Vite explained that the main efforts were to control sales expenses and meet sales quotas. Accounting supplied data on historical sales expenses along with a "par" established by Gonzalez and an average for each expense computed by accounting. Vite said, "I treat our salesmen and saleswomen as professionals. I let them know what we are trying to do, give them feedback on how they're doing, and I find that they respond by themselves in almost all cases."

After further discussion, Delphi obtained permission to interview members of the marketing department and left.

HANS EIGENVALUE (ENGINEERING)

Educated in Germany, Dr. Eigenvalue (53) had worked on U.S. satellite programs for nine years. He had been with VDI for eight years and was considered very innovative and avant garde.

"Well, Ms. Jones, what can I do for you?" he greeted her on her visit to his office.

"I'm hoping that I can help you and you will help me with this task," she replied. "I've been assigned to help all managers develop better information systems. As you may know, I was a project programming manager for over five years. I'm wondering if you feel that you need better information for your planning and control."

Hans then explained the problems he was having in tracking and controlling over 100 projects at a time. He was aware of project programming systems, but he never seemed to have time or anybody available to set up such a system. As for change orders and updating of parts lists—this was becoming a nightmare.

JIM GRIMES (MANUFACTURING)

Jim Grimes, 48, had attended a local university for one year and dropped out because he "didn't like theory." After various odd jobs over the years, he had started with VDI as a production clerk. As the company grew he rose gradually over 15 years to become head of manufacturing. He had held this position for ten years.

Grimes greeted Ms. Jones with a big smile. "Hi, little lady, what can I do for you?" Jones sensed that Grimes was not the kind of person she would expect to find picketing for ERA, so she tried to establish a professional relationship at once.

"Good morning, Mr. Grimes. As Mr. Van Dam has informed his staff, my function is to help line management develop an improved companywide information system. Our approach is to identify areas where managers believe they could improve results if they had better information to work with. At this time I would like to identify areas in manufacturing where you believe better reporting would help you. Second, I would like your permission to interview your key personnel to determine the flow of information as it is related to operations."

Grimes' inherent resistance to outside help lessened in view of the growing problems he was having. He remarked that the large Gantt board used for production scheduling appeared inadequate. Jones left feeling that she would get reluctant cooperation.

STEVE NULL (WAREHOUSE)

Steve Null had originally worked in purchasing. As the company developed its lines of stock items, he was put in charge of a small warehouse. Since he had been responsible for purchasing materials and components in his purchasing job, he was given responsibility for inventory control of both incoming goods and finished goods. He felt somewhat uncomfortable with the responsibility for controlling materials for manufacturing.

When Delphi interviewed Null, she found him eager to develop an information system that would allow him to reduce inventory and control costs.

TERESA FULLER (ACCOUNTING)

Teresa Fuller, 38, upon graduation from high school, had gone directly to work for VDI as a clerk in accounts receivable. She took night courses in accounting at the local university over the years to improve her opportunities. Presently she was taking her first course in management.

From an interview, Delphi gained several impressions. First, the local university taught at a very low level. Second, Fuller resented a young woman coming into the company at such a high salary. Third, Fuller was very defensive about her operation. Fourth, she was to going to hang on to the computer and run it her way with her dying breath.

After Jones completed exploratory interviews, she prepared a plan of action:

1. Conduct interviews with lower-level personnel and draw up a description of the information flow within the company.
2. Analyze the forms and reports.
3. Identify principal information needs.
4. Identify operating systems.
5. Prepare a description of the current information system.
6. Design an improved concept of an MIS. Meet with managers to obtain their revisions.
7. Conduct the detailed design of the MIS.
8. Obtain management approval of the detailed design and implement it.

ANALYSIS

Delphi continued with a series of interviews with people at all levels. She identified a set of systems as shown in Fig. 2. All operations in the systems were performed manually except in the accounting and budgeting systems. Engineering obtained some computer time for lengthy routine calculations.

Marketing

Gonzalez obtained reports of sales by product from accounting reports. From time to time, a special study of sales by customer and area was made. This involved manual tabulation of sales orders, so it was not done more than once a year. Gonzalez would have liked to have more current information about customers as well as additional information, such as cumulative sales by customer and by product.

Marketing identified stock items by its own letter and number system because the engineering codes extended to six digits. For example, a certain tachometer was advertised as the T 121 model.

Order Processing

Orders were received from salespeople; from customer by phone, letter, and wire; and from the purchasing and contracts department. In the latter case, contract agents and engineers negotiated the specifications and price for products which required research and development. Thus the order which went to order processing was in the form of a contract attached to the customer's standard purchase order.

The supervisor of order processing prided himself on the simplicity of his system. "We have cut paperwork to the absolute minimum," he boasted. With patient probing, Delphi discovered that there were no flow charts or written

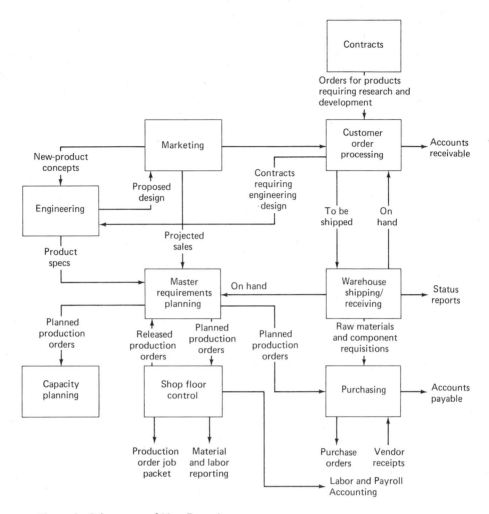

Figure 2 Subsystems of Van Dam, Inc.

procedures for the process. The group issued no reports to management. There was no editing of sales orders going to the warehouse. As a result, the warehouse or manufacturing would often have to trace back the customer's full address, stock numbers, or illegible entries on sales orders prepared by salespersons. The credit department complained that it was overworked to process an average of 180 sales orders a day; many of them were for amounts less than $500.

The open order file was out of date and inaccurate, because there was no system for handling back orders conveniently in updating the file. There was no way to determine the time between receipt of an order or shipment without an individual investigation, so that trends in service went undetected.

Delphi prepared the flow chart of the existing process in Figure 3. A copy of the sales order form is shown in Figure 4.

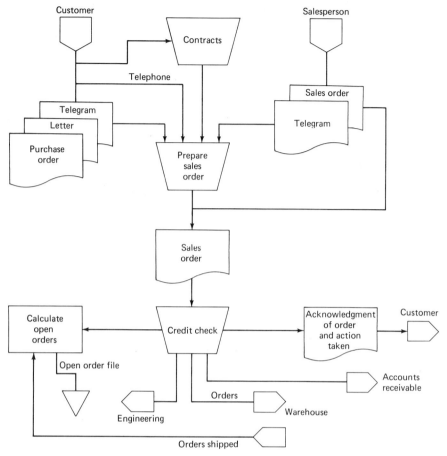

Figure 3 Order processing

Accounting

Ms. Fuller informed Delphi that the computer made it possible to keep the accounts in good order. Payroll, A/R, and A/P were handled promptly and accurately. Delphi asked about the audit trail with the new computerized system. Fuller was momentarily silent. Then she replied, "Now that we have the computer working so well, we don't anticipate mistakes. We don't need to audit the work that the computer does."

One of the flow charts Delphi obtained from Fuller was the payroll system in Figure 5.

Gordie Bell told Delphi that his concern was limited to accounting forms only. He was responsible for the design, analysis, and inventory control of about 53 forms. He estimated that there were about 100 other forms in use throughout the company. These were developed by the supervisors as required. Such forms were often mimeo or ditto runs rather than printed forms. All forms were kept in

Figure 4 Sales Order

```
┌─────────────────────────────────────────────────────────────────────┐
│ VAN DAM, INC.                        Sales Order # _____   │
│ 18422 209th Street                       Date      _____   │
│ Ft. Lauderdale, Florida 33316                                         │
│                                      Salesman # _____   │
│                                                                       │
│ Customer _____        │
│                                                                       │
│ Address _____        │
│                                                                       │
│        City _____ State _____ Zip _____    │
│                                                                       │
│ Phone _____                                         │
├─────────────────────────────────────────────────────────────────────┤
│ If custom designed, attach customer's drawings and specifications.    │
│ Special instructions:                                                 │
│                                                                       │
│                                                                       │
│                                                                       │
├─────────────────────────────────────────────────────────────────────┤
│ For stock items only                                                  │
│                                                                       │
│ Stock No. _____          Terms _____            │
│                                                                       │
│ Description _____          Date required _____      │
│                                                                       │
│ Quantity _____                                            │
│                                                                       │
│ Price/unit _____                                            │
│                                                                       │
│ Total price _____                                            │
├─────────────────────────────────────────────────────────────────────┤
│                           Circle              Customer                │
│ Transportation Method      one    Deliver     pick-up      Install    │
├─────────────────────────────────────────────────────────────────────┤
│ Remarks: _____        │
│          _____        │
│                                                                       │
│ Authorized _____         Approval _____         │
└─────────────────────────────────────────────────────────────────────┘
```

the same stockroom. Many were over ten years old and covered with dust. Inventory control consisted of ordering several dozen boxes of forms when it was obvious that the supply was low.

The workers in accounting prided themselves on getting out reports accurately on schedule. Loafers were not tolerated by the other workers and did not last long with the group. The individuals in accounting mixed very little with other employees.

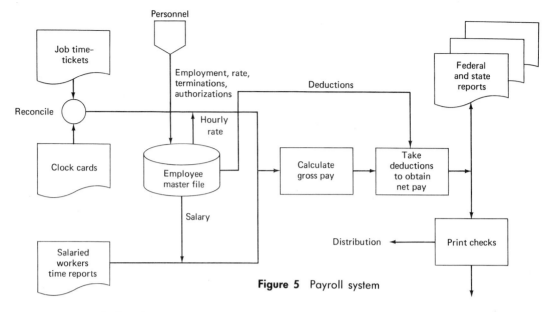

Figure 5 Payroll system

Engineering

Engineering design of components and simple systems was carried out by the Component Design section. For large complex systems requiring significant development work, the Systems Design section first designed the system and issued performance specifications for components. The Component Design group then designed or specified stock items for the components.

In the design of new products, costs can be reduced if the engineer can specify existing assemblies or stock items. At VDI, because of the volume of parts, engineers often specified a new part or assembly rather than trying to find a similar suitable part in the master file of parts. As a result, there was a steady growth in the number of items in the file, manufactured, and stocked which were only slightly different. The fact that parts lists were maintained manually by the

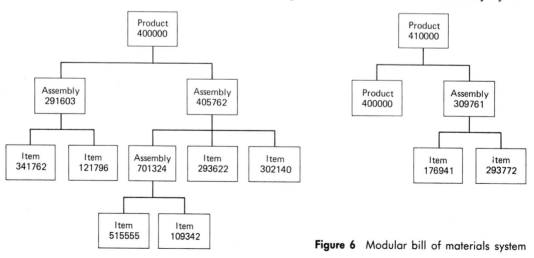

Figure 6 Modular bill of materials system

drafting section made it very time-consuming to search for a suitable part that had previously been designed.

Eigenvalue felt that the product and item identification system was basically a good one, but he had not yet been able to get the numbers into a computer data base available to engineers. The hierarchical system permitted a large range of product variations to be represented by a small number of modular bills of materials (see Figure 6). Nevertheless, engineering change notices were slow in working through the system.

Engineering used a project management system; that is, every job was given a project number. A project plan with Gantt chart was developed for large projects and a task breakdown structure was established. For small projects only a work package description was employed. Because of the many projects, only a semiannual progress report was prepared for management. Hans said, "I have to have a feel for trouble spots and I get some idea of problems at my weekly meetings with engineering section heads."

Eigenvalue believed that the future of the firm lay in its advanced product designs and skilled engineering personnel. A product selection committee composed of five engineering, marketing, and manufacturing representatives evaluated new-product proposals submitted by individuals. Relatively little information about the environment, government regulations, and competition was available to the committee when it made its decisions. Eigenvalue and Gonzalez were concerned about the company's limited outlook in terms of the future.

PURCHASING AND INVENTORY MANAGEMENT

A purchase was initiated by a material requisition form signed by an authorized individual. The warehouse manager, Null, placed requisitions for items and components based upon his current inventory, production plans, and parts lists which he received from manufacturing. For purchases in excess of $50,000, the manager of manufacturing had to cosign the requisition. For purchases over $100,000, Brooks Van Dam was required to sign.

Approximately 450 purchases were in process at a time. In a typical month, 600 purchase orders were placed for 1700 items. About 40% of the orders totaled less than $200. Four copies of the purchase order normally were prepared (see Figure 7). The original was sent to the vendor, one copy was retained by Purchasing, one copy was sent to Accounts Payable, one copy was sent to Null. A flow chart of the purchasing system is shown in Figure 8.

Inventory control for materials and components was based upon the sales forecast for the quarter ahead and the master production schedule for the month ahead. Since changes in the production schedule after the current week were frequently made, Null was forced to keep on hand a wide variety of items that might not be called for during the next year. A lot of time was spent in expediting delivery of components needed within a two-week period because of production and design changes. The value of goods in inventory was growing at a faster rate than sales.

VAN DAM, INC.	PURCHASE ORDER	P.O. NO.	COPY NO.

Table structure of the form:

| VAN DAM, INC. | PURCHASE ORDER | | P.O. NO. | COPY NO. |

SHIP TO — THIS NUMBER MUST APPEAR ON ALL CONTAINERS, PACKING LISTS, INVOICES & CORRESPONDENCE.

VENDOR NO. | CODE

SHIP VIA

DATE | TERMS

F.O.B.

ITEM	QUANTITY ORDERED	DESCRIPTION	UNIT PRICE

REQUESTED DELIVERY SCHEDULE

ITEM ONE	ITEM TWO	ITEM THREE	ITEM FOUR

OUR PART NUMBER AS SHOWN ON THE ORDER MUST APPEAR ON INVOICES, SHIPPING NOTICES AND PACKING SLIPS.

THIS ORDER, INCLUDING THE TERMS AND CONDITIONS ON THE FACE AND REVERSE SIDE HEREOF, CONTAINS THE COMPLETE AND FINAL AGREEMENT BETWEEN BUYER AND SELLER AND NO OTHER AGREEMENT IN ANY WAY MODIFYING ANY OF SAID TERMS AND CONDITIONS WILL BE BINDING UPON BUYER UNLESS MADE IN WRITING AND SIGNED BY BUYER'S AUTHORIZED REPRESENTATIVE.

SELLER WARRANTS COMPLIANCE WITH ASPR CLAUSE "NON-DISCRIMINATION IN EMPLOYMENT" EXECUTIVE ORDER 10925.

By _____

Figure 7 Purchase order

Management Reports

Management reports were developed to meet specific needs of managers as the company grew. As a result, there was considerable overlap among reports. At the same time, most reports could only be issued quarterly because the data were collected manually for the reports. Only accounting could boast of issuing frequent, regular, and accurate reports.

Figure 8
Purchasing
systems and
inventory
control

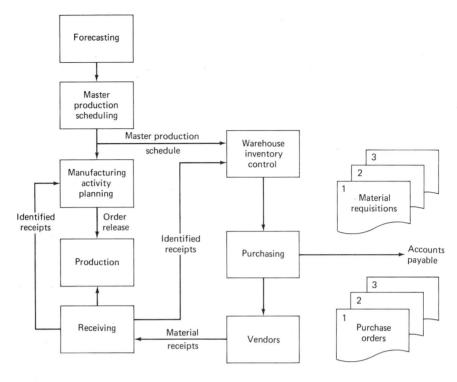

The following reports were received by the key managers:

Executive	Report	Frequency
President	Earnings and Balance Sheet	Semiannually
	Budgets	Annually
	Budget Variances	Monthly
	Sales Forecast and Analysis	Monthly
	Cash Flow	Monthly
	General Management Activity Report	Monthly
Marketing Manager	Earnings and Balance Sheet	Semiannually
	Marketing Budget	Annually
	Budget Variances	Monthly
	Sales Forecast and Analysis	Monthly
	Sales by Product and Salesperson	Monthly
	Shipping Summary	Monthly
Production Manager	Sales Forecast	Monthly
	Manufacturing Budget	Annually
	Master Production Schedule	Weekly
	Production Summary	Weekly
	Quality Control Summary	Monthly
	Shipping Summary	Monthly
	Work-in-progress Inventory	Monthly
	New Products	Quarterly
	Manufacturing Costs	Monthly
	Backlog	Quarterly

Executive	Report	Frequency
Engineering Manager	Engineering Budget	Annually
	Section Engineering Progress Report	Monthly
	Project Analysis Report	Monthly
	Budget Variances	Monthly
	Proposed Projects List	Quarterly
Warehouse Manager	Master Production Schedule	Weekly
	Raw Materials Inventory	Monthly
	Finished Goods Inventory	Monthly
	Shipping Summary	Monthly
	Warehouse Budget	Annually
	Budget Variances	Monthly
Purchasing Manager	Purchasing Budget	Annually
	Budget Variances	Monthly
	Prime Vendor Report	Quarterly
	Receiving Report	Monthly
	Open Orders	Monthly
	Open Contracts	Monthly
Personnel Manager	Budget for Personnel Section	Annually
	Personnel Section Budget Variances	Monthly
	Absenteeism	Monthly
	Number of Employees, Hires, and Terminations	Monthly
	Vocation List by Employee	Monthly
	Open Positions	Monthly

Office Space

Approximately 2200 square feet of office space were either unoccupied or used to pad the area of some workers' offices beyond the dictates of company policy. About 800 square feet were immediately available on the second floor of the building, whose plan is shown in Figure 9.

Figure 9
Plan of existing facilities at Van Dam, Inc.

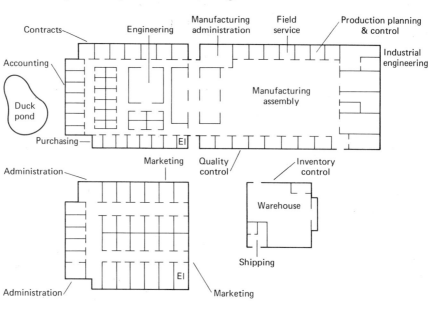

2nd Floor

Chapter 1

1. Give five examples of information described in the case.

2. Set up a table similar to that in Table 1.3 of Chapter 1 for the following systems: (a) order processing, (b) inventory control, (c) purchasing.

3. Identify three operating systems in the case.

4. Discuss the MIS in the case. Who is in charge of the MIS? Is the MIS computer-based?

5. What managers do you believe are using the "systems approach" to managing? Give your reasons for your selections.

6. To whom at Van Dam should Delphi report on a permanent basis?

Chapter 2

1. For the five basic principles of classical management, relate the management of VDI.

2. What is a clique that can be identified in the case?

3. Give an example of a group norm.

4. Give an example of the grapevine in action.

5. Give an example of authority (a) by personal acceptance, (b) by sanctions, (c) by authority of the situation, and (d) by organizational relationship.

6. Identify an important decision made at VDI by an individual and not a group.

7. Identify a set of group decisions that will be made at VDI in the near future.

8. In what organization at VDI is motivation apparently based on need for affiliation?

9. Identify two organizations where Herzberg's "motivators" and "hygiene" factors probably play a dominant role in motivation.

10. Where in VDI might we see a clear application of Skinner's operant conditioning as a basis for behavior?

11. Describe, by narrative and/or diagram, how a management information system would interact with the expectancy model (Fig. 3 of Chapter 2) to play a part in the motivation of (a) Gonzalez, (b) Eigenvalue, and (c) Fuller.

12. Set up a table in which the first column is a list of the following managers: Van Dam, Gonzalez, Grimes, Eigenvalue, Null, Fuller, and Buffun. Entitle the second column "Possible Reasons for Resisting a New MIS." Complete the table by indicating which of the nine reasons for resisting change, as given in this chapter, might apply for each manager.

13. Identify three different types of leaders and discuss their styles as you infer them from the case.

Chapter 3

1. Is the present computer system appropriate for the present limited application to accounting? Why or why not?

2. Would the present computer system be adequate for a computerized MIS for the entire company? If not, what modifications would you recommend?

3. Although Delphi, at this analysis stage, has only a vague idea of an appropriate computer system, she jotted down in her notes the following configuration for production and administration.

   a. Harris S 240 CPU utilizing virtual memory with main memory capacities
   b. Two 80-megabyte disk drives
   c. Two magnetic tape units for a rate of 74 ips
   d. One 300-megabyte disk drive
   e. One 1000-card/minute reader
   f. A 600- and a 900-line/minute printer
   g. Twelve CRT terminals located throughout the plant.

   The hardware configuration for engineering development was sketched as:

   a. Harris S 120 CPU with main memory capacity as 128K word storage
   b. Two 80-megabyte disk drives
   c. One 45-ips magnetic tape unit
   d. One 300-card/min card reader
   e. One 200-line/min line reader
   f. One 200-line/min line printer
   g. Ten remote CRT terminals

   Evaluate Delphi's hardware system configuration.

4. Discuss the use of the following and give an application relative to the hardware Jones is thinking about (Question 3).

   a. Batch processing
   b. Multiprogramming
   c. Multiprocessing
   d. Timesharing.

5. Develop the MIS and the DP organization for VDI and relate these to each other.

6. Develop a computer system configuration using distributed processing with minicomputers and no large central processor.

Chapter 4

1. What is the basic form of organization of VDI? Show an alternative organization structure that is systems-oriented and identify cost centers, phase systems, and resource systems.

2. Compare the differences between Delphi's flow chart of operations, Fig. 2, and Fig. 7 of Chapter 4. What major systems appear to be missing? How would you restructure the company to include all the systems of Fig. 4.7?

3. Draw a detailed flow chart for an engineering and production control system for VDI. (Refer to IBM's COPICS manuals or Fig. 12 of Chapter 4 for a good start.)

4. Develop a description of a good human resources management *system* including a flow chart of procedures.

5. Refer to Table 4.3 of Chapter 4 and check each system listed there if it is present at VDI.

6. Discuss whether Fig. 15 of Chapter 4 would describe a good order-processing system for VDI. What modifications would you recommend?

7. Relate Fig. 19 of Chapter 4 to VDI. Check each item on the figure that definitely is present at VDI. Check items that you think VDI has at present but which are not discussed in the case.

8. When manufacturing turns over a finished product for stocking to the warehouse manager, the transaction should involve authorization, execution, recording, and accountability. Describe how each of these parts of the transaction is, or should be, carried out at VDI, including listing or general description of forms and records required.

Chapter 5

1. VDI's special competences are its engineering and marketing personnel. Is there any indication in the case that the company prepares a strategy based upon these competences?

2. In view of VDI's products, what are ten important factors in the environment that VDI should monitor?

3. Sketch, in about two pages, a strategy for VDI to be implemented over the next five years.

4. What kinds of information could an MIS supply to help develop a complete strategy for VDI?

5. How could MIS improve short-range (operating) planning at VDI?

Chapter 6

1. Treat the inventory activities as a system and draw a block diagram to show the type of control used. List the type of control applied: feedback, feedforward, steering, or yes-no.

2. Prepare a table listing the managers Van Dam, Gonzalez, Grimes, Fuller, Eigen-value, Null, and Buffun in the left column. As column headings across the top, list (a) product lines (b) inventory, (c) cash, (d) capital assets, (e) new-product planning. If a manager appears, from the case, to be getting adequate information to exercise control over one of these systems, place a check in the appropriate cell.

3. Prepare a hierarchical system of reports on sales that computerized MIS could supply to the hierarchy of salesperson, sales manager, marketing manager, and president (see Fig. 12 of Chapter 6 as a guide.)

4. Design an Operations and Strategic Planning Room for VDI, assuming that the most modern MIS and equipment are available to you. Show where you would locate the room in the building.

5. Prepare a plan for an operations audit of VDI.

6. Describe what you would do to audit administrative and accounting control at VDI.

1. Give five specific reasons for developing a strategic plan for MIS development at VDI.

2. List three possible strategic objectives of MIS development

3. Identify five possible MIS projects and rank them in the order that you would initiate them at VDI.

4. Whom would you name to a steering committee for MIS development?

5. Prepare a work breakdown structure for the development of a companywide MIS.

6. Prepare a work package (with hypothetical estimates of resources) for the analysis of present company reports. This task would be concerned with studying the number of reports, purposes, overlaps, etc.

7. Prepare a PERT network for the development of an MIS at VDI. (You may limit the events to 15 to 30 and estimate activity times simply as guesses.) Find the critical path.

8. Prepare a project proposal for the development of an inventory planning and control information system. This should include the output reports to management.

Chapter 8

1. List the operating systems in the restructured organization you described for Question 1, Chapter 4, above.

2. Referring to the restructured organization you described for Question 1, Chapter 4, list each manager and five to ten principal items of information each will need to perform his or her job. Be sure to include Ms. Nording, Supervisor of Quality Control, and Ms. Viking, Manager of Purchasing and Contracts, in your list.

3. What constraints do you anticipate will be imposed on a computerized MIS at VDI?

4. Prepare an information flow chart for VDI similar to Fig. 7 of Chapter 8. Remember, only *managerial-type* information is to be listed.

5. Prepare a matrix which lists managers in a vertical column and proposed files across the top. Place a check in each cell which indicates that a manager uses a particular file.

6. Sketch a proposed computer configuration for VDI which simply shows components and their location on the floor plan. (In the next chapter you will be asked to detail the characteristics of the components.)

7. Show in tabular form the inputs and outputs of the following proposed systems at VDI:

   a. Quality control
   b. New-product planning
   c. Engineering change notice
   d. Environmental scanning system
   e. Human resources planning system
   f. Sales forecasting system.

8. List five possible trade-offs for the conceptual design of the new MIS being proposed for VDI.

9. Prepare a complete list of reports suitable for the reorganized Van Dam company.

Chapter 9

1. In two pages, summarize where you would stand after completing the conceptual design and as you are prepared to embark upon the detailed design.

2. Identify some dominant criteria that you think might exist in developing the MIS design.

3. Give an example of a possible trade-off relationship involved in the MIS design.

4. For a manager, as assigned by your instructor, prepare a position description, a list of information needs, an identification of the level of aggregation or summarization of information appropriate to the position level, and typical reports with their frequency that he or she would receive.

5. For an information subsystem, as assigned by your instructor, prepare or list:

   a. The subsystem objectives
   b. A system flow chart showing both operations and information or document flow
   c. A record layout
   d. Source data for a computer application program identified with the system
   e. Possible computer programs used by the subsystem, if any
   f. Output forms and reports and their distribution.

6. Draw a flow chart to describe an improved system for your new organization and computer-based MIS at VDI for the following systems:

   a. Order processing
   b. Purchasing
   c. Payroll
   d. Inventory control
   e. Accounts payable.

7. Design the following forms:

   a. Sales order form
   b. Order acknowledgement form
   c. CRT format for response to an inquiry about the bill of materials for a component
   d. CRT format for weekly sales by salesmen
   e. Manufacturing order release form
   f. Job ticket
   g. Travel authorization request form
   h. Engineering development proposal form
   i. Capital equipment request form
   j. New-product proposal evaluation form.

8. Give a proposed retention period for the following forms or records:

   a. Copies of invoices sent to customers
   b. Packing slips for goods received

c. Annual earnings statements for VDI

d. Travel expense report

e. Machine downtime reports

f. Quality control reports

g. Engineering monthly progress reports.

9. Prepare a written procedure for

a. The preparation of the monthly marketing report by the marketing organization for Van Dam

b. Preparation and dissemination of an engineering change notice

c. Accumulation of charges in the manufacture of a custom-designed instrument system.

Chapter 10

1. Develop an implementation plan for a new MIS at VDI. (Include a time schedule.)

2. Sketch a training program for the implementation.

3. Describe how software might be prepared or purchased. Describe who would have responsibility for software acquisition. Where would software of various kinds be stored?

4. Develop a layout for the MIS group and the computer systems personnel. Show where you would place these organizations on the plant layout.

5. Describe how you would convert from the old situation to the new MIS.

6. Describe a testing program you would recommend.

7. Describe how you would evaluate the new MIS.

8. Identify three areas of the MIS that would require maintenance on a regular basis.

9. Describe a maintenance program that you recommend VDI adopt.

Chapter 11

1. Prepare a data or information matrix for the following:

a. Report vs. data sources (see VDI, Question 9, Chapter 8, above.)

b. Reports vs. user

c. File vs. data source

d. File vs. user

e. Computer application program vs. departments using.

2. Prepare a table or form for making a job-station analysis of positions at VDI.

3. Prepare a decision table for the preliminary screening of new-product concepts.

4. Devise a coding for customers to identify important characteristics.

5. Prepare an outline for the documentation of the new MIS to be developed at VDI.

6. Make appropriate assumptions for the queues and simulate a two-stage operation such as (1) log incoming orders, and (2) transfer order information to order forms or to data base. (The advanced student may wish to simulate an entire subsystem.)

Chapter 12

1. Identify the most important forms and CRT formats; then estimate the total of these required for VDI.

2. Devise an inventory control system for forms.

3. Show the organization that includes responsibility for forms design, analysis, and control and prepare a position description for the person responsible for these activities.

4. Prepare an outline of the monthly report which Van Dam should receive covering the entire business.

Chapter 13

1. List three problems at Van Dam. Give two alternative solutions. Give three pieces of information helpful in making a decision in each case. (Answer in the form of a table.)

2. Give an example of (a) group decision making at VDI and (b) individual decision making.

3. Give an example of how an MIS could (a) provide decision support and (b) make programmed decisions.

4. Set up a factor analysis table and evaluate two computer-system alternatives for VDI.

5. Formulate the principal problem faced by Ms. Jones by identifying the elements, the present state, the desired state, constraints, and criteria for the solution.

Chapter 14

1. Show how Delphi could apply the information processing model of Fig. 12 of Chapter 14 to marketing's need for better sales forecasting in the development of the MIS.

2. a. For the data which go into an engineering progress report, trace their life cycle according to the model of Fig. 2 of Chapter 14.
   b. Do the same for the monthly sales forecast.

Chapter 15

1. Show who in VDI will have responsibility for (a) administering the data base, (b) developing the data-base scheme, (c) implementing the data-management program, (d) developing query-language programs, and developing application programs for the new MIS.

2. Show a linked-list structure for finished goods in the warehouse at VDI.

3. For the computer system that you propose, describe security and privacy measures that you will install.

4. Very approximately, about how many megabytes of data do you estimate will be stored initially in the data base for your proposed system?

1. Describe how Delphi would apply the systems approach to the development of the MIS.

2. Identify and describe in a few paragraphs:

   a. Three possible planning models for VDI
   b. Two control models.

3. Prepare a simple engineering information system description similar to that shown in Fig. 1 of Chapter 16.

INDEX

A

ABC principle, 185-87
Access methods, 479-80
Accountability, 233-34
Accounting control and auditing, 196-98
Accounts receivable system, 131-34
Ackoff, Russell L., 416n
Acquisition, 315-17
Adaptive control, 179, 180
Adaptive systems, 507
Administrator, data-base, 472, 489-90
Aguilar, F. J., 441
Airline operations, 122, 123
Allocation of resources, 94
Alter, Steven, 427
American Accounting Association, 461
American Institute of Certified Public Accountants (AICPA), 196-97
Analog models, 520
Analytical problem-solving, 413
Applications software, 95
Archival program, 491
Argyris, Chris, 53, 183n, 185n
Arnoff, E. Leonard, 416n
Assembly languages, 91-92
Atkinson, J. W., 42, 43
Authority, 38-40

B

Bank operations, 119, 121
Barnard, Chester I., 53, 54

Barrow, Jeffrey C., 47, 48
Batch processing, 89
Behavioral decision theory, 421, 422
Behavioral theory, 35-41, 46
Bench marks, 366
Bench-mark simulation, 369
Bertalanffy, Ludwig von, 516
Bill of Material Processing Subsystem, 287-88
Binary number system, 71-72
Binding, 476
Binstock, Jeanne, 5
Birnbert, Jacob G., 420n
Bits, 72
"Black-Box" concept, 522, 526-27
Blake, Robert R., 47, 53
Block diagrams, 260, 261, 263, 345, 522, 526
Blocking criteria, 158, 159
Blumenthal, Sherman C., 213-14
Boundaries, 512-13
Bounded rationality, 40
Bray, D., 421n
Brooks, Frederick, 94
Budgeting, 231
Bureaucratic model, 421, 422
Burnett, Gerald J., 86n

C

Cannon, J. Thomas, 147n
Capital budgeting system, 110, 111
Capital equipment purchases, 157-59